CAMBRIDGE

Brighter Thinking

A/AS Level Computer Science for OCR

Student Book

Alistair Surrall and Adam Hamflett

CAMBRIDGE
UNIVERSITY PRESS

University Printing House, Cambridge CB2 8BS, United Kingdom

One Liberty Plaza, 20th Floor, New York, NY 10006, USA

477 Williamstown Road, Port Melbourne, VIC 3207, Australia

314–321, 3rd Floor, Plot 3, Splendor Forum, Jasola District Centre, New Delhi – 110025, India

79 Anson Road, #06 -04/06, Singapore 079906

Cambridge University Press is part of the University of Cambridge.

It furthers the University's mission by disseminating knowledge in the pursuit of education, learning and research at the highest international levels of excellence.

www.cambridge.org
Information on this title: www.cambridge.org/9781108412711 (Paperback)
Information on this title: www.cambridge.org/9781108412742 (Paperback + Cambridge Elevate enhanced edition, 2 years)

First published 2017

20 19 18 17 16 15 14 13 12 11 10 9 8 7 6

Printed in Great Britain by CPI Group (UK) Ltd, Croydon CR0 4YY

A catalogue record for this publication is available from the British Library

ISBN 978-1-108-41271-1 Paperback
ISBN 978-1-108-41274-2 Paperback + Cambridge Elevate enhanced edition

All exam-style questions that appear in this publication have been written by the author.

This resource is endorsed by OCR for use with specifications H046 OCR AS Level Computer Science and H446 OCR A Level Computer Science. In order to gain OCR endorsement, this resource has undergone an independent quality check. Any references to assessment and/or assessment preparation are the publisher's interpretation of the specification requirements and are not endorsed by OCR. OCR recommends that a range of teaching and learning resources are used in preparing learners for assessment. OCR has not paid for the production of this resource, nor does OCR receive any royalties from its sale. For more information about the endorsement process, please visit the OCR website, www.ocr.org.uk.

Contents

Introduction

What is Computer Science?

Computer Science provides a fascinating insight into the digital world. Through studying it, you will learn how to solve problems in a structured way and be able to apply logic and mathematical principles. Computer programming is a practical application of problem-solving skills. It is also a very creative and absorbing process. Learning how to design, write and test code well are very valuable skills that will be of benefit in the world of work.

About the course

The Advanced Level Computer Science course consists of two examinations and one Non Examined Assessment. The Computer Systems unit (Component 01), provides a broad and balanced study of all aspects of the subject. Algorithms and Programming (Component 02), focuses on the computational thinking principles and the development of code.

Applications of Computer Science

There are many job roles that require the skills and knowledge of Computer Science. Computer hardware can take many forms from traditional computers to mobile phones, tablets and embedded control systems. Technology evolves rapidly and a thorough understanding of system function allows this to be exploited. Networked systems are vulnerable to attack which could lead to theft of valuable data and loss of business. Understanding threats and mitigation techniques is an exceedingly valuable skill set. The ability to write code is perhaps the most fundamental skill of a computer scientist. There is a plethora of different languages following a number of paradigms. A good programmer will have mastered the art of writing well-crafted code in a similar manner to writing poetry or painting a picture. A logical approach to problem solving will help you in many aspects of everyday life from trying out a new recipe to mending a bicycle. Be logical, be creative and enjoy learning Computer Science!

How to use this book

Throughout this book you will notice particular features that are designed to aid your learning. This section provides a brief overview of these features.

Specification Points

A list of the specification points that will be covered in a particular chapter.

Specification points

1.1.1 Structure and function of the processor

- The Arithmetic and Logic Unit (ALU), Control Unit and Registers (Program Counter (PC), Accumulator (ACC), Memory Address Register (MAR), Memory Data Register (MDR), Current Instruction Register (CIR). Buses: data, address and control. How computer architecture relates to assembly language programs.

Learning Objectives

A short summary of the content that you will learn in each chapter.

Learning objectives

- To know the different parts of a computer's processor and their purpose.
- To know about different types of processor architecture.
- To understand the term 'machine code' and how it relates to software.
- To understand the FDE cycle and the special purpose registers involved.
- To be able to describe pipelining and explain how it improves efficiency.

Tip

Useful guidance about particular types of code or software, as well as common errors to avoid and tips to help you prepare for exams.

Tip

Machine code and assembly code form the main focus of another part of the course, and questions based on these topics may not appear in questions linked to the processor and the **FDE cycle**. However, the terms 'opcode' and 'machine code' are key in answering questions in this section successfully.

Activities

Questions and exercises designed to help you practice what you have learnt throughout the resource.

Activity 1.3

Visit a website that sells computers and find two computers: one with a single core and one with multiple cores. What is the difference in cost? Do you think the extra performance is worth the money? Explain.

Computing in Context

Provides examples of how the concepts you are learning fit within real-life scenarios.

Computing in context: overclocking

Most GPUs are capable of running at a faster speed than the manufacturer specifies. Manufacturers try to strike a balance between getting a good performance and not burning the card out, so the speed they set for the card is a compromise, which means the graphics are not as good as they could be, but the card will last for a reasonable length of time before it stops working.

End-of-Chapter questions

Questions designed to test your learning of the material in the chapter you have just studied.

End-of-chapter questions

1 Describe the following components of a CPU.

- **a** Control unit [2]
- **b** Arithmetic logic unit [2]
- **c** Memory unit [2]

A Level only icon

This icon indicates where material is specific to the A Level only. The green line extending from the icon shows you clearly where the A Level only content starts and finishes.

1.1.2 Types of processor

- The differences between, and uses of, CISC and RISC processors.
- A GPUs and their uses (including those not related to graphics).
- Multicore and parallel systems.

Summary

A short summary to recap on the key concepts and topics and that you have learnt in that chapter.

Summary

- A CPU is made up of the following components:
  - ALU – arithmetic logic unit
  - MU – memory unit
  - CU – control unit.

Further Reading

A list of additional sources where you can find further information on a particular topic.

Further reading

Von Neumann architecture – www.cambridge.org/links/kose5151
EDVAC computer –https://www.thocp.net/hardware/edvac.htm
Zargham, M. (1996) *Computer Architecture*, London: Prentice Hall, Ch 2.

Chapter 1
Structure and function of the processor and types of processor

Specification points

1.1.1 Structure and function of the processor

- The Arithmetic and Logic Unit (ALU), Control Unit and Registers (Program Counter (PC), Accumulator (ACC), Memory Address Register (MAR), Memory Data Register (MDR), Current Instruction Register (CIR). Buses: data, address and control. How computer architecture relates to assembly language programs.
- The fetch–decode–execute cycle, including its effect on registers.
- The factors affecting the performance of the CPU: clock speed, number of cores, cache.
- Von Neumann, Harvard and contemporary processor architecture.
- A The use of pipelining in a processor to improve efficiency.

1.1.2 Types of processor

- The differences between, and uses of, CISC and RISC processors.
- A GPUs and their uses (including those not related to graphics).
- Multicore and parallel systems.

Learning objectives

- To know the different parts of a computer's processor and their purpose.
- To know about different types of processor architecture.
- To understand the term 'machine code' and how it relates to software.
- To understand the FDE cycle and the special purpose registers involved.
- To be able to describe pipelining and explain how it improves efficiency.

Figure 1.1: Clean room.

Introduction

At the centre of all modern computer systems is an incredible device referred to as the central processing unit (CPU), microprocessor or simply the processor. The processor is the brain of the computer; it carries out all the mathematical and logical operations necessary to execute the instructions given to it by the user. It is one of the most expensive parts of a computer system, and upgrading a computer's processor remains one of the best ways of increasing a computer's performance.

Today, processors can be found in anything from smartphones and tablets to washing machines and microwaves. Without them, modern life would look very different.

As you might expect, processor designs are extremely complex and the way they are constructed (their architecture) changes rapidly. Innovations in specialist materials and improved design techniques are utilised to make them faster and more efficient.

To create a processor's architecture, specialists will first design the necessary circuitry. Silicon discs are then produced by melting sand, refining it and finely slicing the resulting crystals. Next, the circuit diagrams are transferred to the silicon discs, resulting in the creation of thousands of minute transistors; these are joined together using copper to create small integrated circuits. Finally, these are packaged with the pins necessary to connect the processor to a computer's motherboard. This process takes place in a 'clean room' (Figure 1.1), which is a controlled and sterile environment; the smallest amount of dust could ruin the silicon. This is a very basic overview of the extraordinary manufacturing process used to create CPUs. It is well worth using the 'Further reading' section at the end of this chapter to find out more.

A processor is made up of a number of key parts, which work together to execute instructions. Despite this, the processor still requires software to perform tasks. In this chapter you will learn about machine code, assembly code and their relationship with high-level programming. We also explore how the processor transfers instructions from main memory to the processor and how this process can be made more efficient through the use of **pipelining**.

Machine code instructions

When code is written in languages such as Python or Visual Basic .NET, the code is readable and understandable by humans and is known as source code. Processors have no understanding of source code and cannot execute it directly unless it is translated into machine code. A compiler is the name given to a piece of software that takes source code and converts it to machine code (see Chapter 4 for more details). Source code, written as a text file, allows software to be created without the need to understand the inner workings of the instruction set of the target processor. The programming language hides a lot of the complexities of the processor, such as memory addressing modes (Figure 1.2).

Each processor architecture (for example, ARM or x86) has its own set of instructions. The compiler must specify the target architecture before compiling, as the differing architectures are not compatible with all computers. Each line of source code can be compiled into many lines of machine code.

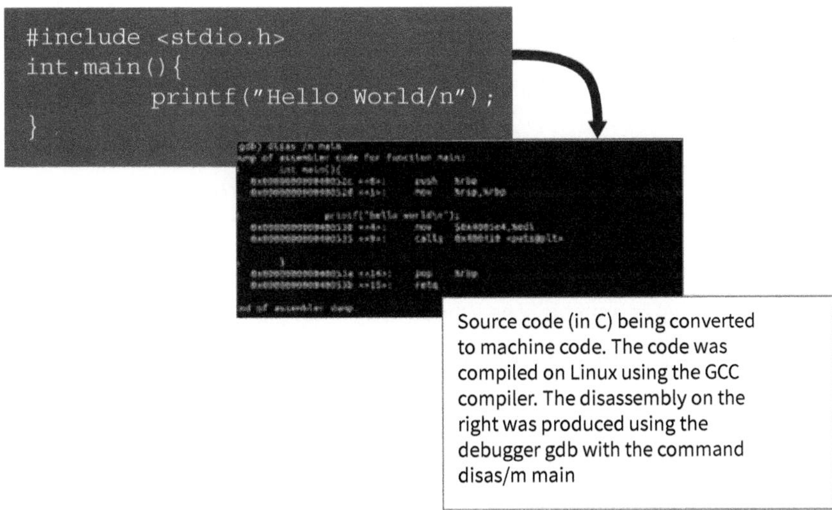

#include <stdio.h>
int.main(){
printf("Hello World/n");
}
Source code (in C) being converted to machine code. The code was compiled on Linux using the GCC compiler. The disassembly on the right was produced using the debugger gdb with the command disas/m main

Figure 1.2: Source code being converted into machine code.

Structure of machine code

Machine code is the binary representation of an instruction, split into the opcode and the instruction's data. Assembly code uses text to represent machine code instructions, or mnemonics. Each processor architecture has a set of instructions that it can run; this is known as the instruction set. Table 1.1 shows the basic structure of an instruction:

Bits 1–6	Bits 7–16
Opcode	Data

Table 1.1: Basic structure of an instruction.

The size of instructions differs from architecture to architecture and can even differ between instructions. In the example above, the instruction is 16 bits in size. Every instruction available, in a given instruction set, will have a unique binary value known as the opcode. When an instruction is executed by the processor, it uses the opcode to determine which instruction to run. Table 1.2 shows an example instruction set, which is not based on any real-life processor and should be treated as an example only. Note that ACC stands for accumulator, a special purpose register.

Opcode	Assembly mnemonic	Description
000 001	MOV	Moves a value to a register
000 010	ADD	Adds a value and stores in ACC
000 100	SUB	Subtracts a value and stores in ACC
001 000	MUL	Multiplies a value and stores in ACC

Table 1.2: Table showing example machine code instructions and their respective opcodes.

Each opcode represents a different instruction and mnemonics are used to make development in assembly language easier, as dealing with binary can get very complex. As an example, Table 1.3 shows a simple program that will perform the calculation $(4 + 5) \times 2$:

	Opcode	Data	Value of ACC
MOV value 0 to ACC	000 001	0000 0000 00	0000 0000 0000 0000
ADD 4 to ACC	000 010	0000 0001 00	0000 0000 0000 0100
ADD 5 to ACC	000 010	0000 0001 01	0000 0000 0000 1001
MUL 2 to ACC	001 000	0000 0000 10	0000 0000 0001 0010

Table 1.3: Table showing an example of how the computer sees the opcode and data as binary.

Some instructions take up more than one word. A word is a complete unit of data for a particular computer architecture. In the above example, the MOV instruction has two arguments, the first being the register to use. In this case ACC (accumulator) is represented by register 0. The value to move into ACC is stored in the second word. ADD and MUL both store the value to add or multiply in the data part of the instruction, which is known as immediate addressing. However, we could just as easily store it separately. Placing data in the second word of a double-word instruction allows the full 16 bits to be used, thus supporting larger numbers.

Tip

Machine code and assembly code form the main focus of another part of the course, and questions based on these topics may not appear in questions linked to the processor and the **FDE cycle**. However, the terms 'opcode' and 'machine code' are key in answering questions in this section successfully.

Relationship between machine code and assembly code

Assembly code is the step above machine code, allowing the coder to write code using mnemonics, which represent machine code instructions. Each assembly code instruction has a one-to-one mapping with a machine code instruction. This is unlike source code, which has one-to-many mapping. When translating assembly code to machine code an assembler is used. Assembly language is directly related to the instruction set of the processor, and the assembler acts upon this. The processor in a desktop computer will use a different assembler to a Raspberry Pi, for example.

Components of a processor

A processor is a small and complex device. Internally, the processor is made up of a number of key components, which include the ALU, CU and MU (Figure 1.3). Each component does a different job. One type of simple model processor is called the Von Neumann architecture.

Arithmetic logic unit

The arithmetic logic unit (ALU) is responsible for carrying out calculations and logic operations. Calculations include floating point multiplication and integer division, while logic operations include comparison tests such as greater than or less than. The ALU also acts as a conduit for input and output to and from the processor.

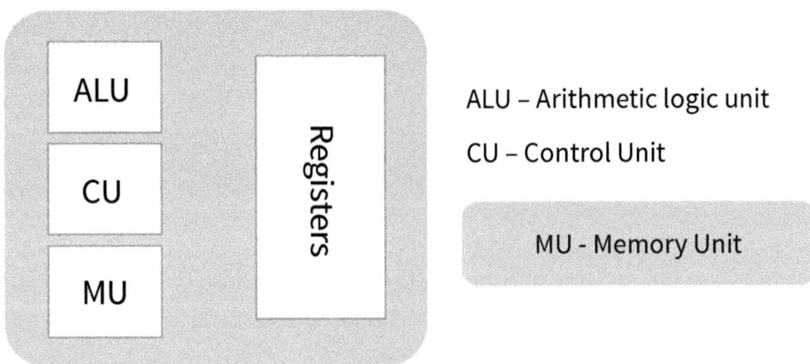

Figure 1.3: Overview of a processor.

Control unit

The control unit (CU) is a key part of the processor. It manages the execution of machine code by sending control signals to the rest of the computer. Control signals are sent via a control bus to connected devices, such as hard drives or the graphics card. Part of the job of the CU is to synchronise instructions by using the processor's internal clock. This will be based on the clock speed and is known as a clock cycle. Some instructions may take less time than a single clock cycle, but the next instruction will only start when the processor executes the next cycle.

Memory unit

A processor must pull instructions and data from main memory into the registers for that data to be processed. An instruction can only operate on data that is inside a register. The memory unit (MU) stores currently running programs, current files and the operating system. The fetch–decode–execute cycle describes the whole process of executing a single instruction.

Control bus

The control bus carries control signals around the CPU. These are generated by the control unit and coordinate the fetch–decode–execute cycle.

Address bus

This carries memory addresses from the processor to primary memory.

Data bus

The data bus in a Von Neumann processor carries data and instructions to and from the CPU and RAM.

Processor speed

Processor speed is measured by the number of clock cycles that the processor can perform in a second and is measured in hertz (Hz). A clock cycle is one increment of the CPU clock. During a clock cycle the processor can fetch, decode and execute a simple instruction, such as load, store or jump. More complex instructions take more than one clock cycle.

It is easy to calculate the amount of time it takes to run one cycle for any speed of processor. The calculation for a 2 gigahertz (GHz) processor is shown below:

The number 2 000 000 000 is obtained by converting GHz to Hz.

$$\textit{Frequency} = \frac{1}{\textit{Time}}$$

$$\textit{Time} = \frac{1}{\textit{Frequency}}$$

$$\textit{Time} = \frac{1}{2\,000\,000\,000}$$

$$\textit{Time} = 5.0 \times 10^{-10}\text{s}$$

Figure 1.4: Calculating the time taken to complete one clock cycle on a 2 Ghz CPU.

 **Tip**

You do not have to be able to calculate clock speed in the exam.

Processors have progressed to a level where it is hard to increase speed. When the number of clock cycles per second is increased, the transistors within the processor have to switch faster, which generates more heat. Unless the heat is drawn away from the processor, it can easily overheat. A processor can reach temperatures in excess of 300 °C degrees, which is hotter than an oven, in a matter of seconds. If you open up a desktop computer, you will see a large heat sink and fan attached to the processor (Figure 1.5), which has the job of pulling all of this heat away from the processor. You should never run a system without a heat sink, as this could cause permanent damage to both the processor and the motherboard. It could also pose a severe fire risk.

Figure 1.5: Heat sink and fan alongside a processor.

Processor manufacturers, such as AMD or Intel®, try other methods to increase the performance of their CPUs. This can include increasing the number of cores (processors) in the CPU, making existing circuitry more efficient, or developing new instructions. Modern processors contain at least one level of cache memory, which stores recently used instructions and data. This speeds up the fetch process, as cache memory is closer than RAM. You can read more about cache memory later in this chapter.

In order to make a fair comparison of the effects of modifying processors, they would need to be subjected to standard benchmark tests.

 **Tip**

You must be able to describe the **three** types of bus and the type of information sent over each of them.

Little Man Computer

The Little Man Computer (LMC) is a simple architecture designed to help you understand the concepts of machine code and instruction sets. Unlike real instruction sets, LMC has a very limited number (shown in Table 1.4 along with their opcodes). An xx in the opcode refers to the data part of the instruction (only if required, as not every instruction needs data). For example, in order to add, you first need to know what you are adding. To keep things simple, the LMC has only two registers, ACC and PC. Data and instructions are stored in memory locations known as mailboxes; this is directly synonymous with a standard von Neumann-based computer (see the 'Computing in context: von Neumann bottleneck' later in this chapter). Conceptually a mailbox represents one single byte of memory. Mailboxes can be referred to directly or indirectly, through the use of labels. A label is a text symbol that represents a mailbox, making coding in LMC easier. When a label is used to represent a mailbox, the LMC assembler assigns a suitable mailbox as the code is assembled.

Opcode	Name	Data	Explanation
1xx	ADD	The number to add	It will add a value from a register to the current value of the ACC
2xx	SUB	The number to subtract	It will subtract value from a register to the current value of the ACC
3xx	STA	Stores a value into a register	Will take the contents of the ACC
5xx	LDA	Loads a value from a register	Will take a value from a register and store it in the ACC
6xx	BRA	Line number to 'jump' to	Unconditional branch. Will jump to the given instruction number

Opcode	Name	Data	Explanation
7xx	BRZ	Line number to 'jump' to	Branch if zero. Will only jump if the ACC is zero
8xx	BRP	Line number to 'jump' to	Branch if positive. Will only jump if the ACC has a positive value **or is zero**.
901	INP	Input from the user	Will input a value and store it in the ACC
902	OUT	None	Will output the contents of the ACC

Table 1.4: Table showing the instructions available in the LMC.

```
0          INP
1          STA   FIRST
2          INP
3          ADD   FIRST
4          OUT
5          HLT
6  FIRST   DAT   0
```

Figure 1.6: Sample LMC program to add two numbers together.

The simple LMC program on the right will add two numbers input by the user. Each line of the code is converted into an LMC machine code instruction and stored in a single mailbox, as shown in Table 1.5. Line 1 is converted to '901', which is stored in mailbox 0. Line 2 stores the value in the accumulator in mailbox 6, which is represented by the LMC code as the label FIRST. The fully assembled code is shown in Figure 1.7.

POS	0	1	2	3	4	5	
Value	901	306	901	160	902	0	12

Table 1.5: An LMC program and its mailboxes.

```
0              LDA   ONE
1              STA   COUNT
2              OUT
3   LOOPTOP    LDA   COUNT
4              ADD   ONE
5              OUT
6              STA   COUNT
7              SUB   TEN
8              BRP   ENDLOOP
9              BRA   LOOPTOP
10  ENDLOOP    HLT
11  ONE        DAT   1
12  TEN        DAT   10
13  COUNT      DAT   0
14
```

Figure 1.7: Sample LMC programme to display the numbers from 1 to 10.

This program will display the numbers from 1 to 10, but could easily be updated to perform actions on any sequence of numbers. Assembly code, regardless of **CPU** architecture, does not have control statements such as IF or WHILE. Instead, the flow of execution is changed by conditional jump commands. In LMC, jumps are referred to as branches. It is possible to represent any programming control statement through branches and jumps.

Branches allow decisions and loops to be coded in LMC. Figure 1.8 is a diagrammatic representation of the LMC code to add the numbers 1 to 10. The line **BRA LOOPTOP** does an unconditional jump back to the top of the loop. **BRP ENDLOOP** breaks out of the loop once the ten numbers have been added. BRP will only branch if the value in the accumulator is positive, which is why 10 is subtracted from the current count. Initially the count will be

LDA ONE
STA COUNT
OUT OUT
LDA COUNT
ADD ONE
OUT OUT
STA COUNT
SUB TEN
BRP ENDLOOP
BRA LOOPTOP
HLT
DAT DAT ONE
DAT DAT TEN

Pos	0	1	2	3	4	5	6	7	8	9
Value	511	313	902	513	111	902	313	212	810	63
Pos	10	11	12	13	14	15	16	17	18	19
Value	0	1	10	10	0	0	0	0	0	0

Figure 1.8: Diagram showing the LMC code required to add the numbers 1–10.

Tip

LMC is studied more formally in Chapter 6, but is introduced here as a practical way to help you understand machine code and how the processor works, and more specifically, how opcodes and data work together. It is advisable to try out some basic LMC programs to get a working understanding for yourself.

1; so 1–10 will result in a negative number. One gets added to the count and we branch unconditionally. This continues until the count becomes 10, as zero is considered to be a positive number. Rather than having a command that loops only if the accumulator is negative, we can use simple mathematics to remove the need for the command entirely.

Activity 1.1

Using an LMC simulator, enter the following code.

```
            LDA   ONE
            STA   COUNT
            OUT
LOOPTOP     LDA   COUNT
            ADD   ONE
            OUT
            STA   COUNT
            SUB   TEN
            BRP   ENDLOOP
            BRA   LOOPTOP
ENDLOOP     HLT
ONE         DAT   1
TEN         DAT   10
COUNT       DAT   0
```

Run this program to ascertain its purpose. Once you understand it, write the code out in a high-level language or in pseudocode.

Consider this Python code:

```
x = 0
total = 0
while x<10:
    total = total + x
    x = x + 1
print total
```

Rewrite this code using the Little Man Computer simulator.

Computing in context: von Neumann bottleneck

John von Neumann was a Hungarian-American mathematician, born in 1903. He is widely considered to be one of the fathers of modern-day computing. In his career he also made many contributions to areas of mathematics such as game and operator theory.

In 1945, while consulting for an engineering group developing the EDVAC computer, von Neumann released a paper entitled 'First draft report on the EDVAC'. To give the report context, it is important to understand the EDVAC computer and generally how computing was achieved in the 1940s. The majority of computing systems in use today are based on the von Neumann architecture, named after him.

Most modern computers share the same critical problem as a result of using the von Neumann architecture. Because of the speed mismatches between memory, secondary storage and the processor, most of the processor's time is spent idle. This is known as the von Neumann bottleneck.

John von Neumann

Harvard architecture

Harvard architecture, named after the Harvard mark I, differs from the standard von Neumann architecture with regards to how instructions and data are stored. Instructions are stored separately from data, meaning that there is no need to share common attributes between the two. For example, you could set the address bus to be 32 bit for instructions and 64 bit for data. Conversely, in the von Neumann architecture instructions and data share the same address space meaning that they must share the same properties.

Aspects of the Harvard architecture are in use in modern CPUs to help overcome some of the problems with fetching instructions from memory before execution (FDE cycle). Modern CPUs will employ a split cache that essentially reserves part of the cache for instructions. If the CPU accesses instructions from the cache then it operates under the Harvard architecture. However, if the instruction is not located in cache, it will have to access instructions from RAM and therefore act under the von Neumann architecture.

Some embedded systems, where the software can be programmed into ROM, will make use of the Harvard architecture.

Registers

A processor contains many registers, some reserved for specific purposes while others are used for general-purpose calculations. A register is a small block of memory, usually 4 or 8 bytes, which is used as temporary storage for instructions as they are being processed. This temporary storage runs at the same speed as the processor. Machine code instructions can only work if they are loaded into registers.

General purpose registers are used as programs run, to enable calculations to be made, and can be used for any purpose the programmer (or compiler) chooses. Special purpose registers are crucial to how the processor works. Values are loaded in and out of registers during the execution of a process. Some of the key special purpose registers are:

- program counter
- memory address register and memory data register
- current address register
- accumulator.

Program counter

The **program counter** (PC) always contains the address of the next instruction to be executed.

Programs, in order to function, need to be loaded into memory by the operating system (Figure 1.9). As memory is referenced using memory addresses, the start of any given program has a specific memory address. It is not possible to know where exactly in memory a program will be loaded, as this is managed by the operating system. Each instruction of the program is assigned an address in memory. The program counter contains the address of the first instruction of the program, not the actual instruction.

As the process is run, the instruction to which the PC is pointing is loaded into the **memory address register** (MAR) so that it can be fetched from memory into the processor, and the PC is incremented so that it points to the address of the next instruction. The value added to the PC is calculated from the size of the instructions for the given instruction set.

Sometimes the value of the PC changes as the result of an instruction being executed. This tends to be when a JUMP or BRANCH instruction is run. These instructions are used to provide the functionality of procedures, IF statements and iteration.

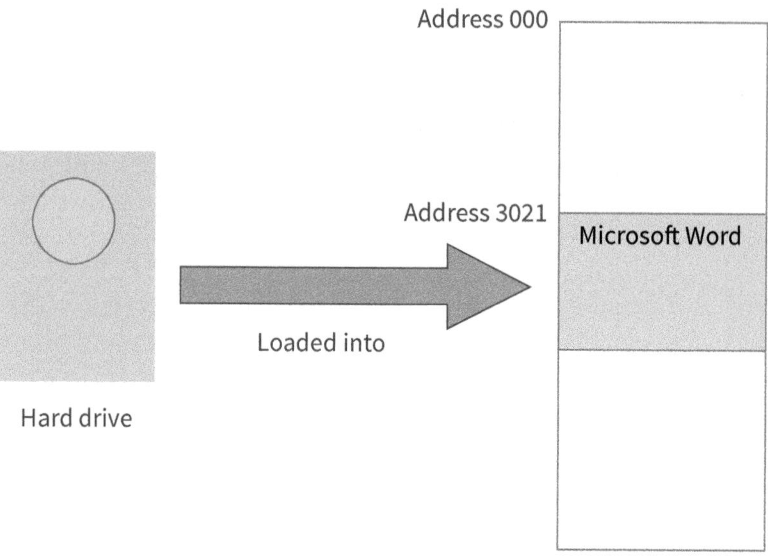

Figure 1.9: Microsoft Word is loaded into memory by the operating system.

Memory address and memory data registers

Currently running programs are stored in memory, which means that they must be loaded into registers. This process is known as fetching and makes use of two special registers, the MAR and the **memory data register** (MDR). The MAR contains the address of the instruction or data to be fetched, and the fetched instruction or data is stored in the MDR. Fetching instructions from memory can be a slow process, so the processor will try to fetch one instruction ahead of the one it's currently working on. So, while one instruction is being executed, the next one is being fetched. This process of looking ahead is known as **pipelining** and will be explored later.

Current instruction register

Once an instruction has been fetched, it's copied into the **current instruction register** (CIR) for executing. As the instruction in the CIR is being decoded and executed, the next instruction is being fetched into the MDR.

Accumulator

Any instruction that performs a calculation makes use of the **accumulator** (ACC). Many instructions operate on, or update, the ACC. If a subtraction instruction is run, it performs the subtraction using the data part of the instruction and stores the result in the ACC. Calculations take a step-by-step approach, so the result of the last calculation is part of the next. Some instruction sets, like LMC, use ACC as part of the calculation. Only one value needs to be given in the data part of the instruction. This is shown in Table 1.6.

Instruction	ACC
Initial value	0
ADD 4	4
ADD 2	6
SUB 1	5

Table 1.6: Table showing how the value of the ACC changes when instructions are executed.

Cache

For a program to work, it loads instructions and data from main memory (RAM) by using the FDE cycle. As memory runs a lot slower than the processor, the processor is likely to have to wait for main memory to fetch data, which results in wasted clock cycles. The overall efficiency of the computing system is reduced, due to a lot of time being wasted as a result of the speed mismatch between the memory and the processor (the von Neumann bottleneck). Caches help solve this problem by acting as a 'middle man' between the processor and the memory. Cache memory runs much faster than standard memory and sits in between RAM and the processor (Figure 1.10). Data and instructions that are used regularly are copied into the cache. When the processor needs this data, it can be retrieved much faster. Cache memory size is small (normally a few megabytes) owing to its high cost. It would not be cost-effective to use cache memory as RAM, as such a machine would have a cost running into the tens of thousands, if not more.

Figure 1.10: Cache memory sits between RAM and the CPU.

The processor always tries to load data from the cache, but if the data it needs is not there, it is copied over from RAM. If the cache is full already, the least recently used data in the cache is thrown out and replaced with the new data. There are a number of algorithms that can be used to ensure that the cache contains the most regularly used data. This is a lot easier than you might expect, owing to the 80/20 rule. Programs tend to spend most of their time in loops of some description, which means that they will be working on the same instructions for a lot of their execution time. The 80/20 rule states that 80% of a program's execution time is spent in only 20% of the code. This proves to be fairly accurate in most cases.

When the processor requests data that is not in the cache, this is referred to as a **cache miss**. If a system has a high incidence of cache misses, the overall speed of the system will be substantially reduced. Whichever algorithm is employed to manage the cache, the primary focus is to minimise cache misses. Data that has been requested and is found in the cache is termed a **cache hit**.

Tip

It's important that you understand the relative speed of devices compared to one another. The processor is the fastest, followed by cache, then RAM, with secondary storage being the slowest.

Fetch–decode–execute cycle

When instructions are to be executed by the processor, they must be loaded into the processor one after another, via a process known as the fetch–decode–execute (FDE) cycle. Previously, you were introduced to a number of special purpose registers used during the FDE cycle (Figure 1.11) and here you will see how they work together. It's important to remember that a single processor can execute only a single instruction at once from the current instruction register. By using a large number of registers, the whole process can be made more efficient using a system called pipelining.

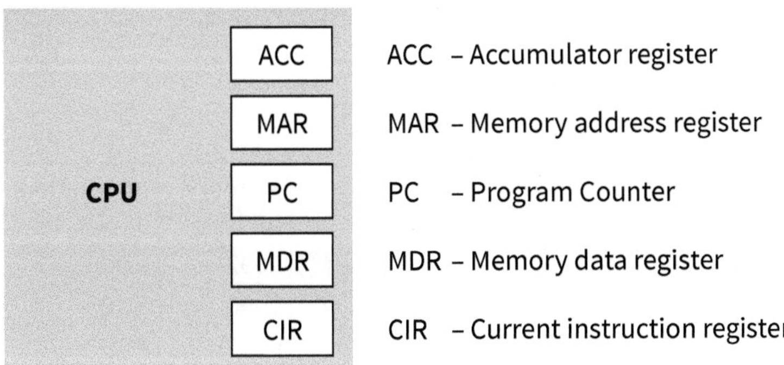

Figure 1.11: Specialist registers used during FDE cycle.

In Figure 1.12, the address stored in the PC is 0092. The first part of the cycle is to fetch the next instruction for processing. The PC is copied over to the MAR and then the PC is incremented. Most programs, unless a control instruction such as a jump is encountered, will run serially, so by incrementing the PC it is highly likely that it will be pointing to the next instruction to be fetched.

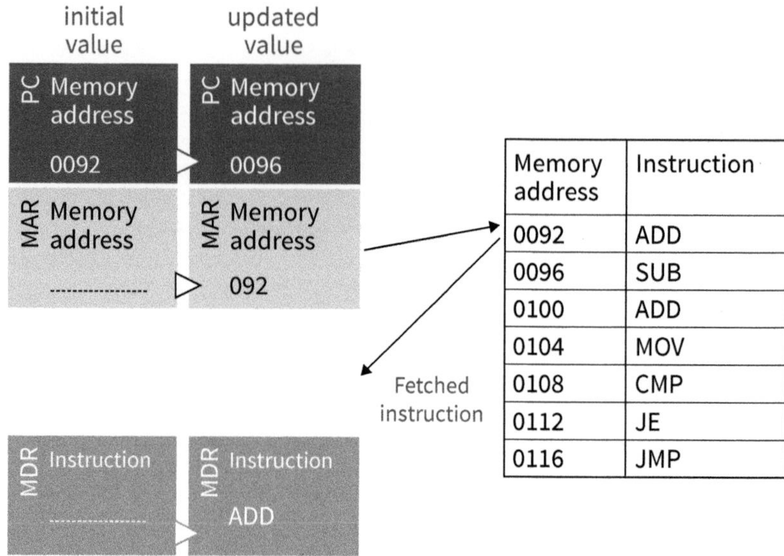

Memory address	Instruction
0092	ADD
0096	SUB
0100	ADD
0104	MOV
0108	CMP
0112	JE
0116	JMP

Figure 1.12: The content of registers change during the FDE cycle.

Figure 1.12 shows how the registers are altered in the first step of the cycle and sets up the fetch part of the cycle. In order to fetch, the address found in the MAR is looked up in memory and the contents of that memory address are loaded into the MDR. As memory is much slower than the processor, the fetch could take a number of clock cycles to complete and depends on whether the data is found in cache memory. One of the key design goals of the FDE cycle is that when one instruction is being fetched, the previous one is being decoded and executed. This is why it is necessary to have separate registers for fetching and executing instructions.

In order for the processor to execute the instruction after the fetch, it must decode the **opcode** part of the instruction. The contents of MDR are copied over to the CIR. From here the instruction can be decoded and then executed, and as this is happening the next instruction can be fetched. Figure 1.13 shows what the registers look like during the second stage of the FDE cycle. As the first instruction, ADD, is being decoded, the second one is being fetched while the PC is pointing to the third. That way, the processor is always trying to be one step ahead of itself in order to make efficient use of memory and clock cycles.

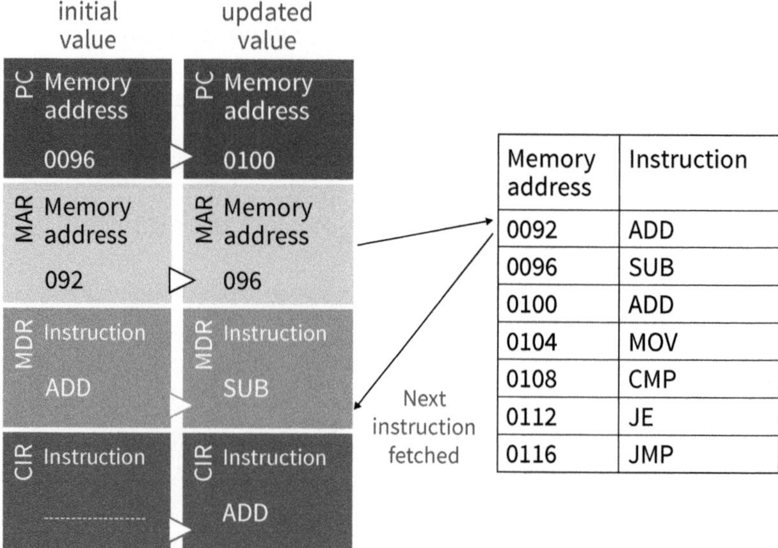

Memory address	Instruction
0092	ADD
0096	SUB
0100	ADD
0104	MOV
0108	CMP
0112	JE
0116	JMP

Figure 1.13: Registers during the second stage of the FDE cycle.

The cycle is designed to perform as many actions of the processor concurrently as possible, thus improving the overall speed of execution.

In nearly any program, at some point a control instruction that will force a jump from one instruction to another that is not in sequence will be encountered. The most common such instruction is a jump. A jump breaks the FDE cycle and forces it to start again from scratch, because the next instruction that has been fetched, the next one in sequence, is not the next instruction that should be executed. Consider the instruction JE 0092 (jump if equal to address 0092) and the CMP command has returned true for equality (Figure 1.14), executing this instruction will cause a break in the linear flow of the program and will update the PC to be 0092.

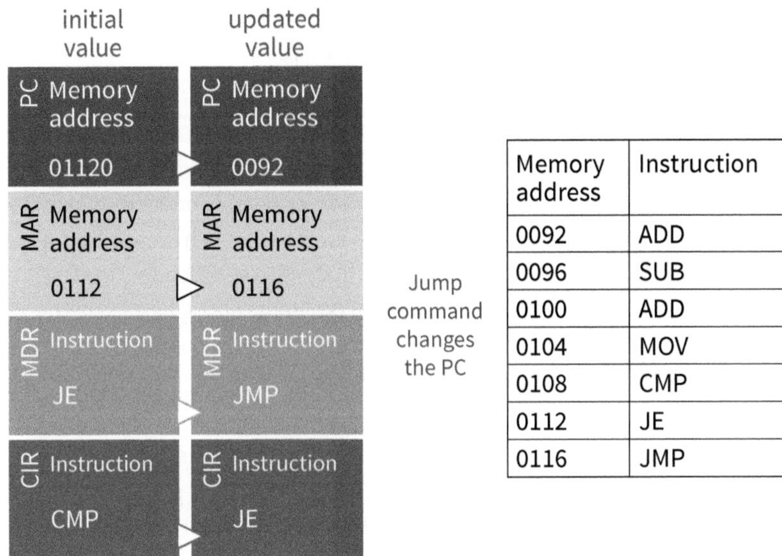

Memory address	Instruction
0092	ADD
0096	SUB
0100	ADD
0104	MOV
0108	CMP
0112	JE
0116	JMP

Figure 1.14: A jump command changes the PC.

Jumps slow down the processor by losing the benefits of pipelining. When programming in assembly, or when a compiler optimises code, it is important to limit the number of jump commands.

Pipelining

Pipelining can be compared to an assembly line for a car, where certain parts have to be assembled before others can be added. If each car is built independently, parts of the assembly line will be idle for the majority of the time. By having a continuous assembly line, where each section of the line is always working on something, the overall efficiency is increased. The assembly line does not increase the speed of production of a single car, but does mean that more cars can be produced in the same amount of time. Processor pipelines work in the exact same way, with each part of the processor working at the same time, fetching the next instruction while executing the last one. However, some instructions may take longer than simple ones. For example, a jump instruction will take longer to perform than addition. This creates a delay in the pipeline called a bubble. Bubbles lead to inefficiency because the pipeline is not being fully utilised in every clock cycle. One solution is to use a branch predictor, which attempts to guess the target of a jump instruction. For example, a loop may be executed more than once so the branch predictor will base its guess on the previous target address. Sometimes, an instruction in the pipeline depends on the output of the previous instruction, which may not yet be available. In this case, the processor can insert a no operation or NOOP instruction, which creates a slight delay in the pipeline. An alternative is called scoreboarding. This uses a flag bit to indicate when registers have been written to after the decode stage. This removes the need to insert a NOOP instruction into the pipeline.

Types of processor

You have seen one type of processor architecture (von Neumann), but there are many other types of architecture and many different ways of implementing them. Generally, however, computer architectures can be categorised as either RISC or CISC.

Reduced instruction set computer (RISC)

RISC architectures support only a small number of very simple instructions, which can be completed in a single clock cycle. This means that individual instructions are executed extremely quickly, but more instructions are needed to complete a given task.

RISC processors were developed in the 1980s when it was realised that most computer programs use only a very small number of the available instructions (around 20%). Creating an architecture that used only the most popular instructions meant much more efficient processing. A side effect of the simpler instructions set is that RISC architectures need a greater number of registers to provide faster access to data when programs are being executed.

Complex instruction set computer (CISC)

CISC architectures support a large number of complicated instructions. This means that instructions can take many clock cycles to complete, as a single CISC instruction might be made up of a number of smaller RISC-type instructions. Thus, CISC processors operate with higher clock speeds than RISC. However, they can support a much wider range of addressing modes. When many programs were written in assembly language, CISC processors were very popular, as writing programs for them is much easier.

RISC and CISC compared

The main difference between RISC and CISC is the CPU time taken to execute a given program. CPU time is generally calculated using the following formula:

$$\text{CPU time} = [(\text{number of instructions}) \times (\text{average cycles per instruction}) \times (\text{seconds per cycle})]$$

RISC architectures seek to shorten execution time by reducing the *average clock cycles per instruction*. Conversely, CISC systems try to shorten execution time by reducing the *number of instructions per program*.

RISC	CISC
Simple instructions	Complex instructions (often made up of many simpler instructions)
Fewer instructions	A large range of instructions
Fewer addressing modes	Many addressing modes
Only LOAD and STORE instructions can access memory	Many instructions can access memory
Processor hardware is more simple	Processor more complex

Table 1.7: Table showing the differences between RISC and CISC.

Activity 1.2

This task requires you to use Linux. This can be done by installing a Linux distribution of your choice, using a Raspberry Pi or using a virtual machine. Note: The commands listed below will not work on a Windows computer.

The following tasks are not designed to teach you assembly programming. It is simply designed to give you a taste of what assembly looks like when applied to a simple C program.

1 Check that the required packages are installed on your Linux box. Run the command **apt-cache policy gcc** . If you see 'Installed: none' then **run sudo apt-get install gcc**.

Run the command **nano helloWorld.c** and enter the code from the code below.

```
#include <stdio.h>
int main(){
printf("Hello World\n");
}

```

2 Compile the program using gcc. The command is **gcc -g helloWorld.c -o helloWorld**

3 Note: The -g option is needed for disassembling.

4 Start the gdb debugger by entering the command **gdb helloWorld**.

5 To view the assembly code you need to disassemble your program. The -g option in gcc adds debugging information, which means that when disassembled it will correlate source code with machine code. Enter the command **disas /m main** – this works on function names.

6 The string helloWorld has been saved at the memory location pointed to by the mov command.

7 Enter the command **x/s 0x4005e4**. (Enter the memory location of your mov command!). Now enter the command **x/4x 0x4005e4**. This will show you the byte (in hex). It should be 6c6c6568 (assuming you used helloWorld as your text). 68 is hexadecimal for 'h' in ascii, 65 is 'e' and 6c is 'l'.

8 Add 9 to the last hex value of the address specified by the mov command. In the example in image 2.1 this would be e4. Adding 9 would make it ec. Now run the command **x/4x 0x4005ec**.

9 Notice that the last byte is 0x00. This is how the computer knows when the string ends. This is known as the null character.

Multicore systems

The classic von Neumann architecture uses only a single processor to execute instructions. In order to improve the computing power of processors, it was necessary to increase the physical complexity of the CPU. Traditionally this was done by finding new, ingenious ways of fitting more and more transistors onto the same size chip. There was even a rule called Moore's Law, which predicted that the number of transistors that could be placed on a chip would double every two years.

However, as computer scientists reached the physical limit of the number of transistors that could be placed on a silicon chip, it became necessary to find other means of increasing the processing power of computers. One of the most effective means of doing this came about through the creation of multicore systems (computers with multiple processors).

Parallel systems

One of the most common types of multicore system is the parallel processor. They tend to be referred to as dual-core (two processors) or quad-core (four processors) computers.

In parallel processing, two or more processors work together to perform a single task. The task is split into smaller sub-tasks (threads). These tasks are executed simultaneously by all available processors (any task can be processed by any of the processors). This hugely decreases the time taken to execute a program, but software has to be specially written to take advantage of these multicore systems.

Parallel computing systems are generally placed in one of three categories:

- Multiple instruction, single data (MISD) systems have multiple processors, with each processor using a different set of instructions on the same set of data.
- Single instruction, multiple data (SIMD) computers have multiple processors that follow the same set of instructions, with each processor taking a different set of data. Essentially SIMD computers process lots of different data concurrently, using the same algorithm.
- Multiple instruction, multiple data (MIMD) computers have multiple processors, each of which is able to process instructions independently of the others. This means that an MIMD computer can truly process a number of different instructions simultaneously. MIMD is probably the most common parallel computing architecture. Desktop computers and supercomputers are both examples of MIMD architecture.

All the processors in a parallel processing system act in the same way as standard single-core (von Neumann) CPUs, loading instructions and data from memory and acting accordingly. However, the different processors in a multicore system need to communicate continuously with each other in order to ensure that if one processor changes a key piece of data (for example, the players' scores in a game), the other processors are aware of the change and can incorporate it into their calculations. There is also a huge amount of additional complexity involved in implementing parallel processing, because when each separate core (processor) has completed its own task, the results from all the cores need to be combined to form the complete solution to the original problem.

This complexity meant that in the early days of parallel computing it was still sometimes faster to use a single processor, as the additional time taken to coordinate communication between processors and combine their results into a single solution was greater than the time saved by sharing the workload. However, as programmers have become more adept at writing software for parallel systems, this has become less of an issue.

Co-processors

Another common way of implementing a multi-processor system is by using a co-processor. Like parallel processing, this involves adding another processor to the computer, but in a co-processor system the additional processor is responsible for carrying out a specific task, such as graphics processing or advanced mathematical operations. The co-processor and the central processor operate on different tasks at the same time, which has the effect of speeding up the overall execution of the program. This is one of the reasons why computers with graphics cards run computer games much more smoothly than those without. However, the co-processor cannot operate in its own right, whereas a CPU can.

Some common examples of co-processors are:

- Floating point units (FPU) – these are built into the main CPU and run floating point mathematical operations. These tend to be more processor intensive than standard arithmetic.
- Digital signal processor (DSP) – commonly used to process sound effects and merge sound channels so that they can be output in stereo or surround sound.
- Graphics processing units (GPU) – most modern computers have a GPU installed, either on the motherboard or on a separate card. These perform the massively complex 3D calculations needed for games, transparency effects used to make the user interface look good, and so on. You will learn more about GPUs in the next section.

Advantages and disadvantages of multicore systems

Advantages	Disadvantages
More jobs can be done in a shorter time because they are executed simultaneously.	It is difficult to write programs for multicore systems, ensuring that each task has the correct input data to work on.
Tasks can be shared to reduce the load on individual processors and avoid bottlenecks.	Results from different processors need to be combined at the end of processing, which can be complex and adds to the time taken to execute a program.
	Not all tasks can be split across multiple processors.

Table 1.8: Table showing the advantages and disadvantages of a parallel computer.

GPUs and their uses

A graphics processing unit (GPU) is a type of processor (similar to the traditional CPU) that is dedicated to performing the very complex calculations necessary to render graphics. They are a common example of a co-processing system.

GPUs are usually located on a separate graphics card and most require their own heat sink to function properly. The two most common makers of GPUs are NVIDIA and ATI, with each company using its own hardware design and specialist programming techniques to try to ensure that its graphics cards provide the biggest increase in performance.

The quality of graphics produced by different GPUs and their associated graphics cards varies hugely. For example, the standard integrated graphics chip that you might get on a netbook is suitable for using Microsoft PowerPoint but won't be able to handle more complex tasks such as running the latest computer games.

As GPUs have become more powerful they have attracted attention from those outside the traditional gaming and graphics editing communities. Today, GPUs can run faster and more cost-efficiently than CPUs in a huge number of areas, ranging from medical

Activity 1.3

Visit a website that sells computers and find two computers: one with a single core and one with multiple cores. What is the difference in cost? Do you think the extra performance is worth the money? Explain.

and scientific research to oil and gas exploration and financial modelling. One firm specialising in high-performance financial computing has even found that running financial models on a GPU produced results almost 700 times faster than running the same analysis on a CPU alone.

Activity 1.4

Bitcoin mining is one area where GPUs were widely used. Have a look at newer methods and try to find out why GPUs have become a less popular option.

Computing in context: overclocking

Most GPUs are capable of running at a faster speed than the manufacturer specifies. Manufacturers try to strike a balance between getting a good performance and not burning the card out, so the speed they set for the card is a compromise, which means the graphics are not as good as they could be, but the card will last for a reasonable length of time before it stops working.

Most serious gamers are prepared to take more risk than the manufacturers in a quest for better graphics, so they will improve their GPU's performance by manually setting the clock speed to the highest possible rate. This activity is called overclocking and, while it results in better graphics processing, it almost certainly voids the manufacturer's warranty.

As you might expect, overclocked GPUs produce much more heat than those running to the manufacturer's specification. They therefore require extra cooling systems, such as larger heat sinks and fans, to stop damage occurring.

Overclocking used to be a very technical activity carried out by elite gamers, but these days most graphics cards' control panels contain some sort of overclocking functionality.

Summary

- A CPU is made up of the following components:
  - ALU – arithmetic logic unit
  - MU – memory unit
  - CU – control unit.
- Machine code instructions are written in binary and are made up of an opcode and data.
- Little Man Computer is a simplified architecture used to help learners understand the basics of low-level programming.
- The fetch-decode-execute (FDE) cycle will fetch instructions from memory to be run on the CPU. During the cycle the following registers are used:
  - MAR – memory address register, which stores the address of the instruction to fetch
  - MDR – memory data register, which stores the data or instruction once fetched
  - PC – program counter, which stores the address of the next instruction to fetch
  - CIR – current instruction register, from where the instruction will be decoded and executed.
- Cache is fast memory that sits between memory and the CPU. It is used to help remove the impact of the von Neumann bottleneck.
- Processors, to improve the throughput of instructions, perform parts of the FDE cycle concurrently, which is known as pipelining.
- Reduced instruction set (RISC) processors use a small set of simple instructions.
- Complex instruction set (CISC) processors use a large set of complex instructions.
- A multicore system is a common architecture where processors have more than one core allowing multiple processes to be run concurrently.
- Parallel systems are made up of multiple processors in order to perform multiple operations concurrently. Code must be written in such a way as to take advantage of any parallelism.

- Co-processors take the burden off the main processor by performing certain tasks on the processor's behalf.
- Graphics processing units (GPU) are used to process complex 3D graphics calculations to improve the performance of graphics-intensive processes such as games.

End-of-chapter questions

1 Describe the following components of a CPU.

a Control unit [2]

b Arithmetic logic unit [2]

c Memory unit [2]

2 Assembly code allows developers to produce programs using mnemonics.

a Explain the relationship between mnemonics and machine code instructions. [2]

b Explain how machine code instructions are structured. [2]

3 Most computing devices will contain cache memory.

a Explain the purpose of cache memory. [2]

b Describe how cache memory can help overcome the von Neumann bottleneck. [4]

A **4** Describe how the FDE cycle is used by the CPU and how pipelining can be used to make the process more efficient. [8]

5 Describe the relationship between assembly code and a high-level language of your choice. Give examples of when you may use assembly code over a high-level language and vice versa. [8]

6 What are the main characteristics of a RISC architecture? [4]

7 What are the main characteristics of a CISC architecture? [4]

8 In a multicore system what is the purpose of a co-processor? [2]

9 In a multicore system what is meant by parallel processing? [2]

A **10** Other than graphics processing, give one use of a GPU. [1]

Further reading

How AMD make CPUs – search on Youtube for 'How a CPU is made' on the HadronMesons channel.
How Intel make CPUs – search the Intel Newsroom website for 'From Sand to Silicon: The Making of a Chip'
CISC and RISC architectures – Search for RISC architecture on the Stanford Computer Science website (cs.stanford.edu)
Parallel processing – search the Princeton website for 'Parallel processing'
Von Neumann architecture – search for Von Neumann architecture on c-jump.com
EDVAC computer – search for EDVAC on 'The History of Computing' website.
Zargham, M. (1996) *Computer Architecture*, London: Prentice Hall, Ch 2.

Chapter 2
Input, output and storage

Specification points

1.1.3 Input, output and storage

- How different input, output and storage devices can be applied as a solution of different problems.
- The uses of magnetic, flash and optical storage devices.
- RAM and ROM.
- Virtual storage.

Learning objectives

- To understand the main components of a computing system.
- To understand the key features of systems software and how they differ from application software.
- To have an overview of the key internal hardware that is essential in any computing system.
- To understand key input devices and how they could be used in a computing system.

Introduction

In this chapter you will explore the main components and concepts of standard computing systems. Many of the ideas shared in this chapter are expanded in later chapters. By the end of the course you will get the chance to build your own computing system following the systems lifecycle and a methodology appropriate to your chosen user. It is crucial that, by the end of the project, you have an appreciation of the scope of computing and that you understand that every computing system, regardless of its complexity, contains the same components.

Computing systems may differ, but they all have the same basic structure as shown below.

Software

Software comprises a series of instructions, which are executed by the microprocessor. It is written by programmers to perform a variety of tasks for the user of a computing system. In order to perform any task, from writing a document to playing a game, software is required.

Software type	Overview
System	Will manage both software and hardware and is required in order to run any other type of software.
Utility	Software used to support the operating system and other software. Most utilities are supplied when the OS is installed. However, the user can install more or replace the ones already installed.
Generic	Software, such as a word processor, that can perform multiple tasks and be used to produce different types and styles of document.
Bespoke	Specially built software for a specific purpose. Normally commissioned by a company to support their business. Bespoke software will not be sold on or used for different purposes than it was originally intended.

Table 2.1: Different software types.

Memory

Random-access memory (RAM)

All devices that contain a microprocessor have memory. Memory can store data and programs and it is used to store values currently in use by the computer. Memory access times are much faster than a hard drive, which is why programs are loaded into memory before being executed by the CPU. A memory chip will have a size, which is normally given in either megabytes or gigabytes. Memory is split up into storage blocks, where each block is given a numeric value known as a memory address. The number of available blocks is governed by the size of the memory. Each block can store data or instructions. What the memory is used for will determine what will be stored inside it.

Address	0	1	2	3	4	5	6	7	8
Data	C	O	M	P	U	T	I	N	G

Table 2.2: A small section of memory with addresses and its contents.

Each block inside memory is numbered. This starts at 0 and goes up in fixed sizes until it gets to the end. For example, a 1 GB memory chip contains about 270 000 000 memory addresses. To access or store data, you need to know the address of where it is stored. For example, the 'P' is stored at address 3. If you try to store another value at address 3, it will overwrite the 'P'.

It's common for modern computers to have 4 GB of memory or more. Many people know that more memory means a faster computer. However, not many people know the reasons why. RAM stores what the user is currently working on as well as the operating system and any applications currently open. It is much faster than the hard drive, which is known as secondary storage. The CPU must load instructions and data into its registers in order to work on them. This must be done by loading the programs and data into primary memory first. The CPU then loads instructions and data from main memory into registers.

When the computer is switched off, any information stored in main memory is lost. This is why it is important to save work to secondary storage. Memory that is wiped when power is turned off is known as volatile memory.

Read-only memory (ROM)

 Tip

You must be able to describe the differences between RAM and ROM. Specifically, you must explain how they differ in the type of data they store.

Read-only memory or **ROM** stores essential **systems software** needed for the running of the computer. It stores software that helps begin the computers' start-up and also ensures its smooth running. It does not usually store the operating system except in very simple computer systems such as that in a found washing machine. The OS tends to be stored on the hard drive. The user cannot change settings, as it is read-only memory. It is important that system start-up software is stored in ROM, as it is required the second the computer is switched on. It provides the instructions to the CPU to tell it how hardware should be initialised and how the boot loader is executed. ROM is non-volatile, which is why start-up software is located inside it.

Input and output devices

Input devices allow interaction with a computing system. This could be through a standard interface, such as a mouse or keyboard, or through more advanced interfaces such as a gesture recognition games controller. Once data has been captured by an input device, it must be processed by software before information can be output to the user.

Scanners

Scanners take printed media, a photo or a page of text, and then generate a bitmap image from it. A common use for scanners is to digitise photos (taken with old 35 mm cameras) or to perform optical character recognition (OCR). To scan a document, it is placed face down on the glass and a special sensor travels the full length of the document, converting it into binary data as it goes (Figure 2.1).

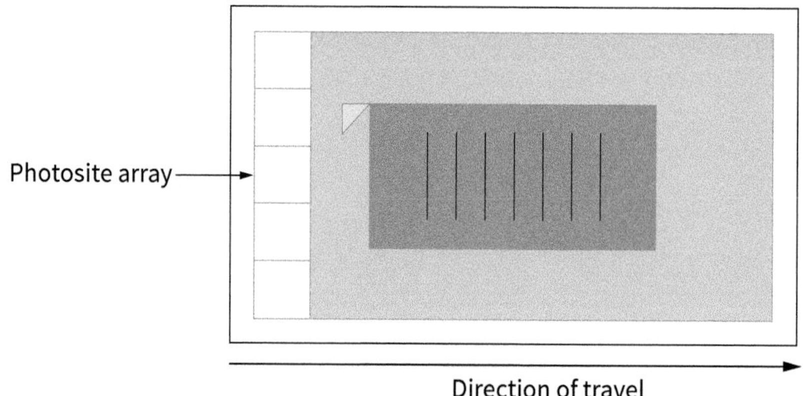

Figure 2.1: OCR scanner.

When an image is digitised, it is converted into a series of dots or pixels (Figure 2.2). The pixels are then stored as binary data based on the colour of the pixel. If the bitmap image being produced is 24-bit, then each pixel will be 3 bytes in size.

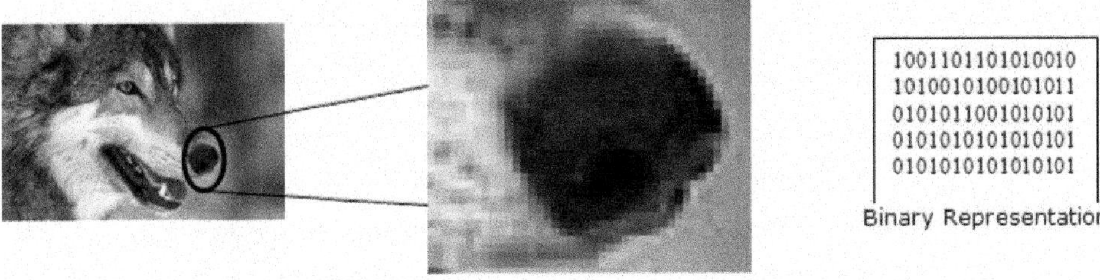

Figure 2.2: Images are made of pixels which contain binary codes representing colours.

Optical character recognition (OCR)

Optical character recognition (OCR) converts printed media into editable text documents using a scanner. Figure 2.3 shows the features of a scanner. . OCR enables the user to change sections of text on a printed document. It also means that old books, for example, can be digitised, allowing them to be published in new formats for new markets such as e-readers.

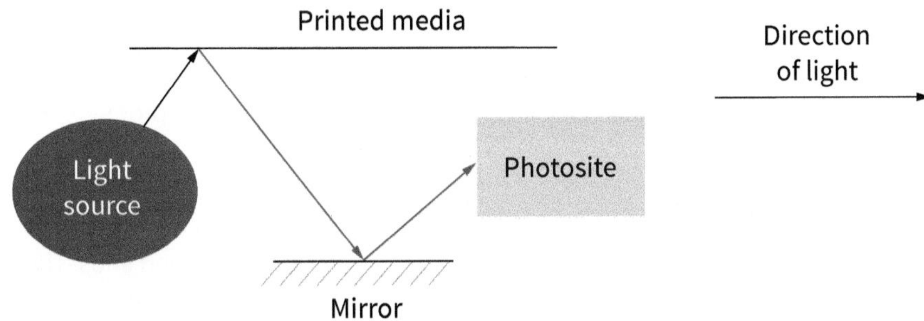

Figure 2.3: Diagram showing how light is reflected onto a document and then read by a scanner.

OCR is a post-processing step that occurs after a document has been scanned. It performs pattern matching by scanning the image for shapes it can recognise as letters, numbers or symbols. This is done by comparing the binary data to an internal database of known character shapes. When a binary shape is found in a document, OCR transforms it (resizes and rotates it) until it matches a known shape from the database. If no match is found, that shape is skipped.

It is very easy for a human to read text from a document but very complicated for a computer to do it. This is why OCR will sometimes get it wrong, so the resulting document must be proofread.

Optical mark recognition (OMR)

Optical mark recognition (OMR) is based around a predefined form, which has areas where someone can mark multiple-choice responses (Figure 2.4). The form has specific parts for someone to fill out by putting a thick black mark on them. A special reader then reads in this form in order to detect the dark marks and note the position of them on the page. As the form is predefined, the scanner knows what option the user has selected. If two marks are made in the same section, the reader accepts only one of the answers, most likely the first one. Also, if the mark does not cover the whole of the rectangle, the reader may miss it. This type of input is used for multiple-choice exams and registers, as they can be automatically marked and processed. It is not suitable for any form of written communication.

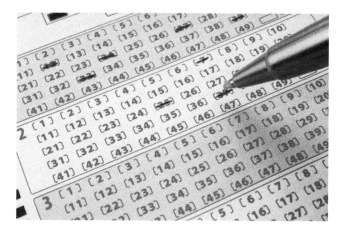

Figure 2.4: A typical input sheet for an OMR reader.

Tip

You will be given computing scenarios where you have to decide which input and output devices would be most suitable. When revising input devices, you should always consider why they are used, as well as how they work.

Barcode scanners

Barcodes are a series of black and white lines, found on the back of most products, which are used to store a unique key for that product (Figure 2.5). The barcode allows devices reading the barcode to look up data about the product on a database. Different values are represented by different thicknesses of lines. At the start and end of the barcode there are terminators that allow the reader to know when the barcode begins and ends. They are slightly different, so when the scanner reads over the barcode it can determine the orientation of the code. This means that the reader can read the code upside down. The number beneath the barcode allows humans to read the barcode.

Figure 2.5: A barcode is a unique identifier for products and information.

A barcode reader runs a laser across the barcode in a line. The laser reflects back to the reader and a different value will be detected depending on whether the laser was reflected from a black or white line. The laser travels at a constant speed across the barcode and looks for the edges of the lines or a change in the reflected value. This information is then used to calculate the length of the bar and thus the numeric value it represents.

In order to ensure that the value read in by the scanner is correct, a check digit validation is used. Check digits are calculated based on the rest of the code and are stored alongside the barcode. When the barcode is read, the reader recalculates the check digit and compares the result with the check digit it read in. If they differ, an error must have occurred and the barcode will be rejected.

A check digit is calculated by:

- Finding the sum of all even digits and adding it to a total.
- Every odd number is multiplied by 3 before adding to the total.
- Dividing the result by 10 and taking the remainder.
- Subtract the remainder from 10 to get the final check digit.

Barcode uses

Each barcode is unique and represents a specific set of data inside a database. In a supermarket, information about price and stock is stored in a database and the barcode allows access to this data. As well as accessing information from the database, it can also be used to update stock levels through an automated stock control system. Every product has a current stock level stored within the database and as products are bought, this value decreases. Most shops have an automated ordering system, which will, if the stock of an item gets too low, order more products using the preferred supplier. When more stock arrives at the shop, the current stock level is increased proportionally.

Warehouses and delivery firms also use barcodes to keep track of deliveries and packages. When a parcel arrives at a warehouse, it is scanned and its location noted in a database. As each parcel has a unique barcode, this system allows individual parcels to be tracked. At every stage of the parcel's journey it is scanned in and out. Online parcel tracking uses this information to let you know when a parcel is out for delivery. It is also used when new stock arrives. In any given situation, barcodes can be used to read data from a database or update values within a database.

Tip

Questions on barcodes tend to carry a lot of marks. They may be based around scenarios, for example, a standard shop and stock control system or a warehouse-based system. Be careful to read the question to find out what type of system it is referring to. Also, notice whether the question is asking how barcodes work or how they are used.

Magnetic ink recognition (MICR)

Magnetic ink recognition uses a combination of ink containing iron oxide and specific fonts so that data written using this ink can be read by a specialist MICR reader. Normal ink does not contain iron oxide, so only the MICR ink will be picked up by the reader, effectively ignoring everything else. This means that regardless of what is written over the magnetic ink, it can still be read by the device.

This is almost exclusively used for cheques because of the high cost of the reader (Figure 2.6). The cheque number and account number are written on the bottom of each cheque using magnetic ink. This can be very quickly read in by the reader, so cheques can be processed quickly by the banks. One of the key benefits of MICR is that it does not have to rely on OCR, which can be problematic.

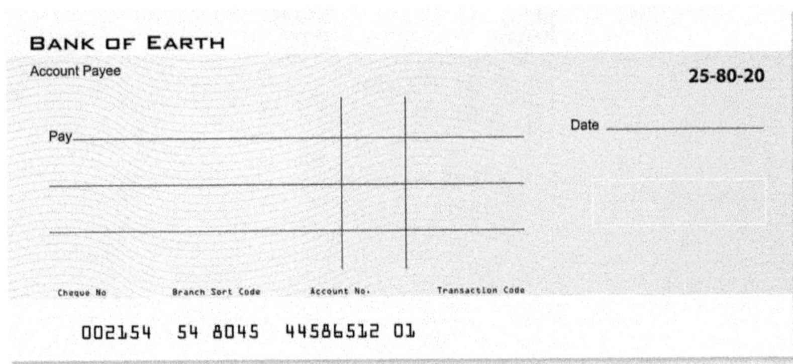

Figure 2.6: A standard bank cheque; notice the number in electronic ink along the bottom.

Sensors and actuators

Sensors can be found in a wide range of devices such as mobile phones, cars, cookers and even games consoles. A sensor records some data from the physical environment.

Common sensors include:

- pressure sensor
- mercury tilt switch or accelerometer
- luminance sensor (light)
- humidity sensor
- infrared sensor.

Data recorded by a sensor must be converted from analogue to digital and then processed by software. For a sensor to work correctly it must either contain an ADC (analogue-to-digital converter) or be connected to one. When the values from a sensor are processed, some form of output will result. This could be using standard output devices, such as a virtual display unit (VDU), but it also can be physical motion. In the case of physical motion, an actuator must be used. An actuator is an output device which can cause physical movement. Examples include conveyor belts on electronic point of sales (EPOS) systems, and automatic doors.

Sensors and actuators form what is known as a feedback loop (Figure 2.7). When a sensor detects a change, it tells an actuator to make a physical change to the system. This could, in turn, cause a change in what the sensors are detecting, which in turn could cause further activation of the actuator.

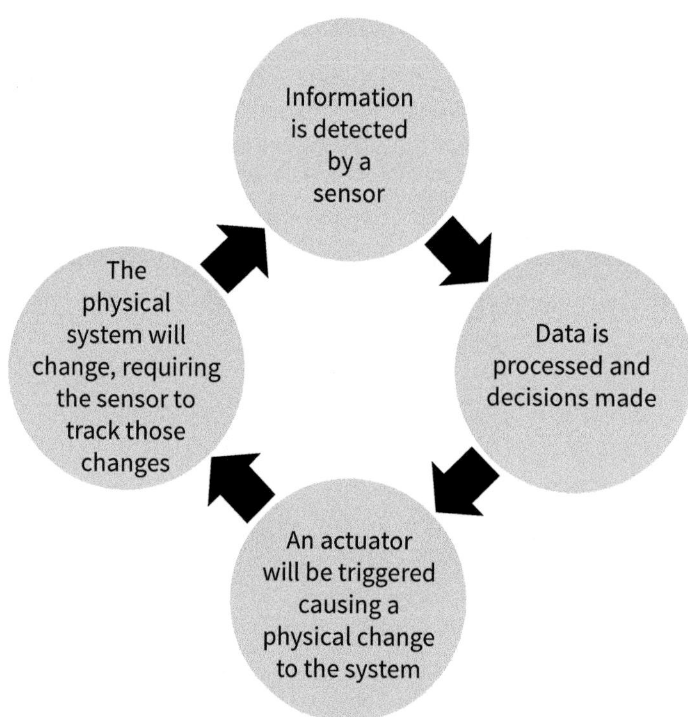

Figure 2.7: Feedback loop.

Tip

Questions on sensors and actuators will always be given in a context. The context may be unfamiliar, but the basic ideas will always be the same. When describing the feedback loop, make sure you relate it back to the question and context given.

Touch screens

Touch screens are very popular in most modern computing devices, especially with the release of Windows 8, which is focused on providing a touch screen interface. Most laptops, desktops and the majority of mobile phones have a touch screen interface. Even satellite navigation and printers have touch screens. There are two types of touch screen, resistive and capacitive; both versions send the X and Y coordinates of the touch to the operating system when a touch is registered. It works using a grid system, with the screen being split up as shown in Figure 2.8 below. The Y-axis increases in value going down rather than up, which is different from what you may be used to in mathematics.

Resistive touch screens are much cheaper and are made up of two thin transparent sheets. When these sheets touch each other, a voltage is recorded at that position. A certain amount of pressure is needed to make the sheets touch, which is why this type of touch screen is known as resistive. These screens do not provide as sharp an image as capacitive screens, nor do they allow for multiple touches.

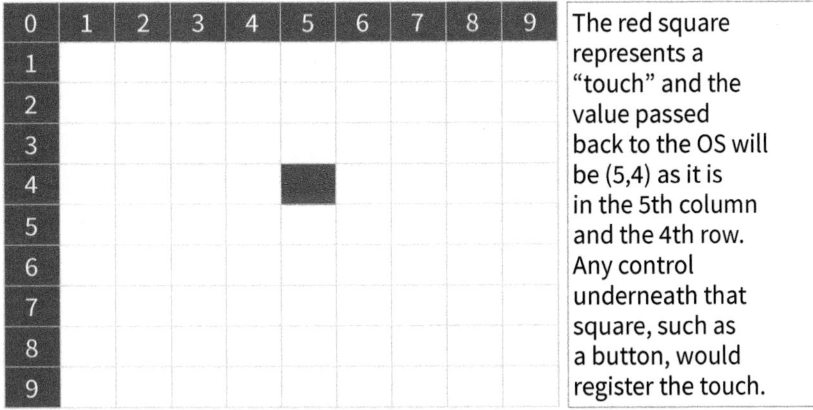

0 1 2 3 4 5 6 7 8 9
1
2
3
4
5
6
7
8
9
The red square represents a "touch" and the value passed back to the OS will be (5,4) as it is in the 5th column and the 4th row. Any control underneath that square, such as a button, would register the touch.

Figure 2.8: A touch screen grid.

Capacitive touch screens allow for a much sharper image and for multiple touch points to be recorded simultaneously, making them superior to, and more expensive than, resistive touch screens. Capacitive touch screens make use of the fact that the human body can conduct electricity; when you touch a capacitive screen you change the electric field of the area you touched. This change in field registers as a click and sends the X and Y coordinates back to the OS. One downside, apart from the expense, is that you cannot make use of a capacitive screen when wearing gloves or using items such as a pen, as they do not conduct electricity.

Storage devices

Computing systems that need to save information in between uses will have some form of storage device. Magnetic hard drives (HDD) are very common in desktop and laptop computers, but increasingly solid-state drives (SSD) are being used. Tablet computers, smartphones and some modern laptops or desktops make use of SSD as their main storage device.

Storage devices in a computing system commonly store:

- the operating system and common utilities
- user applications
- user documents and files.

Magnetic storage devices

A hard drive is a high-capacity storage medium, common in most modern computers. Hard drives are used to store the operating system, software and user data. As hard drives have a fast transfer rate and a fairly fast access time, they provide a good compromise between storage capacity, performance and cost. Their speed does not come close to the speed of memory or the CPU.

Hard drives are a magnetic medium and store data on a hard drive platter (Figure 2.9). Data is read and saved using an arm that has a special read head at the end. As the disc spins, the arm travels across the disc. Each sector of the platter can store data and the movement of both the disc and the read head means that every sector on the hard drive can be reached. In order to read or write data, a small magnetic flux is introduced on the disc. The oxide on the hard drive platter remembers this flux.
Data is then encoded using standard binary techniques, with the flux able to store either a 1 or a 0.

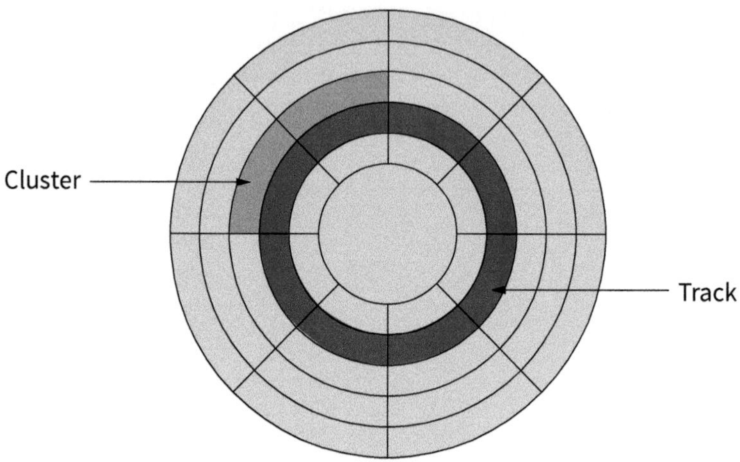

Figure 2.9: Hard drive platter.

The faster the platter spins, the faster data can be read from the disc. This speed is measured in revolutions per minute, or RPM. A common speed for most hard drives is 7200 RPM, but it can vary. Every minute that a 7200 RPM hard drive is in use, the platter will have spun 7200 times. Hard drives can run at 15 000 RPM, but these are expensive and tend to be used in servers rather than in home computers. Laptops use slower drives to conserve power.

As hard drives provide a vital storage for files and programs including the operating system, it is essential that they are well maintained. Hard drives do physically wear and will develop errors over time. These errors are managed by the hard drive and the operating system; however, if there are too many errors, performance can be compromised. Also, these errors can lead to corrupt data. Utilities such as a disc scanner will check for areas of the disc that are causing errors and mark them as bad sectors so that data is not stored in that location.

Flash storage devices

SSDs are becoming more popular in modern computing systems, and use flash memory to store data rather than magnetic discs. They use a special type of memory that can retain its state once power has been disconnected. It is known as EEPROM (electronically erasable programmable read-only memory). SSDs tend to have better performance than hard drives, but also tend to be more expensive and have lower capacity. Performance is increased due to the lack of physical motion. There is no spinning disc or moving read head and thus the time it takes to find data on an SSD is much less. They are also smaller in size and lighter in weight than a magnetic hard drive, so are well suited to use in portable devices such as laptops.

Memory sticks and memory cards, such as secure digital (SD), use solid-state technologies. They all have the same advantages and disadvantages as SSD drives.

Optical drives

Optical drives work by using lasers to store data by burning microscopic indentations into a disc such as a CD. This pattern of indentations is created in a spiral pattern, starting from the middle. Indentations and their absence create pits and lands (Figure 2.10), which are used to store binary data. A laser is aimed at the disc and reflected back, which can cause interference with the original laser. This change in interference is how the optical device can tell the difference between a pit and a land. A DVD uses the same techniques to store data, but the data is stored on two layers. Two lasers of differing wavelength are used to read data from the two layers. Pits and lands are stored closer together, meaning that the laser's wavelength must be shorter.

Optical media tend to be used to store multimedia information or programs, for example DVD movies and music CDs. Programs such as Microsoft Office are distributed on this type of media. The capacity, cost and size of these media make them suitable for storing high-definition data.

Blu-ray follows the same principles but uses a laser with a much smaller wavelength. The laser has a distinctive blue colour, which is why it is referred to as Blu-ray. With a smaller wavelength the pits and lands can be much closer together, allowing more data to be stored.

Figure 2.10: Pits and lands on the surface of a CD.

CD-R and DVD-R can store multimedia or user data onto CDs or DVDs. When a CD is created, it cannot be modified. As such, it is useful for creating a permanent backup over time. As CDs are physically small, they will not take up too much storage space. Rewritable CDs exist; they allow the user to write to them many times.

Storage systems for enterprises

Most of the storage devices considered so far are mainly intended for use by small systems or individual end users. Storage requirements for enterprises, however, are much more demanding. When you have over a thousand people trying to access the same set of files at the same time, some serious hardware is needed. A simple hard drive will not be sufficient.

In order to provide scalability and performance, multiple drives that can be brought together to act as a single drive will be needed. Building a custom network-attached storage (NAS) device can be very expensive. It would be better to bring many disparate devices together and treat them as a single drive. This is known as virtual storage. Before we look at how virtual storage works, it is important to understand a few of the key technologies used for large-scale storage.

Redundant array of independent discs (RAID)

Redundant array of independent discs is one of the most common technologies that run behind the scenes. It can be used with both SSD and HDD, and allows multiple drives to be brought together as a single drive. NASs will commonly support multiple drives and be in some form of RAID array.

Multiple hard drives can sometimes be linked together to improve performance and robustness. Hard drives set up in this way are known as being in a RAID array. This can be in one of the following modes:

- *RAID 0 Striped*: this provides improved performance and additional storage. However, it does not provide any fault tolerance, so any errors on the discs could destroy the RAID array.
- *RAID 1 Mirrored*: each disc provides the same information, which provides some fault tolerance. As data is repeated, read time is increased, but write speed is decreased.
- *RAID 3–4 Striped parity*: this requires three discs in the array. As well as fault tolerance it provides parity checks and error correction. The parity information is stored on a single drive, so the other drives can continue working when one of the drives fails. The lost data can be calculated using the parity data stored on the parity drive.

Storage area network (SANs)

Although RAID offers good storage solutions for most small networks, storage area networks (SANs) offer more features and much greater scalability. Essentially, a SAN acts as a gateway to a series of block devices, such as RAID arrays, and brings them together. A SAN can be seen as a subnet of a network that is solely responsible for serving files. Although the SAN treats each connected storage device as a block-level device, it is possible to run SAN file systems that treat all connected storage devices as a single logical drive.

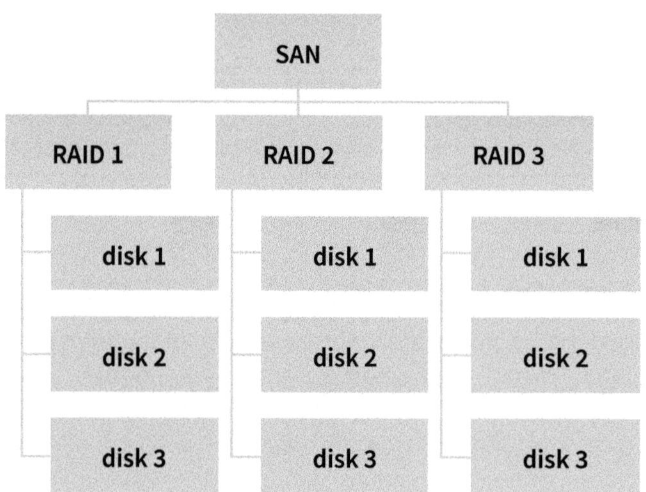

Figure 2.11: SAN with multiple RAID arrays.

Virtual storage

Now, with a basic understanding of RAID and SANs, we can explore the idea of virtual storage or, putting it another way, storage virtualisation. Because SAN and related technologies are very complex, offering an extra layer on top of them to hide their complexity is very desirable for network administrators. Storage virtualisation allows different SANs, RAID arrays and other storage devices to be brought together, offering key services such as backup and archiving. It allows the administration of the individual devices to be done through a central server acting as the virtual storage device. As different SAN technologies could work differently from one another, having a virtual controller that translates generic calls for backup into specific ones understood by the SAN is a great advantage.

Common uses of storage devices

CDs and DVDs

CDs and DVDs are used to install software and store multimedia files. They are not to be used for backup, because once they have been written they cannot be changed.

Tip

You will be given a scenario and have to decide which storage devices should be used, why they should be used and what they will store.

Memory sticks and portable hard drives

Memory sticks are used to transport files from one place to another. They are often referred to as removable media, as they are not permanently installed in the computer system.

Summary

- Random-access memory (RAM) stores the currently running programs, operating systems and user files.
- Read-only memory (ROM) stores the boot-up software required to initialise the hardware, load settings and initiate the operating system (OS).
- Input devices provide data for processing and come in the form of scanners, optical character recognition, optical mark recognition, barcodes, magnetic ink recognition, touch screens and sensors.
- Storage devices store data and programs when the computer is powered down. The main types of storage device are:
  - magnetic – back-up tape and hard drives
  - optical – CD, DVD and Blu-ray
  - solid state – solid-state hard drives, memory sticks and secure digital (SD) cards.
- Redundant arrays of independent discs (RAID) are used in servers and for more data-critical systems. They allow multiple drives to be connected together to form a single drive.
- RAIDs can provide fault tolerance in the form of mirroring and parity bits.
- Storage area networks (SAN) can connect numerous different types of storage device as a single device.
- Virtual storage will abstract the type of storage device in a SAN, allowing devices to be added and removed without having to administer the individual devices.

End-of-chapter questions

1 State what the purpose is of the following buses:

   a Data bus [2]

   b Address bus [2]

   c Control bus [2]

2 State **two** key differences between RAM and ROM. [4]

3 A new coffee shop has opened up and has a self-service coffee machine. You can enter your choices, make a payment and then your coffee is made by the machine. State two input and output devices which could be used by the machine and explain how they would be utilised. [8]

Further reading

VMware virtual SAN explained – search for VMware Virtual SAN on www.networkcomputing.com
How OCR works – search for Optical character recognition on the Explain That Stuff! website.
How to set up a RAID array – search for How to Use Multiple Disks Intelligently on the How to Geek website.

Chapter 3
Systems software

Specification points

1.2.1 Systems software

- The need for, function and purpose of operating systems.
- Memory management (paging, segmentation and virtual memory).
- Interrupts, the role of interrupts and interrupt service routines (ISR), role within the FDE cycle.
- Scheduling: round robin, first come first served, multi-level feedback queues, shortest job first and shortest remaining time.
- Distributed, embedded, multi-tasking, multiuser and real-time operating systems.
- BIOS.
- Device drivers.
- Virtual machines, any instance where software is used to take on the function of a machine, including executing intermediate code or running an operating system within another.

Learning objectives

- Understand the main functionality of operating systems (OS).
- Learn how memory is managed by the OS.
- Learn how scheduling is managed by the OS.
- Learn the main types of OS, including distributed, embedded, multitasking, multiuser and real-time OS.
- Understand the purpose of the basic input/output system (BIOS).

- Understand how devices can be controlled through the use of device drivers.
- Learn how virtual machines work and how different operating systems can be hosted on the same machine.

Introduction

Software can be categorised, with each type responsible for performing a different function. Systems software runs behind the scenes, supported by utility software and applications run on top of it to allow the user to perform tasks. This division of labour means that application developers do not need to worry about how data is saved to the hard drive; they merely have to invoke the OS to perform that task for them. In this chapter, you will look at the role of systems software, with a major focus on the operating system.

Systems and application software

Systems software allows control over the hardware and software of the computer. Systems software is essential in order to perform even the most basic tasks, such as initialising hardware and handling key presses. The two most common types of systems software are the operating system and system start-up software. When considering whether software is system or application, it is important to consider whether that software directly manages the hardware and other software. Some software, such as a camera app on a phone, uses hardware and may seem as if it is managing it. However, it is simply making use of the hardware by interacting with the operating system and hardware drivers.

Application software is software that allows a user to carry out a specific task. For example, Microsoft Outlook® allows a user to send an e-mail. It is essential to make the distinction between commonly used software and the extra software installed with the operating system. Some software bundled with the operating system may be application or utility software. For example, Microsoft Word, although essential for many people, is not systems software; it is an example of generic application software. File Explorer is a utility and not systems software. Other software types will be explored in more detail in Chapter 4.

Overview of the operating system

All software, such as Word® or PaintShop®Pro, makes use of the OS in order to perform basic tasks such as saving files or accessing the hardware. Even opening a new window is handled by the OS. If an application requires a file to be saved, it asks the OS to save it. In order to save the file, the OS needs to make use of a hardware driver, which performs the final save. A hardware driver is utility software that knows how to talk directly to the hard drive. This separation of responsibilities can be seen in Figure 3.1.

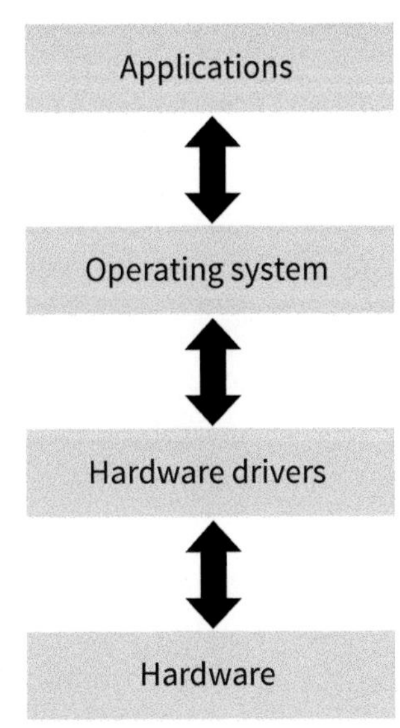

Figure 3.1: The role of an operating system.

The OS is responsible for managing the computer's resources. These include the storage devices, input and output devices, main memory and all software that is running on the computer. When the computer boots up, it will load the main part of the OS into RAM. This part of the OS is responsible for process management, hardware management and other key low-level tasks, and is known as the **kernel**. Once this has been loaded, the user interface part of the OS is loaded alongside key utility software.

The OS is split into different layers and modules in order to perform its key responsibilities (Figure 3.2). Each key module is responsible for a different task under the OS remit. Although every OS shares the same modules, how they perform their tasks can differ significantly. Some of the key modules are listed below:

- *Memory manager* – responsible for splitting RAM into chunks called segments and assigning them to different processes based on need. It is also responsible for handling virtual memory.

- *Process manager/scheduler* – responsible for managing processes, dealing with multitasking and deciding the order in which processes should be run.
- *File manager* – responsible for managing the file systems of secondary storage devices.

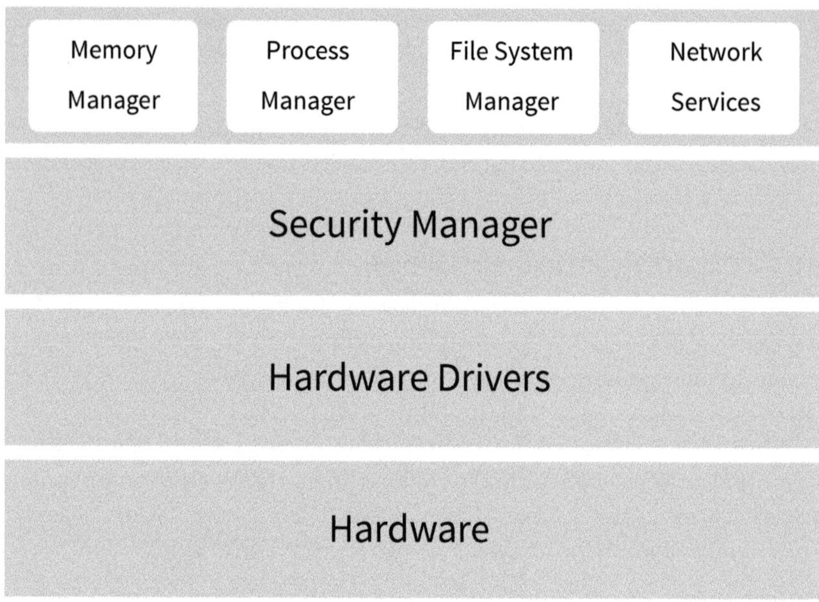

Figure 3.2: The layers of an operating system.

Memory management

A standard computer contains memory (RAM) that is shared between processes and managed by the OS. The instructions of a process must be stored in RAM as well as any data that is being worked upon. The OS must also have the kernel, the essential part of the OS, in memory, together with any modules required to allow management of the system at a given moment. With all of this data located in RAM, it can get overloaded very quickly, which is one of the key reasons why a memory manager is essential. Before we look at how the memory manager works, we must understand some of the key design goals for memory management:

- Allocate enough memory so that each process can run.
- Split memory up so that it can be allocated to processes (paging/segmentation).
- Ensure security so that other processes cannot access each other's data.
- Allow efficient sharing of memory.
- Extend memory by using virtual memory.

The memory manager must split RAM into workable chunks and allocate these to processes in a fair manner. As processes start and stop at different times and have different memory demands, keeping track of what memory is free becomes a challenge. Allocation of RAM can be done through two managing techniques that will be explored in this chapter, both employing a table to monitor which process has been allocated which chunk of memory. This allows RAM to be shared without worrying about any processes

> **Tip**
>
> Systems software in this course refers to start-up software and the OS. As such, systems software is *not* the OS; rather, the OS is an *example* of systems software.

accidentally overwriting each other or gaining unauthorised access, as their access will be strictly monitored by the OS.

Security is a core concern for memory management. If processes could inspect or change each other's memory, this could bypass many security protocols put in place to protect user data. For example, if a process could inspect the data from your web browser, it could very easily manipulate what you see on screen. When a program decrypts something, the plain text will be visible inside that process's memory, making it easy pickings for spyware. Finally, the last consideration is the use of virtual memory to extend memory beyond what is physically available.

RAM will hold:

- the OS
- currently running programs
- current files and data you are working on.

Memory addressing

In order to understand memory management, you need to understand the basics of memory addressing, which is how an individual byte of data can be found in RAM. Instructions and data are all stored in the same memory space. Each byte in memory is numbered, starting from 0, and this number is referred to as an address. In the table below, the text 'hello' is stored, with each letter having its own individual memory address. Memory addresses are essentially the position of a specific byte of data in RAM.

0	1	2	3	4	5	6	7	8	**Address**
H	E	L	L	O					**Data**

Figure 3.3: Data stored in memory.

In the above example, the text starts at address 0 and ends at address 4, using 5 bytes to store the whole word. If a computer has 128 MB of memory, it has a memory address range of 0–134 217 728. This address range is calculated by converting the megabytes to bytes, or 128 × 1024 × 1024 = 134 217 728 bytes. Most modern computing devices have 2 GB, 4 GB or even more. The memory range for 2 GB is 0–2 147 483 648, and 4 GB is 0–4 294 967 296.

When we talk about addresses, we are normally talking about where to find data in RAM. It is not possible on a modern computer to hard-code memory addresses, as you have no way of knowing beforehand where data will be stored by the OS. The memory manager has the job of allocating memory addresses when a process wants to load or save data, so programs make use of virtual address spaces, which will be explored later.

Paging

When the memory manager uses paging, it allocates fixed-size blocks of memory to processes. These blocks of memory are known as pages. Each process has its own private view of pages and each memory access is made up of two parts: the page number and the offset within that page. All processes have access to a virtual memory space and are not aware of their location in physical memory, i.e. the page frame, nor are they aware of other processes and where their **pages** are stored in virtual memory. They will use their own memory address space, known also as **logical address space**. It is the job of the memory management unit to translate between physical addresses of pages in RAM and logical addresses of pages in virtual memory. In Figure 3.4 there are two processes, each with its own virtual memory space. A paging table will translate the virtual page number to the physical page frame held in memory. For example, page 1 of process 1 stores the text 'utin' and the paging table shows that this data is actually stored in page 5 in physical memory.

Process 1

Virtual address space	
Page	Data
0	Comp
1	utin
2	g is
3	Fun.

Page Table	
Virtual page	Page Frame
0	0
1	5
2	6
3	3

Process 2

Virtual address space	
Page	Data
0	I li
1	ke c
2	hees
3	E :)

Page Table	
Virtual page	Page Frame
0	1
1	2
2	4
3	7

Physical memory	
Page Frame	Data
0	Comp
1	I li
2	ke c
3	Fun.
4	hees
5	utin
6	g is
7	E :)

Figure 3.4: Two processes using virtual memory.

Individual processes view memory as a continuous block, even though this may not be the case. Page to frame translation is done transparently to the process; if a process attempts to access addresses outside its paging table, an error occurs. When a page is accessed, the page number requested acts as the index to the paging table to get the real page frame.

In order to calculate the physical memory address of a single byte, we must make use of the physical page number and the size of an individual byte. The simple formula below can be used to find out the address of a byte:

$$address = page\ number * page\ size + offset$$

For example, the ':' from page 3 in process 2 would be:

$$address = page\ number * page\ size + offset$$

$$address = 7*4 + 3$$

$$address = 31$$

Segmentation

Segmentation is an alternative method of allocating memory to processes, where segments are variable sized rather than fixed. Thus they can logically split RAM into segments of the exact size requested rather than forcing data into fixed-size chunks. This is ideal when storing blocks of code, such as a library, or files where the size is known in advance. In order to allow variable-sized segments, the memory manager must store the length of each segment in the segmentation table.

Segment ID	Start address	Length
1	300	64
2	500	48

Figure 3.5: Example of a segmentation table.

In order to translate memory accesses to physical memory addresses, the segment number and offset are needed. The memory management unit looks for the base address of that segment in a segmentation table, as shown above. If the memory request is outside the segment, a segmentation fault is raised.

$$address = segment\ base\ address + offset$$

One major advantage of segmentation is that memory can be shared between processes, especially when combined with library software. If a block of code used by two processes is needed, it can be loaded into a segment. When a process needs to access code within the segment, all it needs to do is supply the segment ID and the offset.

Virtual memory

When the memory manager sees that some **pages** have not been used recently, it could decide to move these blocks into virtual memory. Quite simply, the pages identified will be placed into a special file on the hard drive, called the page file (Figure 3.6). The memory manager then makes a note of which pages are in virtual memory and the page numbers where the page has been relocated. Virtual memory is commonly used to extend memory and allow programs to run, even though there may not be enough memory physically available. Image manipulation programs, for example, can use massive amounts of memory. Consider a high-definition image of size 4000 × 3000 in 32-bit colour. Each pixel will need 4 bytes to store, so:

$$4 \times 4000 \times 3000 = 48\ 000\ 000\ bytes\ or\ 45.7\ MB$$

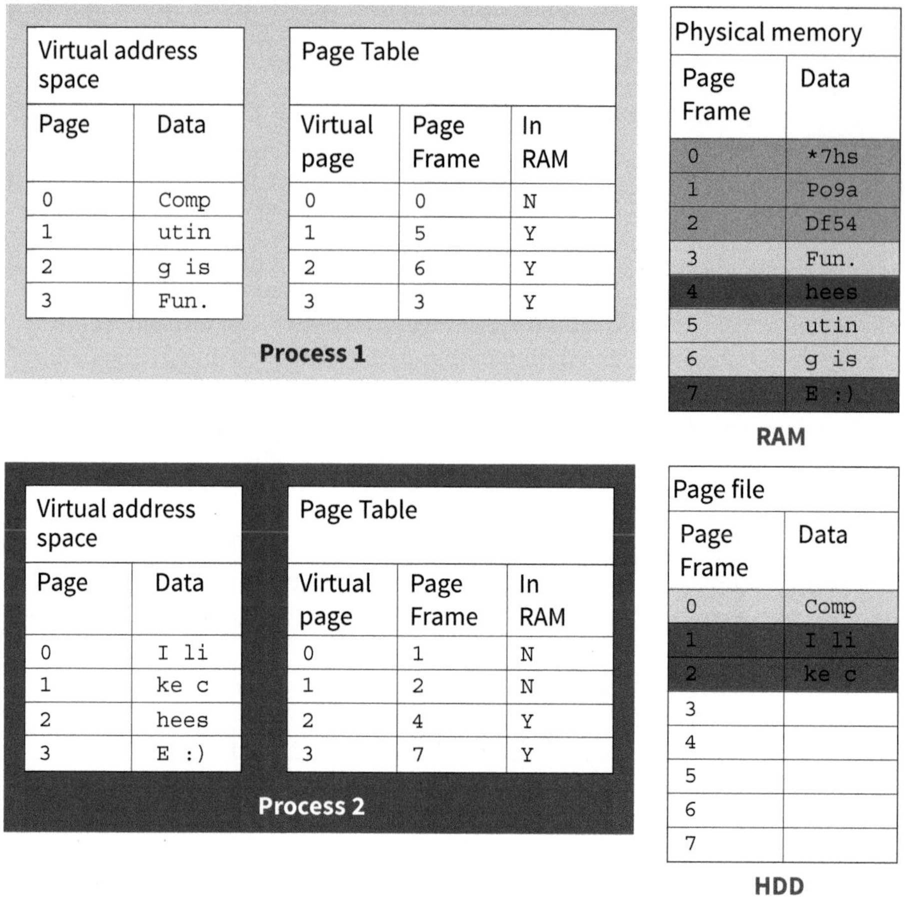

Process 1

Virtual address space	
Page	Data
0	Comp
1	utin
2	g is
3	Fun.

Page Table		
Virtual page	Page Frame	In RAM
0	0	N
1	5	Y
2	6	Y
3	3	Y

Process 2

Virtual address space	
Page	Data
0	I li
1	ke c
2	hees
3	E :)

Page Table		
Virtual page	Page Frame	In RAM
0	1	N
1	2	N
2	4	Y
3	7	Y

RAM

Physical memory	
Page Frame	Data
0	*7hs
1	Po9a
2	Df54
3	Fun.
4	hees
5	utin
6	g is
7	E :)

HDD

Page file	
Page Frame	Data
0	Comp
1	I li
2	ke c
3	
4	
5	
6	
7	

Figure 3.6: Page file.

Image manipulation programs always end up using double or triple the amount of memory for each image (for processing purposes and undo). So we could need over 150 MB just for one image. It is not hard to see how programs will very quickly use up available memory. As the hard drive is much slower than main memory, the choice of which pages should be swapped is very important. If poor choices are made, there will be a significant reduction in system performance. Until the page is loaded back into main memory, that process is effectively blocked. A process which has been swapped into virtual memory is known as suspended. When poor choices are made, lots of pages are continually swapped in and out of main memory, leading to unresponsive processes; this is known as **thrashing**. This situation can be improved by either updating your OS or getting more RAM, which will result in a lower reliance on virtual memory.

In order to implement virtual memory, page entries in the page table hold a flag that specifies whether that page is located in RAM or saved into the page table. When a page located in the page file is accessed, the memory unit will raise a page fault to the OS. Owing to the speed mismatch between the hard drive and memory, the OS must load the page back into RAM and update the page tables. There is no guarantee where in memory the OS can place the page, so it must update not only the flag but the frame number into which the page has been loaded.

If process 1 requires page 0, which is currently stored in the page file on the HDD, it must swap out another page and update the page tables. Figure 3.7 shows the changes (marked in pink). As process 2 had a page swapped out, its page table needed to be updated along with the page table for process 1. Should process 2 need that page immediately, it would have to be loaded back into RAM and the page tables updated, which would cause a delay. If repeated, this could lead to thrashing.

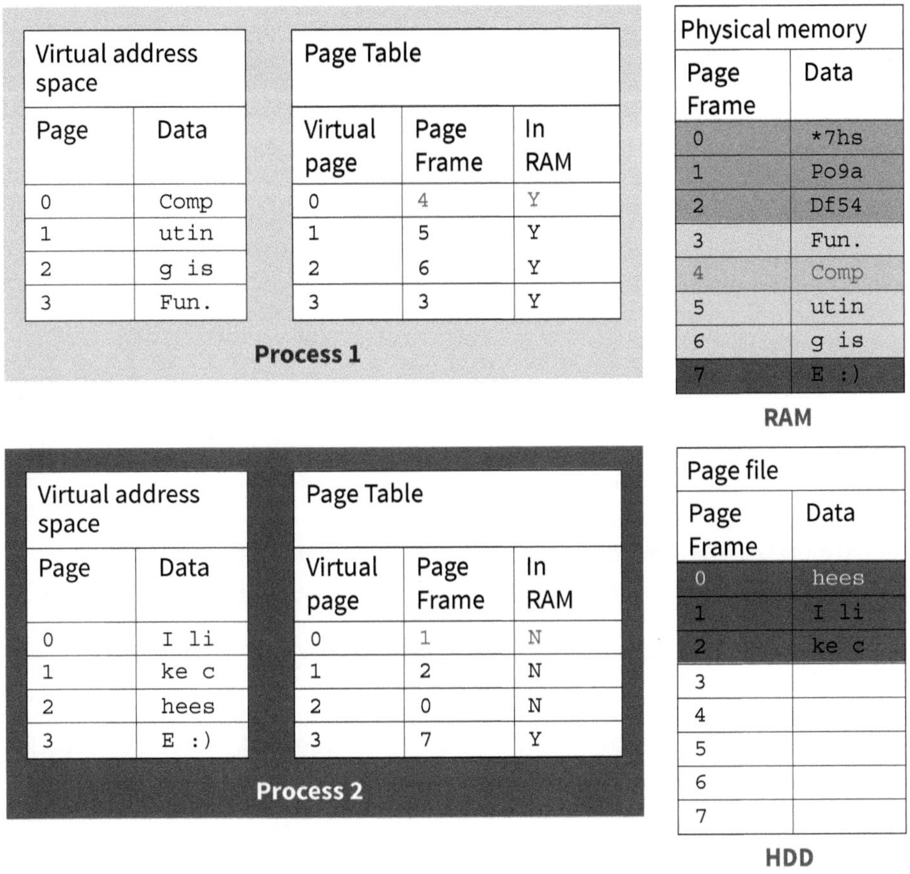

Process 1

Virtual address space	
Page	Data
0	Comp
1	utin
2	g is
3	Fun.

Page Table		
Virtual page	Page Frame	In RAM
0	4	Y
1	5	Y
2	6	Y
3	3	Y

RAM

Physical memory	
Page Frame	Data
0	*7hs
1	Po9a
2	Df54
3	Fun.
4	Comp
5	utin
6	g is
7	E :)

Process 2

Virtual address space	
Page	Data
0	I li
1	ke c
2	hees
3	E :)

Page Table		
Virtual page	Page Frame	In RAM
0	1	N
1	2	N
2	0	N
3	7	Y

HDD

Page file	
Page Frame	Data
0	hees
1	I li
2	ke c
3	
4	
5	
6	
7	

Figure 3.7: Changes to the page table.

Interrupts

Process scheduling is handled by the OS and decides when a process will run and for how long. However, it also needs to respond to input devices and other system-wide events, for example when the hard drive is ready to serve another request or the user has pressed a key on the keyboard. The OS needs to be made aware of these events in order to decide which course of action to take. These signals, sent from hardware to the CPU, are known as interrupts. Software can also generate interrupts during normal execution.

When an interrupt occurs, the CPU will, on the next instruction cycle, run some special OS code to inform it of the interrupt. The currently running process will be suspended so that this event can be handled. It is important for the OS to make this decision as it will know more about the context of what the user is doing. The OS, if it chooses, can ignore interrupts. When an interrupt occurs, the CPU has the role of informing the OS rather than dealing with the interrupt itself.

Here is a list of common interrupts:

- Hard drive ready for more data to save or it has retrieved requested data.
- Timer interrupt has occurred.
- Key has been pressed.
- Peripheral requires more data (for example a printer or a scanner).
- The on/off button has been pressed.
- Hardware failure or problem encountered.

In order to understand the role of an interrupt, it may help to consider an example. A user wishes to save a 30 MB file onto the hard drive. In order to do this, the file will need to be stored in small chunks of 1 MB. Using the buffer and **interrupt** system, the first chunk is sent to the hard drive, which, in turn, writes it to the disk. While this is occurring, the CPU will continue doing other tasks, such as dealing with keyboard interrupts or playing music.

Once the hard drive has finished saving the file, it sends an interrupt to the CPU requesting more data, which is duly sent by the CPU. This cycle will continue until the file has been saved: all 30 MB. It is important to remember that the CPU is much faster than any other part of the computer, including the user. If the CPU waited for the hard drive to finish saving before it did anything else (i.e. was synchronous), a lot of CPU cycles would be wasted. Interrupts allow the CPU to make much better use of time.

Buffers and interrupts

A buffer is a small block of memory inside hardware devices such as printers, keyboards and hard drives where work currently being handled by that device is stored. When a keyboard key is pressed, for example, an interrupt is sent to the CPU and the key stroke stored in the keyboard's buffer. However, sometimes the OS may not be ready to deal with the keyboard stroke and more keys may have been pressed. Instead of losing the key strokes, the buffer stores the values until the OS is ready. If that buffer overflows, the motherboard warns the user by sounding a beep. Hard drives also contain a buffer; by utilising a buffer the CPU can send a block of data to be saved without having to wait for the data to be physically stored onto the disk. This increases system performance by allowing the CPU to work on other tasks.

When data is stored on or loaded from any device, buffers will be used. There is a very specific algorithm used to deal with buffers and interrupts when saving data to a slower device:

- A chunk of data is sent by the CPU to the device and stored in a buffer.
- The device will slowly save the data while the CPU is free to do other tasks.
- When the buffer is empty, an interrupt is sent to the CPU.
- At the start of the next FDE cycle the interrupt is processed by informing the OS.
- More data is sent to the device and the cycle repeats. This will continue until all data has been saved.

Interrupt service routines

Hardware and software can trigger interrupts and these are then dealt with by calling an interrupt service routine (ISR). When a device driver loads, it will register interest in a specific interrupt so that when the interrupt occurs the code within the device driver will be executed. The ISR does not continuously check the status of the device. As ISRs are part of the device driver, the OS is effectively using the driver to process the interrupt.

Multitasking

Multitasking is the process of swapping applications in and out of the CPU, giving the illusion that they are running in parallel. Most modern OSs have the ability to run more than one program at once. The user is led to believe that the computer is doing many things at once, such as playing music, editing a document and performing a virus scan. A single-core CPU can only process one instruction at a time. In order to implement multitasking, the OS ensures that each process is swapped in and out of the CPU so that the user is under the impression that all processes are running at the same time. This illusion can easily be shattered if a process causes the system to become unresponsive, as this will stop all other processes from running.

Scheduling

Scheduling is the term the OS uses to define how and when a process is swapped in and out of the CPU, thus enabling multitasking. Each OS has a different way of performing scheduling. Many of the specifics on how scheduling occurs in an OS is kept secret from the public, which is especially true of Mac OS X and Windows. A process is a piece of software that is currently being managed by the scheduler inside the OS; this definition allows us to make the distinction between software and running software.

Scheduling must not be confused with interrupts, which are hardware signals sent to the CPU to inform it that an event, external to the CPU or generated by software, has occurred. Interrupts are initially handled by the CPU before being passed over to the OS. This differs from scheduling, which makes decisions on which process should be run next or which ones should be interrupted, known as **pre-empting**.

Process states

Only one process can be run at once on a single CPU core. This process will be in the 'running state' or just 'running'. Other processes will be either in a 'ready-to-run queue', waiting for their turn with the CPU, or in a **blocked** state:

- *Running*: when the process has control of the CPU.
- *Ready-to-run*: a process is in a queue waiting for the CPU.
- *Blocked*: a process is waiting on an I/O operation such as the hard drive.

When a process is waiting for a device or external operation to complete, we say that this process is **blocked**. A process should never be held in the ready-to-run queue while waiting for an I/O operation to complete, but should relinquish control to another process by placing itself into a blocked state. Consider the state diagram shown in Figure 3.8.

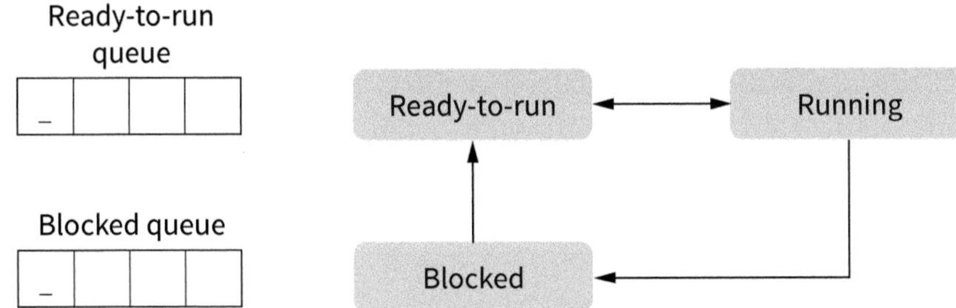

Figure 3.8: Process states.

The OS will have different queues to monitor these three states. Imagine an internet browser which has requested data from the internet on a 56 kbps connection. That process could potentially be blocked for a few seconds, which, in processor terms, is a lifetime. If that process was in the ready-to-run queue, a situation could occur where the process is brought into the running state while still waiting for a device. This would waste CPU cycles, as all the process could do is place itself back into the ready-to-run queue. A process will only become unblocked when an interrupt occurs, and will always go back into a ready-to-run state. For example, if a process is waiting for the hard drive it will remain in the blocked state until the hard drive sends an interrupt to the CPU. The process manager will then change the state from blocked to ready-to-run and the process will join the ready-to-run queue.

Ready-to-run queue

A new process is created when the user, or another process, loads an application from the hard drive. Once loaded into memory, the process becomes live and is added to the ready-to-run queue rather than being placed into the running state. It is the job of the scheduler to decide on which process to run next using a **scheduling algorithm**, and not that of the recently loaded process. However, the scheduler will also decide in what position in the queue the new process should be added. If the new process has a high priority, it may be added higher up in the queue or the scheduling algorithm may decide that the new process should be placed behind others.

Running process

In a standard single-core CPU, there will be only one process running at any given time. This process will be given a certain amount of time to run called a time-slice, based on the scheduling algorithm. A running process has a number of options while running:

- *Complete the task (and close)*: this removes the process from **scheduling** completely and is the equivalent of the user clicking on quit. A process can elect to stop itself or it may have completed the processing. It is important to remember that not all processes are GUI-based applications and could be batch processes running in the background.
- *Be interrupted by the scheduler*: not to be confused with interrupts, which will stop a process so that the OS can deal with an event. This is where the scheduler has decided that the process has had enough CPU time and will swap it for another process. The currently running process is then placed in the ready-to-run queue based on the scheduling algorithm. When a process is stopped it is said to be pre-empted, which tends to cause schedulers to reduce the priority of the process to ensure system stability.
- *Become blocked*: in this situation, the process is moved to the **blocked** queue immediately. This is to prevent wasting CPU time.
- *Give up CPU time*: a process could voluntarily give up CPU access with the view of getting it back in the near future. A process which does this is known as a well-behaved process and tends to be given higher priority in most modern scheduling algorithms (see the section on multi-level feedback queues).

Process swapping

When a process is running, it will have full access to the CPU. The state of the running process is represented by the data stored in the registers. When the process is swapped out, it is important that the values in the registers are saved. A data structure known as the **process control block** (PCB) is created, and is used to store the contents of the registers.

The PCB will contain the following pieces of data:

- *The PC (program counter) register*: this is so that it will know exactly what point it reached in the task and can continue from that exact place when restored.
- *General purpose registers*: these are temporary values used by the process. Another process could overwrite them, which could potentially change the result of calculations. As such, it is imperative that they are saved.
- *ACC*: the accumulator stores the result of the last calculation and would be needed as the starting value for the next calculation that process needed to perform.
- *Variables and state of the process*: any variables linked to the process in memory must be recorded.
- *Priority and process ID*: used by the scheduler for process administration.

Once a process has had a PCB created and saved into primary memory, the registers of the next process are loaded. These will overwrite the current register values. The next **fetch-decode-execute-reset** (FDER) cycle will then run the new process instead of the old. One key role of the scheduler is to ensure that registers are copied from the CPU first and then overwritten with the values of the new process.

Deadlock and starvation

Processes sometimes arrive at a situation where they can no longer perform their tasks. This tends to be due to them waiting for some system resource that is currently not available. This problem is called deadlock. Another problem is when a process keeps being pre-empted or never getting a chance to run, caused by higher-priority processes running on the system. This is called starvation. One of the key design goals of the scheduler is to minimise the chance of deadlock and starvation occurring.

Deadlock is when a process is waiting for a system resource that is currently held by another process. This process, in turn, is waiting for a resource held by the other process before it can complete. Each process has locked a resource needed by the other, which means that neither can go any further. Deadlock occurs when a process gains access to a system resource, such as the internet, but is waiting for a second resource, such as a printer, in order to proceed. Imagine that another process is trying to do exactly the same thing but it has access to the printer but not the internet. Unless one of the processes relinquishes control of its resource, neither of the processes will be able to complete. As such, both processes will be blocked indefinitely, which, as far as the user is concerned, means they will hang and require a restart of one, or both, processes.

Starvation is when a process never gets a chance to run, or not enough CPU time to complete in a timely manner, owing to high-priority processes always gaining an advantage over it. This normally happens as the result of poor **scheduling**. If the scheduler is being fair, all processes should eventually get a chance to run. Most modern OSs will have procedures in place to prevent starvation.

Activity 3.1

This task requires you to use Linux. This can be done by installing a Linux distribution of your choice on a computer, using a Raspberry Pi or a virtual machine such as VirtualBox. Note: the Linux shell commands listed below will not work on a Windows computer.

1. Open a terminal window and run the command '**ps**'. This command will list out processes running in the current terminal.
2. Enter the command '**ps c -u <your username>**'. This will list out all of the processes currently running by that user. The STAT column shows the current status of that process.
3. Look at the main state codes (shown as capital letters). Which of these states can you see in the results of the ps command? You may wish to save the results to a file so you can look in more detail. For example, for a username of 'mrh', the syntax would be: **ps c -u mrh > result.txt**.
4. Which of the main Linux states match the blocked state described in this chapter?
5. What does it mean when a process is sleeping? Why is this important for multi-level feedback queues?

Code
D Uninterruptible sleep (usually IO)
R Running or runnable (on run queue)
S Interruptible sleep (waiting for an event to complete)
T Stopped, either by a job control signal or because it is being traced
X dead (should never be seen)
Z Defunct ('zombie') process, terminated
but not reaped by its parent
< high-priority (not nice to other users)
N low-priority (nice to other users)
L has pages locked into memory (for real-time and custom IO)
s is a session leader
l is multi-threaded (using CLONE_THREAD, like NPTL pthreads do)
+ is in the foreground process **group**

Process codes to show the state of a process while using the ps command.

Recording interrupts

When an **interrupt** occurs, a signal is sent to the CPU via a control bus or, in the case of a software interrupt, a flag is set. A special register, known as the interrupt register, is then updated by flipping a bit to 1. Each bit in the interrupt register represents a different interrupt and is referred to as a flag. When a flag is set to 1, it represents an interrupt that needs to be processed. Initially the interrupt register will have all flags set to 0 (Table 3.1).

IRQ flag	Device	Flag
0	Timer	0
1	Keyboard	0
2	Programmable	0
3	COM 1	0
4	COM 2	0
5	Term 2	0
6	Floppy	0
7	Term 2	0
8	RTC timer	0
9	Programmable	0
10	Programmable	0
11	Programmable	0
12	Mouse	0
13	Co-processor	0
14	ATA/IDE 1	0
15	ATA/IDE 2	0

Table 3.1: Example IRQ flags used by an interrupt register.

The binary value of 0 shows that the interrupt has not occurred, while if a value of 1 is detected, the processor will need to perform an action. When the interrupt is sent to the CPU, the corresponding flag is set. This does not mean that the interrupt will be dealt with immediately, but that the interrupt has been recorded. If the same interrupt happens twice before it is dealt with, only the first one is recorded. The Table 3.2 shows that a timer interrupt has occurred:

Sometimes more than one interrupt can be sent to the CPU at the same time, or before the CPU has had a chance to deal with the previous interrupt. This is handled by simply setting multiple flags, but only if they are for two different interrupts. If more than one of the same interrupt is generated before the CPU has had a chance to deal with it, the second and subsequent interrupts are ignored. This is a fairly common occurrence for low-priority interrupts such as I/O) tasks or timers.

Each interrupt will be assigned a priority depending on how critical it is to the system. Timer events have the highest priority so will always take precedence over lower priority interrupts such as the user moving the mouse.

Dealing with interrupts

At the end of a fetch-decode-execute (FDE) cycle, the CPU will check if an interrupt has occurred by looking at the interrupt register to see if any flags have been set. If an interrupt has occurred, the priorities of the currently running process and the interrupt are compared.

If the interrupt has a higher priority than the currently executing process, the process must be swapped out by the processor and the interrupt handling code loaded instead. Priorities are checked to ensure that a high-priority process is not being interrupted by low-priority interrupts. If more than one interrupt must be processed, the one with the highest priority will always be selected first, as only one interrupt can be processed at a time. Swapping out an interrupted process requires all of the registers and the state of the process to be copied and saved onto a stack data structure. This includes the program counter (PC), accumulator (ACC) and all general purpose registers. The program counter effectively keeps track of where the process was in its execution because it points to the address of the next instruction. A stack data structure stores all register values of the interrupted process so that the OS can resume the previous process, or handle another interrupt. When restoring a process, the PC, ACC and general purpose registers must be copied back to the CPU so that it can resume from the exact point it was interrupted.

When an interrupt is to be processed, the OS has specific code which is run for each type. For example, if a timer interrupt occurs, every process that depends on timing must be informed. In most operating systems, such as Windows or Linux, there will be a number of running processes which make use of a timer event. In order to ensure that all running processes get to respond to the interrupt, the OS must send an event to each of these processes. The processes do not get a chance to do anything about it at this stage – they are merely informed so that when they next get a chance to run they will have the option of dealing with that event. Event-driven programming is based around the OS sending events to processes, and interrupts are abstracted by the OS as system events. To stop every process having to deal with every interrupt, a focus system is used, meaning that only the active window will get the interrupts unless they are running in the background.

IRQ flag	Device	Flag
0	Timer	1
1	Keyboard	0
2	Programmable	0
3	COM 1	0
4	COM 2	0
5	Term 2	0
6	Floppy	0
7	Term 2	0
8	RTC timer	0
9	Programmable	0
10	Programmable	0
11	Programmable	0
12	Mouse	0
13	Co-processor	0
14	ATA/IDE 1	0
15	ATA/IDE 2	0

Table 3.2: An interrupt register with a single flag set.

In order for the correct OS code to be executed when an interrupt is processed, there is a vector (array) of memory addresses set up, each pointing to the OS code designed to deal with that interrupt. Figure 3.9 below represents this vector.

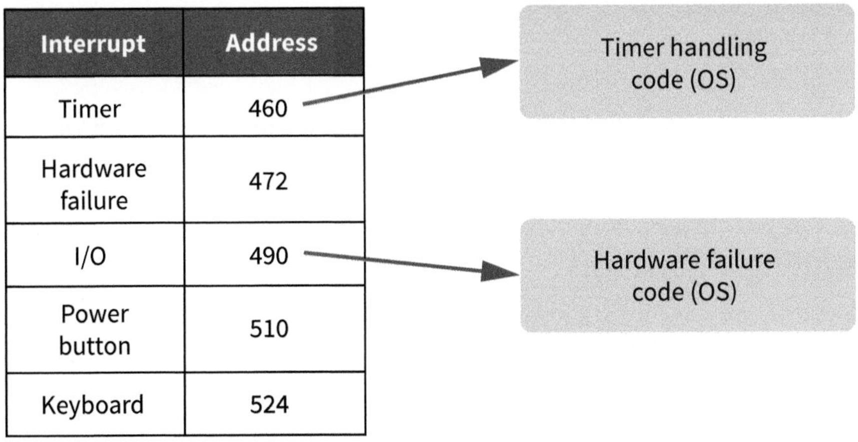

Interrupt	Address
Timer	460
Hardware failure	472
I/O	490
Power button	510
Keyboard	524

Timer handling code (OS)

Hardware failure code (OS)

Figure 3.9: Vector.

To find the correct interrupt handler the CPU will use the indexed addressing mode (see Chapter 6):

$$\textit{Interrupt handling code} = \textit{Base address} + (\textit{index} * 4)$$

The base address is where, in memory, the vector exists and the offset is defined by the interrupt that has fired. As such, if the timer interrupt occurs, the offset will be 0, while if the keyboard interrupt occurs, the offset will be 16 (assuming 32-bit addresses).

Stacks and processing interrupts

A stack data structure is key to how interrupt handling occurs. It is a fairly common scenario when an interrupt is being dealt with by the OS and a higher-priority interrupt is received in mid-process. In this case the interrupt handler must itself be interrupted, by using a stack data structure the OS will know where it needs to jump back to. Figure 3.10 demonstrates how interrupts can be restored.

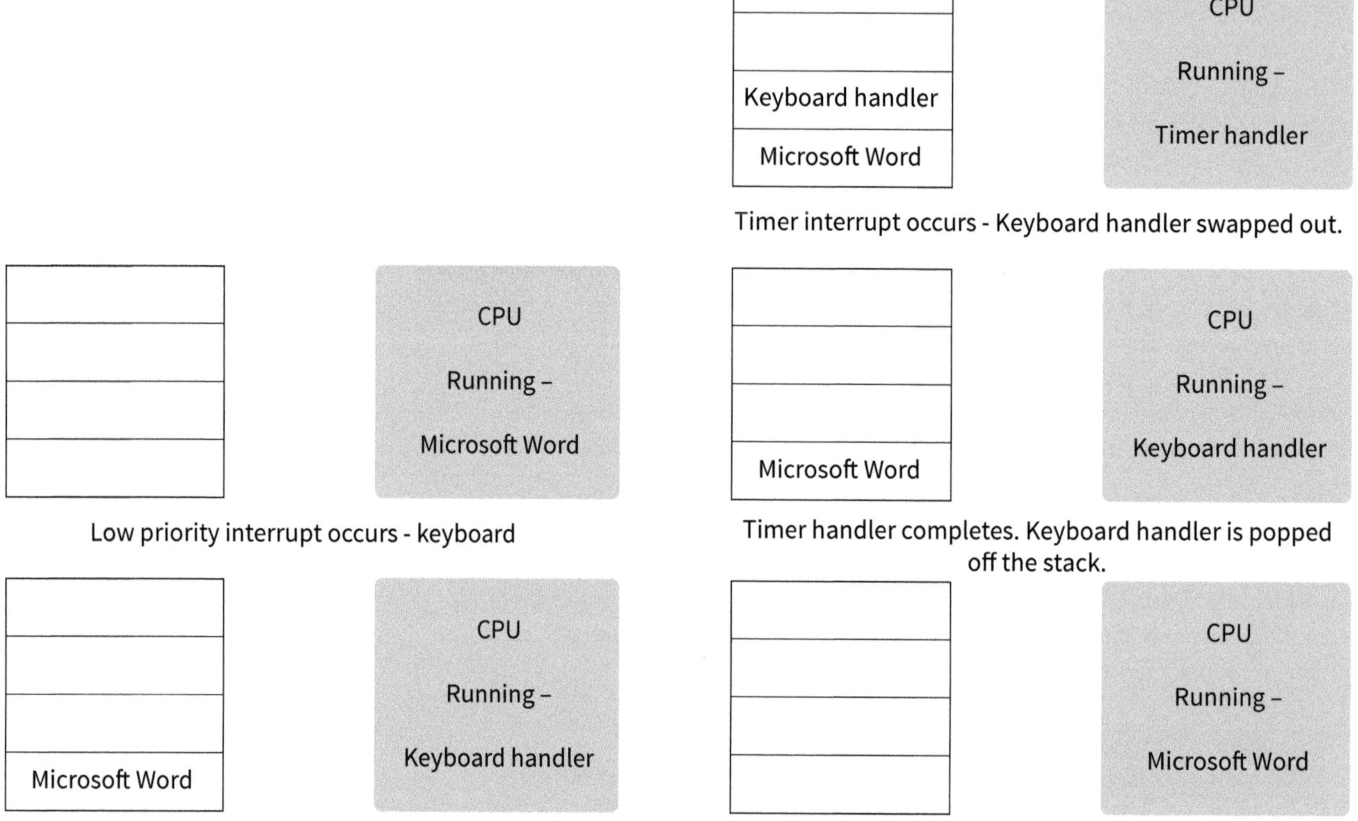
Keyboard handler
Microsoft Word
CPU
Running –
Timer handler
Timer interrupt occurs - Keyboard handler swapped out.
CPU
Running –
Microsoft Word
Low priority interrupt occurs - keyboard
Microsoft Word
CPU
Running –
Keyboard handler
Timer handler completes. Keyboard handler is popped off the stack.
Microsoft Word
CPU
Running –
Keyboard handler
Microsoft Word is added to the stack and keyboard handler loaded.
CPU
Running –
Microsoft Word
Keyboard handler completes and Microsoft Word is restored by popping the stack.

Figure 3.10: Handling interrupts.

Scheduling algorithms

The scheduler is part of the OS and has the job of deciding in what order processes should be executed. It is separate from the interrupt handlers. The main design goals of the scheduler are to:

- Minimise starvation of processes.
- Eliminate deadlock.
- Ensure high throughput of processes (i.e. processes can be completed as quickly as possible).
- Ensure fairness for all processes (linked to starvation).
- Ensure reasonable response time (to enhance user experience).

The choice of **scheduling** algorithm is key to ensuring that these goals are met. In order to understand the scheduling algorithms described in this chapter, you must be familiar with the concept of execution time for a process. Most operating systems keep an historic record of the behaviour of processes in order to predict future operation.

Execution time

Each process will require a certain amount of time to perform its task. These tasks may be bounded (such as converting a CD to MP3 format) or unbounded (such as playing a game). Unbounded processes will continue needing CPU time until the user stops the application; these types of process are the most common, but they are also the most predictable. They tend to need the CPU for short bursts of time; for example, playing music requires the decoding of part of an MP3 file and sending that decoded data to the sound card. Once that has been done, the process sleeps until the sound card is ready for the next part of the MP3 to be decoded. This repeats until the song has been played. The execution time of unbounded processes is measured by these bursts of CPU time rather than overall execution. After all, there is no way the OS can predict how long you decide to listen to music. When describing how much CPU time a process needs, we will be referring to a single burst rather than how long the process has been running.

Round robin

Round robin is a simple **scheduling** algorithm designed to ensure fairness. Each process is given a fixed time to run, called a time slice, and is pre-empted if the process has not completed before the end of that time. If the process has not completed, it is sent to the back of the ready-to-run queue and the head of the queue is swapped into the CPU. This process continues until all processes have completed. A process can decide to end, give up its time or be interrupted. In these cases, the next process, or the interrupt handler, will be swapped to the head of the queue before the time slice is over. Below is the pseudocode for round robin:

```
REPEAT
IF Ready to run queue is NOT empty THEN
    Restore the process at the head of the queue
END IF
Run process for fixed length of time
IF process is NOT complete
    Add process to the back of the queue
UNTIL ready to run queue is empty
```

Figure 3.11: Round robin pseudocode.

Round robin analysis

Round robin is a fair algorithm and processes are always guaranteed processor time, which limits the chance for starvation. Owing to the simplicity of the implementation, it does not take priorities into consideration. This means that the quality of user interface interactions could be impacted on a system where there are many processes running. If each process gets 10 ms of time to run and there are 30 processes running, each process will have to wait 300 ms each time it wants to use the CPU. Most computers have many more processes running than that. Figure 3.12 shows how many processes are running on a MacBook under low load; 91 processes means that each process waits 910 ms, which is almost 1 second. This does not include the time taken to swap processes (which is not instant).

Round robin, therefore, is not suited for applications that have interactive interfaces. The lag time between doing something on screen and the process being able to handle it would be noticeable with only a few hundred processes running. Round robin is best suited for situations where only a few simple processes are running at any given time.

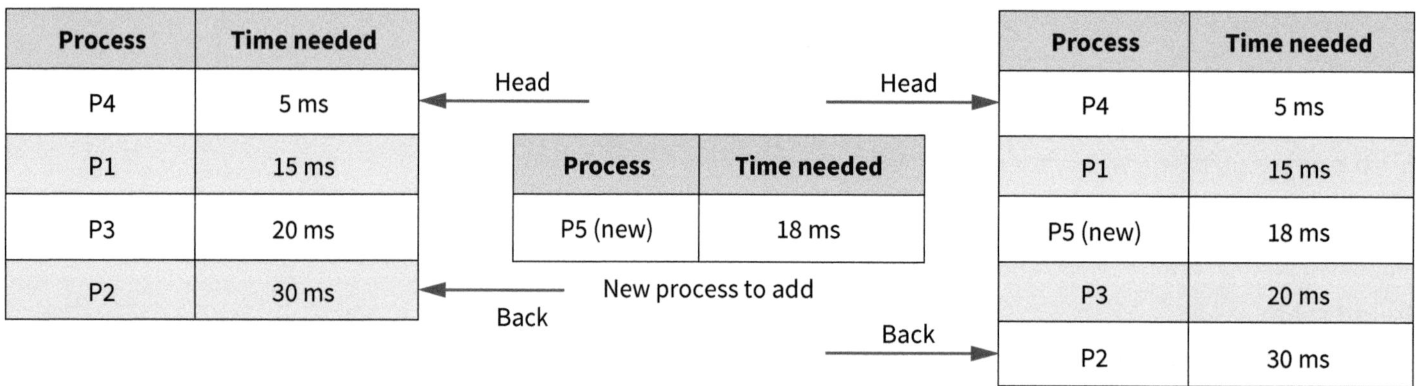

Process	Time needed
P4	5 ms
P1	15 ms
P3	20 ms
P2	30 ms

Process	Time needed
P5 (new)	18 ms

Process	Time needed
P4	5 ms
P1	15 ms
P5 (new)	18 ms
P3	20 ms
P2	30 ms

Figure 3.12: Running a new process.

Shortest job first

The shortest job first (SJF) algorithm relies on knowledge of how long a process requires, in order to complete its task. Most processes are unable to supply this information, so it is up to the OS to take an educated guess based on historic data. As the burst time of most processes is predictable, this task is not too difficult to accomplish, as the OS gathers statistical information on processes being run. The algorithm works in a similar way to round robin, except that processes are not pre-empted after a set amount of time, but rather allowed to complete. Processes are completed in the order they arrive in the ready-to-run queue. What sets SJF apart is where the process is placed in the ready-to-run queue initially. Shorter jobs are always added to the queue at the front, while longer jobs are added to the back (Table 3.3).

SJF analysis

Segment ID	Start address	Length
1	300	64
2	500	48

Table 3.3: Table showing some example segments.

SJF ensures that user-interface-based processes will be run before other, more processor-intensive tasks. It can do this because dealing with simple mouse clicks or keyboard strokes is easy to accomplish and tends to require much shorter CPU bursts. SJF cuts down the average waiting time for these processes, as they are always prioritised over other processes. Waiting time is defined as the amount of time a process must wait before getting access to the CPU, which includes the time taken to swap processes. By reducing the average waiting time for interface and I/O processes, we increase the responsiveness of the system and increase throughput. To aid comparison, it is worth examining waiting times of a simple first come first served (FCFS) algorithm to SJF (Figure 3.13):

Process	Time needed	Wait time
P4	5 ms	0 ms
P1	15 ms	5 ms
P5	18 ms	20 ms
P3	20 ms	38 ms
P2	30 ms	58 ms

SJF average waiting time = 11.6 ms

Process	Time needed	Wait time
P1	15 ms	0 ms
P2	30 ms	15 ms
P3	20 ms	45 ms
P4	5 ms	65 ms
P5	18 ms	70 ms

FCFS average waiting time = 14 ms

Figure 3.13: A comparison of the waiting times between SJF and FCFS.

FCFS does not order processes by their execution time; it simply does them in the order they arrive, and the amount of time each process takes is exemplified in the above tables. Although the time difference is small, this would be amplified greatly if there were more processes to deal with and if some of those processes had larger burst times. SJF requires the OS to keep track of how much time each process is taking, which adds extra overhead when swapping processes. Although we have not considered swap time, it is considered constant and must be added on for each process swap.

Round robin tends to swap processes more often, but the algorithm is simple, which keeps the swap time low. SJF does not swap as much, but owing to the statistical nature of the algorithm, it has more processing to perform at each swap. It needs to manipulate queues to ensure that processes are added at the correct position, which also adds to the complexity. One other criticism of SJF is that longer processes could become starved, as shorter processes are always being added and run as high priority. It is entirely feasible for processes with a long burst time to always be beaten to the CPU by shorter processes.

Shortest remaining time

Shortest remaining time (SRT) is very similar to SJF, with the biggest difference being that when a process is interrupted or pre-empted, the time remaining on that process is looked at and then the process is added ahead of any other processes that have longer time left to run. This is to prevent longer processes suffering from starvation. As time progresses, processes that require a lot of CPU time will slowly get a chance to run and the time they require will reduce. This, in turn, increases their priority and increases their chances of running, thus reducing the risk of starvation. Swapping becomes more expensive, however, as all processes (not only new ones) must be placed correctly in the ready-to-run queue and new burst times must be calculated. A key design goal is that at all times the queue must be in shortest time order, not just when a process is added.

It is worth noting that the SJF and SRT algorithms are very similar and work in exactly the same way if pre-empting is not allowed. However, it is very common for the OS to pre-empt processes, and the longer a process runs, the higher the chance of this occurring. SRT has advantages over SJF if the OS is actively pre-empting longer-running processes.

Multi-level feedback queues

So far we have been using a single queue for **scheduling**, the ready-to-run queue. Multi-level feedback queues (MFQ) make use of three queues of differing priority instead of a ready-to-run queue. Level 0 (high priority) will always have processes run before level 1 (medium) and level 2 (low). Each queue works on an FCFS basis, but the head of level 0 is always run before level 1 and level 2.

In Figure 3.9 there are six processes queued for execution and the scheduler always selects the head of level 0 if a process exists. As such, P1 and P2 will run ahead of the other processes. If no process exists in level 0, it will try the head of level 1 and so on. It is easy to see how having three priority queues could lead to starvation, so MFQ implements a promotion and demotion system for processes as shown in the following rules:

- New processes are always added at the tail of level 0.
- If a process gives up the CPU of its own accord, it will be added back into the same-level queue.
- If a process is pre-empted (stopped by the scheduler), it will be demoted to a lower queue.
- If a process blocks for I/O, it will be promoted one level.

Head	1	2	3	
P1	P2			level 0

Head	1	2	3	
P3	P4			level 1

Head	1	2	3	
P5	P6			level 2

Figure 3.14: Example MFQ.

Multi-level feedback queues analysis

Each process is given a fixed amount of time to run, as in round robin. If a process uses the full amount of time, it will be stopped by the scheduler. This is known as **pre-emptive scheduling** and for MFQ it will result in the process being demoted, unless it is already in level 2. A process that requires pre-emptive action is not considered to be well behaved and could end up monopolising the CPU if allowed to stay at level 0. It could be a CPU-heavy process or one that is poorly programmed. A well-designed program will always give up CPU time to ensure overall system liveliness. **Blocked** processes waiting for I/O will always be promoted and this is done for several reasons. First of all, they will have had to wait a certain amount of time already before they could become unblocked, so it makes little sense to make them wait any longer. Secondly, to ensure that I/O devices are used at maximum efficiency, a process must be ready to send more data as soon as an interrupt has occurred. Thirdly, sending data to an I/O device is not a

CPU-intensive task and requires only a short burst of time. Thus giving a blocked process a higher priority would not negatively impact on other processes and would increase the throughput of other processes.

Activity 3.2

Code

```
processNames = ["word", "excel", "MP3", "movie player"]
processTimes = [20, 40, 30, 50]
time = 5
while len(processNames) > 0:
  processTimes[0]  = processTimes[0] - time
  tempTime = processTimes.pop(0)
  tempName = processNames.pop(0)
if tempTime < 0:
  print tempName, "has completed"
else:
  print tempName, "has run with", tempTime, "remaining"
  processNames.append(tempName)
  processTimes.append(tempTime)
print "All done"
```

The above code simulates the round robin scheduling algorithm. Using this code as a template, implement shortest job first and shortest remaining time. You may wish to add some random element which will interrupt or pre-empt a process.

Hardware drivers

When an application asks the OS to save a file or access any connected device, it needs to make use of a hardware driver. Hardware drivers are simply software that understands how to talk directly to a given piece of hardware. Drivers are normally produced by the manufacturer of the hardware, but can also be produced by OS manufacturers and even the open-source community. As all devices are different, the OS needs to have a generic way of talking to devices of the same type. This generic communication is not understood by the hardware itself and requires translation into the correct binary control signals. Hardware drivers perform this translation from the generic instructions sent by the OS to the specific instructions understood by the device. Drivers are only loaded by the OS if specific hardware has been connected to the PC and requires installation. They are modular in nature and can be loaded on demand. Most OS installations will detect what hardware the user has and try to install the required drivers when the OS is installed. This functionality works by each device having two codes, a vendor ID (VID) and a product ID (PID). When a device is connected, the OS queries the device for these two codes. It then checks its database of known vendors and products to see if a suitable device driver can be found. If not, the user will have to install one before that device can be used.

Sometimes the OS will install generic drivers that will not be able to use the full range of features of the device. When setting up a new OS, you will have to install drivers for every piece of hardware on your PC. To see what drivers your system is currently using, you will need to load Device Manager for Windows or System Profiler on a Mac. On Linux the easiest way to see what devices are installed is to run 'lspci' or 'lsusb' from the command line.

Different OS types

There are many different types of OS available, each with different uses and attributes. Windows, for example, works very differently from Android™ and is used for very different purposes. Devices such as DVD players have a very different OS from a standard desktop computer.

Single-user OS

Single-user operating systems are very common, with early versions of Windows (up to Windows 98) being classic examples. Although these versions of Windows can allow multiple users to have a local profile on a computer, only one of those users can be active at once. Under normal circumstances a user can log into a computer and have sole access to system resources. To help manage different users, a single-user OS creates home directories for each user. Inside these home directories are the user's documents, application settings and browser history, for example. These files are protected by the OS so that only the user and the administrator can have access to them. So if another user logged in after you, they would be unable to access these files.

In Microsoft Windows, there is a folder called 'Users' where all user data is stored. Within this folder, each user has their own folder with their username.

Multiuser OS

Operating systems that run on more powerful computers or servers can allow timesharing of system resources by multiple people simultaneously. Instead of having the standard scenario where someone will physically log in to a single computer, a multiuser OS allows users to log in remotely. Each user then has their own VDU, mouse and keyboard, but is using the internal hardware of the server to which their computer is connected. In order to enable this, the user must use a basic computer that can connect to the network and communicate with the server. An example of a multiuser OS is Unix.

The computer that connects to the server is called a terminal. It can take the form of any networked device. It could be a specialised thin client terminal, a smartphone, another computer or even a tablet. Even though some of these devices are perfectly capable of using their own resources to run applications, their main role is to connect remotely to the server (Figure 3.15) and run applications there. To enable this communication, a number of different technologies can be employed, including secure shell (SSH) and virtual desktop infrastructure.

Multitasking and multiuser OS

Most modern OSs offer multitasking, which was introduced earlier in this chapter. Desktop operating systems such as Linux, Mac OS and Windows have multitasking at their core. The user can have multiple applications open and move between them seamlessly.

Any windowed operating system tends to be multitasking. Android OS also offers multitasking even though the user may only be able to see one application at a time. It is possible for some apps to offer services which run in the background, such as notifications and downloads.

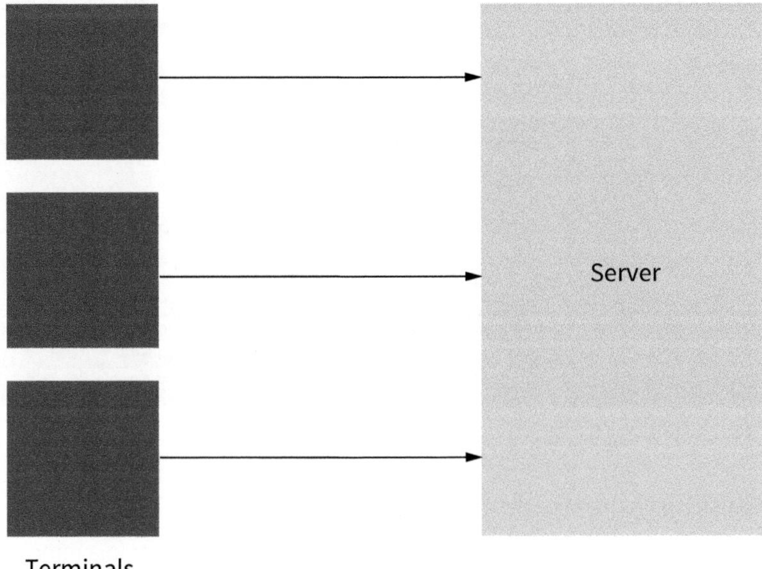

Figure 3.15: Terminals connecting to a server.

Most desktop operating systems offer the ability to have multiple users and can be classed as a multiuser OS. Each user would have their own work area which is protected from other users. In Windows 7 or later, the user's work files would be stored under the 'users' folder followed by their user name. In Linux and Mac OS, it can be found under the 'home' folder followed by their user name. Each user's work files can only be accessed by the user that created them or the administrator for that computer. Mobile devices, such as iOS, do not offer multiuser functionality as they tend to be private devices. For this reason, they are considered to be single user.

Some operating systems allow multiple users to use the same computer at the same time. This is where two or more users would connect to a computer via remote desktop software or secure shell. Multitasking becomes more complicated, as each user could have multiple processes running at once. The scheduler needs to assign processor time to each user first and then schedule the processes for that individual user.

Secure shell

Secure shell, or SSH, makes use of a client to connect to a server through a command line interface (Figure 3.16). This is a very popular method of communicating and running software on servers for network or website administrators. On Windows, you can use some free software called PuTTY to make secure shell connections. Communication is encrypted using a 128-bit key and the user will have to accept the server's host key fingerprint before communication can continue. Once the fingerprint is accepted, it will be checked every time you try to connect, preventing other servers trying to mimic or masquerade as the original.

```
ch208a.cae.tntech.edu - PuTTY
login as: mwr
Using keyboard-interactive authentication.
Password:
Linux ch208a 2.6.8-2-686-smp #1 SMP Tue Aug 16 12:08:30 UTC 2005 i686 GNU/Linux

The programs included with the Debian GNU/Linux system are free software;
the exact distribution terms for each program are described in the
individual files in /usr/share/doc/*/copyright.

Debian GNU/Linux comes with ABSOLUTELY NO WARRANTY, to the extent
permitted by applicable law.
No mail.

Last login: Mon May  1 13:49:31 2006 from ch314c.cae.tntech.edu
mwr@ch208a:~$
```

Figure 3.16: Establishing an SSH connection.

Virtual desktop infrastructure (VDI)

Virtual desktop infrastructure enables users to connect to the server via a remote desktop. Windows has some utility software called Remote Desktop Connection, which allows communication with VDI services. One key distinction to make about VDI and other remote desktop software is that with VDI you are not going to be viewing the server's desktop, but rather you will have your own.

When applications are run under VDI, all processing takes place on the server. In order for the remote client to see what is happening, a live video stream of the desktop is sent over the network. There are many techniques to optimise this stream, but it will still require a high bandwidth. Most VDI servers can support only a certain number of users, owing to the extra processing required to broadcast live desktop streams. Also, when implementing a VDI system, networking resources must be taken into consideration. Regardless of how powerful the server or how fast the network is, VDI technology is inherently slow and user interface actions can be sluggish.

Resources within a multiuser OS are time shared, especially the CPU, in order to ensure fairness to all connected users. Each user is given time to make use of the CPU in the same way that multitasking works in a single-user OS. As each user could potentially run more than one application, the OS has more to do when managing multitasking. Modern software solves this problem through the use of virtualisation technology. Each user will be allocated one or more virtual CPU (vCPU) to execute their tasks within a symmetric multiprocessing virtual machine (SMP VM). A software utility called the hypervisor manages how processes are scheduled across multiple virtual CPUs. This ensures that each user's processes run in their own execution space. This type of scheduling was originally developed for scientific applications running on parallel processors and is known as coscheduling. Virtualisation software is now very popular with organisations to centralise services. VMware is a company that produces a popular range of desktop virtualisation software.

Tip

Questions relating to multiuser OSs will normally ask you to explain the idea of time sharing between users. It is important, although technically the CPU is just multitasking, that you relate your answer to multiple users.

Real-time OS

Real-time operating systems must respond to system inputs within a short amount of time, sometimes considered to be immediate, in order to output information from the system. Owing to the speed of computing systems, it is feasible to develop software that can respond to user requests *so* quickly that it seems immediate. In truth, a few milliseconds would have elapsed. When developing a real-time OS, consideration must be taken away from general computing needs and focused on very specific applications. You would not expect to run a real-time OS on a desktop computer, owing to the unpredictability of the software applications the user may install. No matter how good the OS is, a webpage could not load in real time because of the broadband connection bottleneck. Real-time OSs run only on very specific, usually mission-critical, systems.

Some examples of systems that require a real-time OS are nuclear power stations and aircraft systems. If a decision or action were delayed because of software running slowly in a nuclear reactor, it might explode, which would be a disaster. A real-time OS must always respond quickly, so it is crucial that it focuses only on the job of managing the power plant. Some transaction-based systems are also considered to be real-time, for example travel agents with multiple stores across the country. If one store books the last seat of a cut-price holiday, it should no longer allow any other store to book. The transaction needs to happen fast enough to stop multiple bookings from occurring and thus is considered to be real time.

Embedded OS

Many devices contain simple processors, RAM and ROM in order to provide their services. DVD and Blu-ray players, printers and even washing machines all have basic hardware internally and can be considered to be specialised computing systems. In order to run the device, an OS is required. Embedded operating systems are used in these circumstances rather than using a generic desktop equivalent which would be too large and complex.

Devices that make use of an embedded OS need to provide very specific services, such as wash clothes or play a DVD. Most features of a desktop OS, such as process and user management, networking and file storage, are not needed. An embedded OS provides just the exact services needed to perform the device's task, and by stripping out any features that are not required it can run on much more limited hardware. Most embedded OSs are custom-built for the device, but some are based on more generic operating systems such as embedded Linux and Windows IoT.

Computing in context: database transactions

Databases form the backbone of almost every enterprise and are essential for any form of website that sells products or services. Most ticket-based systems run over the internet and have a website interface with a database running in the background. Owing to the nature of the internet, it is impossible to purchase tickets in actual real time. To prevent duplicate attempts to buy the same ticket, the database uses transactions.

Transactions are a crucial part of ecommerce systems, but they are also very technical. On their most basic level, a series of database transactions are collected together into an all-or-nothing approach. For example, say a customer bought an item that required two actions: reducing stock and taking money. If only one of the actions was successful, the database would be an inconsistent state and you could potentially have either a very happy or a very angry customer, depending on which action was successful. If one action fails, both actions should be undone, which is known as a **rollback**. Both of these actions could be combined into a transaction. If the actions are successful then the transaction can be committed, which means that the database is updated. This gets even more complicated when more than one database is involved: for example, the bank and the shop would have separate databases.

To prevent other clients changing data that is currently being worked on in a transaction, locks can be used. A lock can be placed on any record in the database, preventing anyone else from writing to it until the lock has been removed. This is a simplification of what happens 'under the bonnet', but it does give an idea of how tickets can be sold successfully outside of a real-time system.

Distributed OS

When faced with a project that requires a highly scalable and powerful computing system, a distributed system is the most logical choice. When more power is needed, more computers, known as nodes, can be added to the network. From the user's perspective this network of computers is logically presented as a single computing device. In order to ensure that the nodes work together, a distributed OS is needed. Although a distributed OS requires **scheduling**, memory management and all of the other classic elements of an OS, it is much more complicated owing to the fact that these services will be spread over a number of different nodes. Part of the distributed OS's job is to synchronise nodes and ensure timely communication of data. As such, network communication is at the heart of a distributed OS.

Each node in the distributed OS has a small set of key features, known as a **microkernel**, so that it can access the hardware of that node. This will include basic device management, network communications and a way to manage the node's RAM. All of the distributed features, such as application **scheduling** and file management, sits on top of, and makes use of, the microkernel (Figure 3.17).

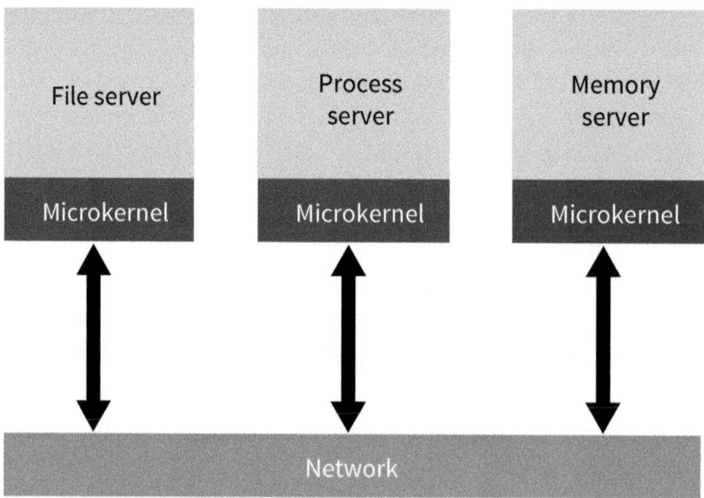

Figure 3.17: File, process and memory servers all use the microkernel to connect to the network.

Distributed OSs have a major disadvantage owing to the requirement for synchronisation across the network, which impacts on performance. User-space programs (i.e. anything outside the kernel) are a key part of the distributed OS model. Services that would normally reside inside a monolithic kernel, such as device drivers, are moved out of the kernel and into user space. This allows greater modularity and flexibility without impacting the core services provided by the kernel. In a distributed setting, it means that nodes can offer different services easily without having to provide them all. User processes can be split across the nodes and be managed by the distributed OS without having to specify which node the process should run on.

BIOS

BIOS stands for **basic input/output system** and it is the systems software that is the first program that is run when the computer is switched on. It is loaded from ROM and performs the following tasks:

- Initialises and tests hardware by running the POST (power-on self-test).
- Selects the first boot device based on information collected in the POST.
- Tries the boot loader of that device and, if successful, runs the OS.
- Moves on to the next boot device if unsuccessful. Repeats until all boot devices have been tried.
- If no boot devices have suitable boot loaders, the system will stop.

The BIOS also comes with a setup utility, which allows basic configuration of the boot process and low-level configuration of devices. Some motherboards, where the ROM is located, allow the user to overclock the CPU through the setup utility. Some users do this to increase the speed of their system, however this could cause the computer to overheat and damage the hardware. This is an example of why you should never change BIOS settings unless you know exactly what you are doing.

When the BIOS first starts, it runs the POST. This sends an initialisation signal to every device and instructs each to run internal tests. Devices then return their current state and may not be permitted to function if they return an invalid state. Although it may seem as if the POST is determining whether devices are fully functioning, this is not the case. Tests run are very basic and there is no guarantee that the device is 100% functional. It is possible to see the results of the POST through diagnostic information displayed on screen (Figure 3.18), but most computer manufacturers hide this information behind their logo during start-up. An interested user could easily disable this logo to view POST output. Once the POST is completed, it knows which boot devices are available to try.

```
                         Phoenix Technologies, LTD
                           System Configurations

 CPU Type          : AMD Athlon(tm) XP   Base Memory      :     640K
 CPU ID            : 0681                Extended Memory  :1047552K
 CPU Clock         : 2000MHz             L1 Cache Size    :     128K
                                         L2 Cache Size    :     256K

 Diskette Drive A  : 1.44M, 3.5 in.      Display Type     : EGA/VGA
 Pri. Master Disk  : LBA,ATA 100,40822MB Serial Port(s)   : 3F8 2F8
 Pri. Slave  Disk  : LBA,ATA 100,40062MB Parallel Port(s) : 378
 Pri. Master Disk  : DVD,ATA 33          DDR DIMM at Rows : 2 3 4 5
 Sec. Slave  Disk  : CHS,PIO 4,  512MB

PCI device listing ...
Bus No. Device No. Func No. Vendor/Device Class Device Class              IRQ

   0        2         0      10DE   0067  0C03  USB 1.0/1.1 OHCI Controller 10
   0        2         1      10DE   0067  0C03  USB 1.0/1.1 OHCI Controller 11
   0        2         2      10DE   0068  0C03  USB 2.0 EHCI Controller      5
   0        9         0      10DE   0065  0101  IDE Controller              14
   0       13         0      10DE   006E  0C00  Serial Bus Controller       10
   1        8         0      1106   3043  0200  Network Controller          11
   1        9         0      1102   0002  0401  Multimedia Device           11
```

Figure 3.18: POST testing results.

Devices such as the hard drive will have an OS installed on them. It is possible to install an operating system onto a DVD, known as a live disc, or a memory stick. If a device can have an OS loaded from it, it is known as bootable. It is common in the setup utility (Figure 3.19), to have multiple boot devices set up in a priority order. Normally the top priority is CD/DVD drives, followed by USB connected devices and finally hard drives. The HDD is last because if it were first, new OSs could not be loaded from DVD or USB drives unless the priority list was changed. If a device is undetected by the POST, or does not have a boot loader, the BIOS will move on to the next device.

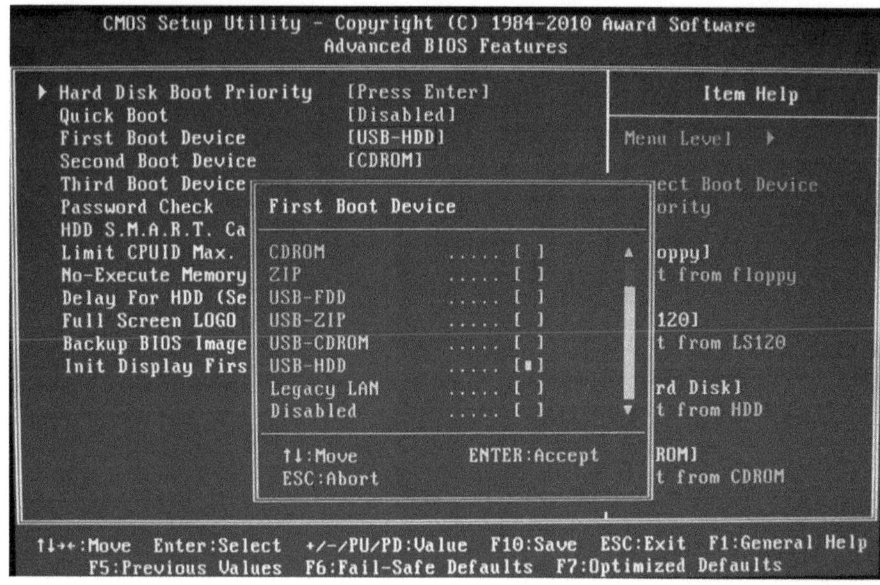

Figure 3.19: A typical BIOS interface.

Bootable storage devices contain a special sector known as the **boot sector**, which points to the boot loader on that device. If the boot sector is not set, that device will be skipped. Boot loaders execute OS code that, in turn, starts the OS loading. Sometimes the boot loader offers a number of choices if more than one OS is installed. GRUB (GRand Unified Bootloader), used by Linux, allows multiple OSs to be invoked and can be configured to automatically boot these and even provide runtime parameters (Figure 3.20).

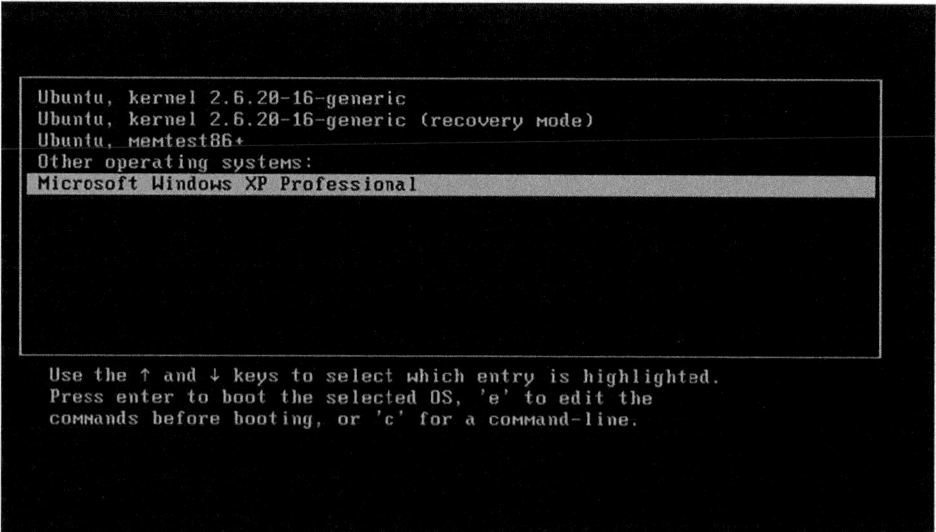

Figure 3.20: Choosing which OS to use.

Virtual machines

Sometimes it is desirable to be able to install a new operating system without having to wipe your hard drive completely or to install them side by side. It may be that you want to be able to try out a new OS, run two side by side or run them in a sandboxed environment. Virtual machines allow you to perform all three of these tasks through the use of virtualisation. A virtual machine is simply a general-purpose computer that will emulate the hardware of your system, including its own RAM, processor and hard drives. Computers that run virtual machines are known as the **host system**, while the virtual machines themselves are known as guests.

Virtual machines are essentially sandboxed environments where the guest OS has no knowledge that it is being run inside a virtual machine. It has full access to memory assigned to it and makes use of its own memory manager and scheduler. Hardware provided by the host is emulated as generic hardware by the virtual machine, meaning that the guest machine has no need to install device drivers. The host has the ability to assign system resources to the virtual machine, such as the amount of memory and whether or not the guest can have access to USB devices. As the guest OS is running in a sandboxed environment and has no direct access to the host system, there is little chance that the guest can damage the host.

There are many applications, both free and paid for, that provide virtualisation services. One of the most commonly deployed is Oracle's VM VirtualBox, which is free. As previously mentioned VMware produce a range of virtualisation products for the enterprise. It is common for companies to set up servers as virtual machines to provide better security and to allow multiple servers, including virtual desktops, to run on the same computer. By isolating each server to a separate virtual machine, the network manager can bring them up and down without impacting the rest of the network. Virtual machines also allow for snapshots to be taken, where their current state is recorded, which means that the administrator can roll back to previous snapshots if disaster strikes. This means that there is no need to completely reinstall a server should one fail; they just have to restore a snapshot. Another key advantage of virtual machines is that they can be copied and migrated at a touch of a button. If you need ten servers based on a Windows server, you can set up one and clone it ten times. These servers can then have their services set up independently. Even though each one is configured separately, a lot of time will have been saved through the cloning process. Also, migrating virtual machines means that a network can be easily scaled up and virtual machines moved around, rather than having to set everything up from scratch.

Smaller virtual machines, which do not emulate full OSs, can be used as well. Java makes use of virtual machines to provide extra security and portability for applications written in the language. Java virtual machines will be explored in Chapter 5 during the discussion of compilers and interpreters.

Intermediate code

Virtual machines, as a computational concept, have been around for a long time. In essence, they represent a logical computer residing within the physical computer that is running it. System virtual machines represent entire OSs, whereas process virtual machines virtualise a single application only. Process virtual machines, as they are known, act as interpreters for generic machine code instructions known as intermediate code.

Process virtual machines, referred to as VMs from now on, run intermediate code that has previously been compiled. Source code is compiled into intermediate code to prevent the incompatibilities that exist when trying to run code on different CPU architectures or OSs. This generic intermediate code cannot be run by a CPU directly and is merely an abstraction rather than a real instruction set. In order to run the code, it must be interpreted by a VM. One example of a programming language that is both compiled and interpreted is Java (Figure 3.21).

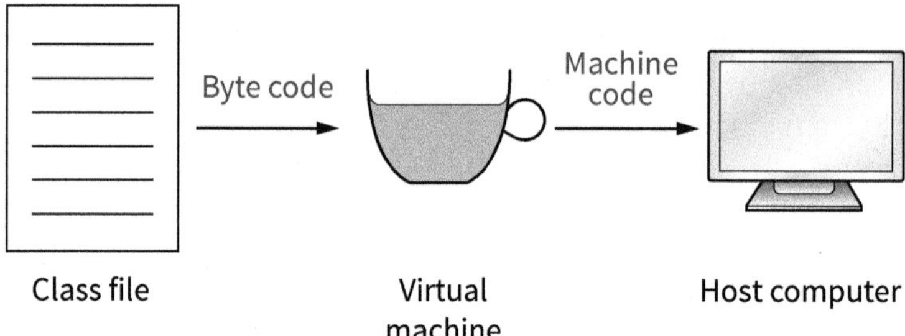

Figure 3.21: Java.

Java is a popular programming language originally created by Sun Microsystems, but now owned by Oracle. Java source code is written in much the same way as other programming languages and bears some comparison, in syntax at least, to C++. Once the source code has been produced, it is compiled into intermediate code (known as byte code in Java), which is a pseudo-executable file (known as a class file). Byte code must then be interpreted by the Java VM when the program is run. This means that for any Java program to run, the Java VM must be installed first.

The host system will not be able to run the intermediate code (byte code) held in the class file directly (Figure 3.22). It would be like someone speaking Russian to you (unless you happen to speak Russian). In order for that person to be understood, their speech would have to be translated by an interpreter. The process VM has the job of translating Java byte code into machine code. As well as managing the translation of intermediate code to machine code, the VM has to trap OS library calls. So when the byte code tries to open a window, the VM makes some system calls to your OS to open a window on its behalf. This applies to any library call, from opening a file to any other library-related task. Libraries will vary considerably between operating systems, so this additional functionality is crucial.

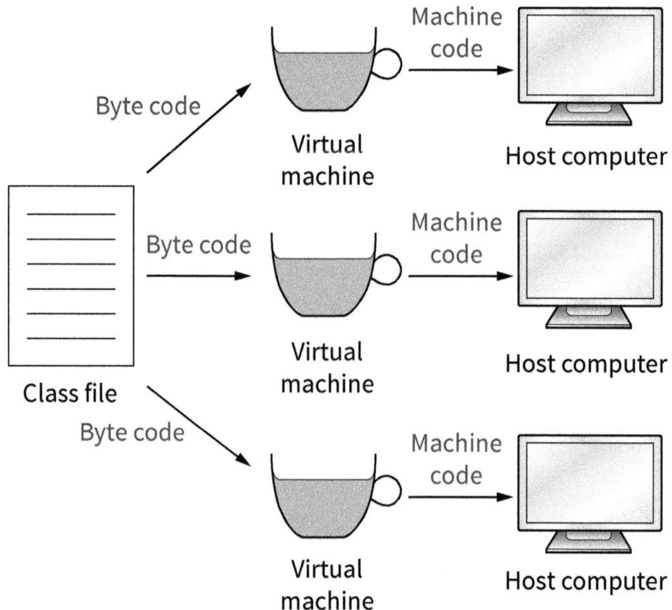

Figure 3.22: This shows the same byte code as Figure 3.21 running on multiple virtual machines.

Process VMs manage their own threads and have their own memory management system. This provides a fully sandboxed environment for the software to run in, which has the main advantage of offering extra security features, such as restrictions on accessing the hard drive or other system resources.

```
outer:
 for (int i = 2; i < 1000; i++) {
        for (int j = 2; j < i; j++) {
            if (i ÷ j == 0)
                continue outer:
        }
        System.out.printin (i):
}
```

```
0:      iconst _ 2
1:      istore _ 1
2:      iload _ 1
3:      sipush 1000
6:      if _ icmpge     44
9:      iconst _ 2
10:     istore _ 2
11:     iload _ 2
12:     iload _ 1
13:     if _ icmpge     31
16:     iload _ 1
17:     iload _ 2
18:     irem
19:     ifne    25
22:     goto    38
25:     iinc    2, 1
28:     goto    11
31:     getstatic       #84: System.out.PrintStream:
34:     iload _ 1
35:     invokevirtual #85: //Method printin:
38:     iinc    1, 1
41:     goto    2
44:     return
```

Figure 3.23: Disassembled exemplar byte code.

The above Java code (left) would be compiled into byte code (right). Byte code does not run on any known computer and requires a Java VM to run it. Intermediate code acts in the same way as normal machine code, but is not architecture-specific.

Java is an example of a programming language that is both compiled and interpreted. First of all, source code is compiled into intermediate code (for example, Java byte code) and then interpreted by a VM. There are a number of advantages of doing this:

- Code can be run on many different host OSs without the need to recompile.
- Intellectual property is protected, as source code is not released.
- Code can be optimised by both the compiler and the interpreter.

Summary

- System software manages the hardware and software of the computer.
- The operating system is responsible for memory management, process management and managing devices.
- Memory management is done through two mechanisms: paging and segmentation.
- Pages are blocks of memory of fixed size that are referenced through a paging table. The paging table contains the page number and offset to physical memory.
- Each process has a virtual address space which is translated by the memory unit to physical addresses by the formula

  address = page number * page size + offset

- Segmentation allows blocks of memory to be used, which are variable in size.
- Each segment is stored in a segmentation table and will record the ID, start address and length for each segment.
- Segments are commonly used to store library software or other blocks of data that are shared across multiple processes.
- Virtual memory is where the hard drive is used as additional memory in order to increase the number of processes that can be active at once.
- When a process is saved into virtual memory it is suspended. When loaded back into RAM for processing it is restored.
- Page tables will record which processes are located in RAM or in virtual memory.
- An interrupt is an electronic signal (hardware interrupt) or a process-generated signal (software interrupt) that is sent to the CPU to inform it that a device or process requires attention.
- Common interrupts include storage devices, timers, peripherals, power, and software and hardware failure.
- Buffers are used on devices to allow the CPU to perform other tasks while data is being saved.
- Interrupt service routines (ISR) are bits of code that are run when an interrupt occurs; these are normally within a device driver.
- A process can be in one of the following states:
  - running – currently has CPU time
  - blocked – waiting for an operation to complete
  - ready to run – waiting for the CPU.
- Processes are swapped by storing both special and general registers into a process control block. This can then be used to restore the process.
- The main design goal of scheduling is to maximise the throughput of processes. To do this it must minimise starvation and eliminate deadlock.
- There are a number of key scheduling algorithms that can be used:
  - round robin
  - shortest job first
  - shortest remaining time
  - multi-level feedback queues.

- There are a number of different types of operating system:
  - single-user
  - multiuser
  - real time
  - embedded
  - distributed.
- Virtual machines allow hardware to be abstracted and provide system-level emulation. They come in two forms:
  - system virtualisation – where a full operating system is virtualised on the host PC
  - process virtualisation – where intermediate code can be executed through a virtual machine.

End-of-chapter questions

1 In order to function, all computing devices require an operating system.

  a Describe the purpose of memory management in the operating system. [3]

  b Describe the purpose behind process scheduling in the operating system. [3]

2 Describe how page tables are used by processes to manage their memory address space. [6]

3 Describe, using an example, how and why a process may become suspended. [4]

4 Describe how buffers and interrupts are used when saving a large file to the hard drive. [6]

5 Describe how a distributed operating system works and how micro kernels are used. [6]

Further reading

What are virtual machines? – search What is a Virtual Machine on the Make Use Of website.
Successor to BIOS – unified extensible firmware interface – search for UEFI BIOS explained on the Alphr website.
Comparison of OS scheduling algorithms – search for the piece by Neetu Goel and Dr. R.B. Garg on the Cornell University Library.

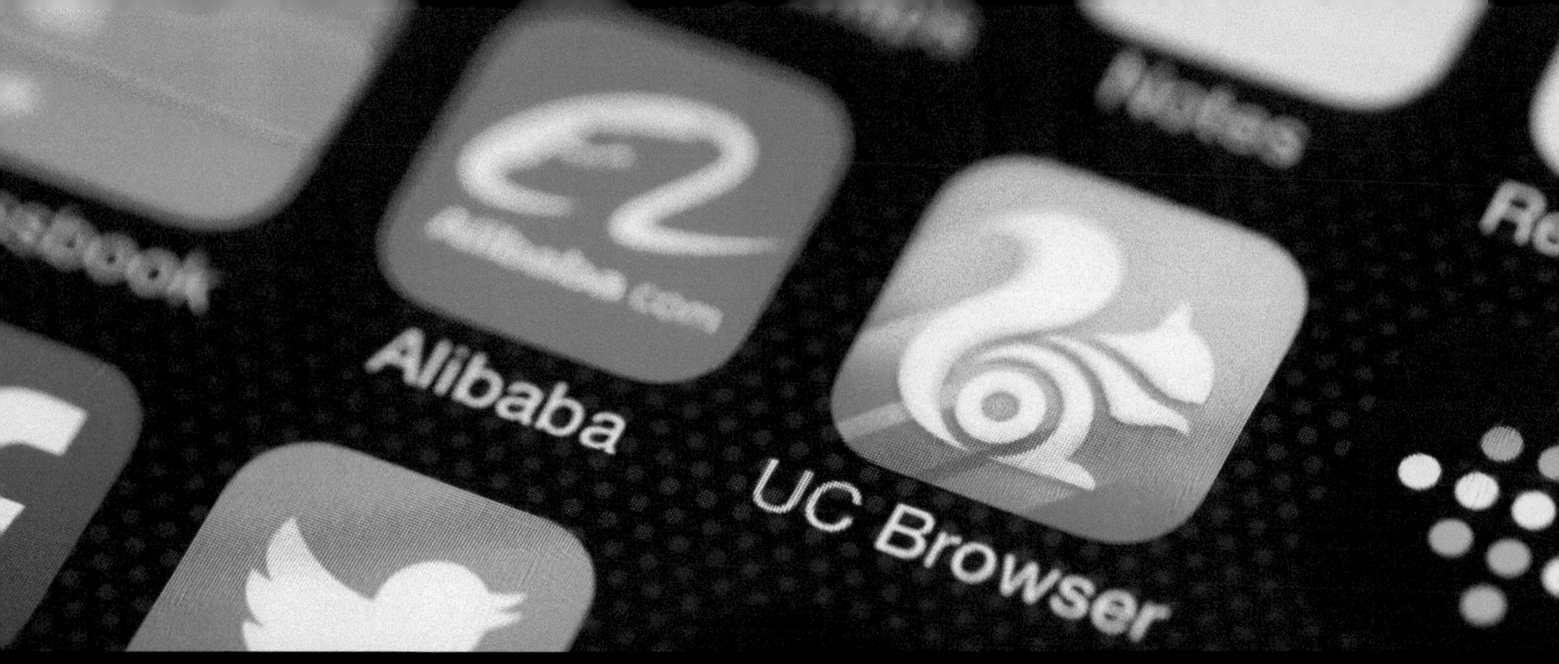

Chapter 4
Applications generation

Specification point

1.2.2 Applications generation

- The nature of applications, justifying suitable applications for a specific purpose.
- Utilities.
- Open source versus closed source.
- Translators: interpreters, compilers and assemblers.
- Stages of compilation (lexical analysis, syntax analysis, code generation and optimisation).
- Linkers and loaders and use of libraries.

Learning objectives

- To understand the nature and variety of application software.
- To describe and understand the purpose of utility software.
- To know the difference between open and closed source software.
- To understand the differences between the three main types of translator: compiler, interpreter and assembler.
- To understand the different stages of compilation, including lexical analysis, syntax analysis, code generation and optimisation.
- To describe the roles that linkers and loaders play with regard to translated software.

Introduction

Software has undergone many changes since the advent of personal computers and portable computing devices. In the early days of Microsoft Windows, floppy disks and, later, CDs were the main way of distributing applications and games. Software was mostly closed source (or proprietary) and most people did not have access to the internet in order to download software. Even if they did have internet connections, in most cases the bandwidth would have been too slow to download larger applications. Open-source software became popular after 1997 with Netscape releasing the source code for their web browser Navigator, the basis for Mozilla Firefox. Over the next few years, more software was released under the open-source agreement, meaning that people could not only download software for free, legally, but also make changes to the code.

This brings us to 2008, when the Apple App Store opened its virtual doors for the first time. Although mobile phones had applications before this, the Apple App Store delivered software to the masses in easy-to-consume packages, and smartphones reached critical mass, which led to a surge in simple and single-purpose mobile apps.

More recently, HTML5 with JavaScript and CSS3 have brought more complex and interactive websites to the user. These web apps can be used on any device without having to install any software other than a modern web browser. Web apps, utilising cloud computing, bring the concepts of mobile apps to the web. As the complexity of the software is being handled on a server somewhere in the cloud, the end user's device can be simple.

Application software can be accessed from portable computing platforms or from a desktop computer via the cloud, meaning that users can access their data and programs wherever they are. Increased internet connection speeds enable fast downloading of apps and allow them to be updated regularly. Digital downloads can be automated so that subscription software is kept up to date without the user needing to remember to renew it. Open-source products have increased in popularity, resulting in well-respected online communities that provide tutorials, documentation, additional libraries and troubleshooting advice.

Tip

Recall from Chapter 2 the distinction between commonly used software and the extra software installed with the OS.

For each major type of application software, you need to know common uses for it and be able to identify the type of scenario for which it would be most suitable. In order to be able to justify your answer, you must remember the key features of each type of software.

Application software

Some application software allows a user to carry out a specific task, such as sending an e-mail. Other applications can be used for many different tasks, and these applications constitute a subset of application software known as generic application software. Examples are word processors and spreadsheets.

Presentation software

Presentation software, such as Microsoft PowerPoint, Google Slides or Apple's Keynote, allows the user to create presentations to convey information. It is designed to be shown on a projector system while a speaker is talking to the audience. Features of presentation software include animations, multimedia, interactive links and speaker notes. Text tends to be large (defaults to size 24–26 point) so that it can be viewed easily at a distance. Simple animations increase the visual appeal of the presentation. By using animations as a form of output, the user can present information in a different way or draw attention to key aspects.

Presentation software is generally used in meetings or in educational environments such as schools or training courses. Each slide contains only a small amount of information, as the bulk of it is delivered by the speaker. Sometimes speakers use notes, which can be displayed to them but not to the rest of the audience, as shown in Figure 4.1.

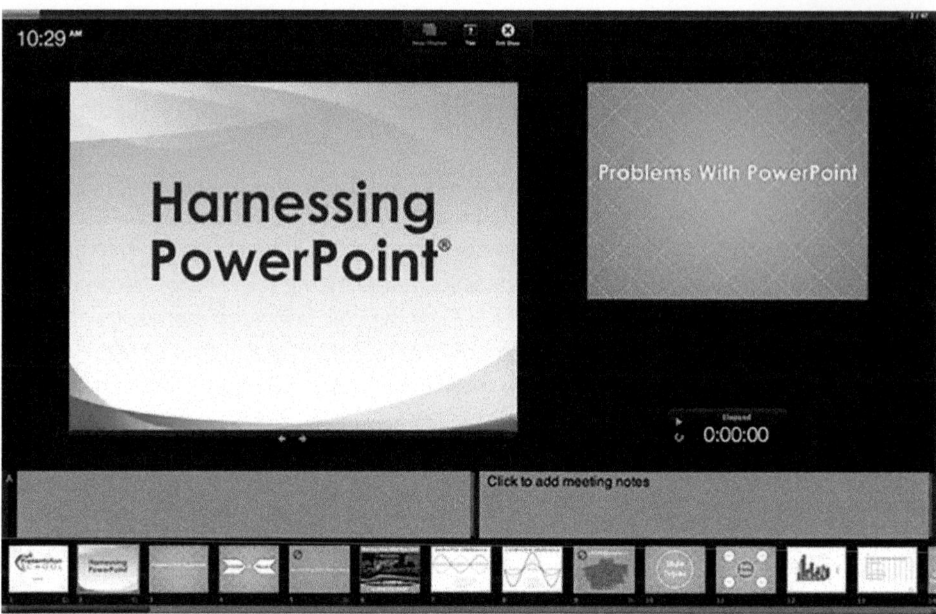

Figure 4.1: Presentation software with user notes, which are hidden from the audience.

Desktop publishing

Desktop publishing (DTP) software, allows the creation of many different types of publication, for example manuals, posters and banners. There is a common misconception that DTP software, such as Microsoft Publisher, is used for the same tasks as a word processor. DTP software allows the user much finer control over the layout of a publication and is not designed to edit large amounts of text. Conversely, word-processing software can be used to produce essays, letters and reports rather than graphical publications. When selecting between DTP and word-processing software, the final result has to be considered. If it is text-heavy, a word processor is more suitable.

Two of the key features of DTP software are templates and the layout of text and images. You can use templates to set up the page size, orientation and basic layout for a variety of commonly used types of publication. It is also possible to set up personal templates for use within a company. This dramatically improves productivity, by allowing you to focus on content instead of setting up document styles.

Spreadsheet packages

Spreadsheet packages are primarily focused on dealing with numbers and financial information. They can be used for storing simple databases, but this is not their primary purpose. A single spreadsheet is known as a workbook and contains one or more worksheets. A worksheet is split into a grid ,with letters representing columns and numbers representing rows. A single box in the grid is known as a cell. The user can reference cells within formulas to perform numeric calculations on values stored in cells. The formulas will automatically recalculate the result when values are changed inside the worksheet; this is one of the most important features of a spreadsheet. An example formula is = A1 + A2, which adds the contents of cells A1 and A2 and displays the result. Any change to the value held in cell A1 or in cell A2 automatically triggers recalculation of the answer.

Drawing packages

Drawing packages come in two main types: bitmap and vector. They both allow the user to draw images, but they do so in different ways. Vector images are made up of lines and shapes that can be dynamically resized without loss of quality. Vector images tend to be used in diagrams for use in publications, including computer science diagrams. Data flow diagrams (Figure 4.2), flowcharts and unified modelling language (UML) diagrams are all examples of vector images. Vector image files store data about the coordinates of the basic shapes that make up the image, which is why, even when resized, there is no loss of fidelity.

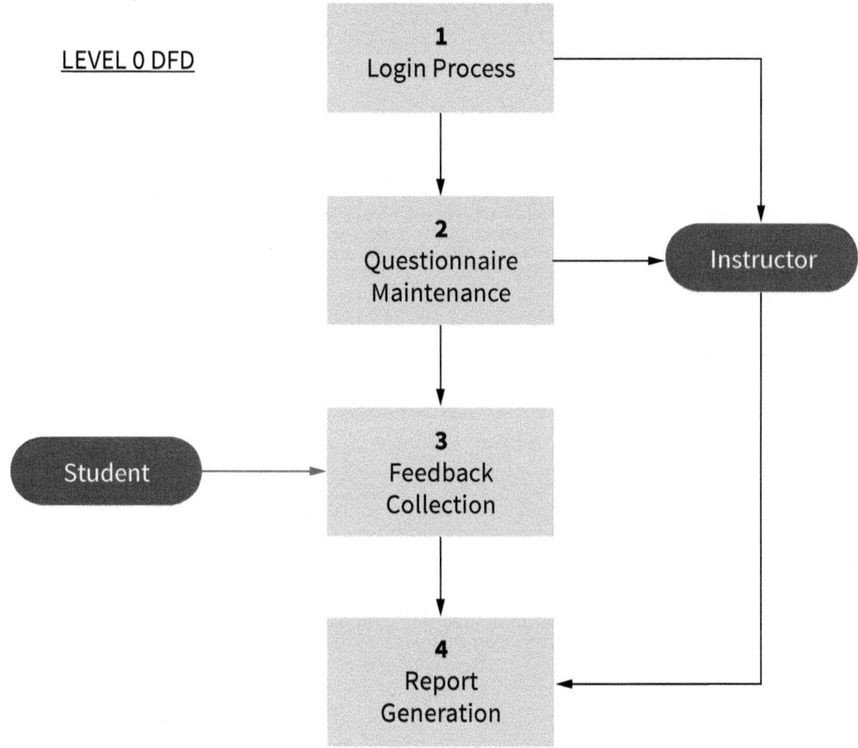

Figure 4.2: Data flow diagram.

Bitmap images are made up of thousands of coloured dots, known as pixels, and when they are resized there is a notable drop in quality. Bitmap image software tends to be used for photos or computer artwork. Software such as Adobe's Photoshop, the GNU Image Manipulation Program (GIMP) or Adobe's Fireworks offer many advanced tools to manipulate bitmaps. To cope with the loss of fidelity as an image is manipulated or transformed, it is important to start off with a high-quality image. Figure 4.3 shows that the closer you zoom in to a bitmap image, the more you notice the individual pixels. However, even this feature can be used to produce pixel art.

The file for a bitmap image contains data relating to the colour of each individual pixel, which is why uncompressed image files tend to be relatively large. The dimensions of an image is measured in pixels too so a large image of a high resolution will have a large file size. Colour bit depth defines how many bits are used to describe the colour of each pixel. 8 bit colour only provides 256 different colour values although file sizes will be smaller. 24 bit colour provides millions of colours but file size will be larger.

Figure 4.3: Example bitmap icons for apps.

Bitmap images are produced by digital cameras and scanners. If you need to edit these, bitmap drawing tools are your only option, unless you use optical character recognition (OCR) to gather the text from the images.

Bitmap images tend to be high-quality images produced by digital cameras, and the file sizes can be very large. Consequently, compression is required to allow them to fit onto secondary storage media, e.g. an SD card in a camera, or to be downloaded quickly from the internet. A popular image compression format is JPEG (named after the Joint Photographic Experts Group), which uses a lossy compression method to achieve enormous savings in file size. Lossy compression, although very efficient at saving file space, loses some of the overall quality of the image. This is why professional photographers will not take photos in JPEG format, preferring to use the uncompressed RAW format. Compression is covered in more detail in Chapter 7.

Database packages

A database is a structure in which data is organised into tables, fields and records. Databases are used to store vast amounts of data required for specific purposes. Databases form the backbone of most enterprise IT systems, including large-scale websites. For example, your bank records, health details and even the time you register at school are all stored on a database. The BBC website is run entirely from a database, with news stories and images stored in the tables of a content management system. Databases are much better equipped to deal with large amounts of related data, while spreadsheets are better equipped to deal with numeric data.

One of the key features of a database is the ability to search and sort data quickly. This is done by querying the data within the database. Microsoft Access, which is used in schools and small businesses, has a graphical way of generating queries called query by example (QBE), as shown in Figure 4.4. In larger-scale databases, queries are written in a special language called structured query language (SQL). Large organisations such as banks and the owners of substantial websites will use database software such as MySQL, Microsoft SQL Server or Oracle. Microsoft Access can also make use of SQL; the details of SQL are covered in Chapter 8.

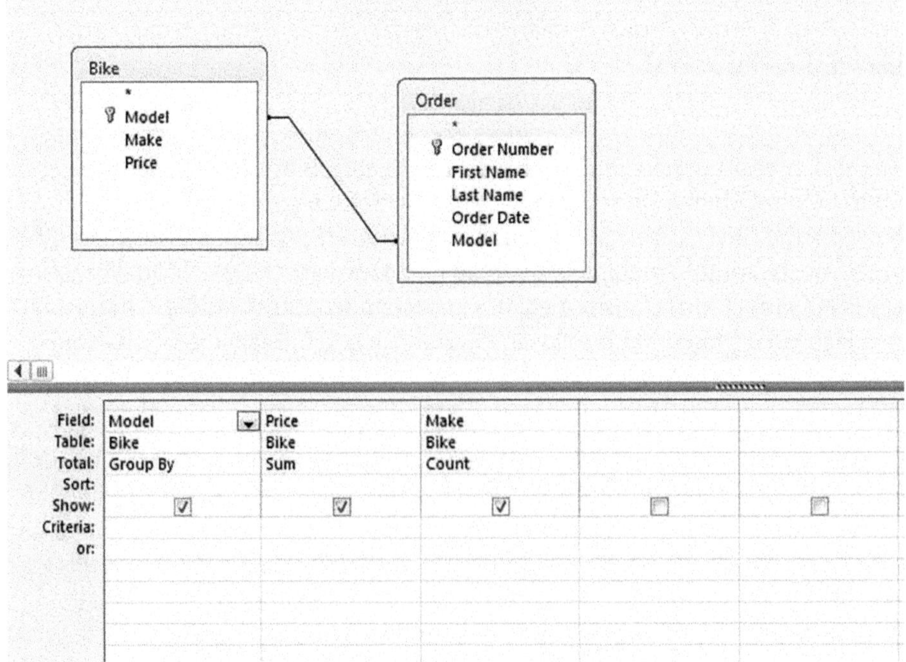

Figure 4.4: Microsoft Access database.

Knowledge-based systems

Using a knowledge-based system, a user can interrogate a vast knowledge base to find a solution. The user enters the information he or she already has, and the knowledge-based system infers an answer. If the system cannot reach a conclusion, it requests more information. This process is continued until either the system has a high degree of confidence that it knows what the solution is, or it is sure that, having exhausted every line of inquiry, it does not know the solution.

Consider a car mechanic who has very specific and detailed knowledge on how to repair cars. For this reason, knowledge-based systems are also called expert systems. The mechanic knows that if a car is exhibiting certain symptoms, it is likely that X or Y is the problem. The process is not always exact and sometimes the mechanic has to look deeper in order to diagnose the issue. The mechanic follows a simple algorithm:

While problem has not been solved:

- Mechanic asks the client questions
- Client responds to the questions
- Mechanic infers what the problem may be based on the information given so far.

A knowledge-based system works in the same way and consists of different parts:

- *Knowledge base*: a database containing expert knowledge.
- *Inference engine*: attempts to work out the answer to the user's query by using the rule base.
- *Rule base*: links knowledge together through facts.
- *User interface (HCI)*: allows the user to communicate with the system. HCI stands for human–computer interface.

- The rule base works by using logic and probabilities. For example, consider a patient who has a headache and a runny nose. It is possible that the patient may have a cold or the flu. Cases of colds are more common but there is a chance that it could be the flu. The rule base sets these links and probabilities for the inference engine to use. Based on the two symptoms, a probability is placed on the two possible outcomes. The more likely scenario, a cold, has a higher weighting. At this stage the inference engine may not have enough information to make a diagnosis, so it could ask for more information, such as 'Does the patient have a fever?' or 'Is the patient fatigued?'
- The inference engine is interactive and will not just take in the input, do some processing and then provide an answer. At any point the knowledge-based system may require more information to help arrive at the correct conclusion.
- The inference engine is responsible for making one of three decisions:
  1. Whether it has enough information to arrive at an answer.
  2. Whether it requires more information.
  3. Whether it cannot reliably come up with an answer.
- Probabilities of which answer is correct are built up over time. Every question eliminates some answers and makes others more likely to be correct, enabling the expert system to make an educated guess.

Tip

Questions on knowledge-based systems can be based around a scenario that requires some form of diagnosis using expert knowledge. You must be able to relate the main parts of a knowledge-based system to the context. Make sure you revise the four main parts.

Computer-aided design and computer-aided manufacturing (CAD/CAM)

Computer-aided design and computer-aided manufacturing (CAD/CAM) is the process of designing a product using a computer, testing it using simulations, and then manufacturing many thousands of copies based on a single design.

Almost all of the things we use in modern life have come from a factory assembly line. From toothpaste to iPads, most products are manufactured using a CAD/CAM process.

CAD software enables designers to try out different designs for a product before physical production. CAD allows the designer to place parts together (some of which may have been pre-designed), scale and rotate in three dimensions, change colour and even run simulations to test how the design might react in the real world. Designers can try out different ideas and styles without having to make physical prototypes until they are sure that the design is sound. It isn't possible to test every aspect of a design using CAD because of the vast number of variables; a prototype will have to be built at some point. By using CAD, the number of prototypes can be kept to a minimum, potentially saving millions of pounds during research and development.

For example, when designing a car it is important, from a safety standpoint, that the design is tested to see how it behaves at different speeds and in different weather conditions. It is not worth creating a prototype that would perform badly at the first sign of bad weather. Running simulations of the car in use through the CAD software allows most problems to be spotted and solved without creating a prototype.

As consumers, we expect everything we buy to be perfect. By enlisting machines to produce our products we can guarantee, within a small error margin, a stable quality level. In CAM, machines make products rather than people making them. Specifications are fed into a CAM system, which drives an assembly line. The specifications say exactly what the product looks like, its materials and the steps required to assemble it. CAM systems rely heavily on sensors and actuators and commonly make use of feedback loops. Sensors are input devices that detect a change in the environment and input this to the computer system. Actuators are output devices that perform an action such as electric motors, valves and solenoids. Feedback loops allow a control system to use an input variable to control output. CAM systems will be able to pick up and move components but to not apply so much pressure that they are damaged. CAM machines offer the following advantages over hand assembly:

- They will always produce products that are exactly the same.
- They do not get tired.
- They do not make mistakes (unless they break down!).
- They can work 24 hours a day, seven days a week and do not require a rest break.

Utility software

A utility program is designed to perform a system task, for example transferring data from one storage device to another, managing the computer's tasks or combating computer viruses. Utility software normally comes bundled with your OS, but can also be installed separately.

File manager utility

A file management utility enables the user to do simple file manipulation. The tasks a file management software can perform are:

- move files from one directory to another
- copy files
- rename files
- list directory contents.

File management software cannot open files, as this is the responsibility of the program associated with the file. For example, in the Windows family of operating systems the .docx file type is associated with Microsoft Word, which will be invoked when a file of this type is double clicked.

Compression software

Compression software is used to compress files to reduce their overall size. When a file has been compressed, it is very close to the minimum size it can be before losing data. Compressing an already compressed file does not result in any further reduction in file size. This is because of the way compression algorithms work and the mathematical theory that underpins them.

When a file is compressed, it becomes unreadable by other software until it is decompressed by the utility originally used to compress it. For example, WinRAR can produce an archive of type RAR. This can only be decompressed by WinRAR or other compatible utilities. So if you receive a Word document that has been compressed using WinRAR, it would no longer be readable in Word until it was decompressed. This is true for any compression utility.

A number of files and folders can be compressed together in order to create an archive using lossless compression. Such a compression utility retains all the file details, names and folder structures. When the file is decompressed, the exact original file, byte for byte, will be reproduced. This is important because when the end user opens the file, they need to be able to view it exactly as it was originally written. Executable programs can also be compressed and decompressed. If any bits were removed by the compression algorithm, the program would no longer be able to run when it is decompressed.

Compression is explored in more detail in Chapter 7.

Task managers

Task managers allow the user to view the processes currently running on a system and see what resources each one is using. This is useful information when trying to find bottlenecks in a system or when killing unresponsive processes. On OS X (Mac) the utility is called Activity Monitor, as shown in Figure 4.5.

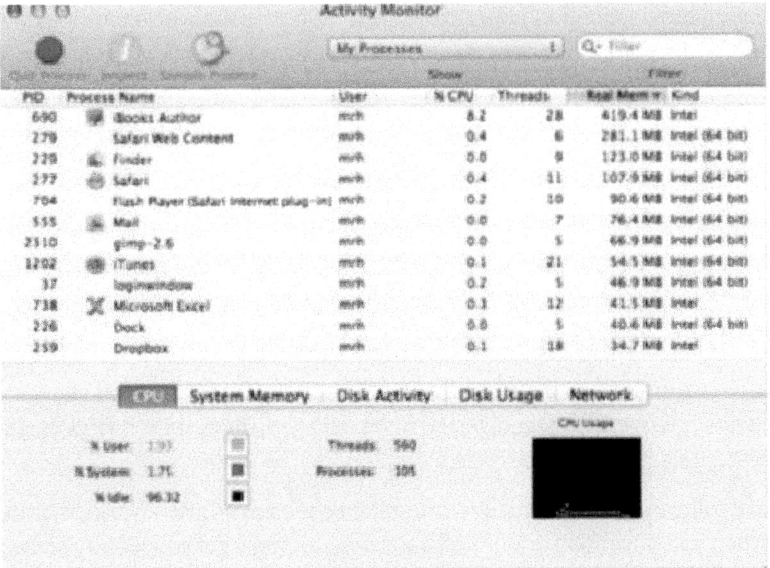

Figure 4.5: Activity Monitor.

Anti-virus software

A virus is malicious code that can infect and spread itself through a user's e-mail, secondary storage drives and social networks. Once a virus has infected a system, it may install software to open up a back door for a hacker, monitor a user's keystrokes or simply just wipe files clean. Viruses are commonly used by criminal gangs to create armies of infected computers known as **botnets**. A criminal can employ botnets to launch denial-of-service attacks, send spam e-mails or offer them to the highest bidder.

Anti-virus utility software can help to protect the user against these threats. It scans every file and all the memory on the user's system, looking for evidence of viruses or Trojans. It has a large database of virus signatures, which it can compare to your files. It also monitors suspicious activity and informs the user if it detects anything untoward. When a virus is found, it can try to remove it, delete it or quarantine the file. It is important that anti-virus software is regularly updated so that the virus definitions stored on the computer are current, as new viruses are being developed frequently.

Tip

There are many different examples of utility software, but those listed in the previous section are the ones most commonly referred to in exams.

Mobile telephone apps

The small but powerful applications (apps) that run on smartphones have revolutionised the way mobiles are used and have given small application developers access to massive marketplaces such as Apple's App Store and Google's Play Store. Apps, which are of low cost to the end user or supported by advertising, have allowed smartphones to become true mobile computing platforms rather than simply something on which to play Angry Birds®.

Unlike desktop applications, mobile apps tend to be small and focused on a number of very specific tasks. Users can download and install apps to enable them to perform the tasks they need. Owing to the menu-based interface on smartphones, small-screen real estate and comparatively low processing power (when compared to desktops), apps are by their very nature simple. It is this reason that has led to their popularity, and many people who do not normally make use of desktop programs happily make use of mobile apps.

Mobile apps are developed in a number of programming languages and environments, depending on the destination platform. Apps for iPhones are written in Objective-C or Swift, apps for Android are written in Java, and apps for Windows 8 are written in C# and use the .NET framework. This poses a problem to software developers, who have to port their programs from one platform to another if they want to reach the widest possible market. In reality, this does not always happen and some apps are available only on the iPhone or Android. There are some programming environments, such as Unity, that enable developers to produce their programs and publish them to all of the different platforms.

Open and closed source software

Source code is produced by developers and defines what they want their software to do. Once software has been produced, tested and packaged, developers have a choice to make: do they release the source code or not?

Proprietary software does not include the source code and is also known as closed source. When you download or buy software, you normally get proprietary software. This means that you will **not** be able to get access to the source code, nor will you be allowed to make any changes to the software. Companies commonly do not release source code because the code may contain trade secrets or patents, which they do not want others to access and use. Similarly, car companies closely guard their new model designs. Companies invest a lot of money in building their software and they want to ensure that people cannot take their intellectual property, which is protected by copyright legislation.. Closed-source software enables developers to protect their knowledge and investments, but it does mean that only they can make changes to the code. So, if a bug occurs in the code, they will be the ones responsible for fixing it. If developers decide not to support the software once released, which is within their right, bugs will not be fixed and will remain forever in the software. A recent example of this is the operating system Windows XP®, which is no longer supported by Microsoft. Even though there are millions of people still using Windows XP, Microsoft will not fix any bugs that emerge or issue updates to prevent security breaches. This means that people either have to upgrade their operating system, which is not always a financial option if they have application software that only functions with that version, or live with software that may have potential security issues.

Closed-source software can be free; it is up to the developers and the business model they are using. Apps are mostly closed source and a lot of them are free to the user. Developers may, however, make money in other ways, such as through advertising or in-app purchases. Sometimes closed-source software is released for free as a trial for a larger, paid, fully featured version of the software. Examples of this are Microsoft Visual Studio Community Edition and Visual Studio Professional. The Community Edition is great for basic programs and learning to code, but for large-scale enterprise applications, built by teams of people, benefit will be gained from the paid version of the software with its additional features such as version control using Team Foundation Server.

Open-source software is the direct opposite of closed source. For software to be open source, you must be able to download the source code to enable you to make changes to it as you wish. There is a big difference between free software and open source. Free software does not make the source code available. Open-source code tends to have a lot of developers working on it for free, or being sponsored by a larger company. Anyone can join the community of developers to make changes to the code and upload their changes for the rest of the world to see. If the changes are good, they will be merged into the main source code and all users can benefit. Some famous examples of open-source software are Mozilla Firefox and the Linux kernel.

Computing in context: software licensing and open software

All software that users can install on their computing devices is covered by some form of software licence. This defines the exact circumstances in which the software can be used, how many times it can be run, the end user's responsibilities and the developer's liabilities. It makes sense that closed-source proprietary software is governed by licences, but the majority of open-source projects are also protected by licences. One of the most common licences is the GNU General Public License (GNU GPL or GPL) (GNU is a recursive acronym that stands for 'GNU's not UNIX').

Richard Stallman

In order to understand why open-source software is governed by a licence, you must take a short look at its history. In 1983 Richard Stallman, shown on the right, started the free software movement by launching the GNU project. He was despondent at the growing trend of companies refusing to distribute source code and felt it was morally incorrect for software developers to impose their view of how software should be used on the people using it. The goal of the GNU project, as well as the free software movement in general, is based around the definition of what free means. Stallman proposed that the ideology behind the word free should be the same as that of free speech. He defines the term 'free software' as:

A program is free software, for you, a particular user, if:

- You have the freedom to run the program as you wish, for any purpose.
- You have the freedom to modify the program to suit your needs. (To make this freedom effective in practice, you must have access to the source code, since making changes in a program without having the source code is exceedingly difficult.)

One issue with open-source software is that someone could take the ideas from the software, legitimately; add it to their code, which is allowed; but then release their version as closed source. This would go against the founding principles of the free software movement, and thus steps had to be taken to counter this danger.

In order to ensure that software released as 'free' is kept free, GPL was born. Those who originally produce the software can release it as open-source, and can enforce the freedoms using GPL. Anyone breaking the licence can be held accountable in the same way as if someone breaks the licence of proprietary software. This prevents unscrupulous people taking advantage of the movement and trying to make a quick profit from other people's ideas and code.

There are a large number of open-source licences, each having their own specific niche. Some insist that any derivations or future versions of the code must be protected by the same licence, while others are more permissive. It is up to software developers to decide which licence they wish to use.

Translators

We use the term 'translators' to cover all the types of software that convert code from one form to another. These comprise compilers, interpreters and assemblers.

Compilers

Compilers convert source code written in a high-level language such as C++, C, Swift and BASIC, into machine code. A compiler produces a standalone executable file, which can be released to others without the need for further compilation. A program is compiled once, but can be run many times. Compiled code protects the intellectual property of the developers, unless they release the source code themselves under an open-source licence. When code is compiled, it will be targeted at a specific platform and CPU instruction set. Programs compiled for Mac OS X will not run on a Windows computer, nor will programs compiled for x86 processors run on ARM-based ones. If software is to be ported to other systems and operating systems, it needs not only to be recompiled, but also most likely changed, as software for different environments tends to be coded differently.

Interpreters

An interpreter handles the job of translating code very differently from a compiler. Instead of producing a single executable, it translates each line of code into machine code, line by line. The interpreter takes the first line of the source code, translates it and executes it before moving on to the next. Any machine code produced while the interpreter is running is not saved, meaning that the interpreter must interpret the code every time the user wishes to run it. Interpreters are commonly used for a number of languages, including, Lisp, Python, JavaScript, Ruby and PHP. In order to be able to run an interpreted language, you must have an interpreter installed on the system. One of the key design goals is that an interpreted language can be run on any system, as long as an interpreter has been installed. There are a number of key advantages and disadvantages of using interpreters:

Advantages

- Source code has to be written only once and then it can run on any computer with an interpreter.
- You can easily inspect the contents of variables as the program is running.
- You can test code more efficiently as well as being able to test single lines of code.
- Code can be run on many different types of computer platforms, such as Macs, a Windows PC, UNIX or Linux machines.

Disadvantages

- You must have an interpreter running on the computer in order to be able to run the program.
- As source code must be translated each time the program is executed, interpreted programs can sometimes run slowly.
- You have to rely on the interpreter for machine-level optimisations rather than programming them yourself.
- Developers can view the source code, which means that they could use your intellectual property to write their own software.

Compilers and interpreters are contrasted in Table 4.1 below:

Feature	Compiler	Interpreter
Source code	Hidden from other developers and users. Intellectual property protected.	Shown to all developers and users. Intellectual property at risk.
Multiple platforms	Compiled code will only run on CPUs which have the same instruction sets. Also the OS has to match.	Will run on any platform from the same source code base. An interpreter is required to run.
Distribution	Executable files can be easily distributed on CD or over the internet.	Systems need to be set up before the code can be run. This can include installing library files as well as the interpreter.

Table 4.1: Table comparing compilers and interpreters.

Assemblers

In the early days of computing, programmers wrote machine code to run directly on the CPU. As programs became more complicated, it became apparent that writing binary machine code was not an efficient way to write lengthy programs. To make low-level programming more manageable, they designed a language called Assembly.

Assembly language is a step above machine code, allowing the developer to write code using mnemonics which are short, English-like acronyms such as ADD, SUB, LDA (load) and STA (store). Each assembly code instruction has a one-to-one mapping with a machine code instruction. This is unlike source code, which has a one-to-many mapping. Machine code, as already stated, is a binary representation of an instruction that can be run on a specific CPU architecture. Writing machine code directly in binary would be very time-consuming and prone to errors. The translator that converts assembly language code to machine code is known as an assembler.

Opcodes and data

A machine code instruction has two parts, the opcode and the operand. The image below shows how a 16-bit instruction could be split. An opcode is a specific binary value that represents a single instruction from the processor's instruction set. In order for the instruction to be executed correctly, it requires an operand or data, which is the second part of the machine code instruction. Sometimes the operand is split over multiple bytes, meaning that the next set of bytes fetched to the CPU will actually be the data from the last instruction, rather than the next instruction to be processed. Also, machine code instructions differ between architectures, so an ADD instruction on an x86 processor may look completely different from the ADD instruction on an ARM processor. The binary opcode values used are not comparable on different CPUs , which is one of the key reasons why assembly language programs written for one architecture will not run on another.

Opcode	Operand
10010011	11001010

Table 4.2: Structure of a machine code instruction.

Mnemonics

Assembly languages assign a mnemonic to each opcode in order to make it more readable for humans. It also makes use of labels and other features to make low-level coding simpler for the developer. Some example mnemonics are:

- ADD – add numbers together.
- MOV – moves data from register or memory to another location.
- SUB – subtracts numbers.
- JMP – jump to a memory address and start executing at that point.

Assembly code also uses labels to represent variables and memory addresses.

Assembly language for x86 processors

So far we have considered assembly language and machine code in the general sense, but from this point forward we consider the x86 Assembly language. This chapter is not designed to teach you Assembly, but rather to give you an idea of how Assembly is structured and written. To get a better understanding of writing Assembly code, try developing Little Man Computer (LMC) code, which is covered in Chapter 6.

```
mov ax, 1
add ax, 5
```

Figure 4.6: Example code.

The example code in Figure 4.6 will first move (mov) the value 1 into the accumulator referenced as 'ax' and then add 5 to it. This code makes use of the immediate addressing mode (covered in Chapter 6). x86 Assembly language represents numbers and memory addresses as hexadecimal values rather than decimal. In this case, although the values of 1 and 5 in hex do represent 1 and 5 in decimal, this will not always so. Both of the instructions above have two operands in the data part of the instruction, and these are encoded as part of the instruction when assembled.

Translating assembly language to machine code

Assembly code has a one-to-one mapping between the mnemonic instructions of the language and their binary code equivalents. It may appear that translation seems almost trivial, but this is not the case. Due to the inclusion of variables and labels, there is still a lot of work to be done and a two-phased approach must be taken. In the first phase, labels are converted into memory addresses and stored in a symbol table. Symbol tables in assembly language work differently from those used during lexical analysis (covered later) and should not be regarded in the same way. The second phase of translation involves converting the mnemonics into their binary representations and combining them with the binary representations of the data.

Symbol table

When a label or variable is encountered during the translation process, an entry is made in the symbol table. This maps the label or variable to a memory address. Variables map to a memory location that will be used to store its value, while labels map to the exact position of the instruction that it needs to jump to. Consider the code below:

Address	Mnemonic	Op1	Op2
0	mov	count	10
1	mov	ax	0
2	loop: add	ax	count
3	sub	count	1
4	CMP	count	0
5	JNE	loop:	

Note: mov stands for 'move', CMP is 'compare' and JNE means 'jump not equal'.

Symbol	Address
Count	6
Loop	2

Table 4.3: An example of a machine code program and the resultant symbol table.

The assembly code on the left performs the calculation sequence 10 + 9 + ... + 1 and stores the result in the 'ax' register. Next to each line of code is the instruction's memory address. A symbol table (Table 4.3) is produced as the assembler works through its first phase. In order to store the count in memory, an address has to be set up, for example the first available memory address after the program. This decision about the memory addresses that variables are assigned is up to the assembler. When a label is encountered, the memory address of where it was defined is placed in the symbol table; in the above example that would be address 2. Once the symbol table has been produced, as shown in Table 4.3, the assembler goes over the code and replaces every variable or label with the memory address stored within the table. Table 4.4 shows the same program with the symbols replaced:

Note that memory addresses (not[/immediate values) are represented by surrounding them with square brackets ([ ]).

Address	Mnemonic	Op1	Op2
0	mov	[6]	10
1	mov	ax	0
2	add	ax	[6]
3	sub	count	1
4	CMP	count	0
5	JNE	[2]	

Table 4.4: Machine code instructions after labels have been replaced with memory addresses.

Stages of compilation

Compiling is a complicated process and requires a large amount of processing time. To make the task simpler, compiling is separated into a number of phases. Each phase produces something for the next phase to work on. Some of the tasks that the compiler must perform are:

- parsing source code (lexical analysis)
- analysing syntax
- checking types
- generating machine code
- sequencing code blocks
- allocating registers
- optimising
- linking of libraries.

Some of these operations have been simplified for this course and the key phases that you may encounter are summarised in Figure 4.7.

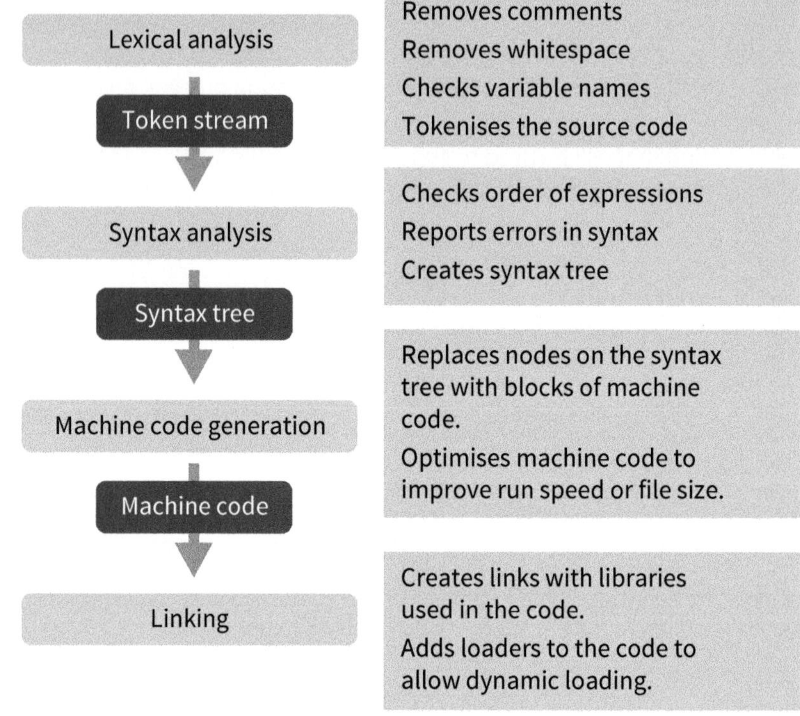

Figure 4.7: Key stages in compilation.

Lexical analysis

When a compiler receives source code, it parses or checks it, and decides whether each line contains keywords, variables, constants or anything else accepted by the language. It converts the source code into a token stream. A token is a numeric representation of a keyword or identifier. Identifiers, such as variables and function names, must be treated independently. Each token represents a different identifier and if that identifier is seen again, the same token is used. As a token is just a single number, extra information about it, such as the name of the identifier, is stored in a symbol table. Lexical analysis makes use of spaces, newlines or atomic values to separate tokens. Atomic values are core parts of a language such as operators or keywords. It removes anything deemed unnecessary by the compiler, such as comments and white space (tabs, newlines etc.). Anything that does not match the pattern for a keyword, operator, literal (a data value) or identifier is flagged up as an error. The lexical analysis phase does not check the syntax or the order of keywords and operators; it simply prepares the code for syntax analysis.

The lexical analyser does not pick up typing mistakes. The example shown here should read: IF Y A = 1 THEN PRINT "moo", but it has been mistyped:

Code

```
IFFY A=1 THEN PLINT "moo"
```

The lexical analyser would not pick up IFFY and PLINT as errors, but assume they were identifiers. Both IFFY and PLINT are perfectly acceptable identifier names, but where they are placed is clearly wrong.

Lexical analysis will not pick up any errors in the ordering of expressions.

Code
`IF 1=A PRINT THEN "moo"`

Again, the lexical analyser would accept this code, even though the order of the expression is invalid; as long as each atomic part of the code matches an identifier, literal or keyword.

In order to tokenise source code, which is the key design goal of the lexical analyser, it must read each individual character and then try to match it to something it recognises. For example, the expression $2 \times 3 + 4$ would be converted to a stream of tokens such as:

- NUMBER <2>
- MULTIPLIES
- NUMBER <3>
- ADD
- NUMBER <4>

A token would normally be represented as a number, which would be assigned by the lexical analyser through the use of a symbol table. To make the process a bit more human friendly, the above token stream is represented by words to aid understanding.

Regular expressions

The lexical analyser searches through the code looking for specific patterns of letters, numbers and symbols. These are called regular expressions. Consider the lines of Python code in Figure 4.8.

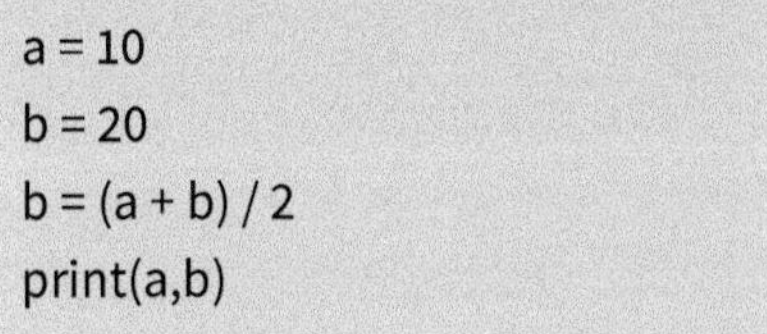

```
a = 10
b = 20
b = (a + b) / 2
print(a,b)
```

Figure 4.8: Python.

In this code you can see examples of variables, assignments, operators and keywords. In order to tokenise this code there needs to be a regular expression for each. Table 4.5 below shows what these regular expressions would look like. At first they may seem confusing, but they are in fact very straightforward. For example, variables must be made up of lowercase or uppercase letters only.

Token	Regular expression
print	print
variable	[a-z]|[A-Z].+
assignment	=
operator	+|-|*|\

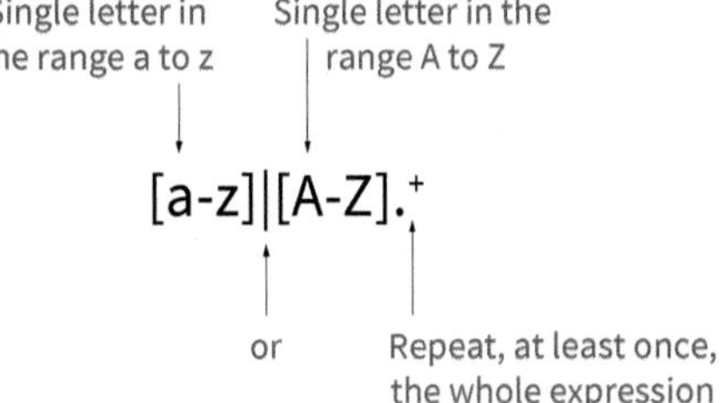

Table 4.5: Simple regular expressions representing common tokens.

A lexical analyser recognises identifiers, keywords, operators and literals, and each one has its own regular expression. These are then applied to the source code to generate the stream of tokens.

Symbol	Description	Example	Possible input
.	Represents any character, digit or symbol	.at	cat hat mat bat zat 3at
*	Repeats the symbol immediately to the left. Can be empty.	ab*	a ab abb abbb abbbb
[a-z]	Range of characters. Accepts a single character in the range specified inside the [] brackets.	[a-c]+	abc aabbcc caba bbaabbccaaa
[^a-z]	Character is NOT in the range specified in the [] brackets.	[^a-c]+	uyd hythytd popodd qqwtyuw
a|b	A choice between two or more items.	+|-+	+ - -- --- ----

Table 4.6: Example regular expression operators.

Regular expressions can be represented as diagrams known as automata or state machines. Although we will not look at automata in any great detail, it is useful to know that they can be converted directly from regular expressions. When developing a lexical analyser, a finite deterministic automaton is created for each expression and combined to enable the analyser to make the right choice of token at any given point during parsing. This forms the internal representation of the language in the compiler (Figure 4.9).

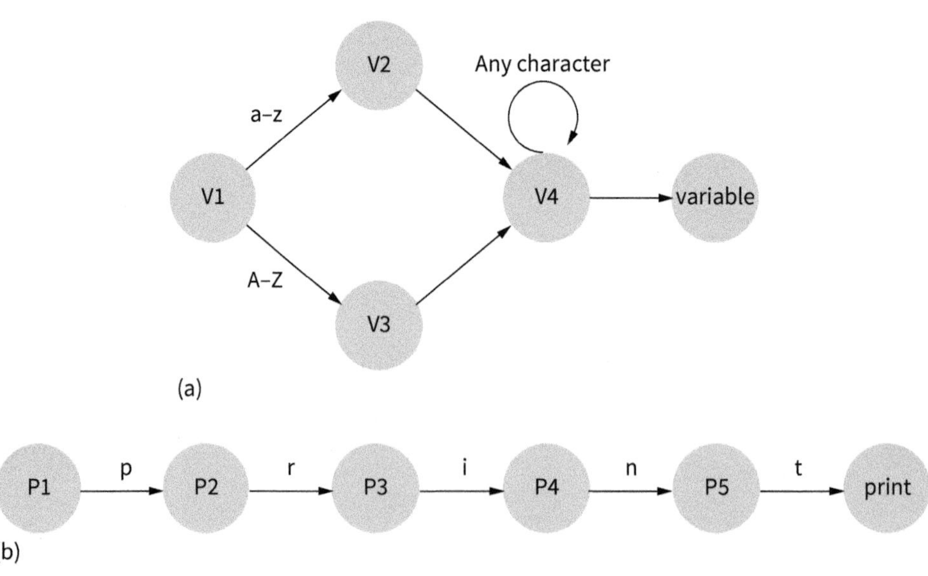

Figure 4.9: Finite deterministic automata for print keyword.

Each circle represents a state of the analyser, each line a transition between states, and the text on each line shows which transitions are legal. Normally each transition (each line) represents a single letter rather than a group. Groups of characters have been added to make the diagram more compact and readable. One issue we currently have is that at the moment we have no idea which automaton to use if we see the input 'p'. It could be 'print' or it could be 'pad' – one is a keyword and the other is an identifier. Because we need to know about future input, we call this a non-deterministic finite automaton (NFA). A parser cannot be written based on an NFA because for every given input we could potentially have more than one transition to take. In order to create a lexical analyser we must convert the non-deterministic automaton to a deterministic automaton. How this works is outside the scope of this course, but is well documented on the web for the interested reader.

Symbol table

A token may have a value, for example a variable name, procedure name or a constant. In addition, the language may also define some tokens to represent keywords and operators. Both language-defined tokens and user-defined tokens must be stored in the symbol table. Identifier names can be made up of many characters and are descriptive in order to help the developer. A compiler does not need to make use of long names to help it understand the code, and by replacing long identifiers with a simple token it can reduce the amount of work to be done by the syntax analyser. Each element of the code is replaced with a token that will provide an index to the symbol table. The symbol table stores:

- an index or identifier
- the name of the token
- data type
- scope and restrictions.

Comments and white space are removed at this stage. Spaces, carriage returns and comments are simply there to aid the programmer and have no relevance to the compiler. Indentation aids readability but is irrelevant to a **compiler**. Consider the following code snippet:

Code

```
//comment
IF A>5 THEN A = A * 2
ELSE A = A * 3
A = A + 2
```

This code produces the following tokens.

IF VARIABLE GREATER_THAN THEN VARIABLE EQUALS
VARIABLE MULTIPLIES LITERAL ELSE VARIABLE EQUALS
VARIABLE MULTIPLIES LITERAL VARIABLE EQUALS VARIABLE
PLUS LITERAL

It will also produce the symbol table shown in Table 4.7.

The code and symbol table would produce the following token stream:

1 2 3 4 5 2 6 2 7 8 9 2 6 2 7 10 2 6 2 11 8

When an error is found during compilation, it will be returned to the developer via translator diagnostics. During lexical analysis, the errors found will be due to incorrect

Token code	Type	Lexeme
1	IF	–
2	Variable	A
3	>	–
4	Literal	5
5	THEN	–
6	=	–
7	*	–
8	Literal	2
9	ELSE	–
10	Literal	3
11	+	–

Table 4.7: Example symbol table after lexical analysis.

identifier naming. For example, consider the statement 1Var = 10. Looking at this as a human, we can guess that the developer wanted a variable called '1Var' and to assign the value 10 to it. However, the lexical analyser does not have such an easy task reading this and it would not match the correct regular expression. When a number is the first part of an expression, the lexical analyser has to make a choice between a number and an identifier.

A simple identifier that would allow numbers at any point in a regular expression would be [0-9a-zA-z] .*, while a regular expression for integer literals could be [0-9] .*. In a regular expression, characters, including numbers, are represented within the square brackets. The dot after the square bracket represents a single character and the * means that it may be repeated one or more times or not at all i.e. we only have a single character.

Now consider the expression 123 = 50. According to the regular expression we have written so far, '123' could be either a variable or a number. At this point the lexical analyser has a choice to make, which can result in ambiguity and incorrect compilation. We could say that because there is an equal sign after it, we should match to an identifier. However, the number 123, anywhere else in the code, would then always match to an identifier. Effectively we have an ambiguous set of regular expressions and this would lead to code being misinterpreted and some very complex bugs to fix. It is common that languages do not accept a number as the first part of a variable definition. A common (simple) variable definition would look like this:

Expressions – any set of programming code that will result in a value being produced.

With this definition, the lexical analyser would report an error for 1Var through translator diagnostics.

Activity 4.1

```
%{
int lineNumber =1;
%}
if if
letter [a-zA-z]
digit [6-9]
id {letter}({letter}|{digit})*
number {digit}+
%%
{if} printf("<IF>");
^{id} {dispNewLine(); printf("<ID>");}
{id} printf("<IF>");
^{number} {dispNewLine(); printf("NUMBER");}
{number} printf("<NUMBER>");
[^a-zA-Z0-9 \t\n]+ printf("the rest is \\%s\\",yytext);
%%
dispNewLine(){
printf("%d : ", lineNumber++);
}
```

1 Install the lexical analyser flex using **'sudo apt-get install flex'**

2 Enter the code shown above and save the file as 'exampleLex.lex'

3 Run the **lex** command to produce the c source code for the lexical analyser.

4 **lex -t exampleLex.lex > exampleLex.c**

5 Compile the scanner using **gcc. gcc exampleLex.c –o exampleLex -ll**

6 Run your scanner by executing the command **./exampleLex**

7 Try a number of lines of code to see what happens. See if you can work out which rules are being run. Press CTRL-D to exit.

8 Edit 'example.lex' to include more keywords and operators such as brackets and mathematics. Each change you make you must regenerate the source (run lex) and then compile (gcc).

9 The **ldd** command in Linux will show what libraries a program currently uses. In order to view which libraries are linked you must find the binary executable (not rely on the $PATH environment variable). Enter the command **cd /bin** to navigate to a directory containing some common Linux binary files.

10 Enter the command **'ldd echo'**

11 Research what each of the libraries do for the echo command. A library tends to have the extension '.so'

12 Navigate to the folder '/usr/games' by using the command **'cd /usr/games'** – list the contents of this directory using the ls command.

13 Run ldd on any file in this folder. Why do you think there are so many extra library files? What do some of these extra ones do?

A notation for defining a language's syntax

Every programming language has its own syntax, just as a human language such as English or Swahili does. Syntax is the way the components of a language are put together to form meaningful statements. It can be very useful in a computing context to formally define and document the syntax of a programming language. One way of doing this is to use the Backus Normal Form or Backus–Naur Form (BNF) notation. This system is named after its two inventors, John Backus and Peter Naur. It defines the rules that must be followed in order for source code to be syntactically correct. Consider the following IF statement, which is syntactically incorrect:

Code

```
IF ELSE a > 10 THEN
END IF
a = 1
```

ELSE should never follow immediately after an IF. The syntax rules of most languages state that a comparison expression should follow the IF keyword, such as '> 10'. The correct syntax for an IF statement could be represented using BNF. Rules defined in BNF define valid syntax within the compiler.

How it works

Figure 4.10 shows a simple rule that defines a single digit from 0–9.

Reading it from left to right:

Let the rule **digit** be defined (or assigned) as being the terminal: 0 or 1 or 2 or 3 or 4 or 5 or 6 or 7 or 8 or 9.

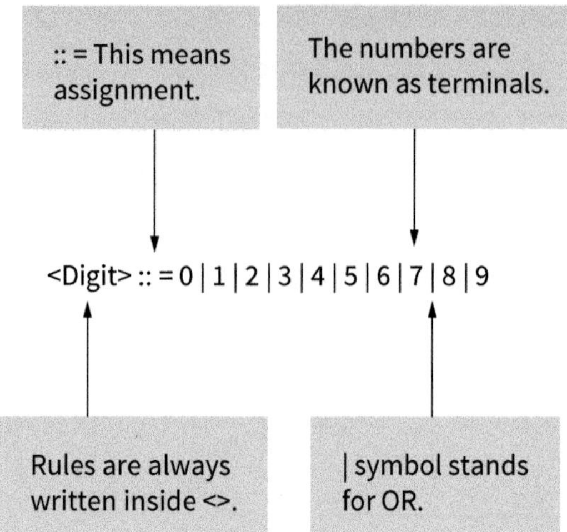

Figure 4.10: Example BNF.

Terminals cannot be evaluated any further and take the form of symbols, characters or digits. The | (pipe) symbol represents OR (disjunction or choice). If terminals or non-terminals are next to each other, this is considered to be concatenation (conjunction), which means they are added together. Rules can be combined by referring to the name of one rule within another. When a rule is used in this way, it is known as a non-terminal. This is because we have to evaluate it further before we can accept the input.

<Two_Digit_Number>: : = <Digit> <Digit>

The rule <Two_Digit_Number> has been made up of a <Digit> followed immediately by a second <Digit> using concatenation. We already know that a <Digit> is a single-digit number from 0 to 9, so by combining two digits we can match any two-digit number.

Rules can be evaluated (or tested) with specific values. Consider the number 54. <Digit> is a non-terminal and must be evaluated further. By replacing <Digit> with 0 | 1 | 2 | 3 | 4 | 5 | 6 | 7 | 8 | 9 we have terminals for that part, as shown above. The digit 5 can be compared to one of these terminals, which means that the first part of the rule passes. The second <Digit> is evaluated in the same way.

<Two_Digit_Number> : : = <Digit> <Digit>
<Two_Digit_Number> : : = 0 |1 | 2 | 3 | 4 | 5 | 6 | 7 | 8 |<Digit>

At this point we have run out of input, which means that the number 54 matches the rule and is accepted as valid input. However, the evaluation of 5A would cause issues for the 'A', as this has not been defined in the existing syntax.

Recursion

So far our grammar is not very practical. For example, imagine being able to store numbers that can have up to 200 digits. We could define a rule for every possible set of digits from 1 to 200; three of the rules are shown below:

<Number> : : = <Digit>
<Number> : : = <Digit><Digit>
<Number> : : = <Digit><Digit><Digit>

This is clearly impractical; we need a single rule that can define any number of digits. Thankfully, this can be accomplished by using recursion within BNF. Below is the recursive rule for a number of variable lengths of digits:

What we are saying here is that we can either have a single digit or we can have a digit followed by another number, which in turn can be another digit. Consider 5983:

<Number> : : = <Digit> | <Digit> <Number>

First of all the 5 is evaluated; this is clearly a digit so it can match to either <Digit> or <Digit><Number>. As there is more input left, we cannot match to the first rule part of the disjunction. This process continues until we reach the end of the input, when the final three matches <Digit>, which ends the recursion.

Context-free grammar

In order to create a token parser for syntax analysis, we must first write down the specific rules of the language. One such way of writing the rules of a language is by using BNF, which was introduced in the previous section. This provides us with a rich toolkit to sequence tokens together to define the syntactic rules of the language.

<assignment> : : = <variable> | "=" <expression>

Let us take a simple assignment expression, <assignment>, where <variable> variable and <expression> is an expression.

<expression> : : = <term> | <expression> "+" <term>
<term> : : = <factor> | <factor> "*" <term>
<factor> : : = "(" <expression> ")" | <variable> | <literal>
<variable> : : = <letter> | <letter> <variable>
<literal> : : = <digit> | <digit> <literal> | <letter> | <letter> <literal>
<digit> : : = 0 | 1 | 2 | 3 | 4 | 5 | 6 | 7 | 8 | 9
<letter>: : = A | B | C | D | E | F | G | H | I | J | K | L | M | N | O | P | Q | R | S | T | U | V | W | X | Y | Z

Remember, anything in BNF that is surrounded by < > refers to a rule, so we need to define a rule for expressions. To keep things simple, here we use only simple arithmetic expressions. We consider literals to be numbers or strings. A variable must have letters in its identifier in our definition although in real languages, it may include a number after the first letter.

Although writing BNF rules to implement a programming language is outside the scope of this course, it is useful to have an idea of how syntax analysis works.

When all of the rules are in place, a parser can be constructed. One such parser, recursive descent, is simple to implement and demonstrates how the token stream can be read efficiently. The program reads one token ahead and checks this against its grammar rules. If it does match the rule, it continues reading the next one. Python code for a simple recursive descent parser is shown below. Assume that the token stream is a list and that tokens are represented by numbers. In this simple example, error handling has not been specified, but could easily be added. Parsers can be fairly complicated to write, and there are tools available that will generate them for you based on some BNF definitions.

Code

```
var_token = 1 # token represents a variable
lit_token = 2 # token represents a literal (number)
assign_token = 3 # represents an assignment token
open_bracket = 4 # represents an open bracket
close_bracket = 5 # represents a closed bracket
plus_op = 6 # represents addition
minus_op = 7 # represents subtraction
mult_op = 8 # represents multiplication
div_op = 9 # represents division
# represent the following sum res = 3 * (2 + 1)
token_list = [1, 3, 2, 8, 4, 2, 6, 2, 5]
a() # start recursive descent
currToken = 0
def accept():
  print "code parsed correctly"
def error():
  print "error with code at" + currToken
def nextToken():
  currToken = currToken + 1
def a():
  if token_list[currToken] == var_token:
    nextToken()
    if token_list[currToken] == assign_token:
      nextToken()
      e()
    accept()
    else: error()
  else: error()
def e():
  t()
  if token_list[curr_token] == plus_op:
    nextToken()
    e()
    if token_list[curr_token] == minus_op:
      nextToken()
      e()
def t():
  f()
  if token_list[curr_token] == mult_op:
    nextToken()
    t()
    if token_list[curr_token] == div_op:
      nextToken()
      t()
```

```
def f():
  if token_list[curr_token] == open_bracket:
    nextToken()
    e()
    if token_list[curr_token] == close_bracket:
      nextToken()
    else: error()
  elif token_list[curr_token] == var_token:
    nextToken()
  elif token_list[curr_token] == lit_token:
    nextToken()
```

Syntax analysis

Once a string of tokens has been generated, the syntax analyser part of the compiler checks whether the sequence of tokens is in an acceptable order. Here are two token streams:

VARIABLE EQUALS CONSTANT
CONSTANT EQUALS VARIABLE

The first is acceptable, the second is not.

The compiler will understand all of the rules of the language. Just as there are rules that must be followed in English, programmers must also follow the rules of the programming language they are using. If they do not, they will be faced with a **syntax error**. A syntax error occurs when the tokens passed to the compiler do not match any rule stored within the compiler. Once syntax has been checked to be 100% correct, the compiler can construct an abstract syntax tree.

Abstract syntax trees

As the code is being parsed, a tree data structure is created, known as the abstract syntax tree, which is passed on to the next phase of compilation. Abstract syntax trees are unambiguous data structures that can be guaranteed to be syntactically correct and only readable in one way, which prevents issues with precedence. Figure 4.11 shows the expression 2 * 3 as an abstract syntax tree.

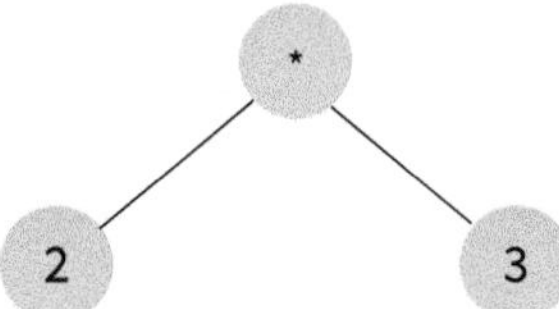

Figure 4.11: 2 * 3 as an abstract syntax tree.

Operators are considered to be the root of a subtree and numbers are considered to be operands; here the operator, *, acts on the two operands, 2 and 3. We put the two operands as children of the root.

Consider a more complicated example, 2 * 3 + 4 (Figure 4.12).

Which operation should happen first? Should the * be done first or should the + be done first? The two trees show the two different ways this code could be interpreted. However, if you read the trees, it is clear what is meant and there is no room for ambiguity. The first tree adds 4 to the subtree 2 * 3, while the second multiplies the subtree 3 + 4 by 2. Trees are unambiguous, unlike source code, which must rely on operator precedence to achieve the same goal. Removing the ambiguity in the code simplifies code generation.

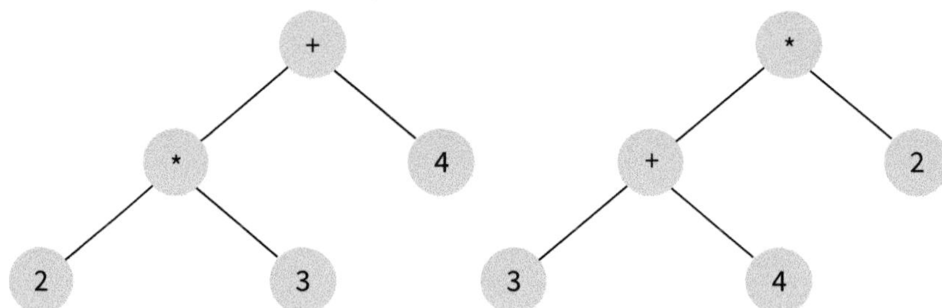

Figure 4.12: 2 * 3 + 4 as an abstract syntax tree.

Machine code generation

Machine code generation occurs once the abstract syntax tree has been created and checked against the rules of the language. It is important to understand that there is no point in generating machine code if the program has any syntax errors. In order to do code generation the compiler will perform three tasks:

- Convert elements of the abstract syntax tree into machine code.
- Allocate registers to minimise memory access.
- Optimise the machine code to improve efficiency.

Machine code templates

Machine code generation is done by mapping parts of the abstract syntax tree to blocks of machine code. You can think of these blocks as machine code templates. Consider a simple line of code:

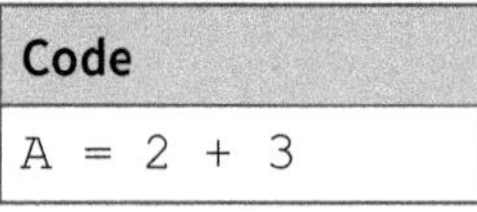

Code
`A = 2 + 3`

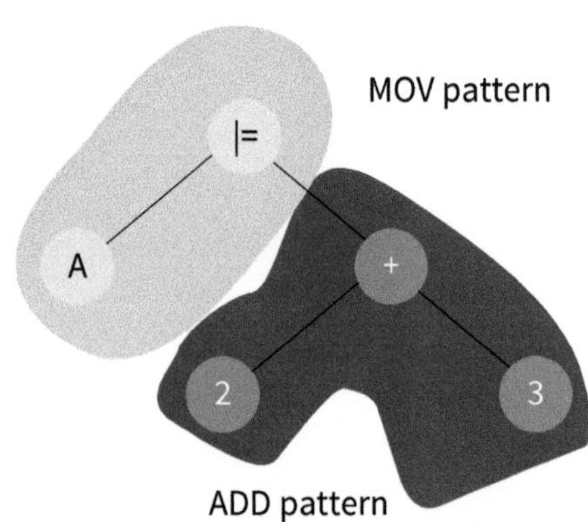

Figure 4.13: Matching parts of a syntax tree.

Regardless of what the values are within the tree, we know that we need to perform an assignment and an addition. These are both common tasks in programming and machine code templates can be easily assigned. Code mapping is done by finding common abstract syntax tree patterns and matching them to blocks of machine code. This pattern-matching process keeps going until the whole tree has been mapped. In Figure 4.13, two patterns have been identified and could have the following Assembly code instructions mapped to them:

```
MOV #LABEL, ACC
```

Matches VAR =

```
MOV ACC, 0
ADD #ID1
ADD #ID2
```

Matches ID + ID

The final machine code from the previous abstract syntax tree would be:

```
MOV ACC, 0
ADD 2
ADD 3
MOV #A, ACC
```

Figure 4.14: Replacing parts of the syntax with machine code blocks.

As machine code makes direct use of general purpose registers then part of the role of machine code generation is to allocate registers. There are a limited number of registers in a single CPU, which means that it is not possible to assign a unique variable to a single register. This means that registers must be recycled as a program executes. Machine code generation, at a given point within the generated code, must decide what registers are assigned to which instructions. The exact mechanics of how this occurs is beyond the scope of this course; however, it is a difficult problem and is considered to be an NP complete problem (non-deterministic polynomial time). NP complete essentially means that solving the problem cannot be done in a reasonable time. To stop compilation from taking an exponential amount of time to complete, a best guess algorithm for register allocation is used which may or may not provide the most efficient generated code.

Optimising machine code

Most programmers write code very inefficiently and as programming languages become more high-level, programmers can become less adept at making their code efficient. Most programmers do not even know, or care, that their code is inefficient. Many compilers perform a number of optimisations for the developer. One way to speed up a program is to limit the number of jumps it has to do. A linear program with no jumps always runs faster than a program with many, for example, one with numerous function calls. IF statements, loops and procedure calls are inherently slow because they reset the FDE cycle, and should be used with some degree of caution. Any break in the flow of the code always carries a speed penalty.

Some short functions can be made inline. What this does is to copy and paste the contents of the inline function whenever it is called, thus reducing the need for jumps. However, there is a space trade-off, as multiple copies of the same function now need to be stored. Another way to optimise code is to make use of any CPU extensions, such as 3D optimisation. These instructions may only be available on certain CPUs and as such the compiler will have to know which ones are available on a given CPU architecture. Overall, the goal of optimisation is to make the machine code run as efficiently as possible.

Linkers and loaders

The process of programming can be time-consuming but can be more efficient if pre-written modules can be used. If we are using these inside our program, they are called libraries. For example, you may use a library in Java to create a user interface.

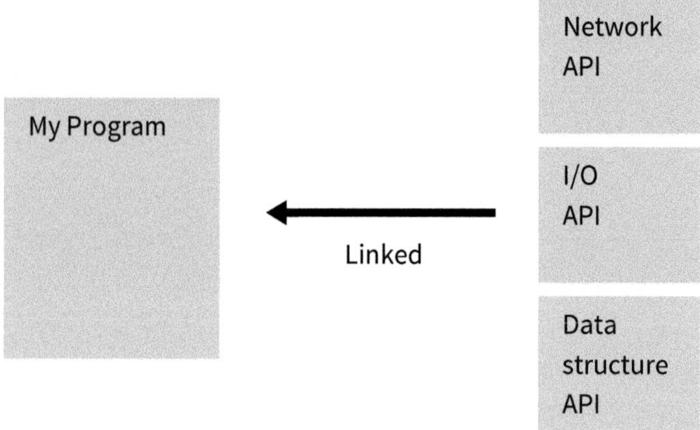

Figure 4.15: Example of how machine code patterns could then be combined into final code.

Library files will have been written to provide specific functionality efficiently and allow for code reuse. This makes writing programs much quicker, and you can be assured that the library code is error-free, as they will have already been compiled. If a call to a library file is made, it will be needed every time the code runs. When making use of library files, a linker will be needed. Linking occurs once code has been compiled, in order to enable access to these libraries. A module can also be used to allow a program to exchange data with an external program. This is called an application programming interface (API). A common use of an API is to allow communication between a program and a web application.

Libraries are linked to your code during the linking phase and linking tells your code how to access the library files, whenever they are used in your program. As library files are separate, for example, provided as a dynamic link library (DLL) in Windows, the linker generates code to allow calls to the library to function correctly. Linking is done in two ways.

1. The library may be directly incorporated into the executable by making a physical copy of the library. The advantage of this is that you do not have to rely on the library being installed on every machine on which the program will be run. The disadvantages are that it will increase the file size dramatically and will not take into consideration any updates to the libraries in the future.
2. The second way is to create a link to the library and keep it separate from the program. This is the most common way to make use of library files and allows file sizes to remain small when the program is distributed. It also allows the code to take advantage of any upgrades to library files that may occur in the future. The biggest disadvantage of dynamic linking is that the library must be available on the target computer for the program to run.

Dynamic libraries are loaded by a small utility known as a **loader**, which has the role of loading a library on request rather than statically linking it at compile time. If a library does not exist when the program is executing, a run-time error will be generated. Loaders need to map memory addresses, depending on where they are loaded in memory, so that they mirror the program. When a library is loaded, the loader makes a note of where it is in memory, referred to as the base address. Every memory request to that library will be offset by that base address. When a library is loaded, it will make use of a logical or virtual address space, which means it assumes it will be loaded as if it were stored in position 0 in memory. To find out the physical address, it just needs to add the base address of where it was actually loaded, which is done by the loader.

Summary

There are a number of generic application types:

- presentation software
- desktop publishing
- spreadsheet software
- drawing packages
- databases.

A knowledge-based system will make inferences based on user input to provide output. It is broken into a number of key sections:

- knowledge base: a database that contains expert knowledge
- inference engine: attempts to work out the answer to the user's query by using the rule base
- rule base: links knowledge and facts together
- user interface (HCI): allows the user to communicate with the system. HCI stands for human–computer interface.

Computer-aided design and computer-aided manufacturing (CAD/CAM) software is used to design, test, model and then mass-produce physical items and devices.

Utility software performs commonplace tasks and normally comes supplied with the operating system. Some common utility software includes:

- file management
- compression software
- task managers
- anti-virus software.

Open-source software is where the source code is included with any executable. This allows the end user to alter and modify the code.

Closed-source software is when the source code is not included. This is common for off-the-shelf software and is used any time a company wishes to protect their intellectual property.

Translators take source code and turn it into machine code. There are three main types: compilers, assemblers and interpreters.

Interpreters will read, translate and execute the code line by line.

Compilers translate the whole program into an executable file once, which can then be run many times.

Assemblers translate low-level code into machine code.

Assemblers will take a two-phase approach:

- phase one – turn symbols into memory addresses and store this in a symbol table
- phase two – convert assembly mnemonics into machine code.

Compilers perform the following phases:

- lexical analysis – removes comments and white space before producing a token stream
- syntax analysis – checks the order of expressions using the token stream
- machine code generation – matches parts of the syntax to machine code; it will optimise the generated machine code
- linking – links the generated machine code to library software; it will add loaders to the code to enable dynamic library linking.

Backus–Naur Form (BNF) is a way of representing syntax as a context-free grammar. BNF contains a number of key elements:

- the rule written as <rulename> : : =
- concatenation: elements of the BNF are written next to each other

  <IF> : : = IF <expression> THEN <statement>

- disjunction: elements are separated by the | symbol and effectively offer a choice of options

  <digit> : : = 0 | 1 | 2 | 3 | 4 | 5 | 6 | 7 | 8 | 9

- recursion: allows rules to be iterative

  <number> : : = <digit> | <digit> <number>.

End-of-chapter questions

1 A careers advisor has just installed a knowledge-based system for students to use when they are in school. Explain the purpose of the following parts of a knowledge-based system.

  a Knowledge base [2]

  b Inference engine [2]

  c Rule base [2]

2 Describe the following utility software.

  a Compression [3]

  b Anti-virus [3]

3 Discuss the difference between open source and free software. [8]

4 Explain the purpose of a virtual machine when using a programming language that is both compiled and then interpreted by a virtual machine. [6]

5 There are a number of stages which must be followed when compiling code. For each of the stages below, explain their purpose and what they produce.

a Lexical analysis [3]

b Syntax analysis [3]

c Machine code generation [3]

d Linking [3]

Further reading

Lexical analysis in detail - search for Lexical Analysis on the Stanford Open Classroom website.
Building a compiler – Lexical and syntax analysis – search for The Compiler I: Syntax Analysis article on the Computer Science and Engineering section of the Hebrew University of Jerusalem website.

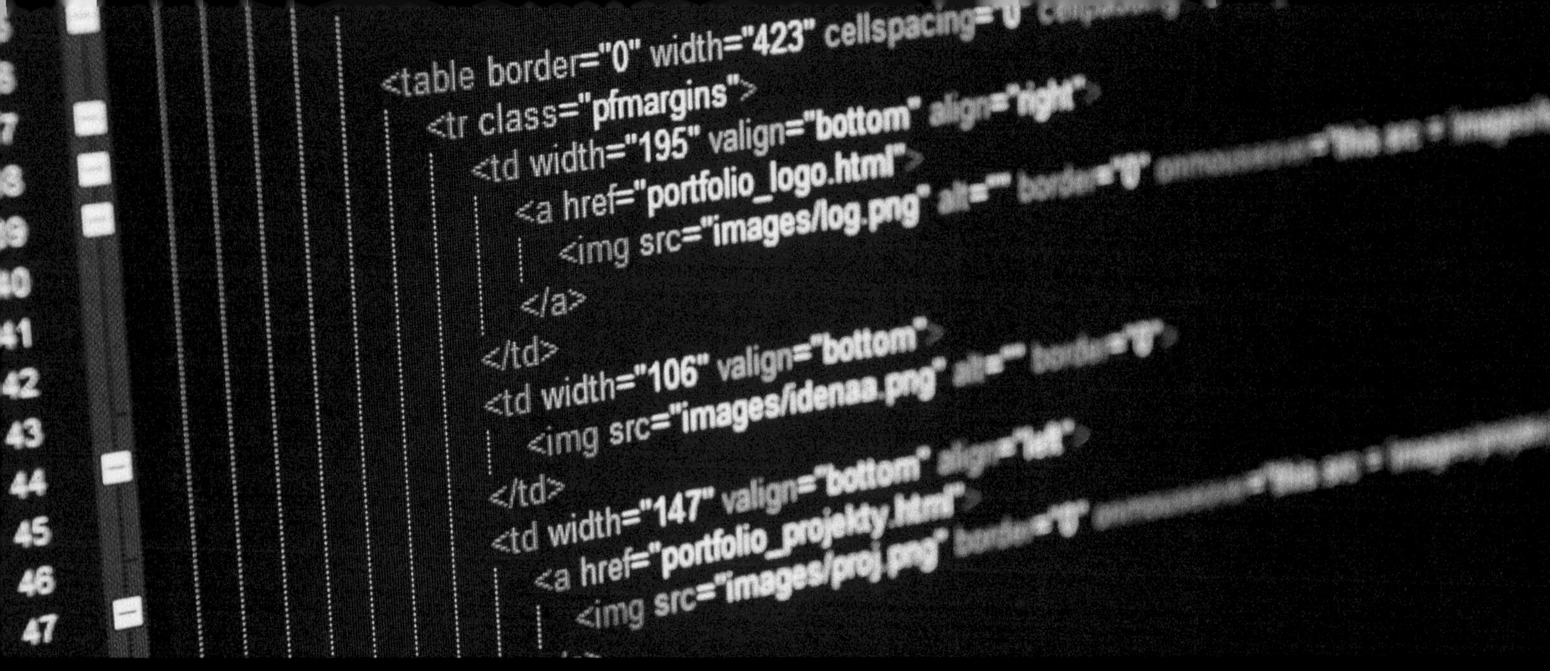

Chapter 5
Software development

Ⓐ **This chapter contains A Level content only**

Specification points

1.2.3 Software development

- Understand the waterfall lifecycle, Agile Methodologies, Extreme Programming, the spiral model and Rapid Application Development.
- The relative merits and drawbacks of different methodologies and when they might be used.
- Writing and following algorithms.

Learning objectives

- To understand the systems lifecycle and what the main phases are.
- To understand different methodologies that can apply to the systems lifecycle, including the waterfall cycle, Extreme Programming, the spiral model and rapid application development.
- To learn about the different merits and drawbacks of different methodologies and when they might be used.

Introduction

Software is not cheap to build, mainly due to the high cost of employing developers and the time that projects can take to complete. Larger programs, such as accounting systems, can take two or three years to make and involve hundreds of staff. Even games can take a lot of time and money to produce. For example, in 1999 a game called *Shenmue* produced by Sega® for the Dreamcast games console cost $47 000 000 to develop. Most of the cost of development goes towards paying for software developers and other staff rather than hardware. When dealing with massive projects involving hundreds of people and millions of dollars, it is crucial that formal methods are followed to ensure that projects are developed with as few issues as possible. All software projects, to a greater or lesser extent, make use of the systems lifecycle. However, how they choose to follow the lifecycle depends on the methodology chosen. In this chapter you will learn about the key phases of the systems lifecycle as well as the key methodologies used in modern software development. It is important to note at this stage that there is no one methodology that is better than any other. Each one comes with its own set of merits and drawbacks, meaning that the methodology chosen should depend on the projects being attempted.

Software projects and application systems

The purpose of an ICT development project is to create an application system, which is a combination of software and hardware that meets the needs of a given set of users or purposes. Application systems (or systems for short) tend to be commissioned when there is a perceived need or when improvements to a current system are required. Take care to distinguish between application systems (which enable users to achieve some purpose) and systems software, which is the software that runs in the background on computers, providing a base platform on which applications are run.

It is easy to think that new ICT systems always take an old manual system and automate it with ICT; however, this is increasingly not the case. Computing systems have been around for a long time. There are systems in use that were originally developed many years ago and are referred to as legacy systems. These systems use old technology and may be archaic by modern-day standards. They could be upgraded, but the cost of replacing legacy systems can run into the millions and so not all of them get replaced. Where the legacy system is retained, the company or organisation concerned might build a new front-end for it, that is, a new way of interacting with it, that uses modern technology, such as the world wide web.

Reasons to commission a new system could be company expansion, old systems being too slow compared to modern alternatives, lack of support for old software or a desire to capitalise on new technologies. Systems could also be built if a new business venture has been identified. There is always a reason for building a new ICT system and this is driven by the needs of the organisation. It is worth mentioning at this point that building a new ICT system requires much more than programming skills; it also needs business experts, analysts, project managers, testers, technical authors, marketing specialists, etc. The project team must include people who have a good awareness of business methods, people skills and creative problem solving.

Regardless of whether an existing ICT system is in place, some formal methodology will be followed in order to produce it. When a new system, or an upgrade, is commissioned, a series of steps will be followed, known as the systems lifecycle. Each project will go through several of the phases shown in Figure 5.1, but they do not have to use all of them. The way in which the lifecycle is implemented is known as the methodology. This will govern which phases are used and their relative importance. Methodologies are covered in more depth later in this chapter.

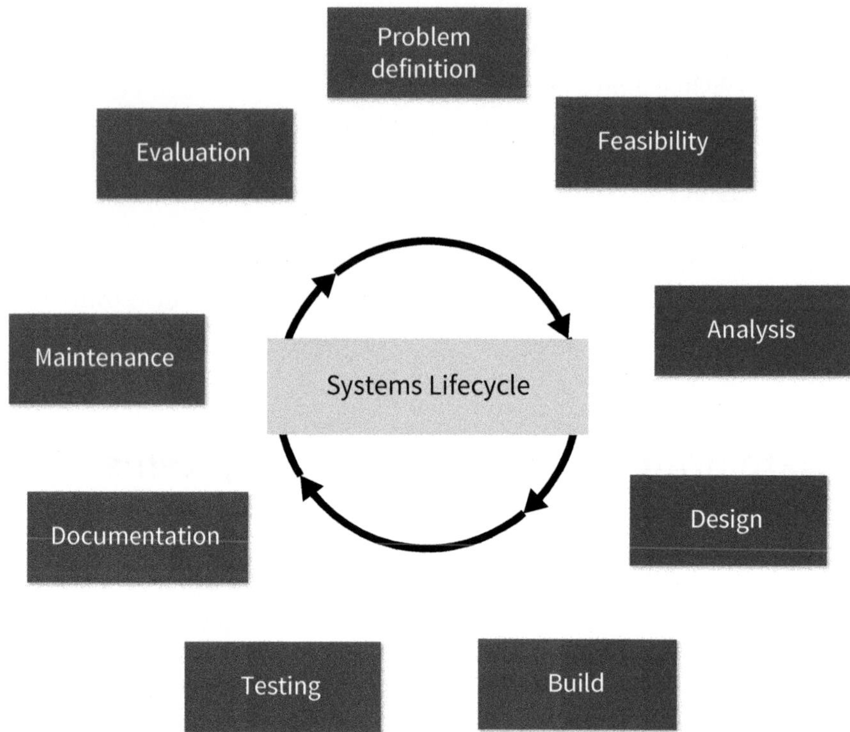

Figure 5.1: The systems lifecycle.

Stakeholders

A stakeholder is someone, or a group of people, with a vested interest in the new system being built. They may be passive stakeholders, meaning that they will not be involved in production, or active stakeholders who have a part to play in the system to be built. Under normal circumstances, a new system involves two main companies: one that requires a system to be built, known as the client, and one that will develop it. In the real world this simple distinction cannot always be drawn, as there may be many other companies involved in the project. For example, the suppliers of hardware, which may be custom-built; contractors providing specific technical skills not currently available in the development company; externally contracted development teams and even legal representatives. Some development companies outsource the work if they do not have the required technical skills or staff. Staffing on a large-scale project is expensive, with some software developers earning over £50 000 per year. Any cost saving that the development company can make, for example sending some of the development work offshore, will enable it to increase its profit margins. In any software development project, staffing is the single biggest cost.

Users

The user is not the same as the client. The client requires the new system to be built but the user is the person who will be interacting with it. It may seem an odd distinction to make, but it is important. Consider an automatic teller machine (ATM). The people who use ATMs are the general public. Apart from owning an account with the bank, they are not directly involved with the development or maintenance of it. So in this case the user is not the person who has initiated the new system. The bank has asked for the new system to be built and is therefore the client.

It is crucial to consider the users, as they are the people who will be interacting with the system on a daily basis. If the system does not meet their needs, it will fail.

Programmers

Programmers, or developers, are the people building the system. They take information passed to them by the systems analysts and use it to develop the system. They will have specialist knowledge of usually several programming languages and will be able to make an informed decision as to which will be the most suitable to use to develop the software based on the requirements. They rarely have direct involvement in the analysis or design of a system, but they do have a vested interest in the success of the project. They are usually the people who spot the more subtle problems with the new system and their input is invaluable to the systems analysts. It is common for a systems analyst to talk to the lead programmer during the whole of the lifecycle, to get the thoughts and ideas of the programming team.

Project managers

Project managers have a critical role to play in the project. It is their responsibility to monitor progress and allocate resources to the project. There is normally a project manager on both the client side and the developer side. The reason for this is straightforward: both parties want to ensure that there are no nasty surprises coming up, for example the project falling behind or new requirements needing to be introduced. The two project managers work very closely together.

In order for project managers to plan out the project successfully, they need to understand how well their teams work and what skills they have. It is normal for different members of staff to have different sets of skills and to be able to tackle certain problems or tasks at different rates. It is the project manager's job to ensure that they know as much as possible about their team. It is also important that they can produce realistic estimates for different tasks. That way, they can monitor the project and flag up any areas of concern quickly, before they become major issues.

Systems analysts

The role of the systems analyst is simple: to find out exactly what the client wants. This is not as straightforward as it sounds. For a start, most clients are not sure exactly what they want at the start of the project, but have just a vague idea. As a result, analysts have to use their own experience and expertise to fill in the blanks that occur along the way. They are responsible for investigating the organisation's objectives and producing the requirements specification (more on this later). They will also suggest possible implementation methods for the proposed project. They will document the existing system using standard techniques so that it can be clearly understood by the system designer and programmer. They monitor the project, along with the project manager, offering expert knowledge on the system to be built. The systems analyst is the first port of call for programmers if they have a problem with or a query on the requirements specification.

Problem definition

The problem definition phase documents the process of identifying what problems exist in a client's current system or defining what problems a new system could solve. A client will identify problems with their existing system or software to help them to expand their company, for example a mobile app. At this point, very little will be known about the system, other than that there is a perceived need for it. The development company will be called in to have an initial meeting. This meeting is critical for both the client and the development company to discuss fully what is required. This will clarify exactly what is required. It is common for clients to have an unrealistic view on what is required for the new system, so both parties must agree on the scope of the project at this stage. Unbounded projects are guaranteed to fail, as there is no way to differentiate what the client required at the start and what they require six months down the line. Sometimes, when requirements are fluid, the development company may choose a methodology that allows them to change requirements quickly, such as Agile development.

It is important to remember that the analyst is an expert in developing new systems, but not in the client's business. Conversely, the client is an expert in their own business, but not necessarily an expert in systems analysis. This is why they must work together to share information to ensure that the correct problems are solved.

Feasibility study

A feasibility study establishes whether or not the project can be done, given the scope laid out during the problem definition phase. Also, it considers whether it is desirable for the development company to proceed with the project. When embarking on a software project there must be confidence on both sides that the project can be delivered on time and within budget. If this is not the case, the client may choose a different supplier or may become dissatisfied with the work, and the development company could get a poor reputation as a result. In essence, if a project fails to meet the time and financial restrictions, it has failed. Even if a good working product is produced, when a project goes over budget people tend to focus on this fact. From the development company's point of view, if a project is unlikely to bring in much profit or might bring negative attention to their company, they may decide not to proceed.

When deciding on how feasible a new system will be, a number of factors must be considered. These are discussed below.

Economic feasibility

A project has a specific budget, which must include all the costs of the project, including:

- software licences
- hardware
- human resources/wages
- the development company's running costs.

Remember that profit is also an important consideration.

The hardware and software costs are fairly straightforward and are unlikely to change over the course of the project. Human costs are the most variable and account for the majority of the budget. Staffing costs are based on the number of people working on the project, the amount they earn and the length of the project. This cost can vary considerably, for example, what happens if someone gets a pay rise or a developer leaves? You will need to employ a new person, who may be more expensive, or you could engage a contractor. What happens if the project is delayed? It is important, therefore, to know up front how many staff you will need and to have a good idea of the length of the project. It is also important to build in some flexibility, based on a risk assessment. The development company will want to make a profit, not just enough to cover their costs. Economic feasibility considers the overall budget and the overall costs. It then decides if enough profit can be made to make the project worth doing. If the development company makes a loss or just breaks even, it would not really be worthwhile. Some development companies may take a project at cost or even at a slight loss in circumstances where work is scarce. A good reputation may lead to further projects, so it is worth maintaining.

Time feasibility

Late projects result in going over budget because of the cost of developers' wages. It is critically important that projects are delivered on time, as the developing company will make a negative impression if they cannot deliver when they said they could. Sometimes it is even more critical, as the client could well have very pressing business reasons for a project to be delivered by a certain date. Failure to meet the deadline could lead to litigation or a reduced development fee.

In order to decide how long a project will take, the project manager will have to estimate how long their developers will take to complete the required tasks. This requires a balancing act based on cost, resources, skill level and number of staff to bring onto the project.

Once the estimated length of development time has been calculated, based on prior team performance, it is compared with the client's deadline. If it can be done in the given time frame, the project can go ahead.

Technical feasibility

Can the project be done with the technical resources available? Some requirements may not be possible or feasible with current technology. For example, completely accurate speech recognition is not currently possible, nor is being able to perform facial recognition in dark environments. This means that projects that have these requirements are currently not technically feasible. However, what is more likely to cause problems is if the development team does not have the technical skills needed to satisfy the requirements. For example, if you need an expert in SQL for the project, but do not have this resource, the project is either not possible or it will cost extra to buy in the expertise.

Every developer, when they join the company, fills in a skills audit to show what technologies they can work with. The project manager looks through this list when deciding whom to take onto the project. Therefore, if there is no one with the correct skill set available (or if they are already assigned to another project), the project cannot go ahead. Developers update their skills audit as they develop new skills.

Political feasibility

Projects can sometimes have issues that are politically motivated or may go against the beliefs of certain groups of people. Systems such as those used by the NHS, tax systems, other government based computer systems and cyber security come under the direct scrutiny of the general public and media. When these projects go wrong, the national media will undoubtedly report on it and show the development company in a negative light. The development company needs to decide whether the potential positives outweigh the possible negative publicity.

Legal feasibility

Legal feasibility helps decide whether the project will be able to comply with all of the laws that may affect it in the countries where it will be released. File sharing software, although legal in essence, has fallen foul of the law; companies producing or facilitating illegal activity have been sued. Napster, one of the first and most popular file sharing websites, was shut down for a long time, as the courts decided that the company could do more to protect copyright. It then released a paid service, but it was less popular because the company had already lost most of its user base to competitors. Legal feasibility needs to be taken very seriously, as the effects can be very damaging for both the client and the development company. Fines running into millions can be imposed if the software does not comply with the law. In the UK, the Data Protection Act 1998 requires that organisations protect the personal data of individuals. If software is insecure, resulting in data breaches, the company will have broken the law and will be liable to be prosecuted. Also, some countries might ban the use of the software completely if it does not meet basic legal requirements.

Systems analysis

Analysis is the process of finding out exactly what the system will entail by employing various fact-finding methods. It is critically important that the result of the analysis is as complete as it can be. Incorrectly defined requirements can lead to big delays and escalating costs. At the end of analysis, the requirements specification is produced. This is a document that contains the exact requirements of the new system. The four main fact-finding methods used during analysis are:

- observation
- questionnaire
- document collecting
- interview or meeting.

These methods are not meant to be used on their own, but as a collective entity. It is impossible to gather a complete picture of the system by using only one method or talking to only one person. The key to success is to try to understand the business problem from the point of view of the company as a whole, rather than from an individual perspective.

Observation

Observation is where the analyst shadows employees of the customer for a period of time, making notes on how they do their job. They observe employees in their natural environment to see exactly how the business works. One of the biggest advantages of this method is that the analyst sees parts of the system that employees may not realise are important. Some things that we do, especially when they are done every day, may appear insignificant. An outsider often notices these common actions and can include them in the new system, even if they were not part of the original problem definition.

Advantages	Disadvantages
Pick up parts of the system that are not immediately obvious to the client.	Some people may feel threatened while being watched.
Confirm information gathered through different fact-finding methods.	There is no guarantee that some of the more subtle parts of the system will show up during the observation period.

Table 5.1: Advantages and disadvantages of the observation fact-finding method.

Questionnaire

Questionnaires are quite a common method of fact-finding, but can also be one of the most difficult. Designing a questionnaire requires knowledge of the system to be built and the range of people to whom the questionnaire can be sent. This prior knowledge is essential so that the questions can be targeted. It is also important to restrict the number of choices available for each question, as some people may give unexpected responses. This means that questionnaires can give only limited information about very specific parts of the system. Having a small set of response options can be beneficial because these can be analysed to give quantitative data, e.g. 70% of respondents reported slow network connection speeds. Free responses to questions are often considered to be less helpful because they must be analysed individually, which can be time-consuming. However, it does allow users to respond with anything that they might think is important.

Using questionnaires can allow the analyst to get a lot of responses on a specific subset of requirements. As a questionnaire can be given to a lot of people, you will most likely get back a range of responses. For example, consider the idea that employees should use a touch-screen system or swipe card to gain entry to a secure area. This could be set up as a question and the analyst could then see what the users' responses would be. The analyst could then make the appropriate decision, backing it up with hard evidence.

Questionnaires can be issued on paper or, increasingly, using online pages that the user is directed to via a link in an email sent to them.

Advantages	Disadvantages
Can be given to a large number of people at once.	Hard to create and design questions and likely responses.
Can get a large number of different opinions.	Not all questionnaires sent out will be completed.
Targeted responses can allow large amounts of data to be analysed quickly and easily to give quantitative results.	Free responses can be time-consuming to analyse and many give many different opinions to be considered.

Table 5.2: Advantages and disadvantages of the questionnaire fact-finding method.

Document collection

During document collection the analyst gathers any business documents that relate to the new system to be constructed. These include orders, invoices, financial records and any other document that is in use on a regular basis. Documents in use with the current system are a good guide to what is required in the new system. Some key elements which could be inferred from analysis of existing documents are:

- The data they use and what will need to be stored by the new system.
- The analyst can get a very good understanding of the business process by following the trail of documents and seeing the flow of data from start to finish.

One advantage of document collecting is that they cannot lie, distort or misrepresent information. This means that the information found in them can be trusted, unless someone has purposefully gone out of their way to alter the documents. Of course, they do not give a complete picture, but they do help support whatever model the analyst has already built up. They also help the analyst build a data dictionary. However, it is not always obvious how, why or when a document is created. This means that more information is required, which can provide new avenues of investigation for the other fact-finding methods.

Advantages	Disadvantages
Documents are reliable and show most of the data stored in the system.	Documents give a limited view of the system and do not say how they were created.
Document trails help support the analyst's picture of business processes.	Documents may contain sensitive information and there may be restrictions on seeing them.

Table 5.3: Advantages and disadvantages of the document collecting fact-finding method.

Interview or meeting

Interviewing is normally where most analysts start. They will select some key stakeholders of the project (on the client's side) and ask them targeted questions about the current and new system. A lot of information can be gathered in a very short space of time using this method. For example, a questionnaire will only generate a specific answer but when an interview question is asked, the analyst can ask for clarification or can ask further questions on the same topic. However, it is difficult to interview a large number of people because interviews are difficult to schedule and can be time-consuming. If a meeting is arranged with several stakeholders, they may not all be able to attend or may present different opinions about the requirements from their perspective.

Human nature plays a major role in interviews as well, as not everyone is confident when / they do to try to impress the analyst or their superiors. Not everything they say can be trusted, so it must be verified by using other fact-finding methods.

Advantages	Disadvantages
Large amounts of information can be gathered and the analyst can respond to the person to query their responses.	Time-consuming, so only a limited number of people can be interviewed.
Interviews produce detailed responses about key parts of the system.	Interviewees may not be fully truthful, so their responses need to be verified.

Table 5.4: Advantages and disadvantages of the interview fact-finding method.

Requirements

A requirement is a specific feature of the new system and is recorded in a document called a requirements specification. Requirements can be broken down into the following key sections:

- interface requirements
- functional requirements
- performance requirements.

A very important point to make here is that a requirement must be measurable. That is, we must be able to say, without any doubt, that the requirement has been met or not met at the end of the project. This is important contractually so that the development company can be paid, but also to help define the scope of the project. An ambiguous requirement could be interpreted by different stakeholders in different ways, which invariably leads to problems and potentially to conflict.

Interface requirements

The interface of a system is where the end user interacts with it, whether by pushing a button or entering some data or viewing a report. In most cases, the interface of computer systems is mainly driven by software. However, many new systems also include a hardware interface. Consider a game such as Guitar Hero®. The game comes with a software element, namely the game itself, and a hardware element, which is the custom controller. In this case, the interface requirements must take both the software and hardware interfaces into consideration.

Interface requirements depend on the end user and also the complexity of the new system. As such, it is imperative that detailed analysis has already been carried out on what the user may require. A common mistake is to confuse interface requirements with interface design. At this stage the development company is not worried about what the interface will look like or how the user will interact with it. The decision to have three or five buttons on a game controller is not important at this point. What we are interested in is the standard to which the interface must conform in order to be considered suitable by the end user. So Guitar Hero's interface requirements would be, for example, 'the hardware must be durable, with large accessible buttons suitable for use by people with less manual dexterity' or 'the software interface must be immediately accessible for a beginner'.

Functional requirements

Functional requirements detail what the system will do and what key features it will have. An example of a functional requirement for Guitar Hero would be the scoring and combination mechanisms. Looking at a more work-based scenario, Microsoft Word could be considered. Some of the functional requirements would be auto correction, word count, spell check and formatting. The key is what they do when the user clicks on them. The requirements do not dictate what the features should look like. In fact, it is very common for features described to have no possible user interface. What the functional requirements focus on is simply what they need to achieve in order to be considered successful.

Performance requirements

Performance requirements cover such things as response times and throughput. They have to be specific, for example 'the user interface must respond to a request from the user in a bounded time of *x* seconds'. Bounded, in this context, means a reasonable maximum time agreed by both the client and the development company. An Adobe Photoshop® performance requirement might be 'the user interface must respond in a reasonably bounded time'. The requirement is not 'everything will run fast', because a lot of what the system does is mathematically very complicated. It is therefore meaningless to say that actions such as resizing a very large image will occur quickly. What if a user runs it on a slower computer? Should it be required always to run at the same speed? Clearly that is unrealistic.

Real-time systems, such as those found in a hospital intensive care system, must respond to a system input in the shortest possible time. Indeed it is critical that they do so. In these systems, response time would be a very important requirement.

Performance is very important in a system, but the requirements set out must be clear, realistic and measurable. Failure to do so could lead to differing opinions between the customer and the development company.

Requirements specification

Once information has been gathered, it is time to place all of the accrued knowledge into a single document, known as the requirements specification. This document provides not only the basis for design, but also a fundamental reference for all other phases, most notably the evaluation phase.

In order to ensure that the requirements specification is correct, it is essential to follow a template. This template may vary from company to company and from methodology to methodology. Below is a sample template, adapted from the IEEE standard 830-1998:

- *Introduction*
  - Purpose
  - Scope
  - Definitions and abbreviations
  - References
  - Overview
- *Overall description*
  - Product perspective
  - Product functions
  - User characteristics
  - Constraints
  - Assumptions and dependences
- *Specific requirements*
  - Interface requirements
  - Functional requirements
  - Performance requirements.

Although, for the purpose of the course, it is not important to understand exactly how a requirements specification is written, it is useful to be aware of it. There are a number of key elements to the template that are necessary for understanding its purpose:

- Purpose and scope: every project must have a scope. Putting it simply, if a project is unbounded, how will you know when you have finished? By stating exactly the expected outcomes and limitations of the new system, you can prevent misunderstandings. The purpose of the system is also crucial. If this is misunderstood by any of the stakeholders, there will be problems when it comes to project sign-off.
- Product functions and perspective: this describes where the system fits into the larger picture, or its role within the business.
- User characteristics: this is where the end user's experience of the system is documented. Remember that this is key when writing the user interface requirements. If you do not produce a system that is accessible for the end user, the system may not be used correctly and will ultimately fail.
- Constraints: these are the key boundaries and limitations to which the new system must adhere. They are related to the scope of the project and to the feasibility study.

Design

Design is the process of taking the requirements of a new system and deciding what it will look like, how it will store and process data. The design phase can only go ahead once the requirements specification has been completed.

Each requirement then needs to be incorporated into the design. The design includes a number of areas:

- hardware and software choices
- data
- output design.

Input

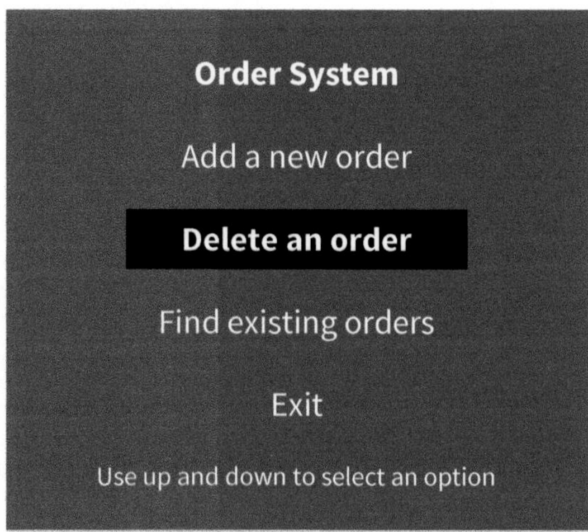

Figure 5.2: Interface design.

This is also known as the interface design (Figure 5.2). Interface design shows how information will be input into the new system and also how it will be displayed after processing. It does not describe how that information will be processed, nor does it look at the functional requirements other than to show interaction.

Output

Output design is carried out in a very similar way to input design. The first thing to think about is what triggers the output. Normally, an output design is triggered by something the user has done on an input screen. Figure 5.3 shows a simple example.

In this example, an invoice output is triggered when a new order has been entered into the system. Triggers may include entering new data into the system, clicking on specific buttons or even the completion of a scheduled batch process. There are no hard and fast rules on what designates an output trigger, but there must always be one for every output designed. If a trigger cannot be identified, that output will never be seen.

Data structure design

Data structure design is fundamental to how a system will work. It dictates what data needs to be stored and how that data will be organised. This then has a direct impact on how the rest of the system will work. It is almost impossible to produce an input or output design without knowing exactly what data will be stored.
The data structure design process tends to start with listing all of the data that is required by the system. This information will have already been gathered

Orders page

NPM

Order number

Item type

Quantity

Submit Reset Home

Example GUI input design

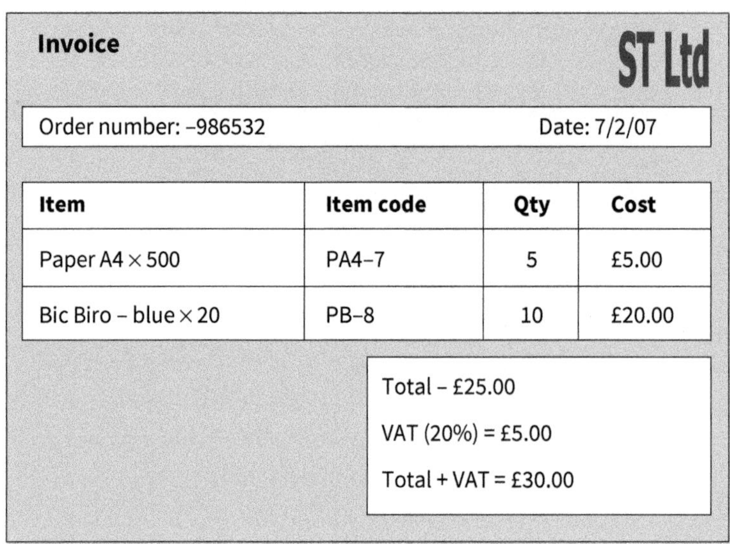

Invoice

ST Ltd

Order number: –986532 Date: 7/2/07

Item	**Item code**	**Qty**	**Cost**
Paper A4 × 500	PA4–7	5	£5.00
Bic Biro – blue × 20	PB–8	10	£20.00

Total – £25.00

VAT (20%) = £5.00

Total + VAT = £30.00

Figure 5.3: Output design.

during analysis and placed into a data dictionary. A data dictionary stores every item of data, the size, the data type, validation requirements and a comment to explain what that data means. An example:

Name of field	Data type	Description
Surname	String	The surname of a client.
Forename	String	The forename of the client.
DVD NAME	String	The full name of a DVD.
DVD owner	String	The name of the client who owns the DVD.

Table 5.5: Example data structure design.

Once the data dictionary is completed, decisions are made on how the data will be saved. This could be stored in a file, or in the case of a larger-scale system, a database. If a database is used then normalisation must also be carried out to prevent redundancy (duplicate data). (See Chapter 8).

Building the system

Development is the planning, writing and alpha testing of the software – and any hardware required. It also includes the writing of the user and technical documentation (see later in this chapter). It is usually the longest part of the process of creating new applications.

Approaches to software development are described later in this chapter.

Testing

Untested or poorly tested code tends to result in unstable applications and incorrect output, leading to dissatisfied clients and users. Most developers find it very difficult to find bugs in their own programs, not because of the complexity of testing, but because they make subconscious assumptions and use their software in the way they believe others will. However, other people may take a very different approach to using the software, which can result in them finding bugs or problems that the developer did not. This is why developers pass their code on to another person to test. There are a number of testing strategies that can be used and it is common to use more than one. The better-tested software is, the more robust it will be. Problems found later on in the system's lifecycle are harder and more expensive to fix.

White-box testing and unit tests

White-box or glass-box testing is where the structure of the code is tested. It requires knowledge of how the code was developed. Every time you have a control statement such as IF, you effectively create a new path through the system. Each path must be tested in order to be sure that the code will run as expected. These sorts of tests tend to be carried out by the developer, as they understand the code. They know what sort of values should trigger a certain path through the code. Consider the example shown in Figure 5.4.

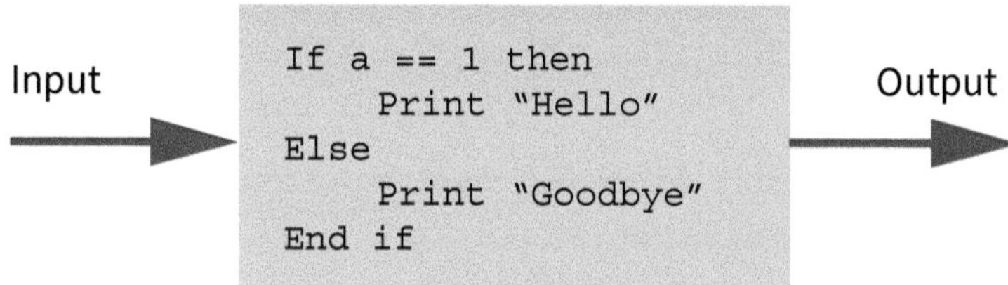
Input
If a == 1 then
Print "Hello"
Else
Print "Goodbye"
End if
Output

Two possible paths through this code

Figure 5.4: Example of white-box testing.

There are two possible paths through the code: 'A equals one' and 'A does not equal one'. In order to check the code, the programmer needs to run two tests.

Programmers normally create some unit tests to ensure that the code they have written is working as expected. Unit tests run the code with various sets of input, usually using an automated script that can be run on a regular basis.

As most code within a large system is coupled with other parts, it is entirely plausible that changes made by one developer can impact code written by another. What unit tests allow us to do is fast regression testing of existing code, so if changes made downstream introduce bugs, this will be picked up by the unit tests.

Unit tests are written by the developer under the guidance of the **methodology** being employed on the project. As a minimum, unit tests should use valid, invalid and extreme values to ensure that the code can handle different inputs in the expected way.

Here is a simple function written in Python:

Code

```
def findMaxNumber(listToCheck):
  max = listToCheck[0]
  for v in listToCheck:
    if v > max:
      max = v
  return max

print findMaxNumber([5,1,9,5,3,10,14,3])
```

This is a simple test using a single set of values for the function 'findMaxNumber', but running the test will not guarantee that the code is correct for all values.

Below is a sample unit test for the function 'findMaxNumber'.

Code

```
import random
import unittest
def findMaxNumber(listToCheck):
  max = listToCheck[0]
  for v in listToCheck:
    if v > max:
      max = v
  return max
print findMaxNumber([5,1,9,5,2,10,14,3])
class findMaxUnitTest(unittest.TestCase):
  def setUp(self):
    print "set up unit test for findMaxNumber"
  def test_norma9lValue(self):
    # generate a list of numbers
    l = []
    for a in range(1,100):
      l.append(random.randint(1,100))
    # add the value 101 in the middle
    l.insert(50,101)
    # run test
    self.assertEqual(findMaxNumber(l),101)
  def test_invalid(self):
    l=["a", 13, "b"]
    # this should raise a type error
    self.assertRaises(TypeError, findMaxNumber,l)
```

```
    def test_empty(self):
        l=[]
        self.assertEqual(findMaxNumber(l), False)
suite = unittest.TestLoader().loadTestsFromTestCase
(findMaxUnitTest)
unittest.TextTestRunner(verbosity=2).run(suite)
```

```
======================================================================
ERROR: test_empty (__main__.findMaxUnitTest)
----------------------------------------------------------------------
Traceback (most recent call last):
  File "max.py", line 37, in test_empty
    self.assertEqual(findMaxNumber(l), False)
  File "max.py", line 4, in findMaxNumber
    max = listToCheck[0]
IndexError: list index out of range

======================================================================
FAIL: test_invalid (__main__.findMaxUnitTest)
----------------------------------------------------------------------
Traceback (most recent call last):
  File "max.py", line 32, in test_invalid
    self.assertRaises(TypeError,findMaxNumber,1)
AssertionError: TypeError not raised

----------------------------------------------------------------------
Ran 3 tests in 0.000s

FAILED (failures=1, errors=1)
```

Figure 5.5: Corrected unit test code.

Two of the tests failed to produce the required output. One caused a runtime exception, which was not expected, and the other failed to work as expected. Unit tests are a great way for the developer to do alpha testing in a systematic way and continue to test their code throughout the lifetime of the project. Most development departments run all unit tests at the end of the day as a batch process and the developers spend the first part of the following day chasing up any errors encountered.

Unit tests are defined differently depending on the language chosen, but they normally make use of object-oriented programming (see Chapter 6). Most of the unit-testing framework is based on inheriting the testing features of a base class, in Python's case the class 'TestCase'. Each test is allowed to set up data by overriding the 'setUp' method and tear down data by overriding the 'tearDown' method. Each test is defined by adding the text 'test_' in front of the method name.

Below, in Figure 5.6, is the corrected code, which will pass the unit tests defined above:

Black-box testing

In black-box testing (Figure 5.6) we do not have knowledge of the code and are testing the functionality of the program based on the requirements specification. We take valid, invalid and extreme input data and compare the output to what we expect should happen, based on the design and requirements specification. If the output is correct, the test will pass. We are not interested in which paths were followed to get to the result; what we are interested in is whether the code does what it is supposed to.

```
def findMaxNumber(listToCheck):
    if len(listToCheck) ==0:
            return False
    max = listToCheck[0]
    for v in listToCheck:
        if not isinstance (v,int):
            raise TypeError("test")
        if v > max:
            max = v

    return max
```

```
test_empty (__main__.findMaxUnitTest) ... set up unit test for findMaxNumber
ok
test_invalid (__main__.findMaxUnitTest) ... set up unit test for findMaxNumber
ok
test_normalValue (__main__.findMaxUnitTest) ... set up unit test for findMaxNumb
er
ok

----------------------------------------------------------------------
Ran 3 tests in 0.000s

OK
```

Figure 5.6: Black-box testing.

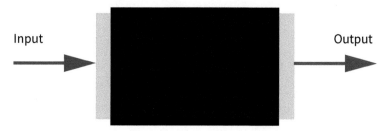

Figure 5.7: Black-box testing diagram.

Black-box testing is commonly done by people who are not directly involved in development and is carried out in a very systematic manner. For example, it is not acceptable just to play around with the software to see if it works. Testers use a test script, which enables them to test every element of the system and allows tests to be reproduced. Should a test fail, the developer will need to be able to reproduce the bug in order to fix it.

Alpha and beta testing

Testing is carried out in phases and by different people. The two most obvious phases are alpha and beta. These terms relate to alpha and beta builds of the software. Alpha builds tend not to be stable and may lack functionality or even not work in all circumstances. It is important that an alpha build is not given to the customer or users, as they may feel that this is the level of quality they will get once the system is complete. Alpha tests are always carried out by the developer or by their in-house testing team.

Beta builds are more complete and are created later in the development cycle. They should be more stable than alpha builds, since all of the main functionality has been already tested, but may contain bugs and problems. Beta builds are stable enough to give to the client for testing. The client carries out beta testing as if they were using the code in a live situation. The intended end user tests the system using real data. All faults found are, of course, returned to the development team for correcting.

Acceptance testing

Acceptance testing is the last testing phase, and it occurs before the client agrees to pay for the final system. The goal of acceptance testing is for the customer to ensure that what the developer has produced meets the requirements specification. Acceptance marks the end of the contract to develop the system, and if successful, the development company will be paid.

Documentation

During the life of the project a lot of documentation is produced. This includes the design documents, diagrams and the requirements specification. However, this is all internal technical documentation and is mainly of interest to the development company.

The focus of this phase in the development cycle is documentation for the customer and end user. Technical authors write user documentation, working alongside the developers and using the same design documents, chiefly the requirements specification. Writing good documentation is not easy, and this phase needs to happen in parallel with software development to ensure that it is completed at the same time. The documentation needs to be planned, designed and tested, and there are normally at least two rounds of commenting before final versions are ready.

User documentation

Every application system has a user interface, which enables the end user to interact with it. The user will, in most circumstances, require training in order to use the system. So there may well be a training course, with an accompanying manual. In addition, there should be a full set of documentation for use after the training is completed. It will also be used for users who start to use the system sometime after its initial launch.

User documentation should be very carefully targeted towards the readers and their needs. There should be material suitable for the novice user that is straightforward and avoids the use of technical terms. The user should be able to find out how to perform any task by consulting this document.

The user documentation could include some or all of the following, depending on the type of application system:

- step-by-step 'getting started' guides or tutorials for the main features of the system
- installation guide
- user guide focusing on typical tasks
- reference manual
- online help, at the level of both individual controls such as input fields and at the task level
- error messages and troubleshooting guide
- frequently asked questions (FAQs) detailing common questions and problems
- glossary.

Technical documentation

If the new system is a bespoke product for a company, rather than an off-the-shelf product such as a game, there needs to be at least one person in the company who can ensure that it runs smoothly once it has been implemented. That person is normally ICT literate and has a good understanding of technical ideas and concepts. Their role is to ensure that the system is set up and configured correctly, and to ensure the smooth day-to-day running of the system. It is not likely to be someone who was involved in developing the system, but may have been involved during analysis.

They need to know installation processes, how the system can be configured, the minimum hardware specification required, and maintenance and backup routines.. They also need access to the design documents and code so that they can get a deeper understanding of the system. Technical documentation includes:

- any form of diagrams used in analysis and design
- the data structure
- source code
- design documents
- hardware and software requirements
- configuration guide and options.

Implementation

Implementation (for bespoke systems) is the process of installing the new system at the client site and putting it into use. It occurs after the software and documentation have been produced by the development team. If the new system is a bespoke product for a company, implementation is carefully managed. It normally includes both hardware and software components.

There are a number of ways to manage the implementation of a new system; four of them are discussed below.

Direct changeover

Direct changeover is the simplest option, but can be very dangerous and should only be used if there is no old system or if the old system is broken or unworkable. For example, releasing a mobile app where one did not exist before.

New systems invariably have problems, for example bugs, lack of training or lack of understanding of the new system. Just swapping over to the system straight away could mean a loss in productivity or, worse, if the new system fails completely, a complete shutdown of the business. Even though the system will have been tested, there is no guarantee that it will work as expected when using live data.

Phased changeover

Big projects are normally split into many smaller chunks, known as modules. This is a natural part of systems analysis and forms the basis for implementation. This type of implementation works best with certain methodologies, such as rapid application development. Initially, only part of the new system is used, the rest still being based on the old system. As such, if there are problems with the first implemented component, the remainder can be delayed and the old system used until the problems are cleared. This does mean that the old and new systems must be able to work together, which is not always possible. If they are completely incompatible with one another, a phased approach cannot work.

The phased approach works best when a small company is upgrading an existing system. It is not suitable for companies with many different premises because of the difficulties in coordinating and managing the phased change.

Pilot changeover

Companies, especially larger ones, tend to have more than one business site. For example, Sainsbury's has hundreds of shops across the country. Each one is likely to be doing a very similar, if not identical, job to the other shops. This is the perfect environment for a pilot changeover. In a pilot, just a small number of shops run the new system while the rest rely on the old one. That way, if the system is faulty or if there are problems, only a few shops will be affected. This is an ideal model for any business that has many similar branches. It is not suitable for companies spread across many sites, with each one doing something different, or for companies with only a small number of sites.

Parallel changeover

If you cannot afford for the system to fail at any time, parallel changeover is usually the best method to use. In parallel changeover, the old and new systems are run at the same time, causing duplication of all tasks, while the new system is checked to ensure consistency. Thus, if one fails, there is a backup to take over immediately. This does mean that the employees could potentially be doing double the amount of work. For every order that arrives, they need to enter and process it through two systems. This can become very tiresome and inefficient, so it is highly undesirable to do this for too long. Parallel changeover is the safest type, but also requires the most work. It is best reserved for critical systems such as those used by banks, where the loss of even a single transaction could be catastrophic or for those where safety is a key feature.

Maintenance

After implementation, a system is formally handed over to the customer, and then enters the maintenance phase. There are two aspects to maintenance covering two main ideas: fixing problems and adding new functionality.

The customer, at this stage, normally expects one of the following maintenance arrangements for bug fixes:

- The developing company will fix any problems for a period of time after the product has been released (rather like a warranty for software). This will take the form of a rolling maintenance contract or an upfront payment.
- The developer will charge for every fix that is produced for the software rather than pay a maintenance contract. This can be thought of as a 'pay as you go' scheme.

Where new functionality is concerned, the customer normally expects the development company to provide updates.

Maintenance is rarely free. It is almost always paid for, even if the price is included in the original bid. The reason for this is that maintenance is very expensive for developers and requires a team of people working to support a product. We already know that problems found later on in the systems lifecycle are harder and more expensive to fix. Clearly, all bugs found during maintenance have the potential to be costly to fix.

Because maintenance is so expensive, it is critical that it is well defined for both the customer and the developer for example, via a service level agreement. Problems and bugs can cause the system not to operate as intended, and range from simple spelling mistakes to serious issues with incorrectly defined requirements. Bug fixes do not add any extra functionality but merely ensure that the system meets the original specification.

Extra functionality should never be added unless the updates have been commissioned and have gone through the full systems development lifecycle. This is to ensure that the original functionality is not broken and that the client does not get any nasty surprises.

There are three approaches to providing maintenance: adaptive, corrective and perfective. The approach is normally agreed in the contract between the client and development companies.

Adaptive maintenance

In adaptive maintenance the development company fixes bugs and also adds extra functionality to the system. It is common for companies to purchase systems that come in multiple versions. These multiple versions can be basic, standard and professional. Clients can implement the basic version first, since it is likely to be available first, then upgrade to a higher level of functionality later. This way they can get something up and running quickly in order to support their business. New features tend to be added based on external needs, for example the recent change in law making companies more accountable for cookies. Complying with this requires adaptive changes to any web-based system.

Corrective maintenance

Corrective maintenance simply fixes problems as they arise to ensure that the system closely matches the original specification. Normally the customer will take out a support contract that asks the developer to work on corrective maintenance. Their mandate will be clear: they are to fix problems without breaking the system or adding functionality.

Perfective maintenance

A perfect system is one that completely matches the original specification with no problems at all. There should be a direct mapping from requirements to implementation. So perfective maintenance is maintenance performed with the aim of achieving a perfect system. In order to make the system perfect, it will be necessary to fix all problems. If new or changed requirements are identified and agreed, the development company must also provide upgrades to implement them.

There should always be a current scope for the product and a way of describing what the perfect system should be. Perfective maintenance is expensive and very time-consuming. It should only be used on very small systems or on critical systems. Systems such as air traffic control or nuclear power facilities fall into the latter category. Perfective maintenance also requires that performance is improved when possible. A perfect system is only as perfect as the testing carried out on it. So although you may fix all the bugs you encounter, this does not mean there are no more bugs left in the system.

Evaluation

Evaluation is contractually very important, as it allows the development company and the client to decide whether the project was successful. Evaluation is important to the client because they must be sure that what they are buying is exactly what was specified in the requirements specification. However, evaluation is also important to the developer, as it will determine whether they will be paid. To reduce arguments and the chance of litigation, there are a number of specific criteria that need to be considered before the system is designated a success, which are requirements, performance, usability, robustness and cost:

1. Requirements: Does it meet the functionality set out in the requirements specification? It must meet every requirement in order for the system to be considered a success. This is why each requirement laid out in the specification must be objective and measurable. If a requirement can be interpreted in more than one way, there is a chance for conflict.

2 Performance: Does it respond in a timely manner for the user? This can be subjective, so performance criteria are normally put in place to ensure that there are fewer areas of conflict. Certain complicated processes will be given a time frame in which they must respond, or defined to have progress bars. For example, a search of a database should not take longer than 30 seconds.

3 Usability: It is crucial that the software produced is useable by the end users. This is dependent on the skill level of the end user as well as the nature of the solution. For example, a mobile app would tend to be menu based and be aimed at the novice user. Software to support a network administrator, on the other hand, could be command line based.

4 Robustness: There is nothing worse than software that crashes all the time or is bug ridden. Robustness is a fundamental requirement for all systems. The level of robustness depends on the type of software to some extent. For example, if a word processor crashes it is annoying, but not critical, as users should be saving their work regularly. If an air traffic control system fails, the effects could be devastating.

5 Cost: Has the project come in on or under budget? Systems that cost more than expected are rarely seen as successful. Extra costs are normally carefully negotiated and might have to be absorbed by the developer.

Writing and following algorithms

In any software oriented project, the implementation phase will involve writing and following the algorithms mapped out during the design phase.

You can discover the basics of writing and following algorithms in:

Chapter 6: Types of programming language
Chapter 20: Programming techniques

One of the key tasks during development is to design, create and test algorithms. During the analysis phase a number of key algorithms will be identified. In design, these algorithms will be written down in the form of a diagram or pseudocode.

Tip

Exam questions can sometimes focus on the advantages and disadvantages of the waterfall model, so make a point of highlighting these in your notes. Also, don't be afraid to draw diagrams of different methodologies (particularly spiral and waterfall models) in your exam. These are often worth marks.

To successfully answer exam questions on the systems life cycle you should be able to recommend a particular model over the others for a given project and justify your decision in terms of its relative advantages and disadvantages.

Techniques and methodologies

Program development techniques cover the various approaches to the design, writing and testing of programs, while systems lifecycle methodologies are the different ways in which stages of the systems lifecycle can be combined and implemented. Each methodology has its own set of advantages and disadvantages, so a particular methodology may be perfect for one project but completely inappropriate for another. Which model or methodology to use is decided by the project manager and can have a critical impact on the successful implementation of the solution.

Program development techniques

Before looking at some of the methodologies and models available to project managers, it is worth familiarising yourself with some of the more common program development techniques. Just as many different methodologies use the same stages from the systems lifecycle, there are a few key development techniques that are also shared by most methodologies.

Incremental development

In **incremental development**, the entire system is designed before being divided into separate modules or subsystems. These modules are then programmed one after the other, with each module being designed in detail, implemented and tested before being added to the existing release.

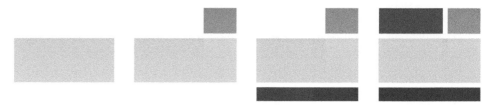

Figure 5.8: Incremental development example showing how a sample program would be built under this approach.

This approach has a number of benefits. Software is generated quickly, so users get a chance to give feedback on the work so far. This in turn means that the development team can be more flexible and are better able to react to changing requirements, for example the release of a new operating system. New functionality can easily be added to the existing product if the client decides they would like the software to do something extra. Development can also be carried out by specialists, and as modules can be created by different teams with different areas of expertise, they could even be written in different programming languages.

Incremental development also encourages very thorough testing, as each individual module is tested before its release using the methods described in this chapter, especially unit testing, meaning that the system is less likely to fail later on.

However, incremental development also has some inherent weaknesses. In order to be properly subdivided a problem must be well understood and the major requirements clearly defined, which isn't always possible at the start of a project. In addition, extensive integration testing needs to be carried out to ensure that the separate modules work well together, which requires very clearly defined programmatic interfaces.

Iterative development

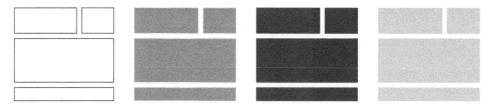

Figure 5.9: Iterative development example showing how a sample program would be built under this approach.

Iterative development models deliver a fully working system up front but then build on this functionality with every additional release. For example, Microsoft Word has gone through many iterations since it was first released. Each release improves and extends the functionality of the last iteration.

Iterative development enables customers to experience the system from an early stage in development and to provide feedback on changes they would like to be made. The model also allows developers to spot problems early on and fix any bugs in the next iteration. Models based on iterative development work particularly well for large projects where the requirements are fully understood. However, projects can suffer if requirements are not substantively met by the initial release, as after this the focus is very much on refining existing functionality rather than adding new areas.

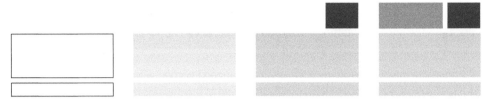

Figure 5.10: Prototyping development example showing how a sample program would be built under this approach.

Prototyping

Prototyping seeks to combine the iterative and incremental development models by providing a cut-down version of the final product on which the client can give feedback. This initial prototype can then be improved or have extra functionality added to it in order to produce a next prototype. This cycle is repeated (iterated) until the client is happy with the final product.

Prototyping allows a system to be quickly built in order to demonstrate ideas and concepts to the customer. Used properly, prototyping can provide a high degree of flexibility and enable developers to react quickly to changing requirements. However, prototyping can also make projects difficult to manage, as there are few concrete deadlines and mission creep can set in, with developers constantly refining the product, adding less and less relevant functionality.

Systems lifecycle methodologies

Each of the lifecycle methodologies described here implements the systems lifecycle in a different way. This means that each has its own set of advantages and disadvantages that make it suitable for different projects.

Tip

To successfully answer exam questions on this topic you should be able to recommend a particular model over the others for a given project and justify your decision in terms of its relative advantages and disadvantages.

Waterfall model

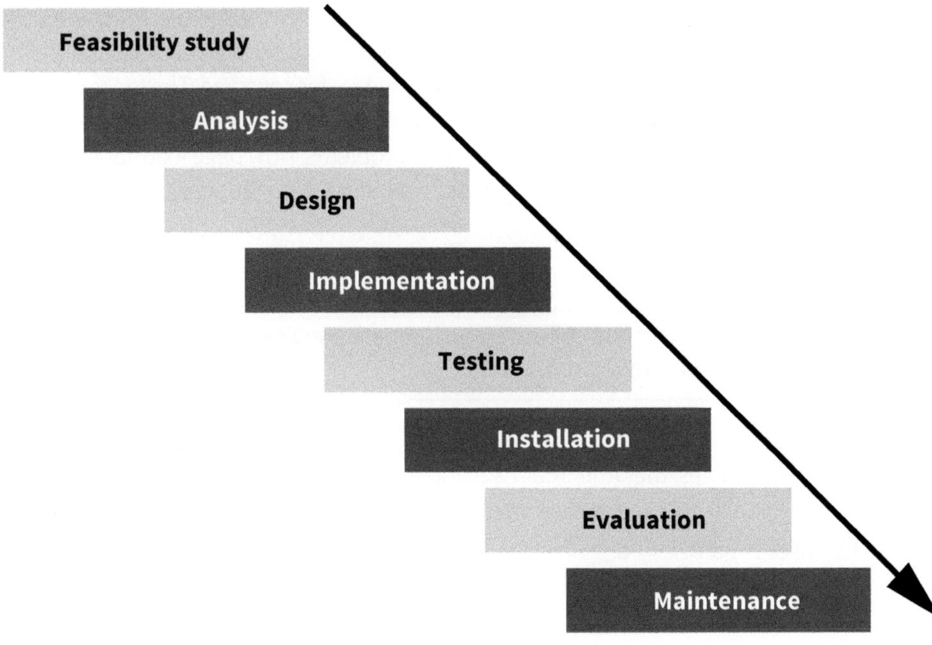

Figure 5.11: Waterfall model.

The waterfall model is probably the most famous incarnation of the systems lifecycle. It was initially designed for use in manufacturing and engineering environments where the products being created were based around hardware rather than software. Since then, the waterfall model has been successfully employed across a range of industries and sectors. Its linear nature and the fact that deliverables are produced at the end of each stage made it popular in the early days of software engineering.

In the waterfall model the different stages are arranged in order, with each stage cascading down to the next. It is impossible to begin one stage of the development until the preceding one has been completed. This linear approach to development is both the biggest strength and the Achilles' heel of the waterfall model.

Each stage in the waterfall model ends with a deliverable document, produced to inform the next stage. For example, at the end of the design stage the design documentation is produced, detailing exactly what is to be created during the implementation stage. These deliverables can be shown to clients or used internally within the company. It is very important that these deliverables are detailed and accurate, as it is possible that the team that builds the system will be completely different from the team who implement the project; both rely on the design documentation. At the end of each phase, some testing of the deliverables occurs to make sure that they meet the overall requirements of the project and that nothing has been omitted.

These deliverables constitute a major advantage of using the waterfall model, as they can be used to provide concrete deadlines, called milestones, for the project, which helps build client confidence. These regular deadlines also bring a level of discipline to a large project that can be lacking in some of the more flexible models and methodologies you will see later.

Computing in context: high-profile failure of the waterfall model

In 2010, the American President, Barack Obama, set out to reform healthcare in the USA. He aimed to provide health insurance to US citizens who couldn't afford the expensive premiums charged by private healthcare companies and were therefore very vulnerable if they fell ill. An important part of the reform was the creation of healthcare.gov, a federal website that was to serve as a marketplace where people could compare insurance plans, learn about the new subsidies and sign up for coverage. The federal portal was plagued with technical glitches from its rollout, including long sign-in wait times, log-in difficulties, insurance account creation problems, slow page loads and outages. One source claimed that of the 20 million people visiting the site, just half a million were able to access it.

Senior aides publicly blamed the waterfall development model for the poor quality of the site, believing that the project would have been much better implemented by the 'adoption of modern, incremental software development practices, like a popular one called Agile, already used in the private sector'.

Aside from the deliverables, the other main advantage of the waterfall model is that it forces developers to consider the requirements of the system thoroughly, rather than diving straight into programming. A detailed, thorough design reduces the possibility of mistakes later on. In addition, the model is relatively simple and easy to understand.

This makes it attractive to clients who don't understand software development, as it helps them grasp long, technical projects.

However, despite its popularity the waterfall model has some important disadvantages that make it unsuitable for certain types of project. In particular, the waterfall model is much less flexible than the alternatives you will see later on. Most importantly, following the waterfall model makes it very difficult for systems developers to react to changes or problems that crop up during any of the later stages. If a problem is discovered during the implementation stage, it may be necessary to go right back to the top of the waterfall and revise the requirements.

It is also very difficult for software engineers or their clients to completely understand the requirements of a system at the start of development. It is common for the requirements of a project to evolve over the course of development, as the programmers grow to understand the area in which they are working and the client better understands what the software might be capable of. This problem is amplified by the length of time that the waterfall model can take to implement; it is perfectly feasible for the process to take so long that, by the time the project has been completed, the requirements have changed dramatically.

Tip

Exam questions can sometimes focus on the advantages and disadvantages of the waterfall model, so make a point of highlighting these in your notes.

Waterfall model summary

- The different stages are arranged in order, with each stage feeding into the next.
- No stage of the development can be begun until the preceding one has been completed.
- Each stage ends with a deliverable or handover document produced to inform the next stage.
- It is simple to understand and suitable for large projects where the requirements are clearly understood.
- It is very bad at reacting to changing requirements and is not suitable for projects where the requirements may not be fully understood at the start.

Spiral model

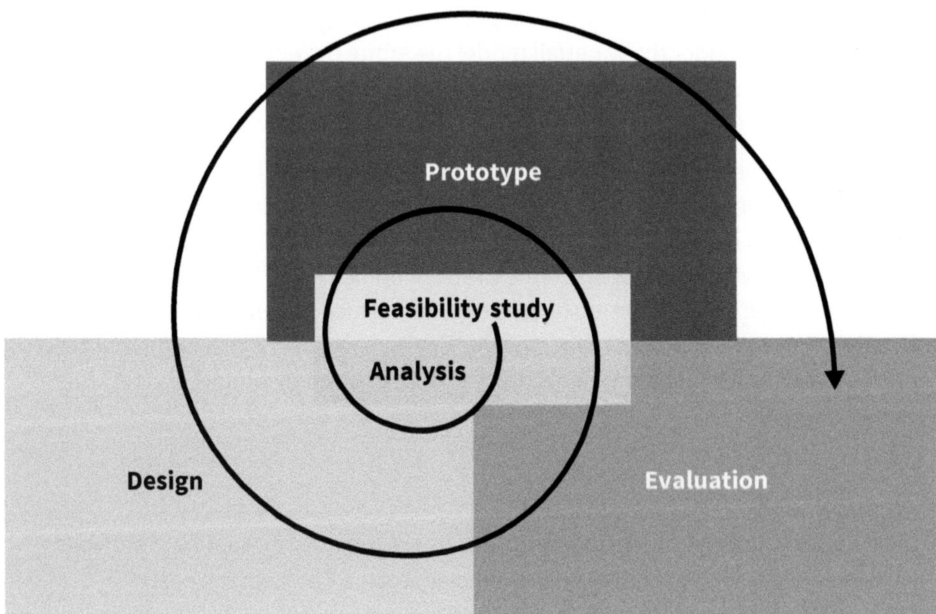

Figure 5.12: Spiral model.

The spiral model is much less linear and constrained than other development methodologies such as the waterfall model. In the spiral model, a reduced number of stages are visited and revisited in a constant quest for perfection. This approach is iterative and each completed cycle is referred to as an iteration of the development.

Development begins with an initial feasibility study and analysis to get an idea of what it is that needs to be achieved. A possible solution is then quickly designed by the developer in order to meet the user requirements. Next, this design is implemented in the form of a prototype, which means that it is a rough, partially incomplete version of the final product. This prototype is then shown to the client, who evaluates it and decides what functionality they would like to be added, removed or improved. At this point, the stages are repeated by analysing the new requirements, designing any modifications that need to be made and improving the prototype. This process is repeated as many times as necessary, with development 'spiralling' towards the final product. Often the prototypes can be built very quickly because it isn't necessary to implement all the functionality of a full product.

The spiral model can be successfully employed in large and small projects and is a good choice when it is likely that the systems requirements will change as the project develops. This makes it ideal for software engineering, as requirements can change a great deal over the course of a project. This ability to adapt to changing requirements means that the spiral model has a number of advantages over less flexible alternatives, such as the waterfall model. Estimates about the resources needed for the project, such as time, staff and budget, get more accurate as the work progresses, because developers have a better idea of what needs to be done and have the experience to make more accurate predictions. Using prototypes also makes the spiral model better at adapting to unforeseen circumstances. For example, if a new version of Windows is released, the developer simply needs to ensure that the next prototype runs on that version as well. Using prototypes also means that the model is better able to cope with changing user requirements. If the user decides they want additional functionality they didn't specify at the beginning, it is simply added to the next prototype. Under the waterfall model the entire development process might need to be started again or the new requirements dealt with through maintenance, which is costly.

Tip

Ensure you are happy with comparing and contrasting the spiral and waterfall models. You can prepare for this by making sure that you are able to contrast the advantages and disadvantages of one with the advantages and disadvantages of another for a given project.

However, despite these many advantages, the free-flowing nature of the spiral model can also lead to problems. It can be difficult to follow for large projects where lots of people are involved in developing a product. This in turn makes it very hard to explain to customers exactly what will happen during the development right from the beginning. There are no regular deliverables, so deadlines can be difficult to enforce and projects can easily fall behind without proper management. Finally, because the requirements phase may not be complete initially, problems that cannot be solved by simply adapting the prototype can arise.

Spiral model summary

- Software is produced by repeatedly designing, creating and evaluating prototypes.
- The evaluation of each prototype is used to inform the design of the next.
- It is an excellent model for reacting to changing requirements and adding new functionality.
- With this model it can be difficult to plan ahead and provide deadlines to clients, particularly in large projects.

Rapid application development (RAD)

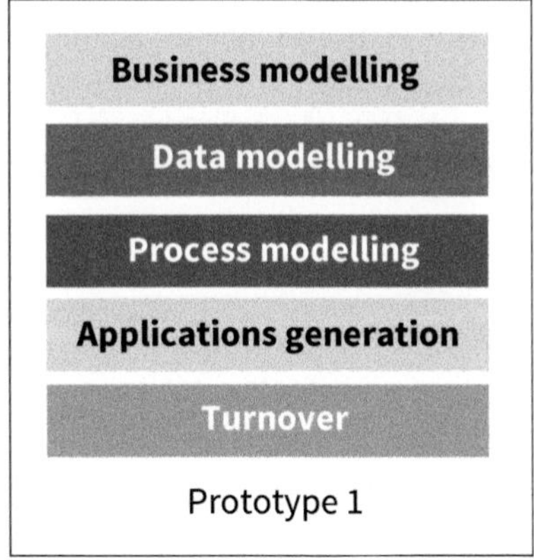

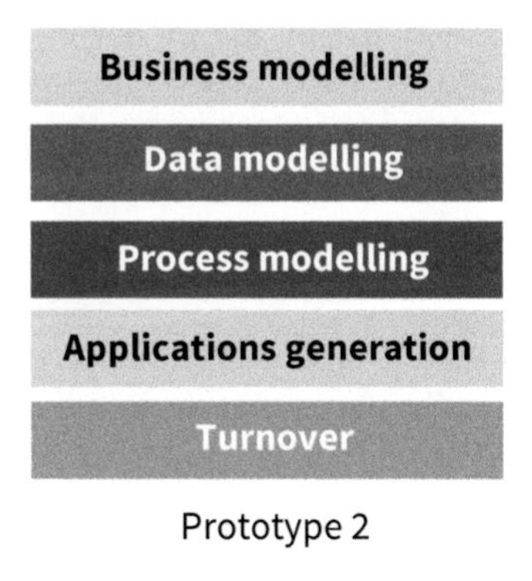

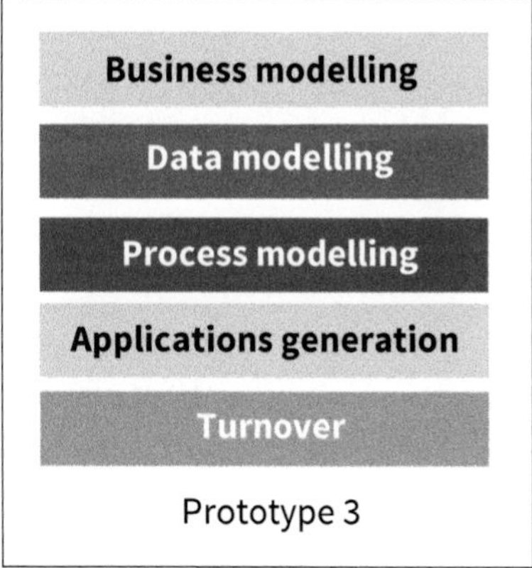

Figure 5.13: RAD Using three separate prototypes for inclusion in the final product.

Rapid application development is essentially a much quicker version of the spiral model. Once the user's requirements have been ascertained through analysis, a modular design is drawn up. Development is then entirely focused on prototyping and re-prototyping until the final product is created. The prototypes created must be reusable for RAD to work, as it relies more than other models on repurposing and developing the existing prototype in order to create the next one.

The RAD model typically breaks the analysis, design, implementation and testing stages into a series of very short (rapid) development cycles, with stages entitled business modelling, data modelling, process modelling, application generation and turnover:

- Business modelling: the business model describes the flow of information around the system using data flow diagrams and flowcharts.
- Data modelling: during this phase, the results of the business modelling are analysed and used to produce datasets or objects that are needed for the system to function.
- Process modelling: in this phase, descriptions are added to the data objects explaining whether data is to be added, deleted or edited.
- Application generation: the actual system is created by combining the process and data models to create a prototype.
- Turnover: the prototype is tested at the end of each cycle. Later on, more testing will be required as modules are linked together in order to ensure that they function properly in conjunction with each other.

RAD has a heavy focus on modular design, because modules can be created in parallel by separate teams and combined together to create prototypes. This iterative and incremental approach enables RAD developers to create functional prototypes very quickly. It is this speed of development that gives RAD its name. The use of special software called a CASE (computer aided software engineering) tool can help to develop a solution quickly. High-level programming languages with an integrated GUI development tool, such as Microsoft's Visual Studio suite, became very popular because prototype user interfaces could be developed within minutes and program functionality built in afterwards.

A secondary advantage of RAD is that it encourages a great deal of collaboration between the developers and the client. Constant client feedback on the previous prototype is obtained in order to develop each new prototype. This collaboration is made possible by the speed of development, as clients are able to see working versions of their system very early on. This in turn means that the client always feels engaged with the project and any changing requirements can be incorporated into the next prototype, something not possible in less flexible models. Another advantage is that the speed at which prototypes are developed means that any new requirements arising from client feedback can be quickly taken into account.

There are, however, a number of potential problems in using RAD. The same lack of upfront planning that makes it easier to incorporate changing requirements can also be a disadvantage, as insurmountable problems may be encountered very late in the project. RAD is not workable if a project cannot be subdivided into modules, as it is not possible to create prototypes fast enough to ensure regular user input. The reliance on modularisation also means that RAD development may require many more developers, as code needs to be created in parallel if the speed of development is to be maintained.

Tip

Questions about rapid application development tend to require fairly short answers and their mark schemes usually focus on the use of prototypes. Prepare by making sure you have fully understood the prototypes section.

RAD summary

- Creates a quick succession of prototypes, which swiftly develop into the final solution.
- Encourages collaboration between developers and clients as well as being quick to react to changing requirements.
- Without detailed analysis and design, it is possible to encounter insurmountable problems very late in development.

Agile programming

Agile methods were developed in the 1990s to provide a flexible alternative to the more structured development models, such as the waterfall model. There are many different types of Agile development, but they are all based on the same founding principles outlined in the 'Agile Manifesto'. RAD and the spiral model could both be said to be forms of Agile development; other popular incarnations include Extreme Programming (XP) and Scrum, which will be discussed later.

Agile techniques value collaboration and people over processes and tools. There is a strong focus on providing programmers with the tools and resources they need, then trusting them to solve the problem set as efficiently as possible. Teams are trusted to organise and manage themselves, with a focus on regular meetings and interactions rather than the documentation-heavy approach favoured by the waterfall model.

This focus on collaboration is also extended to customers and clients. Agile programmers spend much more time meeting regularly with clients to discuss the system's development. This is radically different from the waterfall model, in which clients must rely on a few large meetings to negotiate contracts or finalise requirements.

Agile programmers favour using their time to produce software rather than detailed, comprehensive documentation. They prefer their projects to be judged on how well their software works, rather than on how well its development has been documented. This means that they are able to deliver well-written software far faster than programmers working to more rigid development models. This reluctance to produce lengthy documentation, combined with the high level of client contact, allows agile programmers to focus on responding to change rather than simply following a plan. One of the founding principles of the Agile Methodology is that it is impossible to know all of the user's requirements at the start of a project, something that is hotly disputed by proponents of the waterfall model. All this means that agile projects are able to quickly adapt to changes, for example a competitor releasing a new product or a new operating system becoming available.

There are a number of different implementations of the Agile Methodology, each sharing the tenets of the Agile Manifesto but implementing them in different ways. The most common are Extreme Programming and Scrum.

- Extreme Programming emphasises four areas of Agile development: communication, simplicity, feedback and courage. Communication means between individual programmers and teams as well as regular communication with clients and customers. Simplicity encourages programmers to adopt the most straightforward solution to a client's problems rather than providing an overly complex or unnecessarily detailed one. Opportunities for regular feedback are also built into the development process, with programmers often working in pairs. This is known as paired programming, with one developer coding while the other observes and offers advice.
- Like other Agile methods, Scrum focuses on regular iterations to create functional prototypes quickly. Scrum programmers focus on having fixed-length iterations (for example, 30 days) called sprints. A Scrum project will be worked on by several teams at the same time, with each team focusing on a different piece of functionality. These teams will hold regular meetings, called scrums, to update each other on their progress and give feedback on any problems they have encountered.

Agile Methodology summary

- Has various implementations, including Extreme Programming and Scrum.
- Focus on communication, simplicity, feedback and courage makes it possible to develop very well-written programs quickly.
- Some Agile techniques such as paired programming are not popular among developers, and a lack of documentation and specific deadlines can lead to problems with customers who are unfamiliar with the approach.

Summary

A stakeholder is anyone who has a vested interest in the development of a system. Common stakeholders include:

- user
- programmer
- project manager
- system analyst.

Analysis of a computing system will include:

- problem definition: the current problems with the system will be investigated and initially agreed upon
- feasibility: an investigation to ensure that the project is achievable by checking the following factors:
  - economic: is there enough money to pay for the system?
  - time: can the project be done in the timescales allowed?
  - technical: is the technology and expertise needed to produce the system available?
  - legal: will the project comply with the laws of the countries it will be released in?

Activity 5.1

One way to maximise marks on your computer science exams is to have a mastery over the keywords used in each section. To this end, you should design and develop an app to support students in learning their keywords. Pick a methodology which is best suited and then use it to help develop the app. To make this more meaningful, you may wish to work in small teams of developers.

Activity 5.2

Use the internet to find a technology company that uses Agile development. What are they creating? Why do you think they have chosen this methodology?

Activity 5.3

Follow the waterfall model to create a simple hangman game in Python. Analyse the problem then design a solution before coding your program. Evaluate the methodology you used: did it help or hinder your games development?

- fact finding: gather information needed to accurately define the new system to be built, using the following methods:
  - observation
  - questionnaire
  - interview
  - collecting documentation.

requirements specification will be produced at the end of analysis.

- Design is based on the requirements specification and is broken down into input, output, processing and storage design.
- Testing is where the system is put through its paces to ensure that it has met the requirements and most of the bugs have been fixed.

Part of the deliverables of a project include documentation:

- user documentation: a manual on using the system provided to the end user
- technical documentation: information to allow the system to be maintained.

When a project is implemented, one of the following methods is used:

- direct
- phased
- pilot
- parallel.

Once the system has been deployed, it must be maintained through one of the following methods:

- corrective
- adaptive
- perfective.

When developing systems, different methodologies will be used to implement the systems lifecycle.

Program development techniques cover the various approaches to the design, writing and testing of programs. Some of the more common ones are:

- Incremental development is where the entire system is broken down into modules which are designed, implemented and tested before being added to the final product.
- Iterative development will provide a full system upfront but then build upon the functionality as time goes on.
- Prototyping is where only a small number of features are implemented, combining both incremental and iterative approaches.

Systems lifecycle methodologies are the different ways in which stages of the systems lifecycle can be combined and implemented:

- The waterfall model is a linear approach to the systems lifecycle where each phase is completed fully before moving on to the next.
- The spiral model is an iterative approach where a prototype is built, evaluated and then improved.
- Rapid application development (RAD) is an incremental approach where modules are prototyped with reuse in mind.
- Agile development is focused on producing software rather than documentation and places value on communication and collaboration. Team meetings are favoured over documentation.

End-of-chapter questions

1 Describe what happens during analysis and what document is produced at the end. [8]

2 The spiral model is a common methodology used to produce software.

  a Explain how prototypes are used during the spiral model. [3]

  b Describe a single iteration of the spiral model. [4]

  c State **one** advantage of using the spiral model over the waterfall model. [1]

3 Describe how prototypes used in rapid application development (RAD) differ from those used in the spiral model. [6]

4 Discuss how the Agile Methodology can deal with changing requirements. [6]

5 Pick and justify which development methodology would be best suited for creating an app to support students making their GCSE options. [6]

6 In the waterfall model, what is handed to the client at the end of each stage? [1]

7 When is it not suitable to use the waterfall model? [4]

8 What is a prototype? [2]

9 Agile development methodologies focus on what, instead of the copious documentation produced by the waterfall model? [4]

10 The different ways of implementing the systems lifecycle are referred to as what? [1]

Further reading

Teach ICT system lifecycle – search for it on the Teach-ICT website.
Manifesto for Agile programming – go to agilemanifesto.org
RAD – search for Rapid Application Development on the SQA website.
Software development methodologies – search on the Code Project website.
Unit testing from Extreme Programming – search on extremeprogramming.org
Unit testing in Python – search on Jeff Knupp's website.

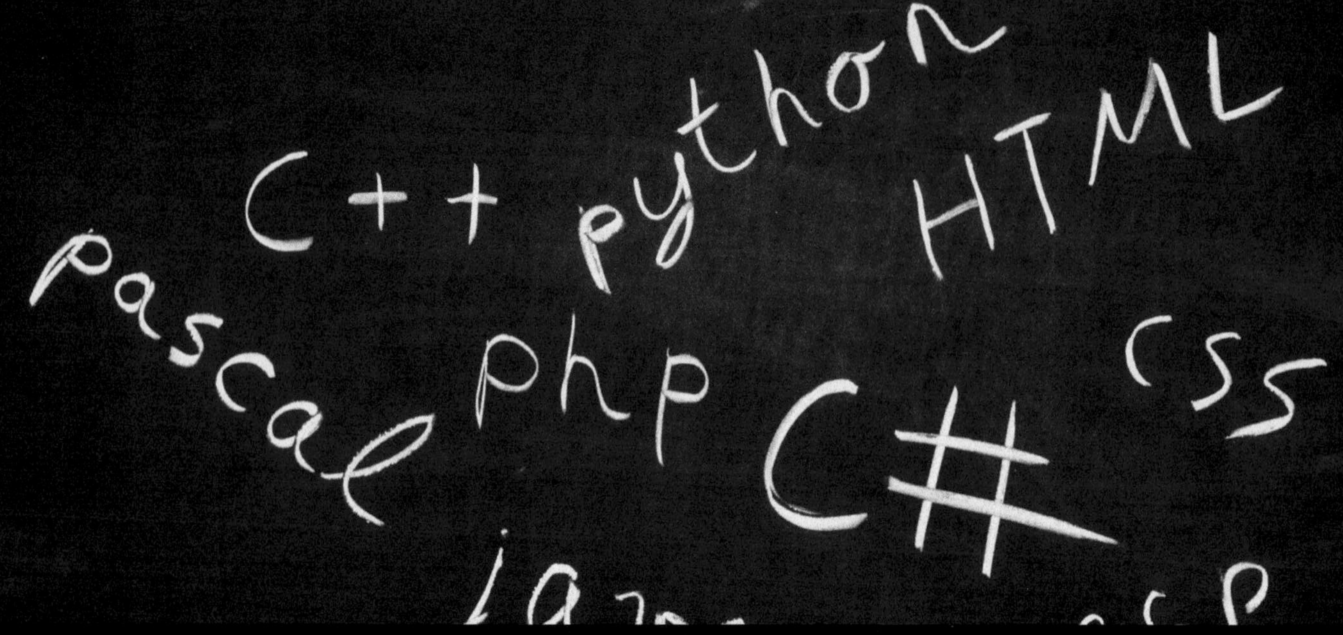

Chapter 6
Types of programming language

Specification points

1.2.4 Types of Programming Language

- Need for and characteristics of a variety of programming paradigms.
- Procedural languages.
- Assembly language (including following and writing simple programs with the Little Man Computer instruction set).
- A Modes of addressing memory (immediate, direct, indirect and indexed).
- Object-oriented languages with an understanding of classes, objects, methods, attributes, inheritance, encapsulation and polymorphism.

Learning objectives

- To understand what is meant by the term 'procedural languages'.
- A To be able to read and understand object-oriented pseudocode, based on Java, including:
  - defining classes
  - instantiating objects
  - methods and attributes
  - inheritance
  - encapsulation
  - polymorphism.
- To learn and write basic Assembly code, using Little Man Computer (LMC), as well as understanding the basics of how real Assembly code works.
- A To learn the different memory addressing modes, including immediate, direct, indirect and indexed.

Introduction

Any programming you have done so far is likely to have been procedural. Procedural programs consist of statements that tell the computer exactly what to do and are executed line by line. The basic module of a procedural program is the procedure which is a section of code that performs a task. Functions are also modules of code found in procedural programs but unlike a procedure, they return a value. What you may not have been aware of is that procedural is just one of several paradigms (styles) of programming. In this chapter you will explore not only the procedural paradigm, but also two other paradigms, assembly language or low-level programming and, for A Level students, object-oriented. This chapter is not exhaustive and there are other paradigms in use by computer scientists. One notable omission from this course is declarative languages, popular with artificial intelligence and knowledge-based systems. If you are interested you may wish to conduct some individual research into the programming language Prolog to see how declarative languages work.

Computing in context: culture of innovation

Google employs many experienced programmers. They insist that their programmers spend at least 20% of their time working on personal projects that are unrelated to their current work. They believe that this keeps their staff passionate about their jobs as well as creating a culture of innovation. Some huge Google services like Gmail and Google News started life as pet projects devised by staff during this 20% time.

Procedural languages

Fledgling programmers commonly use procedural languages, because such languages enable them to focus on the logic of a program rather than worrying about high-level concepts such as software reuse. A procedural language, such as C, has a number of key features:

- Code is run serially, one line after another.
- The language supports selection, iteration and assignment.
- It uses identifiers for variables, constants and procedures.
- It uses procedures and functions.
- Variables have either local or global scope.

It is important to note that a lot of languages are not intrinsically procedural, but can be used in that way. Some languages support multiple paradigms, meaning that you can code in either procedural or in an object-oriented fashion. Python is an example of this, as you will see in this chapter.

This section does not go into detail on selection, iteration and assignment techniques, identifiers and constants, and procedures and functions, since it is assumed that you are already familiar with these features of the procedural paradigm.

The scope of a variable refers to its lifetime in a procedural language. If a variable is defined outside of a procedure, it is known as a global variable. Global variables can be used and updated by any part of the program and will exist until the program is closed. Local variables, that is, those defined within a procedure or function, exist only while it is running. Once it returns to the calling procedure, the local variable will no longer exist. Local variables cannot be used outside of the procedures in which they were defined. The code sample below, written in Python, shows the difference between local and global scope. The program illustrates variable scope, although it is not considered good practice to declare a global variable inside a procedure or function. Consider why this is the case.

Code

```
z= "hello" # global scope
def myProc():
  global z # python requires globals to be explicitly
  defined as globals inside procedures
  y = "world" # local scope
  print z,y
def mySecondProc():
  global z
  print z,y # this line of code will fail, y is not defined
  as it is not within scope
myProc()
mySecondProc()
```

Object-oriented programming

Object-oriented programming (OO), has gained popularity among the programming community. Most languages offer some form of OO support, including languages that were originally designed to be procedural. OO allows programs to be well structured and offers the potential for reusable code, which is much sought-after in modern programs.

Most modern programming projects use the object-oriented paradigm, so it is important, once you understand the basics of procedural languages, to move on to OO. Few languages are 'pure OO' but one example is the language called Smalltalk. Although it isn't very popular, it is interesting because any value in the program is also an object of a class. Learning a language such as Smalltalk encourages programmers to use OO principles correctly.

Selection, iteration and assignment, along with identifiers for variables and constants, all basic to procedural programming, are also available in the object-oriented paradigm. This makes moving from procedural to OO much more straightforward than it would be otherwise. One of the key differences, however, is that in OO languages, procedures are replaced by classes, objects and methods, and the whole code is structured and designed differently. Classes and procedures both offer modularity of code, but classes allow the developer to produce more reusable code and relate their design more closely to reality.

Three characteristics define an OO language:

- encapsulation
- inheritance
- polymorphism.

These are explained later in this chapter.

Objects, classes and methods

In OO programming, code is developed around objects and classes. An object is a combination of data and the actions that can operate on that data. A class is the definition of an object; it embodies all the information needed to create and manipulate objects of a particular type (Figure 6.1). For example, there are many types of cars, which may differ, but fundamentally they share common descriptions and actions. If you saw a car coming down the road you would immediately classify it as a car before noticing the make and model. A car is an example of a class while a specific car, such as a Jaguar, is an example of an object.

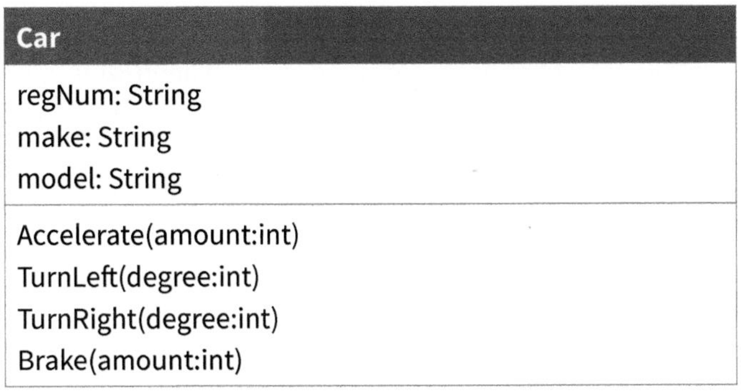

Car
regNum: String make: String model: String
Accelerate(amount:int) TurnLeft(degree:int) TurnRight(degree:int) Brake(amount:int)

Figure 6.1: Class diagram for a simple car.

A class has two main sections:

- a description (attributes)
- actions (methods).

Methods are fundamental to OO languages. A method is a piece of code that implements one of the behaviours of a class. For example, the car class could have the method 'turnleft'.

In order to identify an individual car, it must be described, and in OO this means creating an object. The process of creating an object is known as instantiation. The code below shows how an instance of the class car could be instantiated. The notation used in the pseudocode below is common to many different OO languages. When an object is created, a blank version is generated on the heap (a large pool of memory) and a reference to it is returned. The new keyword is responsible for instantiating a class and allocating memory. Once instantiation has occurred, a reference to the object will be created, pointing to the location of that object in memory.

Code

```
ford = new Car()
ford.regNum = "YR99REG"
ford.make = "Ford"
ford.model = "Fiesta"
print ford.make, ford.model
```

To set an attribute of a class, you need to use the reference created during instantiation. Attributes are treated as variables within the object and are accessed by using a full stop between the object name and the variable. You can assign attributes or use them in other expressions in the exact same way you would any other variable. Accessing attributes is shown in the code above. Here we are setting up three attributes for our Ford car: the make, registration number and the model. The last line uses the class's print method to print two of these attributes as an example of how they can be used. It is important to note that setting the attribute for one object does not impact any other car object. Each object is distinct from each other, even if they share the same class.

Encapsulation

Encapsulation is the hiding of the implementation of a class and controlling access to its methods and attributes. Classes can hide how they work from developers who may wish to use them in their programs. Anyone using the class needs only to understand the interface to the class, i.e. its methods and attributes.

Using encapsulation to implement data structures

One common use of OO programming that relies on encapsulation is the implementation of data structures, such as stacks. Here is some pseudocode showing how a stack structure could be implemented in OO:

Code

```
CLASS Stack
  start = -1
  list = []
  FUNCTION pop()
    oldstart = start
    IF start == -1 THEN
      RETURN "error - queue empty"
    ELSE
      start = list[start].next
      list[oldstart].next = free
      free = oldstart
    END IF
    RETURN list[oldstart]
  END FUNCTION
  FUNCTION push(value)
    temp = NEW Node()
    temp.data = value
    temp.next = start
    start = free
    free = list[free].next
    list[start] = temp
  END FUNCTION
END CLASS
```

The pop() and push() methods are held within the class structure. The diagram in Figure 6.2 shows how the class will be presented to developers.

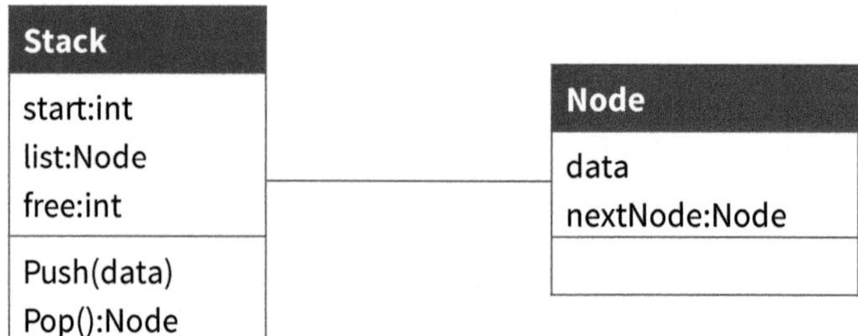

Figure 6.2: Class diagram for stack.

Code

```
test = new Stack()
test.push("Bert")
test.push("Sally")
print test.pop()
print test.pop()
print test.pop()
```

If this stack class was placed within a library file, developers would only need to import it in order to use the stack functionality.

Inheritance

In the real world, inheritance has a very specific meaning. We inherit genes from our parents, and in some cases money from relatives. The idea is that something is being passed down through some form of relationship. **Inheritance**, in OO, follows the same principle.

Consider the two classes shown in Figure 6.3.

Car	Van
Accelerate(amount:int) Brake(amount:int) CurrentGear():int Gearup() Geardown()	Accelerate(amount:int) Brake(amount:int) CurrentGear():int Gearup() Geardown()

Figure 6.3: Class diagram for different road vehicles.

They are clearly different classes. A van is much larger than a car and has more storage space. However, they both have very similar operations. They accelerate, brake and turn. It makes little sense to write the same code twice, so the methods they have in common can be taken and placed into a new class called RoadVehicles (Figure 6.4). This new class will contain all of the shared methods and attributes of both class Car and class Van.

Car and Van now inherit from class RoadVehicles. They no longer define the methods themselves; rather, they inherit them from class RoadVehicles. RoadVehicles is said to be the superclass of both Car and Van, while Car and Van are subclasses of RoadVehicles. RoadVehicles is also a base class, that is, the first class within a hierarchy of classes. Subclasses can have methods of their own, which are specific to them. Consider the following classes.

The class diagram shown in Figure 6.5 shows a basic calculator superclass. All calculators, regardless of the type, offer these core services. Scientific calculators offer more services, such as *sin* and *cos*. Tax calculators might offer extra functionality such as percentages. These two types of calculator are subclasses, each having methods of their own.

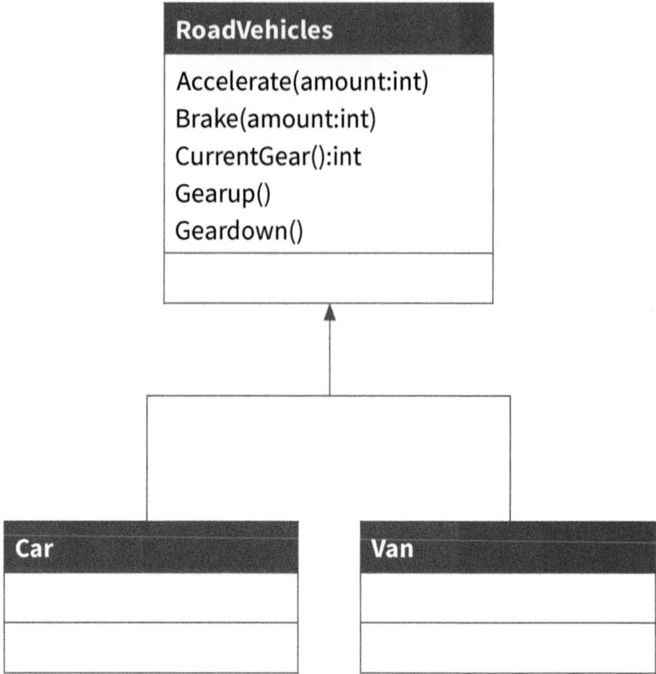

Figure 6.4: Class diagram for road vehicles using inheritance.

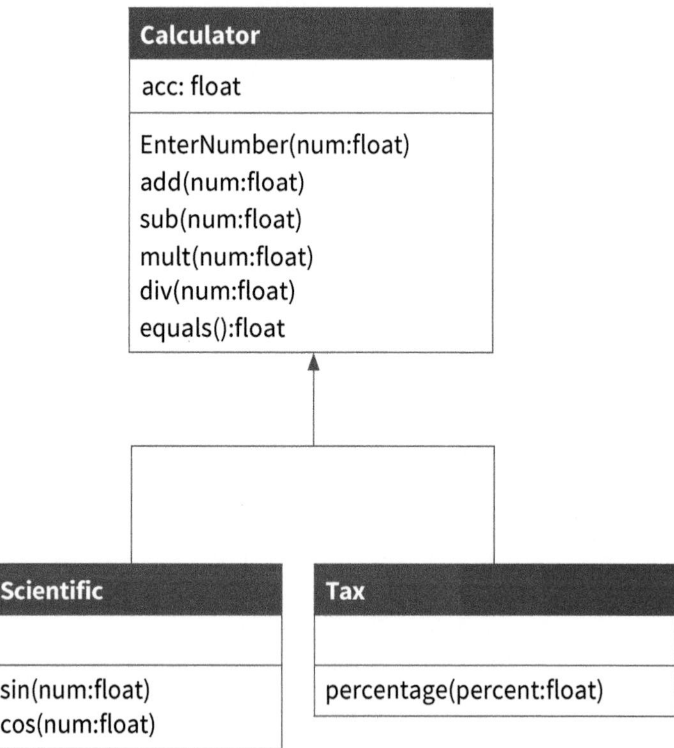

Figure 6.5: Class diagram showing how inheritance can be used to extend functionality.

Here is the pseudocode for the Calculator and Scientific classes:

Code

```
CLASS Scientific INHERITS Calculator
  FUNCTION sin(num)
    acc = Math.sin(num)
  END FUNCTION
  FUNCTION cos(num)
    acc = Math.cos(num)
  END FUNCTION
END CLASS
CLASS Calculator
    acc = 0
    FUNCTION enterNumber(num)
      acc = num
    END FUNCTION
    FUNCTION add(num)
      acc = acc + num
    END FUNCTION
    FUNCTION sub(num)
      acc = acc - num
    END FUNCTION
    FUNCTION mult(num)
      acc = acc * num
    END FUNCTION
    FUNCTION divide(num)
      acc = acc / num
    END FUNCTION
    FUNCTION equals()
      RETURN acc
    END FUNCTION
END CLASS
sci = new Scientific()
calc = new Calculator()
sci.enterNumber(45)
sci.sin()
print sci.equals()
calc.enterNumber(45)
calc.sin()
```

The Scientific calculator class inherits all of the attributes and methods of the Calculator base **class**.

The Scientific class can use any method from the Calculator class. However, Calculator cannot use any of the methods from the Scientific class. Subclasses can inherit functionality only from their superclass. It is not a two-way process. In the code sample above, the line calc. sin() fails because 'calc' is an object of type Calculator, which does not have the sin() method.

Polymorphism

Polymorphism is the ability for an object of one class type to appear to be used as another. When you instantiate an object it has a specific data type, which is based on the class from which it was originally created. Three classes are defined in the code below:

Code

```
CLASS Shape
  FUNCTION draw()
  FUNCTION move(x_amount, y_amount)
CLASS Circle INHERITS Shape
  FUNCTION circle(radius,x,y)
  FUNCTION resize(radius)
CLASS Triangle INHERITS Shape
  FUNCTION triangle(x1,y1,x2,y2,x3,y3)
  FUNCTION movePoint(pointNumber, new_x, new_y)
```

The Circle and Triangle classes inherit from the Shape class. If an object were created using the code Circle myShape = new Circle(50,0,0), myShape would have the data type of Circle. As Circle inherits from Shape, it has access to the methods of Shape as well as its own.

In the above example, rather than treating Circles and Triangles as different classes, it would be better to treat them as Shapes. When classes inherit from one another, they get more than just the superclass's methods and attributes. Because of polymorphism, they get the data type of the superclass's object. This **inheritance** of data type is one-way only. So a Circle is a Shape, but a Shape is not a Circle. Being a bit more formal, the subclass can be referenced as its superclass, but not vice versa.

Code

```
Shape polymorphicCircle= new Circle(50,0,0)// valid data
type assignment
polymorphicCircle.draw() // this line of code works!
polymorphicCircle.resize(100) // this line fails
```

Consider the example code above. A Circle object is instantiated in the normal way, but this time is stored in a variable of data type Shape. Due to polymorphism, this is allowed and the Circle can be referenced as a Shape. Making a call to the draw() function works perfectly, as Shape has a draw method. However, the call to resize fails, as the Shape class does not have a resize method. Even though the object may be a Circle, if we use a polymorphic reference we are bound by the data type of the reference and not of the actual object. We can, however, cast the object back to a Circle reference using the line of code below.

Code

```
((Circle) polymorphicCircle).resize(100)//this now works
```

Polymorphism at first may seem pointless. Why would we want to reference an object through a different data type? To aid understanding, it is easier to look at an example:

Code

```
List myShapeList = new List()
myShapeList.add(new Circle(50,100,100))
myShapeList.add(new Triangle(0,0,30,30,10,10))
Shape s = null
  while true
    for s in myShapeList
      s.move(1,0)
      s.draw()
```

The two Shapes are now being stored in a list. Thanks to polymorphism, it does not matter what type of Shape is in that list: because they all share the common methods of move() and draw(), they can be treated as Shapes. With only two Shapes this example may seem trivial, but what if we had hundreds of Shapes making up a complex background in a game? The loop would not need changing at all, as each item in the list will always be a Shape.

Inheritance allows classes to share common methods, but also to have their own specific methods. Polymorphism allows us to treat related classes as the same, in order to make more effective use of their shared methods. This is possible because objects referenced through polymorphism inherit from the same base class.

To end the discussion on polymorphism, we can have a look at a common OO method, 'instanceof'. This operator will test an object to see if it is a subclass of a given class, that is, whether the object and class are polymorphic.

Object instanceof class – will return true or false depending on whether or not they are polymorphic.

Code

```
Circle myCircle = new Circle(50,100,100)
Triangle myTriangle = new Triangle(0,0,30,30,10,10)
Shape myShape = myCircle
myCircle instanceof Circle // true
myTriangle instanceof Circle // false
myCircle instanceof Shape // true
myTriangle instanceof Shape // true
myShape instanceof Circle // false
myShape instanceof Shape // true
```

OO in Python

So far we have look/ed at how object-oriented programming works in general, using pseudocode. This is loosely based on Java syntax. Even though the syntax is different in Python, the ideas and concepts are the same. Java and Python are syntactically different, but semantically the same.

Creating a class

Classes in Python are defined using the class keyword and indentation. The **class** keyword starts the class block with the name of the class immediately afterwards. Methods are created using the **def** keyword, in the same way functions are. The biggest difference is that all methods must have at least one parameter called **self** and be inside the class indentation block. Self enables functions in Python access to the attributes and methods of the class. A lot of OO languages do this automatically (for example, the **this** keyword in Java can be omitted), but in Python you have to be explicit about the object's reference to itself.

Code

```
class foo:
  def method(self):
    print "hello class"
myFoo = foo()
myFoo.method()
```

Using attributes

Attributes must be defined in order for them to be part of the class. This occurs in the __init__(**self**) method. This is a special method, which is called when the class is instantiated. It is known in OO terms as a constructor. To use attributes, you must use the self-reference as shown in the code example below. When an object is instantiated, the **self**-reference is exactly the same as the object reference. In the code example below, the value is 100 and an error will be printed. **self.x** refers to the attribute inside the foo class, which was instantiated to 10 during construction.

Code

```
class foo:
  def __init__(self):
    self.x = 10
  def method(self):
    print self.x * 10
myFoo = foo()
myFoo.method()
```

Inheritance in Python

In Python, the base class must be defined first. To inherit, you simply put the name of the class in brackets after the name of the subclass. You will then have full access to the methods of the superclass as shown in newMethod(self).

Here is the Python code for the Calculator and Scientific classes described earlier:

Code

```
class Calculator:
  def __init__(self):
    self.acc = 0
  def enterNumber(self,num):
    self.acc = num
  def add(self, num):
    self.acc = self.acc + num
  def sub(self,num):
    self.acc = self.acc - num
  def mult(self,num):
    self.acc = self.acc * num
  def divide(self,num):
    self.acc = self.acc / num
  def equals():
    return self.acc
class Scientific(Calculator):
  def sin():
    self.acc = math.sin(self.acc)
  def cos():
    self.acc = math.cos(self.acc)
```

In the example code below, a ball class is defined. It encapsulates how a ball moves, draws and its location. It uses a library called pygame.

Code

```
import sys, os
# pygame allows access to drawing and animation tools
import pygame
from random import *
# init's the pygame engine
pygame.init()
class ball:
    def __init__(self):
      self.x = randint(50,400)
      self.y = randint(50,400)
      self.dx = randint(1,3)
      self.dy = randint(1,3)
    def update(self):
      self.x = self.x + self.dx
      self.y = self.y + self.dy
      if self.x<0: self.dx = self.dx * -1
      if self.x>500: self.dx = self.dx * -1
      if self.y<0: self.dy = self.dy * -1
      if self.y>500: self.dy = self.dy * -1
```

```
  def draw(self):
    pygame.draw.circle(screen,(255,255,255),
    (self.x, self.y), 20)
# set up screen
size width = 500
height = 500
size = width, height
screen = pygame.display.set_mode(size)
# set up screen size
width = 500
height = 500
size = width, height
screen = pygame.display.set_mode(size)
myBall = ball()
while 1:
# this code will stop the animation.
  for event in pygame.event.get():
    if event.type == pygame.QUIT: sys.exit()
  screen.fill((0,0,0))
  myBall.update()
  myBall.draw()
  # show the newly drawn screen (double buffering)
  pygame.display.flip()
  # short delay to slow down animation.
  pygame.time.delay(5)
```

Assembly code

Assembly code was introduced in Chapter 1 and you should ensure you understand this prior knowledge before proceeding with this section.

Mnemonics

Assembly language code assigns a mnemonic to each **opcode** to make it more readable (for humans). Some example mnemonics, that we have come across already, are:

- ADD – add a number to the accumulator.
- SUB – subtract a number from the accumulator.
- MUL – multiply a number to the accumulator.
- JMP – jump to a memory address and start executing from there.

Assembly code also uses labels to represent variables and memory addresses. When the program is assembled, these labels are converted into memory addresses with the help of a symbol table.

The x86 assembly language

From this point onwards we discuss assembly language using the x86 instruction set (introduced in Chapter 4).

Addressing modes

Assembly languages use various addressing modes. An addressing mode is the way that data is referenced.

Immediate addressing mode

Immediate addressing is when a constant is used as part of the instruction itself. No memory or register access is required. An example of immediate addressing is:

Code

```
mov ax, 4
```

Direct addressing mode

With direct addressing an instruction has a memory address included in it, enclosed within square brackets. At run time the data pointed to by the address must be fetched before it can be operated on.

The example below loads the value stored at memory address 321 and copies it to the accumulator. It then adds d3 (a hexadecimal value) to it and finally copies the result back. This is an example of instructions using direct addressing and immediate addressing modes.

Code

```
mov ax, [321]
add ax, d3
mov [321],ax
```

Tip

Note: **ax** and **eax** are both accumulators. You may see eax used more on websites. The difference between them is that ax is a 16-bit register while eax is 32-bit.

Indirect addressing

Indirect addressing works like two direct memory fetches. The final data is pointed to by the address contained in the memory block pointed to by the indirect address stored in the instruction.

The example code below uses indirect addressing. A memory address exists in a register dx (data register), which points to a block of memory that contains the actual value to move. Memory address manipulation, using registers, is a common assembly code technique.

Code

```
mov ax, [dx]
add ax, d3
mov [dx],ax
```

Relative addressing

In relative addressing, a specific number of bytes are added to or subtracted from a base address in order to access the data. In the example below, the memory address 33a has 2 added to it, resulting in the address 33c. The data from 33c is fetched. It is common for relative addresses to use variables.

Code

```
mov ax, [33a] + 2
(Example of direct addressing)
```

Indexed addressing

In indexed addressing, an incremental counter is used in a similar way to relative addressing to look up a memory address from a base address. Memory addresses are calculated using index and base registers. Indexed addressing is used to handle arrays. The size of an individual element within an array is also used in the calculation.

Code

```
Index Address = base + (index * size)
```

Using variables in assembly language

You can use variables in assembly language. This allows you to perform calculations without having to worry too much about memory addresses. The code below sets aside a memory block one byte in size and sets its value to be 5. Whenever the variable val is accessed, it will be replaced with the memory address for val using direct addressing.

Code

```
val byte 5
mov ax, val
add ax, ax
```

Jumps and compares

Jumps and compares allow flow control within the assembly language program and provide the basic functionality of loops and decision statements and functions, as found in high-level programming languages. (When high-level languages are compiled, these statements are converted to jumps and compares.)

Jump instructions allow control to move to a different part of the program specified by accessing a memory address. There are two types of jump command: unconditional, which always jumps; and conditional, which makes use of a compare instruction to decide whether a jump should occur.

The example codes below show a simple bit of pseudocode and the assembly code equivalent. Notice the use of CMP (compare) and JE (jump if equal).

Pseudocode version

Code

```
val = 5
if val = 3 then
  val = val + 10
else
  val = val + 12
end if
```

Assembly version

Code
`val byte 5`
`CMP val, 3`
`mov ax, val`
`JE trueIF`
`add 12,ax`
`JMP final`
`trueIF: add 10,ax`
`final:mov val,ax`

Labels are used to specify the destination of a jump instruction. In the above example we jump to the label trueIF should the comparison for equals be true. JMP is an unconditional jump.

A jump command needs to have a label in order to know exactly where in the code it must jump to. Labels must be converted into memory addresses during assembly. This process will be looked at in more detail in the next section.

32-bit versus 64-bit registers

There are two sets of registers on a 64-bit processor; 32-bit registers start with e, while 64-bit registers start with r. A 32-bit processor has one set of 32-bit registers. Some commands cannot work on 32-bit registers. Also, the way system calls work differs from 32-bit to 64-bit. The code listing you will see later in this section works on both 32-bit and 64-bit.

Common 32 bit registers

Register	Purpose
eax	**Accumulator** – used for arithmetic, interrupt calls and I/O port access
ebx	**Base** – used for memory access and some interrupt returns
ecx	**Counter** – used for loops, shifts and passing data to interrupts
edx	**Data** – used for I/O, arithmetic and interrupts
esi	**Source index** – used for string and array copying
ebp	**Stack base** – points to the base address of the stack
esp	**Stack pointer** – points to the top of the stack
eip	**Index** – instruction pointer

Table 6.1: Common 32-bit registers.

Common 64 bit registers

Register	Purpose
rax	**Accumulator** – used for arithmetic, interrupt calls and I/O port access
rbx	**Base** – used for memory access and some interrupt returns
rcx	**Counter** – used for loops, shifts and passing data to interrupts
rdx	**Data** – used for I/O, arithmetic and interrupts
rsi	**Source index** – used for string and array copying
rbp	**Stack base** – points to the base address of the stack
rsp	**Stack pointer** – points to the top of the stack
rip	**Index** – instruction pointer

Table 6.2: Common 32-bit registers.

Stack contents for command **myProgram foo bar**

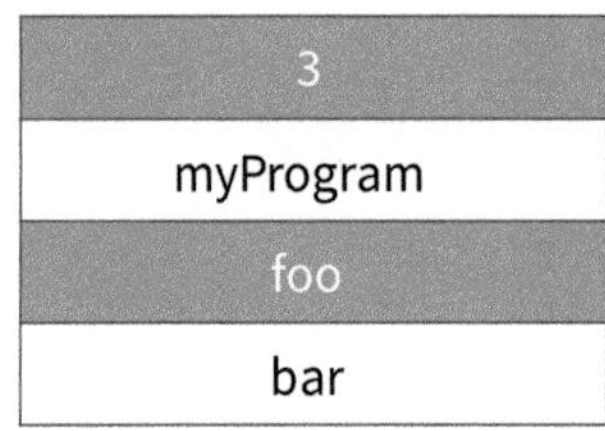

3
myProgram
foo
bar

Table 6.3: Contents of the call stack when running a command-line program.

Calling the kernel

In assembly language programming, it is necessary to invoke kernel code in order to perform tasks such as file handling, printing to stdout or doing system administration tasks. An invocation of kernel code is known as a system call. Each system call (syscall) requires you to put values into specific registers and then make a software interrupt (32-bit) or issue a syscall (64-bit). A unique number or code is assigned to each interrupt or system call, so the coder must make extensive use of reference manuals. The accumulator (eax or rax) is used to hold the code for the interrupt or system call. On 32-bit systems, sys_write has the code 4 while sys_exit has the code 1.

As the kernel is responsible for dealing with interrupts, it catches the software interrupt and deals with it accordingly. This is how 32-bit assembly code communicates with the kernel. Software interrupts on 32-bit can be fairly slow, as they have to perform a number of memory lookups. The syscall method in 64-bit assembly language code uses specific registers to speed up invocation, and incorporates other improvements.

Programs that use syscall do not work on 32-bit architectures.

The following code illustrates the use of interrupts:

Code

```
; 32 bit
; sys_write(stdout, message, length)
mov edx,len; Length of message (variable)
mov ecx,msg; set message (variable)
mov ebx,1; set to be stdout
mov eax,4; invoke sys_write
int 0x80
extern printf; link to the printf C function
section .text
global main
main:
mov rbx, 2; argument for the path
cmp rdi, rbx; rdi stores the arg count
jne.error; display error msg if problem
; rsi points to the start of the stack
mov rdx, qword [rsi+8]; 8 bytes into the stack
mov rdi, format; needed by printf
mov rsi, rdx; the text to display
mov rax, 0; no floating point
call printf; execute the c function printf
; this code will sys_exit
mov ebx, 0; exit code 0
mov eax, 1
int 0x80; send interrupt
jmp .end; skip error code
.error
mov edx,len; Length of message (variable)
mov ecx,errorMsg; set message (variable)
mov ebx,1; set to be stdout
mov eax,4; invoke sys_write
int 0x80; send interrupt
; exit with error code 1
mov ebx,1
mov eax,1
int 0x80
jmp .end
.end
ret; return from main function
```

```
section.data
errorMsg db "Only accepts one argument",0xa
len equ $ - errorMsg
format: db "%s", 10, 0
```

Stacks

When an assembly language program is loaded, a stack that contains information about the command-line options is created. The stack is stored in memory and can be manipulated by using the registers DI, BP, SI, SP or by the instructions push and pop. When a program loads, the stack will contain any command-line argument. For example, the stack below contains four values for the command 'myProgram foo bar':

The number of items in the stack is always one or more, even if no arguments were supplied, since the name of the program is always added to the stack. To access items on the stack, it is common to use offsets rather than push and pop.

Label	Mailbox	Is variable?
CURRENT	7	Yes
START	0	No
END	6	No

Table 6.4: An example LMC symbol table.

Little Man Computer

In Chapter 1 you were introduced to the basic concepts of the Little Man Computer (LMC). In this section, you will consider the relationship between assembly language code and the LMC, as well as looking at some more complicated examples of programs. The LMC is considered to be a reduced instruction set computer (RISC), as it has a very limited number of instructions. These are shown in Figure 6.5.

Opcode	Name	Data	Explanation
1xx	ADD	The number to add	It will add a value from a register to the current value of the ACC
2xx	SUB	The number to subtract	It will subtract value from a register to the current value of the ACC
3xx	STA	Stores a value into a register	Will take the contents of the ACC
5xx	LDA	Loads a value from a register	Will take a value from a register and store it in the ACC
6xx	BRA	Line number to "jump" to	Unconditional branch. Will jump to the given instruction number
7xx	BRZ	Line number to "jump" to	Branch if zero. Will only jump if the ACC is zero
8xx	BRP	Line number to "jump" to	Branch if positive. Will only jump if the value held in the ACC is positive or zero.
901	INP	Input from the user	Will input a value and store it in the ACC
902	OUT	None	Will output the contents of the ACC

Table 6.5: Opcodes for LMC instructions.

Each instruction has a simple opcode and makes use of direct addressing mode. Data is stored and used within programs using variables, which resolve to mailbox values (memory addresses). LMC uses the term mailbox to be equivalent to memory. The FDE cycle is not used explicitly. There are various versions of the LMC that may display few or more registers. Every version will at least display the program counter (PC) and accumulator (ACC).

Opcodes in the LMC

In assembly language code, opcodes are represented as the first bits of the instruction, depending on the architecture. For the LMC, the opcode is represented by the first digit. Unlike assembly language, the LMC uses the first digit for the opcode and the last two digits for the data. For example, the instruction '206' consists of an opcode of '2' and data of '06'. The opcode '2' represents a SUB command and the '06' represents the mailbox '06', which will store the data needed when the command is executed. As there are only two digits available for mailboxes, the maximum number of mailboxes is 100, ranging from 0 to 99.

Like assembly language, labels and variables are allowed and it is the job of the assembler to assign mailboxes. Figure 6.6 shows an example program with a corresponding symbol table.

```
start inp
brz end
add current
out
sta current
bra start
end hlt
current dat 0
```

Label	Mailbox	Is variable?
CURRENT	7	Yes
START	0	No
END	6	No

Figure 6.6: Sample LMC code with the resulting symbol table.

The BRZ command, branch if zero, has an opcode of 7 and data of 6, since that is the mailbox assigned to the END label. Therefore, the whole LMC instruction is 706.

Using branches (jumps)

The LMC program below (Figure 6.7) adds up a series of numbers entered by the user until the value 0 is entered:

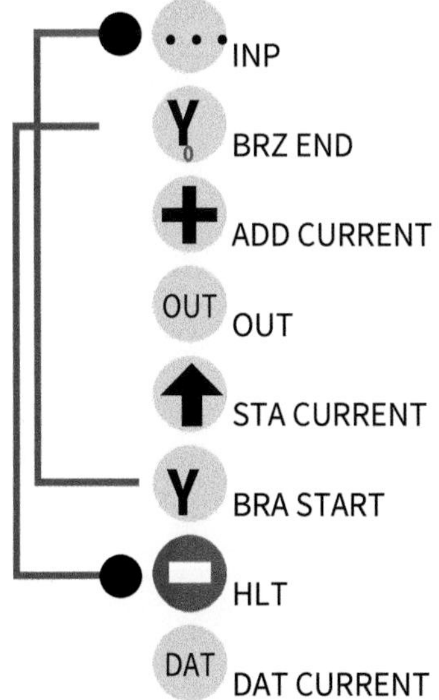

INP
BRZ END
ADD CURRENT
OUT
OUT
STA CURRENT
BRA START
HLT
DAT
DAT CURRENT

Figure 6.7: LMC for value 0.

Iteration and selection in procedural languages are implemented in machine code by using branches (jumps). In order to implement the condition for a while loop, we need to make use of two branches, one to loop back to the start of the iteration and the other to break the iteration. The condition x! = 0 is handled by the BRZ command. Normally in LMC, an unconditional branch, BRA, is used to return to the start of the loop.

Compare the Python code and LMC program in Figure 6.8. Two branches are used to implement the full selection structure. The first branch tests the initial condition and, if it is false, jumps to the ELSE clause. This is different from how many people think of selection statements, but logically it creates the same result. The second unconditional branch skips over the FALSE clause should the TRUE clause be executed. LMC, unlike assembly code, has only two conditional branches: branch if the value in the accumulator is positive or zero. This may seem restrictive, but any logical condition can be encoded into it by making use of the other commands. In the LMC program below, you can see that 10 is subtracted from the initial number being tested. This is the same as testing if $x - 10 < 0$. All we have done is a bit of simple equation balancing to ensure that one side of the condition is 0.

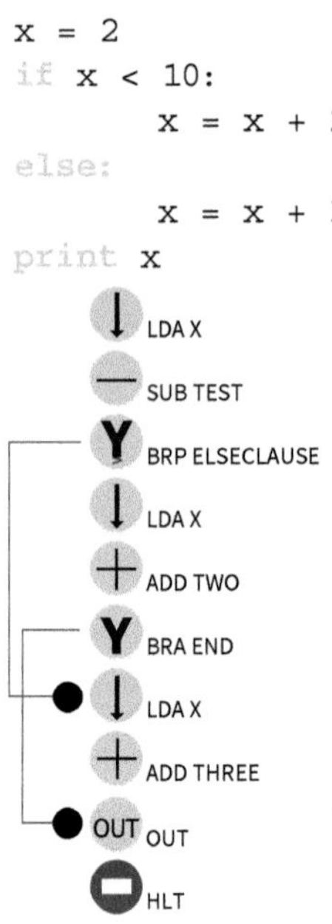


```
LDA x
SUB test
BRP elseClause
LDA x
ADD two
BRA end
elseClause LDA x
ADD three
end OUT
HLT

x dat 2
test dat 10
two dat 2
three dat 3
```

Label	Mailbox	Is variable?
X	10	Yes
TEST	11	Yes
TWO	12	Yes
THREE	13	Yes
ELSECLAUSE	6	No
END	8	No

Figure 6.8: LMC program.

Summary

- There are many different programming paradigms, each with its own strengths and weaknesses.
- Procedural programming languages describe the solution to a problem as a sequence of steps. Procedural languages describe which steps to take to solve a problem and how to complete each step.
- Assembly language instructions consist of two distinct sections: operators, such as ADD or SUB, and operands, which are usually memory addresses.
- The Little Man Computer is a very simplified version of a computer which uses inputs, memory and outputs as well as a very small set of instructions to replicate the workings of a simple processor.
- There are many ways of accessing a computer's memory; these are called addressing modes.
- In immediate addressing the operand is the data that will be processed.
- In direct addressing, the operand is the address of the memory location holding the data that will be processed.
- In indirect addressing the operand is the address that holds the memory location holding the data that will be processed.
- In indexed addressing a counter (index) is combined with the operand to calculate the memory location holding the data that will be processed.
- In relative addressing, a specific number of bytes are added to or subtracted from a base address in order to access the data.
- Object-oriented languages describe the solution to a problem by creating objects that represent real-world entities.

- Classes are templates for real-world objects which have attributes and methods.
- Objects are instances of classes and represent a real-world object.
- Methods are actions that classes or objects can perform, for example SpinWheel().
- Attributes are properties of a class or object such as radius or colour.
- Classes can inherit attributes and methods from other classes. For example, a Car class might inherit the attributes and methods from a Vehicle class. In this example, Car would be a derived class and Vehicle a superclass.

End-of-chapter questions

1 Define the following object-oriented terms

a Class [2]

b Object [2]

c Inheritance [2]

d Encapsulation [2]

e Polymorphism [3]

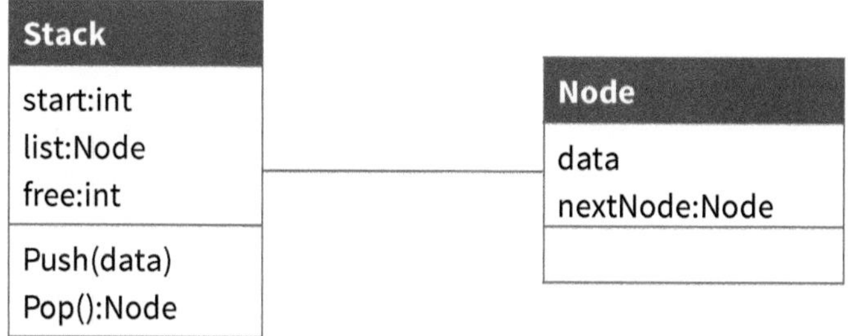

Figure 6.9

2 The class diagram above shows the abstract data type for a stack.

a Show code to instantiate an object and assign it to a variable called "myStack". [1]

b Add the data items "Football" and "Drawing" to this object. [2]

c Using the keyword "print", write the code and show the output if the "pop" operation was run. [3]

3 A sprite class has the following definition

```
CLASS Sprite
X : int
Y : int
moveLeft(amount : int)
moveRight(amount : int)
moveUp(amount : int)
moveDown(amount : int)
END CLASS
```

a If you were developing a platform game, explain why you may wish to use inheritance on this class. [4]

b Why would using polymorphism make rendering a single frame in the game (drawing the screen) more efficient? [6]

4 Explain the following addressing modes.

a Indexed [3]

b Indirect [2]

c Relative [2]

5 Describe how an 'if statement' could be represented in assembly code using jumps and compare commands. Use examples to help clarify your answer. [8]

Further reading

HTML tutorial – search on w3schools.com.
HTML and CSS – search on the Codeacademy website.
JavaScript tutorial – search on w3schools.com.
JavaScript – search on the Codeacademy website.
Linux system calls – go to syscalls.kernelgrok.com

Chapter 7
Compression, encryption and hashing

A This chapter contains A Level content only

Specification points

1.3.1 Compression, encryption and hashing

- Lossy versus lossless compression.
- Run length encoding and dictionary coding for lossless compression.
- Symmetric and asymmetric encryption.
- Different uses of hashing.

Learning objectives

- To understand lossy compression and lossless compression.
- To understand run length encoding and dictionary coding for lossless compression.
- To understand symmetric and asymmetric encryption.
- To appreciate the different uses of hashing.

Compression

In computing, compression means reducing the amount of storage space in bits that a given file takes up. This can be done in a number of ways but they all achieve the same end goal, which is to remove unnecessary bits to reduce the overall size of the file. In the past, compression was important because computer memory was expensive. Today, memory is much cheaper but compression remains important because of the volume of information we transmit over networks including the internet. A smaller file size means fewer bits to transmit so it is faster to transfer a file, whether this is a television programme being streamed from the internet or an email attachment being downloaded on a LAN.

Computing in context: 7-Zip

7-Zip is a piece of open-source compression software that uses multiple compression and encryption algorithms to reduce the size and increase the security of files. As 7-zip uses multiple compression algorithms, it is able to achieve very high compression ratios. Its website states that the authors were able to compress 15 684 168 bytes of Mozilla Firefox files into just 4 621 135 bytes, a compression ratio of 0.2.

The level of compression is measured by its **compression ratio**. The compression ratio is the size of the compressed file divided by the size of the original. The ratio will be a number between 0 and 1; the closer the ratio is to 0, the tighter the compression. Different pieces of compression software, such as WinZip, WinRAR and 7-Zip, achieve slightly different compression ratios in different datasets.

The 256-bit encryption used also means that the compressed data can be transmitted securely across the internet.

Lossy and lossless compression

As you might expect, there are many different compression algorithms. These all try to reduce the number of unnecessary bits in a file and use a wide range of methods to do this. However, all these algorithms fit into one of two broad categories: lossy and lossless.

- **Lossy compression** means that the file is compressed to a smaller size but some information is lost during the process. The original file cannot be perfectly reconstructed.
- **Lossless compression** techniques are able to reduce a file's size without losing any information. The original file can always be perfectly restored.

Lossless compression may seem preferable to lossy compression, but if the lossy algorithm can provide a much better compression ratio and the lost data is not important, the choice may not be so clear-cut. This is particularly true when compressing images: it may be possible to remove a huge amount of information without noticeably reducing the quality of the image.

Run length encoding for lossless compression

- Run length encoding is a popular and widely used method of lossless compression. In some files a single character will be repeated many times in a row (this doesn't happen in English text but will happen in many other situations, for example DNA sequencing).
- Run length encoding replaces a sequence of repeated characters with a flag character, followed by the character itself and the number of times it is repeated. Using this method BBBBBBBBB would become $B9 (the $ is the flag) and so the file size is reduced from 9 bytes to 3, a compression ratio of 0.3. Any other characters that are not repeated would not be compressed and just included in the file as normal. So AAAAAANNNBBBBBBBBUUBYE becomes $A6NNN$B8UUBYE, giving a compression ratio of 0.69.
- Notice that we don't compress sequences of letters shorter than four; this is because our notation for highlighting repeated characters is itself three characters long, so the pay-off between the time taken to compress and the compression ratio achieved makes it unnecessary.

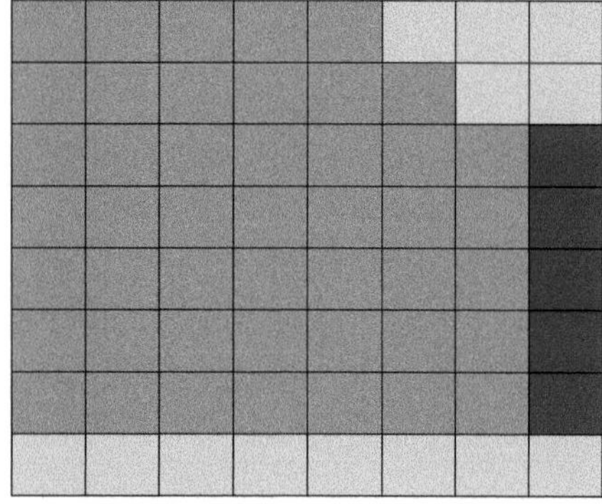

Figure 7.1: A simple image made from 64 pixels.

Look at the bitmap images shown in Figures 7.1 to 7. 4; many of the pixels are the same colour, which leads to long sequences of identical values. By using run length encoding it is possible to reduce the number of letters needed to represent the image from 64 to 34, a compression ratio of 0.5.

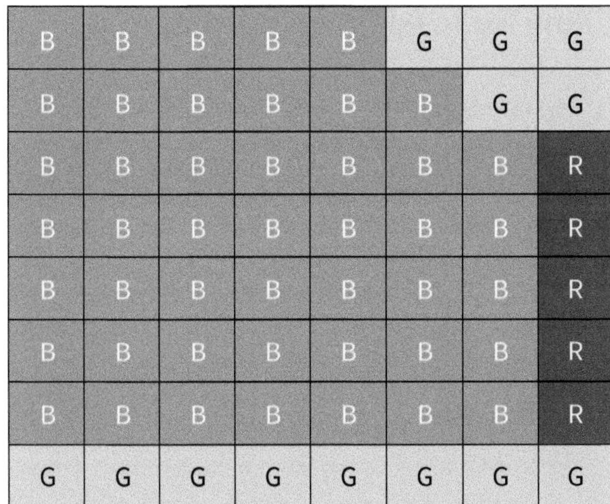

Figure 7.2: A simple image made from 64 pixels.

8	B	B	B	B	B	G	G	G
8	B	B	B	B	B	B	G	G
8	B	B	B	B	B	B	B	R
8	B	B	B	B	B	B	B	R
8	B	B	B	B	B	B	B	R
8	B	B	B	B	B	B	B	R
8	B	B	B	B	B	B	B	R
8	G	G	G	G	G	G	G	G

Figure 7.3: A simple image made from 64 pixels. The column on the left shows the number of bits required to represent each row.

6	$B5	G	G	G
5	$B6	G	G	
4	$B7	R		
4	$B7	R		
4	$B7	R		
4	$B7	R		
4	$B7	R		
3	$G8			

Figure 7.4: Run length encoding reduces the file size.

Dictionary coding for lossless compression

Dictionary encoding is another form of lossless compression. There are many different types of dictionary compression, but they all work on the same principle. A dictionary of commonly occurring sequences of characters is created. In the text these sequences are replaced by pointers to the relevant place in the dictionary. The references are shorter than the words they replace, so the file is reduced in size. Creating the dictionary is simply a case of scanning the document to find the most common words and assigning a reference to each.

Huffman encoding

One of the easiest dictionary encoding methods to understand is Huffman encoding.

In the English language some letters are used far more than others. For example, in most large pieces of text it is likely that the number of As will be larger than the number of Zs. However, computers use the same number of bits to represent both A and Z, which can waste a lot of space. Huffman encoding uses a dictionary to store all the letters that occur in a piece of text. Each letter is then given a unique code, with the most commonly occurring letters being given a shorter code than less used ones.

Huffman code	Letter
00	G
01	O
010	L
011	E

Table 7.1: An illustration of Huffman encoding.

For example, if we wanted to write the word GOOGLE using 8 bits for each letter, the word would take up 48 bits. But if we used the Huffman dictionary below and replaced each bit sequence with its Huffman code, it would be just 14, giving a compression ratio of 0.2.

The important thing to notice is that the most commonly used characters (G and O) have the shortest codes, which helps to maximise the file's compression.

Compression algorithms will have a proportionally greater impact on longer pieces of text, as there will be more instances of repeated letters.

 **Tip**

It is unlikely you will have to explain the inner workings of the different algorithms (e.g. RSA) but you should be able to describe what they do.

Encryption

Encryption is simply the act of scrambling a piece of plain text into cipher text so that it cannot be easily understood. Decryption is the process of unscrambling the encrypted message to reveal the original piece of plain text. The piece of information needed to decrypt the message is commonly called the **key**.

Encryption has been carried out for thousands of years. Julius Caesar is thought to have been one of the first people to use encryption when sending messages to his supporters and generals. As his messages were encrypted, it didn't matter if they were intercepted, as whoever stole them couldn't read them anyway!

The Caesar cipher (or shift cipher) is a very simple one to understand, so it makes a useful example as shown below.

First you write out the alphabet in the top and bottom rows of a table:

A	B	C	D	E	F	G	H	I	J	K	L	M	N	O	P	Q	R	S	T	U	V	W	X	Y	Z
A	B	C	D	E	F	G	H	I	J	K	L	M	N	O	P	Q	R	S	T	U	V	W	X	Y	Z

Then *shift* the bottom alphabet along a random number of places. You can choose any number you want, and that number becomes your ***key***.

In this example we have shifted the bottom alphabet along two places, so the key to this message is two; notice that we wrap around letters from the end of the alphabet so that they don't get lost:

A	B	C	D	E	F	G	H	I	J	K	L	M	N	O	P	Q	R	S	T	U	V	W	X	Y	Z
Y	Z	A	B	C	D	E	F	G	H	I	J	K	L	N	M	O	P	Q	R	S	T	U	V	W	X

The next step is to write out your message using normal English. Finally you encrypt this message by replacing each letter with its shifted equivalent, so all the **A**s become **Y**s, **B**s become **Z**s and so on:

C	O	M	P	U	T	I	N	G		I	S		B	R	I	L	L	I	A	N	T
A	N	K	M	S	R	G	L	E		G	Q		Z	P	G	J	J	G	Y	L	R

You can now send your message 'ANKMSRGLE GQ ZPGJJGYLR'. Only someone with the key knows how to decrypt it. To do this, they need to know the key.

Of course, in modern terms the Caesar cipher provides very weak encryption. A computer could break this code in milliseconds simply by trying all possible combinations (brute-force hacking), but in 30 BC this was thought to be a very effective method of encryption, as many people were unable to read, let alone having the time to decrypt the message.

Encryption in the modern world

For hundreds of years, encryption was only really used by the military. However, with the rapid increase in the use of electronic communication encryption is becoming more and more important in everyday life. At the same time, powerful computers can crack most traditional forms of encryption (such as the Caesar cipher) in seconds.

You can read about the social and ethical impact of electronic encryption in Chapter 14.

During the Second World War, Turing worked as a code breaker at Bletchley Park in Buckinghamshire. For the duration of the war the country house and its grounds were requisitioned by the military and used to house a top-secret code-breaking unit called Station X. The code breakers were successful in breaking a number of enemy ciphers and their work is thought to have shortened the war by a number of years.

Breaking encryption required a great deal of complex and repetitious mathematics, which Turing thought could be more accurately carried out by a machine. Together with the other code breakers and engineers at Bletchley Park, he designed and built a computer known as the Bombe to decrypt messages encoded by Enigma machines. Later, a team led by Post Office engineer Tommy Flowers developed a new computer known as the *Colossus*, an electronic computer capable of rapidly and accurately breaking the incredibly complex Lorenz codes. This was able to use a technique developed by Turing to adjust settings ready to decrypt the message. Turing also performed cryptoanalysis of the Lorenz cipher to gain a deep understanding of its operation. After the end of World War II, the Colossus computers were destroyed but in 2007, a replica was unveiled at the National Museum of Computing at Bletchley Park. This marked the culmination of an historic project led by Tony Sale, who continued to demonstrate its operation to visitors until his death in 2011.

Symmetric and asymmetric encryption

Symmetric encryption means that the process of decryption is simply the opposite of the process used to encrypt. For example, in the Caesar cipher the message is encrypted by replacing each letter with another one a set number of places down in the alphabet. Decrypting the message is simply a case of swapping each letter in the encoded message with another that is a set number of places up the alphabet. As the process of decryption is just the opposite of the process used to encrypt the message, the Caesar cipher is a **symmetric encryption algorithm**.

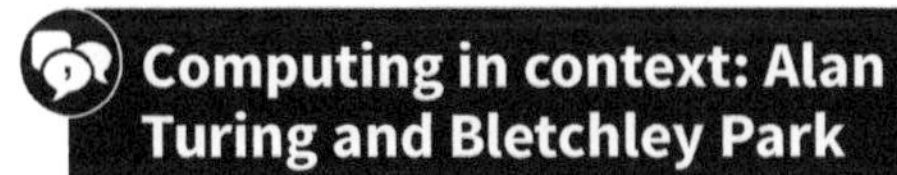

Computing in context: Alan Turing and Bletchley Park

Alan Turing is often referred to as a pioneer of modern day cryptography. He is responsible for many of the ideas and concepts that still underlie modern computing.

As well as writing a number of ground-breaking academic papers on computing, he was largely responsible for the creation of the world's first electronic computer.

Symmetric encryption algorithms have the advantage that they are quick to set up and easy to execute. Every encryption algorithm created before 1975 was essentially a symmetric technique. The problem with symmetric algorithms is that they are very easy for modern computers to crack. A computer can crack an encrypted message simply by trying thousands of different alternatives and in a very short amount of time.

In **asymmetric encryption algorithms** the encryption and decryption keys are different. If someone knows the encryption key, they can encrypt information but not decrypt it. Likewise, if someone possesses the decryption key, they can read the information they receive but can't encrypt their response using the same algorithm. Asymmetric algorithms were almost impossible for computers to crack, and until the 20th century nobody had thought of the concept, much less implemented it. When the American computer scientists Whitfield Diffie and Martin Hellman invented the asymmetric key in 1975, it was a discovery that revolutionised the fields of cryptography and electronic warfare. Their pioneering work was developed into the protocol for key exchange known as Diffie-Hellman.

Asymmetric encryption is also called **public key encryption** and is best explained using an example.

Suppose Adam wants to send Charlotte a message. Charlotte keeps her decryption key secret (this is referred to as a private key), but publishes her encryption key on the internet (this is referred to as a public key). When Adam wants to send Charlotte a secret message, he simply uses the public key (which anyone can find out) to encrypt the message and then sends it to Charlotte.

It doesn't matter if anyone intercepts the message because only Charlotte has the private decryption key, so only she can read the message.

The system sounds simple but in reality it is incredibly complex. It requires the creation of a one-way mathematical function that can only be reversed under a single circumstance. In fact, when Diffie and Hellman first came up with the idea of asymmetric encryption it seemed likely that no such mathematical functions even existed.

Fortunately, within two years of their discovery, three American mathematicians, Ron Rivest, Adi Shamir and Leonard Adleman, developed such a function. Called the **RSA cipher** (based on the inventors' initials), it went on to become the foundation of all modern encryption techniques.

In the 'Computing in context' box below is a short overview of how the RSA cipher works, adapted from Simon Singh's *The Code Book: the Secret History of Codes and Code Breaking* (Fourth Estate, 2002).

Computing in context: mathematics of the RSA cipher

1. Charlotte picks two large prime numbers, w and q. These should be massive, but for simplicity's sake we'll say $w = 17$ and $q = 11$.
2. Charlotte multiplies these numbers together to get N. In our example $N = 187$. She then picks another number, e; let's say $e = 7$.
3. Charlotte now publishes e and N on the internet. These become her public key.
4. To encrypt a message it must first be converted into a number M, for example by adding together the ASCII (American Standard Code for Information Interchange) codes that make up the message.
5. M is then encrypted to create cipher-text C using the formula $C = M^e(MOD\ N)$

Example

If Adam wants to send Charlotte a single kiss (X), he converts this to its ASCII value 1011000, which is the equivalent to the denary number 88. So $M = 88$.

He then calculates the value of C using the formula $C = 88^7(\text{MOD } 187)$. So $C = 11$. He then sends this to Charlotte.

Exponents in modular arithmetic are one-way functions, so it is incredibly difficult to work backwards to the original message unless you know the private key.

6 The private key d is calculated by Charlotte using the formula $e^*d = 1(\text{MOD}(w-1)^*(q-1))$. In our example this eventually gives us $7^*d = 1(\text{MOD } 160)$ or $d = 23$.

7 To decrypt the message Adam has sent her, Charlotte simply uses the following formula: $M = C\text{^}d(\text{MOD } 187)$. This resolves as $M = 11^{23}(\text{MOD } 187)$ or $M = 88$, which is X in ASCII.

The brilliant part is that the function can be personalised by choosing w and p. Therefore only the person who knows these values can decrypt the message.

Diffie and Hellman released their asymmetric encryption algorithm for free on the internet, which meant that everyone in the world suddenly had access to incredibly strong, military-grade encryption. Many governments, not least the American government, were deeply upset by Diffie and Hellman's actions; you can read about their reactions in Chapter 14.

Hashing

There are some problems with public key encryption. For example, someone could intercept Adam's message and randomly remove chunks of the encoded message before passing it on to Charlotte. In this situation she wouldn't know if she had received the correct message. This problem can be resolved by using hashing.

A hash is a unique string of data. In public key encryption a hash is created when the original message is put through a hash function. This process is called hashing.

In public key encryption, the hash resulting from putting an encrypted message through a hash function is unique to the original message and can be used to confirm the integrity of the information sent. It is almost impossible to work out the original message from the hash, and a change of a single bit in a message will create a completely different hash. Since a hash creates a unique signature for the original message, it can be used to determine whether a set of data has been changed.

The sender generates a hash of the message, encrypts it and sends it with the message itself. The recipient then decrypts both the message and the hash, produces another hash from the received message, and compares the two hashes. If they're the same, the message they have received is the one that was sent.

Hashes are sometimes called one-way hashes because once they are created they can never be reversed. This means that a hash cannot be deciphered to determine the contents of the original message; they can only be used to compare data received with the data that was sent. Public key encryption can use hash numbers that could be one of 3 402 823 669 209 384 634 633 746 074 300 000 000 000 000 000 000 000 000 000 000 000 000 possible combinations.

Tip

Look at the amount of time you have for the exam paper and divide it by the number of marks available. This will tell you how long you should spend on each question.

Activity 7.1

Download some different types of free encryption software. Use each one to encrypt the same set of files. How different are the resulting file sizes?

Activity 7.2

Find and install some free encryption software. Do you think the hassle of using it is outweighed by the enhanced security?

Digital signatures

Digital signatures are commonly used for software distribution, financial transactions and in many other cases where it is important to detect forgery or tampering. They provide authentication that the message being sent has been written by (or agreed to by) the person with the signature. Likewise, it is confirmation that the sender actually sent the message. This is known as non-repudiation.

One of the most common digital signature mechanisms is the digital signature algorithm (DSA). DSA lets one person with a secret private key 'sign' a document so that others with a matching public key can verify that it was signed only by the holder of the private key. Digital signatures are usually applied to the hash of a message to add another layer of security.

It is not necessary for you to know the exact operations used to produce a digital signature, but it is a fascinating subject, and you can find out more in the 'Further reading' section at the end of this chapter.

Summary

- Lossy compression reduces the size of a file but results in data being lost.
- Lossless compression reduces the file size without losing any data.
- Run-length encoding replaces a sequence of repeated characters with a flag character, followed by the character itself and the number of times it is repeated.
- In dictionary encoding a dictionary of commonly occurring sequences of characters is created. In the text these sequences are replaced by pointers to the relevant place in the dictionary. The references are shorter than the words they replace, so the file is reduced in size.
- In symmetric encryption the process of decryption is the opposite of the process used to encrypt the message. The Caesar cipher is an example of symmetric encryption.
- In asymmetric encryption algorithms the encryption and decryption keys are different.
- The process of creating a hash (a unique string of data) is called 'hashing' and is achieved using a hash function. Hashes are also widely used as digital signatures on electronic documents.

End-of-chapter questions

1 Explain the difference between lossy and lossless compression. [2]

2 What is meant by symmetric encryption? [2]

3 Give **one** example of a symmetric encryption algorithm. [1]

4 What is meant by asymmetric encryption? [2]

5 Other than encryption give **one** use of a hash function. [1]

Further reading

Encryption – search for How Encryption and Digital Signatures Work on www.tatanka.com.
Asymmetric encryption – go to openpgp.org.
Hash and signature algorithms – search for Hash and Signature Algorithms on the Windows Dev Center website.
Hash functions – search for Cryptography Lecture 8 on the Informationskodning page of the Linköping University website.
7 zip compression – go to the 7zip website.

Chapter 8
Databases

Specification points

1.3.2 Databases

- Relational database, flat file, primary key, foreign key, secondary key, entity relationship modelling, normalisation and indexing.
- Methods of capturing selecting, managing and exchanging data.
- Normalisation to 3NF.
- SQL – interpret and modify.
- Referential integrity.
- Transaction processing, ACID (atomicity, consistency, isolation, durability), record locking and redundancy.

Learning objectives

- To understand relational database, flat file, primary key, foreign key, secondary key, normalisation and indexing.
- To understand entity relationship modelling.
- To understand methods of capturing data.
- To understand normalisation to 3NF.
- To understand SQL.
- To understand referential integrity.
- To understand transaction processing, ACID (atomicity, consistency, isolation, durability), record locking and redundancy.

Introduction

What is a database?

'Big data' is a popular term used to describe applications or situations when trillions of pieces of data may be collected together. The ability to hold vast amounts of information is one of the reasons why computer systems have become so widely used. Imagine how many products, customer details and financial transactions the ecommerce businesses Amazon or eBay must hold. Think about how many individual posts, comments, images and links the social networking site Facebook has to store.

Before the advent of computers, this data would need to be held on paper records in filing cabinets. Entire buildings were dedicated to storing important records for companies or governments. Teams of office workers were paid to find information and distribute it to those who needed it. Accessing the records held in another town or country was very time consuming.

Computers can store the equivalent of thousands of text documents on a single chip in a USB memory stick, smaller than a fingernail. Just being able to store this much data is only part of the solution. Data is only useful if you can access it quickly and know that it is correct. Databases are permanent, organised structures that hold vast amounts of data in a way that makes it easy to modify and search. Databases are used to hold product details, customer information, financial records – even your school attendance record. Many websites include a user interface for a database, allowing users to search for products and store their personal details for use later on. However, storing all this data in one place has led to a number of concerns about privacy and data theft (you can read more about these issues in *Chapter 14*).

Data capture

Before you can start to organise data you need to collect it. There are many different methods for collecting or capturing data that can be stored in databases.

One of the most convenient ways of capturing large volumes of data, is optical mark recognition (OMR) technology. OMR can be used for marking multiple-choice tests and collecting the results of surveys or questionnaires. The user will fill out a form by shading in the box they want to select usually with a pencil. An OMR scanner uses a light which is shone at the paper. As the mark made by the user reflects less light than the empty boxes, the software can work out which answer was selected. This data can then be stored in a database.

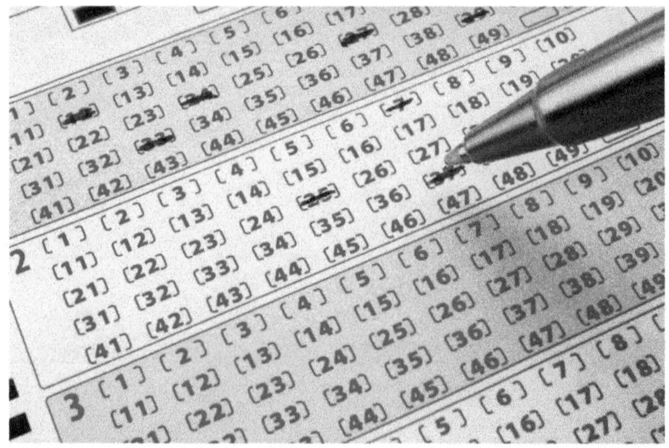

Figure 8.1: Lottery tickets use optical mark recognition.

An alternative to OMR is optical character recognition (OCR) (Figure 8.1). This technology is used for converting paper-based hardcopies, often handwritten, into editable, digital versions of the same document, for example, converting a letter into a Microsoft Word document. OCR works by scanning in the character. then comparing the marks scanned in to a look-up table that holds all possible values. When a match is found, the character has been recognised and the equivalent ASCII value is placed in the digital file.

Today, because of the prevalence and affordability of electronic devices, these traditional methods of data capture are becoming obsolete. For example, rather than being stopped in the street and asked to fill out a paper survey, you are much more likely to be asked a series of questions by someone who enters your answers straight into a database using a tablet. However, OCR is still a very valuable technology to blind and visually impaired users because it allows them to scan handwritten documents which can then be processed by text-to-speech software.

Other automatic methods for capturing data include the use of barcodes and QR codes. These are often used in stock control systems. Sensors can also be used to automatically capture data, for example temperature and air pressure in a weather station. This is called data logging and allows data to be captured automatically for prolonged periods without the need for human intervention.

Data can be entered into a database manually, for example, by completing a web form. However, there needs to be a mechanism to check that all of the required data items have been entered and that it is in the correct format. This type of checking is called validation.

Database key terms

Flat-file database

In a flat-file database, information is held in a single table. Each column in the table is called an attribute and each row is a record:

Student ID	Student name	Gender	DOB	Course ID	Course name	Teacher ID	Teacher name	Teacher specialism
67678	Jim Donaldson	M	30/01/2000	GY51	Mathematics	4445	Mr Surrall	Mathematics
67677	Jane Jones	F	02/01/2000	FU451	Physics	4445	Mr Surrall	Mathematics
67678	Jim Donaldson	M	30/01/2000	F41052	Computer Science	4433	Mr Smith	Physics
67222	Lucy Kid	F	08/03/2000	GY51	Mathematics	4445	Mr Surrall	Mathematics

Table 8.1: An example of a flat-file database.

Flat-file databases are generally used for very small amounts of data that has a simple structure, because as they get larger they develop a big problem called *data redundancy*. Data redundancy simply means that lots of data is replicated. Look at the table above and you will see that the same information about Mr Surrall, his ID, name and specialism, is repeated three times. Jim Donaldson has his ID, name, gender and date of birth (DOB) repeated twice. This repetition has occurred in a really small database. You can imagine how much repetition would occur in a database with thousands or millions of records. This increases the amount of storage space required, which, for a large database, can be significant.

Redundancy is a problem for many reasons. Imagine that Mr Surrall changes his specialism to Physics. At the moment that information would need to be changed in three separate places. In a large database it would be easy to miss a record and the data being stored would be inaccurate. This could potentially even cause legal problems with the Data Protection Act because it requires that data held about a person must be accurate (see Chapter 14). If we decide that we want to store some extra data, such as student e-mail addresses, using a flat-file will require us to enter the same information over and over again.

In order to solve problems caused by flat-file databases, we need to structure the data differently by creating a relational database.

Relational databases

Relational databases were created to remove the problems that can occur when using flat-file databases. They are made up of smaller tables linked together using primary and foreign keys. When properly designed, this will remove the redundancy that is such a big problem in flat-file databases, but it does mean that the databases are more complex to create and maintain.

The example below (Figure 8.2) shows how, by placing the teachers' details in a separate table, we can remove the redundant data:

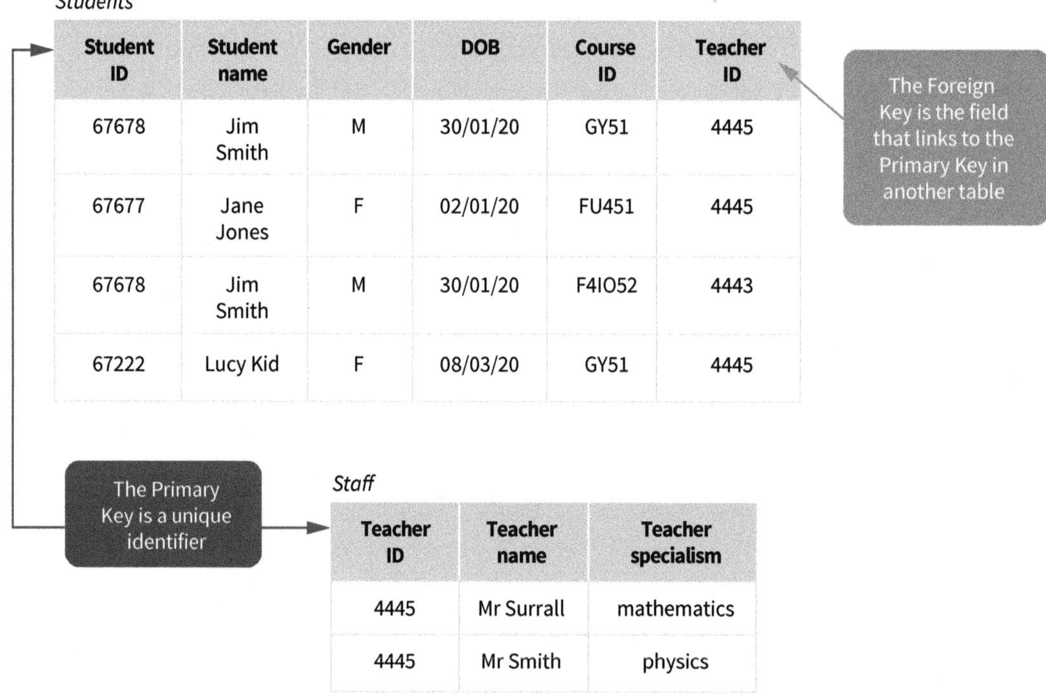

Students

Student ID	Student name	Gender	DOB	Course ID	Teacher ID
67678	Jim Smith	M	30/01/20	GY51	4445
67677	Jane Jones	F	02/01/20	FU451	4445
67678	Jim Smith	M	30/01/20	F4I052	4443
67222	Lucy Kid	F	08/03/20	GY51	4445

Staff

Teacher ID	Teacher name	Teacher specialism
4445	Mr Surrall	mathematics
4445	Mr Smith	physics

The Foreign Key is the field that links to the Primary Key in another table
The Primary Key is a unique identifier

Figure 8.2: Relational databases contain multiple tables linked together by primary and foreign keys.

Of course, now the data is stored in separate tables we need some way to associate the students' records with their teachers' records. For this we need to use the primary and foreign keys.

Primary key

In a database a **primary key** is a piece of data in each record that uniquely identifies it. Primary keys are usually ID numbers generated especially for that purpose. This is because finding unique information about records is not very easy; for example, there may be lots of people with the same first name, postcode and DOB. Any time you are given an account ID or user number, you can be sure that it is the primary key in a database somewhere.

Primary keys are vital in creating relational databases. By using the primary key of one table we can link two tables together. In the example above, the primary key of the Staff table is 'Teacher ID', so by including 'Teacher ID' in the Students table we can indicate which teacher is responsible for teaching which student.

Foreign key

In a database a **foreign key** is any field in a table which is the primary key in another table. In our example, the 'Teacher ID' field in the Students table is a foreign key because it links to the primary key in the Staff table.

Secondary key

The secondary key is an additional key (sometimes called an **alternate key**), which can be used to search for a record in a database. Unlike the primary key, it does not need to be unique to a particular record. Account numbers are often difficult to remember so, by using a secondary key, sometimes in combination with another field, we can still locate a particular record.

A

Normalisation

Normalisation is the formal process of converting a flat-file database (with a single table) into a relational database (with many tables). There are various levels of normalisation that remove data redundancy to a greater or lesser extent. You will look more at normalisation in a future section.

Indexing

An index is a data structure used to shorten the length of time it takes to search a database. For example, the index might contain the 'surname' column of a database. This would mean that when you are searching for a student, if you know their surname and their student ID you can find the information you want much faster.

Normalisation to 3NF

As you have already seen, normalisation is the process of converting a flat-file database to a relational database, that is, going from a database with a single table to one with many tables. The different levels of normalisation are called 'forms' and you need to know the first three of them.

First normal form

A table is in first normal form if each field contains only one piece of data and all the attributes in a table are dependent on the primary key.

Look at this flat-file database:

Student ID	Course ID	Teacher ID	DOB	Gender	Postcode
ST6, James	67TY, 67UI, 67PM	TYM1, TYM3, TYM8	30/01/2000	M	OX68TY
ST7, Charlotte	67TY, 67UI, 67PM	TYM1, TYM3, TYM8	12/05/2000	F	CA80GH
ST8, Julie	67TY, 67UI, 67PM	TYM1, TYM3, TYM8	03/10/2000	F	WR168UY

Table 8.2: A table that is not in first normal form (1NF).

Student ID, Course ID and Teacher ID all have multiple values in each cell. To fix this we need to expand the table:

Enrolment ID	Student ID	Student name	Course ID	Teacher ID	DOB	Gender	Postcode
E1	ST6	James	67TY	TYM1	30/01/2000	M	OX68TY
E2	ST6	James	67UI	TYM3	30/01/2000	M	OX68TY
E3	ST6	James	67PM	TYM8	30/01/2000	M	OX68TY
E4	ST7	Charlotte	67TY	TYM1	12/05/2000	F	CA80GH
E5	ST7	Charlotte	67UI	TYM3	12/05/2000	F	CA80GH
E6	ST7	Charlotte	67PM	TYM8	12/05/2000	F	CA80GH
E7	ST8	Julie	67TY	TYM1	03/10/2000	F	WR168UY
E8	ST8	Julie	67UI	TYM3	03/10/2000	F	WR168UY
E9	ST8	Julie	67PM	TYM8	03/10/2000	F	WR168UY

Table 8.3: A table with a single piece of data in each field, not yet in first normal form (1NF).

Now that each attribute contains just one piece of data, it is much closer to being in first normal form.

The next requirement for being in first normal form is that all the attributes in a table are dependent on the primary key. This is not true for our current table, as the teachers, courses and students are not uniquely associated with the Enrolment ID; for example, the same Teacher ID appears in many enrolments.

Look at the tables below:

Enrolment ID	Course ID	Student ID	Teacher ID
E1	67TY	ST6	TYM1
E2	67UI	ST6	TYM3
E3	67PM	ST6	TYM8
E4	67TY	ST7	TYM1
E5	67UI	ST7	TYM3
E6	67PM	ST7	TYM8
E7	67TY	ST8	TYM1
E8	67UI	ST8	TYM3
E9	67PM	ST8	TYM8

Table 8.4: The database is now in first normal form (1NF).

Student ID	Student name	DOB	Gender	Postcode
ST6	James	30/01/2000	M	OX68TY
ST7	Charlotte	12/5/2000	F	CA80GH
ST8	Julie	3/10/2000	F	WR168UY

Table 8.5: The database is now in first normal form (1NF).

Course ID	Course name	Teacher ID	Teacher's name	Postcode
67TY	Mathematics	TYM1	Mr Smith	CA80GH
67UI	Computer Science	TYM3	Mrs Jones	WR168UZ
67PM	Physics	TYM8	Ms Pratt	WR168UB

Table 8.6: The database is now in first normal form (1NF).

This new layout has removed nearly all the repetition from the tables. Notice that primary and foreign keys are essential for linking the tables together, so they don't count as repeated attributes.

Second normal form

A table is in second normal form if it is in first normal form and it contains no partial dependencies. For example, in our enrolment table our Teacher ID is only partially dependent on the Course ID, so can be removed.

Enrolment ID	Course ID	Student ID
E1	67TY	ST6
E2	67UI	ST6
E3	67PM	ST6
E4	67TY	ST7
E5	67UI	ST7
E6	67PM	ST7
E7	67TY	ST8
E8	67UI	ST8
E9	67PM	ST8

Table 8.7: The database is now in second normal form (2NF).

Student ID	Student name	DOB	Gender	Postcode
ST6	James	30/01/2000	M	OX68TY
ST7	Charlotte	12/5/2000	F	CA80GH
ST8	Julie	03/10/2000	F	WR168UY

Table 8.8: The database is now in second normal form (2NF).

Course ID	Course name	Teacher ID	Teacher's name	Postcode
67TY	Mathematics	TYM1	Mr Smith	CA80GH
67UI	Computer Science	TYM3	Mrs Jones	WR168UZ
67PM	Physics	TYM8	Ms Pratt	WR168UB

Table 8.9: The database is now in second normal form (2NF).

Now our tables are in second normal form.

Third normal form

A table is said to be in third normal form if it is in second normal form and contains no transitive dependencies. Transitive dependency is tricky to understand; basically, if A is dependent on B and B is dependent on C then A is transitively dependent on C. In our example the course is dependent on the Course ID and the teacher is dependent on the course. So the teacher is transitively dependent on the Course ID and must be placed in a separate table.

Enrolment ID	Course ID	Student ID
E1	67TY	ST6
E2	67UI	ST6
E3	67PM	ST6
E4	67TY	ST7
E5	67UI	ST7
E6	67PM	ST7
E7	67TY	ST8
E8	67UI	ST8
E9	67PM	ST8

Table 8.10: The database is now in third normal form (3NF).

Student ID	Student name	DOB	Gender	Postcode
ST6	James	30/01/2000	M	OX68TY
ST7	Charlotte	12/05/2000	F	CA80GH
ST8	Julie	03/10/2000	F	WR168UY

Table 8.11: The database is now in third normal form (3NF).

Teacher ID	Teacher's name	Postcode
TYM1	Mr Smith	CA80GH
TYM3	Mrs Jones	WR168UZ
TYM8	Ms Pratt	WR168UB

Table 8.12: The database is now in third normal form (3NF).

Course ID	Course name	Teacher ID
67TY	Mathematics	TYM1
67UI	Computer Science	TYM3
67PM	Physics	TYM8

Table 8.13: The database is now in third normal form (3NF).

Our database is now in third normal form.

Tip

Long-answer questions can often require you to describe how a given flat-file database could be normalised. A good way to remember the requirements of the first three levels of normalisation is that each field must depend on: 'the key (1NF), the whole key (2NF) and nothing but the key (3NF)'.

Entity relationship modelling

In a database context, entities are real-world objects about which data is being held. For example, in a database for a mobile veterinary practice, pets, owners, vets, vans and appointments could all be entities.

Entity relationship modelling is the process of drawing up an entity-relationship (ER) diagram that describes the relationships between these entities.

There are three types of relationship that can be displayed on an ER diagram (Figure 8.3).

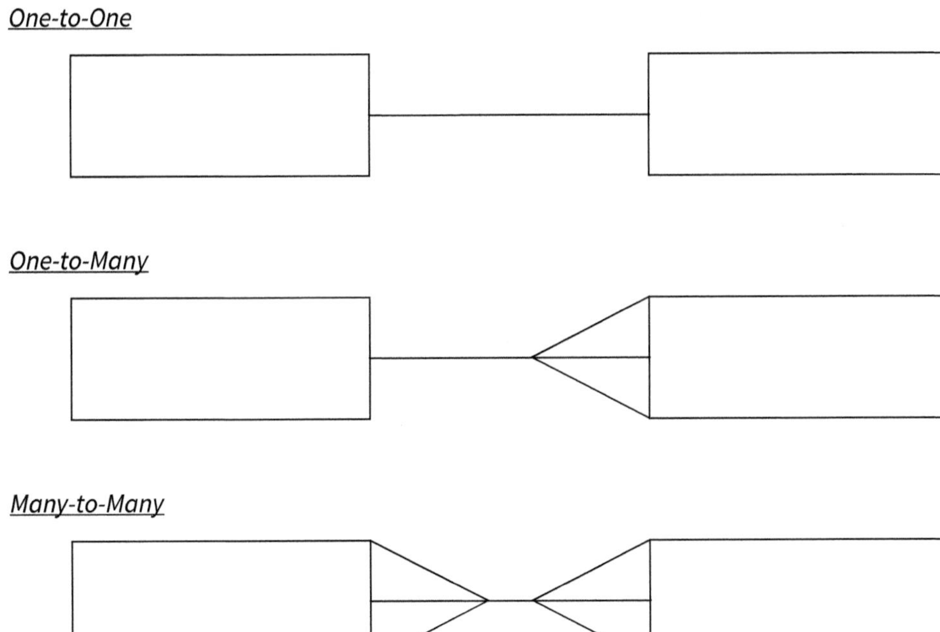

Figure 8.3: Possible relationships between entities.

In our example, the link between owners and pets would be one-to-many, as one owner can have many pets but a pet can only have one owner.

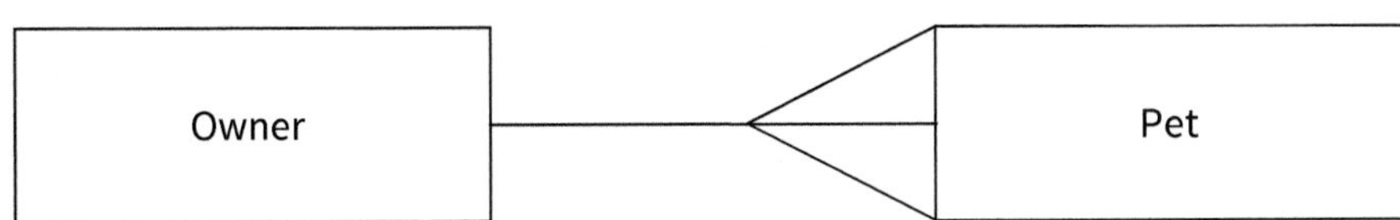

Figure 8.4: Link between owners and pets.

The relationship between vets and pets is many-to-many as a vet will see many pets and a pet might be seen by multiple vets.

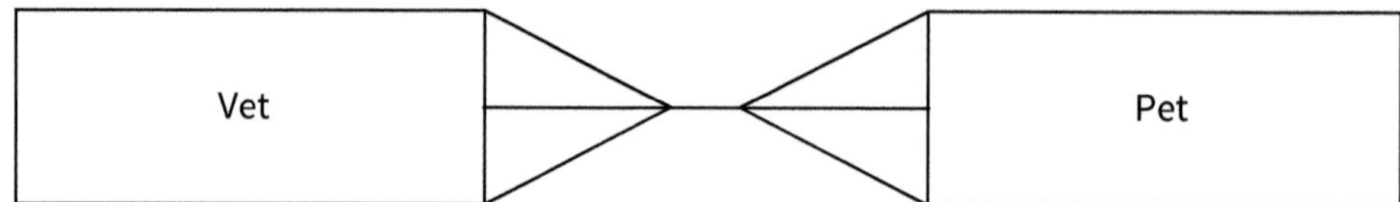

Figure 8.5: A vet sees many pets and a pet may be seen by many different vets.

The relationship between a vet and the van they use to travel between appointments would be one-to-one as each vet only drives one van and each van only has one registered driver.

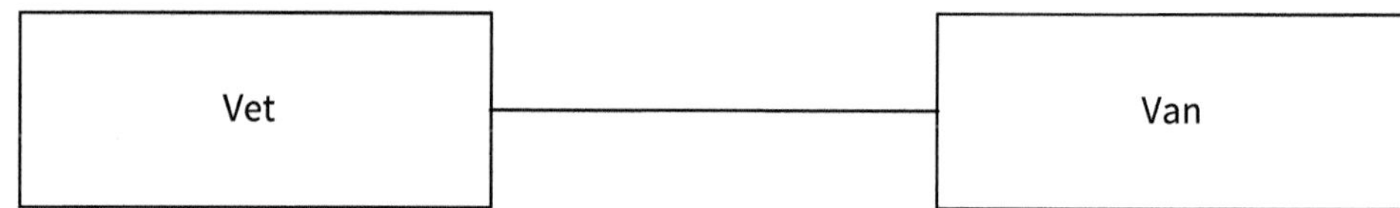

Figure 8.6: Each vet owns one van and a van is only driven by one vet.

These separate ER diagrams are then combined to create an ER-diagram for the whole database.

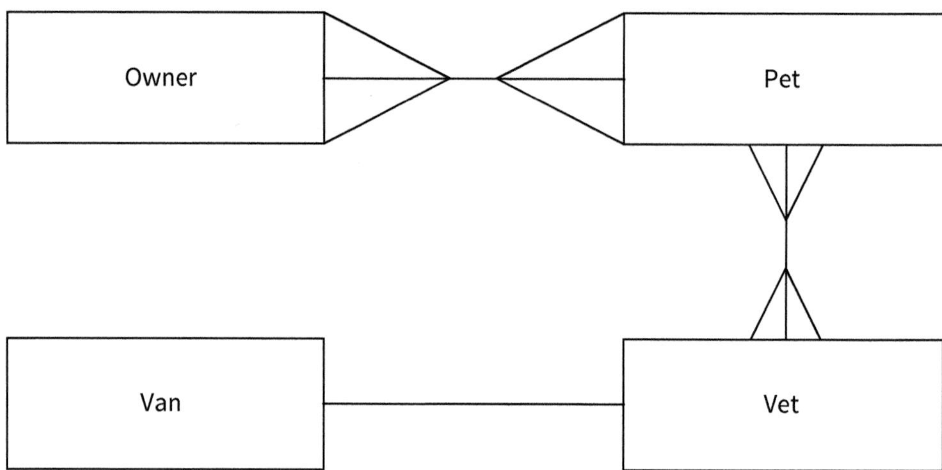

Figure 8.7: The individual relationships are combined to describe the whole database.

ER diagrams are very useful in the early planning stages of a database, as it is likely that each entity will be a table in the database and the attributes of that entity will become fields. It also makes it easy to spot when a database is in 3NF, as no database which contains a many-to-many relationship can ever be.

To remove a many-to-many relationship it is necessary to insert another table (sometimes called a link table) that breaks the relationship into two one-to-many relationships. In our example this can be achieved by including an appointments entity. A pet can have many appointments but each appointment is only for one pet. A vet will have many appointments but only one vet will be present at each appointment.

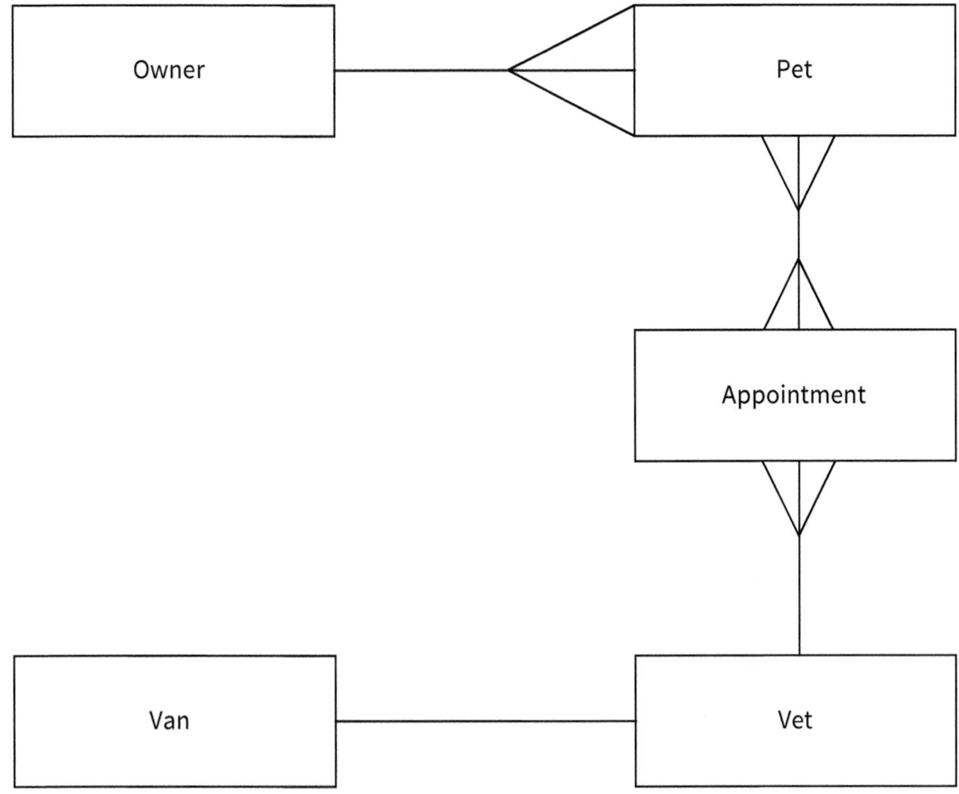

Figure 8.8: A linking table is added to break up the many-to-many relationship.

SQL: Interpret and modify (list of keywords)

Databases become very useful when we are able to search for specific information held within it. We call a database search a query.. A query may return one or more fields from one or more tables. In the early days of computing there were many different types of database. Each had a different way to query the data. This meant that it was very difficult to transfer skills from one database to another. There was no standardisation, which meant that developers were locked into specific database implementations.

Databases often formed the cornerstone of computerised systems in a business, and therefore the demand for skilled database operatives was high. It became clear that there needed to be a standard way of interacting with databases. A committee called the ANSI-SQL group produced the standard for querying a database. SQL stands for structured query language. A query is written in SQL and sent to the database query engine as plain text. The database then executes the query and returns the results in the form of a table. The following examples show some basic SQL commands and their results.

SELECT query

The SELECT command returns a specified piece of data from a database. It can return whole rows and columns or the data from a single field.

Student ID	Student name	DOB	Gender	Postcode
ST6	James	30/01/2000	M	OX68TY
ST7	Charlotte	12/05/2000	F	CA80GH
ST8	Julie	03/10/2000	F	WR168UY

Table 8.14: A table called Students containing student details.

SQL example	Result
SELECT * FROM Students	Returns the entire table with everything in it.
SELECT StudentID FROM Students	Returns the StudentID column from the students table.
SELECT * FROM Students WHERE StudentID = "ST6"	Returns the whole of the record where the StudentID is ST6.
SELECT Studentname, DOB FROM Students WHERE Gender = "F"	Returns the name and date of birth of all the students who have their gender recorded as F.
SELECT Studentname, DOB FROM Students WHERE Gender = "F" ORDER BY DESC Studentname	Returns the name and date of birth of all the students who have their gender recorded as F. The list returned will be sorted in descending order by student name.

Table 8.15: Selecting information from a database using SQL.

You can use familiar logical operators in SQL statements such as AND, OR and NOT.

INSERT

As well as retrieving data from an existing database, SQL also lets you add records using the INSERT command.

SQL example	Result
INSERT INTO Students (StudentID, Studentname, DOB, Gender, Postcode) VALUES ("ST9", "Adam", "29/01/2001", "M", "OX69TG")	Inserts a new record in the students table.

Table 8.16: Inserting data into a table using SQL.

Be aware that when inserting a record you must include a value for the primary key (in this case StudentID). If you try to insert a new record with the same primary key as an existing record, the database will reject the query.

UPDATE

The UPDATE command is used to edit or modify existing data in the database.

SQL example	Result
UPDATE Students SET Studentname = "Joseph"	Sets every students' name in the database to James.
UPDATE Students SET Studentname = "Joseph" WHERE StudentID = "ST6"	Will find the record where the StudentID is ST6 and set the student's name to Joseph.

Table 8.17: Updating data in a table using SQL.

DELETE

As well as adding and editing data, SQL also enables you to delete data from a database using the DELETE command.

SQL example	Result
DELETE FROM Students WHERE Studentname = "Joseph"	Will delete every record where the student's name is Joseph from the database.

Table 8.18: Deleting data from a table using SQL.

Creating and removing tables

SQL commands are not just focused on manipulating records. You can also use SQL to create new tables, delete tables you don't want and edit the properties of existing tables.

SQL example	Result
DROP Students	Will delete the entire Students table and everything in it.
CREATE TABLE Parents (ParentID VARCHAR(4) NOT NULL, Parentname VARCHAR(20) NOT NULL, DOB DATE PRIMARY KEY (ParentID))	Creates a new table with three columns called ParentID, Parentname and DOB. ParentID is the primary key and can be up to four characters long, Parentname can be up to 20 characters long and DOB must be a date. NOT NULL indicates that a field must be set when inserting a record.

Table 8.19: Deleting and creating tables using SQL.

Referential integrity

In a relational database every foreign key must correspond to the primary key in another table. For example, there is no point including the TeacherID TYM9 in our courses table if there is no record in the teachers table with TYM9 as a primary key.

Teacher ID	Teacher name	Postcode
TYM1	Mr Smith	CA80GH
TYM3	Mrs Jones	WR168UZ
TYM8	Ms Pratt	WR168UB

Table 8.20: To maintain referential integrity all foreign keys must relate to primary keys.

Course ID	Course name	Teacher ID
67TY	Mathematics	TYM1
67UI	Computer Science	TYM3
67PM	Physics	TYM9

Table 8.21: Referential integrity not maintained.

Making sure that each foreign key refers to an existing record is called maintaining referential integrity. Records with a foreign key that do not link back to a primary key are sometimes called orphan records.

There are some specific commands included in SQL to help ensure that a database maintains its referential integrity.

SQL example	Result
CREATE TABLE Parents (ParentID VARCHAR(4) NOT NULL, Parentname VARCHAR(20) NOT NULL, DOB DATE, StudentID REFERENCES Students (StudentID) ON UPDATE CASCADE, PRIMARY KEY (ParentID))	This creates a new parents table with a foreign key linking it to the students table. The ON UPDATE CASCADE instruction means that if we update the StudentID in the students table, the foreign key in the parents table will be automatically updated to match.

Table 8.22: Maintaining referential integrity using SQL.

Just as referential integrity is used to ensure that the links between tables remain correct, record locking is used to ensure that the data itself is correct. Record locking ensures that two people cannot try and update the same piece of data at the same time and thus override each other's changes.

Tip

Make sure you are comfortable with SQL code, as you may have to write or annotate SQL code in the exam.

Transaction processing, atomicity, consistency, isolation, durability

Transaction processing

Transaction processing means taking multiple smaller operations and grouping them together in a single 'transaction' operation. If any of the smaller operations fails then the transaction as a whole must fail. The aim of transaction processing is to ensure that complex operations are not left partially complete by hardware or software failures.

For example, imagine transferring £12 000 from one bank account to another. This operation is made up of two smaller ones (removing £12 000 from one account and adding £12 000 to another). If either of these smaller operations is not successful, the operation as a whole must fail; if it does not then £12 000 could just disappear.

There are four properties of a successful transaction: atomicity, consistency, isolation and durability (ACID):

- *Atomicity*: either every part of the transaction is successful or none is.
- *Consistency*: all parts of the transaction must be in line with the database rules; for example, they do not create duplicate keys.
- *Isolation*: ensures that even if different transactions are happening at the same time, the results are the same as if they were happening one after the other.

- *Durability*: once a transaction has been successfully completed, its actions are not undone. This involves ensuring that the data is saved to a secondary storage device such as a hard drive.

Summary

- Flat-file databases store information in a single large table.
- Relational databases store data in many smaller tables, linked together using keys.
- Primary keys are unique attributes that can be used to identify a record in a table.
- Foreign keys are the primary keys from another table and are used to link tables together.
- Entity relationship models visually describe the relationships between the different entities in a database.
- Optical mark recognition (OMR) is often used to capture data that is to be held in databases. A light is then shone at the paper and, as the mark made by the user reflects less light than the empty boxes, the software can work out which answer was selected.
- Optical character recognition (OCR) is used to convert written words into digital text. It scans in a character then compares the marks scanned in to a look-up table that holds all possible values. When a match is found, the character has been recognised and the equivalent ASCII value is placed in the digital file.
- Normalisation is the process of converting a flat-file database into a relational one.
- An index is a data structure used to shorten the length of time it takes to search a database.
- There are different stages of normalisation. The most common is third normal form. A table is in third normal form if it contains no transitive dependencies i.e. every field depends entirely on the primary key.
- Structured query language (SQL) is used to create, edit and delete data in databases.
- Referential integrity is needed to ensure that the foreign keys in one table refer to a primary key in another.
- Transaction processing uses atomicity, consistency, isolation, durability, record locking and redundancy to ensure that the overall transaction cannot be a success if any one part of it fails.

Activity 8.1

Visit the following website and use the 'Try it yourself' exercises to practise using MySQL: www.cambridge.org/links/kose5038

Activity 8.2

Imagine you have been responsible for creating a database to hold everything in your schools timetable. Draw a diagram showing the tables and fields you would need along with any links between primary and secondary keys.

End-of-chapter questions

1 What is meant by a flat-file database? [2]

2 What is a primary key? [2]

3 What is a relational database? [3]

4 What is the result of running this SQL query: SELECT * FROM Students. [3] 

5 What is the purpose of referential integrity? [2]

Further reading

Flat-file database – search on databasedev.co.uk.
Relational database – search on Oracle's Java Documentation website.
Normalisation – search on sqa.org.uk.

Chapter 9
Networks

Specification points

1.3.3 Networks

- Characteristics of networks and the importance of protocols and standards.
- The internet structure:
    - TCP/IP stack
    - DNS
    - Protocol layering
    - LANs and WANs
    - packet and circuit switching.
    - Network security and threats, use of firewalls, proxies and encryption. (A)
    - Network hardware. (A)
    - Client-server and peer-to-peer.

Learning objectives

- To understand how data is transmitted over networks and other wired connections.
- To understand how protocols work and the difference between physical and logical protocols.
- To learn about protocol stacks and why they are structured in this manner.
- To learn about the key networking hardware, including hardware needed for a wireless network. (A)
- To understand and describe the key differences between circuit and packet switching.

Introduction

Most computing systems are connected to some form of network, most commonly the internet. Computers may be connected through wired, wireless or even satellite links. At its most basic, a computer network is a collection of interconnected computers that have the ability to communicate with one another.

What underpins all communication is the concept of a protocol. Protocols are a set of standard communication rules. No matter what data is being sent or how the various devices in the network are connected, a set of protocols is required to ensure that both the sender and the receiver understand one another.

Characteristics of networks and the importance of protocols and standards

This chapter will introduce many ideas associated with networks and specifically linked to services and protocols. Before these can be explored in depth it is important to take a higher-level view of what defines a network and the importance of standards.

A computer network consists of two or more computing devices connected together to allow communication and resource sharing. Devices can be connected together using cables, wirelessly or a combination of both. The structure and layout (also known as topology) can vary depending on technology used. Two example topologies are shown below, in Figure 9.1.

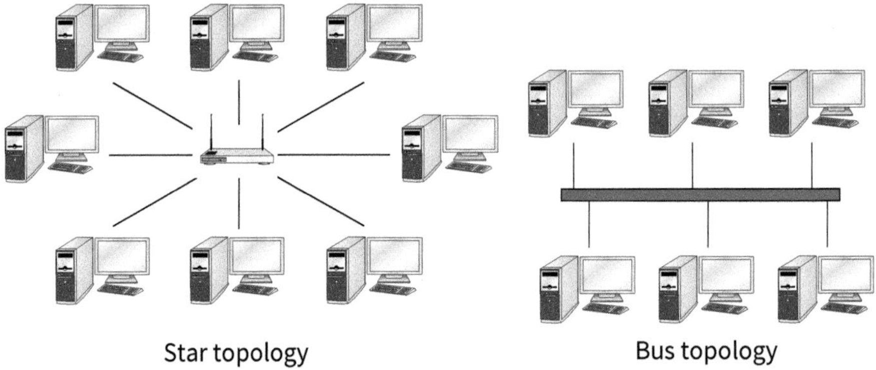

Figure 9.1: Example network topologies.

Some of the key features of a network include:

- Ability to share files through a file server or through peer-to-peer networks.
- Share a single internet connection between multiple devices.
- Share printers and other peripherals.
- Allow communication.
- Enable collaboration though tools and shared resources.

It is very common for a network to contain one or more servers that provide services to the network. This can range from an e-mail or a web server to print managers and file servers. All computers on a network will have the ability, based on the permissions set up by the network administrator, to access these services. A device that uses a network service is called a client.

In order to allow many different types of computing device to communicate effectively, standards must be enforced. A standard is a set of rules that must be adhered to when creating or implementing anything intended to be governed by it. Networking has a large number of standards that are used to ensure smooth interoperability between devices. This is useful because if a hardware manufacture wants to ensure that their device will be compatible, they can follow the standard exactly and be assured that it will. In Chapter 10, you will be introduced to a number of web standards that are used when developing web apps or websites.

Protocols and standards must be followed, otherwise, communication between devices can fail due to incompatibility. This can be exemplified by some web browsers supporting plug-ins that others do not. This can result in a frustrating experience for users when they try to load their favourite website in a browser that no longer supports its features. For a business, the impact may be more serious and could result in loss of business. For this reason, if developers stick to the HTML standards developed by the W3C, their sites can be viewed in any compatible browser.

Types of network

Before computer networks were common in organisations, users would have had to transfer files by walking from one office to another and transfer them using a medium such as a floppy disk. The was termed 'sneakernet'. Networked computers have the advantage of being able to share files, offer services and communicate with each other, for example, through the use of email or instant messengers. Businesses can save money by sharing devices such as printers across a network. The internet is a global network of computers and devices.

When services are distributed over a network, this is also called a **distributed** system. This enables different computers to share the load of providing services which can improve reliability and speed of access. Networks differ in size depending on where they are located. At home, you will most likely have a small network. This is referred to as a local area network (LAN). Schools have a bigger network than at home, with many more computers connected together. Even though the size of a school network is massive when compared to a home network, it is still referred to as a LAN. Local refers to the computers being near each other geographically rather than the number of computers connected to the network. The maximum span of a LAN is 2 km.

The internet is a worldwide network of connected computers, which means that you can access websites, or more specifically web servers, in any country in the world. As the geographical distance between computers on the internet is very great, the internet constitutes a wide area network (WAN). A WAN is defined as a network greater than 2 km in span. Many of the technologies used on WANs are based around the telephone network called the POTS (plain old telephone service).

LANs are inherently more secure than WANs because they are usually owned by one organisation and secured on the boundary between it and the internet. In a LAN, all networked devices are likely to be managed by a small group of network administrators who manage access to resources by assigning permissions, whereas WANs involve many different organisations whose security arrangements may not always be known. Data travelling over a WAN is likely to travel over many different networks owned by many different organisations, so there is potentially a much higher risk of data being intercepted on its journey between sender and recipient. This form of threat, known as a man-in-the-middle attack, means that unencrypted data could be stolen or altered. This is why you should be careful about what information you send over the internet and why you should also make sure that you only use sites that encrypt your personal data before sending.

Structures for networked services

Two common structures for networks are client–server and peer-to-peer.

Client–server structure

Most networks work on the client–server model (Figure 9.2). Services, such as file storage, are made available on servers to which clients connect in order to access the services. Web servers host sites and clients use web browsers to access the webpages held on the server.

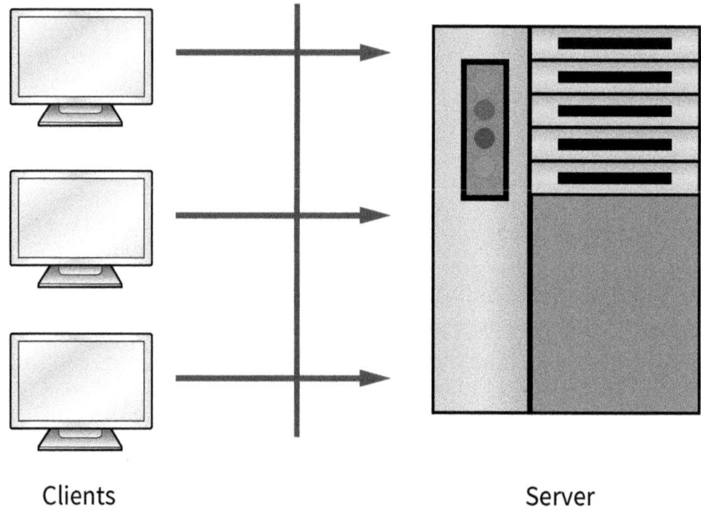

Figure 9.2: Client–server model.

Servers use the model of centralised computing, as services and processing power are held at a central point on a network rather than using the distributed model, where resources are spread across a set of peers.

Clients and servers make use of a request–response model. Clients request a service or resource from the server. The server responds either with a security challenge or with the requested resource. If the server fails for any reason, the service cannot be provided by that server but may be provided by another offering the same service.

Peer-to-peer networks

In a peer-to-peer network, each computer, or peer, has the same status as the others. No computer acts solely as a server, meaning that peers must work together to fulfil the required task. Peer-to-peer networks use the distributed model of computing, as tasks are shared between different computers on the network. One of the most common uses of peer-to-peer networking is file sharing. A file required by a number of peers is downloaded in parts. Initially each peer downloads parts of the file, known as leeching, until they have enough of the file to start sharing. Other peers on the network then start downloading the parts of the file from the peers that have already downloaded them, until each peer has full access to every part of the file. As soon as a peer has the whole file, it becomes a seed and continues to share the file until that peer is taken out of the network. Peer-to-peer networking allows very large files to be downloaded efficiently without the need for a powerful server.

Peer-to-peer technology can also be used to share the processing load for complicated calculations. This form of peer-to-peer networking is known as distributed processing. Difficult problems that require extensive processing time are split up into smaller chunks and these chunks are shared with peers. Each peer then solves part of the problem and returns the result to the peer that is responsible for consolidating and coordinating the calculations.

Data transmission

When data is transmitted, regardless of whether over a network or not, it is sent in the form of a packet. A generic data packet is split into three main parts: the message, a header and a footer (Figure 9.3).

Figure 9.3: Packet structure.

A packet has a maximum amount of data that it can transmit, defined by the protocol currently in use. Protocols enforce and provide services to enable data transmission and govern the rules that apply. As packets are limited in size, a large file needs to be split into multiple packets. Each packet, therefore, contains only part of the original file. For example, if a file is 6000 bytes in size and the maximum packet size is 1500 bytes, the file must be sent in four separate packets (Figure 9.4). Ethernet is a well-known LAN protocol that has a maximum transmission unit (MTU) size of 1500 bytes.

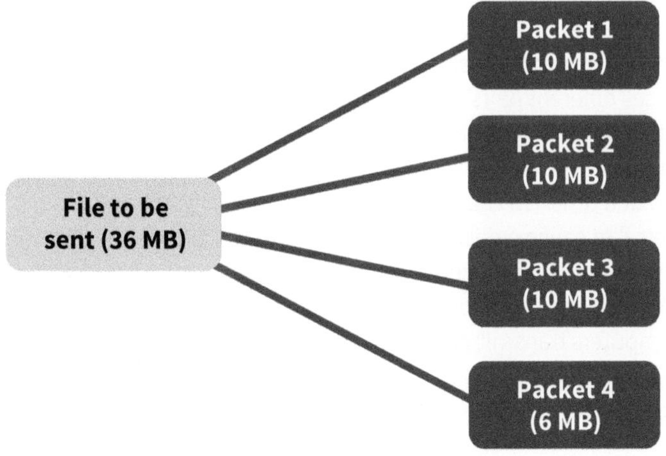

Figure 9.4: Files are transmitted as multiple packets.

Packets can be thought of as being like an envelope, with critical information about the destination and sender written on the outside of it. Information required to transmit the packet to the correct destination, such as source and destination IP address, must be added to the header. Each protocol employed during the transmission of data adds information to the packet's header or footer. Exactly how this process works is looked at later in this chapter.

When a network is set up, the parties involved need to decide how data will be transmitted between computers; in other words, which protocol is to be used. They must also decide which transmission mode to use. There are three main transmission modes (Figure 9.5): simplex, half duplex and duplex (or full duplex).

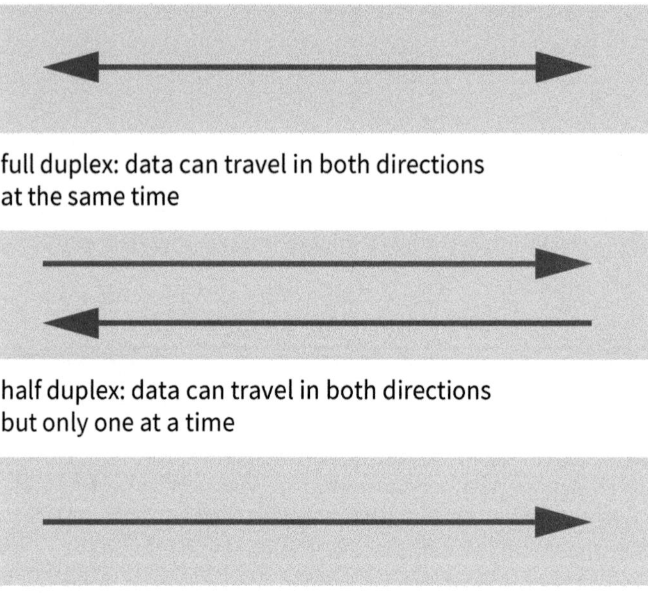

full duplex: data can travel in both directions at the same time
half duplex: data can travel in both directions but only one at a time
simplex: data can travel in only one direction

Figure 9.5: Types of transmission mode.

Simplex data connections send data in only one direction, so no return packets are allowed. Satellite connections for TV use simplex mode, as satellite dishes can only receive data from a satellite – they cannot send messages back. Full duplex, and half duplex, makes use of separate cables to send data back and forth. A twisted pair cable, such as CAT6, uses different pairs of twisted copper wires for sending and receiving data (Figure 9.6). In this way, packets travelling in opposite directions do not interfere with each other. Half duplex allows communication in both directions but only allows packets to be sent one way at a time. On shared network media, e.g. backbone cables, it is possible that data packets can cause a data collision. When this occurs, the packet needs to be retransmitted. On early Ethernet networks, it was considered normal to lose some traffic to collisions and this did impact on performance. Any network that has shared media, which two or more computers transmit data through, can only be configured to operate in half duplex mode. Early Ethernet networks used a shared backbone cable configured in a bus topology discussed later in this chapter. Full duplex allows simultaneous transmission and receiving of data. This is more efficient because the two processes, sending and receiving, can be happening at the same time.

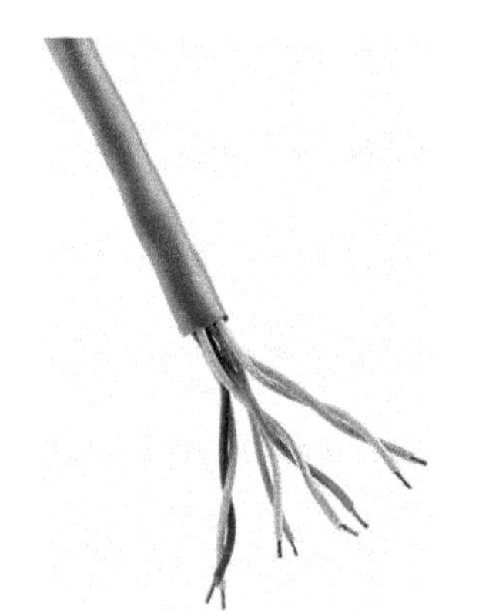

Figure 9.6: Twisted pair copper network cable.

Data can be transmitted as serial or parallel. Traditionally, serial transmission was slower, as bits are sent one after the other down a single link. Serial communication was originally developed for longer-distance communication but now, because of improvements in transmission speed, it is used for many shorter links too, e.g. USB and PCI X. Serial connections always send one bit after another in order. Parallel transmission sends many bits simultaneously over several wires. Originally this was much quicker than serial but, as more wires are needed in a parallel cable, it takes up more physical space and synchronisation can be an issue. It was originally designed for short distance links e.g. buses on a computer motherboard, between storage devices and printers and the computer. Serial and parallel are independent of the communication link being one or two way, meaning that you can have combinations such as serial full duplex (but using one wire for transmit and one to receive), or parallel simplex.

Tip

It is important to be able to distinguish between different modes of transmission clearly. Compare serial and parallel transmission, simplex, half duplex and full duplex in a table so you have a clear understanding and a useful resource for revision.

Bandwidth and bit rate

Bandwidth is not a measure of speed as many people think, but a measure of how much data can be fitted onto a cable at any point in time. A useful analogy is to compare the bandwidth of a cable or wireless link with the traffic carrying capacity of a road. If you counted the number of cars travelling down a small country lane in ten minutes, even at the busiest time of the day, it still only has one lane so the number of cars would be quite small. If we counted cars on a busy motorway such as the M25, we would quickly lose count because there are more lanes so the traffic carrying capacity is much higher. High bandwidth in a network cable means that there is more room for data than there is with a low-bandwidth connection. Data still flows at the exact same speed along that cable. Consumers often confuse bandwidth as being the same as speed. Bandwidth is the theoretical data carrying capacity and is measured in megabits per second (Mbps) or gigabits per second (Gbps). In reality, this is the absolute maximum. If we were to count the cars travelling on the M25 at rush hour, we might find the traffic moving very slowly indeed. The motorway still has three lanes in each direction but it is congested so the actual traffic moving is much lower. We call this measurement throughput. Most domestic broadband connections are shared, which means that when the network is busy, the throughput is less so the link appears to be slower.

Bit rate is a way of expressing a piece of software's data transfer requirements. High-bit-rate connections are required when a large amount of data must be sent in a short period of time. Video conferencing needs to send a lot of data, which must arrive in a timely manner otherwise the video will buffer frequently, which is frustrating for the viewer. In order to have a high-quality video stream, a high bit rate is required. When small files, such as Word documents or simple webpages, are going to be sent, a low bit rate is sufficient. Connections capable of supporting high bit rates are more costly, so when purchasing a broadband package, consumers need to think about the activities that they want to use it for.

Tip

Bit rate and bandwidth can be thought of as similar concepts. There are technical differences, but this is not covered in the exam.

Table 9.1 shows examples of applications and gives an indication of whether a low or high bit rate would be advisable.

Application	Low or high	Reason
Sending a text-based e-mail	Low	E-mails tend to only be a few kilobytes in size.
Streaming a video	High	Video sends a lot of data per second, depending on the quality of the video.
Connecting to a file server	High	File servers have a lot of requests for files arriving and need to process them fast. The higher the bit rate, the shorter the amount of time needed to send each file.
Browsing the web	Low	Most webpages, even those with multimedia-rich content, tend to be small in size. They do send a lot of data out, but it tends to be spread out over a period of time. Also, your connection is limited to the speed of the web server you're connecting to. One exception to this is if the website makes heavy use of video.

Table 9.1: Bit rate required for various common tasks on the internet.

Error detection

When data is sent across a network, errors can be introduced due to changes in the signal. Errors can come from many different sources, for example the cable might be damaged, there might be interference from other electrical devices or the cable might be too long and the signal has become weak. When the signal is altered, this may cause a changed data packet that can make it unreadable or unable to be delivered. It is impossible to predict when errors will occur, nor is it possible to stop them occurring altogether.

Error detection mechanisms allow communicating computers to know when an error has occurred. The data in a packet, consisting of a series of binary digits, can become corrupted at any point in the transmission. In the example shown in Figure 9.7, a binary stream has been sent over a connection medium and some bits have been changed. The data is no longer valid and if the error is not spotted, the data could be interpreted incorrectly by the recipient.

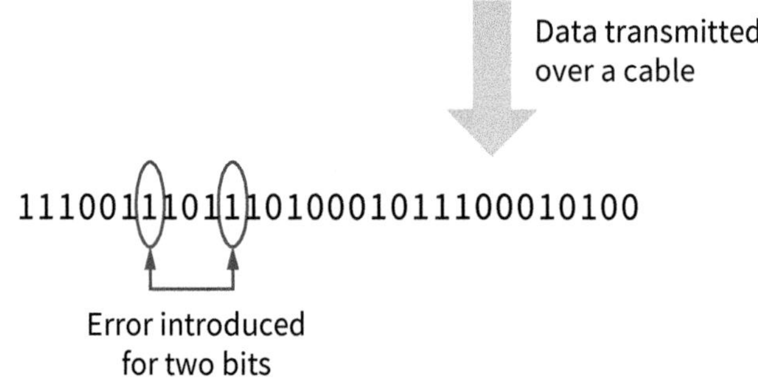

Figure 9.7: Example of how data in a packet can become corrupted.

Tip

You need to be able to explain how each of the three error detection methods works, as well as the error correcting method. Explaining how checksums are calculated is not required.

Due to the unpredictable nature of errors, error detection methods need to be employed. Upon detection of an error, the sender has to retransmit the packet. Below are three methods used to detect errors. Only one of these methods is used at any one time.

Echo error detection

Echo error detection is very simple to implement. First, a packet is sent from the source computer to the destination computer and the destination computer sends the packet straight back, or echoes it (Figure 9.8). The source computer compares this packet with the one it originally sent. If they are the same, nothing happens. However, if there is a difference an error must have occurred and the message is resent. This method can pick up all errors, as every bit is compared and if just one is in error, the message is resent.

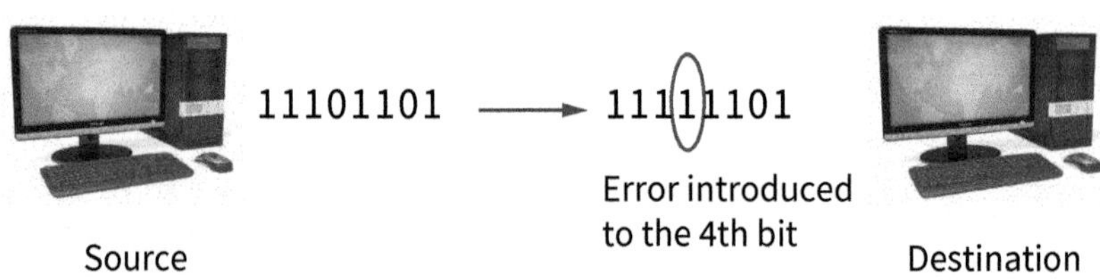

Figure 9.8: Echo error detection.

There are two major problems with the echo technique:

- Echo dramatically increases network traffic because each packet must be sent at least twice, effectively doubling the amount of data being transmitted.

- Errors can be introduced as the packet returns to the source. In this case the destination computer did receive the packet correctly, but its response to the source has become corrupted. There is no way for the source computer to know this, so the message still has to be resent. Ultimately this means that there is more chance for errors to be introduced, thus reducing the efficiency of the system.

Checksum

A checksum is the most common way of detecting errors over a network. It has a good trade-off between the amount of extra data being sent over the network and the ability to spot most errors. A checksum, like a check digit on barcodes, adds extra bits to the packet, calculated from the original data. This calculation produces the checksum, which is only a few bytes in size regardless of how big the data is. When the data is sent, the checksum is added to the packet's header, and the destination computer performs the same calculation. If the checksums produced by both calculations do not match, there must have been an error during transmission and the packet is requested again.

The most common checksum in use today is the cyclic redundancy check (CRC), which is used in many network protocols. CRC is effective and picks up over 99% of all errors. This is why, when files are being do/nloaded from the internet, they can sometimes be corrupted. It is rare, but can happen.

Parity bits

It is possible to send extra information to help the destination computer decide whether an error has occurred. One of the most basic methods is to add a parity bit to the data. The parity method can be either odd or even (Figure 9.9), and this decision is made prior to transmission.

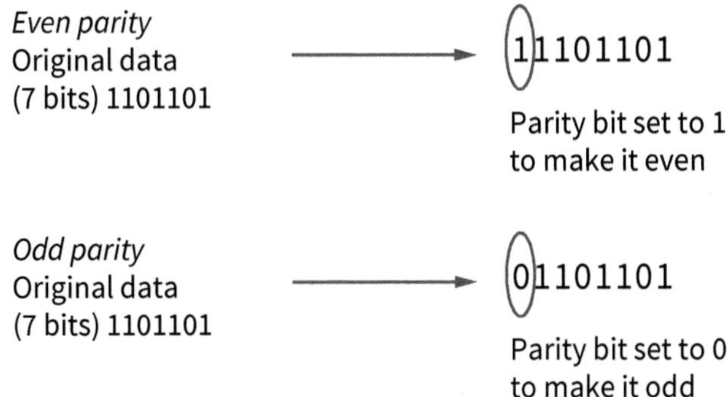

Figure 9.9: Parity.

In the case of even parity, if the message contains an odd number of 1s, the parity bit is also set to 1, so that the entire data transmission (message plus parity bit) contains an even number of 1s. If the message already contains an even number of 1s, the parity bit is set to 0. When data is transmitted, both the message and the parity bit are sent. The receiver recalculates the number of 1s in the message to check that parity has not changed. If the parity has changed, for example an odd number of 1s is encountered, an error is sent back to the sender and the packet is resent.

Here is a complete example. Some data needs to be sent across the network, so a parity bit is added to ensure even parity (Figure 9.10).

Figure 9.10: Creating an even parity.

During transmission, an error is introduced: the fourth bit is flipped to a 0. The number of 1s is counted by the destination, giving an odd number, 7, which means that the message no longer has even parity (Figure 9.11). This is an error, so the source will have to resend the packet.

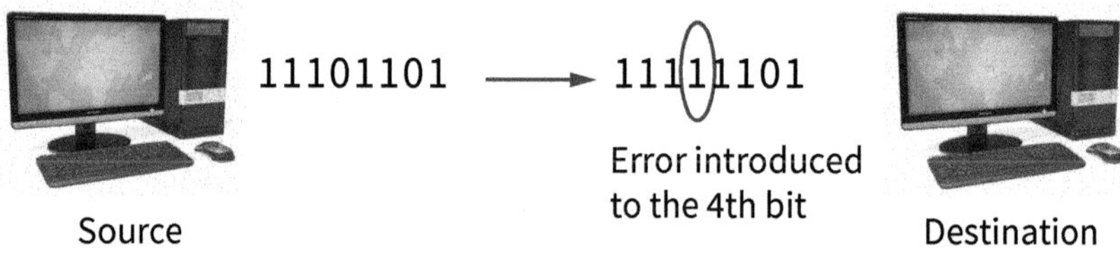

Figure 9.11: Parity error.

The parity method cannot spot all errors and cannot be relied on for accurate data transmission over a network. If errors occur in two bits, this can result in the message being changed in such a way that it still has the correct parity. For example, if we have the message 1100, a parity bit of 0 would be added to make it even, 11000. As the packet is transmitted two errors are introduced, and we still get the message 11110 at the destination. This has an even number of 1s, so the errors are not noticed.

Parity bits in grids

Parity bits can be used not only to detect but also to correct errors in transmitted packets. We can thus save network bandwidth, as we will not have to request that the packet be retransmitted. Parity bits are arranged in such a way that every bit in the message has at least two parity bits assigned in a grid system. In networking terms, correcting a bit means flipping it.

Consider the following four bytes of data with a parity bit (even) added to the end of each line:

1101 0011 **1**

1100 1111 **0**

1001 1001 **0**

0110 0011 **0**

The next step is to add eight more parity bits to represent parity on every bit place or column. This is sent as a separate byte of data, at the end of the message.

1101 0011 **1**

1100 1111 **0**

1001 1001 **0**

0110 0011 **0**

1110 0110

The next step is to consider the case when an error is introduced into the data. The error is shown, below.

1101 0011 **1 Byte 1**

1100 1111 **0 Byte 2**

1001 0001 **0 Byte 3**

0110 0011 **0 Byte 4**

1110 0110

The parity for bytes 1, 2 and 4 are ok, meaning that the error must be in byte 3. Only column 5's parity does not calculate correctly, which means that the error must be in column 5. With these two pieces of information, it is trivial to work out which bit was in error and it can be solved by flipping the bit, thus getting the original message back.

Protocols

When talking to someone who does not speak English as their first language, it is possible that you may have difficulties being understood. At some point you will have to make a decision to aid communication. Maybe they speak a little so you decide to use simple English, or maybe you speak a little of their language. It might be possible to mime what you want to say or even to try to draw or use symbols. If you're lucky, you might have a translator handy who could act as a go-between. However you decide to communicate, you will have needed to make a conscious choice of the communication style and decide on a set of rules to govern future communication. Computers, when they transmit data, can do this in many different ways. As such, it is crucial that each computer not only follows a set of rules, but ensures that both sides use the same ones. In Computer Science, a set of rules that governs communication is known as a **protocol**.

In the early days of computer networks, there were many different LAN protocols developed by different. At that time, there were a number of protocol stacks including Apple's Appletalk, Novell's IPX/SPX and the internet standard, TCP/IP, which was adopted by Microsoft for their LANs. It is not possible for a computer using IPX/SPX, for example, to communicate with another computer using TCP/IP without making use of special hardware or software to translate, known as a bridge. IP version 4 addresses take the form of four sets of numbers ranging from 0 to 255, while IPX uses a 32-bit hexadecimal address. This is why the choice of protocols is so important: if each computer knows exactly how data should be sent over the network, when it arrives the computer will know exactly how to process it.

Tip

A classic exam question is to define a protocol and then explain why they are combined with other protocols in a protocol stack such as TCP/IP.

Handshaking

In order to set up a communication link, both devices need to agree on a set of protocols to use. This must occur before a single byte of data is sent and is known as **handshaking**. The handshaking signal is sent from one device to the other and is acknowledged by the second device. It is entirely possible that the second device may not support the choice of protocols, so either another set must be chosen or communication will fail.

During the handshaking process, the two communicating devices must agree the bit rate, the type of error correction to use and the format of the packet.

Tip

The exam will normally focus on handshaking for communication over a cable rather than a network.

Physical and logical considerations

When a choice of protocol has to be made, there are many aspects to consider, both physical and logical.

Physical aspects include:

- wired or wireless
- serial or parallel data transmission
- synchronous/asynchronous
- copper or fibre optic
- simplex, half duplex or full duplex mode.

Logical aspects include:

- bit rate
- error detection
- packet size
- ordering of packets
- routing
- compression and encryption
- digital signatures.

Tip

Physical protocols relate to the properties of the transmission medium. Logical protocols relate to software layers of the protocol stack.

Protocol stacks

There are many different tasks that need to be carried out when sending a packet over a network. How will the packet get there? How will the packet be formatted? Do the packets need to arrive in a specific order? What happens when an error is introduced during transmission? Some protocols relate directly to the characteristics of the transmission medium such as how an electrical signal on a copper wire can be changed (modulated) to carry data. These are the physical protocols. Others relate to the encryption processes, routing and compression for example, which are implemented in software. These are the logical protocols. One single protocol could not possibly cover the entire process. Instead a 'stack' of protocols, sitting on top of one another, describes the whole communication process. The best known and most widely implemented is TCP/IP.

Protocol stacks have many advantages:

- Manufacturers of hardware only need to concern themselves with physical layer protocols.
- Upper layer protocols do not directly depend on the ones beneath them so it does not matter what routing protocol is used on a wireless or a wired network, for example. The important part of any protocol is how it interfaces with the protocol beneath it and above it. Changes in one layer, should not affect those in another layer. Development can be quicker because different organisations can develop protocols for different layers.

The TCP/IP protocol stack is a widely implemented example. It is covered in detail in the next section.

The TCP/IP protocol stack

The TCP/IP protocol stack, which is used in most modern network transmission, is named after two of the protocols it contains, although it also contains many others. The diagram in Figure 9.12 shows the four key layers of the TCP/IP stack:

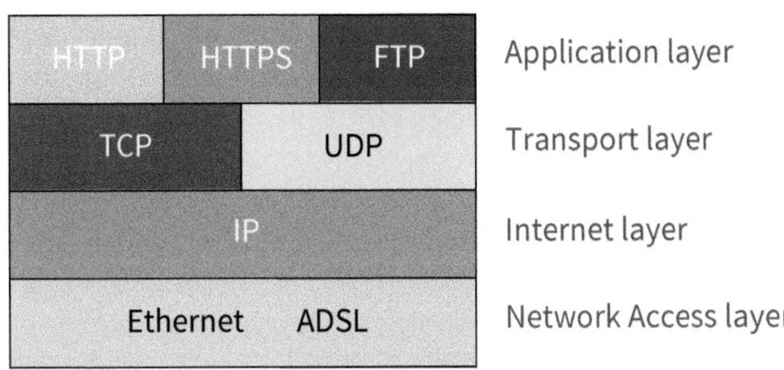

Figure 9.12: TCP/IP protocol stack.

At each layer there is a choice of which protocol to use. Each choice provides a different service, which will add different information to the packet before it is sent.

The top layer has a large number of protocols and is called the application layer. Protocols used in this layer provide network services to software and users. For example, hypertext transfer protocol (HTTP) is used to transport webpages, while file transfer protocol (FTP) is used to send files over a network. The transport layer has two protocols in the TCP/IP stack: the transmission control protocol (TCP) and the user datagram protocol (UDP). The difference between these is that TCP provides reliable delivery of packets, whereas UDP is unreliable but with fewer overheads. HTTP and FTP packets are both delivered reliably using TCP. The internet protocol (IP) sits at the internet layer. It is responsible for delivering packets and providing a logical addressing system, the IP address. Routing also occurs at this layer. The lowest layer known as network access. All physical protocols sit at this layer, including ADSL and Ethernet.

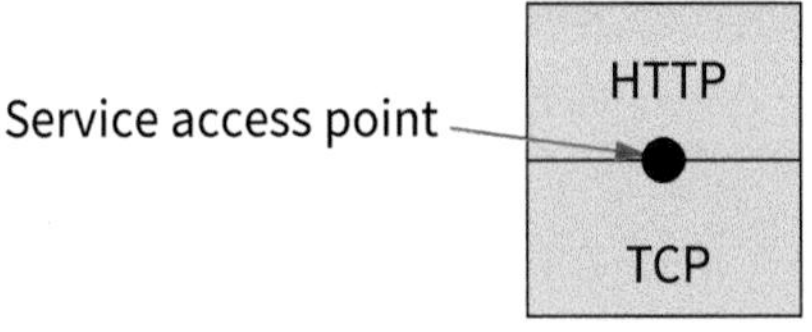

Figure 9.13: SAP.

A service access point (SAP) is a logical point in a layer that allows one protocol to request the services of a protocol in the adjacent layer. This acts as an interface between layers.

Figure 9.14 shows how elements of the TCP/IP protocol stack communicate. The principle applies equally to other protocol stacks.

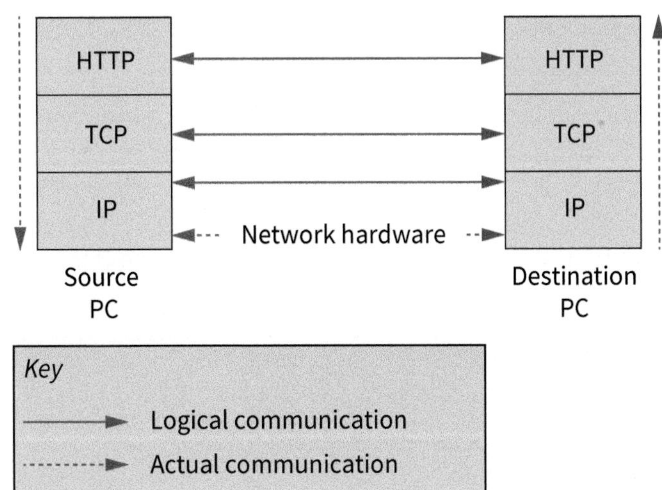

Figure 9.14: Packets travel through different layers of the stack.

Each protocol considers that it communicates directly with its counterpart on the destination machine, and it does so by adding data to a packet's header for its counterpart to read. However, what actually occurs is that information is passed down each protocol, with data being added to the packet's header as it goes, before being placed on the network medium, which transports it. At the destination, the packet is passed back up the protocol stack, with each protocol removing a part of the header. The actual path that a packet will travel is denoted by the dashed line shown in Figure 9.14.

Application layer

The application layer contains the most protocols which provide a wide range of network services. They also mark the interface between the network and the client device's software. For example, a web browser is the software that a user will access to use HTTP to retrieve web pages from a server.

HTTP

HTTP allows web pages, including their text and images, to be transmitted over the network. Each page is identified using a URL (uniform resource locator), and is transmitted using TCP port 80. HTML pages are downloaded using HTTP along with any resources identified within it. The web browser then interprets the HTML code and displays the webpage. HTTP is a stateless protocol, meaning that each HTTP request is independent. No data is recorded between requests. This makes interactive websites and web apps more difficult to program, which is why other technologies, such as sessions and AJAX (Asynchronous JavaScript and XML), are becoming common on websites, as they overcome this shortcoming of HTTP.

When an HTTP request is sent, it is structured in the following way:

- initial line
- header line 1
- header line 2 ...
- optional message.

The initial line is different if this is a request to, or a response from, the server. When a request for a resource is sent to the web server, it might look like the line below:

Code

```
GET /path/to/file/index.html HTTP/1.0
```

'GET' instructs the server to send a file, which is pointed to by the path, which is the URL with the host name taken off. The last part refers to which version of the HTTP protocol should be used. The server may respond with a code. Should a problem arise when it tries to send the resource back, this code can be used in diagnosis. Some of the more common codes include:

- 200 – OK!
- 404 – File not found
- 302 – Resource has moved
- 500 – Server error.

Header information is sent, which includes information about the browser and other general-purpose information that will be used by the server. A lot of this information is used for statistical purposes by the web server, such as recording the most common browser type. The message is the data to be sent back, which will be the contents of the file.

HTTPS

Hypertext transfer protocol secure (HTTPS) is the secured version of normal HTTP. Before communications can start, the data stream must be encrypted. HTTPS works over port 443 and uses public key 128-bit encryption to secure the data being transmitted. In order to make the process secure, it makes use of SSL (secure socket layer) and certificates.

Certificates are issued by a trusted third party to web servers to correctly identify that server. The certificate includes the public key of that server and is used for verification purposes. The process for SSL is:

1. The user makes a request over port 443 and the server sends its public key back.
2. The browser checks the public key against the certificate for that site. This may include connecting to a third party to request the certificate.
3. If the keys match, the user sends its own public key to the server.
4. The server generates a number using the user's public key and again, separately, using the server's private key. Both are sent back to the user.
5. The user then decrypts both messages using its own private key and the public key from the certificate. If the decrypted numbers match, the secure connection will have been established.

Communication, after SSL has been established, will make use of public keys for transmission of data and private keys for decrypting. At no point will the private key from either the user or the server be sent over the internet.

FTP

FTP (file transfer protocol) is used to transfer data from a server to a client or vice versa. FTP remembers information about the state of the connection; that is, each subsequent request makes use of information sent in previous requests. FTP uses port 21.

A common FTP conversation may look like this:

>> OPEN ftp.example.com

<< Which account do you want to access

>> USER bert

<< That account requires a password

>> PASS my password

<< welcome

>> CD my directory

<< DIR changed

>> LIST

<< Contents of directory myfile.txt

>> RETRIEVE myfile.txt

<< File sent

Transport layer

The transport layer focuses on how packets will be transported, without looking at the route they will take. There are only two options at the transport layer and they are very different from one another. Most data communication occurs using TCP, for reasons that will become clear.

TCP

TCP provides reliable and error-checked streams of packets over a network and is the core transport protocol for HTTP. Each set of data sent using TCP, known as an octet, contains a checksum generated using CRC. A sequence number is also included, so that the stream of packets can be reorganised in the correct order at the destination. Port numbers, both source and destination, are included, so that the packet can be correctly delivered to the corresponding application. For example, HTTP uses port 90, SMTP (Simple Mail Transport Protocol) uses port 25 and FTP uses ports 20 and 21. Client connects are dynamically assigned port numbers which uniquely identify the connection.

In order for a packet to be accepted, an acknowledgement field is included in TCP. This is simply the highest sequence number of the last accepted packet. This enables the source to resend data should packets get lost or damaged.

UDP

The user datagram protocol (UDP) provides an unreliable communication channel with a minimal level of features. There is no error checking, ordering of packets or resending of lost packets. UDP is commonly seen as a fire-and-forget protocol. On face value, this may not seem very useful, but UDP has a number of advantages. As it does not use any checksums or ordering, less data has to be sent with each packet, which makes better use of the bandwidth. Also, as there is less processing involved, data will be passed back to the application much faster. Applications that require data fast, but are not concerned about losing data along the way, are better served by UDP. An example protocol that uses UDP is the routing information protocol (RIP). Routers send regular updates about networks that they have learned about. These are sent by default every 30 seconds. If one RIP message gets lost, another will be sent in 30 seconds' time, so reliability is not a priority. For this reason, RIP uses UDP at the transport layer.

Internet layer

The internet layer consists of just one protocol, the internet protocol (IP). IP uses an end-to-end principle wherein each node and link is considered to be unreliable. Each node on the network will take part in routing, with no single central routing device. If one router goes down, the current host will try to route the packet along a different path. IP uses packet switching.

Network access layer

This layer provides data transfer across the physical link (see the next section on networking hardware).

IP address

In order for computers to talk to one another, each one must have a unique address, known as an IP address. An IPv4 address is made up of a set of four octets (group of 8 binary bits) represented by decimal numbers between 0 to 255, such as 192.168.0.1. This format is called dotted decimal. When data is transmitted over a network, the IP address of both the sender and the receiver must be included in the data packet. The destination IP address is needed to ensure that each packet can be routed to the correct destination. The source IP address must be included so that information can be sent back. Most networking communication takes the form of a request and a response, so without the source IP the response can't be sent back to the correct destination.

Computing in context: running out of IP addresses

Each device connected to the internet must have a unique IP address. This uniqueness applies across the world, not just in a single country, which raises a massive problem: there are a limited number of IP addresses available. Version 4 of the internet protocol (IP), which uses four bytes to represent a single address, has a maximum of 4 294 967 296 or 2^{32} unique addresses. This value may seem huge, but considering that the world population is about 7.15 billion (7 150 000 000), not everyone on the planet can be connected at the same time. Matters are made much worse by the fact that an individual may be using multiple devices connected to the internet at the same time, and every computer at work or at school must also have an IP address; it is easy to see how the number of addresses can run out.

This problem has been known for some time and steps have been taken to resolve it and to enable more devices to be connected, for example, smart home appliances:

- *Dynamic IP addresses*: Most devices connected to the internet do not have a fixed IP address, known as a static address, but rather a dynamic one. When a device connects to the internet, an IP address is assigned to it by the internet service provider (ISP). ISPs have a set of addresses assigned to them, which they use for their clients. A request is sent to a DHCP (dynamic host configuration protocol) server, which assigns an IP address. By issuing IP addresses on demand and leasing them for a limited time period, they can be recycled.
- *Network address translation (NAT)*: Private LANs can share a smaller number of external IP addresses sufficient for their servers and router ports to connect to the internet by using network address translation, also known as IP masquerading. Each private LAN has an internal IP address range, allowing it to use as many IP addresses as needed using ranges within the reserved or private address space. These include the entire 10.0.0.0, 172.16.0.0 and 192.168.0.0 networks. These are not permitted for use on the internet and are reserved for private LAN use. When connecting to the internet, these addresses must be translated to the external IP address. This WAN address is usually provided by an ISP. A router holds a table of these IP address translations so that responses can be mapped to be returned to the sender. This effectively allows an entire LAN, such as a school might have, to share a single IP address. This is also called NAT with overload or port address translation (PAT). Modern home routers also use NAT to allow a single IP address to be shared by all connected devices. The additional advantage of NAT is that the internal addresses are hidden from the internet, as only the WAN port address is visible. This can enhance security.
- NAT with overload works by changing the TCP/UDP port numbers of the source IP address. In the image below, three computers in a private LAN each have their own IP

addresses. When they connect to the internet, these addresses are translated using NAT into the external IP, with each computer having a unique port number. When the response comes back, NAT uses the unique port numbers to translate the address back to the original private IP address.

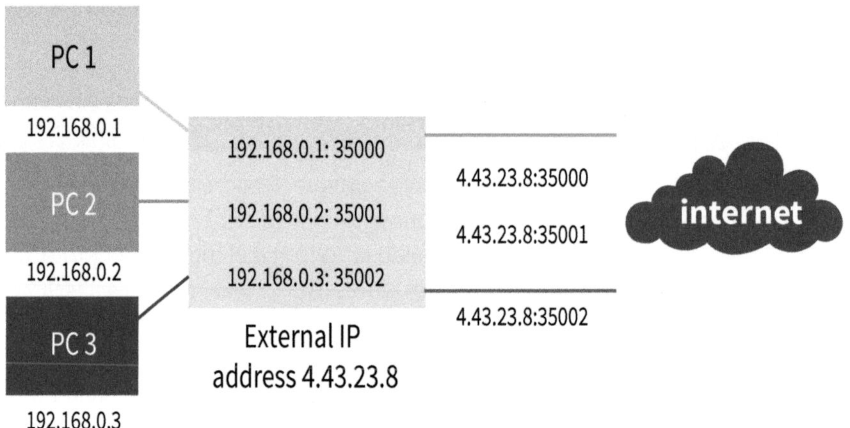

IP version 6: Unfortunately, even with the use of NAT with overload and reserved addresses, the internet is still running out of IPv4 addresses. The solution has been to develop a version of IP with a much greater address space. IPv6 uses 128-bit addresses (compared to IPv4s 32 bits). This gives a maximum IP address range of 3.4×10^{38} as opposed to 4.3×10^{9}. This may seem like an obvious solution, but the problem is that devices that use version 4 do not necessarily work with version 6. Protocols have been developed to translate between the two versions to allow networks to adapt to the changeover. On a LAN this is a relatively simple process, as a DHCP server can easily be switched to run IPv6 and routers can be configured to support both address formats. On the internet, this is potentially a must bigger problem to solve. As we write in 2016, just less than 25% of addresses assigned in the UK are using IPv6.

Activity 9.1

This task requires you to use Linux. This can be done by installing a Linux distribution of your choice, using a Raspberry Pi or using a virtual machine. The commands listed below will not work on a Windows computer.

1. Run the command **ifconfig -a** and write down the MAC address and the IP address of your current computer.
2. Run the command **dig ocr.org.uk +short**. What does this command do?
3. Install **traceroute** (**sudo apt-get install traceroute**).
4. Run the command **traceroute www.ocr.org.uk.** Explain the output of this command.
5. Run the command **netstat -a**. Explain the result of this output.

Read over the tutorial here for programming sockets in Python. A socket is a programming term for making and using a network connection.

Domain name system (DNS)

When accessing webpages or other internet-based resources it is common to use a URL (uniform resource locator). This is useful for humans because remembering the IP addresses of your favourite websites is rather onerous. However, an IP address is usually in the format of decimal numbers which represent their binary equivalent that is readable by computers. A typical URL can be broken down into a number of key parts, as shown in the diagram below. It is much more intuitive to use a URL when accessing internet resources.

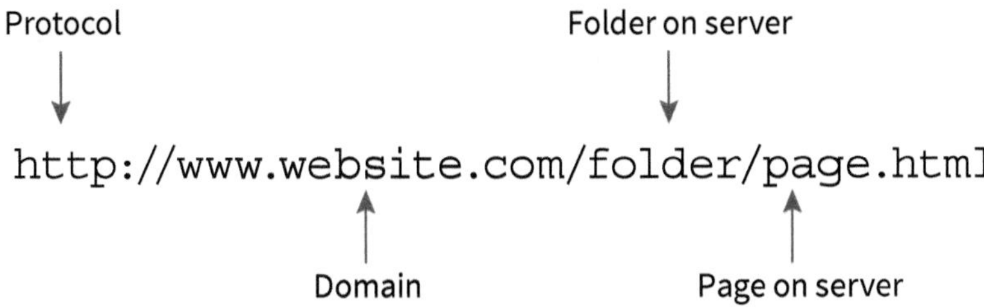

Figure 9.15: The component parts of a URL

When computers communicate over the internet they will use IP addresses. Every time a URL is typed into the address bar of a user's web browser, for example www.ocr.org.uk, it must be converted into an IP address before network communication can occur. This is done by using the protocol DNS (domain name system).

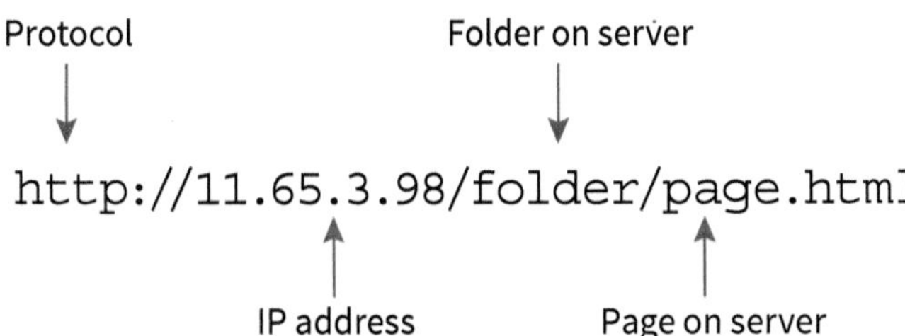

Figure 9.16: URL after domain name lookup has occurred.

In order to understand how the domain name system works it is important to understand the structure of a domain name. Top-level domains can be geographic, like UK or FR (France), or could be non-geographic, for example COM or ORG.

Domain name resolution, is done through distributed computing. If there was only one domain name server in the world then it would quickly become overloaded and if it failed, the world wide web would become inaccessible to anyone who did not know the website's IP address. When you connect to a website at home, the first DNS server that will be contacted will be owned by your ISP. Every ISP has one or two name servers, which are already configured into your broadband router. If by chance the ISP DNS server cannot resolve the domain name, it can forward the query to another server. In this way, a hierarchical structure of DNS servers supports user requests from around the web. Of course, if the user made a mistake and typed in www.ocrr.org.uk this could not be resolved to an IP address. When the final DNS server in the hierarchy has been queried and the domain name still cannot be resolved, an error is reported.

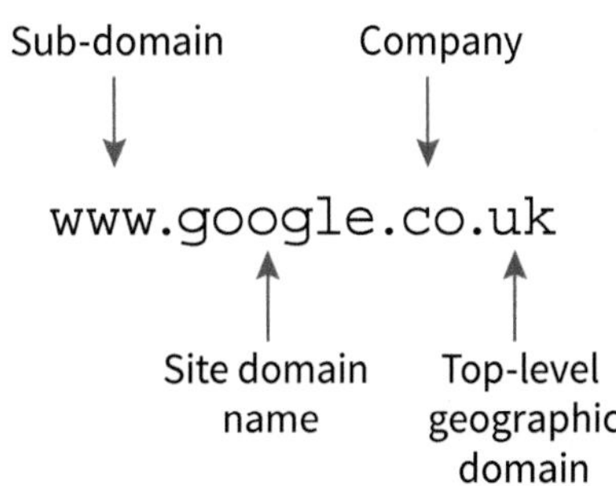

Figure 9.17: The anatomy of a domain name.

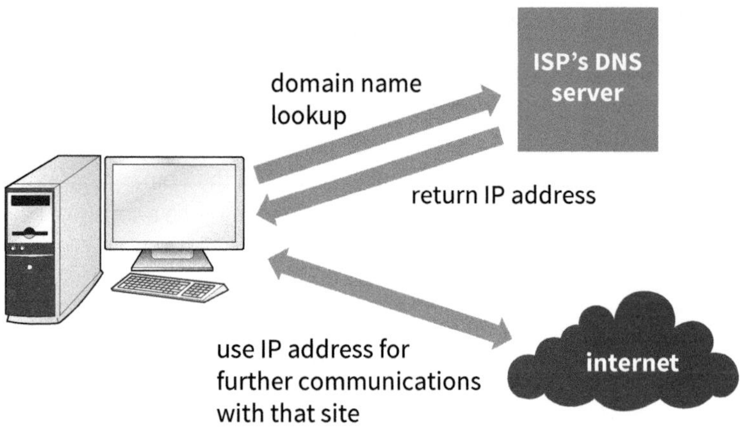

domain name lookup
ISP's DNS server
return IP address
use IP address for further communications with that site
internet

Figure 9.18: Finding the IP address of a website.

Every domain name system server will contain a database of domain names and associated IP addresses. If the server has the domain you are trying to look up in its database then it will immediately return the IP address (Figure 9.18). However, there is a chance that the server does not have the domain in its records. This could be because it is not accessed very often, the website is new or the IP address has changed. When a DNS server does not have the domain name then it will contact another DNS server and then cache the result for a limited time. It could also be the case that the cache entry for that lookup is stale.

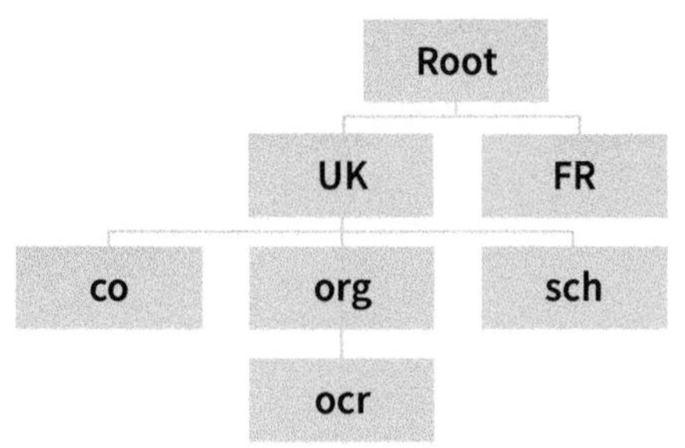

Root
UK
FR
co
org
sch
ocr

Figure 9.19: DNS, a hierarchy of servers.

Domain servers can cache each other's results but are also responsible for maintaining lists of domains themselves. The primary DNS server for a particular domain is called the authoritative name server and will have a record in its database called the state of authority (SOA) record, which gives information about the domain to other DNS servers. When a DNS server needs to contact another server to help with the resolution of a domain name then it could contact the top-level domains, which are also known as root servers, or it can contact the domain's authoritative name server and access the SOA record. The DNS server structure can be thought of as a hierarchy of servers, as shown in Figure 9.19. DNS resolution starts at the bottom of the hierarchy and will work its way up to the root server. If no server has a record of the domain being looked up then the lookup will fail.

Consider the resolution of www.ocr.org.uk. If the ISP DNS server did not have a record of this domain then the authoritative name server's SOA record at ocr.org.uk should have it. If that server also did not know about the domain, eventually we will reach the root server that maintains all UK records.

It is not the case that the higher up the hierarchy you go the more domains are stored in their databases. Each server is responsible for managing a set of domains, which is why they are referred to as a start of authority. In practice this means that a resolution may need to contact multiple servers. This is very common when sub-domains are used. A sub-domain is where a domain can be split into multiple smaller domains to allow quicker access to specific resources or services.

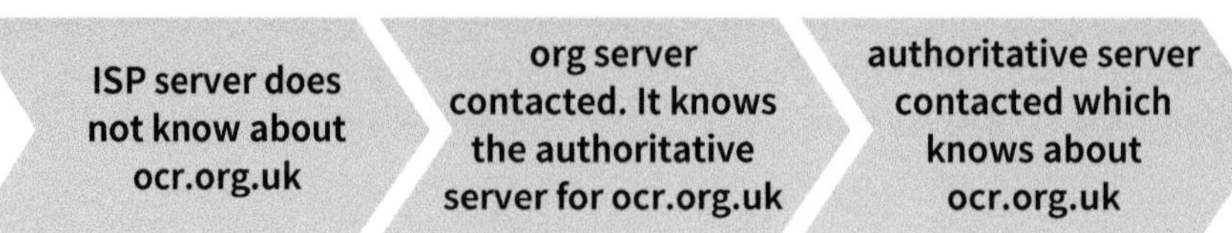

ISP server does not know about ocr.org.uk
org server contacted. It knows the authoritative server for ocr.org.uk
authoritative server contacted which knows about ocr.org.uk

Figure 9.20: Order of DNS requests for sub-domains.

Once the SOA record is found for a specific domain then it can be interrogated to find out about the sub-domains. It is only when we get to the SOA record from a domain's authoritative name server, which contains details of the sub-domains, that we arrive at the final IP address.

Networking hardware

In order to connect computers together into a network, certain hardware is required.

Network interface card

In order for a computer to connect to a computer network, it needs a special piece of hardware called a network interface card or NIC. This hardware is responsible for placing packets onto network cables in the form of electronic signals, or pulses of light if the cable is optical. NICs produce electric signals that are changed (modulated) to encode the data onto it based on the physical protocol being used on the network. One of the most common data transmission systems used on LANs and the internet is Ethernet. NICs tend to be built into most modern motherboards, so extra hardware is not needed.

Wireless interface cards, or WICs, are needed if the connection to the network is wireless. Most devices have WICs built onto their motherboards, with the exception of desktop computers. Wireless networks make use of the 802.11.x protocol, often called WiFi, rather than Ethernet. Again, this is a physical protocol and uses electromagnetic waves in the radio frequency band to transmit data. Every network adapter, whether it is wired or wireless, will contain a unique physical address or MAC address. MAC stands for media access control. This consists of 48 bits written as 12 hexadecimal digits. Half of the bits indicate which company made the adapter and the other half form a unique serial number.

Hub

A hub allows more than one computer to be interconnected in a network by connecting them all into one central device. When using a hub, each computer uses a single cable to connect, which ultimately creates a path between each computer. If a single cable breaks, it affects only the computer connected to the hub rather than the entire network. When a packet is sent to a hub, it will broadcast it to all other connected devices. A single hub can have up to 48 computers connected (more if stacked together). If 48 computers were connected to a single hub, then, when a packet arrived, that packet would be repeated to all connected computers.

Hubs work well for small networks with low network traffic, but the more computers connected, the more traffic will be generated. The area shared by all connected computers is called a collision domain. Within this area, packets can and do collide. This happens when two computers transmit data at the same time. A part of the Ethernet protocol called carrier sense multiple access with collision detect (CSMA/CD) detects that this has occurred and a jam signal is sent. Both transmitting computers back off and wait for a random amount of time before attempting to transmit again. On busy networks, collisions can cause a serious reduction in network throughput. For this reason, it is always advisable to keep collision domains as small as possible.

Switch

One solution to the problem of collisions was to use an intelligent hub called a switch. Rather than repeating the network signal out of all ports, the switch learns the MAC addresses of all devices connected to it. It then examines the destination MAC address in the packet header and decides which port it needs to forward it out of. In this way, it is as if the two devices were directly connected together and the collision domain only consists of each computer's connection. As a result, ports on a switch can be configured to operate in full duplex mode, which allows packet to be sent and received at the same time, increasing throughput even more. Modern LANs are based around switches.

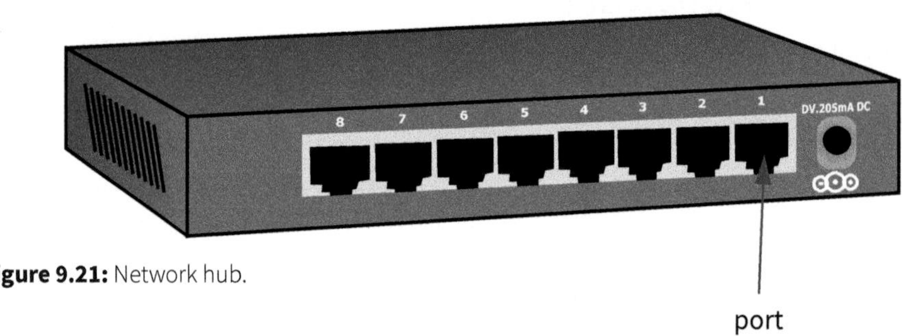

Figure 9.21: Network hub.

Port number	MAC address
1	00:00:AE:3B:09:FF
2	00:00:4B:BC:00:E1
3	00:1A:D7:B6:CA:F2

Table 9.2: Table showing the MAC address of devices connected on various ports of a switch.

When a new switch is connected to a network, its MAC address table will be empty. When it boots up, a switch will read the source MAC address of packets it receives and associate that address with the port that it received it on. It continues this process until it has learned what it connected to each port. This is why it is possible to unplug one device from a switch port and immediately plug in another. Within a fraction of a second, the switch will have learned its address. A sample table is shown in Table 9.2.

Router

Switches connect computers to the network but routers connect networks to other networks. They perform two actions: to determine the best route that a packet should take and to switch the packet from the inbound port to the outbound port. Routers store information about which networks are connected to its ports in a routing table. Routers share their routing table with other routers by sending out updates regularly. One routing protocol that is part of the TCP/IP protocol stack is called the routing information protocol (RIP), which sends out updates every 30 seconds by default. In this way, routers learn about more networks other than those that are directly connected. Your home router only really needs to know how to connect to your ISP. This is called a static route because it will be configured into the router and no updates are required.

Routers perform routing on IP addresses rather than MAC addresses. In a larger enterprise network, sections of a network, known as IP subnets, can be assigned ranges similar to IP address ranges to create a hierarchical address structure for routing internally. When routers have learned about a large number of networks, they need to perform calculations using a routing protocol, to decide which is the best path to choose. RIP counts how many routers away the destination network is in 'hops'. Where there is a choice of paths to the destination, RIP will always choose the lowest number of hops as the preferred path.

> **Tip**
>
> One of the key differences between a switch and a router, which is covered in the exam, is the fact that routers connect networks to other networks (or subnets) but switches connect computers to a LAN. Routers base forwarding decisions on IP addresses, whereas switches use MAC addresses.

Wireless interface card

A wireless interface card (WIC) connects to a wireless access point (WAP). A WAP is a device that allows wireless devices to connect to a wired network using Wi-Fi or similar standard. A WAP has a maximum number of devices that it can support and a physical broadcast range where connections are possible. It is possible to pick up a wireless network by sitting outside a company's premises, which is why security on a wireless network is a top priority.

Wireless networks use encryption and require a special key in order to stop unauthorised people accessing the network. Home routers are also known as integrated services routers (ISRs) because they normally offer a wireless connection and tend to have security set up by default. This is intended to protect data sent over the network but the level of protection is only as strong as the encryption methods used. Some wireless security protocols, such as wired equivalent privacy (WEP), uses a static key and originally only 40-bit encryption, which can be can be cracked very easily by a determined hacker using easily available software. WiFi Protected Access version 2 (WPA2) is one of the more secure wireless protocols available at present for home use, as it uses a key that changes in value making it very difficult for a hacker to break. Additionally, WPA2 allows the use of 256-bit encryption using the Advanced Encryption Standard (AES), which is very difficult to crack.

Wireless networks minimise the amount of cable needed, but can be tricky to set up to provide a consistent, high-quality connection in all areas. Distance from the router, interference from other devices and even bad weather can impact the speed and quality of connection. When a wireless signal is low quality, packets may contain errors and the data will need to be resent.

There are two main wireless technologies in use currently, 802.11 (WiFi) and Bluetooth. Both have their uses, but only 802.11 is used for networking. Bluetooth is used for connecting external devices, such as wireless handsets, to other devices to form a short distance personal area network (PAN)

Packet and circuit switching

A WAN such as the internet is formed of a collection of interconnected networks (Figure 9.22). There are so many connections that it will be possible for a packet to find more than one way to reach its destination. This is very similar to our road system. There are many different ways to get from one place to another. Some ways are quick and some are slow. One of the key benefits of having multiple routes is that if one route is down, because of road works or traffic, alternative routes can be found. Networks have the exact same properties and packets can have a choice of how they are routed. Packet and circuit switching are two methods of sending packets across a network with multiple paths.

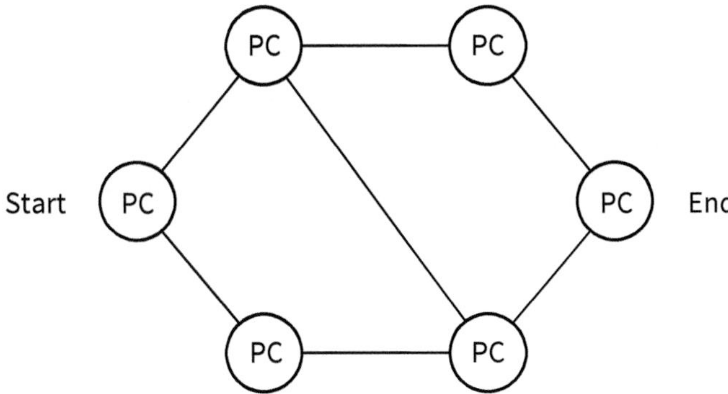

Figure 9.22: The internet.

Due to its many links, the internet is very resilient to broken lines or faults. If one line is broken, another one can be used. One issue with having so many paths is that a route needs to be worked out in order to get from one computer to another efficiently. A single packet can travel down the network in a number of different ways. Two of those ways are shown in Figure 9.23 (links travelled are shown in purple).

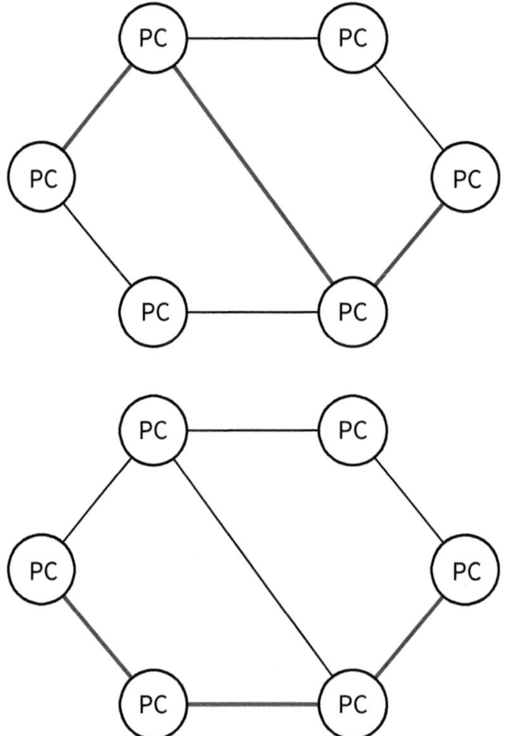

Figure 9.23: Routes of a single packet.

Originally, internet traffic used POTS technology including its hardware, which used circuit switching technology. In circuit switching, a route across the network is set up in advance and all packets are then sent down the same route. All packets, on arrival, will be in order, but the circuit is vulnerable because if any part of the route is broken, the whole circuit will fail. When a link fails, a new circuit has to be set up before further communications can take place, which could cause issues. One of the most common uses of circuit switched networks is our telephone network. When a number is dialled, a circuit is set up so that voice data can pass along it. If that link breaks, the conversation has to end and the number redialled. Another issue is that bandwidth can be wasted, as once a connection has been established, no other device can use the circuit until it is free. This is why you get an engaged tone when someone you are trying to call is already on a call. If the link is being utilised well, this may not be so much of an issue, but this is rarely the case. Lost bandwidth in a networking context can lead to slower services overall.

Packet switching allows packets to take independent routes through the network. The key device in a packet-switched network is a router. Communication using packet switching is much more resilient to failed links, because if one route is brought down, the router will seek alternatives. Packets may travel down different routes to the destination.

However, packets may not arrive in order, meaning that extra processing is required to reassemble the final message. Each packet has to be labelled with a sequence number and the destination computer will reassemble them in order to recreate the original message. This is handled by the protocol TCP. Bandwidth can be used more efficiently using packet switching, as traffic is shared between all available paths.

Tip

When considering questions on packet and circuit switching, you will normally have to explain the differences. These relate to the order of packets, how the routes are set up, how resilient they are and their use of bandwidth.

Network security

According to a government report, in 2011 the cost of cybercrime to the UK stood at £27 billion. Networking has a large number of advantages, which have already been discussed, but it also has one key drawback, which is potential security risk. There are many threats which face users of a network, and each year these threats become more and more sophisticated. Some of the key threats are:

Viruses – these are self-propagating malicious code, which can infect the target machine. When a virus strikes it can destroy files, install other malicious software or even encrypt files for ransom purposes.

Spyware – this will monitor the activities of a computer and report back to the hacker with the goal of stealing passwords and account details.

Ransomware – software that creates a scenario where the user is at a disadvantage for the purposes of extracting money from them. This could take the form of making the user believe they have a virus or slow computer and installing the hacker's software will fix the problem, or encrypting key documents so that the user cannot access them without making a payment.

Botnet/zombie computer – one of the common payloads of viruses is to install a back door to the user's computer that is kept hidden until the hacker requires use of the computer. A computer under the influence of a hacker is known as a zombie. These can be brought together to form a botnet, which the hacker can use to execute more sophisticated attacks.

Denial of service (DoS) – a hacker bombards a server with requests that prevent it from responding to legitimate requests. Whilst this attack does not steal data, it can cause inconvenience and loss of business.

Distributed denial of service (DDoS) – a botnet will flood the target server with so much data that it is forced offline. A distributed attack will be controlled by a hacker, although the owners of the zombie computers may not be aware that they are involved. The combined traffic is far more effective than a single DoS attack.

Man-in-the-middle attack – this type of attack is where a hacker intercepts data transmitted across a network. They may use software that allows them to perform packet sniffing (read the data within packets). Any data in clear text will be visible and readable. Wi-Fi links in public hotspots such as cafes and railway stations are particularly vulnerable because data may not be encrypted. Anyone accessing the network will be able to use packet sniffing software to see what interesting data is being transmitted, in particular usernames and passwords. With all of the threats linked to network use, it is important to consider how best to secure it. Most companies will employ a combination of technical solutions and employee policies. Social engineering is the process of extracting key information from a person with a view to using it to launch a hacking attack. It may be as simple as looking over a person's shoulder while they input their password or asking key questions about how a network is configured and the timing of particular routines. It is therefore crucial that companies have clear policies and training for staff so that these risks can be reduced. Additionally, security permissions including network access need to be assigned based on need and regularly reviewed.

Firewalls

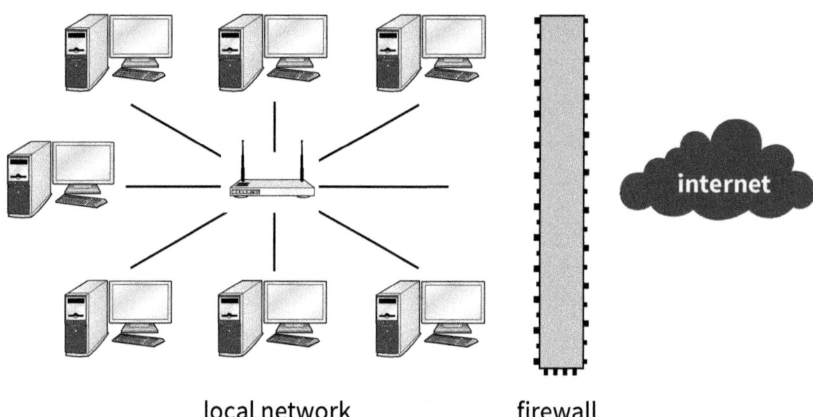

Figure 9.24: Firewalls can sit between a LAN and the internet.

A firewall is a common security precaution used by most networks and users' computers. It can take the form of software or hardware depending on the size of the network being protected. It will sit between the local network and the internet and monitor all data being sent and received. It acts as a specialised filter which will permit or deny packets.

Firewalls operate by enforcing rules, which packets must adhere to. This will include looking at:

- The source IP address.
- The protocol in use by the packet.
- What port the packet is destined for.
- Which applications are allowed to communicate with the internet.

Most networks will allow HTTP (port 80), SMTP (25) and perhaps also FTP (20 and 21) and the secure shell for secure remote connection SSH (22) packets through. However, they may restrict the applications which use them. For example, it is common for schools to only allow a single browser access to port 80 to prevent students trying to bypass security features.

When data is sent to a firewall, which is then blocked, the firewall will log that security breach. This is a good way for a network administrator to assess threats or check up on users trying to bypass security policies. Firewall rules need to be regularly reviewed to ensure that they are ready to handle new threats.

There are two main methods of packet filtering which are known as stateful (or dynamic) and stateless filtering. So far, filtering rules have been discussed with the assumption of no prior knowledge of the packet and it being treated in isolation. This is known as stateless filtering and does not look for suspicious behaviour between packets. Stateful filtering will look at packets in context and will ensure that the rules will be followed, and any packet that is exhibiting unusual behaviour will be automatically blocked. For example, when TCP connections initiate they perform a three-way handshake and then become established. One type of denial of service attack is called syn flooding.

This prevents a TCP connection from ever becoming established by continually requesting acknowledgements. Stateful packet filtering will detect this unusual behaviour and block the connection.

Proxies

Figure 9.25: Proxy servers sit between the user and the web resource they want to access.

A proxy server sits between the end user and the web resource they wish to access. The user will send requests to the proxy, which will then forward on the request. When the message returns, the proxy will pass the data back to the end client. As far as the web server is concerned the request came from the proxy, which in effect hides the details of the end user. It is possible to use proxies to bypass filters set up in a local network (Figure 9.26).

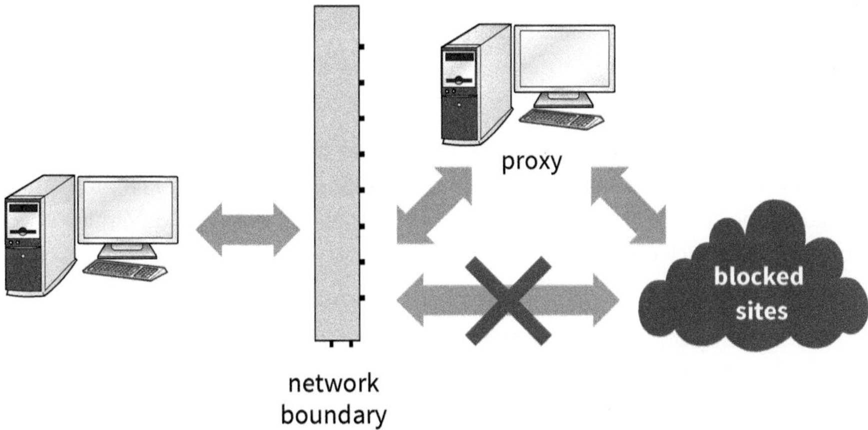

Figure 9.26: Using a proxy server to access blocked sites.

There are millions of proxy websites on the internet but they all have the same key drawback. As it is a server which is outside of your control, it can open up security threats to your network. A lot of proxy sites will inject advertisements into the sites you view as well as potentially carrying malware. They can also monitor traffic and act as spyware. It is not advisable to use proxy websites on the web.

Proxies do have a number of legitimate uses within a network. They allow network administrators to filter and monitor internet traffic easily. All data that passes through the proxy can be blocked or be logged. Proxies allow for greater internal network security by preventing users from accessing known sites which contain viruses or inappropriate material (Figure 9.27).

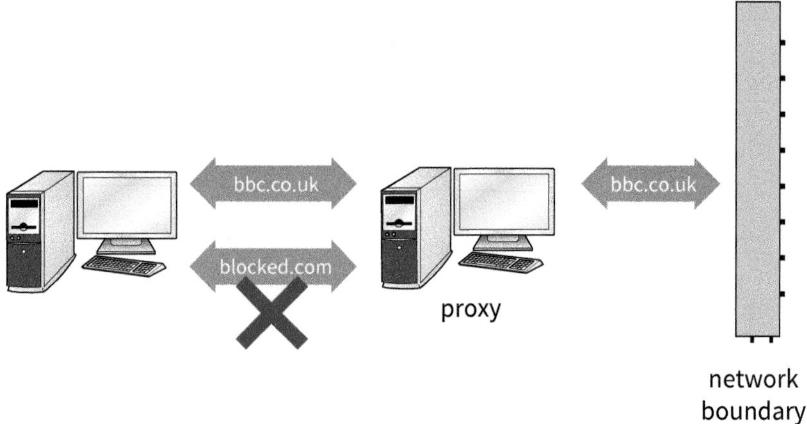

Figure 9.27: Proxy servers can be used to filter network traffic.

Encryption

This section will explore how encryption is used on a network and why it is important rather than how encryption works. In order to fully understand encryption it is advised you read Chapter 7.

When accessing the internet it is common for packets to travel across numerous networking devices. This means that every packet sent over the internet is susceptible to a man-in-the-middle attack. When information is sent via plain text then any device in the route can read and potentially exploit the data. This can be a serious issue if the rogue computer not only reads the data, but also changes it on the way back. That could potentially give the end user false reports on their bank statements, for example.

Encryption, as you will have read in Chapter 7, hides the plain text and sends cipher text instead. Without the key it is not possible to turn the cipher text back to plain text without trying to guess the key using a brute force attack. The size of the key will determine how long a brute-force attack will take.

Encryption can only work if the sharing of keys is kept secret. The second the key is sent over the network, any computer along the route will potentially have access to it. To solve this issue asymmetric encryption is used. This uses a public and private key. Although the public key is sent across the internet, the private key is never transmitted. The most common way of securing data over the internet is to use secure socket layers (SSL). To learn more about SSL, read the section in this chapter about HTTPS.

Summary

- Networks rely on the use of protocols and standards to ensure that communication between devices can occur even if those devices were produced by different companies.
- Client–server-based architecture is where a powerful computer (known as a server) provides functionality to the rest of the network (a service). This can include providing files, websites or databases.
- Peer-to-peer networks have no server; rather, each computer has the same status as the other. These networks are commonly used for file sharing.
- When data is transmitted over a network it is broken down into packets. Each packet will have a header and footer attached which is generated by the protocols employed to transmit that packet.

- Transmission mode signifies which direction packets can travel at any given time:
    - full duplex: transmit and receive simultaneously
    - half duplex: transmit and receive but only one way at a time
    - simplex: one direction only.
- Bit rate is the measure of how much data can be transmitted in a second. Measured as Mbps, or megabits per second.
- Error detection ensures that packets arrive at their destination without corruption. Common error-detection methods include:
    - parity bits: adding additional bits to make the number of ones odd or even, depending on the type chosen
    - echo: packets are returned from the destination and then compared by the sender
    - checksum: calculations are performed on the packet generating a value that is sent with the packet; this calculation is repeated upon receipt and the checksums compared.
- Protocols are a set of rules that govern communication.
- Handshaking is a process that devices undertake when a connection is set up. This is where the set of protocols to be used is agreed.
- Protocol stacks describe the whole communication process but each layer has different protocols that can be used. The interface between layers passes data up the stack. Packets have data added by each layer in a header or footer.
- Transmission control protocol/internet protocol (TCP/IP) stack is the most common protocol stack used in networking.
- Hypertext transfer protocol (HTTP) is used for the transmission of webpages and webpage components. HTTP uses port 80.
- HTTPS (secured) is a secure version of HTTP and communicates over port 443. Certificates and the secure sockets layer (SSL) protocol are used to secure communication.
- File transfer protocol (FTP) uses ports 20 and 21 and allows files to be transmitted.
- The transport layer of TCP/IP uses either TCP or UDP:
    - TCP provides reliable communication with error detection, ordering of packets and confirmation that packets have been received.
    - UDP (user datagram protocol) is a fire-and-forget approach with minimal protections.
- IP is a network layer protocol that provides logical addressing. IP is unreliable and relies on routing protocols to determine the best path to the destination. The domain name system (DNS) will translate uniform resource locators (URL) into IP addresses.
- Domain name resolution is done through a hierarchical set of servers. Requests start at the bottom of the hierarchy and work their way up until a server knows about the domain being looked up.

- Common networking hardware includes:
    - network interface card: allows a computer to connect to the network
    - hub: connects multiple computers and packets are broadcast to all connected devices
    - switch: allows multiple devices to be connected and provides switching by media access control (MAC) address
    - router: connects different networks together and uses IP addresses for routing; commonly used to connect to the internet.

- Packet switching is where each packet will take an independent route through a network.
- Circuit switching is where all packets will follow the same route.
- Firewalls come in the form of either software or hardware. They will block access to certain ports and IP addresses and are used to restrict network access.
- Proxy servers sit in the middle of communication and redirect traffic. Destination computers will be unaware that a proxy was used.

End-of-chapter questions

1 Explain the purpose of each of the following networking hardware.

a hub [2]

b switch [2]

c router [2]

2 Describe, using examples, how bit rate can impact the downloading of files. [4]

3 Explain the following data transmission modes.

a simplex [2]

b duplex [2]

c parallel [2]

4 A set of bytes have been sent across a network using an error correcting code.

0101 1111 **0**

1100 1001 **0**

1110 1000 **1**

0110 0111 **1**

0100 1001

a Explain, using an example in the data above, how parity bits are calculated. [2]

b One of the bits is wrong. Which bit contains the error and describe how this error correcting code works. [2]

5 Describe, using specific protocol examples, the TCP/IP protocol stack. [8]

Further reading

OSI model (reference model for networking) – search on the Tech FAQ website.
HTTP protocol (request fields definition) – search on w3.org.
Microsoft introduction to TCP/IP – search on the Microsoft TechNet website.
Socket programming introduction in Python – search on the Codingtree website.

Chapter 10
Web technologies

Specification points

1.3.4 Web technologies

- HTML, CSS and JavaScript.
- Search engine indexing.
- PageRank algorithm.
- Server-side and client-side processing.

Learning objectives

- To appreciate the difference between the world wide web and the internet.
- To have a basic understanding of HTML, CSS and JavaScript.
- To understand search engine indexing and the PageRank algorithm.
- To understand server-side and client-side processing.

What is the world wide web and how does it work?

The world wide web (WWW) is a collection of all the webpages on the internet. The WWW is not the same as the internet; the internet is a network of interconnected computers which supports the WWW, among other things. The web is just one of the components of the internet. You can learn more about how the internet works in Chapter 9.

Webpages on the internet are stored on servers. These are essentially powerful computers, parts of the file system of which are publicly accessible. Files or objects such as images, videos, sounds, animations and webpages are all available from servers via unique addresses.

Tip

There is a lot of crossover in this chapter with the networking technologies covered in Chapter 9. Make sure you can link the relevant aspects together.

To access a webpage from a personal computer, you need a web browser such as Google Chrome or Mozilla Firefox. Web browsers are used to fetch webpages from a server and present them to the user. Different web browsers work in different ways, which is why some websites look different depending on the browser you are using to view them.

Web browsers communicate with servers using HTTP (Figure 10.1). HTTP defines how clients must ask for objects and how servers must respond. HTTP uses TCP/IP as its underlying protocol (see Chapter 9 for more details).

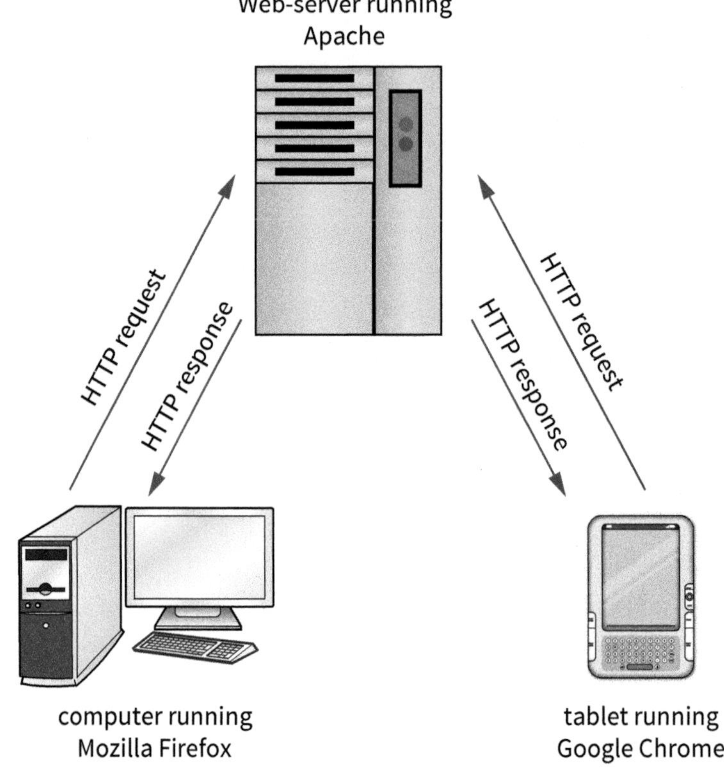

Figure 10.1: Web browsers can be used to access content from web servers.

When you enter the unique address of a website, called a URL, in your browser, it first finds the server, then the individual file on that server and returns it to your machine. Look at this address: http://www.ocr.org.uk/index.html

The first part of the address tells the browser what protocol to use, the 'www' that begins the second part tells the browser that it should look in the world wide web, the rest of the second part points to the server and the final part to the html file that you want.

The part of the web address that follows 'www' (in this case 'ocr.org.uk) is called the domain name. Domain names are stored in a huge look-up table on a name server, a component of the domain name system (DNS). The DNS record holds the domain name and the IP address of the server holding that website. When you enter a domain name, your browser first asks the name server for the IP address related to the domain name, then accesses the server using the address it receives. You could access the server directly by entering the IP address (192.149.119.226) straight into your browser, but 'ocr.org.uk' is easier to remember.

Computing in context: Tim Berners-Lee

Tim Berners-Lee is a British computer scientist who invented the world wide web while he was working at CERN in the late 1980s, to enable him to share information with other researchers. He was the first person to use HTTP to share information between a client and a server. The world's first website was the CERN website and mainly contained information about how to create other webpages.

Shortly after inventing the web, Tim Berners-Lee decided that its standards should be based on royalty-free technology, so that they could easily be adopted by anyone. He went on to establish the World Wide Web Consortium (W3C) to educate people about the web and its uses. This is still one of the most valuable resources for anyone trying to learn web development.

Building the web

You have already seen that the world wide web is a collection of webpages hosted on servers and accessible to clients via HTTP. Webpages are made up of many different file types, from images and videos to JavaScript files and formatting sheets. In this section you will look at three of the main technologies used to create websites. If you would like to learn more about web development, visit the W3Schools website (https://www.w3schools.com/html/), which contains thousands of editable examples from many different web-based languages.

Hypertext markup language (HTML)

Every webpage on the internet is created using a markup language called hypertext markup language (HTML). Markup languages are not programming languages. A programming language is made up of a set of instructions telling a computer's hardware what to do, while a markup language simply defines how text and images should be displayed in a web browser.

There are lots of different versions, but HTML5 offers a huge amount of extra functionality compared to its predecessors, including the ability to create animations and games without needing plugins such as Adobe Flash®.

Look at Figure 10.2. If you were given a sketch like this and asked to create a website with the same appearance, you would have no idea what to make. What fonts would you use? Which images and colours?

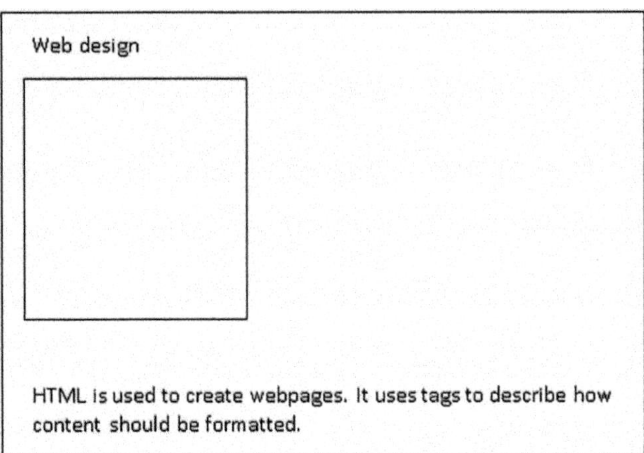

Figure 10.2: A sketch with no labels.

Now look at Figure 10.3; the image is the same but this time it is labelled. Now you have a much better idea of what needs to be created and in a better position to create the correct product. Figure 10.4 shows what the client wanted.

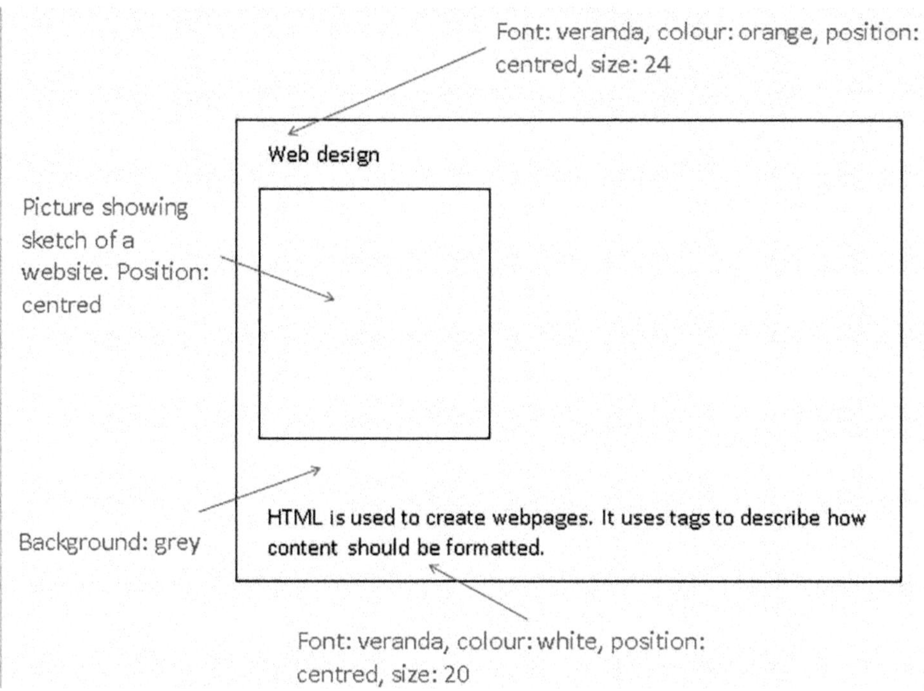

Figure 10.3: A sketch with labels.

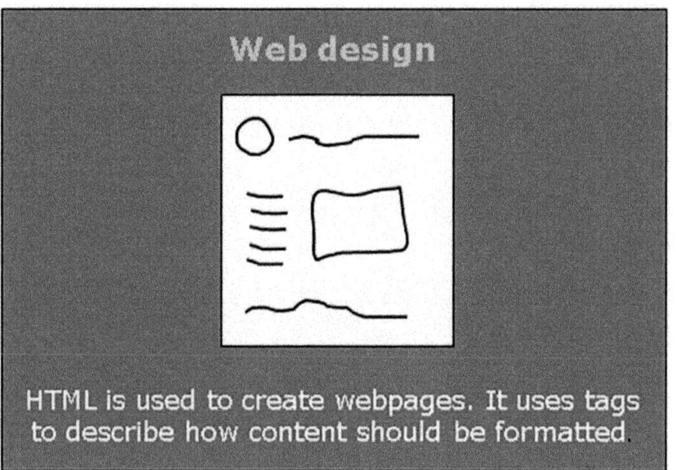

Figure 10.4: The final product.

HTML works in the same way as Figure 10.3. It is used to label text and images, telling the browser how those items should look and where they should be placed. In HTML the labels on Figure 10.3 are called tags and they surround the items to which they should be applied.

Compare the webpages in Figures 10.5 and 10.6. The webpage in Figure 10.5 contains all the information but no formatting. By adding in some HTML tags to the webpage in Figure 10.6 we are able to show the same information but formatted completely differently.

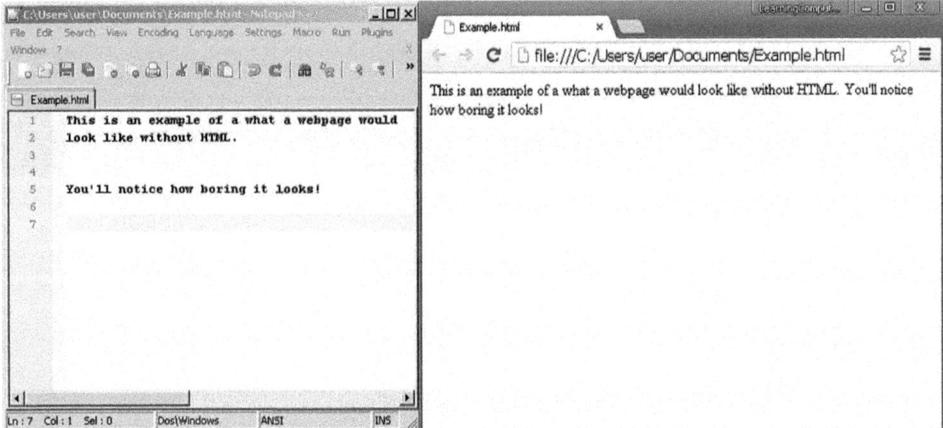

Figure 10.5: A webpage without HTML, even simple formatting is impossible.

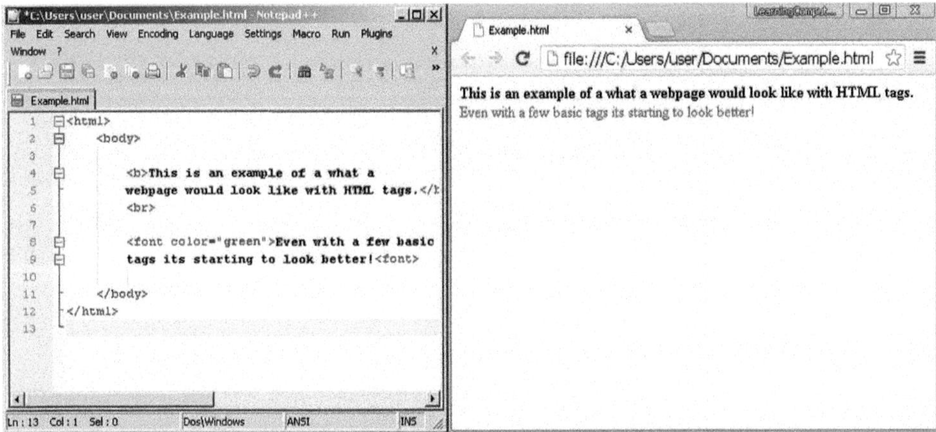

Figure 10.6: A webpage with a few HTML tags is much easier to read.

Example webpage

All HTML documents have the same structure and include the same basic elements:

Code

```
<!DOCTYPE html>
<html>
  <head>
    <meta charset="utf-8" />
  </head>
  <body>
  </body>
</html>
```

The first line in the file tells the browser that this file has been created using HTML, as shown in the code above. Most modern browsers will work this out anyway, but it's good practice to include it.

Notice that each element is opened with a *tag*, for example <html>, and closed by repeating the same tag with a forward slash in front of the letters, for example </html>.

The first tag, <html>, confirms to the browser that what follows is written in HTML. The second set of tags, <head> </head>, contain the webpage's header information.

Tip

It is unlikely that you will have to write the HTML code for an entire webpage in your exams but you should be able to identify key aspects (like tags) from a given sample.

This can contain the character set being used and links to any other files that the webpage needs. The third and final set of tags, <body> </body>, contain the webpage's content.

The order of these tags is important but white space is not; you should use white space to lay out the code in a way that is easy to read. Notice that it is good practice to indent your HTML, just as you would if you were writing in a programming language such as Python.

If you copy this HTML and save it as a webpage (.html), you'll see that nothing appears on the page when you view it in a browser. This is because all these tags are just used to provide structure to the webpage and you haven't added any content to the body, as yet.

Adding text

The HTML code in Figure 10.7 creates the webpage in Figure 10.8; notice how the <font> tags on line 9 and 11 have been used to change the appearance of the text.

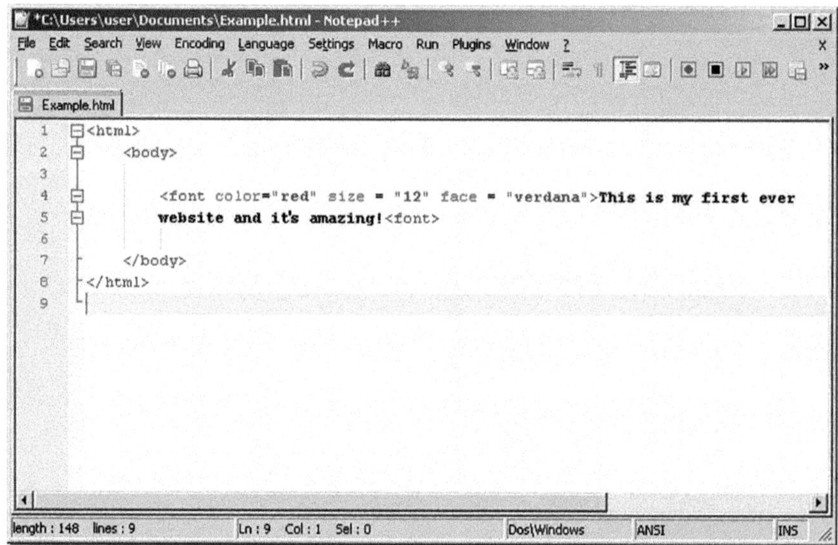

Figure 10.7: HTML code.

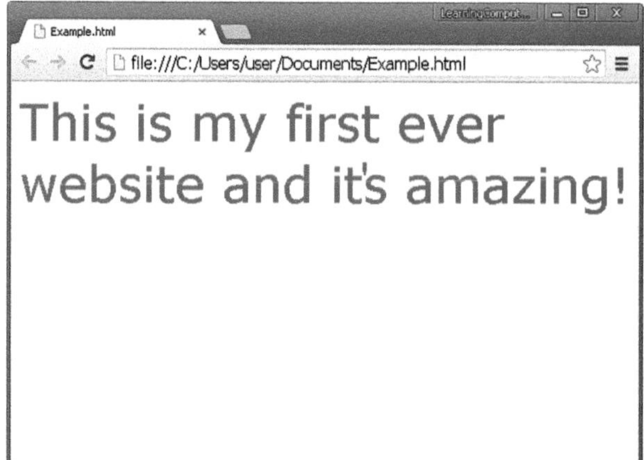

Figure 10.8: A simple webpage formatted using HTML.

Adding links to other webpages (hyperlinks)

You can add **hyperlinks** (a link to another document, usually a webpage) to your text using the <a href="site to link to">link text</a> tags.

Line 12 in Figure 10.9 creates a hyperlink to http://www.google.com.

```
<html>
    <body>

        <font color="red" size = "5" face = "verdana">This is my first ever
        website and it's amazing!<font>

        <a href="http://www.google.com">Search</a>
    </body>
</html>
```

Figure 10.9: Creating a hyperlink.

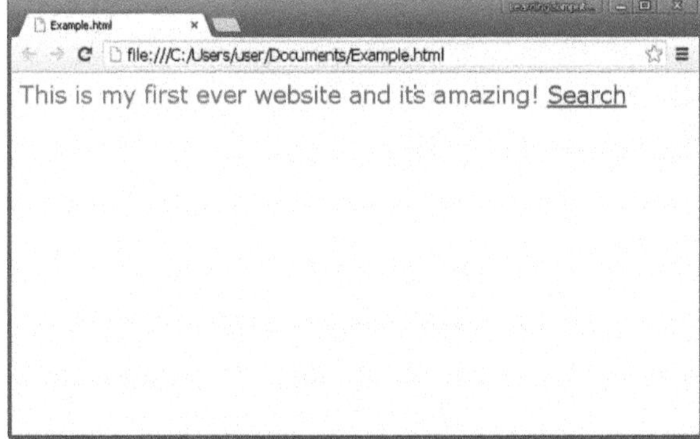

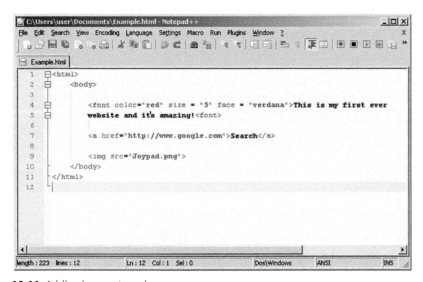

Figure 10.10: A simple webpage with a hyperlink to another page.

Adding images

You can add images to your page using the <img src="url" alt="some_text"/> tag (Figure 10.11). The URL can be the name of a file on your computer or the web address of an image online. The alternate (alt) text will be displayed if the image fails to load.

```
<html>
    <body>

        <font color="red" size = "5" face = "verdana">This is my first ever
        website and it's amazing!<font>

        <a href="http://www.google.com">Search</a>

        <img src="Joypad.png">
    </body>
</html>
```

Figure 10.11: Adding images to webpages.

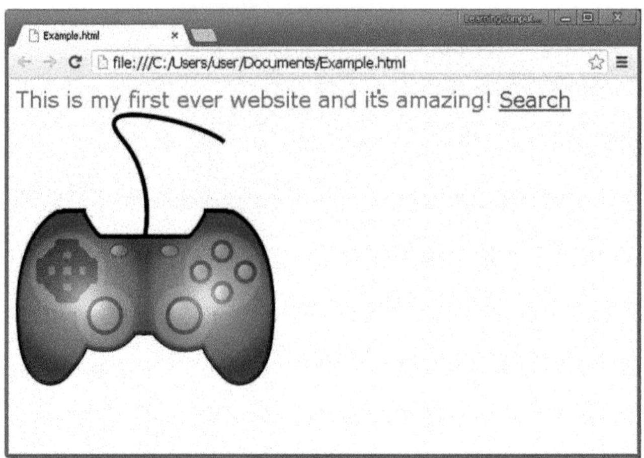

Figure 10.12: A simple webpage containing some images.

It is important that the image is in the same folder as the webpage or the site won't be able to find and display it.

This section gives you a brief overview of HTML and the structure of a typical webpage. You can learn more by following the links in the 'Further reading' section at the end of this chapter.

Cascading style sheets (CSS)

HTML has two main drawbacks. Imagine you have a website made up of hundreds of pages and you want to change the colour of the title on every page. Using HTML, this would involve loading every page individually and changing the title's colour hundreds of times – not ideal. HTML is also not great at laying out pages: you can use line breaks and alignments, even tables, but these don't give designers much flexibility. The solution to both these problems is to use cascading style sheets (CSS).

The CSS file is stored alongside the HTML webpages and contains all the formatting information about the website. The HTML tags in the webpages simply point to the relevant section of the style sheet. This means that if you want to change something on every page (for example, the background colour), you only need to change it once in the CSS file and the change will propagate through to every page in the site.

CSS also uses **div** tags to lay out a webpage. Each div tag can have its own size and location on the webpage. Think of div tags like building blocks. First you create a div for your navigation bar, then one for your content and header. Finally you create your site by combining the divs.

Figure 10.13 shows a fairly common layout for a webpage.

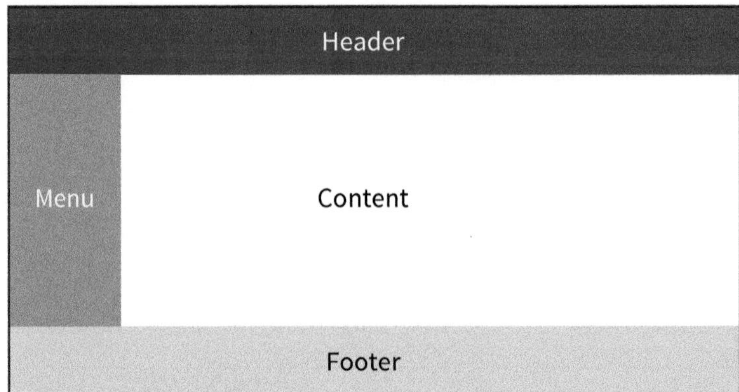

Figure 10.13: A typical website layout.

Divs have the following structure:

Code

```
<div id="name_of_div">
</div>
```

The name_of_div is important because it makes your code easy to read; for example, you could call your div 'header' or 'footer' to describe what it does.

Look at the example in Figure 10.14; notice that there is no formatting information anywhere in the HTML. Each section of the site has its own div; for example, lines 14–19 contain the menu div, which will become the navigation bar.

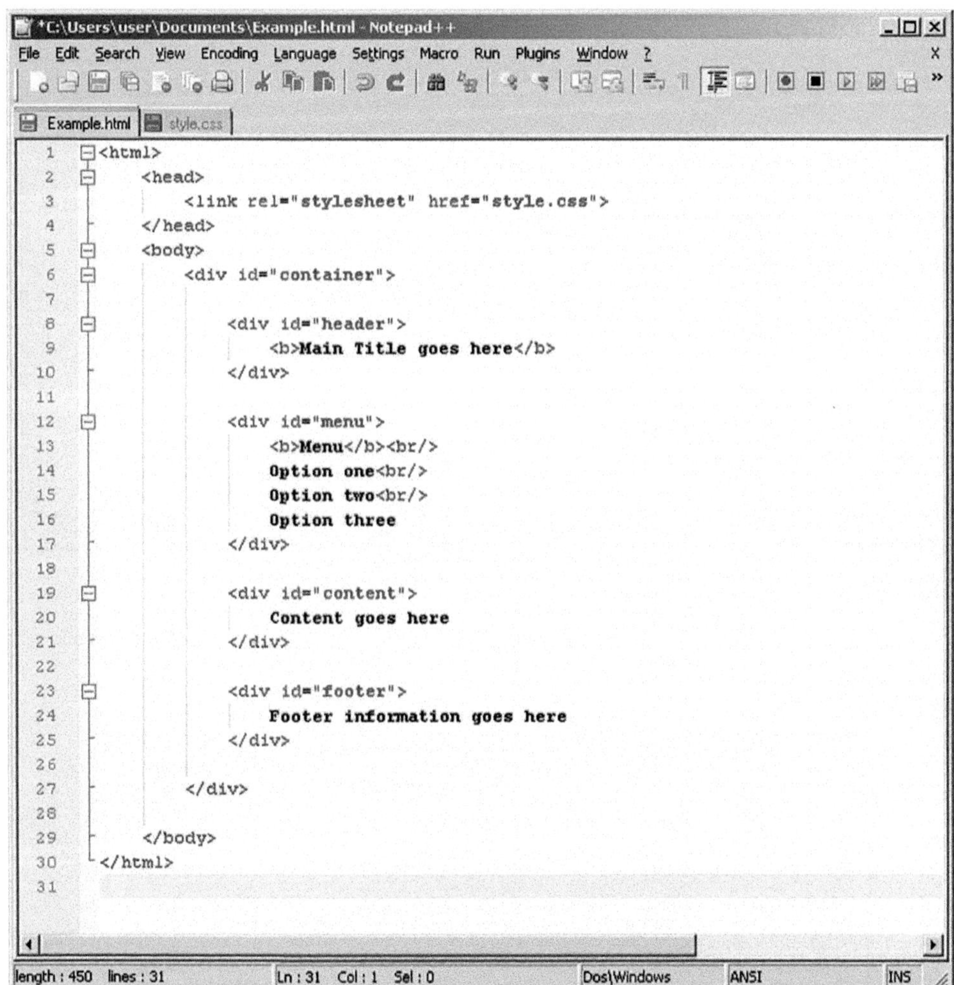

Figure 10.14: HTML webpage with the formatting placed in a CSS file.

Line 5 is important, as it tells the webpage where to look for the CSS file. Our CSS file is called style.css and can be found in the same folder as the webpage. The CSS file for this document can be seen in Figure 10.15.

```
#container
{
    width:500px;
}

#header
{
    background-color:grey;
    text-align:center;
}

#menu
{
    background-color:lightblue;
    height:200px;
    width:100px;
    float:left;
    text-align:center;
}

#content
{
    background-color:silver;
    height:200px;
    width:400px;
    float:left;
    text-align:center;
}

#footer
{
    background-color:grey;
    clear:both;
    text-align:center;
}
```

Figure 10.15: CSS file.

When you open the website in your browser, you'll see a webpage like the one shown in Figure 10.16.

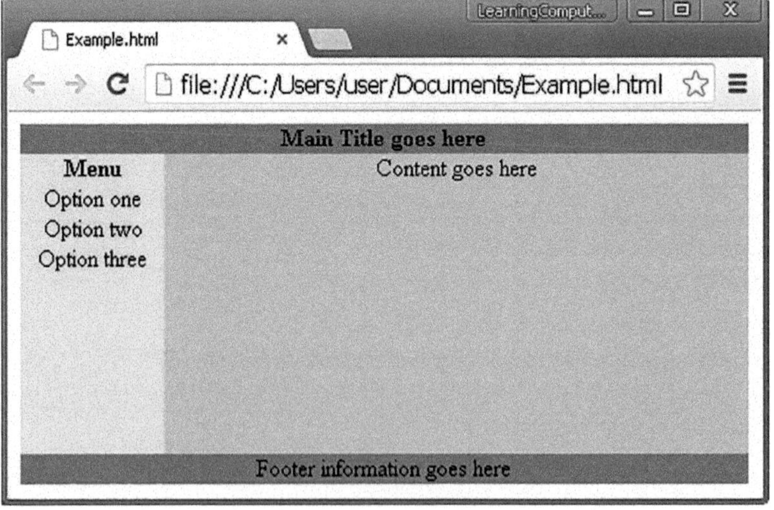

Figure 10.16: The website created by the code in Figures 10.14 and 10.15.

JavaScript

HTML and CSS make websites look great, but they don't add any functionality. If you want your website to do something interesting, such as provide a computer game for people to play, you need to use a web-based scripting language called JavaScript. It contains most of the basic features of a programming language but is interpreted inside the HTML code rather than creating a standalone program in its own right. Its lightweight nature makes it ideal for web programming, where file size and bandwidth can impact on the performance offered by traditional programming languages.

Look at the example HTML file shown in Figure 10.17.

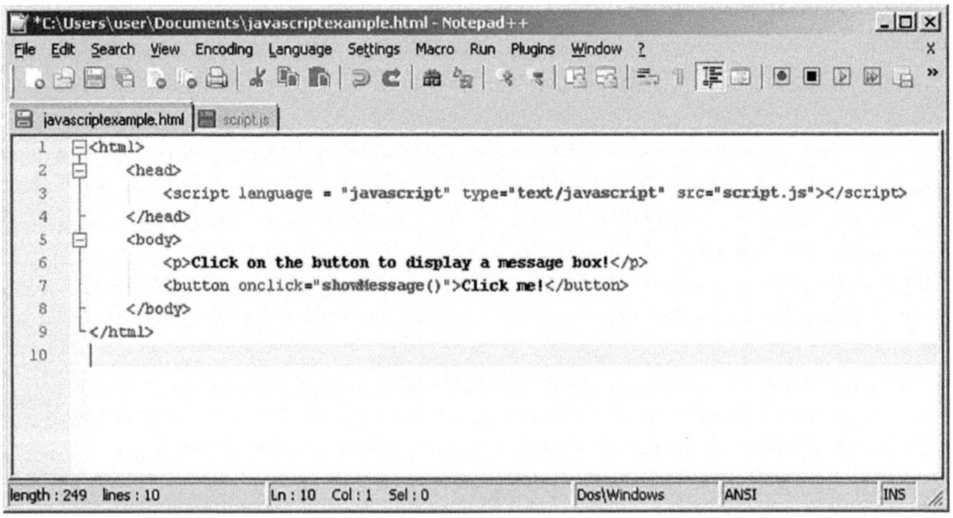

```
*C:\Users\user\Documents\javascriptexample.html - Notepad++
1  <html>
2      <head>
3          <script language = "javascript" type="text/javascript" src="script.js"></script>
4      </head>
5      <body>
6          <p>Click on the button to display a message box!</p>
7          <button onclick="showMessage()">Click me!</button>
8      </body>
9  </html>
10
length : 249   lines : 10   Ln : 10   Col : 1   Sel : 0   Dos\Windows   ANSI   INS
```

Figure 10.17: Example of HTML.

There are two important things here. First, on line 4 it tells the browser that this webpage includes some JavaScript and that this JavaScript can be found in a file called script.js in the same folder as the webpage. It is possible to include the JavaScript code in the same file as the HTML, but this isn't a very good solution, as another webpage can't use the same function. On line 8 we call the function showMessage(), which is located in the script.js file and is shown in Figure 10.18.

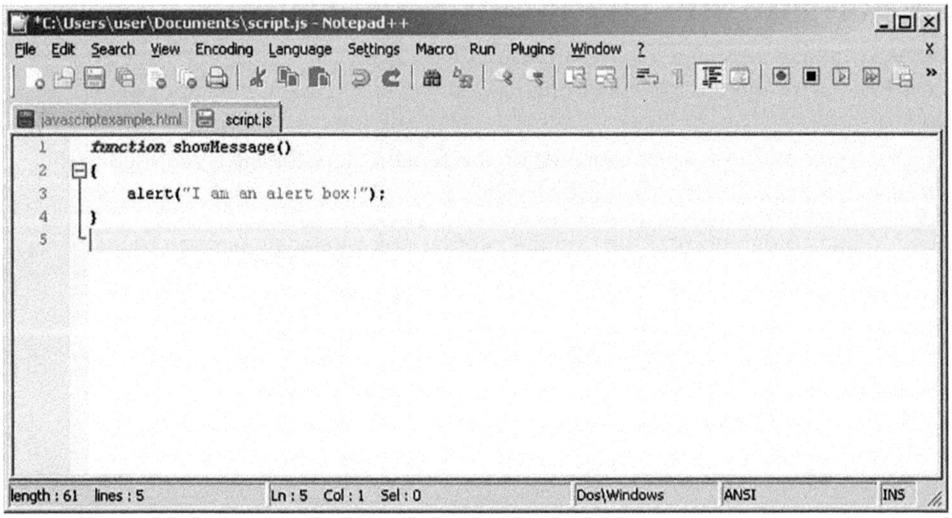

```
*C:\Users\user\Documents\script.js - Notepad++
1  function showMessage()
2  {
3      alert("I am an alert box!");
4  }
5
length : 61   lines : 5   Ln : 5   Col : 1   Sel : 0   Dos\Windows   ANSI   INS
```

Figure 10.18: Example of JavaScript.

Figure 10.19 shows the webpage after the button has been clicked and the message box displayed.

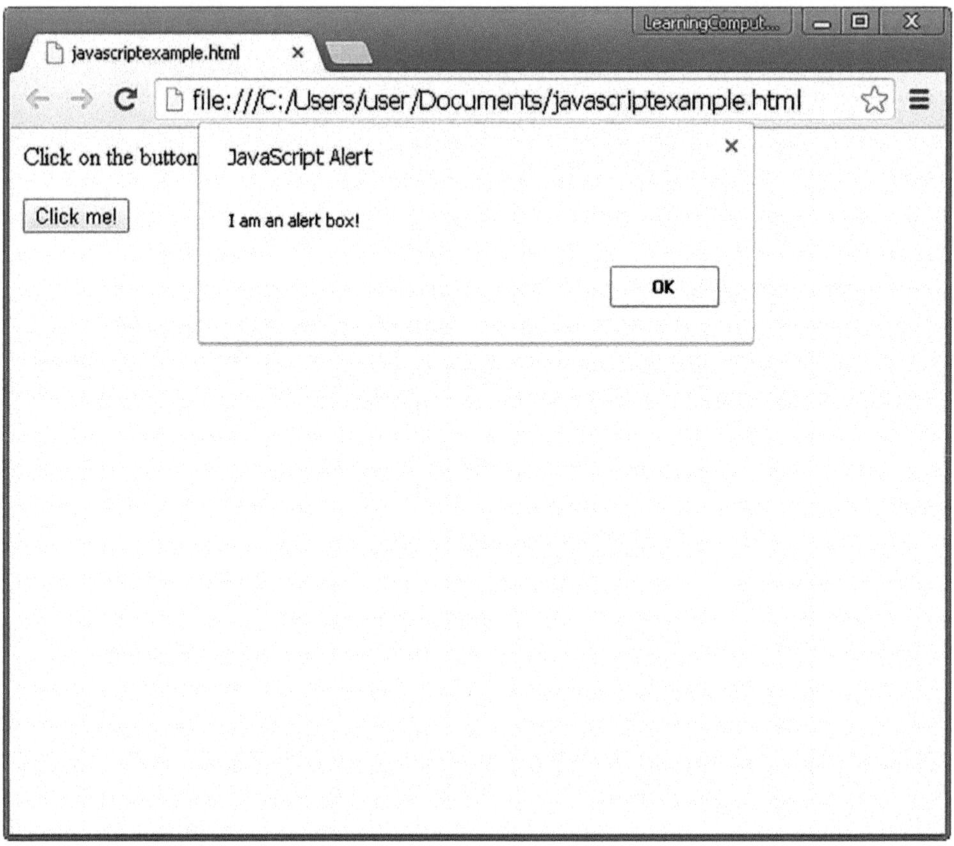

Figure 10.19: An HTML form control is used to execute some JavaScript.

Activity 10.1

Sign up here: http://www.editey.com and use the HTML, CSS and JavaScript tools to create your own website.

JavaScript is a really versatile language and can be used for anything from validating user input to writing animations and games. You can find out much more about JavaScript in the 'Further reading' section at the end of this chapter.

Server-side and client-side processing

You have already seen that the internet stores files on web servers and transfers these to local (client) computers through a web browser. Usually when a browser requests an HTML file, the server sends it to the client. However, if the file contains a server-side script, the script is executed on the server before the file is returned to the browser.

When creating programs that run over the internet, software engineers can choose to run their programs on the client computer or on the server; each approach has its own set of advantages and disadvantages. For example, processing on the client-side reduces the load on the server, important if you're running a *massive multiplayer online role-playing game* (MMORPG). Once the script has been downloaded to the client's computer, it is also faster to run. JavaScript is an example of a client-side processing language.

Server-side scripting can also be used to add a huge amount of extra functionality to a website. It allows you to dynamically edit, change or add any content to a webpage, respond to user queries or data submitted from HTML forms and query any databases held on the server, returning the result to the client. An advantage of server-side processing is that it is not necessary to worry about making code compatible across browsers and you don't have to share all the data you hold with the client's computer.

If server-side processing is necessary, users need a way to pass information from their client back to the server. A common way of doing this is using HTML forms.

HTML forms

Forms (Figure 10.20) can use a wide range of different controls to collect information from a user. All the controls you want to appear on a form must be placed between the <form> tags (lines 11–14 in Figure 10.21).

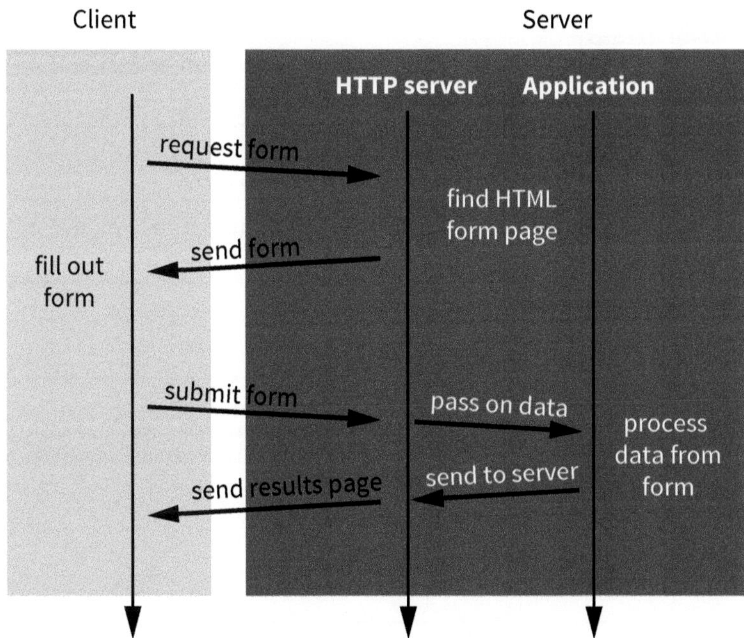

Figure 10.20: HTML forms can be used to pass data back to the server.

```
1   <html>
2
3       <head>
4           <link rel="stylesheet" type="text/css" href="style.css">
5           <script language="javascript" type="text/javascript" src="code.js"></script>
6       </head>
7
8       <body>
9               Log on screen:
10
11              <form>
12                  Username: <input type="text" name="username"><br>
13                  Password: <input type="text" name="password">
14              </form>
15      </body>
16
17  </html>
```

Figure 10.21: <form> tags are used to create HTML forms.

Tables 10.1 to 10.5 demonstrate some of the most popular examples of HTML form controls.

Code	<form>
	    First name: <input type="text" name="**firstname**">
	
	    Last name: <input type="text" name="**lastname**">
	</form>

Example	Username: Alistair E-mail address: asurrall@learningcomputi
Explanation	The text box collects plain text from the user; various settings such as length are available, to customise how the text box appears to the user.

Table 10.1: Plain text.

Code	<form> **Password:** <input type="**password**" name="**password**"> </form>
Example	Password: ••••••••••••
Explanation	The password control is like a text box but it hides whatever is typed into it.

Table 10.2: Password.

Code	<form> <input type="radio" name="OS" value="Android">**Android** <input type="radio" name="OS" value="Windows">**Windows** </form>
Example	Android Windows
Explanation	A user can click on a radio button to choose one from a range of options. Radio buttons always appear in pairs or larg/groups.

Table 10.3: Radio button.

Code	<form> <input type="checkbox" name="OS" value="Android">**Android** <input type="checkbox" name="OS" value="Windows">**Windows** </form>
Example	Android Windows
Explanation	The user can click on a check box to select an option. Multiple check boxes in a group can be selected.

Table 10.4: Check box.

Code	<form action="show.php" method="get"> <input type="submit"> </form>
Example	Submit
Explanation	A submit button is used to pass information from the client to the server. The action = "*show.php*" tells the form what to do when the submit button is clicked.

Table 10.5: Submit button.

PHP

PHP is a widely used and powerful server-side scripting language (PHP originally stood for personal home page, but now it stands for hypertext pre-processor). PHP collects information from users using client-side constructs such as HTML forms or JavaScript, and then uses the information it receives to manipulate information on a server. It is commonly combined with an open-source version of an SQL database called MySQL to create powerful applications (see Chapter 8 for more on SQL).

The screen shot in Figure 10.22 shows a typical HTML form being used to pass information from the client HTML file to the PHP file on a server.

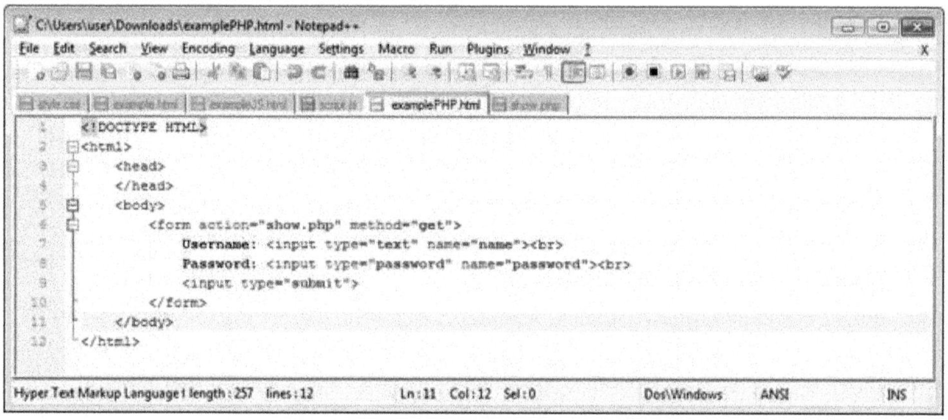

```
<!DOCTYPE HTML>
<html>
    <head>
    </head>
    <body>
        <form action="show.php" method="get">
            Username: <input type="text" name="name"><br>
            Password: <input type="password" name="password"><br>
            <input type="submit">
        </form>
    </body>
</html>
```

Figure 10.22: A form is used to pass information to the PHP file in Figure 10.23.

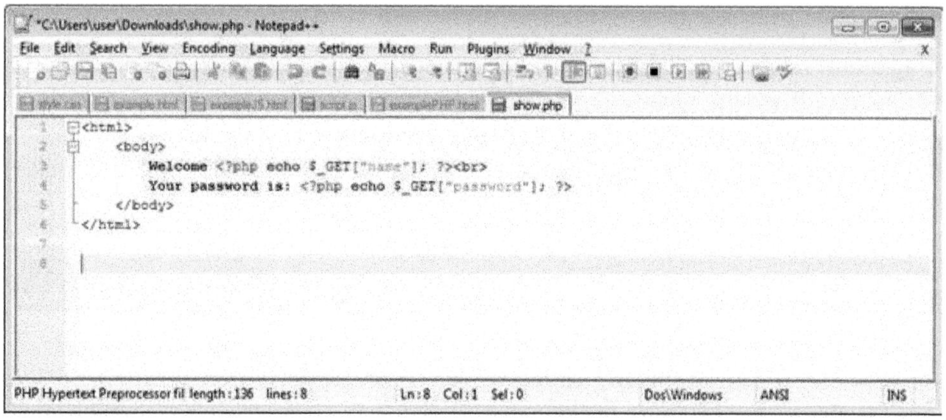

```
<html>
    <body>
        Welcome <?php echo $_GET["name"]; ?><br>
        Your password is: <?php echo $_GET["password"]; ?>
    </body>
</html>
```

Figure 10.23: A PHP file can be used to process the information it receives from a HTML form.

Note: unfortunately, unlike the previous examples, you won't be able to get the example shown in Figures 10.22 and 10.23 working, unless you have a server set up to store the PHP file.

Searching the web

The world wide web consists of billions of webpages spread across tens of millions of servers. This can make finding the exact piece of information you want very difficult. Before search engines appeared on the scene, you had to know the domain name of every website that you wanted to visit, which dramatically cut down the number of websites that you would or could access.

Search engines provide a number of ways for you to find information quickly and efficiently from anywhere on the web. The concept of a search engine is really simple: you type in some keywords and it returns a list of websites that contain those words. The reality, however, is much more complicated. Which websites should go at the top of the list? The first one found, the one that contains your keyword the highest number of times? Early search engines struggled to return relevant, useful results. They could find millions of related sites but you had to trawl through and find the one most relevant to you. Modern search engines use complex indexing and ranking algorithms to ensure that you get instant access to the most relevant websites.

Activity 10.2

Try searching for ocr.org.uk using several different search engines, making a note of any differences in the results.

Search engine indexing

Search engines collect information about webpages using automated **bots** called web spiders. These bots crawl the internet, following links and recording keywords and the addresses where the keywords are found. This information is then transmitted back to the search engine provider, for example Google or Yahoo. The information sent back is then ordered and stored according to an index by keywords, for example. When users are using search engines they are not searching the WWW, they're simply searching the search engine's index of the web. This approach means that results can be returned very quickly.

PageRank algorithm

Search engine companies analyse their indexes using algorithms to ensure they provide the most relevant results possible. The PageRank algorithm is Google's way of ensuring that it returns the best possible webpages in response to users' searches. It was named after its inventor, Larry Page. The PageRank algorithm works by counting the number of links to a page from other websites. This gives Google a rough estimate of how important a website is; more important websites are returned higher up the search results. The information about webpages (like the number of links) is gathered by an automated web spider called **Googlebot**.

The algorithm represents all the webpages as vertices on a directed graph data structure (see Chapter 12) and the hyperlinks between pages are stored as edges within the same structure. Vertices are assigned a numerical value representing their importance (based on the number of links to them). PageRank is no longer the only algorithm used by Google but it was the first and is still the best known.

Computing in context: Google

Google's mission is to organise the world's information and make it universally accessible and useful. Google was founded by Larry Page and Sergey Brin while they were PhD students at Stanford University. The intention was to create a quick reliable search engine to help people find the information they wanted on the internet. Today Google indexes billions of webpages that users can search through using keywords and operators.

Larry Page, who invented Google's PageRank algorithm, is today thought to be worth around $32.3 billion (approximately £21 billion), and the company has used its credentials as a search engine to diversify into a host of other areas, including artificial intelligence and robotics.

Summary

- Hypertext markup language (HTML) is a markup language that describes how items should appear on the computer screen.
- Cascading style sheets (CSS) are used to hold formatting information that needs to be applied to several HTML files.
- JavaScript is used to provide client-side processing on webpages.
- Search engines create indexes of websites. When you use a search engine you are searching their index of the web rather than the web itself.
- The PageRank algorithm is the algorithm that Google uses to decide which websites to display in response to search criteria.
- Server-side languages like PHP process information on a server and only display the results to the user.
- Client-side languages like JavaScript use the user's own computer to process information and display the results.

End-of-chapter questions

1 What is the world wide web (WWW)? [2]

2 What does HTML stand for and what is it used for? [2]

3 What is the purpose of a CSS file? [2]

4 What is the difference between server-side and client-side processing? [4]

5 What is the PageRank algorithm? [2]

Further reading

HTML(5) tutorial – search on the w3schools website.
HTML & CSS – search on the Codeacademy website.
JavaScript tutorial – search on the w3schools website.
JavaScript – search on the Codeacademy website.
CSS tutorial – search on the w3schools website.
PHP 5 tutorial – search on the w3schools website.
PHP – search on the Codeacademy website.
PageRank algorithm – search for the Mathematics of Google Search on the Cornell Maths Department website.
Algorithms – Search for 'How does Google Search work?' on Google Webmasters' Youtube channel.
Crawling and indexing – look for 'How Search Works' on Google Search.

Chapter 11
Data types

Specification points

1.4.1 Data types

- Primitive data types, integer, real/floating point, character, string and Boolean.
- Represent positive integers in binary.
- Use of sign and magnitude and two's complement to represent negative numbers in binary.
- Addition and subtraction of binary integers.
- Represent positive integers in hexadecimal.
- Convert positive integers between binary, hexadecimal and denary.
- Representation and normalisation of floating point numbers in binary.
- How character sets (ASCII and Unicode) are used to represent text.
- A Floating point arithmetic, positive and negative numbers, addition and subtraction.
- Bitwise manipulation and masks: shifts, combining with AND, OR and XOR.

Learning objectives

- To be able to recognise primitive data types including: integer, real/floating point, character, string and Boolean.
- To know how to represent positive integers in binary.
- To understand the use of sign and magnitude and two's complement to represent negative numbers in binary.
- To be able to add and subtract binary integers.

- To be able to represent positive integers in hexadecimal and convert between binary, hexadecimal and denary.
- To understand the representation and normalisation of floating point numbers in binary.
- To understand how character sets (ASCII and Unicode) are used to represent text.
- To understand floating point arithmetic, positive and negative numbers, addition and subtraction.
- To understand bitwise manipulation and masks: shifts, combining with AND, OR, and XOR.

Introduction

Computers use electricity to represent information. An electrical current has two possible states: it can either be on or off. Computers represent 'on' using the digit 1 and 'off' using the digit 0.

The binary number system uses two symbols: 1 and 0. In a computer system, combinations of 0s and 1s can be used to represent anything from a simple number to a film.

Each 0 or 1 in binary is called a bit (short for **bi**nary digi**t**).

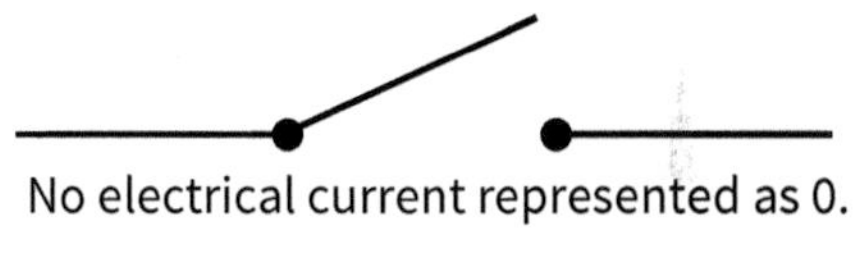

No electrical current represented as 0.
Electrical current represented as 1.

Figure 11.1: Electrical currents representing 0 and 1.

Using binary notation, we need many bits to represent quite small numbers, let alone complex things like games or music files. For this reason, bits are commonly grouped together and given names.

A group of 4 bits is called a nibble and can represent 2^4 (128) combinations. A group of 8 bits is called a byte. A byte can provide 2^8 (256) different combinations of 0s and 1s.

Bytes are grouped together in the following ways:

1 024 bytes = 1 kilobyte (KB) = 2^{10} bytes

1 048 576 bytes = 1 megabyte (MB) = 2^{20} bytes

1 073 741 824 bytes = 1 gigabyte (GB) = 2^{30} bytes

1 099 511 627 776 bytes = 1 terabyte (TB) = 2^{40} bytes

Primitive data types

Nearly all programming languages provide programmers with five primitive (or simple) data types that can be connected together to create more complex (or composite) data types. The five primitive data types are integer, real (or float), character, string and Boolean. These are described in Table 11.1.

Data type	Description	Example
Integer	A whole number.	23
Real/floating point	A number with an integer and a fractional (decimal) part.	12.65
Character	A single alpha-numeric character.	D
String	A sequence of alpha-numeric characters.	Hello
Boolean	Either TRUE or FALSE.	FALSE

Table 11.1: Data types.

The amount of memory that each data type takes up varies from language to language and processor to processor (they take up more bits on a 64-bit system compared to a 32-bit system). A good estimate is that a character takes up 8 bits and an integer 32 bits.

The rest of this chapter will show how binary is used to represent all possible values held using these data types.

Representing positive integers in binary

Binary is a base 2 number system, which means that each value is twice as large as the value before it. Our usual number system is base 10, also known as denary. In denary, each digit is ten times larger than the one before it.

In the denary system, 1011 means one thousand and eleven, because 1000 + 10 + 1 equals one thousand and eleven.

1000	100	10	1
1	0	1	1

In the binary system 1011 means eleven, because 8 + 2 + 1 equals eleven.

8	4	2	1
1	0	1	1

Converting from denary to binary and vice versa

Converting denary to binary is a simple operation. In this example, we'll convert the denary number 121 into a binary number.

Begin by writing a table like this one, with the binary bit place values along the top:

128	64	32	16	8	4	2	1

Next, find the largest number in your table that you can subtract from your number, leaving a positive result. Perform the subtraction and place a 1 in the column corresponding to that number. Here, 64 is the largest number that can be subtracted from 121: 121 − 64 = 57:

128	64	32	16	8	4	2	1
	1						

We repeat this operation over and over again until we are left with 0.

In this example the largest number we have that fits into 57 is 32 (57 − 32 = 25), so our table becomes:

128	64	32	16	8	4	2	1
	1	*1*					

The largest number we have that fits into 25 is 16 (25 − 16 = 9), so our table becomes:

128	64	32	16	8	4	2	1
	1	1	*1*				

The largest number we have that fits into 9 is 8 (9 − 8 = 1), so our table becomes:

128	64	32	16	8	4	2	1
	1	1	1	*1*			

Finally, the largest number we have that can be subtracted from 1 is 1 (1 − 1 = 0), so our table becomes:

128	64	32	16	8	4	2	1
	1	1	1	1			*1*

Now we've reached 0, we just need to fill in the gaps in our table with 0s and the conversion is complete.

128	64	32	16	8	4	2	1
0	1	1	1	1	0	0	1

64 + 32 + 16 + 8 + 1 = 121, 121 in denary is 01111001 in binary.

Converting back is even easier! If you are given a binary number such as 10101001, all you need to do is write out your table, put your 1s in the correct column and add together the values:

128	64	32	16	8	4	2	1
1	0	1	0	1	0	0	1

So 10101001 in binary is 169 in denary, that is, 128 + 32 + 8 + 1.

Representing negative numbers in binary

Binary can also be used to represent negative numbers (−1, −2, −3 and so on). There are two ways in which this can be done and you'll need to read the exam questions carefully to make sure you use the correct method.

Sign and magnitude

Sign and magnitude is the simplest way of representing negative numbers in binary. The most significant bit (MSB) is simply used to represent the sign: 1 means the number is negative, 0 means it is positive. So to represent −4 in 8-bit binary you would write out the 4 in binary, 00000100, then change the MSB to a 1, creating 10000100. In another example, −2 would be 10000010 in the sign and magnitude notation. This notation isn't used very often as using the MSB as a sign bit means that the largest number that can be represented using 8 bits is 127, much less than 255. It also makes it harder to do calculations as different bits mean different things; some represent numbers, others represent signs. Also, their value of zero is represented twice as both positive and negative 0. MSB notation can represent numbers in the range −127 to +127 assuming that only 8 bits are being used.

Two's complement

Two's complement is a much more useful way of representing binary numbers as it allows you to use negative numbers without reducing the range of numbers you can represent . With 8 bits you can represent −127 to + 128.

The easiest way to show a negative number using two's complement is to write it out as a positive number using the usual binary method. Then, starting at the right-hand side, flip each bit (change a 1 to a 0 and a 0 to a 1) and then add 1.

For example, to show −86 in binary, first work out 86. 86 is 01010110 because 64 + 16 + 4 + 2 equals 86:

128	64	32	16	8	4	2	1
0	1	0	1	0	1	1	0

Then start at the right-hand side and flip every bit:

128	64	32	16	8	4	2	1
1	0	1	0	1	0	0	1

Now add 1::

128	64	32	16	8	4	2	1
1	0	1	0	1	0	1	0

So −86 in binary is 10101010 in two's complement notation.

Adding and subtracting of binary integers

Once you can represent positive and negative numbers using binary, the next step is performing arithmetic operations such as addition and subtraction on them.

Binary addition

Binary addition is fairly straightforward. Just remember these simple operations:

Operation	Result
0 + 0 =	0
0 + 1 =	1
1 + 1 =	10
1 + 1 + 1 =	11

To add together two binary numbers, just arrange them above each other in a table. The following table shows the number 42 above the number 18:

0	0	1	0	1	0	1	0
0	0	0	1	0	0	1	0

Then add together each corresponding bit using the operations you saw earlier, **making sure that you start at the least significant bit (LSB):**

					1		
0	0	1	0	1	0	1	0
0	0	0	1	0	0	1	0
						0	0

You can see in the table above the first operation (0 + 0) has produced a 0. The second operation (1 + 1) has produced 10; notice that we record the 0 but carry the 1 to the top of the next column so that the third operation is 1 + 0 + 0 = 1:

					1		
0	0	1	0	1	0	1	0
0	0	0	1	0	0	1	0
0	0	1	1	1	1	0	0

So our final result is 00111100 or 60. We know this is correct because we can check our answer: 42 + 18 = 60.

Tip

In an exam it can be tempting just to work out the answer in denary and then write down the binary equivalent of this number. **Avoid this temptation**, as questions of this type may require you to show your working.

Binary subtraction

Binary subtraction is the same as binary addition except that you convert the number to be subtracted into negative binary (using two's complement) before adding them together. This works because 4 − 2 is the same as 4 + (−2).

For example, if you want to calculate 68 − 33 in binary, the first thing you do is write down the binary for 68:

0	1	0	0	0	1	0	0

Then you work out what −33 is in binary using two's complement and write this beneath it:

0	1	0	0	0	1	0	0
1	1	0	1	1	1	1	1

Finally, you add them together using the same operations as for binary addition:

1		1	1	1			
0	1	0	0	0	1	0	0
1	1	0	1	1	1	1	1
0	0	1	0	0	0	1	1

(Notice that the final 1 that would be carried off the end of the final (8th) bit is just ignored.)

So the answer is 00100011 = 35 and we know this is correct because 68 − 33 = 35.

Representing positive integers in hexadecimal and converting between binary, hexadecimal and denary

Binary can be difficult for people to understand and it's easy to make mistakes when recording larger numbers. To get around this problem we often use a base 16 number system, called hexadecimal, to represent numbers in computing. Examples of its use are MAC addresses, IPv6 addresses, memory address locations and representing colours.

You'll need to know how to convert between denary, binary and hexadecimal. Luckily it isn't very hard.

Hexadecimal uses 16 symbols, the numbers 0–9 and letters A–F:

Denary	Binary (4-bit)	Hexadecimal
0	0000	0
1	0001	1
2	0010	2
3	0011	3
4	0100	4
5	0101	5
6	0110	6
7	0111	7
8	1000	8
9	1001	9
10	1010	A
11	1011	B
12	1100	C
13	1101	D
14	1110	E
15	1111	F

To convert a denary number to hexadecimal, simply convert it to 8-bit binary. Then split your 8-bit binary number into two 4-bit sections and convert each of these to hexadecimal using the table above.

For example, to convert the denary number 31 to hexadecimal you would first convert it to binary:

128	64	32	16	8	4	2	1
0	0	0	1	1	1	1	1

Then split this 8-bit binary number into two 4-bit sections:

8	4	2	1
0	0	0	1

8	4	2	1
1	1	1	1

Finally convert each of these 4-bit segments to hexadecimal:

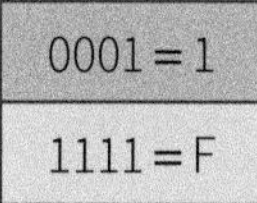

0001 = 1
1111 = F

So 31 in denary is 1F in hexadecimal.

Activity 11.1

Have a look at some of the hexadecimal codes used to represent colours in web programming. Why do you think we use hexadecimal instead of binary?

Floating point numbers in binary

Floating point binary is used to hold really big, really small or really accurate numbers using only 8 bits.

In GCSE mathematics you learned about floating point notation (sometimes called scientific notation). Using floating point, the number 92 can be represented as 0.92×100, which is the same as 0.92×10^2. It is this last part that we refer to as floating point notation. It is called floating point because the number of digits is fixed but the decimal point floats around.

Using the example 0.92×10^2, 0.92 is the *mantissa*, 10 is the *base* and 2 is the *exponent*.

We can represent simple denary (decimal) numbers using our usual binary table:

8	4	2	1	.	1/2	1/4	1/8	1/16
1	0	0	1	.	1	0	0	1

In the example above, 10101001 represents 9.5625 (8 + 1 + 0.5 + 0.0625). But if we use this method, the smallest decimal number we can represent is 0.0625 and the largest number is 15.9375.

Floating point notation allows us to store a much larger range of numbers and store them with much more accuracy.

To show your understanding of floating point notation in binary, you will usually be given two binary values (one for the mantissa and one for the exponent) and asked to convert them to denary.

Mantissa	Exponent
01101	011

- *Step 1*: Convert the exponent to denary, in this example 011 = *3*.
- *Step 2*: The mantissa started as 0.1101. Move the decimal point *3* places left to get 0110.1.
- *Step 3*: Write 0110.1 as denary 6.5 (4 + 2 + 0.5).

Normalisation

The precision of floating point binary depends on the number of bits used to represent the mantissa.

For example, in denary 67849 could be 6.7849×10^4 with 5 digits for the mantissa or 6.785×10^3 with 4 digits for the mantissa.

In order to achieve the most accurate representation possible with the number of bits available for a mantissa, the number should be written with *no leading 0s*. Normalisation is the process of removing these leading 0s.

Mantissa	Exponent
00011	011

- *Step 1*: Convert the exponent to denary, 011 = 3
- *Step 2*: Move the decimal point in the mantissa so that it is before the first 1, so 0.0011 becomes 0.1100. The decimal place has moved 2 places.
- *Step 3*: Because we've just moved the decimal point we need to adjust the exponent to take this into account. As we moved to the right, we subtract the number of moves from our exponent: 3 − 2 = 1. So our new exponent is 1.
- *Step 4*: Our new, normalised, floating point number is 01100 001, which is the same as 00011 011(work it out if you don't believe it!). We now have considerably more space in the mantissa so we can store a much more accurate number if we want to.

Negative floating point numbers

It is also possible to have a negative exponent and move the decimal point to the left. This is achieved by storing the exponent (and mantissa) as a two's complement binary number.

Mantissa	Exponent
01110	110

- *Step 1*: Convert the exponent to denary; in this example 110 becomes 010 or *−2*.
- *Step 2*: The mantissa started as 0.1110. Move the decimal point left 2 places to get 0.001110.
- *Step 3*: Write 0.001110 as denary 0.21875 (0.125 + 0.0625 + 0.03125).

The same method can be used to deal with negative numbers, representing the mantissa using two's complement.

Mantissa	Exponent
11111	010

- *Step 1*: Convert the exponent to denary, 010 = *2*.
- *Step 2*: Convert the mantissa to negative binary by flipping the bits and adding 1, in this example 11111 becomes 0.0001.
- *Step 3*: The mantissa started as 0.0001. Move the decimal point *2* places to get 0.01.
- *Step 4*: Write 0.01 as denary −0.25; don't forget it's negative!

Addition and subtraction

Addition and subtraction of floating point numbers are very similar operations. This example will walk you through adding the two numbers below:

Mantissa	Exponent
01110	**010**
01000	001

- *Step 1*: In order to add two floating point numbers together, their exponent must be the same. We achieve this by changing the exponent of our second number from 001 (1) to 010 (2). Because we've changed the exponent of the second number, we need to adjust its mantissa to take account of this, so the mantissa becomes 00100 (as 00100 010 is the same as 01000 001).
- *Step 2*: Now we can add together the two mantissas using our usual method:

1	1			
0	1	1	1	0
0	0	1	0	0
1	0	0	1	0

- *Step 3*: So the result is 10010 010. You can check this is correct by working out the answers in denary:
  1.0010 010 becomes 100.10 (because the decimal point moves 2 places), which is 4.5. This is the same as 3.5 (our first number) + 1 (our second number).

Subtraction is the same as addition except that you convert the number to be subtracted to a negative number using two's complement.

Mantissa	Exponent
01110	010
01000	001

- *Step 1*: Just like addition, the exponents of the two numbers must be the same. We achieve this by changing the exponent of our second number from 001 (1) to 010 (2). Because we've changed the exponent of the second number, we need to adjust its mantissa to take account of this, so the mantissa becomes 00100 (as 00100 010 is the same as 01000 001).

- *Step 2*: Now convert the mantissa of the second number to a negative one, using two's complement: 00100 becomes 11100.
- *Step 3*: Now we can add together the two mantissas.

1	1			
0	1	1	1	0
1	1	1	0	0
0	1	0	1	0

- *Step 4*: The result is 01010 010. You can check this is correct by working out the answers in denary: 01010 010 becomes 010.10 (because the decimal point moves 2 places), which is 2.5. This is the same as 3.5 (our first number) – 1 (our second number).

Tip

Be prepared for binary subtraction questions. These require you to use conversion, addition and two's complement in a single question.

Floating point binary is one of the few topics in this chapter not covered at GCSE. Make sure you are very familiar with it.

Bitwise manipulation and masks

Bitwise manipulation simply means applying the logical operators (AND, OR, NOT, XOR) to binary. A mask is simply the data that is being used in this operation.

The table below shows the results of the various bitwise operations:

A	B	NOT A (!A)	A AND B (A && B)	A OR B (A || B)	A XOR B (A ^ B)
0	0	1	0	0	0
0	1	1	0	1	1
1	0	0	0	1	1
1	1	0	1	1	0

To carry out bitwise operations on a given mask, simply apply the operations above to each pair of corresponding bits. For example, if you were given the bytes 10111001, 00111010 and asked to carry out an AND operation, the result would be 00111000:

A	1	0	1	1	1	0	0	1
B	0	0	1	1	1	0	1	0
A AND B	0	0	1	1	1	0	0	0
A OR B	1	0	1	1	1	0	1	1
A XOR B	1	0	0	0	0	0	1	1
NOT B	1	1	0	0	0	1	0	1

How character sets are used to represent text

As well as representing numbers, binary can also be used to represent characters. For example, 1100001 might represent the character 'a'. The different representations of letters and symbols in binary are called **character sets**.

The two most commonly used character sets are called ASCII and Unicode.

ASCII

ASCII encodes 127 different letters and symbols using 7-bit binary codes, which is perfect for writing in English. You won't need to know the ASCII value of every character but it's worth taking the time to learn where lowercase letters (97) and uppercase letters (65) start.

Letter	ASCII Code	Binary	Letter	ASCII Code	Binary
a	97	1100001	A	65	1000001
b	98	1100010	B	66	1000010
c	99	1100011	C	67	1000011
d	100	1100100	D	68	1000100
e	101	1100101	E	69	1000101
f	102	1100110	F	70	1000110
g	103	1100111	G	71	1000111
h	104	1101000	H	72	1001000
i	105	1101001	I	73	1001001
j	106	1101010	J	74	1001010
k	107	1101011	K	75	1001011
l	108	1101100	L	76	1001100
m	109	1101101	M	77	1001101
n	110	1101110	N	78	1001110
o	111	1101111	O	79	1001111
p	112	1110000	P	80	1010000
q	113	1110001	Q	81	1010001
r	114	1110010	R	82	1010010
s	115	1110011	S	83	1010011
t	116	1110100	T	84	1010100
u	117	1110101	U	85	1010101
v	118	1110110	V	86	1010110
w	119	1110111	W	87	1010111
x	120	1111000	X	88	1011000
y	121	1111001	Y	89	1011001
z	122	1111010	Z	90	1011010

Unicode

- Languages like Japanese, Arabic and Hebrew all have a much larger alphabet than English. To get around this problem, Unicode was invented. Unicode uses up to four bytes to represent each character (depending on the version). This means that it can represent hundreds of thousands of different characters – more than enough to cope with most of the world's languages. At the time of writing, 128 000 characters have been defined.

Summary

- Programing languages use primitive data types to represent different kinds of data. Integers hold whole numbers, floats hold decimal numbers, characters hold single letters, strings hold sequences of alphanumeric characters and Boolean values can be true or false.
- Binary can be used to represent positive numbers. Each bit in the sequence is worth twice the bit before it.
- Binary can also use sign and magnitude and two's complement to represent negative numbers in binary.
- Binary numbers can be added and subtracted using two's complement: $0 + 0 = 0, 1 + 0 = 1, 0 + 1 = 1, 1 + 1 = 10, 1 + 1 + 1 = 11.$
- Hexadecimal uses a base 16 number system to represent different binary values. The values 0–9 stay the same but the values 10–15 are represented by the letters A–F.
- Binary, hexadecimal and denary numbers are interrelated and it is possible to convert between the different systems.
- Binary can be used to represent floating point binary numbers using some bits as the mantissa and others as the exponent.
- Bitwise manipulation is the application of logical operators to binary.
- Sequences of bits can also be used to represent characters. Unique sequences are assigned to each letter.
- ASCII uses 7 bits to represent 127 different characters. Unicode uses up to 16 bits to represent many more characters.

End-of-chapter questions

1 What is binary? [2]

2 Write the decimal number 17 in 8-bit binary. [1]

3 Add the binary numbers 00001110 and 00100101 together and write the result in binary. Show your working. [2]

4 What is the purpose of sign and magnitude and two's complement? [3]

5 Write the hexadecimal value 24 in decimal. [1]

6 What is the decimal equivalent of the floating point number 01101 011 where 01101 is the mantissa and 011 is the exponent? [3]

Further reading

Binary numbers – search for the Binary System on the Grinnell College website.
Binary addition – search for Binary Calculator on calculator.net.
Binary game – search on the Cisco Learning Network.
Floating point binary – search on Kip Irvine's website.
Unicode – go to unicode.org.

Chapter 12
Data structures

Specification points

1.4.2 Data structures

- Arrays (of up to three-dimensions), records, lists, tuples.
- The properties of stacks and queues.
- A The following structures to store data: linked-list, graph (directed and undirected), tree, binary search tree, hash table.
- How to create, traverse, add data to and remove data from the data structures mentioned above.

Learning objectives

- To understand the principles of using arrays of up to three-dimensions.
- To understand the principles of using records, lists and tuples.
- To understand the principles of using stacks and queues.
- A To understand the principles of using linked lists, graphs (directed and undirected), trees, binary search trees and hash tables.
- To know how to create, traverse, add data to and remove data from the data structures mentioned above.

What is a data structure?

A data structure is simply a way of representing the data held in a computer's memory. There are many different data structures available to programmers but at A Level you only need to understand a few of the most common ones:

- one-dimensional arrays
- two-dimensional arrays

- three-dimensional arrays
- records
- tuples
- lists
- stacks
- queues
- linked lists
- binary trees
- directed graphs
- undirected graphs
- hash tables.

Data structures usually fall into one of two categories: static and dynamic. In static data structures the size of the data structure is set at the beginning of the program and cannot be changed. This is very limiting (and inefficient) because it means that you have to know in advance how large your data structure needs to be. However, static data structures are easy to program and you always know how much space they will take up. Dynamic data structures, on the other hand, do not have a limited size and can expand or shrink as needed, however, they tend to be more complex to implement and can potentially use a lot of memory.

It is also very common for more complex data structures to be made of simpler ones. For example, it is normal practice to implement binary trees using a linked list or create a stack by using an array. It is important to familiarise yourself with the names of each structure, how data is stored within it and the functions used to manipulate data within it.

You will need to perform various operations on your data, such as inserting, sorting or searching .The efficiency of such operations varies depending on the data structure in use. Generally speaking, you want to use the most efficient data structure possible. This is particularly important when you are working with large datasets. Your choice of data structure can have a big impact on the run time of your program. You can find out about the relative efficiency ratings (given using the Big O notation) of the data structures you need for A Level in the 'Further reading' section at the end of this chapter.

One-dimensional arrays

Arrays are the simplest of all data structures (if you did GCSE Computer Science you will already be very familiar with them). An array is a collection of elements of the same data type grouped under a single identifier. Each variable in the array is called an element and is accessed using its position in the array as an index. Arrays are static data structures. It is important to note that, within the Python programming, we generally implement arrays as lists for simplicity. Python does support arrays but only to hold numeric values (you cannot create an array of names using the array class, for example). There are some differences, which are discussed further in this section.

This code shows how to declare a list as an array (holding five names) using Python:

Code

```
Names = ['Sam', 'Lucy', 'James', 'Jack', 'Jane']
```

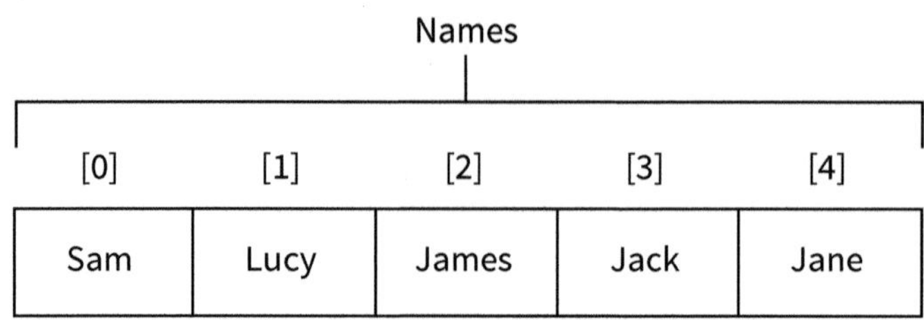

Figure 12.1: A one-dimensional list implemented as an array.

Accessing the data in an array is simple. You simply refer to the element number (index) of the piece of data you want. In Python and many other languages the first index into an array is 0 (this is to ensure the first bit of the indexing integer is not wasted). For example, print(Names[1]) would print the word 'Lucy'. Names[3] = 'Sarah' would change the value of element 3 from Jack to Sarah.

Arrays are static data structures, so once they have been declared they can't grow beyond their initial size. Elements in an array are stored in a sequence of memory address locations (contiguous locations), which is very efficient for searching.

Two-dimensional arrays

You can also create arrays with more than a single dimension. This is an array of arrays. In theory you can have arrays with a huge number of dimensions, but this becomes very hard to visualise and at A Level you only need to go up to three dimensions. We often visualise a two-dimensional array as a table with rows and columns although this is not how the data is actually stored in memory. Three dimensions also does not pose a problem because we can think of a cube with each layer having a depth dimension too. Our analogies crumble when we try to visualise a four-dimensional array. Using a different one, if we think of an array as a book and a two dimensional array as being chapters of the book, we can sub divide chapters into many pages, a page into many paragraphs, a paragraph into many lines, lines into words, words into characters and so on. Each time we are creating a subset of each dimension. If I wish to find the letter z, I would need to search the book, the chapters, each page, every paragraph, line, word and finally letters of words, to locate it.

This code shows how to declare a 2D array using lists in Python:

Code

```
Names = [['Sam', 'Lucy', 'James', 'Jack', 'Jane'],…
['Peter', 'Sarah', 'Adam', 'Karen', 'Verity'],…
['Emily', 'Edward', 'Dominic', 'Justyn', 'Jake']]
```

The implementation of multidimensional arrays differs from language to language. In Python, you simply create an array and then place another array inside each element of it.

They can also be created and populated using list comprehension, as shown below:

table = [[0 for i in range(10)] for j in range(10)]

This is a really useful way of creating an array and populating each element initially with 0 as a placeholder ready for our program to calculate the required value.

Changing or accessing the data in a 2D array is the same as in a 1D array. You simply refer to the element number (index) of the piece of data you want. For example, Print(Names[1]

[2]) would print the word 'Edward'. Names[3][0] = 'Alistair' would change the value of element 3,0 from Jack to Alistair. Notice that for a 2D array, the element index operates in the same way as the coordinates on a map or graph.

Names

	[0]	[1]	[2]	[3]	[4]
[0]	Sam	Lucy	James	Jack	Jane
[1]	Peter	Sarah	Adam	Karen	Verity
[2]	Emily	Edward	Dominic	Justyn	Jake

Figure 12.2: How our two-dimensional array is held in the computer's memory.

Three-dimensional arrays

Three-dimensional arrays are constructed in a similar way to two-dimensional arrays, they consist of an array inside an array which is then inside an array.

This code shows how to declare a 3D array using Python:

Code

```
Alphabet = [[['A', 'B', 'C'], ['D', 'E', 'F'], ['G', 'H', 'I']],
[['J', 'K', 'L'], ['M', 'N', 'O'], ['P', 'Q', 'R']],
[['S', 'T', 'U'], ['V', 'W', 'X'], ['Y', 'Z', '!']]]
```

List comprehension can also be used as for the 2D array:

threeDArray = [[[0 for i in range(5)]for j in range(5)]for k in range(5)]

Accessing data in a 3D array is the same as in a 1D or 2D array. You simply refer to the element number (index) of the piece of data you want. For example, print(Alphabet[0][2][1]) would print the letter 'H'. Alphabet[2][2][2] = '£' would change the value of element 2, 2, 2 from ! to £.

Notice that the element index operates in exactly the same way as the index for a two- dimensional array.

Searching an array

Arrays are static, so you can't increase their size once they've been created, however, you can search through to find any empty spaces and put your new data in there. This has the added bonus that you don't waste memory-reserving space for empty array elements.

This Python function below takes a piece of data and searches through the array until an empty spot is found. If an empty element is found, the data is inserted and the function returns true. If there are no empty elements left, the function returns false.

Code

```
def add_data (data):
  for x in range (0, len (array)):
    if array[x] == None:
      array[x] = data
      return true

return false
```

As you might expect, it is also impossible to remove elements from an array once it has been created. You can, however, set elements to empty or NULL (None in Python) to signify that they are available to store data in:

Code

```
names[1]  = None
```

Computing in context: Big O notation

A

An algorithm's efficiency is usually described using the Big O notation. Big O notation gives an idea of how well an algorithm scales in terms of the space that it takes and the time taken to perform operations such as searching and sorting. For example, how long it will take to search an array of 10 items compared to an array of 10 000 items. Big O notation generally gives the worst-case scenario, that is, the maximum possible number of steps required to complete the algorithm.

If an algorithm always takes the same time to complete regardless of the size of the data set *(n)*, it is said to be ***O*(1)**. For example, reading the first element of an array will be ***O*(1)** because it makes no difference if the array is 10 items long or 100,000 items long. The algorithm will take the same number of steps to complete.

If the length of time taken to complete an algorithm is directly proportional to the size of the dataset, it is said to be ***O*(*n*)**. For example, carrying out a serial search on an array is ***O*(*n*)** because the number of checks carried out is directly proportional to the number of items in the array.

If the time to complete an algorithm is proportional to the square of the amount of data (*n*), it is said to be $O(n^2)$. This is very common in algorithms that have nested loops, such as the bubble sort algorithm. Any function with an exponent of *n* is unlikely to perform efficiently as the size of the dataset grows.

All common algorithms and data structures will have a generally accepted Big O notation efficiency rating. It is up to the programmer to make sure that they choose the most efficient data structure and algorithm for the job.

Activity 12.1

Make a list of some common searching and sorting algorithms. Use Big O notation to find out which is the most efficient

Records

A record is a data structure that allows items of data of different types to be stored together in a single file. Data is stored in different fields and multiple records can be stored together in a file. This is particularly useful to create a set of related data items. A particular record can be searched for by matching a search term to a field value. Records can also be sorted on a particular field too.

Field name	Data type	Maximum size in bytes
CustomerID	String	6
First name	String	10
Gender	Char	1
Age	Integer	2

Not all programming languages support the record data structure. The example below is in Pascal:

Code

```
Type
  StudentRec = Record
    CustomerID, FirstName: String
    Gender: Char
    Age: Integer;
  End;
Var
  Paul: StudentRec;
Begin
  Paul.CustomerID:= '0011CU2'
  Paul.FirstName:= 'Paul'
  Paul.Gender:= 'M'
  Paul.Age:= 19
End.
```

You can see in the example shown above that we first create a template for the record structure specifying the names of fields and the data types. Then we create a new record for Paul and enter in the data we want to hold about him.

Unfortunately, the Python programming language is one that does not implement records in exactly this format. The closest structure is a named tuple which associated fields with a particular key field. However, like all tuples, they are immutable, so once values have been assigned to fields, they cannot be changed.

from collections import namedtuple

Contact = namedtuple("Contact", 'name address postcode')

cookieM = Contact('Mr C Monster', 'Sesame Street', 'USA')

The above example shows the Python syntax for creating a named tuple as an equivalent to a record data structure.

Tip

A common exercise is to be given a number of records and asked to calculate the size of a file. This can be done by calculating the size of each record (by adding together the maximum size of each field it contains) then multiplying this by the number of records.

Tuples

Tuples, like records, are used to group together related values. In appearance they are very similar to one-dimensional arrays. But there are two important differences. First, tuples cannot be edited once they have been assigned (immutable), and second, tuples can contain values of different data types unlike arrays where every item must be of the sametype.

The Python example below shows the creation of a tuple called 'student' which holds a pupil's first name, surname, date of birth and favourite subject.

Code

```
student = ('James', 'Smith', '30/01/2000', 'Computer Science')
```

Retrieving items from the tuple is simple, as elements are indexed in the same way as arrays, print(student[1]) will display the word Smith.

However, trying to assign a new value to the tuple produces an error message telling us that this is not possible, as shown in Figures 12.3 and 12.4.

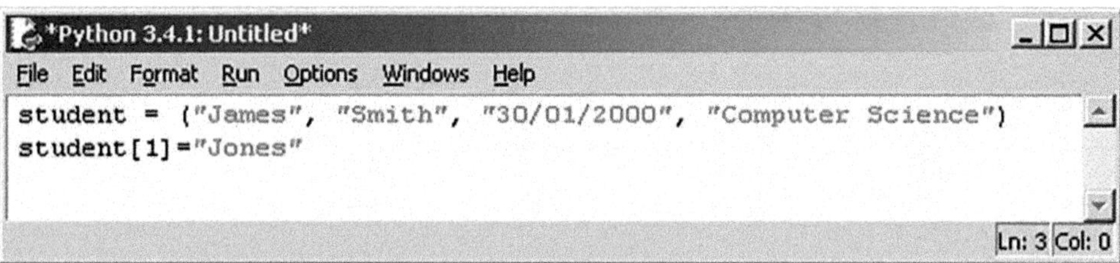

Figure 12.3: Attempting to assign a new value to an element in a tuple.

```
Python 3.4.1 Shell
File Edit Shell Debug Options Windows Help
Python 3.4.1 (v3.4.1:c0e311e010fc, May 18 2014, 10:38:22) [MSC v.1600 32 bit (In
tel)] on win32
Type "copyright", "credits" or "license()" for more information.
>>> ================================ RESTART ================================
>>>
Traceback (most recent call last):
  File "C:/Python34/1203.py", line 2, in <module>
    student[1]="Jones"
TypeError: 'tuple' object does not support item assignment
>>> |
Ln: 9 Col: 4
```

Figure 12.4: This error message is displayed when trying to assign a new value to an existing tuple.

An interesting additional piece of functionality offered by tuples is the ability to assign all values from one tuple to another. The example shows the creation of a new tuple of three variables being assigned the values from our student tuple.

Lists

A list is a simple data structure that is similar to an array. Like tuples, lists can hold a range of data types but like arrays their elements can be edited once they have been initiated (they are mutable). Data types can be mixed within the same list and multidimensional lists can be created in exactly the same way as arrays shown above. In Python, it is more useful to implement arrays as lists because of their flexibility. Lists are dynamic data structures which means that they can grow and shrink in size as data is added or deleted.

Figure 12.5 shows a list containing different data types being created, accessed and edited.

```
Python 3.4.1 Shell
File Edit Shell Debug Options Windows Help
Python 3.4.1 (v3.4.1:c0e311e010fc, May 18 2014, 10:38:22) [MSC v.1600 32 bit (In
tel)] on win32
Type "copyright", "credits" or "license()" for more information.
>>> ================================ RESTART ================================
>>>
James
>>>
                                                                    Ln: 6 Col: 4
```

Figure 12.5: Viewing and overwriting elements in a list using Python.

Linked lists

Linked lists are probably the most common type of dynamic data structure. Being dynamic means that, unlike arrays, they can grow to whatever size is required and their size isn't set when they are declared at the beginning of the program.

Linked lists are made up of nodes, with each node linked to the next node in the list. Linked lists use pointers to indicate the next element as well as the start and end of the list. The use of pointers means that elements do not need to be stored in contiguous memory address locations. They are very flexible, powerful data structures and can be used to implement almost every other type of data structure you need to know about. The use of pointers makes manipulating the data held in a list straightforward although could potentially make searching a large data set take a little more time than an array of the same size.

Nodes in a linked list consist of two things: data and a pointer to the next piece of data in the list (Figure 12.6).

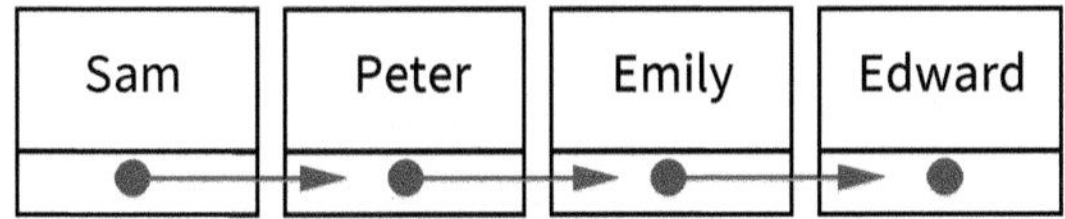

Figure 12.6: A linked list.

The best way to implement a linked list is using an object-oriented language such as C++; this allows the list to be completely dynamic:

Code

```
class Node
{
public:
  Node(string dataInput, Node* next=NULL);
  void setData(string dataValue);
  void setNext(Node* nextNode);
private:
  string data;
  Node* next;
};
```

Each node is made up of a piece of data and a pointer to the memory address of the next node in the list. This information is stored in the private section of the Node class. A node is created by calling the public node constructor and passing it the data value of the node and a pointer to the next node.

Adding data to a linked list

Adding new data to the end of a linked list is easy. The first step is to create a new node:

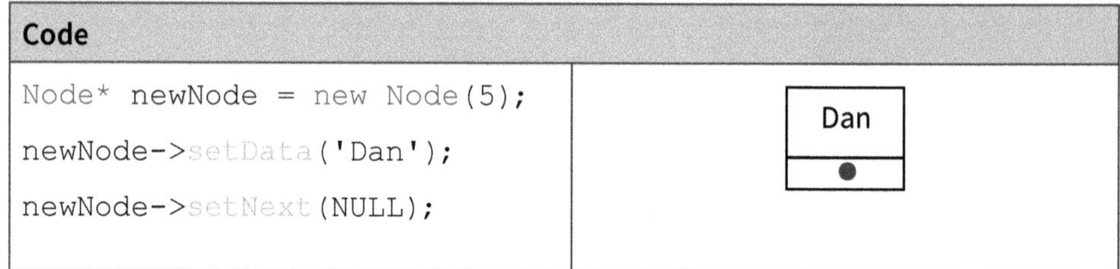

Code

```
Node* newNode = new Node(5);
newNode->setData('Dan');
newNode->setNext(NULL);
```


The second step is to update the last item in the current list so that it points to the new item:

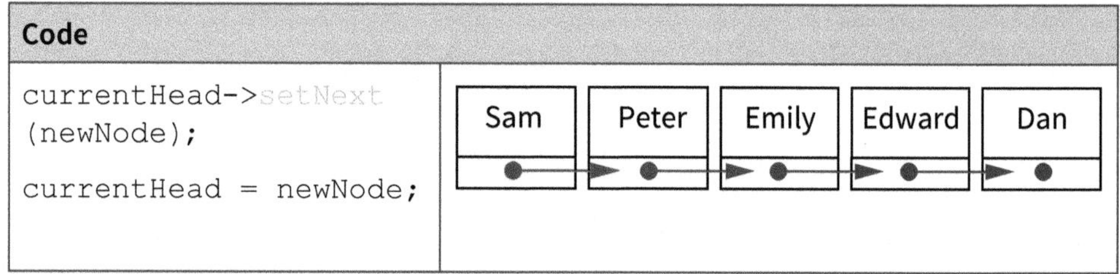

Code

```
currentHead->setNext
(newNode);
currentHead = newNode;
```


Of course, there is no reason why you have to put your new item at the end of the list. Imagine you want to create a linked list that is sorted in a particular order. You can easily insert a new node in the correct place by working out where you want it, adjusting the node that is currently there to point to the new node and then telling your new node to point to the next node in the list (Figures 12.7 and 12.8).

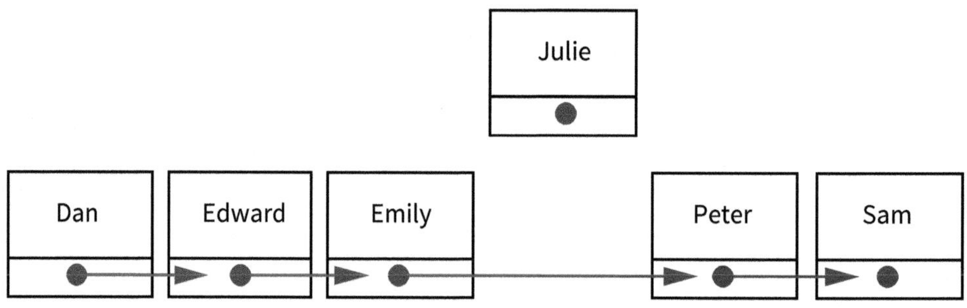

Figure 12.7: Adding data to a linked list.

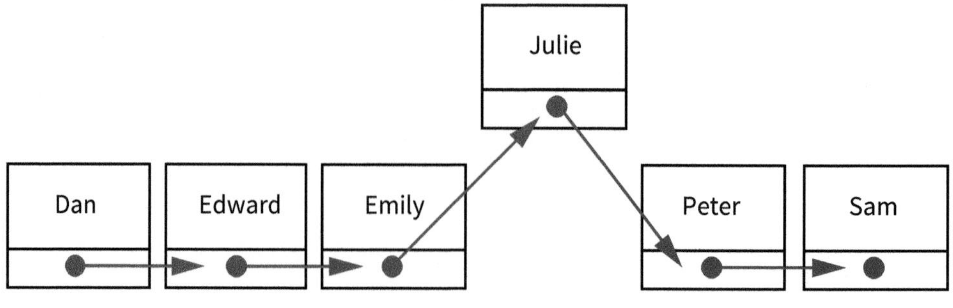

Figure 12.8: Inserting data in to a linked list.

Removing data from a list

It is also very simple to remove an item from a list. We simply need to adjust the item before it in order to point to the item after it. Doing this removes the node from the list and preserves the order of items.

It is also simple to reverse the order of data stored in a linked list. All we need to do is to reverse all of the node pointers and the start pointer becomes the null pointer.

Stacks

Stacks are last-in first-out (LIFO) data structures. This means that the most recent piece of data to be placed onto the stack is the first piece to be taken off of it (Figure 12.9).

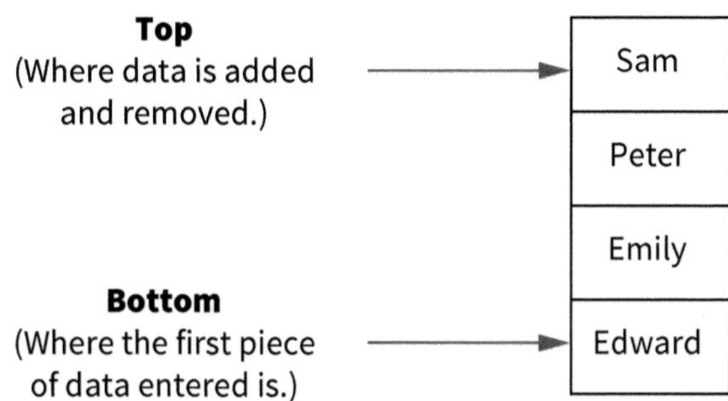

Figure 12.9: Stack.

Think of a stack like a pile of pancakes. The pancake on the top is the last one to be added to the pile and will be the first one to be taken off.

Adding data to the stack is called **pushing** and taking data off the stack is called **popping**.

Stacks are easily implemented using an array or a linked list to hold the data and a variable to point to the top of the stack.

The code below shows how Python could be used to implement a simple stack using a list. Calling the pop function will remove a piece of data from the stack; calling the push function will add some data to the top of the stack.

Code

```
myStack = ['Edward', 'Emily', 'Peter', 'Sam', 'Empty',
'Empty'] # creates a stack
pointerTop = 3 #points to the element at the top of the
stack
def pop( ): #removes the value from the top of the stack
and returns it
  value = myStack[pointerTop]
  myStack[pointerTop] = 'Empty'
  pointerTop = pointerTop - 1
  return value
def push(data): #adds a new piece of data to the top of the
stack
  pointerTop = pointerTop + 1
myStack[pointerTop] = data
```

Queues

Queues are first-in first-out (FIFO) data structures. This means that the most recent piece of data to be placed in the queue is the last piece taken out.

Think of queues like the ones you find at supermarket checkouts. The first person in a queue is the first person to leave it (Figure 12.10).

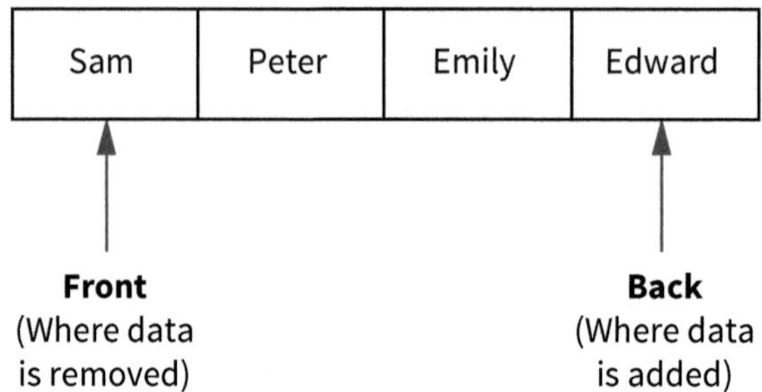

Figure 12.10: A queue data structure.

Queues are easily implemented using the simple Python code shown here. A list and two variables are used. One variable points to the first item in the queue, the other points to the rear of the queue:

Code

```
myQueue = ['Sam', 'Peter', 'Emily', 'Edward', 'Empty',
'Empty'] #creates a queue
pointerFront = 0 #points to the element at the front
of the queue
pointerBack = 4 #points to the element at the back
of the queue


def dequeue( ): #removes the data from the front of the
queue and returns it
  value = myQueue [pointerFront]
  myQueue [pointerFront] = 'Empty'
  pointerFront = pointerFront + 1
  return value


def enqueue(data): #adds a new piece of data to the back of
the queue
  pointerBack = pointerBack + 1
  myQueue [pointerBack] = data
```

Binary trees and binary search trees

Binary tree data structures are composed of nodes (sometimes called leaves) and links between them (sometimes called branches). Each node has up to two others coming off of it, which creates a structure like the one shown in Figure 12.11.

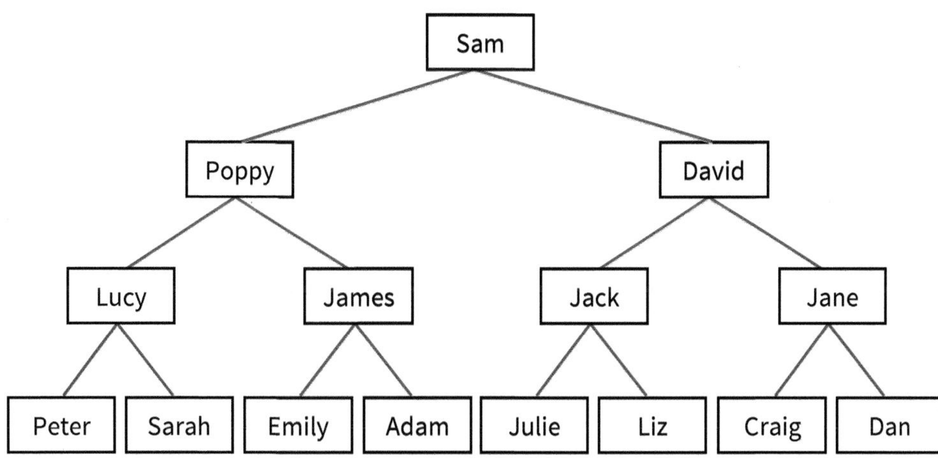

Figure 12.11: A tree.

Activity 12.2

Use Python to create and search queues and stacks.

Trees are used to implement another data structure called a binary search tree. These are identical to trees but have the additional constraint that the data on the left branch of a node must be less than the data in the root node. Likewise, the data on the right branch of the node must be greater than the data held in the root node. All the following trees are also binary search trees. A node in a tree data structure can have any number of child nodes but a binary search tree must have a maximum of two.

A tree structure uses pointers to point from the parent to the child nodes. In a binary search tree, from the root, the left pointer points to the sub tree containing values lower than it and the right pointer points to the sub tree containing higher values.

Unlike stacks and queues, there is a range of different ways to traverse binary tree data structures. Each method will return a different set of results, so it is important that you use the correct one.

We'll use the binary search tree shown in Figure 12.12 to demonstrate the different methods of traversal.

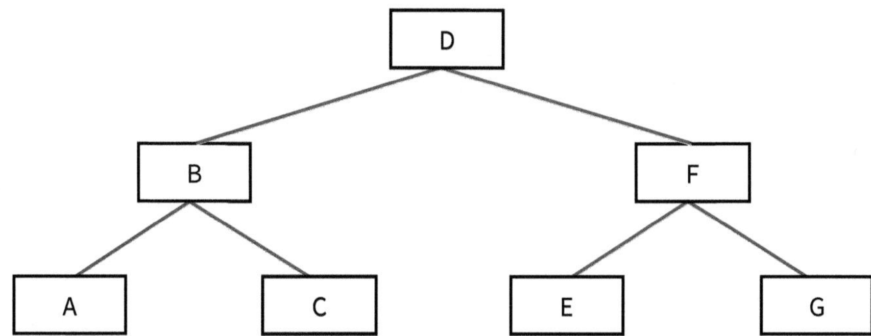

Figure 12.12: A binary tree.

- *Pre-order traversal (depth first search)*: Start at the root node, traverse the left sub tree, then traverse the right sub tree .This would give: *D B A C F E G.*
- *In-order traversal*: Traverse the left sub tree, then visit the root node, and finally traverse the right sub tree. This would give: *A B C D E F G.*
- *Post-order traversal*: Traverse the left sub tree, then traverse the right sub tree, and finally visit the root node. This would give: *A C B E G F D.*
- *Level-order traversal (breadth first search)*: Start at the root node, then visit each sub tree node before descending further down the tree. This would give: D B F A C E G.

Tip

You could be required to write simple search algorithms as well as demonstrating how to add and remove nodes or elements from data structures in the exam so make sure you are prepared for this.

Implementing a binary tree

Just like stacks and queues, it is possible to implement a binary tree using an array or a linked list. It is more useful to use a linked list, as this allows the binary tree to be dynamic and grow to any size.

Using a linked list, the nodes of a tree are made up of a piece of data as well as pointers to the addresses of the nodes on the left and right. It is also sensible to include a pointer to a node's parent (the node above it) to aid in navigation. The C++ code below shows how this can be achieved:

Code

```
class Node
{
public:
  Node(string dataInput, Node* left=NULL, Node*
  right= NULL, Node* parent=NULL);

  void setData(string dataValue);
  void setLeft(Node* leftNode);
  void setRight(Node* rightNode);
  void setParent(Node* parentNode);

private:
  string data;
  Node* left;
  Node* right;
  Node* parent;
};
```

However, binary trees can also be created using a 2D array. The second dimension of array represents the nodes and consists of the data in the node as well as the indexes of the two elements beneath it:

Code

```
myTree = [ ['1', 'D', '2'], ['3', 'B', '4'], ['5', 'F', '6'],
  ['', 'A', ''], ['', 'C', ''], ['', 'E', ''], ['', 'G', '']]
```

Adding data to a binary search tree

You can add data to a binary tree by following these simple steps, starting at the root of the tree:

1. Compare the data you want to add to the current node.
2. If the new data is less than the node, follow the left pointer, otherwise follow the right pointer.
3. Repeat this until you reach the end of the tree.
4. Update the pointers of the last node to point to the new one.

The Python code below gives you an idea of how this can be done.

Code

```
class node:
  def__init__(self, data, parent):
    self.left = None
    self.data = data
    self.parent = parent
    self.right = None

def addToTree (currentNode, data, parent):
  if currentNode = None:
    newNode = node (data, parent)
  else:
    if data < = currentNode.data:
      addToTree (currentNode.left, data, currentNode)
  else:
    addToTree (currentNode.right, data, currentNode)
```

Removing data from a binary tree

Removing data from a binary search tree is more complicated. The method required differs depending on the number of branches the node to be removed has coming off it.

Case 1: A leaf with no branches

If the node to be removed is a leaf with no branches coming off of it, removal is simple. You can delete the node and set its parent's pointer to null. In this example (Figure 12.13), node A is simply removed along with the pointer from node B.

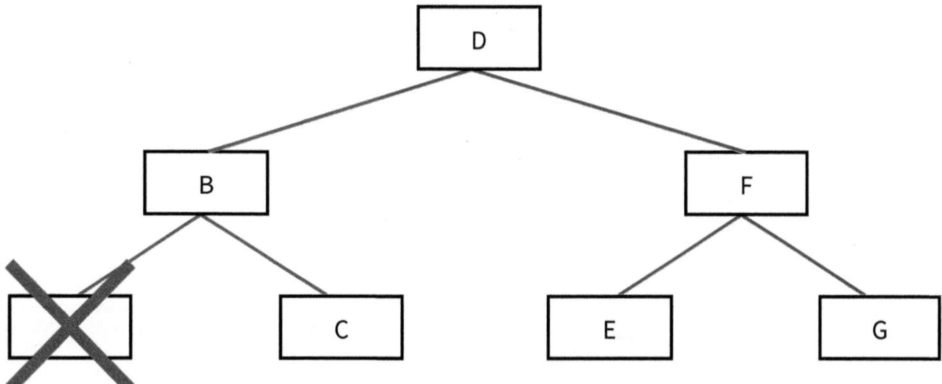

Figure 12.13: A binary tree.

Case 2: A leaf with a single branch

If the node has a single branch, you must update the pointer of the parent to point to the address of the child of the node to be deleted. Then you can delete the node without losing any information. In this example (Figure 12.14), the left pointer of node D is updated to point to node C before node B is deleted.

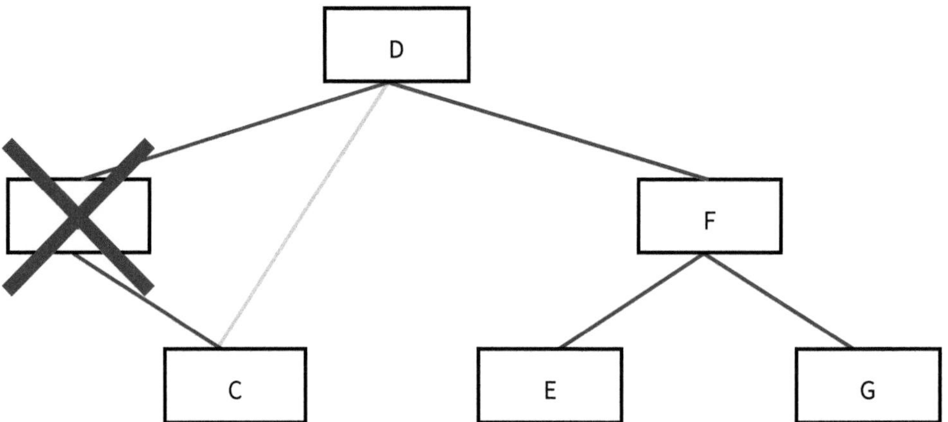

Figure 12.14: An element is removed from a binary tree and the necessary branches are updated.

Case 3: A leaf with two branches

If the node to be deleted has two branches, things are slightly more complicated. First you must use in-order traversal to find the smallest node beneath the one to be deleted, which is known as the successor node. The successor node's left, right and parent pointers are updated so that they are the same as the node to be deleted. Only then can the target node be removed from the tree. Although this may seem complicated, it is vital if the structure of the binary search tree (with small values on the left and large values on the right) is to be preserved.

Graphs

Graphs are made up of two sets of data called vertices and edges. The vertices set is the data you see when you look at the graph. In the example shown in Figure 12.15, the vertices set is {Alistair, Charlie, Lucy, Sarah, Verity}. The edge set contains all the links between these vertices; each edge is made up of the two vertices (and their associated data) being linked. If two vertices are connected by an edge, we say they are adjacent. The edges set for the example below is {(Alistair, Sarah), (Sarah, Lucy), (Sarah, Verity), (Lucy, Verity), (Lucy, Charlie)}.

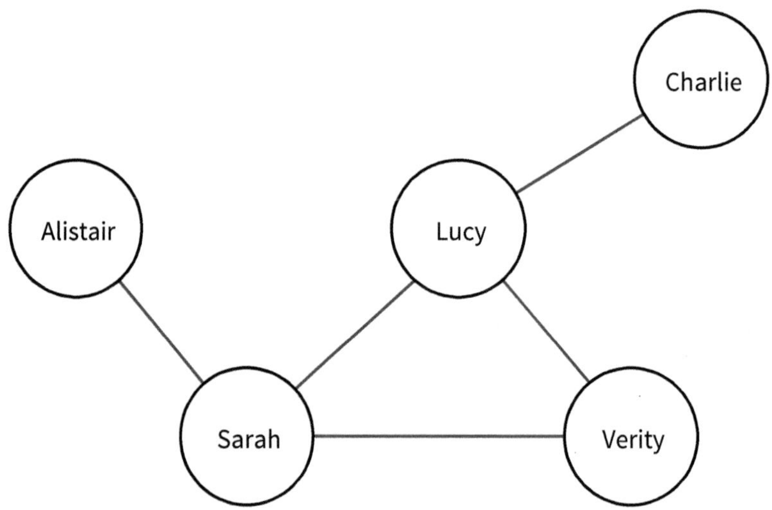

Figure 12.15: An undirected graph.

Undirected graphs

In an undirected graph the order of the pairs in the edges set doesn't matter because the edges go both ways. So if (Alistair, Sarah) is an edge, we don't need to record

(Sarah, Alistair) as an edge as they mean the same thing. Undirected graphs are usually drawn using straight lines with no arrowheads between vertices. The example you have already seen is an undirected graph.

Vertices = {Alistair, Charlie, Lucy, Sarah, Verity}

Edges = {(Alistair, Sarah), (Sarah, Lucy), (Sarah, Verity), (Verity, Lucy), (Lucy, Charlie)}

Directed graphs

In a directed graph the edges only link in a particular direction. This is usually shown on diagrams by using arrowheads to indicate the direction. This has two impacts on the edge set. First, two vertices are said to be adjacent only if their edge is explicitly declared; second, the order of the edges matters, as it indicates the direction of the link. In Figure 12.16, the vertices set remains the same as the previous example but the edges set is very different.

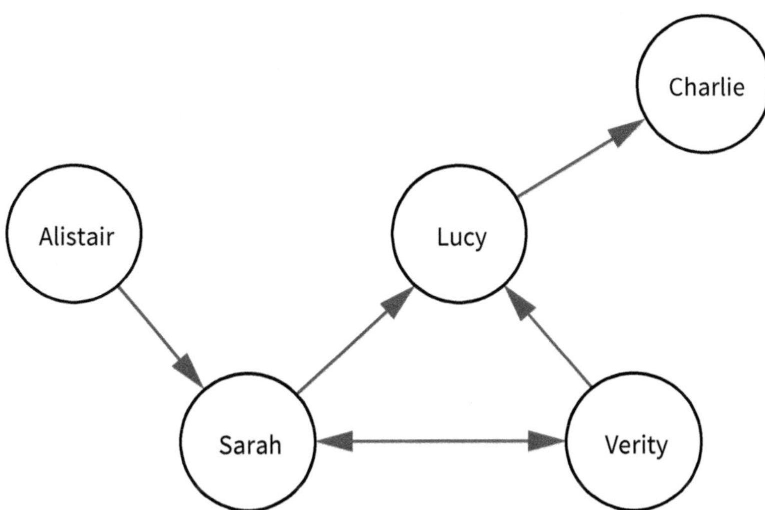

Figure 12.16: Directed graph.

Vertices = {Alistair, Charlie, Lucy, Sarah, Verity}

Edges = {(Alistair, Sarah), (Sarah, Lucy), (Sarah, Verity), (Verity, Sarah), (Verity, Lucy), (Lucy, Charlie)}

Creating graphs

Like most other data structures, graphs can be implemented using linked lists or arrays. This decision is based on a number of factors, including whether you want them to be dynamic or static data structures. The following example uses a 2D array to implement a directed graph. The first element of the second array holds the vertex data and the second and third elements the edge. Using this array means that we are limited to a graph with five nodes and ten edges, but it is easy to understand:

Code

```
graph = [['Alistair', 3, None ], ['Charlie', None , None],
  ['Lucy', 1, None ], ['Sarah', 2, 4 ], ['Verity', 2, 3]]
```

This 2D array represents the directed graph shown in Figure 12.16.

Removing vertices and edges

To remove an edge, you simply find the vertices at the start of the edge and set the edge to null.

The **remove_edge** function below takes a pair of indices representing an edge and removes the link between them:

Code

```
def remove_edge (v1, v2):
  for x in range (1, 2):
    if graph[v1][x] == v2:
      graph[v1][x] = None
```

The **remove_vertices** function replaces a node with an empty node, then searches the rest of the graph and removes any links to it:

Code

```
def remove_vertices (v1):
  graph [v1] = ['empty', None , None]

  for x in range (0, len (graph)):
    for y in range (1, 2):
      if graph [x] [y] == v1:
      graph [x] [y] = None
```

Hash tables

A hash table has two components: a table where the actual data is stored and a mapping function (called a hash function or hash algorithm). The hash function uses the data that is going to be entered in the table to generate the location in the table where the data should be stored.

In this example we want to use a hash table to hold some names. The initial table is the easy part; it looks like any other table:

Index	Name
0	
1	
2	
3	
4	

Next, we need to decide on our hash algorithm; let's say that we will take the length of the name entered and divide it by the size of the table (using the modulo (MOD) operator); the remainder gives the name's index number.
Let's say we want to enter the name 'Sarah' in the table. The length of the string is 5 and so is the length of the table:

Index	Data
0	Sarah
1	
2	
3	
4	

5 MOD 5 = 0

So we'll store the name in index 0:

To insert a new name such as 'Adam', we carry out the same operation (4 MOD 5) and get 4, so the name Adam goes in index 4:

Index	Data
0	Sarah
1	
2	
3	
4	Adam

It's not hard to see that with our simple hash algorithm we'll soon get collisions. If I want to add 'Jane' to the table, her name is the same length as Adam's so the algorithm will try to overwrite Adam to insert Jane. Not ideal! There are many solutions to this problem, the most useful of which is called **separate chaining**.

Separate chaining uses the original table to store a dynamic data structure (like a linked list). When a new item creates the same hash result as an existing piece of data, a new node on the linked list in that location is created to hold the new data. While good at avoiding collision, this technique will slow down finding the data again, as once the hash location has been computed the linked list will need to be searched as well.

Summary

- Data structures are organised stores of data in a computer's memory. Each data structure has its own strengths and weaknesses that make it suitable for a given situation.
- Arrays hold data of a single type in a fixed-size structure; they can have one, two or three dimensions. It is possible for arrays to have more dimensions.
- The different data storage locations in an array are called 'elements' and are accessed using an index (which always starts from 0).
- A record is a data structure that allows related items of data of different types to be stored together in a single file.
- Tuples can hold different data types but cannot have different data assigned to them once they have been created (immutable).
- Lists can hold a range of data types but, as with arrays, their elements can be edited once they have been initiated (mutable).
- Linked lists represent each piece of data as a node which holds the data and a link to the next piece of data in the list.
- Data is removed from linked lists by deleting the node and pointing the item behind it to the item in front of it.
- Graphs are made of sets of edges and vertices. Vertices hold data and edges describe the links between the data.
- Stacks are last-in, first-out data structures that hold data in the order in which it was entered.
- Data is removed (popped) or added (pushed) at the top of the stack.

- Queues are first-in, first-out data structures in which the last piece of data entered is the last piece of data retrieved.
- Tree data structures consist of nodes and sub trees. Nodes contain data and the branches link them together.
- Hash tables use mapping functions to calculate where in the table a new piece of data should be stored.

End-of-chapter questions

1. What notation is used to describe the efficiency of a data structure or algorithm? [1]
2. What is an array? [2]
3. What do the nodes in a linked list contain? [2]
4. Give the name of a first-in first-out (FIFO) data structure. [1]
5. Which **two** datasets are combined to create a graph data structure? [2]

Further reading

Efficiency of data structures – go to bigocheatsheet.com.
Big O notation – search for Big-O notation on Justin Abrahms' website.
Linked lists – search on Stanford Computer Science online library.
Binary trees – search on Stanford Computer Science online library.
Stacks and queues – search for Data Structures on Virginia Tech's Computer Science website.

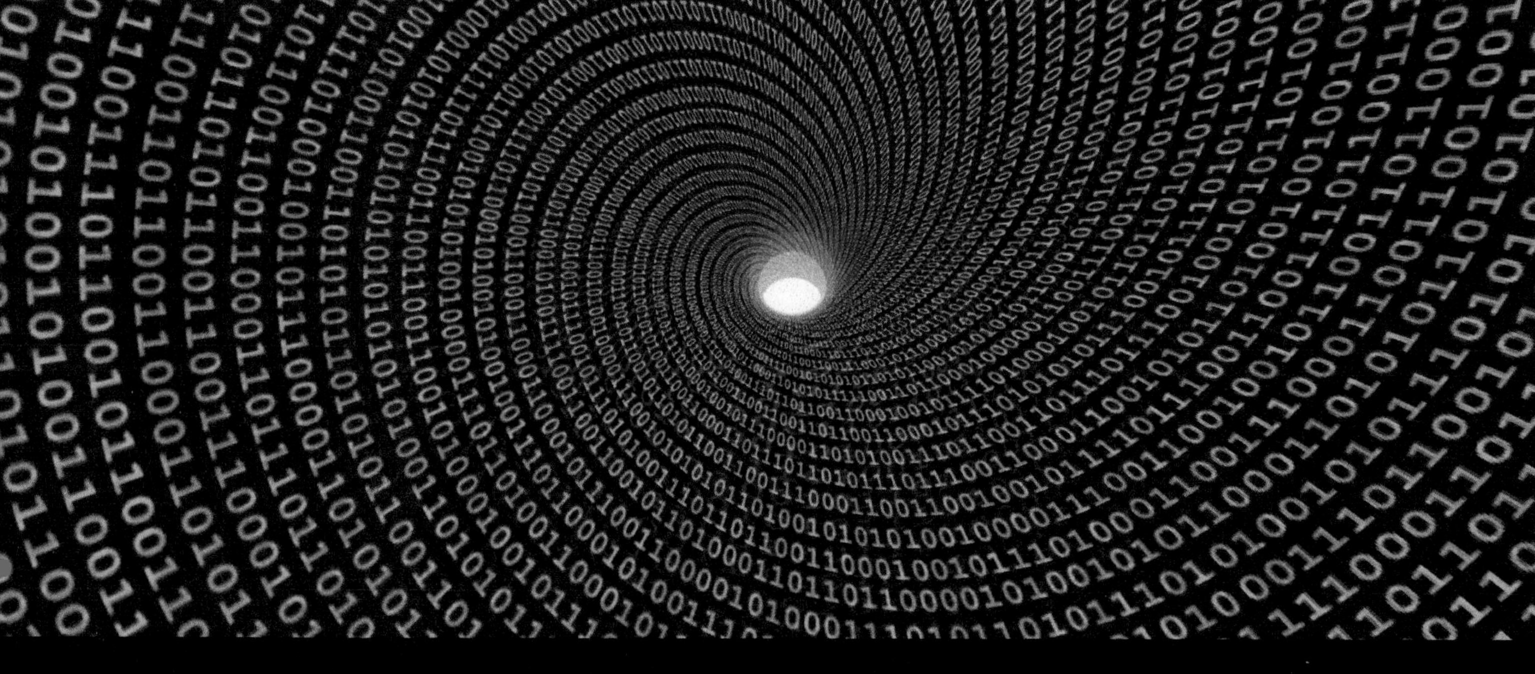

Chapter 13
Boolean algebra

Specification points

1.4.3 Boolean algebra

- Define problems using Boolean logic.
- Manipulate Boolean expressions, including the use of Karnaugh maps to simplify Boolean expressions.
- Using logic gate diagrams and truth tables.
- Use the following rules to derive or simplify statements in Boolean algebra: De Morgan's laws, distribution, association, commutation, double negation.
- The logic associated with D type flip flops, half and full adders.

Learning objectives

- To understand how to read and write Boolean algebra.
- To learn how to define problems using Boolean algebra.
- To understand propositional logic and the related key terms.
- To derive or simplify Boolean algebra using the following rules:
  - De Morgan's laws
  - distribution
  - association
  - commutation
  - double negation.

Introduction

Computers are digital devices, using binary 1 and 0 to represent all data. These two values could also be used to indicate true or false. Boolean algebra examines statements that, when evaluated, will result in true or false. Propositional logic follows mathematical rules that allow manipulation of the statements. This, in turn, allows the logical statements to be simplified or derived. In this chapter, you will learn about propositional logic and some of the tools that can define real-world problems. You will also learn some of the key tools that can be used to derive and simplify these logical statements.

Propositional logic

Let P be 'it is raining'
Let Q be 'I have an umbrella'
Let T be 'I will get wet'

Logical propositions such as 'it is raining' can have either a true or a false value. Statements such as 'what is the weather', which can produce multiple answers, cannot be considered to be logical propositions. A proposition is an atomic value or place holder and is represented algebraically by assigning letters to each proposition. In the statements above, we use P to represent the proposition that it is raining. We have also used Q and T to represent two different propositions. Most of the rules used to simplify logic do not rely on the meaning of the propositions, but rather focus on how a logical statement is structured. It is useful, when defining problems, to give meaning to our propositions to give them more context. It is also possible to allow our propositions to have more of a programming focus by assigning them conditional expressions. For example, we could write 'Let P be $N < 5$' or 'Let Q be $N \geq J$'. These would be acceptable logical propositions, as each one can evaluate to true or false only.

Propositional logic makes use of a number of symbols to represent logical connectives. A summary of these connectives can be seen in the table below. A propositional statement will therefore be a combination of propositions with logical connectives. To aid understanding, colloquial terms have been given to each symbol as well as their formal names. It is important that you learn and use formal names when discussing propositional logic as well as knowing the familiar terms that they relate to.

Symbol	Alternatives	Formal term	Informal term
$\wedge$	.	Conjunction	AND
$\vee$	+	Disjunction	OR
$\neg$	$\sim A$ $\bar{A}$	Negation	NOT
$\rightarrow$		Implication	IF
$\leftrightarrow$	$\equiv$	Biconditional equivalence	Equality
$\veebar$	$\oplus$	Exclusive or	XOR

Conjunction

Consider the conjoined proposition: 'it is raining outside *and* I have an umbrella'. The keyword in this statement is the word 'and'. For this statement to be true, both of the propositions represented by P and Q must be true. If one is false, the whole statement becomes false. Conjunction can be represented in the simple truth table below:

P	Q	P AND Q
T	T	T
T	F	F
F	T	F
F	F	F

When we join two propositions together using conjunction, it is represented by the symbol $\wedge$. If P represents 'it is raining' and Q represents 'I have an umbrella', we can represent the conjunction of these two propositions as the statement $P \wedge Q$.

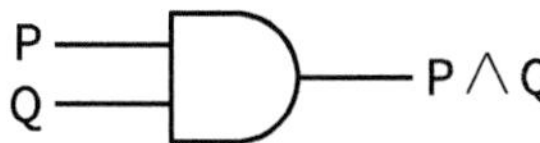

Figure 13.1: Diagrammatic representation of an AND gate.

Disjunction

Sometimes we want to see if one statement or another is true or not. An example would be: 'it is dark or it is foggy'. If either of these propositions is true, my car lights need to be on. Unlike conjunction, we do not require both statements to be true, but if they are, we also need to ensure that 'lights on' is also true. The truth table of two propositions connected using disjunction is shown below:

P	Q	P OR Q
T	T	T
T	F	T
F	T	T
F	F	F

Disjunction is represented by the $\vee$ symbol. To represent the disjunction of two propositions, we would simply write $P \vee Q$.

Figure 13.2: Diagrammatic representation of an OR gate.

Negation

When the negation of a proposition is needed, for example 'it is *not* raining', we can make use of the negation $\neg$ operator, colloquially known as NOT. Negation is a unary operator which means it only requires one operand or statement to act on and will apply to the proposition immediately following it. So if P represents 'it is raining', we can represent the negation by $\neg P$.

P	NOT P
T	F
F	T

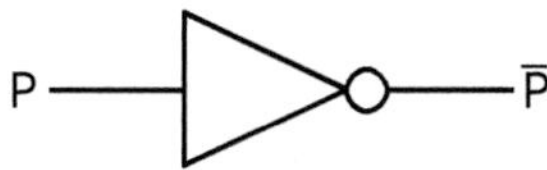

Figure 13.3: Diagrammatic representation of a NOT gate.

Implication

P = *'it is raining'*
Q = *'I have an umbrella'*
T = *'I will get wet'*

When certain propositions are true, we can infer or imply other elements of truth. Consider the proposition $P \wedge Q$. If it is raining and you have an umbrella, we can infer that you will not get wet, or $\neg T$. Implication is represented using the symbol $\rightarrow$, so our keeping dry proposition could be fully written as $P \wedge Q \rightarrow \neg T$. This would be read as 'if P and Q then not T' or 'if it is raining and I have an umbrella, I will not get wet'.

P	Q	P → Q
T	T	T
T	F	F
F	T	T
F	F	T

Tautologies

A propositional logic formula is a tautology if, regardless of what truth values each proposition has, the entire statement will always remain true. Below are some examples of tautologies:

$$x \vee \neg x$$
$$\neg\neg x \rightarrow x$$
$$\neg(x \wedge \neg x)$$

If you substitute truth values for any of the above formulas, they will always evaluate to true. Consider the truth table for $\neg\neg x \rightarrow x$:

x	¬¬x	¬¬x→ x
T	T	T
F	F	T

Replacing a simple proposition, x, with another formula will always result in a tautology. Consider the formula $P \vee Q$. If this formula replaces x for the tautology $\neg\neg x \rightarrow x$, we get the formula $\neg\neg(P \vee Q) \rightarrow (P \vee Q)$. When the truth table is calculated for this, regardless of the truth value of P or Q, the full statement will still evaluate to true. No matter how complicated you make the substitution, the final result will always be the same. Tautologies always evaluate to true and this logical deduction is useful when deriving further formulas.

P	Q	P∨Q	¬¬(P∨Q)	¬¬(P∨Q)→(P∨Q)
T	T	T	T	T
T	F	T	T	T
F	T	T	T	T
F	F	F	F	T

Biconditional equivalence

Biconditional equivalence joins two propositions together using the ↔ symbol, and means that the truth on both sides is equivalent. For example, 'if and only if it is raining will I get wet' can be represented as $P \leftrightarrow T$. It is equivalent because if both sides are true, the whole statement is true, while if they are different, the statement is false. The statement will also be true if both are false, as if it is not raining, I will not get wet, which maintains logical integrity. For biconditional equivalence to be true, both sides must evaluate to the same truth value.

P	Q	P↔Q
T	T	T
T	F	F
F	T	F
F	F	T

Logical laws of deduction

Biconditional equivalence showed that if both sides of the formula are equivalent, the overall formula is true. We can use this property to show the equivalence of formulas and prove that they are tautologies. Boolean algebra has certain laws that can be used to help with further derivations. This section covers association, distribution, commutation and double negation. It is important to remember that each of these equivalencies is a tautology, that is, it is true regardless of what we replace the propositions with.

Commutation

$$P \wedge Q \leftrightarrow Q \wedge P$$
$$P \vee Q \leftrightarrow Q \vee P$$

P	Q	P ∧ Q	Q ∧ P	P ∧ Q ↔ Q ∧ P
T	T	T	T	T
T	F	F	F	T
F	T	F	F	T
F	F	F	F	T

The laws of commutation for both conjunction and disjunction are shown above. Commutation essentially refers to the idea that the order of propositions for both conjunction and disjunction do not matter and they can be interchanged. The truth tables for both $P \wedge Q$ and $Q \wedge P$ are exactly the same. This means they are biconditional.

Association

$$T \wedge (P \wedge Q) \leftrightarrow (T \wedge Q) \wedge P$$
$$T \vee (P \vee Q) \leftrightarrow (T \vee Q) \vee P$$

The order in which we combine multiple conjunctions or disjunctions does not matter. There is a biconditional equivalence regardless of the order, as long as they all use conjunction or disjunction, not a combination. As in standard algebra, statements in brackets are always evaluated first. In the statement $T \wedge (P \wedge Q)$, the conjunction in brackets is evaluated first and the result is conjoined with T. Likewise, in the second statement, $(T \wedge Q) \wedge P$, the conjunction in brackets is evaluated first and then conjoined with P. The resultant truth tables below show that the two statements are equivalent and that they are tautologous:

P	Q	T	P ∧ Q	T ∧ Q	T ∧ (P ∧ Q)	(T ∧ Q) ∧ P	T ∧ (P ∧ Q) ↔ (T ∧ Q) ∧ P
T	T	T	T	T	T	T	T
T	F	T	F	F	F	F	T
F	T	T	F	T	F	F	T
F	F	T	F	F	F	F	T
T	T	F	T	F	F	F	T
T	F	F	F	F	F	F	T
F	T	F	F	F	F	F	T
F	F	F	F	F	F	F	T

Distribution

$$T \wedge (P \vee Q) \leftrightarrow (T \wedge P) \vee (T \wedge Q)$$

$$T \vee (P \wedge Q) \leftrightarrow (T \vee P) \wedge (T \vee Q)$$

This law is a bit more complicated than the others, but distribution for Boolean algebra works in the same way as in standard algebra. Consider the statement $x(y + z)$; this can have x distributed over $y + z$ resulting in $xy + xz$. All we have done is multiplied everything inside the brackets by x. If you consider multiplication to be conjunction and addition to be disjunction, we can see a bit more clearly how the distribution really works.

$$T \wedge (P \vee Q)$$
$$T \wedge P \vee T \wedge Q$$
$$(T \vee P) \vee (T \wedge Q)$$

Brackets are needed to ensure that the resultant equivalency is a tautology and that it is clear in which order the conjunctions or disjunctions must be evaluated. Distribution is not associative, that is, the order of the brackets matters; however, the contents of the brackets are commutative. A simplified truth table proves that the law of distribution is a tautology:

P	Q	T	T ∧ (P ∧ Q)	(T ∧ P) ∨ (T ∧ Q)	T ∧ (P ∨ Q) ↔ (T ∧ P) ∨ (T ∧ Q)
T	T	T	T	T	T
T	F	T	T	T	T
F	T	T	T	T	T
F	F	T	F	F	T
T	T	F	F	F	T
T	F	F	F	F	T
F	T	F	F	F	T
F	F	F	F	F	T

Double negation

$$\neg\neg P \leftrightarrow P$$

You may already be aware that a double negative results in addition. For example, 2 − −2 is the same as 2 + 2. In logic, a double negative always results in the original truth value. So any proposition that is negated twice is the same as simply writing the proposition with no negatives. This equivalency, like all of the others, is a tautology and can be seen in the truth table below. In fact, double negative was one of the statements we saw to explain the concept of tautologies.

P	¬¬P	¬¬P ↔ P
T	T	T
F	F	T

De Morgan's laws

$$\neg(P \vee Q) \leftrightarrow \neg P \wedge \neg Q$$
$$\neg(P \wedge Q) \leftrightarrow \neg P \vee \neg Q$$

De Morgan's laws are named after Augustus De Morgan, who died in 1871. He introduced the laws into propositional logic. De Morgan proposed that the negation of disjunctions is the conjunction of the negations and that the negation of conjunction is the disjunction of the negations. Putting this into plain English, consider an example. If we consider the case that $\neg(P \vee Q)$ is true, this could only come about if both P and Q are false. This is because disjunction, as we know, is true if either proposition is true. This leads to the truth table below, which clearly shows that there is only one case where the statement can be true.

P	Q	(P ∨ Q)	¬ (P ∨ Q)
T	T	T	F
T	F	T	F
F	T	T	F
F	F	F	T

Following through with this logic, we can infer that both P and Q must be false if the entire statement is true. As such, we can say that P must not be true, $\neg P$, and Q must not be true, $\neg Q$. Notice that the word 'and' has been used, which we already know as conjunction. Therefore, once we pull the logic together, we are left with $\neg P \wedge \neg Q$. This is an informal proof of De Morgan's laws; a formal proof is shown below using natural deduction. Note that natural deduction is beyond the scope of A Level, but it is the only mechanism we have to write a formal proof for De Morgan's laws. It is shown below for completeness, with some basic notes on how it works. You do not have to understand this proof, nor will it come up on the exam.

Line	Stage	Logic	Notes
1	Initial premise	$\neg(P \vee Q)$	
2	Assumption for *reductio ad absurdum*	P	Assume that P is true.
3	∨ introduction to line 2	$P \vee Q$	If P is true, adding ∨ Q will still mean the statement is true.
4	∧ introduction to line 1 and 3	$\neg(P \vee Q) \wedge (P \vee Q)$	If you have two propositions, you can introduce a conjunction.
5	*Reductio ad absurdum* for lines 2 and 4	$\neg P$	We assumed P is true, but this has led to a contradiction. P cannot be true as $\neg(P \vee Q) \wedge (P \vee Q)$ can never be true. When we have a contradiction, *reductio ad absurdum* allows us to assume the opposite.
6	Assumption for RAA	Q	Assume that Q is true.
7	∨ introduction to line 6	P ∨ Q	
8	∧ introduction to line 1 and 7	¬ (P ∨ Q) ∧ (P ∨ Q)	
9	*Reductio ad absurdum* for lines 6 and 8	$\neg Q$	
10	∧ introduction to line 5 and 9	$\neg P \wedge \neg Q$	Finally we can combine the two negations as the final step of the proof.

Defining problems using propositional logic

So far in this chapter, you have seen the different notations and laws relating to propositional logic, but mostly in the theoretical sense rather than the practical. What propositional logic enables us to do is to define problems as statements containing propositions and logical connectives. Consider the statement 'If I own an old car which fails the MOT then I can either repair it or buy a new car'. This simple problem can be expressed in propositional logic by first splitting the sentence into propositions. Next, we can analyse the sentence to see what logical connectives we can use. Implication and disjunction are easy to spot using the key words 'if' and 'or'; however, the conjunction is slightly more cryptic. The use of the word 'which' suggests that both of these things must be true for the implication to be true. As we know, if we need two things to be true, we can use conjunction. Sometimes you have to consider the statement in a bit more detail rather than blindly looking for command words.

Consider the statement 'all old cars always fail the MOT and need to be repaired'. It is trivial to spot the conjunction by looking at the keyword 'and', which gives us $X \wedge Y$. However, linking old cars to this statement is a bit more complicated. We are essentially saying that old cars are synonymous with failing the MOT, and we could say 'cars which fail the MOT and need to be repaired must be old'. We have two implications here, as shown by the propositional statements below:

$$W \rightarrow X \wedge Y$$
$$X \wedge Y \rightarrow W$$

When you get a situation where you can reverse the implication and still have a true statement, we have a bidirectional condition. As such, the correct form of this propositional logic is:

$$W \leftrightarrow X \wedge Y$$

It is also possible to bring programming constructs into play. Consider a simple ball, not governed by gravity, bouncing around the screen. When the ball nears the edge of the screen, it needs to reverse direction. We can model this using five propositions, one for each edge and one to reverse direction:

Let A be 'ball is near far left edge, X< = 0'

Let B be 'ball is near far right edge, X> = width'

Let C be 'ball is near the top edge, Y< = 0'

Let D be 'ball is near the bottom edge, Y> = height'

Let R be 'reverse direction'

$$A \rightarrow R$$

$$B \rightarrow R$$

$$C \rightarrow R$$

$$D \rightarrow R$$

$$A \vee B \vee C \vee D \rightarrow R$$

We can combine the initial implications to form a compound disjunction of all four of the initial propositions. Based on the laws of association and commutation, it does not matter in which order we put the propositions, as $A \vee B \vee C \vee D \rightarrow R \equiv D \vee C \vee B \vee A \rightarrow R$.

Using propositional laws to derive and simplify statements

$$\neg(X \wedge \neg Y) \equiv \neg X \vee Y$$

Truth tables are a great way of testing the equivalency of two propositional statements. The $\equiv$ symbol means identity and is used when we want to say that two statements are identical, regardless of the truth values assigned to the propositions. $\neg X \vee Y$ is a simplified version of $\neg(X \wedge \neg Y)$, which can be derived using the propositional laws already encountered:

X	Y	$X \wedge \neg Y$	$\neg(X \wedge \neg Y)$	$\neg X \vee Y$
T	T	F	T	T
T	F	T	F	F
F	T	F	T	T
F	F	F	T	T

Consider the statement $\neg(X \wedge \neg Y)$; it has a negation outside the brackets and looks very similar to De Morgan's law:

$$\neg(P \wedge Q) \leftrightarrow \neg P \vee \neg Q.$$

We can use this law on our original statement, which leaves us with $\neg X \vee \neg\neg Y$. As we know, a double negative is the same as having no negatives at all (the double negation law). We can therefore remove them, leaving $\neg X \vee Y$. When applying both laws, you must set out the simplification as shown below, always stating which law is applied at any given stage:

$\neg(X \wedge \neg Y) \equiv \neg X \vee \neg\neg Y$ De Morgan's law

$\neg(X \wedge \neg Y) \equiv \neg X \vee Y$ double negation law

In the above example, we derived one logical statement from another using propositional laws. It is also possible to make use of the laws to simplify logical statements. In the example below, you can simplify a statement by using the commutation and distribution laws:

$(X \wedge Z) \vee (Y \wedge Z) \equiv (Z \wedge X) \vee (Z \wedge Y)$ Commutation law

$(Z \wedge X) \vee (Z \wedge Y) \equiv Z \wedge (X \vee Y)$ Distribution law

$$\neg(\neg X \wedge \neg Y) \wedge \neg(\neg X \wedge \neg Z) \equiv X \vee (Y \wedge Z)$$

Sometimes, when a statement needs to be simplified, you must break things down into a number of steps. It is not always possible to jump from the statement on the left-hand side to the right in one step. When tackling problems like this, it is important that you know and understand the laws so that you can recognise when they must be used. $\neg(\neg X \wedge \neg Y)$ has a negation outside the brackets, which matches De Morgan's law in the same way that $\neg(\neg X \wedge \neg Z)$ does. $\neg\neg Z$ is a double negation and De Morgan's law has left us with four double negations. As such, the second step will be to remove them. Finally, we are left with *X* distributed over two bracketed statements. The distribution law allows us to remove this from each bracket as long as the conjunctions and disjunctions are correct and match the law. The full derivation is shown below:

$\neg(\neg X \wedge \neg Y) \wedge \neg(\neg X \wedge \neg Z) \equiv (\neg\neg X \vee \neg\neg Y) \wedge (\neg\neg X \vee \neg\neg Z)$ De Morgan's law (twice)

$(\neg\neg X \vee \neg\neg Y) \wedge (\neg\neg X \vee \neg\neg Z) \equiv (X \vee Y) \wedge (X \vee Z)$ double negation (four times)

$(X \vee Y) \wedge (X \vee Z) \equiv X \vee (Y \wedge Z)$ distribution law

X	Y	Z	¬(¬X ∧ ¬Y) ∧¬(¬X ∧ ¬Z)	X∨(Y ∨ Z)
T	T	T	T	T
T	F	T	T	T
F	T	T	T	T
F	F	T	F	F
T	T	F	T	T
T	F	F	T	T
F	T	F	F	F
F	F	F	F	F

The above truth table shows that the two statements have the same truth values, which is not immediately obvious just by looking at them.

Open up the propositional logic calculator here.

Activity 13.1

Enter the formulae found in this chapter to see the truth tables and the expressions' various properties. Use it to test all of the tautologies, which will light up the green 'taut' icon.

Karnaugh maps

Karnaugh maps, or K-maps, offer a mapping method to represent truth tables as well as a method to simplify truth statements. Consider the simple truth table below and the corresponding Karnaugh map. True and false are going to be represented as 1 and 0.

A	B	
1	1	0
1	0	1
0	1	1
0	0	1

	0	1	A
0	1	1	
1	1	0	
B			

The diagram above is constructed by writing the possible values of A in the column headings and B in the row headings. Then the output is written in the squares themselves. At this point, we start looking for sets of 1s, which are next to each other, either vertically or horizontally. These are known as groupings and must be grouped together in powers of 2. So we can have groups of 1, 2, 4, 8 and so on. Legal groupings will be looked at in a later section. Note that we can have multiple groupings and those groupings may overlap. When creating groups, you should always try to make the biggest group possible.

	0	1	A
0	1	1	
1	1	0	
B			

At this point, we can represent the result as a Boolean expression by mapping each row and column to either A or ¬ A and each row to be B or ¬ B. In the first column, A has a value of 0 which is why it is represented by ¬ A. In the second column, A has a value of 1, which means it can be represented by A. The same holds true for the rows.

	0	1	A
0	¬ A	A	
1	¬ A	A	
B			

	0	1	A
0	¬ B	¬ B	
1	B	B	
B			

In the above example, there are adjacent 1s in the first column, which can be represented as ¬ A. There are also adjacent 1s in the first row, which can be represented by ¬ B. These can be put together using a disjunction resulting in the final equation $\neg A \vee \neg B$.

A	B	
1	1	0
1	0	1
0	1	0
0	0	1

Taking a second truth table, the same method can be applied to determine the Boolean equation.

Step 1 – Create a Karnaugh map.

	0	1	A
0	1	1	
1	0	0	
B			

Step 2 – Find groupings, which have a 1 (or true).

	0	1	A
0	1	1	
1	0	0	
B			

Tip

When dealing with questions relating to Karnaugh maps, be sure to write out all of the key steps in order to get full marks. You do not have to write out the tables shown in step 3; however, they may help you when deriving the final equation.

Step 3 – Write and simplify the resultant Boolean expression.

	0	1	A
0	¬A	A	
1	¬A	A	
B			

	0	1	A
0	¬B	¬B	
1	B	B	
B			

Result = ¬ B

Simplifying Boolean equations using Karnaugh maps

¬A ∧ (B∨¬A)

A	B	¬A	B∨¬A	¬A∧(B∨¬A)
1	1	1	1	1
1	0	1	1	1
0	1	0	1	0
0	0	0	0	0

Once a truth table of the Boolean equation has been created, you can create a Karnaugh map to simplify the statement.

Step 1 – Create a Karnaugh map.

	0	1	A
0	0	1	
1	0	1	
B			

Step 2 – Find groupings, which have a 1 (or true).

	0	1	A
0	0	1	
1	0	1	
B			

Step 3 – Write and simplify the resultant Boolean expression.

	0	1	A
0	¬A	A	
1	¬A	A	
B			

	0	1	A
0	¬B	¬B	
1	B	B	
B			

Result = ¬ A

Managing three inputs using Karnaugh maps

X	Y	Z	
1	1	1	1
1	0	1	1
0	1	1	1
0	0	1	0
1	1	0	1
1	0	0	1
0	1	0	0
0	0	0	0

When dealing with truth tables, which have more than two inputs, Karnaugh maps can still be used. In the case of three inputs, either the columns or the rows must represent two inputs.

	00	01	11	10	YZ
0	0	0	1	0	
1	1	1	1	1	
X					

It is important that the axes which contain multiple bits do not change by more than one bit. This is why the order of YZ is 00 01 11 10 and not 00 01 10 11 as 01 and 10 require 2 bit changes. This is important as it impacts the resultant groups. The order of the bits along the columns is not random and has been generated using Gray code or reflected binary code. Gray codes, invented by Frank Gray, are a way of representing binary where successive values never differ by more than one bit. To convert normal binary values into Gray codes we need to make use of exclusive or (XOR). Essentially XOR is only true if only one of the inputs is true. If both or neither are true then the result will be false. The truth table for XOR is shown below:

X	Y	X XOR Y
0	0	0
1	0	1
0	1	1
1	1	0

Gray codes follow this algorithm to convert.

- Start at the most significant bit (the bit on the left) and call it B(1)
- Copy that bit to the result.
- For all other bits
- Take the current bit B(N) and perform XOR on the previous bit B(N-1).

Bit position	B(1)	B(2)
Original binary	1	0
Calculation performed	Copy the 1	B(1) XOR B(2) 1 XOR 0
Gray code	1	1

Tip

It does not matter which two values you join together when writing out the Karnaugh map. However, it is important to remember that if you have two or more bits in a single row or column, you should only change adjacent columns/rows by a single bit.

Consider the binary value 10. The first bit is always copied to the result. XOR is then performed on the two bits which results in 1 as only one bit is true. Therefore the Gray code is 11 for the binary value 10. This can be done for any number of bits as shown in the table below.

Bit position	B(1)	B(2)	B(3)	B(4)
Original binary	1	0	1	1
Calculation performed	Copy the 1	B(1) XOR B(2) 1 XOR 0	B(2) XOR B(3) 0 XOR 1	B(3) XOR B(2) 1 XOR 1
Gray code	1	1	1	0

When writing out Karnaugh maps and there are more than 3 inputs, Gray codes must be used. This is to allow the groupings, which is the basis of how they work, to occur. For any position in the map, the adjacent squares will only ever differ by 1 bit.

X \ YZ	00	01	11	10
0	0	0	1	0
1	1	1	1	1

The first grouping to consider is the bottom row or when X is 1. The simplest way to represent this is as X. This can be extrapolated by considering which bits do not change. Y and Z can both have different values, while X always has the value of 1. It can therefore be represented as X.

The second grouping shows both Y and Z to be 1 and can be represented as $Y \wedge Z$. X is variable over the group while both Y and Z stay the same. As they both have a value of 1, they are represented using conjunction $Y \wedge Z$.

Finally, we can bring both of these together using disjunction leading to the final equation $X \vee (Y \wedge Z)$. Consider another example:

X	Y	Z	
1	1	1	1
1	0	1	1
0	1	1	0
0	0	1	0
1	1	0	0
1	0	0	0
0	1	0	1
0	0	0	1

Step 1 – Create the Karnaugh map.

X \ YZ	00	01	11	10
0	1	0	0	1
1	0	1	1	0

Step 2 – Find groupings.

X \ YZ	00	01	11	10
0	1	0	0	1
1	0	1	1	0

Step 3 – Write and simplify the resultant Boolean expression.

There are two groupings in the above diagram which may not be immediately obvious. The first grouping, shown in orange, is fairly clear. The second one, shown in purple, may seem as though it is two groups of 1. However, groupings can loop back on each other meaning that if there is a bit in the first column **and** first row, it is considered adjacent to the bit held in the last column and first row.

When deciding how to write down the equation for a grouping, you should look at which bits are changing and discount them. If a bit is changing, it is not essential in the final truth statement so, in order to get the simplest possible equation, it should not be included.

The orange grouping has a variable Y, while both X and Z stay the same. As such, it is best represented as $X \land Z$. The purple grouping has a variable Y, while both X and Z stay the same. However, both X and Z are 0 for this grouping, so the equation that best represents them is $\neg X \land \neg Z$. The final equation will therefore be $(X \land Z) \lor (\neg X \land \neg Z)$.

Legal groupings for Karnaugh maps

Rule 1 – Vertical and horizontal cells.

AB \ YZ	00	01	11	10
00	1	0	0	0
10	1	0	0	0
01	1	0	0	0
11	1	0	0	0

AB \ YZ	00	01	11	10
00	0	0	0	0
10	1	1	1	1
01	0	0	0	0
11	0	0	0	0

Orange is represented by $\neg Y \land \neg Z$ and purple is represented by $A \land \neg B$

Rule 2 – Square groups.

AB \ YZ	00	01	11	10
00	0	0	0	0
10	1	1	0	0
01	1	1	0	0
11	0	0	0	0

AB \ YZ	00	01	11	10
00	0	0	0	0
10	0	0	0	0
01	0	0	1	1
11	0	0	1	1

Orange is represented by $\neg Y$ and purple is represented by $Y \land B$. To work out the equations for square groupings you must look to see which bits change and which ones remain the same. In the orange group, A, B and Z can be either zero or 1 while Y is always 0. For the purple group, A and Z both change while Y and B are always 1.

Rule 3 – Groups can overlap.

AB \ YZ	00	01	11	10
00	0	0	0	0
10	1	1	0	0
01	1	1	1	1
11	0	0	0	0

AB \ YZ	00	01	11	10
00	0	0	1	0
10	0	0	1	0
01	0	0	1	1
11	0	0	1	1

The orange group is best represented as $\neg Y \lor (\neg A \land B)$. The group of 4 is represented by $\neg Y$ and the row of 4 is represented by $\neg A \land B$ as both A and B have the same value across the row. When bringing two groups together, you always use disjunction.

The purple group is best represented as $Y \land B \lor (Y \land Z)$.

Rule 4 **–** Groups can wrap around the edges.

AB \ YZ	00	01	11	10
00	0	0	0	0
10	1	0	0	1
01	1	0	0	1
11	0	0	0	0

AB \ YZ	00	01	11	10
00	0	1	0	0
10	0	1	0	0
01	0	0	0	0
11	1	0	0	1

The orange group is wrapping around the sides to produce a group of four. In this group of four, only Z stays the same which means that it is best represented as Z.

There are two purple groupings, one of which is a vertical group of two and one which wraps around to produce a horizontal group of two. The vertical group is best represented by $Z \land \neg B \land \neg Y$ and the horizontal group is best represented by $A \land B \land \neg Z$. The final equation is therefore $(Z \land B \land \neg Y) \lor (A \land B \land \neg Z)$.

D type flip flops

One of the most fundamental logical elements in a computer system is the ability to store data or state. To store a single bit of information, a flip flop can be used. In the diagram below, NAND gates are used, which are AND gates with the outputs inverted. A black dot represents when a wire is split into two wires which both carry the same signal. The input D is the data to be stored, and E represents the control signal (or enable), which will change the state of the flip flop to be the data passed through on D. The state of D is only recorded when E transitions from high to low or 1 to 0.

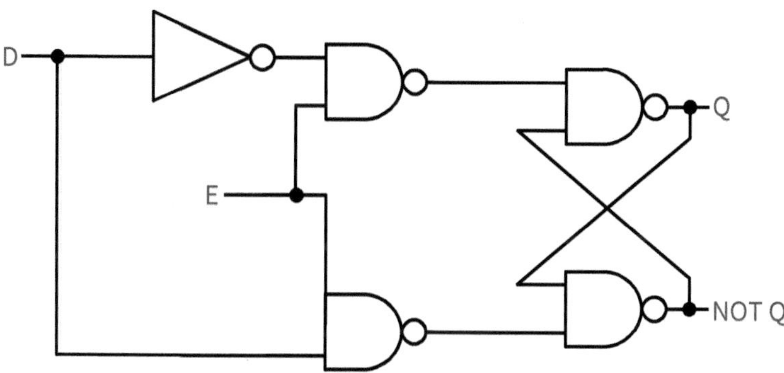

Figure 13.4: D type flip flop.

Consider the input to D to be 1 and E to be 0. To help demonstrate the flow of data, lines carrying a 1 will be turned purple and zero will be turned blue. Q outputs 1 and NOT Q outputs 0.

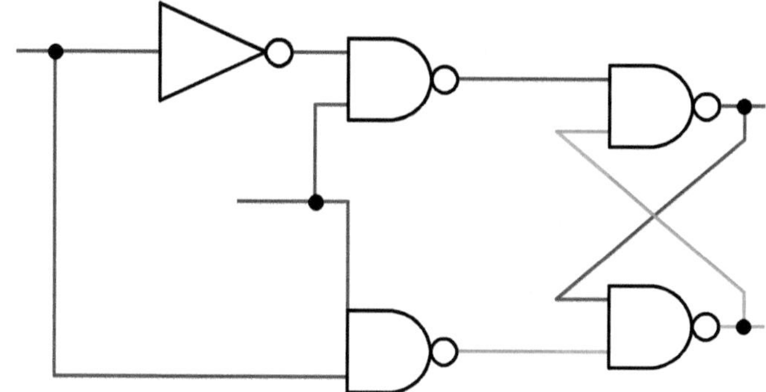

Figure 13.5: D type flip flop.

If both E and D are then set to zero then no change is recorded by the outputs. This is because the top NAND gate requires E to make any change to its output meaning that, regardless of the input from D, no change will occur. The flip flop at the end of the circuit remains unchanged and thus retains the previous value.

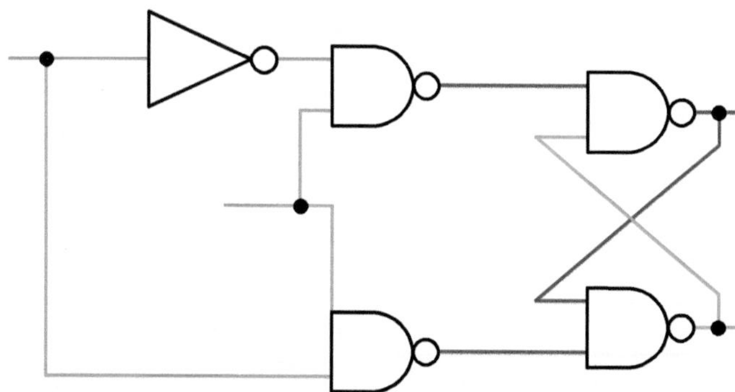

Figure 13.6: D type flip flop.

XOR, half and full adder

Half and full adders allow bits to be added together and form another fundamental part of computing hardware. Before they can be explored fully, the XOR logic gate must be introduced. Exclusive or (XOR) ensures that if both inputs are 1 then the output will be 0.

Figure 13.7: XOR gate.

This is different to normal OR, which would output a 1.

X	Y	X ⊕ Y
1	1	0
1	0	1
0	1	1
0	0	0

XOR can be represented by the following Boolean equation:

$$(\neg X \wedge Y) \vee (X \wedge \neg Y)$$

Half adder

A	B	S	C
1	1	0	1
1	0	1	0
0	1	1	0
0	0	0	0

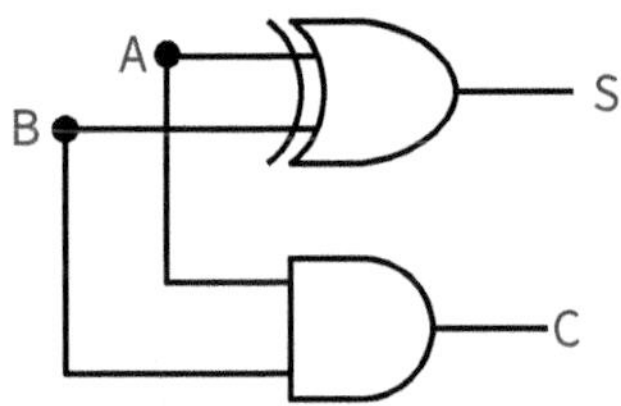

Figure 13.8: Half adder logic circuit.

A and B represent the two inputs to the half adder while S represents the result of the calculation, with C being the carry bit. XOR provides the answer to any 2-bit calculation while the AND gate will output 1 in the case that a carry bit is needed.

Full adder

A full adder not only outputs the correct carry bit, but also takes a carry bit as input. It combines two half adders together in order to allow the three bits to be added. As each half adder can produce a carry bit, these also need to be considered.

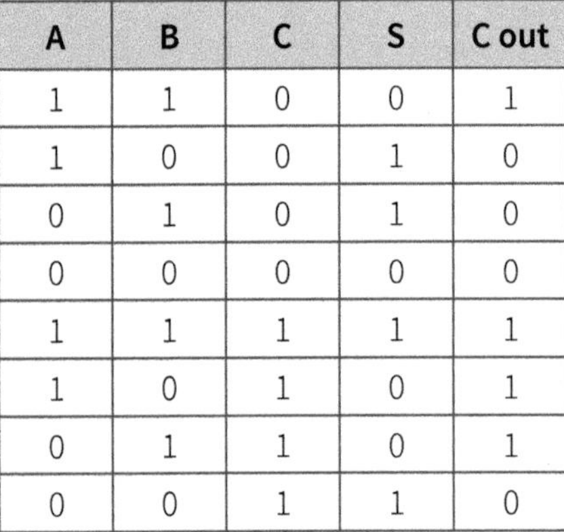

A	B	C	S	C out
1	1	0	0	1
1	0	0	1	0
0	1	0	1	0
0	0	0	0	0
1	1	1	1	1
1	0	1	0	1
0	1	1	0	1
0	0	1	1	0

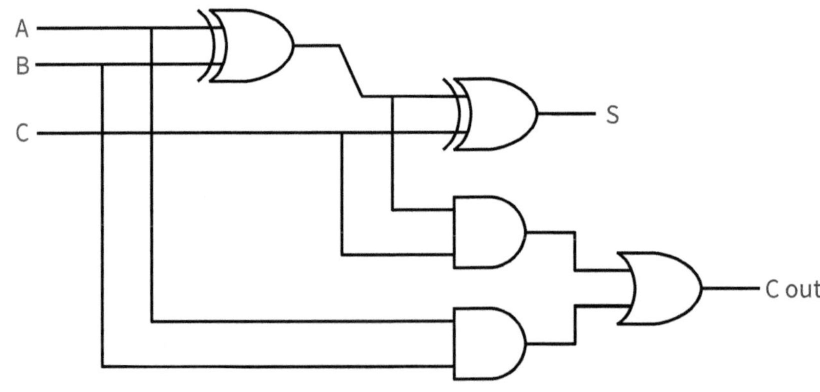

Figure 13.9: Circuit diagram for a full adder.

Summary

- Conjunction: both sides of the proposition must be true.
- Disjunction: either side of the proposition can be true.
- Negation: reverses the truth of a proposition.
- Implication: if something is true then we can infer that something else is also true.

- Commutation: the order does not matter when using conjunction or disjunction.
- Association: the order does not matter when we link multiple conjunctions or multiple disjunctions; this does not hold true if we start mixing conjunctions and disjunctions.
- Double negation: two negations cancel each other out.
- De Morgan's law: the negation of disjunctions is the conjunction of the negations.
- Karnaugh maps are a method of simplifying logical statements.
- Gray code is used to ensure that the bits in a Karnaugh map never differ by more than one bit.

commutation law for conjunction $P \wedge Q \leftrightarrow Q \wedge P$
commutation law for disjunction $P \vee Q \leftrightarrow Q \vee P$
association laws for conjunction $T \wedge (P \wedge Q) \leftrightarrow (T \wedge Q) \wedge P$
association laws for disjunction $T \vee (P \vee Q) \leftrightarrow (T \vee Q) \vee P$
distribution law 1 $T \wedge (P \vee Q) \leftrightarrow (T \wedge P) \vee (T \wedge Q)$
distribution law 2 $T \vee (P \wedge Q) \leftrightarrow (T \vee P) \wedge (T \vee Q)$
De Morgan's law for disjunction $\neg (P \vee Q) \leftrightarrow \neg P \wedge \neg Q$
De Morgan's law for conjunction $\neg (P \wedge Q) \leftrightarrow \neg P \vee \neg Q$
double negative law $\neg \neg P \leftrightarrow P$

Table 13.1: List of rules.

Tip

There are different symbols used for Boolean algebra and it is important to be familiar with all of them, $\neg \leftrightarrow \wedge$.

Symbol	Alternatives
$\vee$	+
$\wedge$	AND
$\leftrightarrow$	$\equiv$
$\neg A$	$\bar{A}$

Make sure you can recreate truth tables for any given Boolean expression. It is worth practising by writing out a logical statement and then creating a truth table for it.

You need to learn the different laws and when they should be applied. Remember that most of them come in multiple formats depending on if disjunction or conjunction was used.

End-of-chapter questions

1 $\neg (P \wedge Q) \leftrightarrow \neg P \vee \neg Q$ is an example of De Morgan's laws. Explain what this law means using examples. [4]

2 Explain, using the correct symbols, what the following terms mean.

- **a** conjunction [2]
- **b** disjunction [2]
- **c** implication [2]
- **d** negation. [2]

3 Using the laws of deduction, show that the following statement is correct. [3]
$\neg (A \vee B) \leftrightarrow \neg B \wedge \neg A$

4 Using truth tables, show the difference between implication and biconditional equivalence. [4]

Further reading

Introduction to propositional logic – search on Math Path's website.
Natural deduction – search on the Example Problems wiki.
Propositional logic (video) – search on the University of Navarra's Youtube channel.

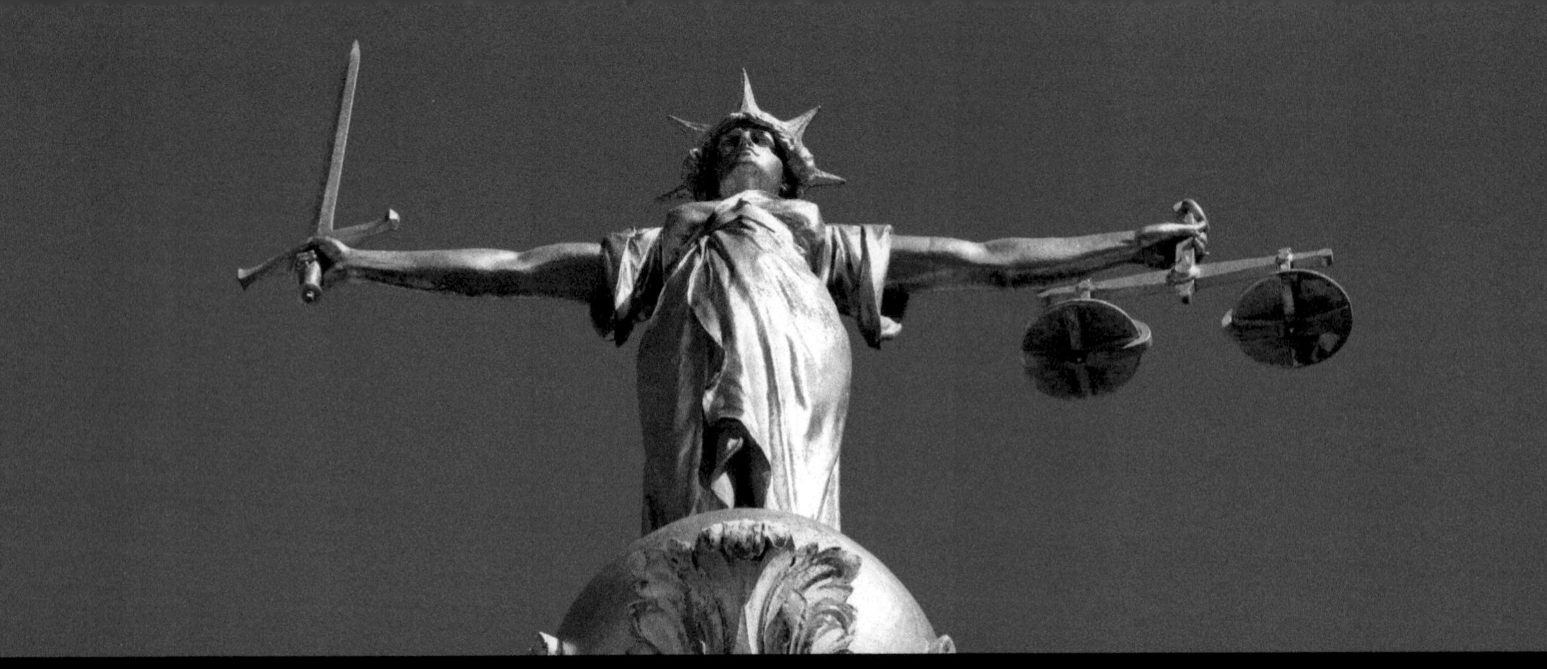

Chapter 14
Legal, moral, cultural and ethical issues

Specification points

1.5.1 Computing related legislation

- The Data Protection Act 1998.
- The Computer Misuse Act 1990.
- The Copyright, Designs and Patents Act 1988; the Regulation of Investigatory Powers Act 2000.
- Regulation of Investigatory Powers Act 2000

1.5.2 Ethical, moral and cultural issues

The individual (moral), social (ethical) and cultural opportunities and risks of digital technology:

- computers in the workforce
- automated decision making
- artificial intelligence
- environmental effects
- censorship and the internet
- monitor behaviour
- analyse personal information
- piracy and offensive communications
- layout, colour paradigms and character sets
- to learn about computer-related laws
- To gain an awareness of the ethical issues raised by the use of computers.

Introduction

The advent of the computer has had an enormous impact on the nature of crimes such as fraud, harassment, and identity and monetary theft. It must also be considered that the internet is a global network and that the source of a crime may not be the same country as the target. This creates a number of legal issues that may result in cybercriminals being extradited to the country where the victim resides. Different countries impose different penalties for particular crimes.

The use of computers also raises a number of ethical issues, including the use of computers in the workplace, artificial intelligence and automated decision-making, environmental impact and censorship.

Computer-related laws

Combating cybercrime or crime involving computers is a complex and difficult task. Technologies evolve at a staggering rate and policing them requires officers to have a high level of technical proficiency. One of the biggest problems in policing computer use has been the speed at which technology has developed, compared to how long it takes to draft and enact legislation prohibiting or restricting their use. This section will introduce you to some of the laws that have been introduced or updated to cope with the influx of new offences. The information contained in this chapter has not been checked by a lawyer and in no way constitutes legal advice. However, what it will do is to provide you with sufficient background in the laws explicitly named in the A level specification.

Data Protection Act 1998

Computers enable companies to store vast amounts of information in a very small physical space. This data can also be transferred instantly across huge distances and between countries with different legal systems. This has led to many problems, not least that private, personal data can be sold on to third parties (such as advertisers or insurance companies). Poorly protected data can be stolen by cybercriminals and poorly maintained data can quickly become out of date.

The advent of cloud computing, in which companies and individuals store all their data online rather than on their own computers, has compounded the problem. Some companies that facilitate information transferring and storage over the internet could be storing your information in another country or even on another continent, often without your knowledge.

The Data Protection Act 1998 was introduced largely to deal with the potential problems of storing sensitive and personal data. However, it must be remembered that it was developed at a time before the internet was used as widely as it is today. The Data Protection Act 1998 gives individuals the right to know what data is stored about them and who is storing it. It even gives people the right to see any data a company is storing about them and have it amended if necessary.

Types of data

One of the first issues tackled by the Data Protection Act 1998 was the question of what constitutes private information. For example, is your name personal, private information? To clarify these issues, the Act places information into two categories: personal data and sensitive data. Personal data concerns living people and tends to be information that is more widely available. Sensitive data includes details that you may not want to be widely known (Table 14.1).

Personal data	Sensitive data
Name Address Date of birth	Ethnic origin Religious views Political opinions Sexuality Criminal records

Table 14.1: Personal and sensitive data.

The eight principles of data protection

The eight principles of the Data Protection Act 1998 describe how those storing data must behave if they are to abide by the law.

1 Personal data shall be processed fairly and lawfully.

This means that those collecting and storing your personal data must have legitimate grounds for collecting and using it. It also prevents them from using the data in ways that have an adverse effect on you.

When collecting data, companies must be transparent about how they intend to use the data, and give individuals appropriate privacy notices. Finally, companies must handle people's personal data only in ways they would reasonably expect and ensure that they do not do anything unlawful with the data.

Example

A bank records information about companies that hold corporate accounts with the bank, including information about individuals who hold shares in those companies. It collects and holds this information to comply with its duties under anti-money-laundering regulations.

Unless the bank had obtained their prior consent, it would be unfair to use this information to send marketing material to the individuals concerned, inviting them to open personal accounts with the bank.

2 Personal data shall be obtained only for one or more specified and lawful purposes, and shall not be further processed in any manner incompatible with that purpose or those purposes.

The second principle means that those collecting your data must be clear from the outset about why they are collecting your personal data and what they intend to do with it. If they change what they want to do with the information, they must inform you and get your approval.

Example

A GP discloses his patient list to his wife, who runs a travel agency, so that she can offer special holiday deals to patients needing recuperation.

Disclosing the information for this purpose would be incompatible with the purposes for which it was obtained.

3 Personal data shall be adequate, relevant and not excessive in relation to the purpose or purposes for which they are processed.

The third principle states that companies hold only personal data about an individual that is sufficient for the purpose for which they are holding it. It also prohibits them from storing more information than they need for their stated purpose.

Example

An employer holds details of the blood groups of all its employees. Some of them do hazardous work and the information is needed in case of accident. For the rest of the workforce, though, such information is likely to be irrelevant and excessive.

4 Personal data shall be accurate and, where necessary, kept up to date.

This fourth principle means that companies must take reasonable steps to ensure the accuracy of any personal data they obtain. In practice, this means that they are responsible for ensuring that any data they are storing is up to date.

Example

A journalist builds up a profile of a particular public figure. This includes information derived from rumours circulating on the internet that the individual was once arrested on suspicion of dangerous driving.

If the journalist records that the individual was arrested, without qualifying this, he or she is asserting this as an accurate fact. However, if it is clear that the journalist is recording rumours, the record is accurate – the journalist is not asserting that the individual was arrested for this offence.

5 Personal data processed for any purpose or purposes shall not be kept for longer than is necessary for that purpose or those purposes.

This is one of the simpler data protection principles. It means that companies must delete information that is no longer needed for the purpose for which it was originally collected.

Example

A customer switches their mobile network provider. The new company needs the customer's details because they have just taken out an 18 month contract with them. The previous company no longer needs to retain the customer's details because their contract with them has ended.

6 Personal data shall be processed in accordance with the rights of data subjects under this Act.

In addition to the eight data protection principles, the Act also gives certain rights to data subjects:

- The right to access a copy of the information comprising their personal data.
- The right to object to processing that is likely to cause, or is causing, damage or distress.
- The right to prevent processing for direct marketing.
- The right to object to decisions being taken by automated means.
- The right in certain circumstances to have inaccurate personal data rectified, blocked, erased or destroyed.
- The right to claim compensation for damages caused by a breach of the Act.

The sixth principle of the Act upholds these rights.

Example

A man is refused a job in the construction industry and discovers that this is because the prospective employer checked his name against a blacklist maintained by a third party.

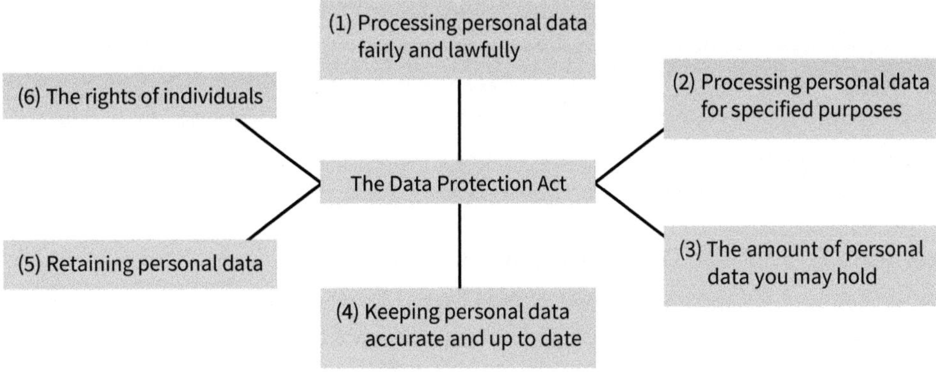

Figure 14.1: Mind map.

The blacklist consists of the names of people who are regarded as unsuitable to be employed in the construction industry because they are trade union activists. The man writes to the person who maintains the blacklist, asking for his name to be removed as it is denying him the opportunity to gain employment.

In these circumstances, the person who maintains the blacklist would have great difficulty in establishing any legitimate basis for processing the man's personal data in this way – because the assessment of 'unsuitability' lacks justification, and because the individuals concerned were not told that their names had been placed on the blacklist. In any event, the man can show that he is suffering damage due to this processing and that this is substantial, as it could continue to prevent him getting a job.

7 Appropriate technical and organisational measures shall be taken against unauthorised or unlawful processing of personal data and against accidental loss or destruction of, or damage to, personal data.

The seventh principle means that companies must have appropriate security and be able to prevent the personal data they hold being accidentally or deliberately compromised. This includes physical security, such as locked doors and windows, as well as cyber-security, such as firewalls and storing data in an encrypted format.

Example

A government employee leaves an unencrypted CD containing benefit claimants' details on a train. As a number of basic security precautions have been ignored, the Data Protection Act has been breached.

8 Personal data shall not be transferred to a country or territory outside the European Economic Area unless that country or territory ensures an adequate level of protection for the rights and freedoms of data subjects in relation to the processing of personal data.

The eighth principle is more complex than it first appears. Although companies must avoid transferring data outside the EEA, they can do so if those receiving the data abide by any relevant equivalent legislation (such as the Safe Harbour agreement in the United States).

Example

A university wishes to transfer its human resources department to East Asia, as data processing would be cheaper to carry out there. As the data being processed could be of a personal nature, the institution would be in breach of the Act.

Key roles in the Data Protection Act 1998

There are three key groups of people mentioned in the Act:

- *The Information Commissioner* is the person whom parliament has empowered to enforce the Act.
- *The data controller* is a person or company that collects and keeps data about data subjects (people).
- *The data subject* is someone who has data about them stored by a third party.

Exemptions from the Data Protection Act 1998

Not all organisations and people need to abide by the Act all of the time. There are specific exemptions for records relating to on-going criminal investigations and matters that could affect national security. Data kept for domestic (personal) reasons, such as a private address book, is also exempt.

Example

A taxpayer makes a data subject access request to HMRC for personal data it holds about her in relation to an on-going investigation into possible tax evasion. If by disclosing the information that HMRC has collected about the taxpayer could prejudice its investigation, it could refuse to grant the subject access. For example, a reason to refuse the request may be that granting access would make it more difficult for HMRC to collect further evidence.

If, however, the taxpayer does not make the data subject access request until some years later, when the investigation (and any subsequent prosecution) has been completed, it is likely that HMRC would have to comply with it.

Computing in context: the Patriot Act 2001

Following the attacks on the World Trade Center on 11 September 2001, the US government felt that it was necessary to update its anti-terror legislation to deal with the increased threat from terrorists and organised crime.

With this in mind, the government introduced the Patriot Act 2001 to increase the powers of law-enforcement agencies. The Act's full name is 'Uniting and Strengthening America by Providing Appropriate Tools Required to Intercept and Obstruct Terrorism Act of 2001'. It contains ten provisions, one of which enables courts to order internet service providers (ISPs) and companies with their headquarters in the United States to hand over information held on their servers anywhere in the world.

It is thought that the Act could be used by US courts to overrule UK and EU data protection legislation, with the result that many companies are now very wary of storing commercially sensitive information on US servers.

Computer Misuse Act 1990

The Computer Misuse Act 1990 was passed in response to a rising level of computer crime and the inability of existing legislation to properly punish those responsible. The Act is lengthy but the four main offences are outlined below.

Section 1: unauthorised access to computer material

Someone is guilty of this offence if they use a computer to secure access to any program or data held electronically if the access is unauthorised and they know this at the time.

The intention to gain unauthorised access need not be directed at any particular program or data; a program or data of any particular kind; or a program or data held in any particular computer.

Anyone found guilty of an offence under this section of the Computer Misuse Act 1990 can face up to 12 months in prison in England and Wales or six months in Scotland. They may also be fined up to a maximum of £5000.

This section of the Act is important, as it was the first time that hacking had explicitly been made illegal in the UK. Simply accessing someone else's computer system without their permission is punishable by a prison sentence, even if nothing is taken.

Section 2: unauthorised access with intent to commit or facilitate commission of further offences

Someone is guilty of an offence under this section if they commit an offence under section 1 ('the unauthorised access offence') with the intention of committing a criminal offence or facilitating the commission of a criminal offence by others.

The Act defines further offence as meaning any activity that is against the law and makes no distinctions between the intention to commit the crime immediately and the intention to commit it at a later date. Importantly, someone could be found guilty of breaching this section of the Act even if they were unsuccessful or it can be proved that they could never have been successful.

Breaching this section of the Act can lead to a prison sentence of between one and five years or a substantial fine.

An example of this might be if you were to hack into a bank's computer with the intention of transferring millions to your own bank account. You could be prosecuted under this section even if the bank's security measures meant that you could never have achieved your aim.

Section 3: unauthorised acts with intent to impair the operation of computer or to delete or modify data and programs.

Someone is guilty of an offence under this section of the Act if they carry out any (knowingly) unauthorised act in relation to a computer with the intention of impairing the operation of the computer or deleting or modifying data or programs. This section also specifically covers any attempt to hinder others' access to programs or data held on a computer. Someone can in fact be found guilty under this section of the Act, even if they did not intend to damage the computer, if their conduct was reckless and therefore likely to lead to damaging the computer or the data held on it.

Breaching this section of the Act can lead to a prison sentence of between one and ten years or a substantial fine.

Section 3a: making, supplying or obtaining articles for use in offence under section 1 or 3

Someone would be found guilty under this sub-section of section 3 if they were to create, adapt, supply or offer to supply any materials with the intention that they be used to commit a crime. This sub-section also makes it an offence to obtain these tools with a view to passing them on.

Computing in context: the Computer Misuse Act 1990

In February 2014, Lauri Love, a 29-year-old British man living in Suffolk, was accused of breaking into Federal Reserve computers. Love allegedly tried to secretly infiltrate the New York Federal Reserve Bank's computer servers in order to steal non-public information and then post that information on the internet.

According to the indictment, in October 2012: 'Mr Love used his unauthorised access to locate and steal certain confidential information residing on the Federal Reserve servers, including the names, e-mail addresses, and phone numbers of users of the Federal Reserve computer system. Mr Love then disseminated that information publicly by posting the information to a website that previously had been hacked and that he controlled.'

Love was accused of breaching the system to steal 'massive quantities' of confidential data, resulting in millions of dollars of losses.

A 2013 US Department of Energy audit report on Mr Love's activities found that personal information on 104 000 people could have been taken. It estimated the fallout of this to cost the United States at least $3.7 million (£2.2 million), including $1.6 million spent on establishing a call centre to deal with people affected by the data breach. Mr Love is accused of working with at least three other people, who have not been named, to breach the security of the US military, the US space agency (NASA), the Environmental Protection Agency and FBI computers.

He was arrested by officers from the UK's National Crime Agency (NCA) under the Computer Misuse Act 1990 and, as of the time of writing in 2016, is still fighting extradition to the United States.

Copyright, Designs and Patents Act 1988

The Copyright, Designs and Patents Act 1988 was not introduced specifically to deal with crimes facilitated by technology. However, the ability of computers to create and distribute thousands of electronic copies of films, books, games and software means that the Act often has to be applied in cases relating to the use of technology.

Copyright law gives the creators of artistic and creative works the right to choose how their material is used. This includes digital artefacts such as games and application software as well as more traditional works such as films, music, dramatic productions, sculptures and books.

Copyright is an automatic right and arises whenever an individual or company creates a work. This means that there is no need to put a copyright symbol on your work. Anything you create is automatically copyrighted to you. Copyright isn't infinite; it lasts for a set period of time. For literary, dramatic, musical and artistic works and films, this is 70 years after the creator dies. For sound recordings, it is 50 years from when the work was first released.

Computing in context: Copyright, Designs and Patents Act 1988

In 2013, UK ISPs were forced by the UK courts to begin blocking access to two sites accused of flouting copyright laws.

The blocks were imposed after the Motion Picture Association (MPA) won a court order compelling ISPs to cut off the Movie2K and Download4All websites. The MPA, which is the international arm of the Motion Picture Association of America, went to court, arguing that the two websites broke the UK's Copyright, Designs and Patents Act 1988. Both the websites let people download or stream copies of recently released movies that have been ripped from DVDs.

The UK's largest ISPs, BT, Virgin, TalkTalk, Sky and EE, are all believed to have complied with the order and stopped their customers reaching the sites.

The British Phonographic Industry (BPI) is believed to be seeking to block many more sites, as it circulates a list of 25 domains it says are involved in pirating popular music. Included in the list are sites such as Grooveshark, Isohunt, Filestube and Monova.

Offences under the Copyright, Designs and Patents Act 1988

Under the Act it is an offence to do any of the following without the consent of the owner:

- Copy the work, for example burning another copy of Microsoft Windows to give to a friend.
- Rent, lend or issue copies of the work to the public, for example making your music collection available to listen to for free online.
- Perform, broadcast or show the work in public, for example show your favourite film to a large group of people without a special broadcast licence.
- Adapt the work. There are exemptions to this, but basically you can't take an existing piece of software, change some icons and sell it on.

Exemptions from the Copyright, Designs and Patents Act 1988

You can, however, do some things with copyrighted works without permission:

- Use works for educational purposes where no profit is being made.
- Replicate works in order to criticise or report on them.
- Copy and lend works (applies only to libraries, but they need a specific licence to operate).
- Record broadcasts for the purposes of listening to, or viewing, at a more convenient time: it's not illegal to record programmes from iPlayer or similar catch-up systems with the intention of watching them tomorrow.
- Produce a backup copy for personal use.
- Play sound recordings for a non-profit-making organisation, club or society.

Sanctions

Sanctions that can be handed down under the Act are wide ranging and depend on the seriousness of the offence committed, but anyone caught breaching the Act could be sentenced to up to two years in prison and receive a large fine. They may also be liable to pay for any damages caused to the holder of the copyright.

Regulation of Investigatory Powers Act 2000

The Regulation of Investigatory Powers Act 2000 was created to make provision for the interception of communications. It particularly focuses on electronic surveillance, the legal decryption of encrypted data and the interception of electronic communications by the security services, the Secret Intelligence Service and the Government Communications Headquarters (GCHQ). Under the Act, they can intercept e-mails, access private communications and plant surveillance devices.

The Act has been controversial since its inception, earning itself the nickname 'the snoopers' charter'. The government argues that it is necessary to allow law enforcement agencies to keep up with the increasingly technologically advanced techniques being used by criminals and terrorists. However, human rights and privacy campaigners are concerned by the lack of oversight and the wide range of the Act's provisions, many of which they feel could be open to misinterpretation. These groups were further alarmed in 2002 when the government requested that a much wider range of government bodies (including local councils and job centres) be given these powers. The request was eventually withdrawn following growing opposition, but the Act remains controversial.

Just 9% of these authorisations have led to a successful prosecution, caution or fixed-penalty notice.

Provisions of the Act

There are ten main provisions in the Act. It:

1 Regulates the circumstances and methods by which public bodies may carry out covert surveillance.

2 Lays out a statutory framework to enable public authorities to carry out covert surveillance in compliance with the requirements of the Human Rights Act 1998.

3 Defines five broad categories of covert surveillance: directed surveillance (includes photographing people); intrusive surveillance (includes bugging); the use of covert human intelligence sources (informants and undercover officers, including watching and following people); accessing communications data (record of e-mails sent, telephone calls made); and intercepting communications (reading the content of e-mails, listening to calls).

4 Allows the Secretary of State to issue an interception warrant to examine the contents of letters or communications on the grounds of national security, and for the purposes of preventing or detecting crime, preventing disorder, public safety, protecting public health, or in the interests of the economic wellbeing of the United Kingdom. This is the only part of the Act that requires a warrant.

5 Prevents the existence of interception warrants, and any and all data collected with them, from being revealed in court.

6 Allows the police, intelligence services and HM Revenue & Customs (and several hundred more public bodies, including local authorities and a wide range of regulators) to demand telephone, internet and postal service providers to hand over detailed communications records for individual users. This can include name and address, phone calls made and received, source and destination of e-mails, internet browsing information and mobile phone positioning data that records the user's location. These powers are self-authorised by the body concerned, with no external or judicial oversight.

7 Enables the government to demand that someone hands over keys to protected information; and makes it a criminal offence to refuse to supply actual encrypted traffic or refuse to disclose an encryption key.

8 Enables the government to force ISPs to fit equipment to facilitate surveillance.

9 Allows the government to demand that an ISP provides secret access to a customer's communication.

10 Makes provisions to establish an oversight regime, creates an investigatory powers tribunal and appoints three commissioners.

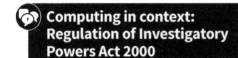

Computing in context: Regulation of Investigatory Powers Act 2000

In March 2009, the government came under increasing pressure to reform the Regulation of Investigatory Powers Act 2000 (RIPA) after it became known that local councils were using the anti-terror legislation to gather information on minor misdemeanours, such as dog fouling and littering.

A survey of more than 180 local authorities found that:

- 1615 council staff have the power to authorise the use of RIPA.
- 21% (or 340) of these staff are below senior management grade.
- RIPA powers have been used 10 333 times in the past five years.

Ethical issues

In the past 30 years, computers have revolutionised the world we live in. We can communicate instantly with people thousands of miles away, we can copy in seconds documents that used to take weeks to type up, and access vast amounts of information from anywhere in the world. These advances have led to huge changes in the way we are educated, do business, work and even meet new people. However, no change this seismic could be without controversy and we have also seen growing concerns about personal privacy. Whether you think the introduction of computers is a good or a bad thing probably depends on how you have been affected by them, but one thing is for certain: advances in technology will continue to present new challenges and ethical dilemmas.

Computers in the workplace

One of the places where computers have had the biggest impact is in the workplace. When you finish school, the chance of you going into a job where you don't need to use computers is minimal. Computers would not have been introduced into the workplace if they didn't provide benefits in excess of the costs associated with them. Consider the case of car manufacturing. Not so long ago, cars were made 100% by hand; each piece of metal, wood and plastic had to be cut and fitted by trained specialists. It took years to train a master craftsman who could consistently produce excellent work and make sure that all your customers received a car that they were happy with. Of course, even the best craftsmen and craftswomen can have bad days and no one can cut metal into the same shape by hand with 100% accuracy every time. Workers also require holidays, days off and lunch breaks, as well as sick and maternity leave. You might spend years training someone only for them to go and work for a rival manufacturer. Finally, of course, if you couldn't provide the working conditions that they wanted, they might go on strike, costing you lost orders and customers.

These days, all but a handful of modern car manufacturing plants use robots. These are expensive to buy initially but they can work 24 hours a day, seven days a week and 365 days a year. Robots don't need lunch breaks, sick leave or holidays and, crucially, every piece of metal they produce is identical to the previous one and the next one. Robots don't join unions to demand better pay and conditions and won't leave you to work for a competitor. These qualities have meant that computers have replaced people in the vast majority of manufacturing jobs, from ship building and mining to car manufacture. While these sectors now employ far fewer people than they did previously, outputs are generally higher than they ever were. This has been great if you own a factory or want to buy a cheap, reliable car, but has meant redundancy (often for life) for people who previously occupied skilled, reliable jobs.

Of course, it's not only industrial workers who have lost their jobs because of the introduction of computers. Consider all the secretaries, typists and office workers whose roles are now redundant. Computers can scan documents, use speech recognition software to take dictation, and even check for spelling and grammatical errors. Computers can scan, in seconds, documents that would take days to type up, even by a skilled typist using a modern word processor. Databases, spreadsheets and effective search algorithms mean that companies no longer need huge pools of secretaries to file and retrieve client records. Think back to the last time you posted a piece of mail to someone. Compare this to the number of e-mails or other electronic messages you have sent today and it's obvious that the number of postal workers required to deliver letters must have reduced significantly since the advent of computers. However, even in a single industry such as the postal service, the picture is blurred. As people buy more and more goods online, the requirement for package delivery is increasing and, with it, the need for postal workers.

In services such as teaching where the introduction of computers has opened up a world of opportunities without costing a significant number of jobs, people are still concerned. Teachers may be worried about their digital literacy skills. Even teachers of subjects other than IT and Computer Science need to be able to use Virtual Learning Environments, take electronic registers and use spreadsheets to manipulate data. In addition, learning to use and integrate new systems can create extra work, which people might not want to do.

Increased reliance on computer systems in the workplace can also cause additional problems. If systems fail, normal business processes will not be possible. This can lead to loss of custom and revenue. The implications of this can be very serious for the business. A solution is to have systems with built-in redundancy in the form of extra hardware and spread the load throughout the entire system. In this way, a hard drive failure is not necessarily an issue, as the data will be stored across a number of discs using the system called RAID (redundant array of independent discs).

Of course, it's not all bad for employees. Computers can automate mundane, repetitive jobs, leaving people free to focus on more interesting, creative tasks, while learning how to use new technology can lead to more qualifications and better pay. In addition, think of all the new jobs directly and indirectly created through the use of computers: systems analysts, programmers, IT technicians and website designers, for example. Many commentators believe that computers have created more jobs than they have ever removed. Using computers also opens up a world of flexible working. Employees can often work from home and submit their work over the internet. This cuts down the cost of commuting and childcare for employees while allowing employers to save money on office space and resources as well as potentially reducing traffic on the roads and the resultant air pollution.

Ultimately, the ethical arguments about computers in the workplace often come down to a conflict between owners and shareholders seeking higher profits, consumers who want cheap, reliable products and workers who simply want reliable, well-paid jobs.

Advantages	Disadvantages
New jobs have been created.	Some jobs have disappeared completely.
Computers speed up the repetitive, boring parts of jobs, leaving people free to do the creative, interesting parts.	People worry about not being able to use new systems, and learning to use them takes time.
Computers are cheaper to run, and so have led to a reduction in the cost of manufactured goods.	Initial purchase and configuring can be very expensive.
Repetitive jobs such as copying documents or stamping metal are carried out more reliably by computers.	Increased reliance on computer systems can make a business vulnerable if they fail and are not repaired quickly.

Table 14.2: Advantages and disadvantages of computers in the workplace.

Artificial intelligence and automated decision making

Artificial intelligence means decision making that has been built into a computer program, enabling it to perform tasks normally undertaken by humans. Alan Turing, the English mathematician, wartime code-breaker and pioneer of computer science, developed the Turing Test to decide whether a computer could be deemed intelligent. The test involved an analyst putting the same question to a computer and a person.

If the analyst could not distinguish which of the answers was supplied by a human, the computer could be said to be intelligent.

Recent developments in computing, especially powerful processors and cheap storage space, have meant that the creation of true artificial intelligence is coming closer to being a reality. However, these developments raise a huge number of ethical concerns. Imagine a car crash between two driverless cars where someone is killed: who is liable? Is it the programmer, the car owner or the manufacturer? Should children and the elderly be allowed to control them? Should such cars have to obey current road rules, such as speed limits?

What about medical robots? IBM's Watson system is currently being programmed to diagnose medical diseases. Doctors and surgeons are required to remember a huge amount of information, work long hours and make life-or-death decisions. A computer would have no problem retaining everything it was told and it wouldn't get tired or hungry. But would you want it to make a decision on whether to operate on a patient?

Robots are already widely used in the military. In November 2012, the US Department of Defense tried to establish guidelines around minimising failures and mistakes for robots deployed to target terrorists. Military robots are not affected by human emotions such as passion or revenge, and so would not make decisions clouded by these feelings. Military robots (particularly drones) have already seen widespread service, in the last few years, in the fight against terrorism. At the moment, drones are controlled by humans, who have the final choice over whether to fire a weapon. However, it is not hard to imagine simply fitting some image-recognition software to a drone and letting it decide what to shoot. Who would take responsibility for civilian casualties, in the event of such an incident? How would families get justice?

Think about robots in general (not just drones). If they are intelligent, do we have a right to demand that they clean our clothes, print our documents or calculate our taxes? Should machines with artificial intelligence be allowed to create new machines with even greater intelligence? Should they be allowed to vote? Is it ethically justifiable to switch off their power or dismantle an intelligent robot? Many people argue that these issues should be addressed before we develop our technology any further. Have a look at an article about this subject here.

Computing in context: Google and driverless cars

Google has been experimenting with driverless cars for some time and they are already legal in three states (California, Nevada and Florida). Google confidently expects to have its driverless car on sale by 2020. The benefits are obvious: no speeding motorists, no crashes because the driver fell asleep and no collisions with stationary objects. Very elderly and very young people could reach their destination safely without the need to pass a test. However, drivers also need to make ethical decisions as well as directional ones! Most drivers will brake to avoid hitting a rabbit, as long as it won't endanger their passengers or fellow motorists. Most of the same drivers would brake much harder to avoid hitting a cat or dog. The balance between not hitting an animal and not harming your passengers is a complex ethical decision, probably based on the individual, the animal involved and who the passengers are. Another example: three small children are crossing a road; two run straight out while the third waits to check if it is safe. If braking wasn't an option, should the driverless car swerve to avoid the two children in the road and risk hitting the one on the pavement?

What about legislation? If a driverless car does kill one of the children who ran in front of it, should the occupant be fined or jailed? What about the programmer or company that developed the car? Should you be allowed to use a driverless car if you are under the influence of alcohol or drugs?

These are all problems that need to be addressed before driverless cars become widespread. Remember, just because something is technologically possible does not mean that it is ethically neutral to do it.

Artificial intelligence and automated decision making

Advantages	Disadvantages
Computers won't react differently based on their mood or lack of sleep.	Computers are unable to make ethical decisions.
Computers can retain a huge amount of information.	Computers are not responsible for their actions, so seeking compensation for mistakes is difficult.
Given the same inputs, a computer always produces the same outputs, offering consistent advice.	Computers are only as good as their algorithms, which are created by people.

Table 14.3: Advantages and disadvantages of artificial intelligence and automated decision making.

Environmental effects

The environmental impact of computers is a complex issue. Many companies are trying to improve their environmental footprint (and their reputations) by going 'paper-less' or 'paper-light'. This approach relies on using e-mails and cloud storage to share information and store documents, which in turn means using less paper. This saves trees and is just one of the ways that companies use computers to soften their environmental impact.

Computers are also being used in the fight against climate change. Computer models and simulations can be used to predict weather and climate patterns, modelling the effects of different initiatives and developments to see which will have the greatest impact.

The introduction of secure internet connections such as VPNs (virtual private networks) to permit flexible working have allowed people to work from home so they commute less. Video conferencing software such as Google Hangouts and Cisco WebEx allows organisations to host meetings from anywhere in the world without any requirement for delegates to travel by air, which would otherwise leave a very large carbon footprint.

Computing in context: coltan

Most people have never heard of coltan and yet it is a key component in almost every electronic device they own. Coltan (short for columbite–tantalite and known industrially as tantalite) is used in capacitors to store charge, and 80% of the world's known coltan reserves are in eastern Congo. However, only about 1% of the metal sold on the open market is Congolese. The reality is that most of Congo's coltan is sold illegally, and the revenue, instead of going towards the country's development, is helping to fund an on-going civil war. The coltan mines in the east are controlled by various armed groups, with civilians, including children, recruited as forced labour. The mortality rate in these mines is high.

The mining by the rebels is also causing environmental destruction. In particular, endangered gorillas are being massacred or driven out of their natural habitat as the miners illegally plunder the ore-rich lands of the Congo's protected national parks.

Have a look at the articles 'Guns, money and cell phones' and 'The Congo's blood metals' in the 'Further reading' section for more information.

However, the issue of new technologies and the environment isn't as simple as it seems. Computers are complex devices and often contain rare metals and minerals that need to be mined from the ground. In fact, a tonne of mobile phones contains more gold than a tonne of gold ore. Computers often contain toxic chemicals that need to be disposed of when consumers decide that they want the latest device. Devices are assembled in huge factories with all their associated environmental costs. Of course, they also require electricity to operate, the vast majority of which is produced by burning fossil fuels. Every server, hub and network switch relies on burning fossil fuels to operate. Anti-virus company McAfee™ recently reported that the electricity needed to transmit the trillions of spam e-mails sent every year is equivalent to powering 2 million homes in the United States and generates the same amount of greenhouse gas emissions as that produced by 3 million cars. Of course, electricity costs money and many large companies are keen to reduce their power consumption and switch to green energy. Google was among the first internet companies to take action to reduce energy consumption at its data centres. It is trying to promote efficient computing and seeking to increase its use of renewable energy.

Computing in context: recycling toxic materials

Properly recycling broken computers is a complex and expensive task. Many computers end up simply being dumped in less developed countries where they cause untold environmental damage.

This is particularly a problem in West Africa, where thousands of discarded computers from Western Europe and the United States end up every day. They are placed in massive toxic dumps where children burn them and pull them apart to extract metals for cash. The people who break open these computers regularly suffer from nausea, headaches and respiratory problems. However, it's not just the human cost that is concerning; fumes from burning old computers creates air pollution and many of the chemicals leak into the ground, contaminating local water supplies.

Environmental impact

Advantages	Disadvantages
Computers can replace paper documents, saving trees and processing time.	Computers are made up of rare chemicals that need to be mined.
Computer networks can be used to send products (such as films or music) that would otherwise need to be shipped in lorries and planes.	Computers are made up of toxic chemicals that are often not properly disposed of.

Table 14.4: Advantages and disadvantages of computers on the environment.

Advantages	Disadvantages
Flexible working allows people to work securely from home using a VPN, reducing the need to commute to work.	Computers use electricity, most of which comes from burning fossil fuels.
Video conferencing allows people to meet from anywhere in the world without increasing their carbon footprint.	Computers require a great deal of intensive manufacture to create, all of which requires burning fossil fuels.

Table 14.4: Continued.

Censorship on the internet and offensive communications

Cheap, unrestricted access to the internet has meant that people can access new ideas and share thoughts with people they would never otherwise have met. Online communities are often referred to as 'communities of interest' because they allow people to connect based on a common interest. In the past a person's community was limited by geography to those who lived nearby. Now, using the internet, people can find communities with similar interests, such as cat animations or a particular political view.

This unrestricted access to information has created a huge debate between those who seek to control what people can access and those who think access to knowledge is a basic human right.

Those who seek to suppress information range from controlling governments to those trying to protect intellectual property by compelling ISPs to block access to illegal download sites. There is also a great deal of support for internet censorship from religious and other groups who seek to prevent people from accessing material that they deem inappropriate, such as pornography or alternative religious views. On the other side of the debate are human rights and privacy campaigners who argue that everyone should be able to access any (legal) material and base decisions to view it on their own moral compass.

One of the factors weighing in support of those who would like the internet to be free of censorship is the composition of the internet itself. The internet predominantly uses packet switched TCP/IP protocols, which (as you saw in Chapter 9) makes it harder for governments and other pressure groups to intercept information. The internet also enables people to distribute new methods for protecting information (for example, encryption algorithms) very quickly and once these are released, it is almost impossible to prevent their use. Of course, this by itself is not enough to prevent censorship of the internet, and many governments have successfully blocked access to material they deem inappropriate. Even when material is not being explicitly blocked, many government agencies, such as GCHQ in the UK and the NSA in the United States, are known to be monitoring a huge amount of electronic communications.

The debate around internet censorship moves at a phenomenal pace and you should make sure that your own knowledge is as up to date as possible; it is, after all, a topic that directly affects your day-to-day life. The 'Computing in context' boxes below outline some of the landmark cases and events in the internet censorship debate.

Computing in context: the UK's internet filter

In February 2014, in response to pressure from 'moral outrage' groups, in particular the right-wing tabloid press, the government introduced new rules that meant ISPs would only allow customers access to restricted sites if they opted into doing so. This was welcomed by some, but seen as a terrifying encroachment on free speech by others.

The arguments surrounding the restrictions are complex and well worth reading about. In simple terms, those in favour of the debate argue that easy access to pornography (particularly extreme pornography) is damaging to children. The National Society for the Prevention of Cruelty to Children (NSPCC) found that almost a quarter of 11- and 12-year-olds had been distressed by an experience online in the past year. It said that, of these, 18% felt upset or scared for weeks afterwards. With pressure mounting to implement a UK internet filter, the then UK Prime Minister David Cameron stated that 'web firms have a moral duty to act but have not been doing enough to take responsibility'.

Those against the censorship argue that such a filter harms free speech and would be impossible to implement properly, leading to restricted sites being accessible and non-restricted sites being banned. These groups also argue that it is up to parents to inform themselves and monitor and filter their children's internet access, rather than relying on a 'nanny state' to do it for them. The major objection to the filter was that once it is possible to filter one website (say extreme pornography), it is trivial to filter others (for example, an anti-government website). Soon after the filter was implemented, these groups had their fears confirmed when sites about sex education and music piracy were also blocked.

Computing in context: WikiLeaks and Bradley (later Chelsea) Manning

In March 2011, the US Army charged Private Bradley Manning with 22 counts relating to the unauthorised possession and distribution of more than 720 000 secret diplomatic and military documents. The most serious charge was that of 'aiding the enemy', a treasonous act that carries the death sentence in the United States. He was found guilty of 20 counts, six of them under the Espionage Act of 1917, but was acquitted of aiding the enemy. He was sentenced to 35 years. Private Manning told the court he had leaked the documents to spark a public debate in the US about the role of the military and about US foreign policy.

Manning downloaded the classified documents (among them was video footage of an Apache helicopter killing 12 Iraqi civilians) to a blank CD, which he hid in a music album case. Manning passed the documents to WikiLeaks, a website with a reputation for publishing sensitive material. At the time, WikiLeaks was run by Julian Assange, an Australian with a background in computer network hacking who released tens of thousands of documents obtained by Manning relating to the war in Afghanistan. The website then went on to disclose thousands of sensitive messages (written by US diplomats) and military records from the Iraq war, causing embarrassment to the US government.

Soon after releasing the documents, Amazon (which hosted many WikiLeaks servers) withdrew its services, soon followed by every DNS which provided the wikileaks.org domain name. WikiLeaks responded by mirroring its site in 14 different countries, making it almost impossible to shut it down, despite US calls for WikiLeaks to be pursued with the same urgency as other suspected terrorist organisations.

WikiLeaks remains controversial, with some believing that it carries out important tasks, exposing government abuses of power and informing the public of what is being done in their name. However, others are outraged and see it as harmful to national security.

Computing in context: Phil Zimmermann and PGP

One of the most important tools against internet censorship and invasion of privacy is access to strong, free encryption technology. It doesn't matter if your government is collecting your e-mail if they don't know what it says or where it is going. Similarly, there is no point in attempting to prevent people accessing websites if all the content is heavily encrypted.

Historically, encryption was only really relevant to military and diplomatic communications. However, in the information age where huge amounts of our personal information and communications are stored online, cryptography becomes essential for maintaining our privacy. Capturing billions of e-mails and scanning them for keywords to find the ones you are interested in is also trivial compared to the effort required to do the same for traditional letters. Unfortunately, true encryption is very difficult and before 1990 had been almost exclusively in the hands of the military, governments and their intelligence agencies.

In 1991, American computer scientist and privacy campaigner Phil Zimmermann created an encryption program called Pretty Good Privacy (PGP) and released it for free on the internet. PGP is based on existing public–private key encryption (see Chapter 7 for more detail), but also includes a range of other techniques, such as digital signatures. The important things are that it is simple to use, free, and provides a high level of encryption. It was soon being used around the world.

The US government was not amused to say the least, since it includes encryption software in its list of military technologies (alongside tanks and cruise missiles). As a result, Zimmermann was accused of being an international arms dealer, became the subject of a grand-jury investigation and found himself pursued by the Federal Bureau of Investigation (FBI). Eventually, the case was dropped allowing PGP to be 'exported' around the world. Zimmermann's philosophy was simple: 'It's personal, it's private and it's no one's business but yours.' He was inducted into the Internet Hall of Fame in 2012 by the Internet Society.

Like all the issues surrounding internet censorship, the debate about people's right to encryption technologies continues. On the one hand are those who point out that these technologies can be used by criminals and terrorists to hide their activities. On the other hand are those who point out that encryption is vital for protecting the rights of repressed peoples and the privacy of everyone who communicates using the internet.

Source: Simon Singh (2002) *The Code Book: The secret history of codes and code-breaking* (London: Fourth Estate).

Advantages and disadvantages of unrestricted access to the internet

Advantages	Disadvantages
People can share and access information that would be very difficult for them to obtain without the internet.	Automated filters make it easy for governments to monitor millions of citizens.
People can spread news of atrocities and corruption very quickly, ultimately helping to bring those responsible to justice.	Computer networks are ultimately owned by governments and large corporations that can control the knowledge to which people have access.

Advantages	Disadvantages
	It is easy to disseminate false information or unconfirmed rumours.
	People can access vast amounts of illegal information and products such as extreme pornography.

Table 14.5: Advantages and disadvantages of unrestricted access to the internet.

Monitor behaviour

The ability of governments to collect communications information and use this to monitor the behaviour of its citizens is another area where technology is causing controversy. In 2013, Edward Snowden released classified files that showed the US and UK governments were collecting vast amounts of information without people's consent in the name of national security.

Computing in context: Edward Snowden

On 9 June 2013, 29-year-old Edward Snowden revealed himself as the source of one of the biggest leaks in Western intelligence history. Snowden had been an intelligence analyst working as a contractor for the NSA. He used his position (and passwords provided unwittingly by his colleagues) to access classified material and leak it to the world.

Snowden began leaking information by e-mailing the columnist Glenn Greenwald, from the Guardian newspaper, insisting he install PGP encryption software on his laptop. Once they could communicate securely, they arranged to meet in Hong Kong to exchange information.

Snowden's initial leak contained around 20 documents, most of which were stamped 'Top Secret'. At a glance, it suggested that the NSA had misled Congress about the nature of its domestic spying activities, and quite possibly lied. Greenwald described the documents as 'unbelievable', and 'enough to make me hyperventilate'.

To date, Snowden's leaks have revealed that the NSA and GCHQ are using a secret program known as PRISM to collect foreign communications traffic from the servers of nine leading US internet companies, namely Microsoft, Google, Yahoo, Facebook, PalTalk, YouTube, Skype, AOL and Apple. Of particular concern to UK citizens was the amount of internet traffic being monitored by the UK's security service GCHQ: up to 600 million communications every day.

Snowden has also revealed that the NSA and GCHQ are using apps such as Google Maps and Angry Birds to record people's locations, websites visited and contacts. In addition, the NSA was shown to be monitoring the location of 5 billion mobile phones around the world. It was also revealed that it had used these capabilities to spy on foreign leaders and diplomats at the 2009 G20 summit. The most recent leaks have highlighted the NSA's plans to develop a quantum computer capable of breaking all forms of encryption currently in use.

UK and US government reaction to the leaks has been extreme, including detaining Greenwald's partner without charge for nine hours and confiscating all his electronic devices. In one particularly sinister response, the Guardian's London offices were raided and all the hard drives relating to the leaked files were destroyed. Of course, the action had little impact, as copies of the leaked files exist on servers around the world.

Many people consider Edward Snowden to be something of a hero. Currently hiding in Russia, he was recently elected Rector at Glasgow University and runs regular VoIP and Twitter sessions explaining his motives for leaking such highly classified material. It's worth noting that some of the government activities he has highlighted may turn out to be illegal, and all are controversial. Others are disgusted by his conduct and say that by revealing US and UK intelligence capabilities to the world, he is harming national security.

The intelligence community argued that this information was a vital and effective tool for monitoring the behaviour of people who might pose a threat to those around them. However, many people are against this kind of mass surveillance and monitoring, believing that it gives the state too much power.

In 2013, Fusilier Lee Rigby was murdered outside Woolwich army barracks. During an inquiry into his death, it was revealed that his murderer had discussed his intention to kill a soldier on Facebook but this information had not been passed on to the security services. The security services were already aware of the killer and it is possible that had they known of his Facebook exchange they could have taken action to prevent the murder. This case underlines the difficulty in striking the right balance between the need of the state to protect its citizens and the needs of citizens to be protected from the state.

Analyse personal information

You have already seen how computers can use databases to store vast amounts of information and complex searching algorithms to quickly select the information they need. These properties can be combined to allow companies and governments to collect huge amounts of information and analyse it for their own purposes.

Store cards can be used to track which products you purchase and tailor the advertising leaflets sent to your home. E-mails can be searched for key phrases that might reveal potential criminal or terrorist leanings. There is such a wealth of publicly available information that political parties are using to target regions where they may be able to make the marginal gains that will help them win the next election.

Some people find this level of analysis invasive but many others find it very useful. If your local food store can stock food and drink that they think you are most likely to want then they won't lose stock to wastage and you are more likely to find the brands that you want.

Computing in context: Mosaic

Mosaic is a postcode-orientated information system. It takes data from a range of sources such as the electoral roll, census and the DVLA, and uses this information to make predictions or assumptions about people who live in a particular area. Mosaic is used by political parties to target voters, department stores to decide what to stock in their shops and even travel agents to decide which holidays to market in a given area.

Upon being given any postcode in the country, Mosaic is able to make predictions about likely consumer habits and lifestyles. This information is very detailed, covering favourite products, media platforms consumers are likely to respond to, even most likely names. This information is very valuable to a range of businesses, not least retail chains, who want to ensure that their shops stock items local people want to buy. Mosaic can even tell you which other areas of the UK have a similar consumer profile – useful if you have a successful retail business and are looking to expand.

More and more political parties are also getting in on the act. The information provided by Mosaic can be used to highlight key types of voters in marginal constituencies. For example, if you know that voters in a particular postcode are sympathetic to your ideas and might be persuaded to vote for your candidate, you could focus resources on that area rather than others where the chance of success is much lower.

Piracy

Piracy has long been a problem for film and record producers but the advent of digital technology, in particular computer networks, has led to an explosion in the amount of pirated material available. Computers make it simple to instantly copy and share copyrighted works and almost impossible to track those who are committing the crime. With so many people accessing copyrighted material for free on the internet, many otherwise law-abiding people simply do not view it as a criminal offence.

Computing in context: the Pirate Bay

The Pirate Bay is a website that provides links and torrent files which enable peer-to-peer file sharing using BitTorrent.

The site was founded in 2003 by Gottfrid Svartholm and Fredrik Neij. The site made it easy to access thousands of copyrighted works and police estimated that the owners made around £109 000 a year through advertising on the website. Since 2009, many ISPs have been ordered to block access to the website though the site is still easily accessible via proxies established by supporters all around the world. In 2009, the site owners were prosecuted for 'assisting in making copyright content available', found guilty and fined nearly £4 million, as well as being sentenced to one year in prison.

The cost of piracy is difficult to gauge but the Motion Picture Association of America estimates that piracy costs the US movie industry around $20.5 billion (£13.3 billion) per year. However, others question these figures; if someone watches a film they have downloaded illegally but would never have gone out and bought that film, has the film industry actually lost any money?

You have already seen some of the penalties for piracy in the section on Copyright, Design and Patents Act 1988, as well as how creative industries are joining with governments and ISPs to try and block access to pirated material. The difficulty is the sheer number of people who indulge in piracy. It is costly to track down and prosecute individual file sharers, many of whom are children and teenagers without any means of paying a fine.

A possible solution for performers is to release material openly on the internet. In 2007, Radiohead released their In Rainbows album for download from the internet. They allowed people to pay however much they wanted for the work, including paying nothing. This was a risky initiative that drew both acclaim and criticism. It should be remembered that if people enjoyed the album, they may wish to see the band in concert, buy a T-shirt and their back catalogue. Rather than fighting the internet, Radiohead chose to embrace it. Prior to the release of their ninth album in 2016, they deleted their entire internet presence in a move that would once again draw attention.

Many musicians and other performers have found recognition through their YouTube channel and welcome copying and sharing of their work.

The internet has provided a wealth of opportunities for users to showcase their work but for large media corporations wishing to protect their products, the threats are considered more significant.

Layout, colour paradigms and character sets

To people from different cultures, the same piece of information can mean many different things. There are many examples of brands that failed when they translated their famous slogans in order to target an overseas market; a quick search online for 'slogan translation mistakes' will reveal many examples where poor translation impacted on a product's success. This is particularly a problem if you are marketing a product or providing a service using a medium as international as the internet.

The internet has also allowed disabled people access information and communicate more easily by using adaptive hardware and specialist software. Websites should be constructed so that they function well with text-to-speech software so that they can be easily used by blind people, although it is estimated that 70% of them still fail to meet accessibility baselines.

Layout

Even something as simple as website layout will be interpreted differently by different cultures. For example, English speakers read left to right. Therefore, websites built for these audiences tend to have important navigation items (like home buttons) on the left, text tends to be left aligned and the largest, most important articles appear on the left-hand side of the page. Arabic speakers, however, read right to left and websites built for this market tend be completely the opposite, text is right aligned, important articles appear on the right of the page and logos and home buttons appear on the top right rather than top left. If you want your product to sell in the Middle East then you need to ensure that your target audience finds your website as easy to read and navigate as possible. Simply translating the content of the page may not be enough.

The layout of a website should also work well with text-to-speech software so that it is easily navigable for blind users. Some sites may choose to use a second accessible site, but ideally the main site should work with a text-only browser such as Lynx.

When developing a software or hardware interface, the needs of the user should always be fully considered, for example a program to be used by young children will have a simple layout with minimal text. It will probably also use icons to represent actions and bright colours to attract their attention and be fun to use. A business product would need to have a simple, functional interface, branded with the company logo and house style.

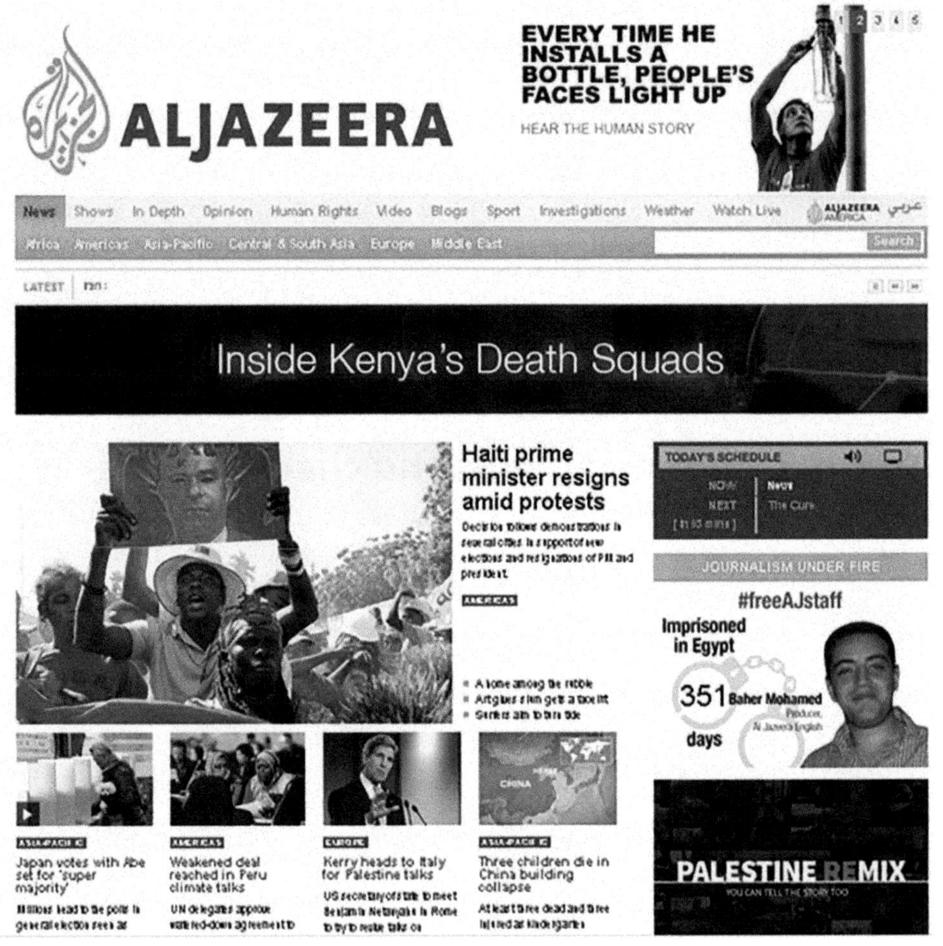

Figure 14.2: AlJazeera.com aimed at an English-speaking audience.

AlJazeera.com is aimed at an English-speaking audience. Notice the position of the search bar on the right, left alignment of text and order of navigation buttons with popular options being leftmost on the page.

AlJazeera.net is aimed at an audience that speaks Arabic. Notice the position of the search bar on the left, right alignment of text and order of navigation buttons with popular options being rightmost on the page.

Colour paradigms

Colours are particularly prone to cultural interpretation. This is important to know if you have one website that you are using to target lots of different markets. In Western Europe, for example, the colour pink is commonly associated with femininity. In Japan, however, there is no such distinction and in Thailand pink is simply the colour of Tuesday. Yellow in Western Europe can have connotations of caution, alarm or even cowardice but in China it is considered a royal or imperial colour and is seen as being particularly masculine. Of course, cultural interpretations of colour are liable to change over time and may not have a particular stronghold on the cultural psyche. Use the 'Further reading' section at the end of this chapter to find out more about the cultural associations applied across different cultures.

Certain colour combinations are more easily accessible for visually impaired users, for example, primary blue and yellow are often very effective.

Figure 14.3: AlJazeera.net aimed at an Arabic-speaking audience.

Character sets

You will already be familiar with the two most common character sets ASCII and Unicode. ASCII uses 7 bits to represent 128 different characters. This is fine for the English language but is nowhere near enough if you want your product to be translated into Japanese or Arabic. This is one of the major reasons behind the prevalence of Unicode on the internet. Unicode compensates for its larger file size by making it possible to represent hundreds of thousands of characters.

However, simply being able to properly display the characters used by your target audience isn't enough. The way in which even simple information, such as a person's name, is recorded varies hugely between different cultures. Imagine you have created a website and want your users to register before they are given access to the content. In England, it is traditional practice for a person to have a single given name (e.g. Charlotte), perhaps a middle name and a surname they have inherited from their father. So, a form which requires the user to enter their first name and surname with an optional field for middle name is reasonably likely to be successful. However, what happens when someone from China wants to sign up for your site? In China, names are typically split into three parts, for example, Mao Ze Bao. The final word Bao is actually the given name, the first word Mao is the family name and the middle name is a generational name, which is also shared with siblings, so the same field layout is obviously not appropriate. In Iceland, a person's surname is generally just their father's name with 'sson' added to the end of the name for a son or 'sdóttir' for a daughter. It would be very unusual to call someone by their

Tip

Questions on this topic are more likely to be long-answer questions. Use bullet points for the main aspects of your answer first to make sure you include them all.

Long-answer questions will also assess your spelling and grammar, so take time to check.

Activity 14.1

Join Twitter and follow technology correspondents from major news outlets. Retweet anything you are sent that involves technology and the law.

Activity 14.2

Find a recent case where someone has been jailed for their use of technology. What laws were used to prosecute them?

surname as it has no cross-generational significance and is very unlikely to be unique. If you want to appeal to all these groups a general 'full name' field is probably going to be more suitable, or even just 'family name', or 'given name'. It's also important that your database field lengths are able to cope with the number of characters entered. Many people assume that some cultures or countries (for example, Spanish) have longer names than others but there are so many variations within these that it is impossible to make any useful generalisations. A good rule of thumb is to aim for slightly over the average and then add 10% so we could say that a first name field should be able to hold up to 20 characters.

Summary

- The Data Protection Act sets out how those who collect personal and private data may use it. It also covers where this information can be sent and how long it can be kept for.
- The Computer Misuse Act makes it illegal to access a computer without consent as well as establishing the penalties for doing so.
- The Copyright Design and Patents Act sets out who has the right to make money from a particular creative work and how long those rights last.
- The Regulation of Investigatory Powers Act sets out the rules that govern how the UK government can collect information on its citizens.
- Computers have had an enormous impact on almost every work place imaginable. Some see this impact as a negative one costing jobs and reducing wages. Others see it as a very positive one that has created whole new industries.
- Advances in artificial intelligence have given rise to the prospect of automated decision making. Many are happy that impartial machines will make decisions formerly made by fallible humans; others are dismayed by the idea that a computer could make life-or-death decisions.
- Computers have made it easier to publicise the environmental impact of the actions of industries and individuals. However, computers themselves require huge amounts of electricity and rare minerals to create and maintain.
- The internet has provided a wonderful forum for debate and free exchange of ideas. However, some governments view this freedom of expression as a threat and seek to censor it.
- Computers allow us not only to hold vast amounts of personal information, but also to analyse it to spot trends and patterns. For some this is useful, for others it is a serious invasion of privacy.
- Piracy and offensive communications began long before the invention of the computer but the advent of the internet means that it is quicker and easier than ever before to distribute offensive and illegal materials.
- The internet has made the world a much smaller place. This presents a unique set of challenges to those who are trying to communicate with everyone in this vast global marketplace.

End-of-chapter questions

1 The Data Protection Act 1998 contains eight principles – what are they? [8]

2 What is the purpose of the Computer Misuse Act 1990? [2]

3 In the context of computer-related laws, what does RIPA stand for? [1]

4 Which piece of legislation is used to prosecute those who illegally download music? [1]

5 Who is responsible for enforcing the Data Protection Act 1998? [1]

Further reading

Computer Misuse Act 1990 – search for 'What is Computer Misuse?' on sqa.org.
Sebastian Thrun, Google's driverless car, TED – search on TED's website.
Kristi Essick, Guns, Money and Cell Phones, The Industry Standard Magazine, Global Issues, June 2001
Caroline Sourt, The Congo's Blood Metals, The Guardian, December 2008
Richard Wray, Breeding toxins from dead PCs, The Guardian, May 2008
James Chapman, Blocks on internet porn to begin in new year: 20million families will have to make a Yes or No choice on access to filth, The Daily Mail, November 2013
Laurie Penny, David Cameron's internet porn filter is the start of censorship creep, The Guardian, January 2014
Jane Wakefield, Wikileaks' struggle to stay online, BBC, December 2010
Ed Pilkington, Bradley Manning may face death penalty, The Guardian, March 2011
Patriot Act 2001 – search on the US Department of Justice website.
Profile: Private First Class Manning, BBC, April 2014
The Eight Principles of Data Protection – search on the Information Commissioner's Office website.

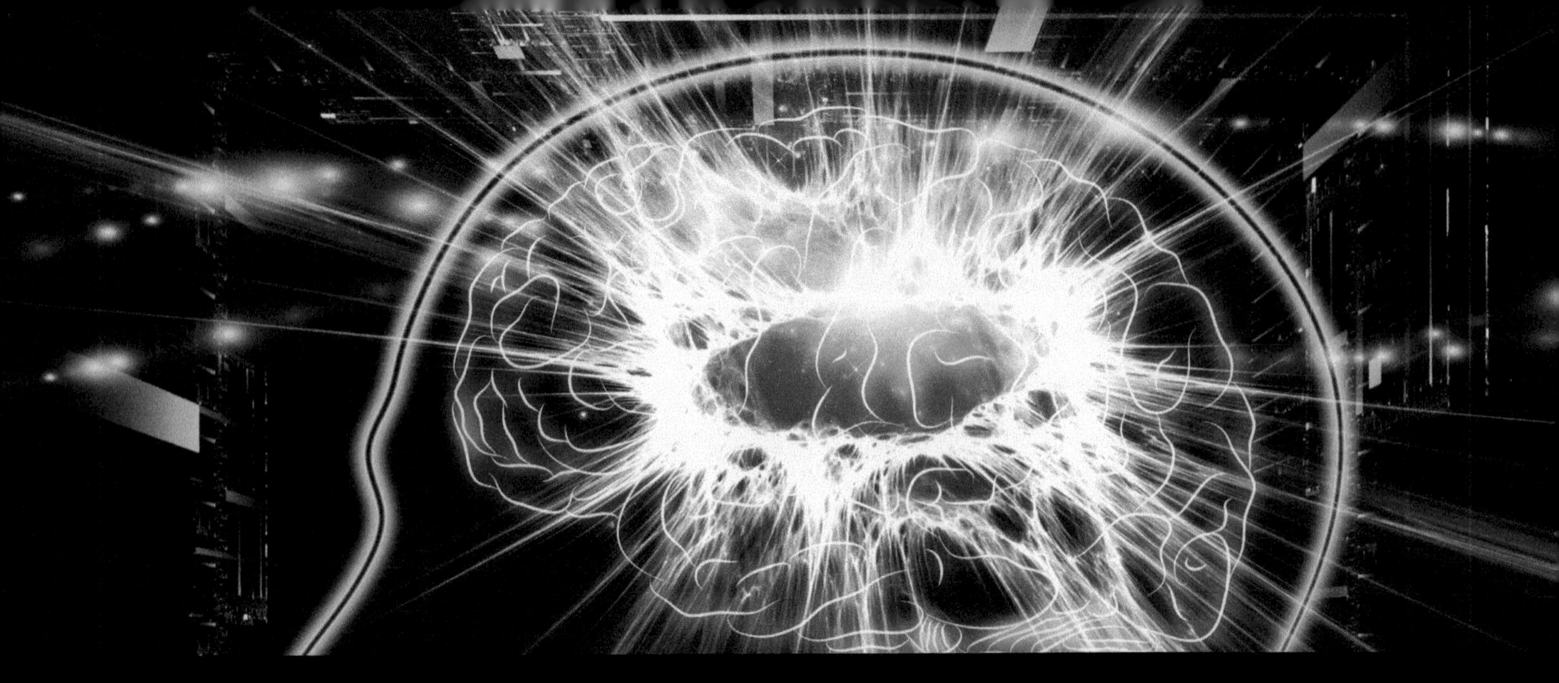

Chapter 15
Thinking abstractly

Specification points

2.1.1 Thinking abstractly

- The nature of abstraction.
- The need for abstraction.
- The differences between an abstraction and reality.
- Devise an abstract model for a variety of situations.

Learning objectives

- To understand the nature of abstraction.
- To understand the need for abstraction.
- To know the differences between an abstraction and reality.
- To devise an abstract model for a variety of situations.

What is abstract thinking?

When a solution is presented for a given computing problem, we say that we have a concrete solution for that problem. However, sometimes our solutions can be generalised so that they can provide part of the solution to other problems. For example, if I produced code that e-mails people who passed an online computing test, then it makes sense that the same code could be adapted to work with other tests. **Abstraction** is the process of separating concrete instances of a solution from the ideas that were used to solve them. For example, queues are used to store print jobs in a print manager as well as to determine the next process to run when using round-robin scheduling (see Chapter 3). They both use the abstract idea of a queue.

When dealing with an abstract idea, the semantic meaning behind the idea must be separated from the details of how it will work or be implemented. Abstraction for computer science can be split into two main parts:

- **Control abstraction** hides actions and programming control, such as if statements. The basic premise behind high-level programming languages is control abstraction – hiding the details of machine code from the developer.
- **Data abstraction** hides how bits are organised for primitive data types such as floating point or dates.

Abstract data types such as stacks and queues (not to be confused with primitive data types) are an example of abstraction. Only the operations performed on them and any constraints on the data type are defined. For example, a stack would define what push and pop do (see Chapter 12) while an ordered set would define that items must be held in a logical order.

One of the most important skills for a developer to cultivate is the ability to think in abstract terms. This allows you to consider the ideas behind an algorithm or a system without getting bogged down with the implementation details. When abstracting, it is possible to generalise in layers. Each layer will hide more of the key implementation details than the last.

Example: Abstraction layers

Abstraction is about generalising the idea of how to solve a problem away from any specific implementation detail. Abstractions can be combined into multiple layers enabling more and more of the concrete implementation to be generalised. So far, you have already come across two ideas that make use of abstraction layers: networking protocols and the operating system.

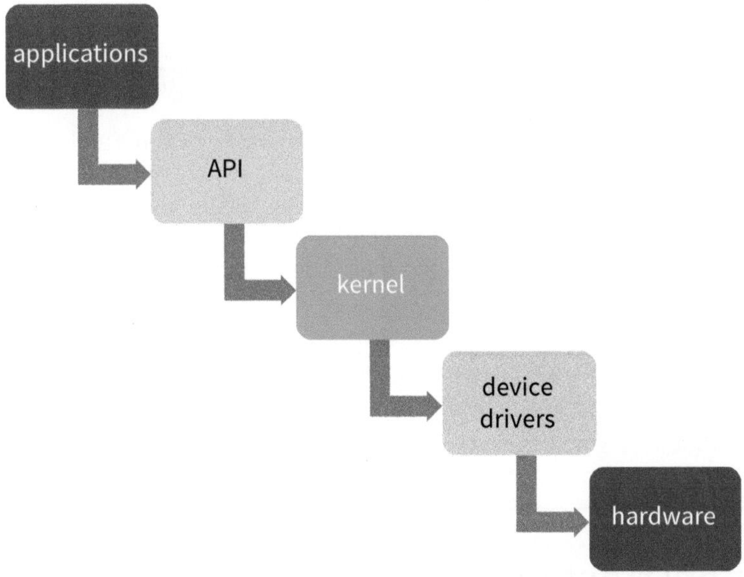

Figure 15.1: Abstraction layers for a typical operating system.

Figure 15.1 represents an example of abstraction layering for operating systems. Consider a simple application that opens a file and saves some text to it (see code below). The first abstraction is the idea of opening, writing and closing a file. The program makes use of some built-in Python functions. The details of how open, write and close work are hidden or abstracted, because the developer is not interested in how Python will perform these actions. The problem for the developer is not how to write a series of bits to the hard drive, but rather that the text 'hello world' must be saved.

Code

```
f = open("test.txt","w")
f.write("hello world")
f.close()
```

Python has a set of built-in functions, or **application programming interfaces (APIs)**, which have been written by its developers. They will have written the functions open, write and close to make a call to the **kernel**. All file access goes through the kernel, as seen in Chapter 3, which again hides how the files are actually accessed. All Python is doing is providing a convenient way to access the kernel. At this level, knowledge of the kernel is required, as all hardware actions must go through the operating system.

In order to manage files, the kernel must make use of device drivers. Not all devices of a similar type work in the same way. Memory sticks, plugged into a USB port, use different drivers to internal hard drives. However, if you were saving a file in an application, you would just consider them to be different drives rather than concerning yourself with how the device is connected to the motherboard. Device drivers abstract the implementation details of how any device interacts with the operating system. More information about device drivers can be found in Chapter 3.

Finally, the hardware level provides an example of the lowest level of abstraction. In this situation, knowledge of exactly how a file should be edited is required. At the highest level of abstraction, we are simply concerned with the overall idea. As we approach the lowest level of abstraction, then more knowledge of how devices *physically* work must be known. For example, to determine exactly which sector a file is saved to on the hard drive is something that the kernel and hard drive device driver would have to decide.

Computing in context: Java 3D

Java programs are meant to work homogeneously on different operating systems and devices. Three-dimensional (3D) graphics tend to be displayed using either DirectX (Windows®) or openGL (Linux, Mac®). DirectX and OpenGL work very differently; code written for one would not work for the other. They are separate libraries, so under normal circumstances a developer would have to port their program from one to the other. This is not a simple process.

Java 3D attempts to abstract the underlying choice of graphics library away from the developer. When displaying 3D objects in Java 3D, the underlying mechanisms will detect what graphics libraries are available and hide this complexity from the developer. Although this example is about 3D graphics, Java uses this type of abstraction for a lot of libraries, for example those used in creating graphical user interfaces.

The need for abstraction

Abstraction allows the key ideas of a problem to be considered without having to get bogged down with the exact nature of the implementation. Most problems in computer science are complex, so unless they are simplified, they may be too complicated to solve as a whole. If the entire problem is considered all at once then there may be too many variables and special cases to worry about. By abstracting the problem and only considering the most important aspects, we can simplify it and start to work towards a solution. It may be that later on we introduce different levels of abstraction to fully solve the problem.

One of the key advantages of abstraction is that, because we are not concerned about how the idea will be implemented, we can always improve the implementation later. Consider binary search as an abstraction (see Chapter 8). For binary search to work properly, the list of items to be searched must be sorted first. However, the abstract idea behind binary search does not take sorting into account, so when it comes to implementation, the numbers may need to be sorted before the search can be run. This raises another level of abstraction: which sort method to use. We might start with **bubble sort**, but if we found it too slow for our needs, we could replace it with **quick sort**. In this example, the sort method we choose does not change the way we are using binary search, but swapping between sorting algorithms speeds up the system, making the search more efficient. So having an abstract idea of a problem enables us to swap implementations in and out when more efficient models are found, without impacting the functionality.

X = 5 is a very simple programming command, assigning a single value to a variable. This is a control abstraction, which hides the mechanics of how variables and assignment work at the machine code level. The developer is using a high-level language. If they had to work out how X = 5 is translated into machine code, it would make their programming much more complicated. Abstraction is therefore necessary to enable the developer to focus on the problem at hand.

Tip

Next time you use your mobile phone, have a look through all of the apps and consider what abstractions each have used. One of the key skills you need to develop is the ability to spot when abstraction is used and use it for yourself. This is best learned through considering different scenarios.

Abstraction versus reality

Abstract ideas generalise reality by focusing only on the key attributes and actions of the concept being abstracted. For example, if designing a racing game, an abstraction of how a car handles is key to efficient development. Rather than developing a separate handling code for each car to be represented, the developer would simply create a generic model of a car that could be altered to simulate different cars. In reality, cars behave differently from each other, even if they are the same type of car. For example, their performance is dependent on the state of their tyres, how well the engine has been maintained, whether the correct quality assurance procedures were followed when the car was built, and a million and one other factors. When abstracting the concept of car handling for the game, a lot of these subtle factors are simply ignored. They are important in real life, but not for game development.

Abstractions, especially in object-oriented coding, may sometimes not even represent something from real life. They make up an 'abstraction layer' to deliver functionality to other **classes** through **inheritance**, but are not meant to be used on their own. Consider the example below for Java abstract data structures.

Example of abstraction in Java

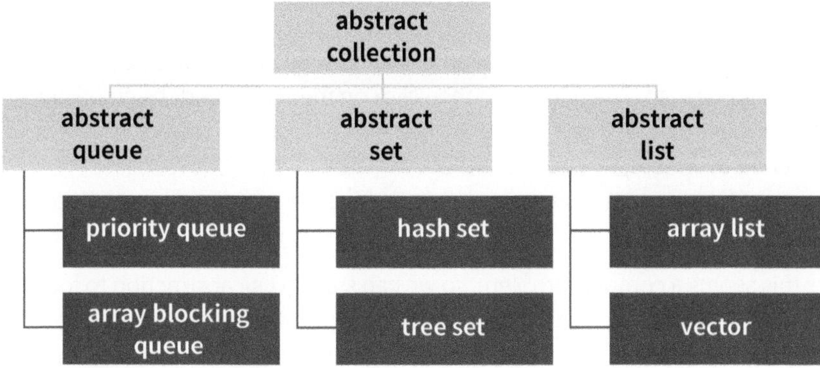

Figure 15.2: Abstraction layers for Java's abstract data types.

Tip

In the exam you will be shown different real-world scenarios where abstraction can be used. You need to be able to spot that abstraction is required and then come up with examples of how it can be implemented. The best way to practise this is to consider different scenarios that you encounter in real life and then use computational methods to consider a possible solution. It is not necessary to produce a solution, but you should be able to describe one.

The classes shown in green represent abstract classes, while the purple ones are concrete implementations. AbstractCollection, which is at the root of the inheritance tree, provides basic functionality to create an abstract data structure. It is designed for developers who wish to speed up the process of making their own data structures. AbstractQueue, AbstractSet and AbstractList expand on the AbstractCollection by implementing code more specific to that type of data structure. The concrete implementations differ from their abstract counterparts and may provide subtle differences. For example, HashSet implements a set using a hash table and provides no guarantees on the order of items when iterating over them. TreeSet, backed by a tree, provides natural ordering. However, both are examples of a set and so inherit mutual characteristics from AbstractSet.

Abstraction allows us to capture concepts rather than worrying about specific implementation details. When combining abstraction layers and the power of object-oriented code, abstraction provides us with a way to share fundamental building blocks. The interested student should read up on how Java uses abstraction – see the 'Further reading' section for a link.

An example of abstract thinking: point-and-click adventure game

The problem: to find a way for a character to move around on screen, avoiding obstacles, when a position on the screen is clicked.

Figure 15.3: A point-and-click game – Beneath a Steel Sky.

Initial abstraction

Point-and-click adventures will have a controllable character with interactive items placed around the game map. The player can then click on the screen and the character will either move to that point, or interact with the item when it has been selected. Part of the map will not be traversable, which means that the character must move to find the best route, if any exist, to where the player has clicked, therefore avoiding any potential obstacles.

On face value, this seems a complex problem, so we can start to use abstraction to focus on the key details. The game map, including what parts of the map are traversable or not, is one of the key aspects of the game. Drawing out the game map in a 2D grid, we can start to represent traversable areas in one colour and blocked areas in another. 2D grids can be represented as a 2D array, multiple colours can be represented as different numbers (values of which are not important, they just need to be consistent) and finding the correct path can be done using standard algorithms such as A*. Most 2D game screens can be represented as 2D arrays and any situation where players or computer-controlled objects move around a map is known as route finding. What was once a complex problem, thanks to abstraction, has now become much more manageable. More importantly, we now have a template to solve a whole raft of similar problems. Let us now explore how this solution may unfold in more detail using object-oriented programming.

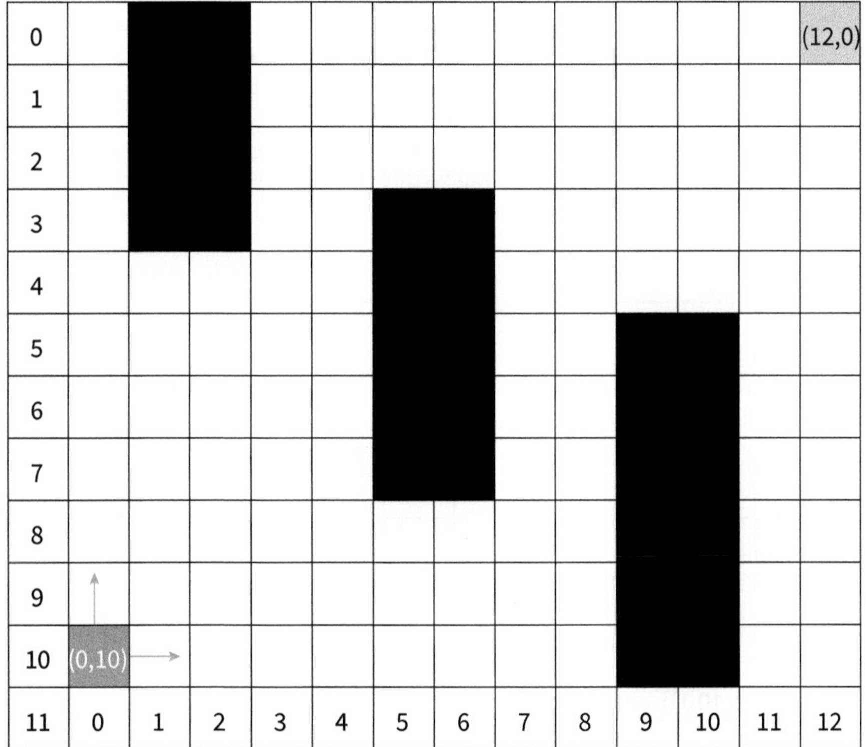

Figure 15.4: Abstraction of a map.

The above grid represents the game map; white squares are passable and black are blocked. The grey square represents the player (P) and the green square represents the destination (D). The problem is to find a path between P (0,10) and D (13,0) avoiding obstacles. At any given point in time, the player can move one square vertically or horizontally. Two classes can be deduced from the above description, the player and the grid. Assumptions are made that all obstacles are rectangular.

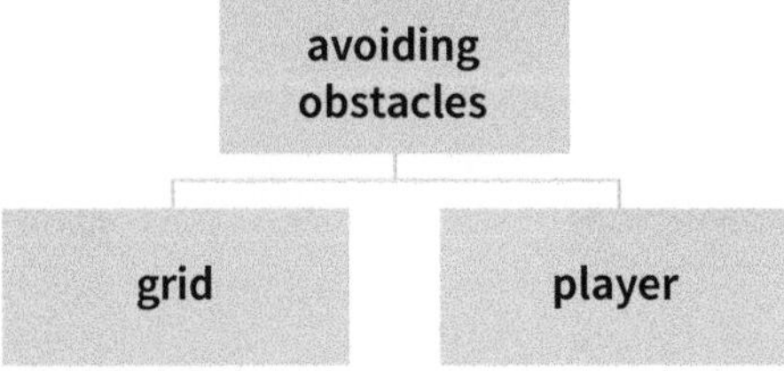

Figure 15.5: The main objects involved in a pathfinding problem.

Code

```
Class Map:
  public map(maxX, maxY)
  public setObstacle(x,y, width, height)
Class Player:
  public player(startx,starty)
  private makeValidMove(x,y)
  public travelToDestination(dx, dy, map)
```

Note: the class is called 'Map', as the abstract idea represented is that of a map. When implementing the solution a *grid* will be used to represent the map. When coding in object-oriented code it is important to name classes after the abstract idea and not the specific implementation method. This is also known as **encapsulation** (see Chapter 6).

At this level, no decisions have been made on how to represent the grid or how travelToDestination will work. The basic idea will be that travelToDestination will perform the algorithm below. How the next step is determined will be looked at in the next level of abstraction.

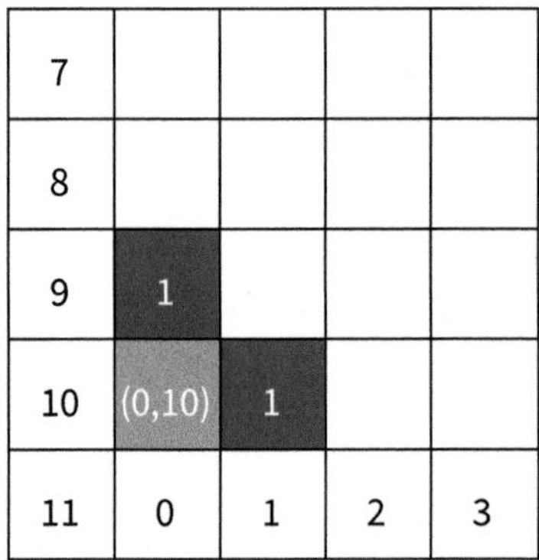

[(0,10,0), (0,9,1), (1,10,1)]

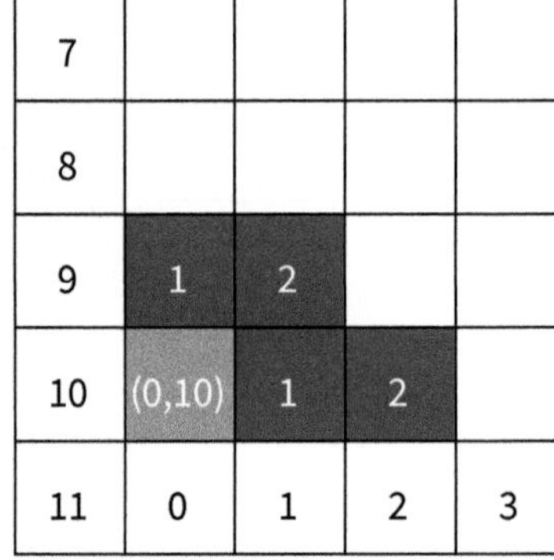

[(0,10,0), (0,9,1), (1,10,1), (1,9,2), (2,10,2)]

Figure 15.6: Initial steps of pathfinding.

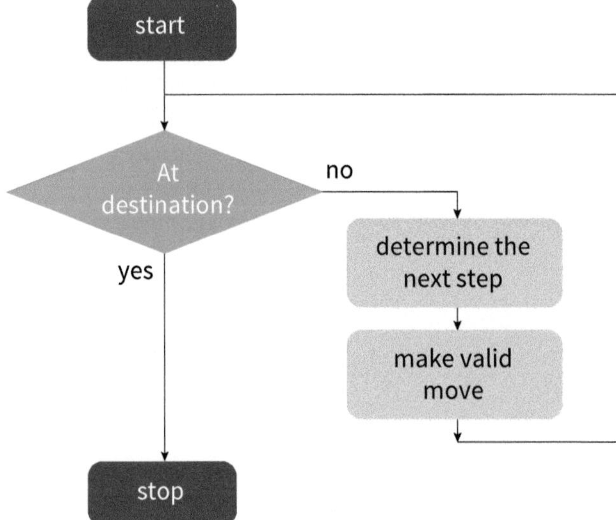

Figure 15.7: Flowchart showing the high-level abstraction for solving pathfinding.

Second layer of abstraction – pathfinding

Now that the problem has been represented in a more simplified manner, the task of performing the pathfinding will commence. At this stage, no consideration has been given to how the grid (level) will be displayed or stored. In Chapter 8 you will be introduced to **Dijkstra's** and **A*** pathfinding algorithms. It is worth reading over these algorithms to help give context to the following explanation. As we have abstracted the method travelToDestination, we can pick and choose which pathfinding algorithm we use. In fact, should we wish, we could swap them at a later date. For this example we will use Dijkstra's algorithm:

1. Add the start position to a list with a counter initialised to zero.
2. For each valid move:
   a. take the current counter and add one to it
   b. add the move to the list if it is not there already with the new counter.
3. Move on to the next item in the list until the destination has been reached.

0	10			13	14	15	16	17	18	19	20	21	(13,0)
1	9			12	13	14	15	16	17	18	19	20	21
2	8			11	12	13	14	15	16	17	18	19	20
3	7			10	11			14	15	16	17	18	19
4	6	7	8	9	10			13	14	15	16	17	18
5	5	6	7	8	9			12	13			18	19
6	4	5	6	7	8			11	12			19	20
7	3	4	5	6	7			10	11			20	21
8	2	3	4	5	6	7	8	9	10			21	22
9	1	2	3	4	5	6	7	8	9			22	23
10	(0,10)	1	2	3	4	5	6	7	8			24	25
11	0	1	2	3	4	5	6	7	8	10	11	12	13

Figure 15.8: Grid with all path costs shown.

Figure 15.8 shows the calculated distance costs for each square based on the proposed algorithm. The shortest path takes 22 steps and there is more than one solution with the same number of steps (path cost). At this level of abstraction it is not important which path is chosen, as all solutions are a potential shortest path. This algorithm takes an undirected approach to pathfinding and is not the most efficient way of doing it. We could, for example, use A* pathfinding using the **Manhattan heuristic** (see Chapter 8). The key point to note here is that our choice of algorithm will only impact the efficiency of the solution, not whether it is correct. The ability to swap algorithms in and out without changing the solution is one of the key ideas behind abstraction.

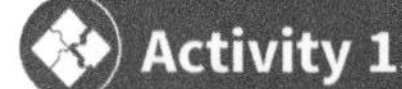

Activity 15.1

You have been asked to create a flash card program to help A Level students study for their exams. Design a possible solution using computational methods.

Summary

- Abstraction is an important problem-solving technique for computer scientists and developers that enables them to focus on key ideas.
- Abstraction is needed to help represent real-world situations as generically and simply as possible by not including information that is not essential.
- Problems can be split into different layers of abstraction, allowing us to choose how to implement each layer without worrying about impacting the rest of the system.
- Abstracted solutions will represent or model reality but may not include every feature. The designer will decide what they deem to be important when abstracting a solution to a real-world problem.
- When designing solutions to problems, it is important to start at the highest level of abstraction and gain an overview of the problem.
- Object-oriented design techniques enable abstraction to be represented through the use of encapsulation.
- Each class represents one idea but hides how that idea will be implemented.

End-of-chapter questions

1 Define the term 'abstraction'. [2]

2 A student decided to create a revision app for his computing exam. His computing teacher thought this was a good idea but felt that he could make his idea more abstract. Explain how the student could use abstraction in this scenario. [4]

3 Sarah produced an implementation of bubble sort for numbers, which she tested. Her boss then asked her to write another function to sort alphanumeric data. Explain how abstraction could help Sarah. [4]

4 Most programming APIs are written abstractly. Explain why it is good practice to do this. [4]

Further reading

Abstract classes – search on the Wide Skills website.

Abstraction – search on the Princeton Computer Science website.

Chapter 16
Thinking ahead

Specification points

2.1.2 Thinking ahead

- Identify the inputs and outputs for a given situation.
- Determine the preconditions for devising a solution to a problem.
- The need for reusable program components
- A The nature, benefits and drawbacks of caching.

Learning objectives

- To be able to identify the inputs and outputs for a given situation.
- To be able to determine the preconditions for devising a solution to a problem.
- To understand the need for reusable program components.
- A To understand the nature, benefits and drawbacks of caching.

What is thinking ahead?

When faced with a problem that requires a computational solution, it is important to tackle it using the skills outlined in Chapter 15. Thinking ahead, which is the focus of this chapter, requires us to take a step back and consider what the solution might look like, what it will entail, what conditions it will work under and how it will fit in with any wider systems or processes. It also enables us to consider how the solution might be built and start to make some implementation decisions, such as how the project will be broken down into individual components, and what performance enhancements could be utilised.

Some computational problems can be very complex and will require teams of developers to build the final solution. If every developer was asked to build the system in their own way, chaos would ensue unless a systematic approach was followed (see Chapter 5 to see how methodologies can be used to implement larger projects). Thinking ahead is a key part of designing the final application.

Identify inputs and outputs

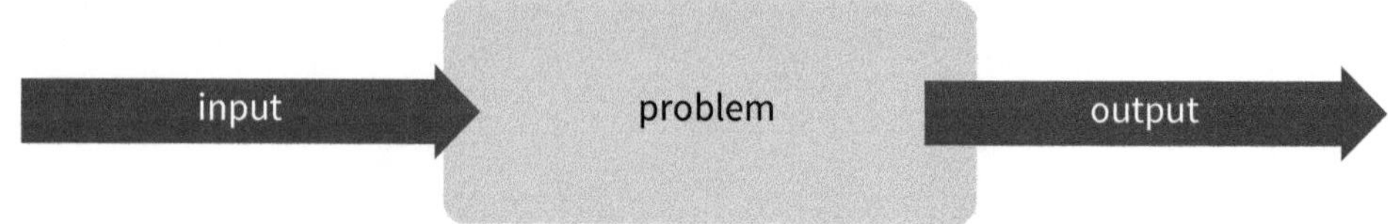

Figure 16.1: Input and output of a problem.

To fully understand the problem at hand, it first must be broken down into smaller problems using top-down design techniques. Breaking the task down into simpler problems allows a modular solution to be developed. For each module, the identification of the inputs and outputs will be the first stage in developing a solution. In Figure 16.2, top-down design is used to break up the problem of building a tic-tac-toe game.

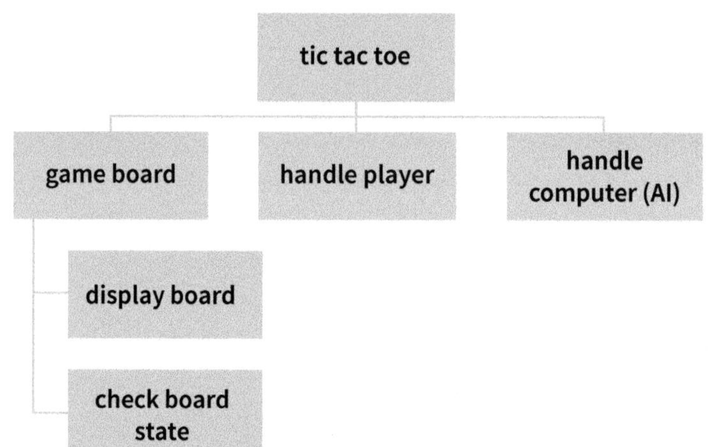

Figure 16.2: Top-down design of a tic-tac-toe game.

There are a number of important considerations to make when deciding the properties of inputs and outputs, which are summarised in the table below.

Consideration	Explanation
Data type	To ensure the correct type of data is passed to the module.
Structure of the data	Will it be a **primitive data type** or a data structure? For example, will the module accept a string or a list?
Validation	Is there a particular format or acceptable range for the data? For example, the program must only accept only numbers from 1 to 10 or a maximum list of 100 elements.

Table 16.1: Considerations when deciding on the input and output of an algorithm.

Consideration	Explanation
Number of arguments	Does the module require multiple parameters to be passed to it? For example, withdrawing money from a bank account will require the amount and the account details.
Where will the input come from or where will the output go?	Will the data input be automatic, e.g. from a sensor, or will it be entered manually (which may require more validation)? Will the data be stored in a database or a simple text file? What output will the user see displayed on the screen?
Are there any preconditions?	Does anything need to have occurred first before the problem can be solved? For example, we would need a digitised map in order to carry out route finding in a navigation system.

Table 16.1: Continued.

As an example, consider the 'handle player' module. The purpose of this module would be to allow the user to decide where they want to take their turn. The input to this module will be the square the player wants to pick. If this is a text-based game then the input will be a number corresponding to the square the user has chosen. The output will simply update the current game board with the player's selection.

Consideration	handle player
Data type	Integer
Structure of the data	The game board will be stored as a one-dimensional array. Each element within the array will be 0 (square is available), 1 for chosen by the player and 2 for chosen by the computer.
Validation	The number must be a valid square starting from 1. If that square is not currently 0, then the player must select again.
Number of arguments	It needs the game board status and the user's selection.
Where will the input come from or where will the output go?	The game board status will be passed through as a 1D array. The user's selection will come from console input.
Are there any preconditions?	The game board array should be pre-initialised. The player and computer should take their turns in order. This module will assume it is the player's go when it is called.

Table 16.2: An example of how the input and output of tic-tac-toe could be considered.

When handling user input, validation will need to be coded into the module to ensure that the data is in the correct format for the program to process it. .It needs to be planned for and designed before the program is coded to prevent incorrect data entering the system. Data input is also the door for security threats, which makes validation crucial in securing a system. If invalid data is input into a module then bugs may occur which could crash the module or allow hackers to bypass security mechanisms. For example, SQL injection allows hackers to run powerful commands by submitting malicious queries through webforms that have poor validation. This is of even greater significance if modules are daisy chained together (e.g. the output of module A provides the input to module B) because a rogue input could be propagated throughout the system.

Determine the preconditions for devising a solution to a problem

Some problems, when broken down into smaller sub-problems, have specific preconditions which must be met and abstracted. When developing a solution to a problem, you should always assume the preconditions have been met. In reality, they may not have been, so we need to code for this eventuality too. It is common for validation rules to be defined in the design phase, but not included as part of the algorithmic design. Abstracting just the basic, required input simplifies the problem. Initialising data structures will be a precondition. For example, in a game of backgammon, the board needs to be set up in a certain way ready for game play to commence. Before applying decision making to calculate the computer's optimum game move, we can assume that the board array has already been correctly set up.

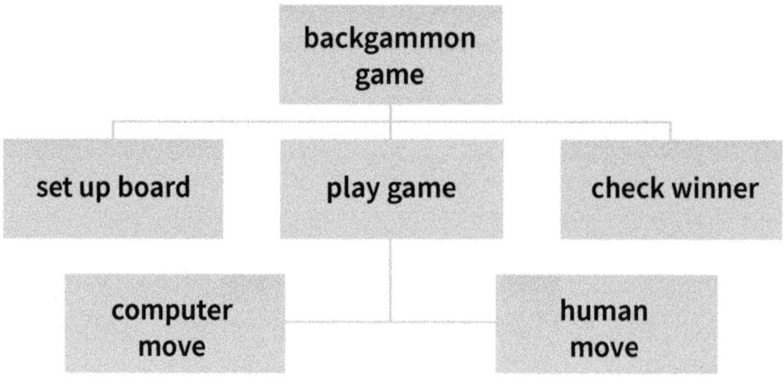

Figure 16.3: Top-down design of a backgammon game.

Tip

Top-down design is a very important skill to master. This will be especially true when you come to work on your project.

Breaking backgammon down logically leaves us with three main elements. Deciding which is the optimum move for the computer to make based on the current game board is one of the elements. The input to the problem will be the current state of the board and the assumptions made are that the board is correctly set up and that it is the computer's turn to play. These assumptions are preconditions to solving the problem.

An example of thinking ahead: Tic-tac-toe game

The problem: to develop a method to enable play against a computer in a tic-tac-toe game. The computer should always try to win.

In order to solve this problem we first need to decide on the inputs, outputs and preconditions.

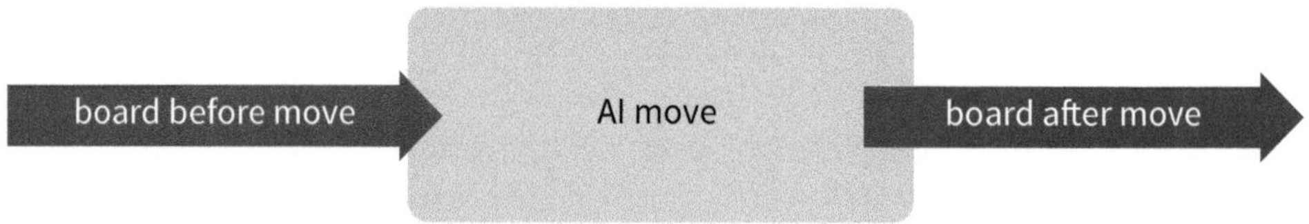

Figure 16.4: AI move module with input and output.

The board will be directly passed to the module and in making the move will update the board rather than returning the position. In order for this to work we must assume that it is the computer's turn and there is a move still available. This means that at no point should a board be passed with no possible moves. In order to solve this problem, the data structure must also be defined. Note that the current state of the board does not fall into the scope of this problem.

The game board will be represented by a 2D array of integers where 0 represents a free space, 1 is an X and 2 is an O.

	0	1	2
0	1	0	0
1	0	2	0
2	0	0	0

Figure 16.5: Example of how a tic-tac-toe board could be represented.

Now that the problem has its inputs and outputs specified and the module domain restricted, the developer can go ahead and solve the problem using the techniques described in other chapters. The interested reader may wish to read up on the minimax algorithm to understand how the solution could be implemented (see 'Further reading').

The nature, benefits and drawbacks of caching

When learning about the CPU and RAM, you will have encountered the concept of **cache memory**. Cache memory, which runs much faster than RAM, is one of the key strategies to overcome the von Neumann bottleneck (see Chapter 1). In this section, we will look at how the concept of caching can be abstracted and used to solve problems.

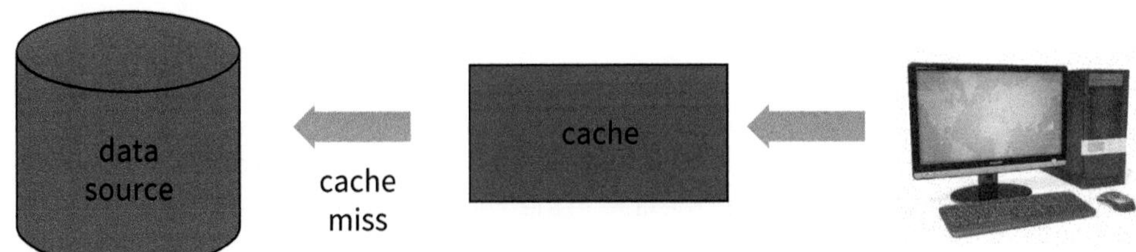

Figure 16.6: Diagram representing how cache is conceptually viewed.

The key idea of caching is that, when requesting data from a data source, the request will go via the cache. The cache will be smaller but faster than the original data source and will hold a subset of the original data. If, when data is requested, it resides in cache, then the copy in cache is returned. This is called a hit. However, if the data does not exist in cache, then it must be copied from the data source into the cache and then returned to the requester. This is known as a **cache miss** and is a much slower operation, even slower than going directly to the data source. As caches tend to be used to speed up a slower resource, their key to success is selecting data that is most commonly accessed and minimising the number of cache misses.

The number of times a cache is missed or hit will determine its overall performance .This can be measured by comparing the number of hits versus misses, known as the 'hit rate' or 'hit ratio', which is expressed as a percentage.

Cache management – reading

When a cache miss occurs, an algorithm will be required to decide which, if any, data entry should be ejected from the cache to make way for the new data. The choice of algorithm for replacing cache entries directly impacts on its efficiency, but can also impact how fast a cache can be managed. Different algorithms to manage a cache perform better in

Activity 16.1

Create your own version of tic-tac-toe using the advice in this chapter. Make sure you take a modular approach to the solution and use functions. When developing the code for the computer you may wish to research the minimax algorithm.

Tip

In the exam you will be expected to be able to identify situations that would benefit from caching. To prepare for this, it is a good idea to make study notes about a number of different real-world caching scenarios. For example, organisations will use a proxy server with a web cache to speed up the load time of commonly accessed webpages.

different scenarios – they are implementation-specific. In this chapter the abstracted ideas of a cache will be discussed, not specific heuristics.

The optimal solution, also known as the **clairvoyant algorithm,** will swap out entries that are not going to be used for the longest amount of time. As this requires information about the future use of the cache, which is why it is known as the clairvoyant algorithm, it is not realistically implementable in a general-purpose system. At any given point in time the clairvoyant algorithm will always make the right choice for a swap to ensure the hit rate is as high as possible. This can be approximated by using statistical analysis of past use of the cache, but it can never be perfectly implemented. What it does provide is a way of measuring performance of any heuristic chosen. Performance of any caching algorithm can be measured by comparing the hit rate to the clairvoyant algorithm.

Another common algorithm is the least recently used (LRU), which will swap out the least recently used page or entry. This uses historic information rather than trying to predict the future. One way to implement LRU is to use a linked list, where the front of the list contains entries that have been recently used and the back contains the entries that have not been recently used.

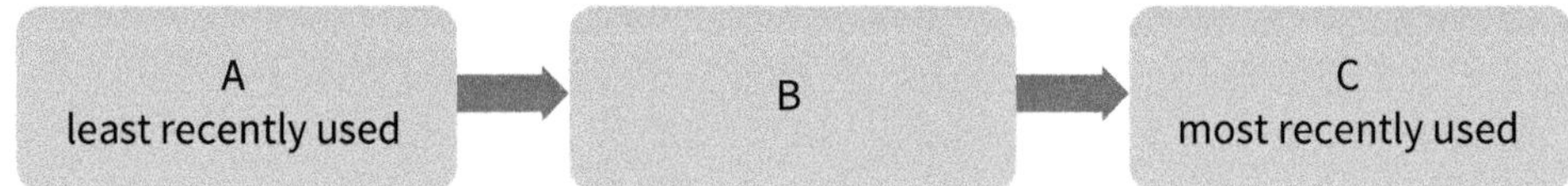

Figure 16.7: A linked list to implement LRU.

Another method is to use a counter which, for every access to the cache, assigns the value of the counter to the entry and then increments it by 1. That way the entry with the lowest counter would be the one to be removed. The interested reader could explore replacement heuristics in more detail by accessing the links in the 'Further reading' section.

Regardless of which heuristic is used, the basic process of reading from a cache is the same, and is shown in Figure 16.8.

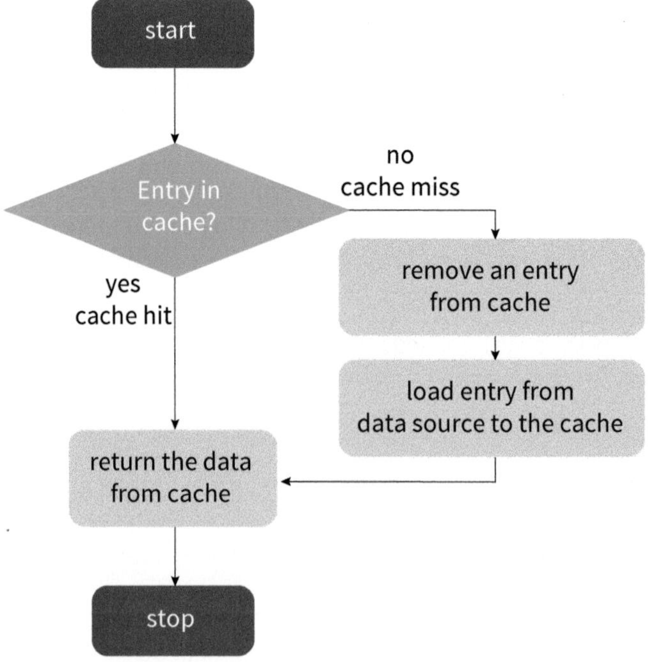

Figure 16.8: Algorithm for dealing with a cache miss.

Cache management – writing

When dealing with making changes to the underlying data source of a cache there are two main strategies. One is to update both the cache and the data source at once (known as **write-through**). The other is to initially update the cache and only update the underlying data source when its data is ejected from the cache (known as **write-back**).

Write-back strategies will perform better if and only if the hit rate is high. To implement write-back, every entry in the cache must be given a **dirty flag**. When an entry is first added to the cache, the dirty flag is set to false. When an update occurs, the flag is updated to true. When an entry is ejected, the dirty flag is checked. Any entry ejected with a dirty flag set to true will need to be saved to the backing store.

Write-through is simple to implement, meaning that no additional complexity must be catered for; however, all data writes will be slow. If a problem requires a lot of data writes then write-through will not be a good option. If the number of times a write occurs is low then write-through can perform better than write-back.

Uses for caching

Caching techniques have three main uses: CPU, disk and web caching. Although these are the three techniques being considered, they are not exclusive and their ideas can be applied to other scenarios. CPU caching was described in Chapter 1.

Disk caching (also known as page caching)

To aid understanding of how page caching works it will be useful for the reader to be familiar with memory paging in the operating system (see Chapter 4). Memory will normally be left idle under light load, allowing it to be available for applications. However, many operating systems take advantage of large amounts of unused memory by implementing a page cache. This will pre-fetch commonly used data from the hard drive, such as regularly accessed applications, and store them as pages in RAM. Any files regularly used or accessed during the current session will also be cached.

As hard drives are much slower than memory, the use of page caching can significantly improve the performance of a computer. Adding more memory to a computer can dramatically improve overall performance as more pages can be cached.

Web caching

Web browsers will cache images, HTML pages and any other files downloaded over HTTP. This helps reduce bandwidth required, as cached files can be accessed from the local computer rather than using the internet. Web browser caches work differently from other caches, as they will store files on the hard drive rather than in memory.

The use of web caches creates an issue with the freshness of the webpage being viewed. For example, if a page was accessed and saved into cache one day then changes the next, it is important that the browser accesses the newer version of the page. This is done through a three-step verification check, which is shown in Figure 16.9. It is possible for the user to manually delete the cache and for web developers to prevent browsers from caching their pages. Websites that change regularly, like news sites, would not want their home pages cached. Less dynamic pages could be cached. The developer of the website can specify how long a file should be kept in the cache, known as 'freshness'.

Web caches follow a similar method to other caches when it comes to ejecting entries, as the size of file space that can be stored in the cache will be capped. A common way to save space on a hard drive is to delete web browser caches or to reduce their cap.

Benefits and drawbacks of caching.

Benefits	Drawbacks
Faster access to data when a cache hit occurs.	Increased complexity when dealing with a cache miss means that accessing backing stores is slower when caches are enabled.
Can reduce bandwidth requirements and load on other resources.	Being given a stale version of data (from cache) when the original source of the data has changed.
A second source of information that can be accessed if the master source fails.	Finding data in a cache is linked to the size of the cache. Larger caches will take longer to search.

Table 16.3: Benefits and drawbacks of caching.

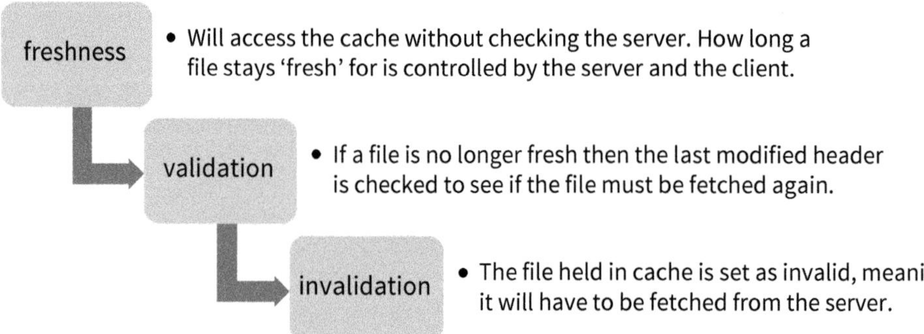

freshness
• Will access the cache without checking the server. How long a file stays 'fresh' for is controlled by the server and the client.
validation
• If a file is no longer fresh then the last modified header is checked to see if the file must be fetched again.
invalidation
• The file held in cache is set as invalid, meaning it will have to be fetched from the server.

Figure 16.9: Key considerations when dealing with a web cache.

The need for reusable program components

When writing programs, we need to think ahead about what reusable components we will use or make to help keep development time to a minimum. Designing programs to take advantage of pre-built code is essential to speed up the development process. Also, designing programs so that code can be reused within the program itself (or in future developments) also helps to speed production.

The following clarifies why it is desirable to use reusable code and the scenarios in which it can be used.

Application programming interfaces – library software

Every programming language has pre-built software routines which can be used within your programs. This can range from performing key algorithms such as sorting, to displaying 3D graphics. Such routines can be included in your programs as library files and can be used by calling their application programming interface (API). Below is an excerpt from the Java API to show what methods are available for the ArrayList class. An **array list** is a special implementation of a list that is backed up by an **array**. If the underlying array is too small for the data being added then the class will automatically resize the array. The code to do the resize is abstracted so developers do not need to concern themselves with how the APIs work but rather how they will best make use of them.

Method Summary	
boolean	add(E o) Appends the specified element to the end of this list.
void	add(int index, E element) Inserts the specified element at the specified position in this list.
boolean	addAll(Collection<? extends E> c) Appends all of the elements in the specified Collection to the end of this list, in the order that they are returned by the specified Collection's Iterator.
boolean	addAll(int index, Collection<? extends E> c) Inserts all of the elements in the specified Collection into this list, starting at the specified position.
void	clear() Removes all of the elements from this list.
Object	clone() Returns a shallow copy of this ArrayList instance.
boolean	contains(Object elem) Returns true if this list contains the specified element.
void	ensureCapacity(int minCapacity) Increases the capacity of this ArrayList instance, if necessary, to ensure that it can hold at least the number of elements specified by the minimum capacity argument.

Figure 16.10: Method summary for the ArrayList Java class.

Example: Using abstraction to create reusable code

Creating modular code is crucial to ensure code is reusable. Each module must have a specific purpose which should be as generic as possible. In Chapter 15 you saw that making code more generic meant that it could be applied to multiple scenarios. Consider a simple game example.

```
import pygame
from pygame.locals import*
img = pygame.image.load('mario_running.gif')

white = (255, 255, 255)
w = 640
h = 480
screen = pygame.display.set_mode((w, h))
screen.fill((white))
running = 1
px = 0
py = 0
dx = 1
while running:
  for event in pygame.event.get():
    if event.type == pygame.QUIT:
      running = False
  screen.fill ((white))
  screen.blit (img, (px,py))
  px = px + dx
   if px > w or px < 0:
      dx = dx * -1
  pygame.time.delay(5)
  pygame.display.flip()
```

The code on the previous page will load up an image and make it move left and right. If a game was being developed, then the code to load, move and display each sprite individually would make the whole program unwieldy and prone to bugs. An improvement would be to take a step back and consider a generic sprite. They all move in a similar way, will be animated, have a screen position, and are represented by an image. Therefore, spending time creating code that will deal with sprites generically allows for it to be reused multiple times within the same program. It also could be used in other programs, allowing the developer to create their games much faster and even share their code for others to reuse.

Pygame is a reusable library that allows Python coders to create games quickly. As it turns out, Pygame has a sprite class, which you can inherit from in order to help speed up development. Other than speed of development, there are a number of advantages to reusing code:

- The code will have been tested and will have a single place to update or fix bugs. This helps make the code base overall more stable.
- Specifically in the case of using library software, the code will have been developed by an expert who will have spent a long time creating the most efficient solution possible.
- Any updates to the reusable code will mean that improvements will automatically be implemented without the need to change any of your code. If the code is dynamically linked as a library then there will not even be a need to recompile the code.

Activity 16.2

Create a module that will sort and search through lists (or arrays) of numbers. You can use Chapter 22 to help you. Once created, you can then use this module in any future code you produce that requires searching or sorting.

Computing in context: Object-oriented design and reusable code

One of the key aspirations for object-oriented programming was that a bank of classes be produced, ultimately leading to more rapid software development. In order to do this, classes have to be produced in a more abstract way, which makes the classes more generic and independent of a specific problem domain.

One way to make classes more abstract is to develop software libraries first and then make use of these to develop multiple applications. During the design phase of development, general classes are produced and refined through the use of subclasses. Some practical ways to achieve object-orientated code reuse come in the form of inheritance, component and framework reuse.

Inheritance reuse allows common methods and attributes of an abstract idea to be placed in a superclass. Classes are then able to inherit the code from these and extend their functionality. For example, when building a mobile Android® app, you may wish to make use of the Activity class. An activity is anything where the user will be interacting with the screen. Most of the setup for an activity, like creating a screen, is handled by the Activity class. To make use of it, you simply inherit the code in your class and override the onCreate() method. All activities, regardless of the app being made, will work in a similar fashion. Accordingly, inheriting from the Activity class dramatically speeds up development time. Activities are an Android abstraction and are not meant to be used directly; rather, you must inherit from them.

Component reuse is when a fully encapsulated set of classes is produced which the developer can use within their code. Pygame uses many components which can be reused by software developers. For example, the pygame.image class encapsulates loading, saving and storing of images in memory. It can handle multiple file types without the developer having to do any additional work. It is possible, due to the elegance of object-orientated programming, to inherit component classes. However, the key difference between inheritance reuse and component reuse is that inherited classes will not do anything unless inherited, whereas components are self-contained.

Framework reuse is more common in larger projects but sometimes used in smaller applications. Essentially, a **framework** is a collection of classes which provide basic functionality for a specific problem domain. **Ruby on Rails**, a framework for building web apps, is written in the **Ruby** programming language and is based on the **model-view-controller** (MVC) design pattern. The framework provides a structure for developing web apps which allows the developer to focus on the key business logic rather than, for example, how they will connect to a database. As most web apps have to solve similar problems, frameworks help speed up development and allow teams of developers to adopt a way of structuring their code.

Summary

- When developing software it is important not to simply jump in and start coding.
- By taking a step back and thinking ahead, you can develop a much more scalable and reliable solution.
- You must consider the input, output and storage requirements of any algorithm before coding it. This includes looking at the data structures to use, validation and how it may change over time.
- Every problem has some preconditions that will impact the overall algorithm. These may be restrictions on the input, assumptions made on the input or linking into other systems.
- Taking into consideration what libraries you will use, or create, during the development process will help reduce the overall development time.
- This, coupled with the increased stability of reusing well-tested code, means that the final solution should have fewer issues and bugs.
- Looking at the input and output of different modules allows you to define interfaces between components, which will aid larger teams of developers to integrate their code to work together.

- Finally, by considering caching and other speed enhancements, the final solutions will be more scalable and will perform better.

End-of-chapter questions

1 Explain how programmers make use of reusable components when developing large systems. [3]

2 Explain what the term 'hit ratio' means for caching and why it is important to keep it high. [4]

3 Explain why it is important to use abstraction when creating reusable components. [4]

4 State two advantages and disadvantages of caching [4]

Further reading

A realistic look at OO reuse – search on Dr Dobb's website
Android coding example: activity inheritance – search on the Android Developers' website.
Example of a component in pygame – go to pygame.org.
Example of a framework in Ruby on Rails – go to rubyonrails.org.

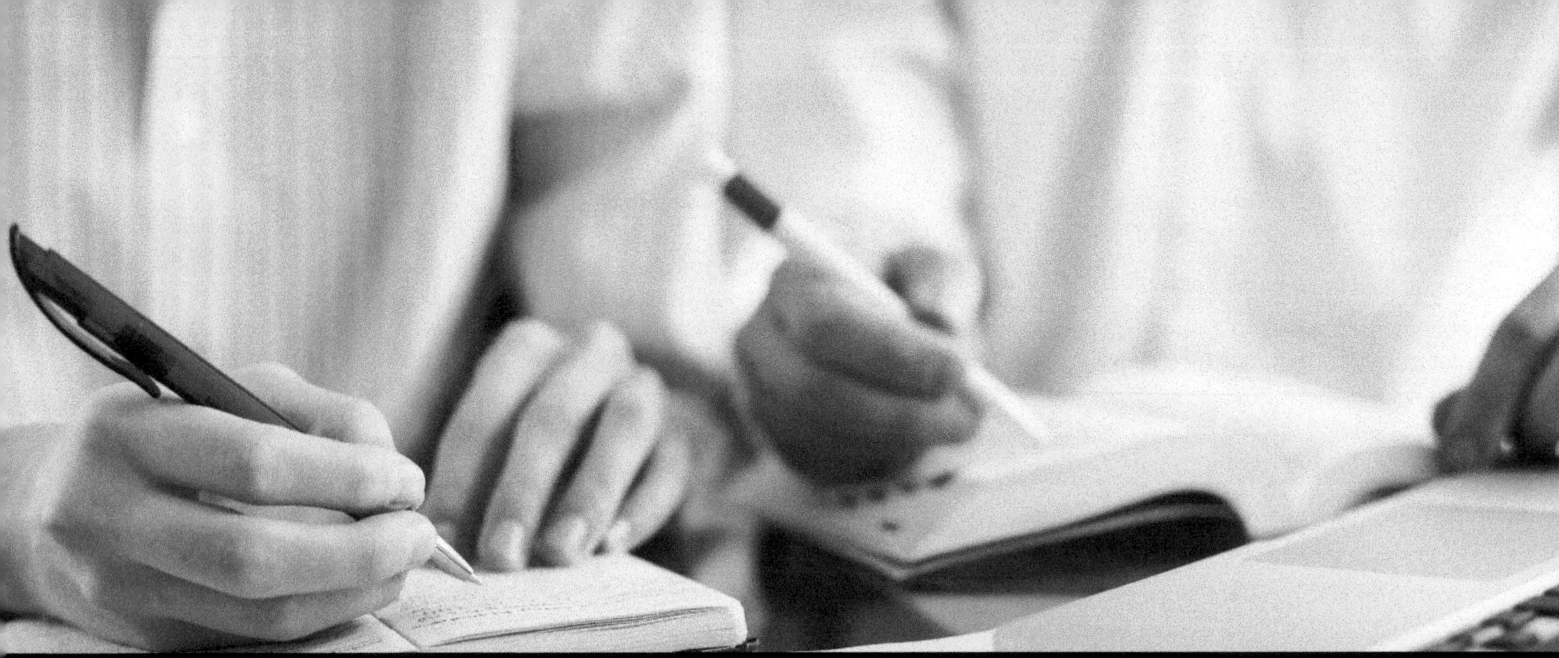

Chapter 17
Thinking procedurally

Specification points

2.1.3 Thinking procedurally

- Identify the components of a problem.
- Identify the components of a solution to a problem.
- Determine the order of the steps needed to solve a problem.
- Identify sub-procedures necessary to solve a problem.

Learning objectives

- To be able to identify the components of a problem.
- To be able to identify the components of a solution to a problem.
- To be able to determine the order of the steps needed to solve a problem.
- To be able to identify the sub-procedures necessary to solve a problem.

What is procedural thinking?

Procedural thinking is the process of thinking through a problem and developing a sequence of steps that can be used to reach a solution. A programmer can describe these steps using a procedural programming language to create a sequence of instructions to be followed by a computer.

A procedural programming language is one that solves problems by executing a sequence of instructions. The order in which steps are carried out is defined by the programmer using three constructs:

- *Sequence* dictates that steps will be carried out in the order they are given – step one first, followed by step two, and so on.
- *Selection* allows the programmer next to choose to execute one of a number of instructions based on a condition that arises during the execution of previous instructions.
- *Iteration* allows the programmer to repeat the same instructions a certain number of times or until a condition is met.

Identifying the components of a problem

Identifying the main components of a problem is a key step towards solving it. The process involves thinking through the problem. What needs to be achieved? What actions would any solution need to carry out? This process is best illustrated by using an example. Imagine you have been commissioned to create a simple, single-player hangman game. The best place to start is by producing a written description of what happens during the game:

> *The computer randomly chooses a five-letter word from its dictionary and displays the appropriate number of _ (underscore) symbols on the screen (each _ represents one letter in the chosen word). The player is then asked to make a guess about a possible letter. If the guess is correct, the _ symbols are displayed again but any _ that represented the letter guessed is replaced by that letter. If the guess is incorrect, then another piece of the hangman drawing is added and displayed to the user. This process is repeated until the whole word is guessed or the hangman drawing is complete.*

This description of the problem should be as detailed as possible, as any information missing from it may cause something to be missing from the solution.

The second step in identifying the components of the problem is to break down the description into the individual sentences. These naturally tend to represent different stages of the problem. Then break these down further by splitting sentences on the keywords AND and OR. Table 17.1 shows how this process has been applied to our description of the hangman problem.

The computer randomly chooses a five-letter word from its dictionary and displays the appropriate number of _ symbols on the screen (each _ represents one letter in the chosen word).
The player is then asked to make a guess about a possible letter.
If the guess is correct, the _ symbols are displayed again but any _ that represented the letter guessed is replaced by that letter.
If the guess is incorrect, then another piece of the hangman drawing is added and displayed to the user.
This process is repeated until the whole word is guessed or the hangman drawing is complete.

Table 17.1: Breaking down a problem.

Tip

Identifying the components of a problem

If you are asked to break a given problem into its component parts, a good place to begin is by underlining the keywords in the question. In the exam, the same mark scheme will be applied to every student, so the examiners would expect all of the solutions to be as similar as possible. As a result, most of the components you will be expected to list in your answer will probably be alluded to in the question.

The statements in this table can then be rewritten as a list of the main components of the initial problem.

1. The computer randomly chooses a five-letter word from its dictionary.
2. The appropriate number of _ symbols are displayed on the screen (each _ represents one letter in the chosen word).
3. The player is asked to make a guess about a possible letter.
4. If the guess is correct, the _ symbols are displayed again but any _ that represented the letter guessed is replaced by that letter.
5. If the guess is incorrect, then another piece of the hangman drawing is added.
6. The hangman drawing is displayed to the user.
7. This process can be repeated until the whole word is guessed.
8. This process can be repeated until the hangman drawing is complete.

Identifying the components of a solution to a problem

Identifying the components of a solution to a problem means identifying which steps need to be followed in order to reach a solution. The best way to identify these steps is by thinking through a possible solution and writing down what actions need to be carried out in order to achieve it.

Having already identified the major components of the problem, you can focus on these individually and produce a list of key steps for each.

Using the example of our hangman game; the first component of the problem was that the computer has to randomly choose a five-letter word from its dictionary. We can identify the components of any solution to this problem by making a list of the steps needed to achieve it:

1. Create a dictionary holding suitable five-letter words.
2. Randomly generate a number between 1 and the number of words in the dictionary.
3. Use the random number to select a word from the dictionary and store it somewhere accessible to the rest of the program.

This process can be repeated for each part of the problem and will give us a complete list of all the components of the solution to each part of the problem.

1. The computer randomly chooses a five-letter word from its dictionary.
   a. Create a dictionary holding suitable five-letter words.
   b. Randomly generate a number between 1 and the number of words in the dictionary.
   c. Use the random number to select a word from the dictionary and store it somewhere accessible to the rest of the program.

2 The appropriate number of _ symbols are displayed on the screen (each _ represents one letter in the chosen word).

   a Create an array called 'guesses' with five elements, each holding a _ symbol.

   b Display the contents of the array.

3 The player is asked to make a guess about a possible letter.

   a Display a message asking the user to enter a letter.

   b Store the letter the user enters in a global variable.

4 If the guess is correct, the _ symbols are displayed again but any _ that represented the letter guessed by the user is replaced by that letter.

   a Compare the user's letter to each letter in the word.

   b If there is a match, replace the _ symbol in the guesses array with the letter.

   c Display the guesses array.

5 If the guess is incorrect, then another piece of the hangman drawing is added.

   a If there is no match, increase the number of incorrect guesses by one.

6 The hangman drawing is displayed to the user.

   a Print an image of the hangman that reflects the number of incorrect guesses the user has made.

7 This process can be repeated until the whole word is guessed.

   a Check to see if the guesses array matches the word being guessed.

   b If it does, display a congratulatory message.

   c If it doesn't, check if the hangman drawing is complete.

8 This process can be repeated until the hangman drawing is complete.

   a Check to see if the number of incorrect guesses is three.

   b If it is, then display a 'game over' message.

   c If it is not, then ask the user to guess another letter.

By identifying the components of a solution to each part of the problem we have also identified the components of the solution to the entire problem.

Key skills: Flowchart symbols

You will already be familiar with creating flowcharts from your KS3 and GCSE studies, but it is worth recapping the process here.

Flowcharts use symbols, connected by arrows, to diagrammatically depict a process. They are particularly useful for giving clear descriptions of complex processes like solving the kinds of problems encountered by computer scientists.

There are many different flowchart symbols and styles, but the majority of the problems you will encounter at A Level can be solved using just four of them.

Terminator	Process	Decision	Arrow
Start/Stop	Process	Decision	→
The terminator, or Start\Stop, symbol, is placed at the beginning and end of a flowchart.	The process symbol is used to hold actions of processes (for example, 'Print letter').	Decision diamonds are used when which action to take next depends on the answer to a question. By convention the question (for example, 'Is there any paper in the printer?') appears within the symbol and possible answers are shown as labels on the arrows leading away from it.	Arrows indicate the direction of flow between decisions and processes. They can be labelled.

Determining the order of the steps needed to solve a problem

In the previous section you saw how to identify the components of the solution to a problem. The next stage is to determine the order in which these steps should be taken, particularly how to move between the different components of the solution. The best way to achieve this is by producing a flowchart that incorporates the steps of each component in the solution.

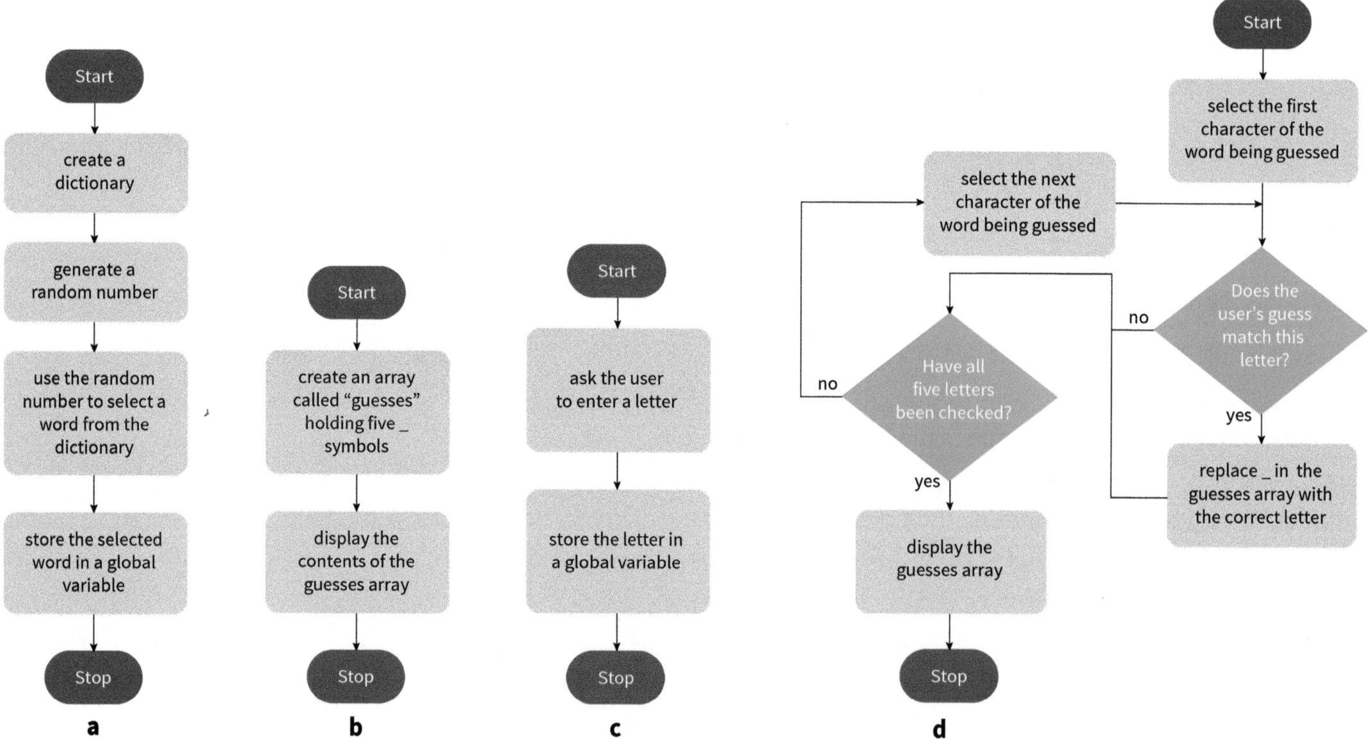

Figure 17.1: A flowchart describing the implementation of a simple hangman game.

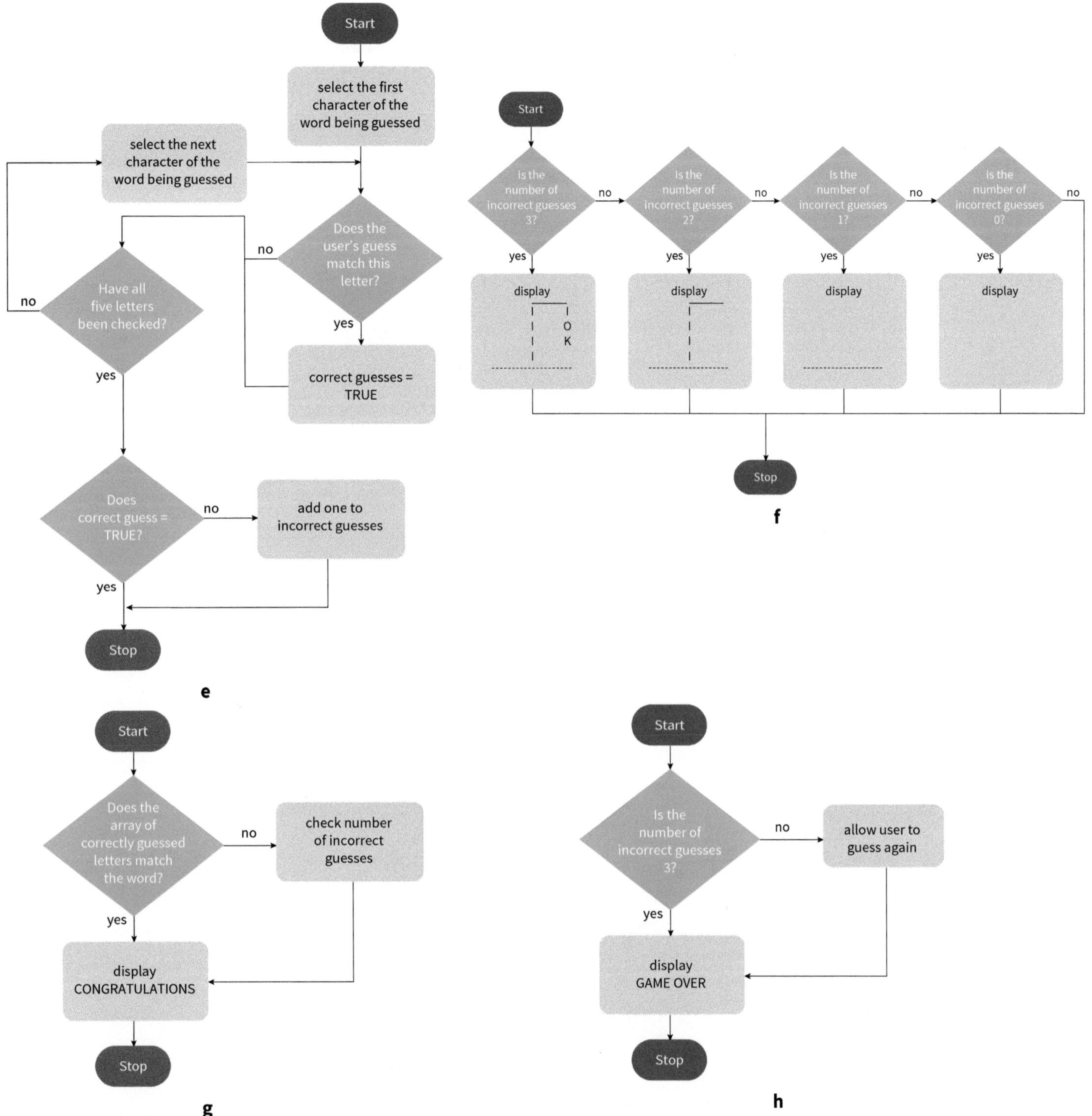

Figure 17.1: Continued.

The final stage is to combine these separate flowcharts to form a complete solution to the problem. Begin by joining together the first two flowcharts and then adding in the third flowchart, and so on until the whole solution is described.

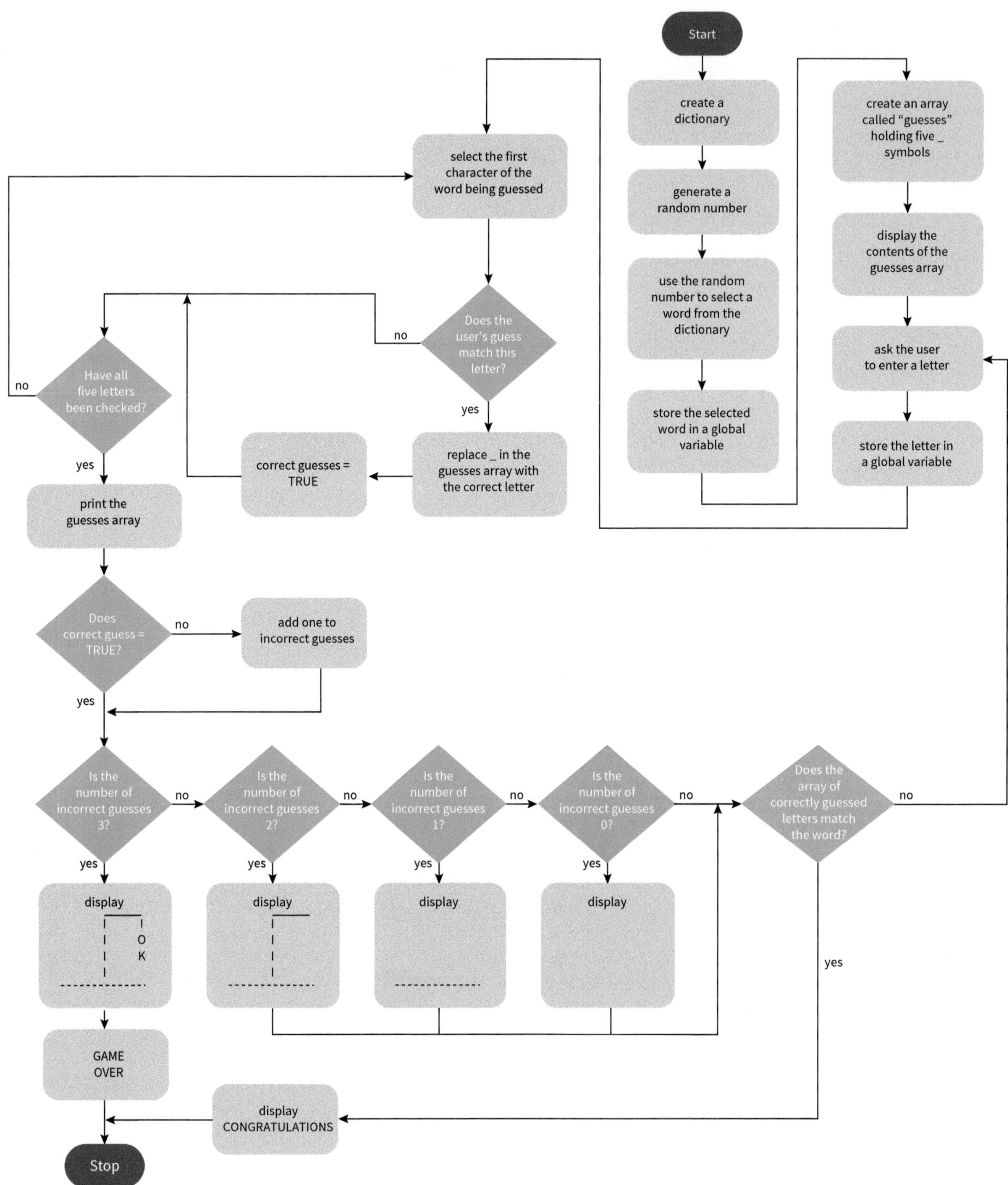

Figure 17.2: A flowchart describing how a simple hangman game could be executed.

The order of the steps required to create our solution is now clear to see. Notice that some of our flowcharts could simply be joined together (for example 1, 2, 3), whereas those that contained very similar functionality were merged together (for example 4 and 5).

Identifying the sub-procedures necessary to solve a problem

A sub-procedure is a sequence of steps grouped together and given its own name. These sub-procedures can then be called (using their name) from the main procedure whenever the functionality they offer is needed.

There are many advantages to using sub-procedures when writing computer programs. For example:

- Once it has been decided which sub-procedures will be needed to solve the problem, each procedure can be worked on by a different programmer. This means that the problem can be solved much faster than if one person had to write the whole program alone (we explore this concept more thoroughly in Chapter 19).
- Sub-procedures can also be coded by programmers who have the most experience in particular areas. They could even be programmed in different languages before being compiled into the final product.
- Sub-procedures help to reduce repetition and the size of the final program because when a sub-procedure has been coded it can be called from anywhere else in the program. This means it is not necessary for each programmer to write their own code whenever they want the functionality offered by the sub-procedure. This also helps make the program behave in a more consistent way.
- Using sub-procedures also makes it easy to debug and maintain a program. It is relatively easy to find which sub-procedure contained the mistake, and fixing it once in the sub-procedure will propagate the improvement throughout the whole program.
- Using sub-procedures also makes your procedure easier to follow, which means you are less likely to make mistakes.

To identify stages in a solution that could be utilised as sub-procedures, look for sequences of steps that are repeated at different points in the flowchart or sequences of instructions that are very similar to one another.

In our example, the most obvious area that would benefit from using a sub-procedure is displaying the image of a hangman. We have the same question ('Is the number of incorrect guesses x?') asked with similar outcomes each time. By separating out this area of the procedure we are able to make it easier to read.

There are no other areas of our procedure that are repeated at different points, so the only benefit to adding in further sub-procedures would be to group the steps logically to make the whole program easier to understand. It is also worth noting that many useful procedures are publicly available for you to use in your own programs. Some (like the print() function in Python) are provided within a programming language, and others are available online for you to download and use in your programs. These publicly available procedures tend to be efficient and well written, so using them could save you a great deal of time.

Tip

Terminology

The idea of a named block of code that performs a specific task will be familiar to you. Traditionally these are called 'subroutines' and you'll recognise them by their flowchart symbol:

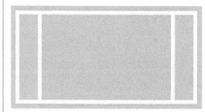

In programming we would normally say that procedures and functions were types of subroutine. A procedure is a subroutine that does not return a value to the main body of code, whereas a function is a subroutine that does return a value.

Procedural thinking as a concept was conceived long before this distinction was important, so for the purposes of this chapter we use the term 'procedure' instead of either 'subroutine' or 'function'.

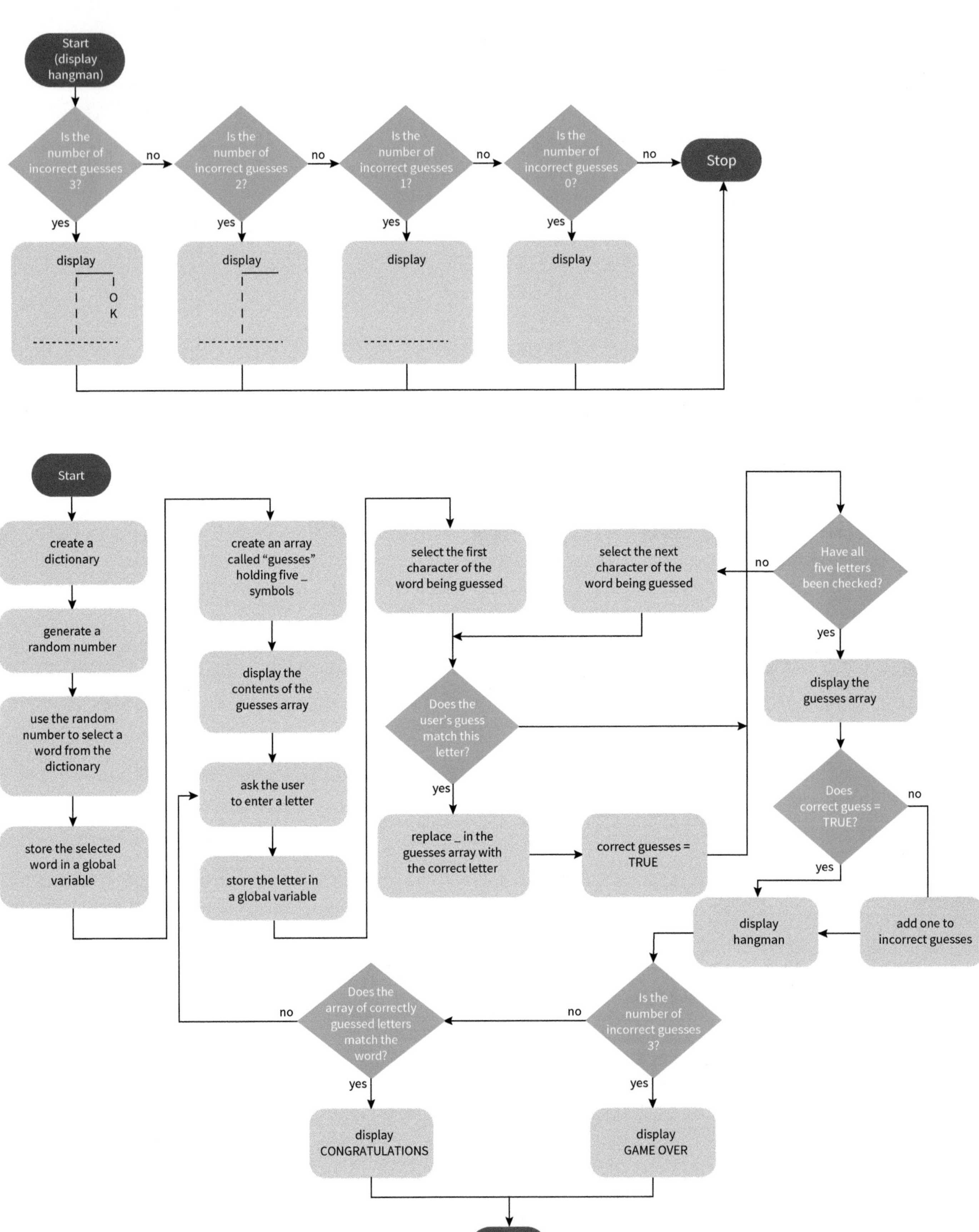

Figure 17.3: A flowchart using a subroutine.

Summary

- In this chapter you've learnt to identify the components of a problem by writing a description of the problem and breaking it down into smaller sub-tasks.
- You've also seen how to identify the components of a solution to a problem by creating a bullet point list describing a possible solution.
- You have reviewed how to determine the order of the steps needed to solve a problem using a flowchart.
- Finally, you've seen how to identify the sub-procedures necessary to solve a problem by identifying repeated sections of the solution and placing them in their own subroutine.
- In this chapter you have learnt that procedural thinking is the process of working through a problem and developing a sequence of steps that can be used to reach a solution.
- Once the components of a problem and its solution have been identified, the order of the steps needed to solve a problem can be determined.
- The key to success is to spend time identifying every possible component of the problem at the start of the process.
- It is never wise to rush to start coding because you could miss a key component or process and end by creating a solution that does not solve the entire problem.

Activity 17.1

Follow the process used in the hangman example in *identifying the components of a problem* to design and code a two-player tic-tac-toe game.

Activity 17.2

Follow the process used in the hangman example in *identifying the components of a problem* to design and code a two-player battleships game.

End-of-chapter questions

1	What is meant by the term 'procedural thinking'?	[1]
2	What is a procedural programming language?	[1]
3	List three constructs found in a procedural programming language.	[3]
4	Explain the difference between a procedure and a function.	[1]
5	List five advantages of using sub-procedures in your code.	[5]

Further reading

Procedural thinking – search on Josh G.'s Notes blog.
Computational thinking – search on Carnegie Mellon's Center for Computational Thinking's website.

Chapter 18
Thinking logically

Specification points

2.1.4 Thinking logically

- Identify the points in a solution where a decision has to be taken.
- Determine the logical conditions that affect the outcome of a decision.
- Determine how decisions affect flow through a program.

Learning objectives

- To be able to identify the points in a solution where a decision has to be taken.
- To be able to determine the logical conditions that affect the outcome of a decision.
- To be able to determine how decisions affect flow through a program.

What is logic?

The exact definition of logic is an area of controversy between computer scientists, philosophers and mathematicians. For our purposes, you can think of logic as the use of logical operators to reason the outcome of a given argument. For example, all possible outcomes of the proposition 'Natasha will go outside if it is sunny and not raining' can be calculated using the expression A = B AND NOT(C) where A represents the statement 'go outside', B represents 'is sunny' and C represents 'is raining'. The value of A (either TRUE or FALSE) can be determined by applying the logical operators EQUALS, AND, NOT to the values of B and C.

A = B AND NOT(C)		
B ('Is sunny')	C ('Is raining')	A ('Go outside')
TRUE	FALSE	TRUE
TRUE	TRUE	FALSE
FALSE	FALSE	FALSE
FALSE	TRUE	FALSE

Table 18.1: A truth table for the proposition A = B AND NOT(C)

The truth table above shows all the possible results of A, and you can see that it confirms the assertion that the only situation in which Natasha will go outside (A is TRUE) is if it is sunny (B is TRUE) and not raining (C = FALSE). For all other possible values and combinations of B and C, A is FALSE. You can see a more detailed list of logical operators in Table 18.1.

Thinking logically is the process of combining logical operators and data sets to produce logical expressions that represent complex arguments and can be used to identify possible outcomes.

In computer science we think of logic in binary terms with any logical operation having one of two outcomes: TRUE (1 in binary, 'Yes' on a flowchart) or FALSE (0 in binary, 'No' on a flowchart). For example, 4>5 would return FALSE because 4 is not greater than 5.

You need to know the basic logical operators and recognise where to use them in your programs. Using these symbols to create and solve propositions is called Boolean algebra and is a fascinating area of mathematics at the very heart of computer science. It's well worth looking through the 'Further reading' section to find out more.

Tip

Practise the basics!

You would be amazed how many A Level students get less-than < and greater-than > signs confused in the exam! It can cost you marks, especially when solving logic problems where one error will change the whole outcome of the program. If this is something you struggle with, find an easy way for you to remember.

Logical operators

Operator	Meaning	Example
>	Greater than	A > B will return TRUE if the value of A is higher than the value of B; otherwise it will return FALSE.
<	Less than	A < B will return TRUE if the value of A is less than the value of B; otherwise it will return FALSE.
<=	Less than or equal to	A <= B will return TRUE if A is the same as or smaller than B; otherwise it will return FALSE.
>=	Greater than or equal to	A >= B will return TRUE if A is the same as or larger than B; otherwise it will return FALSE.
!=	Not equal to	A != B will return TRUE if A is not equal to B but FALSE if A is the same as B.
NOT	The opposite of	NOT(A) will return TRUE if A is FALSE and FALSE if A is TRUE.

Table 18.2: Logical operators.

Operator	Meaning	Example
EQUALS (usually ==)	The same as, equivalent to	A == B will return TRUE if A is the same as B; otherwise it will return FALSE.
AND	Both statements must be true for the argument as a whole to be true	(A == 1) AND (B == 4) will return TRUE if A is 1 and B is 4. It would return FALSE in all other situations.
OR	Only one of the statements needs to be true, or both, for the argument as a whole to be true	(A == 1) OR (B == 4) will return TRUE if A is 1 or B is 4. It would only return FALSE if A wasn't 1 and B wasn't 4.
XOR (exclusive OR)	The argument is false if both statements are true or both statements are false. Otherwise the statement is true	A XOR B would return TRUE if A and B were different values.

Table 18.2: Continued.

Binary logic table

The table below shows the outcomes of nine different logical operations when given two binary inputs, A and B. For example IF A == 0 AND B == 0 then the outcome will be 0.

A	B	OR	AND	XOR	>	<	<=	>=	==	!=
0	**0**	0	0	0	0	0	1	1	1	0
0	**1**	1	0	1	0	1	1	0	0	1
1	**0**	1	0	1	1	0	0	1	0	1
1	**1**	1	1	0	0	0	1	1	1	0

Table 18.3: The results of logical operators on all possible permutations of two values.

Computing in context: Crossing the river

Logical thinking is behind some of the most popular and ancient problem-solving games. See if you can solve this famous example thought to date back to the ninth century!

Once upon a time a farmer went to market and purchased a fox, a chicken and a bag of beans. On his way home, the farmer came to the bank of a river and rented a boat. But in crossing the river by boat, the farmer could carry only himself and a single one of his purchases – the fox, the chicken or the bag of beans.

If left together, the fox would eat the chicken, or the chicken would eat the beans.

The farmer's challenge was to carry himself and his purchases to the far bank of the river, leaving each purchase intact. How did he do it?

Identify the points in a solution where a decision has to be taken

Making decisions in programs happens during selection, when one of a number of alternative statements or paths is chosen based on the condition of a logical operation. It is also used during iteration to decide whether or not to repeat a set of instructions.

The most commonly used forms of selection are IF statements and SELECT CASE. You can read more about these in Chapter 20, together with the most common forms of iteration: FOR and WHILE loops. Reading about these constructs first will make the following examples much easier to understand.

Identifying the points in a solution where a decision has to be taken sounds difficult but can be simplified. As described in Chapter 17, we draw a flowchart that describes the steps required to reach a solution.

When the flowchart is finished, anywhere you see a decision diamond is either going to be a loop or a decision in your final program. These constructs are the only ones that require logical operators to be used.

Consider a program that asks the user to enter two numbers and then tells the user if they entered the same number twice. The first thing to do is draw a flowchart, like the one below.

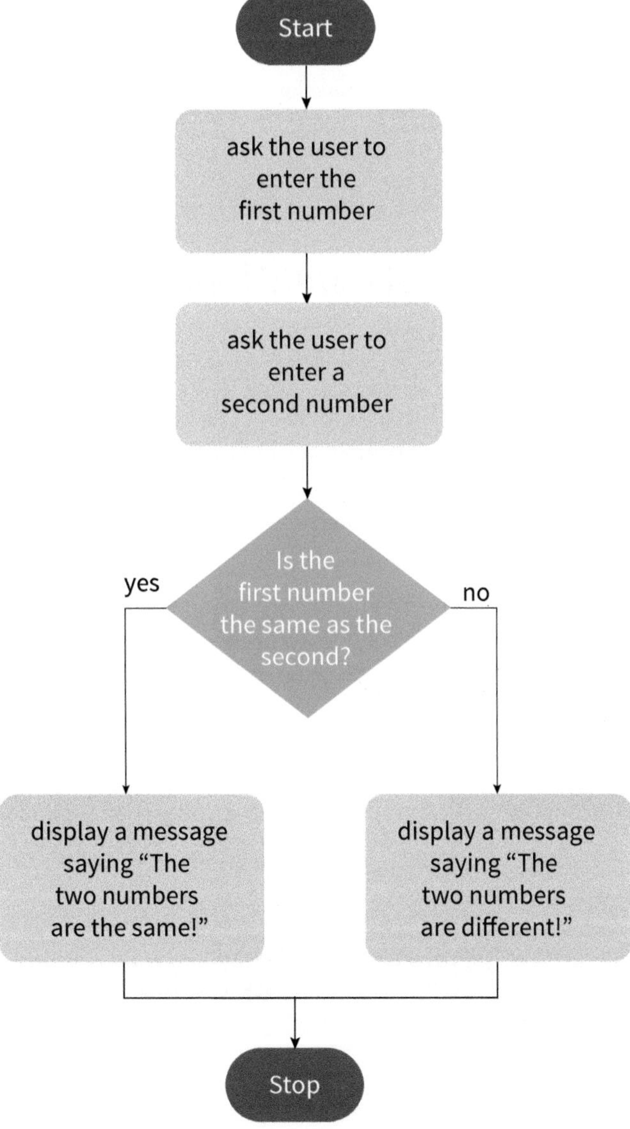

Figure 18.1: A flowchart describing a simple program.

By looking at the flowchart you can see that the logical decision is represented by the blue diamond. You can also see that the decisions must be made after the two numbers have been entered and what should happen for each possible outcome. Converting the flowchart into pseudocode will show you which logical operators to use and where they should appear in the code.

Pseudocode

```
A = first number
IF A == B is TRUE then print "The two numbers are the same"
Otherwise print "The two numbers are different"
```

From here it is straightforward to create a final program:

Code

```
A = input ("Enter your first number")
B = input ("Enter your second number")

if A == B:
  print ("The two numbers are the same")
else:
  print ("The two numbers are different")
```

Determine the logical conditions that affect the outcome of a decision

Determining the logical conditions that affect the outcome of a decision can range from very easy to difficult, depending on their complexity. The basic methodology is to take the problem or conditions that you have been given and write them out in English, then you can rewrite the sentences using the logical operators wherever possible and get rid of any extra text you don't need. This process should leave you with a logical argument that can be turned into selection or iteration construct.

Imagine that Sarah wants to buy a new computer with a graphics card and more than 8 GB of RAM. She doesn't want a sound card but does want either a Linux or Windows operating system. Write a program that takes the specification of a computer and tells her if it is suitable.

Step 1: Write out the conditions again; put them on separate lines if this makes them easier to read.

- She wants a computer with a graphics card and more than 8 GB of RAM.
- She doesn't want a sound card but does want either a Linux or a Windows operating system.

Step 2: Rewrite the sentences using logical operators wherever possible and get rid of any extra text you don't need. Don't forget to put in brackets to make it clear which pieces of data the logical operations apply to.

Pseudocode

```
(GraphicsCard == TRUE) AND (RAM > 8GB) AND
(SoundCard == FALSE) AND (OperatingSystem = "Windows")OR
(OperatingSystem = "Linux")
```

Step 3: You should now be ready to write the logical decision as an IF statement.

Code

```
IF (GraphicsCard == TRUE) AND (RAM > 8) AND
(SoundCard == FALSE) AND ((OperatingSystem = "Windows")
OR(OperatingSystem = "Linux")):
  Print("Specification meets all your criteria")
ELSE:
  Print("Sorry, that computer is unsuitable")
```

Another way to determine the logical conditions that affect the outcome of a decision is to use a flowchart. You can then write the logical operator next to each decision then combine them to give you the correct answer.

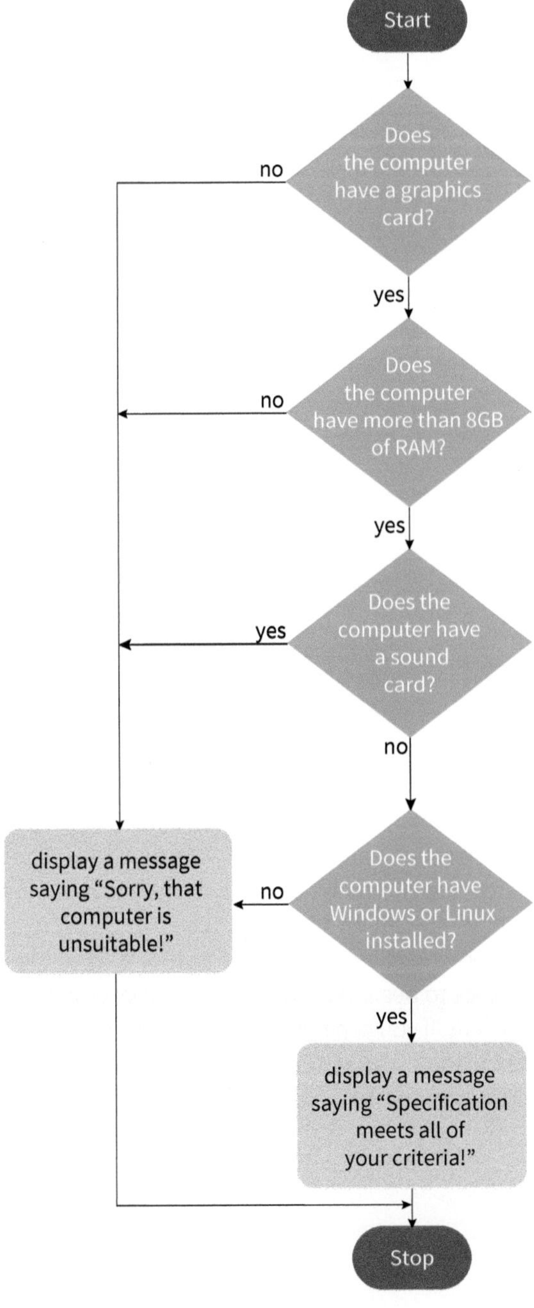

Figure 18.2: A flowchart describing Sarah's decision-making process.

Determining how decisions affect flow through a program

Determining how decisions affect flow through a program is also pretty simple to do once you have created a flowchart. The difficulty comes in how you choose to implement these decisions, as there are usually many possible solutions.

The flowchart in Figure 18.3 shows a game.

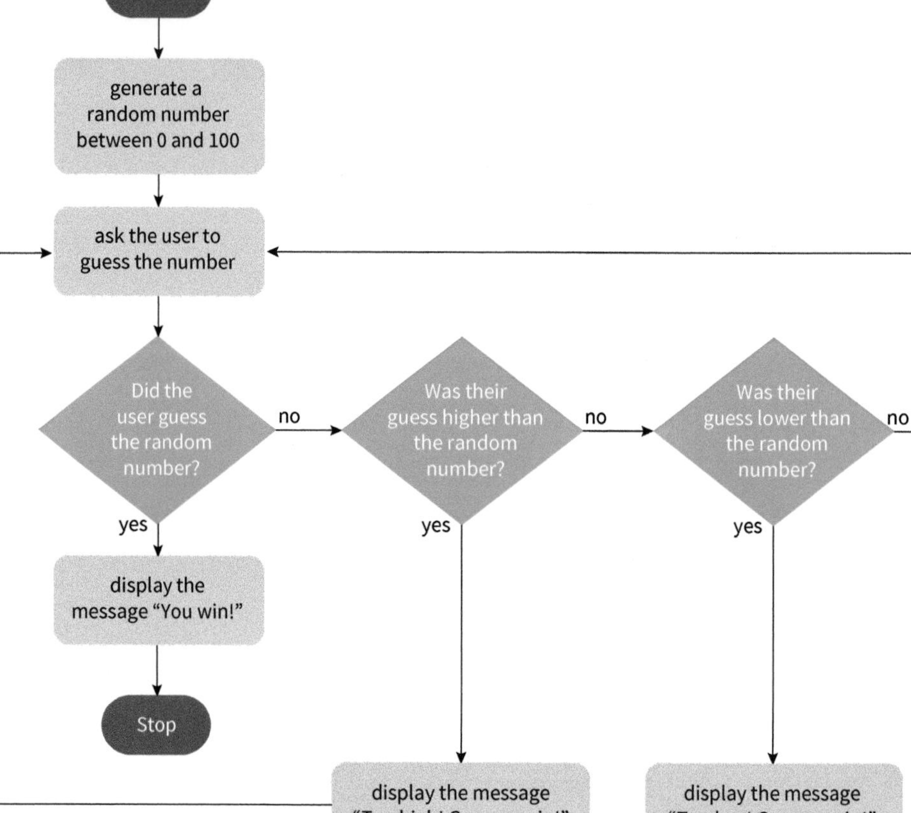

Figure 18.3: Flowchart describing a simple game.

> **Tip**
>
> **Logical decisions**
>
> Don't be afraid to use a sheet of blank paper to draw out a flowchart to help you answer a question. Even complex problems and the decisions within them become easier to tackle once you start to visualise them. You should even do this in the exam.

A selection statement represents a single decision although we can use else if (elif statements in Python) to code alternative values and an else statement to "catch all" at the end of the code block. Selection statements can also be nested to give multiple decisions in sequence. Iteration always involves repetition of code so can be spotted in a flowchart. A good place to begin is by looking for arrows that loop back to earlier instructions in the flowchart. If you can identify a key decision that leads to these arrows it can probably be implemented as iteration. In our example all the arrows that loop back to the start can be traced back to the decision that the user has not guessed the random number.

Pseudocode

WHILE userGuess is NOT EQUAL to randomNumber repeat these steps:

The other two decisions loop back to earlier steps but only because the user guessed incorrectly. It is probable then that these will need to be nested inside our iteration. As their 'No'action will be dictated by the existing iteration we can simply use selection to decide whether or not we want to print out a message.

Pseudocode

```
IF userGuess is higher than randomNumber print "Too high"
IF userGuess is lower than randomNumber print "Too low"
```

By adding in the missing processes we can build up a complete piece of pseudocode that delivers the same outcomes as our flowchart.

Pseudocode

```
Generate randomNumber
WHILE userGuess is NOT EQUAL to randomNumber repeat these
steps:
  Ask the user to guess a number
  IF userGuess is higher than randomNumber
    print "Too high"
  IF userGuess is lower than randomNumber print
    "Too low"
When userGuess is EQUAL to randomNumber print "You win"
```

Code

```
import random
randmNumber = random.randint(0,100)
userGuess = ""

while userGuess!= randomNumber:
  userGuess = int (input ("Please guess a number between 0
  and 100"))

  if userGuess > randomNumber:
    print ("Too high! Guess again!")

  if userGuess < randomNumber:
  print ("Too low! Guess again")
print ("You win!")
```

Summary

- In this chapter you've learnt how to identify the points in a solution where a decision has to be taken by using flowcharts.
- You've also seen how to determine the logical conditions that affect the outcome of a decision by studying common logical operators and combining them with a description of the problem.
- Finally, you've learnt how to determine how decisions affect flow through a program by combining your understanding of flowcharts and logical operators to create a solution using Python.

Activity 18.1

Use the techniques you saw earlier *where a decision has to be taken* to create a flowchart describing a simple game of Higher or Lower in which the computer repeatedly generates a number from 1 to 10 and the player must guess if the next number will be higher or lower than the current number.

Activity 18.2

Use a programming language of your choice to create the game of Higher or Lower that you planned in the last activity.

Activity 18.3

In the 'Crossing the river' problem described earlier in this chapter, how could you represent the objects and their interactions and then solve the problem using logical expressions?

End-of-chapter questions

1 In the logical operation A = B AND C what is the value of A if B = TRUE but C = FALSE? [1]

2 In the logical operation A = B OR NOT(C) what is the value of A if B = FALSE but C = TRUE? [1]

3 In the logical operation A = B what is the value of A if B = TRUE? [1]

4 In the logical operation A = B AND (C OR D) what is the value of A if B = TRUE but C = FALSE and D = FALSE? [1]

5 In the logical operation A = NOT(C) OR NOT(B) what is the value of A if B = TRUE but C = FALSE? [1]

Further reading

Logic in computer science – search on Rice University's Computer Science website.
Boolean algebra – search on Surrey University's Electrical and Electronic Engineering website.
Predicate logic – search on Old Dominion University's Computer Science website.
Propositional logic – search on Old Dominion University's Computer Science website.

Chapter 19
Thinking concurrently

A This chapter contains A Level content only

Specification points

2.1.5 Thinking concurrently

- Determine the parts of a problem that can be tackled at the same time.
- Outline the benefits and trade-offs that might result from concurrent processing in a particular situation.

Learning objectives

- To be able to determine the parts of a problem that can be tackled at the same time.
- To be able to outline the benefits and trade-offs that might result from concurrent processing in a particular situation.

What is concurrent thinking?

In computing, **concurrent execution** refers to systems where computations can be executed simultaneously. You have already been introduced to this concept through the parallel processing section of Chapter 1. Concurrency is becoming more and more important in modern computing. Game servers that communicate with thousands of players and multicore computers that tackle complex mathematical operations are now commonplace. Concurrency is also widely used in **Big Data Analytics** where it is necessary to quickly process massive data sets, terabytes or even petabytes in size. These large data sets exist everywhere from astronomy and healthcare to Netflix and supermarket loyalty cards. They are used to research the history of the universe, genetics, customer choices and preferences.

Concurrent systems are incredibly complex; however, this extra complexity can be richly complemented by a huge increase in processing speeds resulting in a reduction in the time it takes to complete computations.

Concurrent thinking is the philosophy behind concurrent execution. It is the skill of recognising which parts of a problem can be solved at the same time and executed in way that avoids the pitfalls commonly associated with concurrent execution.

Key skill: Threads

A **thread** is a small task running within a process. A process may be made up of multiple threads all sharing the same resources (like memory). Threads are important in concurrency; when computer scientists talk about concurrency, they are generally referring to simultaneously running multiple threads within a single process rather than executing multiple processes at the same time.

The Python examples in this chapter all use threads to demonstrate the advantages and disadvantages of concurrency.

Advantages of concurrent execution

The advantages of (successful) concurrent execution are clear: if you can do two things at once the job gets done twice as fast!

Example: Implementing concurrent execution

In the following basic example a simple program is created that takes a class register and outputs all the children whose names are more than four letters long.

This first solution uses normal, sequential programming techniques.

Code

```
import time

register = ["Anne", "Adam", "Ashley", "Andy", "Barry",
"Beth", "Charlotte", "Charlie", "Douglas", "Dani", "Ellie",
"Frank", "Fred", "Gregg", "Hannah", "Jane", "Kate",
"Katie", "Leon", "Matt", "Nora", "Noah", "Peter", "Ruth",
"Steve", "Tom", "Verity", "Wayne", "Xian", "Zoe"]

def nameLength (reg):

 for name in reg:

  if len (name)>4:

   time.sleep(1.0)

   print (name + "/n")

nameLength(register)
```

The program stores the class list in an array then uses a function call nameLength to loop through it, printing out any name more than four characters long. A 1-second pause has been added to make the readout clearer.

The program prints out the list of names over four characters long and takes 14 seconds to run.

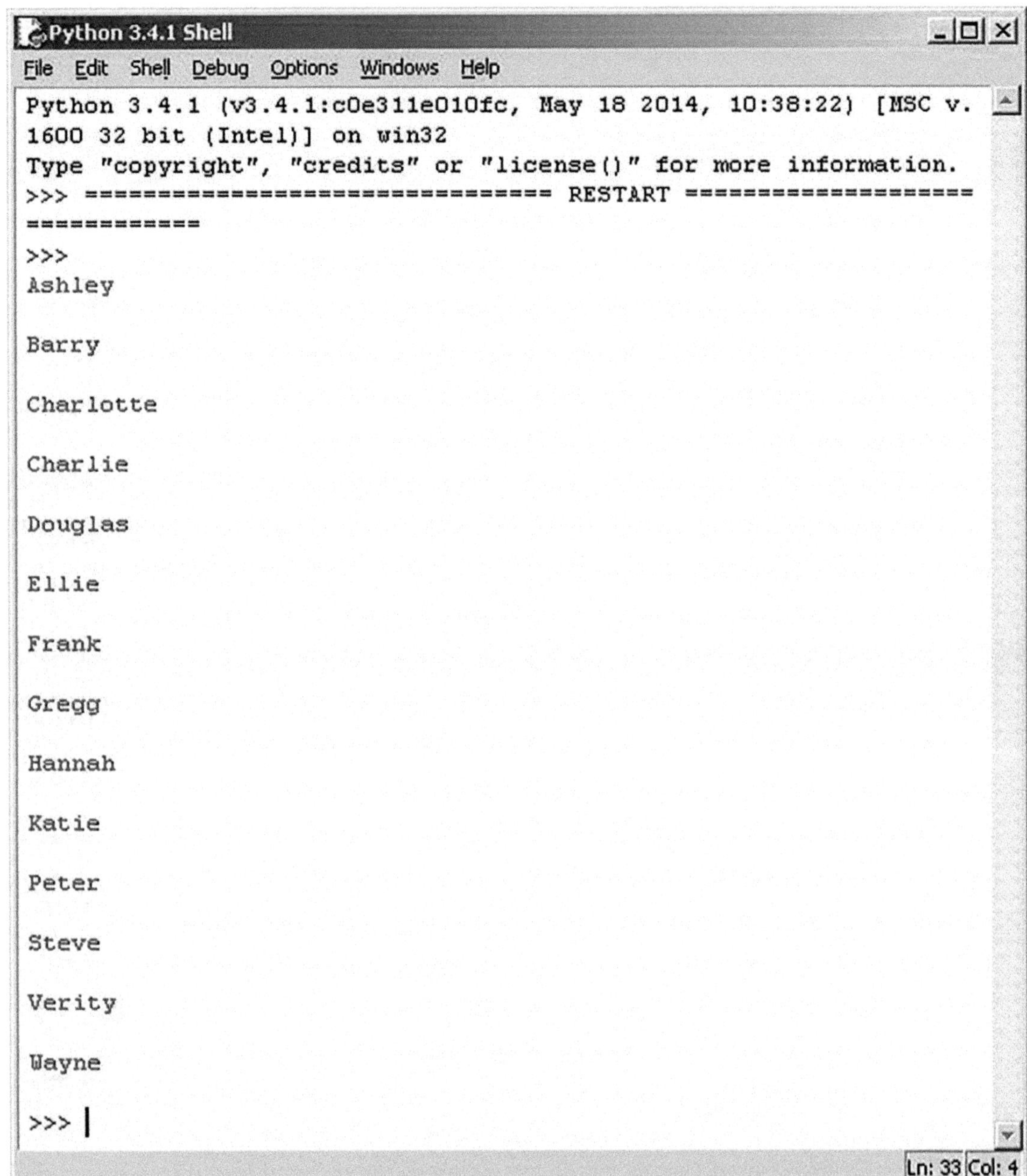

Figure 19.1: The results of running the Python program from code above.

However, if we could split the register in half and search the top half at the same time as the bottom half, we could dramatically reduce the search time.

The modified program does exactly that:

Code

```
import threading
import time

register = ["Anne", "Adam", "Ashley", "Andy", "Barry",
"Beth", "Charlotte", "Charlie", "Douglas", "Dani", "Ellie",
"Frank", "Fred", "Gregg", "Hannah", "Jane", "Kate",
"Katie", "Leon", "Matt", "Nora", "Noah", "Peter", "Ruth",
"Steve", "Tom", "Verity, "Wayne", "Xian", "Zoe"]
```

```
def nameLength(reg):
  for name in reg:
    if len (name)>4:
      time.sleep(1.0)
      print (name + "/n")

t1 = threading.Thread (target=nameLength, args=
([register[0:12]]))

t2 = threading.Thread (target=nameLength, args=
([register[13:30]]))

t1.start(); t2.start()

t1.join(); t2.join()
```

The register is split into two sections; elements 0–12 are searched by the first thread (t1) at the same time that elements 13–30 are being searched by the second thread (t2). This new concurrent program prints the same names in just 7 seconds.

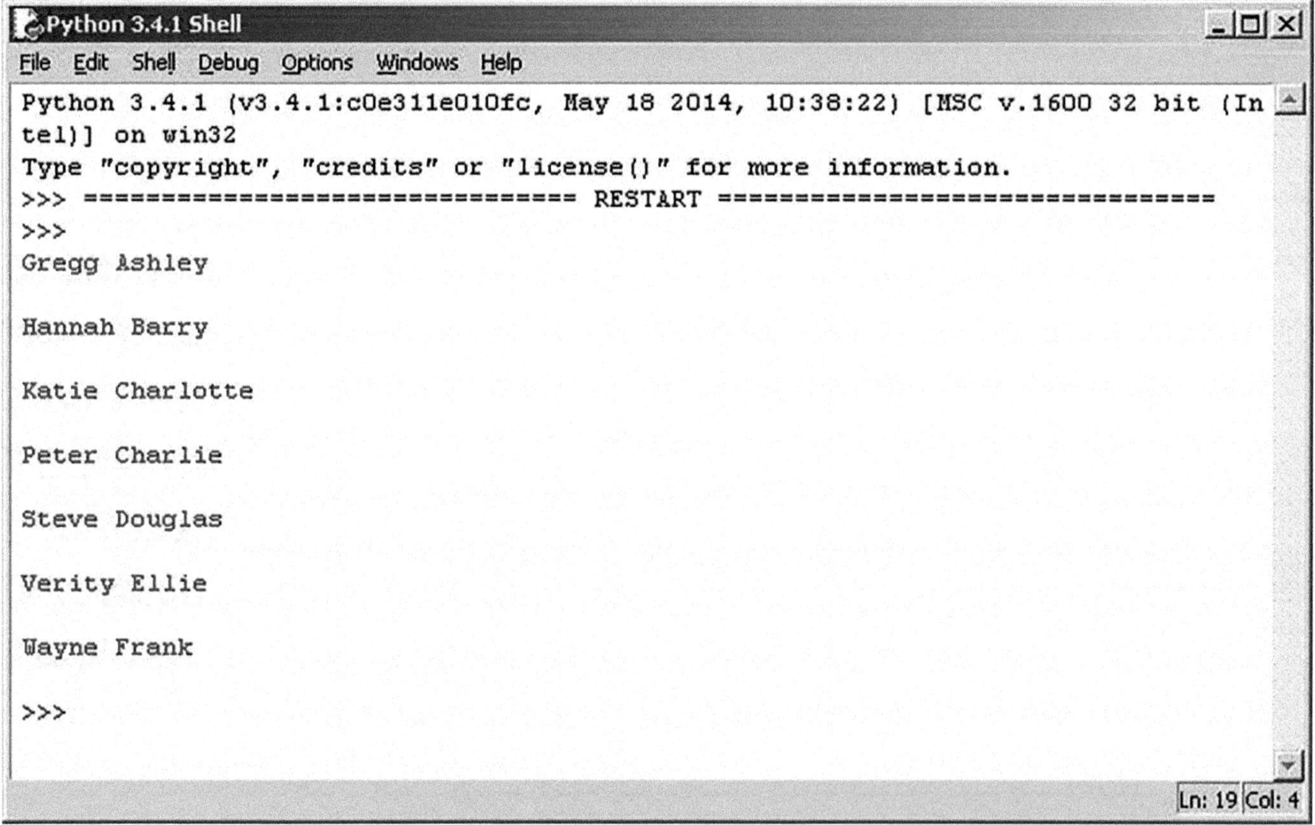

Figure 19.2: The results of running the Python program in code above.

Our concurrent program runs twice as fast as our non-concurrent alternative; in our simple example this saves 7 seconds. In complex, real-world situations, programs are often run in tens or hundreds of parallel threads. The savings could be weeks or even years of processing time.

Disadvantages of concurrent execution

Deadlock

Deadlock occurs when every process is waiting for another to finish; thus, no process is ever able to complete. This is often cyclic, with process A waiting for process B, which is waiting for process C, which is waiting for process A.

For example, in one US state a statute was passed to prevent rail accidents. The statute stated:

> 'When two trains approach each other at a crossing, both shall come to a full stop and neither shall start up again until the other has gone.'

This soon led to a complete deadlock on the state's railways as trains sat opposite each other at crossings, each unable to move until the other had.

There are four conditions (called **Coffman conditions**) that must combine simultaneously for there to be a deadlock – unfortunately they are relatively common in concurrent computer systems:

1. Resources can't be shared. For example, a resource (like a printer) can only be used by one process at a time.
2. A process can hold one resource while requesting another.
3. A resource can only be made available by the process currently holding it. For example, one process can't steal a resource from another.
4. Circular waiting can occur. For example, process A is waiting for process B, which is waiting for process A.

However, the good news is that if you can prevent any one of these conditions from arising then deadlocks can be avoided altogether.

Starvation

Starvation occurs when a process is always denied the resources it needs. Imagine a restaurant in which a busy waiter served food to everyone except you – eventually you would starve. It is easier to avoid starvation than deadlock as it usually occurs when the algorithms responsible for allocating resources are poorly written. Consider two processes that are being executed concurrently and both wish to print. Process A begins printing so B is forced to wait, but before B gets a chance to use the printer a higher priority process C arrives and is allocated the printer ahead of B. If this were to keep happening, process B would be in a state of starvation and unable to move forward. A common solution to this is that the longer a process has been waiting, the higher its priority becomes – eventually its priority is high enough that it gets access to the resource.

Race conditions

Race conditions occur when two processes use the same memory location and the final result depends on the order in which processes are run. Look at the code below and corresponding output in Figure 19.3:

Code

```
Import threading

x = 0

def add():
  global x
  for i in range (1000000): x+=1

def sub():
  global x
  for i in range (1000000): x+=1

t1 = threading.Thread(target=add)
t2 = threading.Thread(target=sub)

t1.start(); t2.start()
t1.join(); t2.join()

print (x)
```

In the program two threads run at the same time. One takes the variable x and adds 1 to it 1 000 000 times. The other takes the same variable and subtracts 1 from it 1 000 000 times.

Even though the same code is run each time, the final value of x is totally different. This is because the two threads are using the same memory location (the variable x) with each one racing to update it. The final value of x depends on which thread 'wins' each encounter.

Expensive resources

Running programs concurrently can require extra CPUs (or multiple cores on the same CPU), more RAM and faster input/output performance. All of this can lead to a need for more expensive servers of a high specification to be able to run programs with a high level of concurrency. For example, services such as Netflix and Spotify use concurrency to manage a large number of people streaming video and audio at the same time. Consequently, they need very large server farms, which are expensive to purchase, administer and run.

Computing in context: The Dining Philosophers problem

The Dining Philosophers problem was created in 1965 as a problem involving simultaneous requests for access to various computer resources such as hard drives and printers; this modern interpretation uses the same concepts but is easier to understand.

A group of five philosophers spend their lives eating and thinking. They sit around a table with a large bowl of rice in the middle. Between each of the philosophers is a single chopstick; a philosopher must use two chopsticks in order to eat the rice. Each philosopher spends time thinking before she picks up the two chopsticks that are closest to her. If a philosopher can pick up both chopsticks, she can eat. After a philosopher finishes eating, she puts down the chopsticks and starts to think.

The challenge is to create a concurrent algorithm that prevents the philosophers from starving. They need to be able to alternate between eating and thinking without knowing when another philosopher will want to eat.

The problem was created to illustrate the problems of deadlock and starvation (remember, deadlock occurs when no progress is possible). Take a look at the following solution:

Step 1: Think until the right chopstick is free then pick it up.

Step 2: Keep thinking until the left chopstick is free then pick it up.

Step 3: When you are holding both chopsticks, eat for 15 minutes.

Step 4: Put the right chopstick down.

Step 5: Put the left chopstick down.

Step 6: Jump to **Step 1**.

On the face of it, the solution looks like a sensible and obvious approach. But what happens after Step 1 if each philosopher is holding the chopstick on their right? They will continue to sit and wait for the left chopstick to become available (Step 2), but as they are all waiting for the same thing this will never happen; the system is deadlocked.

Starvation is also a possibility with this solution: if two very bright and hungry philosophers sit opposite each other they might reserve their two chopsticks while they eat then put them down to think. As they are bright and hungry they want to eat again before the other slower philosophers have had a chance to pick up the chopsticks. So two philosophers get fat while the other three starve!

There are multiple solutions to this problem (you can find some of them in the 'Further reading' section of this chapter). But the original solution is called the 'Resource hierarchy solution' and works like this:

The chopsticks are numbered 1–5 and a philosopher must always pick up her lower numbered chopstick before she picks up her higher numbered chopstick (it doesn't matter what order they put the chopsticks down in). This way, if four out of five philosophers pick up their first chopstick the final philosopher will be unable to pick up the remaining chopstick as it is not her lowest-value chopstick. This will leave a chopstick on the table for the philosopher next to her to pick up and use. So someone is always able to eat.

Identify which parts of a problem can be executed simultaneously

Before you can begin to execute two processes at the same time you must first identify those parts of a problem that can be tackled simultaneously. In order for two parts of a problem to be executed at the same time they must be totally independent of one another. That is, any one process must not depend on the state of another if they are to be carried out simultaneously. Secondly, conditions that will lead to deadlock, starvation and race conditions must be identified and avoided. The easiest way to do this is to identify which areas of the process can be solved separately without the need for a resource to be used by more than one at the same time. A good way to do this is through the use of diagrams like flowcharts. Look at the following example to see this process in action.

Example: Implementing simulations execution

Let's say we want a program that reads through every register in the school and prints out the total number of female students.

The way to do this sequentially is fairly simple:

Code

```
import time

numGirls = 0
mathsRegister = [["Ann", "F"],["Adam", "M"],["Ashley", "F"],
["Andy", "M"],["Barry", "M"],["Beth", "F"],["Charlotte", "F"],
["Charlie", "F"],["Douglas", "M"],["Dani", "F"],["Ellie", "F"],
["Frank", "M"],["Fred", "M"],["Gregg", "M"],[Hannah", "F"],
["Jane", "F"],[ "Kate", "F"],[ "Katie", "F"],["Leon", "M"],
["Matt", "M"],["Nora", "F"],["Noah", "M"],["Peter", "M"],
["Ruth", "F"],["Steve", "M"],["Tom", "M"],["Verity", "F"],
["Wayne", "M"],["Xian", "F"],["Zoe", "F"]]

computingRegister = [["Julie", "F"],["Andrew", "M"],
["Lucy", "F"],["Andy", "M"],["Barry", "M"],["Jane", "F"],
["Charlotte", "F"],["Shaz", "F"],["Douglas", "M"],
["Shannon", "F"],["Katie", "F"],["Justyn", "M"],["Fred", "M"],
["Gregg", "M"],["Hannah", "F"],["Jane", "F"],["Katie", "F"],
["Katie H", "F"],["Joanna", "F"],["Alistair", "M"],["Jade", "F"],
["Noah", "M"],["Peter", "M"],["Sarah, "F"],["Steve, "M"],
["Mark", "M"],["Karen", "F"],["Wayne", "M"],["Xian", "F"],
["Terri", "F"]]

def numFemale(register):
  global numGirls
  for x in range (0, len (register)):
    if register[x] [1] =="F":
      time.sleep(1.0)
      numGirls = numGirls+1

print ("Start time:"+ time.ctime(0)
numFemale(mathsRegister)
numFemale(computingRegister)
print ("Finish time:"+ time.ctime())

print ("The number of girls in the school is: " + str (numGirls))
```

We create a two-dimensional array to hold the name and gender of all the students in a particular class. For the sake of simplicity our school only has two classes, each with one register. We create a function numFemale to loop through a given register counting the number of girls it finds and increasing the global variable numGirls accordingly. We pass this function through each register in turn before printing out the total number of girls in the school.

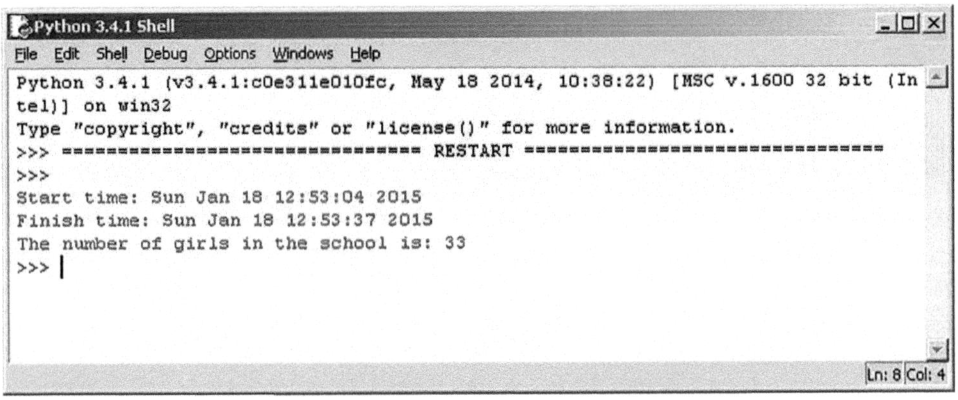

```
Python 3.4.1 Shell
File Edit Shell Debug Options Windows Help
Python 3.4.1 (v3.4.1:c0e311e010fc, May 18 2014, 10:38:22) [MSC v.1600 32 bit (In
tel)] on win32
Type "copyright", "credits" or "license()" for more information.
>>> ================================ RESTART ================================
>>>
Start time: Sun Jan 18 12:53:04 2015
Finish time: Sun Jan 18 12:53:37 2015
The number of girls in the school is: 33
>>> |
Ln: 8 Col: 4
```

Figure 19.3: The results of running the Python program in the code above.

The program produces the correct answer and takes 33 seconds to run.

Now we need to see if we can get the program to run faster by executing any of it concurrently. To do this we need to identify which operations could take place at the same time and whether there are any shared resources that could lead to deadlocks or race conditions.

Operations that could take place at the same time	Shared resources
Counting the number of girls in two separate arrays. As the arrays are different resources they could be accessed simultaneously because the two read operations are independent of each other.	The global variable numGirls is updated each time the function is called, so multiple threads might need to access it at the same time.

Table 19.1: Identifying shared resources.

The global variable that is stored in memory needs to be shared by any threads we create, which could cause a problem. We can overcome this problem by thinking about the operation that is being carried out on the shared memory, which is addition. As we are always adding, getting the correct result doesn't depend on the order in which the operations take place (3+4+7+8 is the same as 7+4+8+3). This means that even if race conditions occur, the final answer will still be the same. Having eliminated this potential problem, we can focus on planning out the processes we've identified as being possible to execute concurrently.

The flowchart in Figure 19.4 shows how we could approach the problem by using two threads, one to search each register. The threads can run concurrently without fear of race conditions occurring as the only resource they share is the **numGirls** variable we've already discussed.

Having identified that the two arrays can be searched in separate threads, we can implement our search using almost the same method we used earlier.

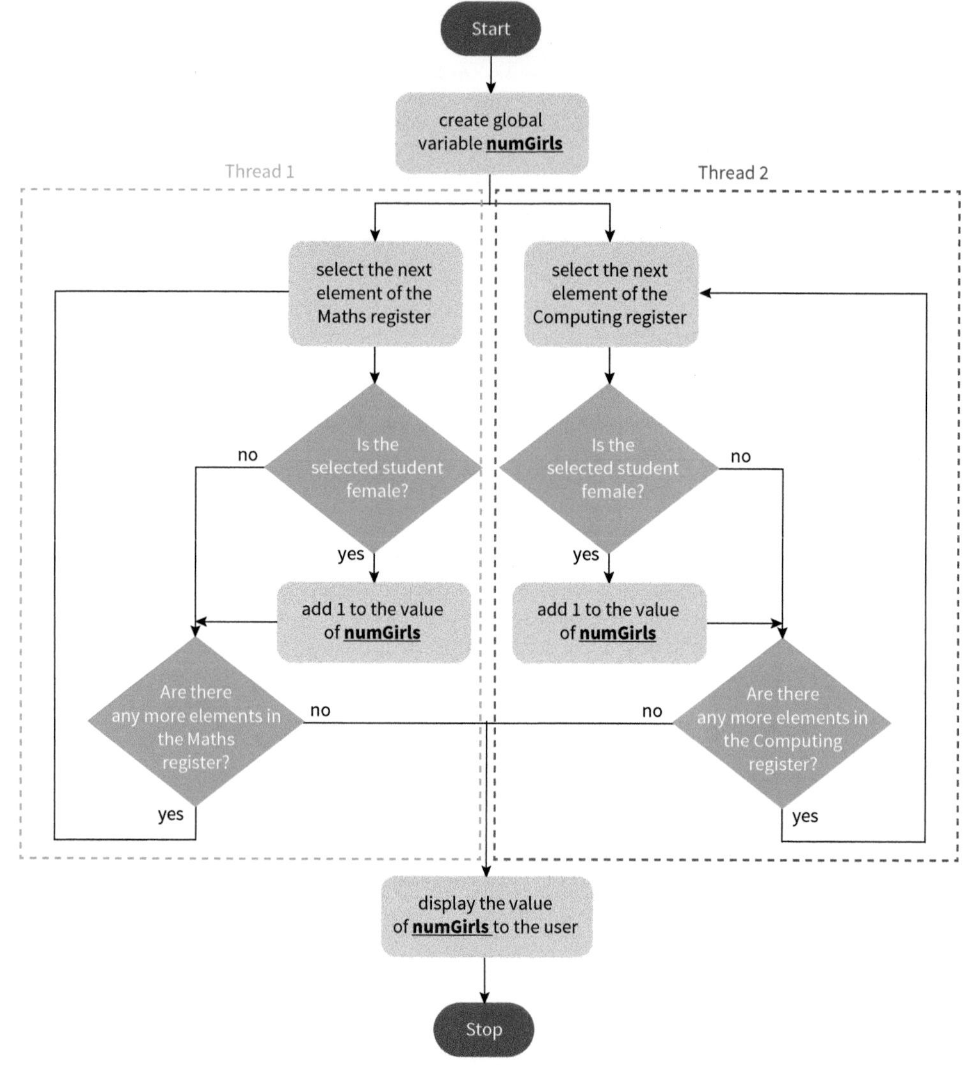

Figure 19.4: Identifying concurrent execution on a flowchart.

Code

```
import threading
import time

numGirls = 0
mathsRegister = [["Anne", "F"],["Adam", "M"],["Ashley", "F"],
["Andy", "M"],["Barry", "M"],["Beth", "F"],["Charlotte", "F"],
["Charlie", "F"],["Douglas", "M"],["Dani", "F"],["Ellie", "F"],
["Frank", "M"],["Fred", "M"],["Gregg", "M"],["Hannah", "F"],
["Jane", "F"],["Kate, "F"],["Katie", "F"],["Leon", "M"],["Matt", "M"],
["Nora", "F"],]"Noah", "M"],["Peter", "M"],["Ruth", "F"],
["Steve", "M"],["Tom", "M"],["Verity", "F"],["Wayne", "M"],
["Xian", "F"],["Zoe", "F"]]
```

```
computingRegister = [["Julie", "F"],["Andrew", "M"],["Lucy", "F"],
["Andy", "M"],["Barry", "M"],["Jane", "F"],["Charlotte", "F"],
["Shaz", "F"],["Douglas", "M"],["Shannon", "F"],["Katie", "F"],
["Justyn", "M"],["Fred", "M"],["Gregg", "M"],["Hannah", "F"],
["Jane", "F"],["Kate", "F"],["Katie H", "F"],["Joanna", "F"],
["Alistair", "M"],["Jade", "F"],["Noah", "M"],["Peter", "M"],
["Sarah", "F"],["Steve", "M"],["Mark", "M"],["Karen", "F"],
["Wayne", "M"],["Xian", "F"],["Terri", "F"]]

def numFemale(register):
  global numGirls
  for x in range (0, len (register)):
    if register[x] [1]=="F":
      time.sleep(1.0)
      numGirls = numGirls+1

print ("Start time:" + time.ctime(0)

t1 = threading.Thread(target=numFemale, args= ([mathsRegister]))

t2 = threading.Thread(target=numFemale, args=([computingRegister]))

t1.start(); t2.start()

t1.join(); t2.join()

print ("Finish time:" + time.ctime())

print ("The number of girls in the school is:" + str (numGirls))
```

Our new concurrent program reaches the same result in just over half the time (17 seconds) used for our first solution.

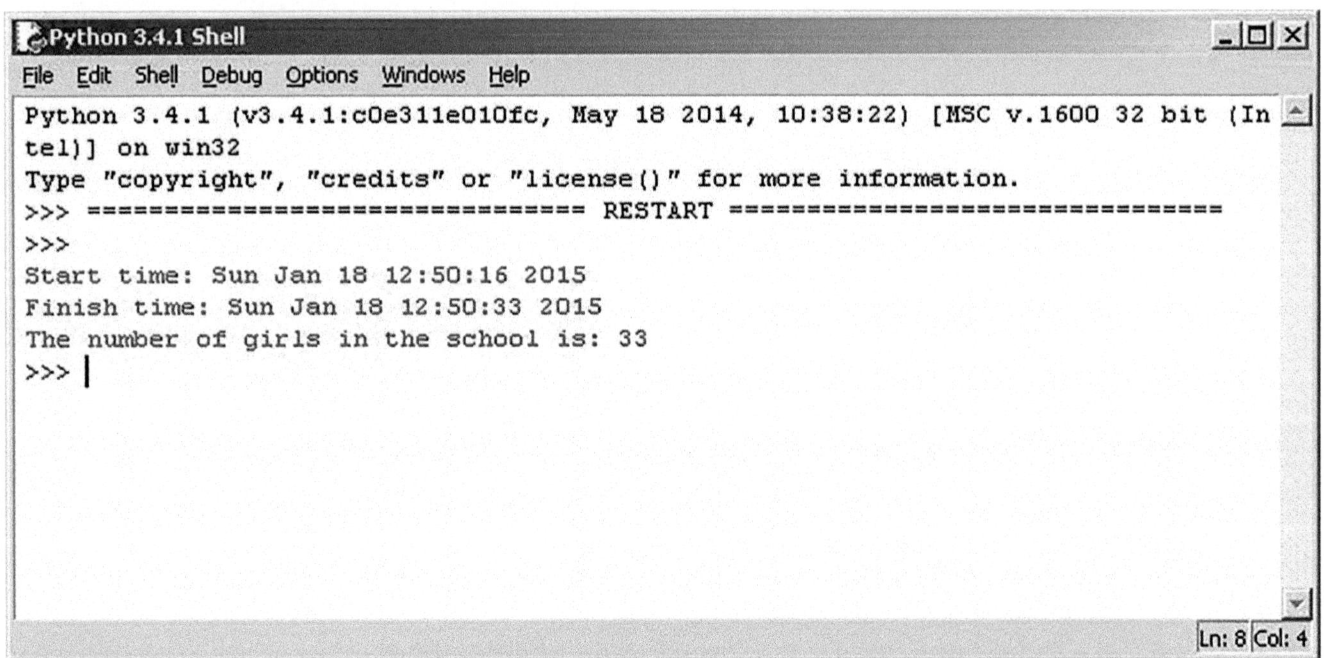

Figure 19.5: The results of running the Python program from the code above.

Key skill: Shared resources

If you are asked how a problem might be solved concurrently, make a list of any shared resources. These could be variables or chopsticks (see the Dining Philosophers problem), but once you've worked out how to share them your job will be much easier.

Make yourself familiar with the solutions to famous concurrent thinking problems (see the 'Further reading' section). They may well be applicable in the scenarios that you are presented with.

Summary

- In this chapter you've learnt how to determine the parts of a problem that can be tackled at the same time by identifying which components of a solution are independent of one another.
- You've also learnt the benefits of concurrent execution, such as faster processing, as well as some of the pitfalls, including deadlock, starvation and race conditions.

Activity 19.1

Use the example in advantages of concurrent execution at the beginning of this chapter to create a program that uses threads to add up the contents of an array holding 100 different numbers.

Activity 19.2

Use the internet to research the concept of hyper-threading. Where is it used and why?

End-of-chapter questions

1 What is the main advantage of concurrent execution? [1]

2 What are the three main pitfalls of concurrency? [3]

3 What condition must be true for two processes to be executed concurrently? [1]

4 True or false? You must have a multicore system to carry out concurrent execution. [1]

5 What programming technique can be used to execute two sets of instructions at the same time? [1]

Further reading

Concurrent thinking – search on Loyola Marymount University Los Angeles' Computer Science website.
Dining Philosophers problem – search on Michigan Tech's Computer Science website.
Cigarette Smoker's problem – search on the University of Maryland's Computer Science website.
Sleeping Barber problem – search for the Oracle Java Combo blog.
Multicore computers – search for million-core supercomputing on Extreme Tech's website.

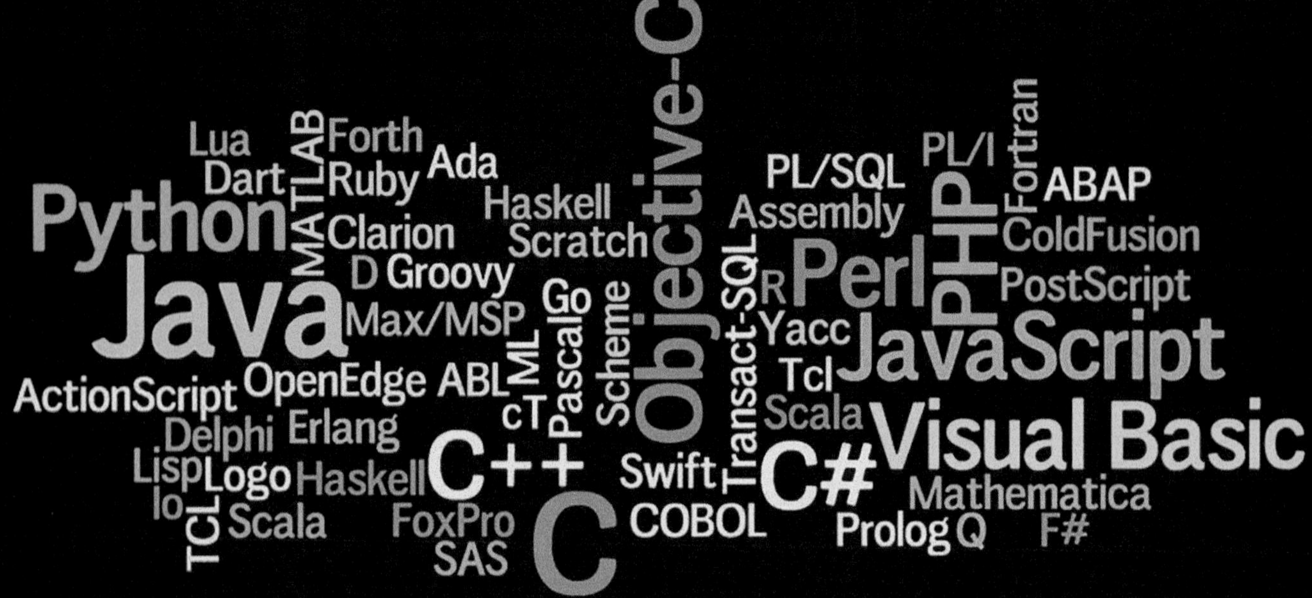

Chapter 20
Programming techniques

Specification points

2.2.1 Programming techniques

- Programming constructs: sequence, iteration, branching.
- Global and local variables.
- Modularity, functions and procedures, parameter passing by value and by reference.
- Use of an IDE to develop/debug a program.

- Recursion, how it can be used and how it compares to an iterative approach.
- Use of object-oriented techniques.

Learning objectives

- To understand the three main programming constructs: sequence, iteration and branching.
- To learn about global and local variables.
- To understand modularity, functions and procedures, and parameter passing by value and by reference.
- To know how to use an IDE to develop/debug a program.

- To understand recursion, how it can be used and how it compares to an iterative approach.
- Use of object-oriented techniques.

Introduction

Programming or coding is the process of creating a set of instructions that can be executed by a computer. The set of instructions can be called 'code', a 'program' or 'software' and could be written in a number of programming languages such as Python, C++ or Java. There are many different programming paradigms, including object-oriented, procedural, functional and declarative, but ultimately they all provide different ways of achieving the same goal: creating a set of instructions that can be executed by a computer. This chapter will use the programming languages Python, Visual Basic and C++ to introduce you to some of the most important concepts in programming.

Programming constructs

Sequence

Sequence is arguably the most fundamental of all programming constructs. Sequence means that each instruction is executed once in the order it is given, just as you are reading this page left to right, top to bottom, reading each word once before moving on to the next. In the same way, a procedural program will be executed beginning with the instructions (also called statements) on line 1 before moving on to line 2 and continuing until all the instructions have been executed. The program in Figure 20.1 shows a sequence of print instructions being used to display a message to the user. Compare the program in Figure 20.1 to its output as shown in Figure 20.2. It's immediately obvious that the first instruction print("Hello") has been the first one executed, followed by the second, and so on until the program was completed.

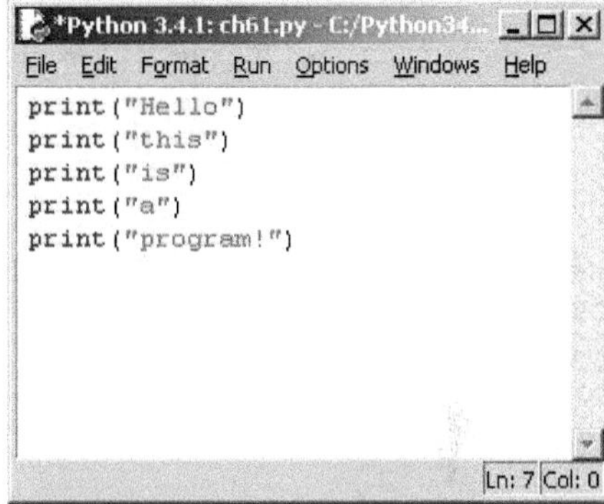

Figure 20.1: This program uses a sequence of print instructions to display text to a user.

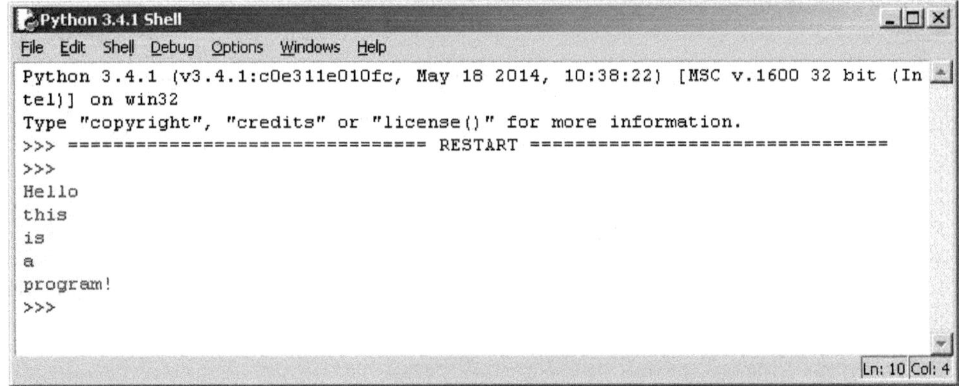

Figure 20.2: The output created when the program in Figure 20.1 is executed.

The use of sequence is even easier to spot when the program is represented as a flowchart (as shown in Figure 20.3). Each instruction in the flowchart must be executed once before moving on to the next, and the flowchart finishes when all the instructions have been executed. Flowcharts are particularly useful for illustrating the path of execution in procedural programs and will be used throughout this chapter.

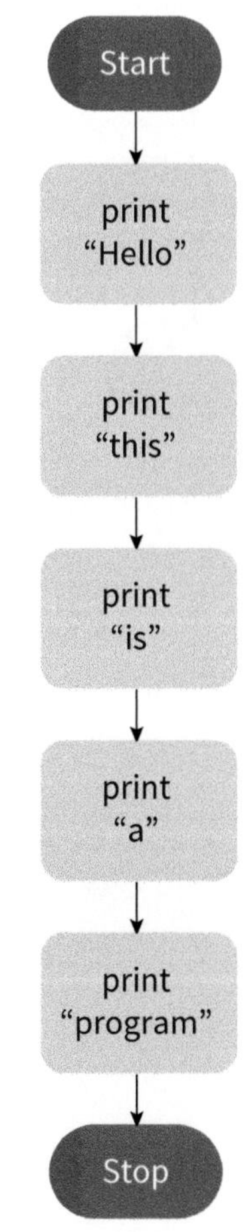

Figure 20.3: A flowchart describing the program in Figure 20.1.

Branching

Sequence is a vital programming construct, but there are many situations in which you won't want the computer to execute every instruction it is given. At some stage you will want to choose which instruction to execute next based on something that happens while the program is being executed. For example, imagine you are creating a simple guessing game in which the computer generates a secret number and the player must try to guess

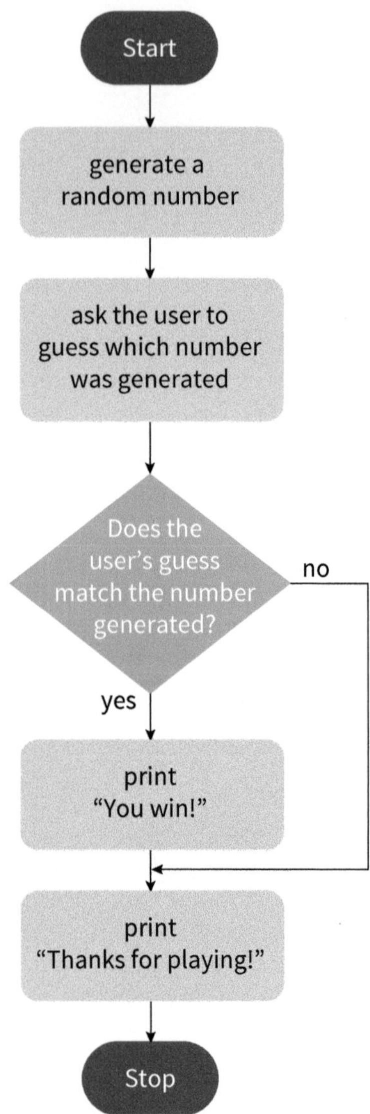

Figure 20.4: A flowchart for a simple guessing game that could be implemented using an IF statement.

what it is. It is important that we have a construct that allows us to print 'You win!' if the user guesses correctly or print 'You lose!' if they do not. When creating a program, this is achieved by using a **branching** construct or selection statement to select which instruction to execute next.

There are three implementations of branching commonly available in programming languages:

- IF statements
- ELIF (ELSE IF) statements.
- ELSE (IF ELSE) statements

IF statements are the most basic form of branching; they check if a condition has been met and, if it has then it's value is TRUE and the program will execute a set of instructions. If the instruction is not met, its value is FALSE and the set of instructions within the IF statement is skipped by the computer, which executes the next instruction outside of the IF statement.

Look at the flowchart in Figure 20.4. The computer compares the random number to the player's guess and, if they match, a message saying 'You win!' is displayed followed by a message saying 'Thanks for playing!' If the two numbers do not match, only the message saying 'Thanks for playing!' is shown to the user. Figure 20.5 shows how this program could be implemented using an IF statement and Figure 20.6 shows the output when the program is run.

Code

```
import random

randomNumber=random.randint(0,10)

playerGuess=input ("Which number am I thinking of?")

if playerGuess == randomNumber:
  print("You win!")

print ("Thanks for playing!")
```

Python 3.4.1: ch63.py - C:/Python34/ch63.py

File Edit Format Run Options Windows Help

```
import random

randomNumber=random.randint(0,10)

playerGuess=input("Which number am I thinking of?")

if playerGuess == randomNumber:
    print("You win!")

print("Thanks for playing!")
```

Ln: 10 Col: 0

Figure 20.5: The output generated by the code above if the user's guess is incorrect.

IF ELSE is an alternative method of branching. It is similar to an IF statement but if the condition necessary to execute the instructions with the IF statement is not met the instructions within the ELSE statement are executed instead. Figure 20.6 shows how our simple guessing game could be implemented using an IF ELSE statement.

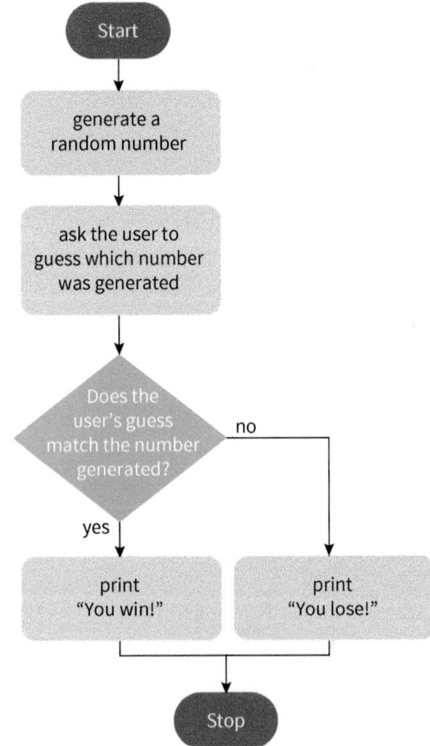

Figure 20.6: A flowchart describing a simple guessing game that could be implemented using an IF ELSE statement.

The value in playerGuess is compared to the value in randomNumber. If they are the same, the message 'You win!' is printed. If they are different, the message 'You lose!' is printed. The difference between this IF ELSE implementation and the IF implementation you saw earlier is that the message 'You lose!' will only be printed if the player's guess is incorrect, whereas the 'Thanks for playing!' message was always printed regardless of whether or not the player's guess was correct.

Code

```
import random

randomNumber=random.randint (0,10)

playerGuess=input ("Which number am I thinking of?")

if playerGuess = = randomNumber:
  print ("You win!")
else:
  print ("You lose!")
```

```
Python 3.4.1 Shell
File Edit Shell Debug Options Windows Help
Python 3.4.1 (v3.4.1:c0e311e010fc, May 18 2014, 10:38:22) [MSC v.1600 32 bit (In
tel)] on win32
Type "copyright", "credits" or "license()" for more information.
>>> ================================ RESTART ================================
>>>
Which number am I thinking of?5
You lose!
>>>
Ln: 7 Col: 4
```

Figure 20.7: The output generated by the code above.

ELIF is an alternative method of branching which combines IF statements and IF ELSE statements (ELIF is short for ELSE IF). If the condition necessary to execute the instructions with the IF statement is not met then the condition attached to the ELIF statement is checked. If the ELIF condition is met then the code within it is executed. This process is repeated until an ELIF condition is met or there are no more ELIF statements or an ELSE statement is reached. Figure 20.8 shows how our simple guessing game could be implemented using an ELIF statement.

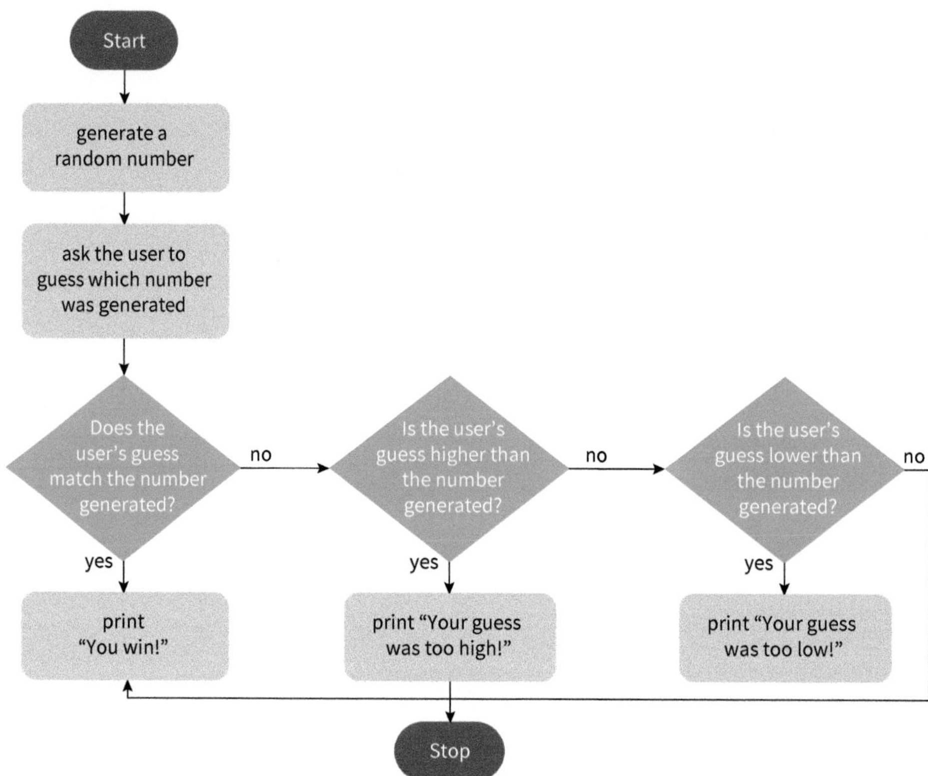

Figure 20.8: A flowchart for a simple guessing game that could be coded using an ELIF statement.

Code

```
import random

randomNumber=random.randint(0,10)

playerGuess=input("Which number am I thinking of?")

if playerGuess == randomNumber:
  print ("You win!")
elif int (playerGuess) > int (randomNumber):
  print ("Your guess was too high!")
elif int (playerGuess) > int (randomNumber):
  print ("Your guess was too low!")
```

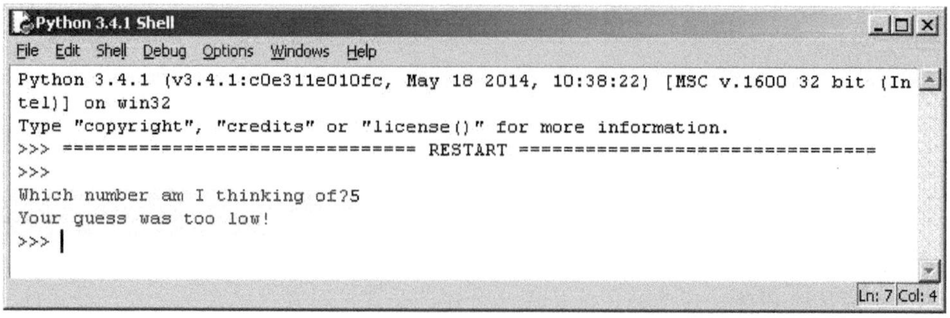

```
Python 3.4.1 Shell
File Edit Shell Debug Options Windows Help
Python 3.4.1 (v3.4.1:c0e311e010fc, May 18 2014, 10:38:22) [MSC v.1600 32 bit (In
tel)] on win32
Type "copyright", "credits" or "license()" for more information.
>>> ================================ RESTART ================================
>>>
Which number am I thinking of?5
Your guess was too low!
>>> |
Ln: 7 Col: 4
```

Figure 20.9: The output generated by the code above.

SELECT CASE

Another common form of selection is the SELECT CASE statement. Although not available in all languages (for example Python doesn't support it) it can be a very useful construct and is well worth knowing about.

Look at the Visual Basic example below:

Code

```
Dim number As Integer = 3

Select Case number
  Case 1
    MsgBox "number is set to one!"
  Case 2
    MsgBox "number is set to two!"
  Case 3
    MsgBox "number is set to three!"
  Case Else
    MsgBox "number is not one, two or three"
End Select
```

SELECT CASE focuses on the content of a variable and has a separate CASE for each outcome. In the example above, a message box saying 'number is set to three!' will be displayed to the user because number = 3.

An important part of the SELECT CASE statement is the CASE ELSE statement (sometimes called a Default statement) at the end of the SELECT CASE. The CASE ELSE will be executed if none of the other cases apply. In the example above, if number was set to any value other than 1,2 or 3 then the message 'number is not one, two or three' would be displayed. If you don't include a CASE ELSE statement and the expression doesn't match one of your CASE statements then nothing will happen.

Using SELECT CASE avoids the need to use multiple nested IF statements which can be difficult to read. As a general rule if you have four or more IF statements all focused on the same variable then it's a good idea to replace them with a single SELECT CASE statement.

Iteration

There are many times when you find yourself using the same sequence of instructions over and over again. This can take a long time and makes your code difficult to read or debug. **Iteration** is used to execute the same instructions a set number of times or until a condition is met. The ability to repeatedly carry out the same instructions is one of the most powerful properties of computer systems.

Programming languages can implement iteration using loops. Most support two types, WHILE loops and FOR loops.

FOR loops execute an instruction (or sequence of instructions) a set number of times. This type of loop is called count controlled. In this case, we create a variable called count and set it to zero. Every time the code inside the loop is executed, count is increased by one. When count reaches the value set by the programmer, the computer stops executing the code inside the loop and moves on to the next instruction outside of the loop. Figure 20.10 shows a flowchart which describes a simple FOR loop which will print out the message 'Hi there!' ten times. Figure 20.11 shows how this could be implemented using Python.

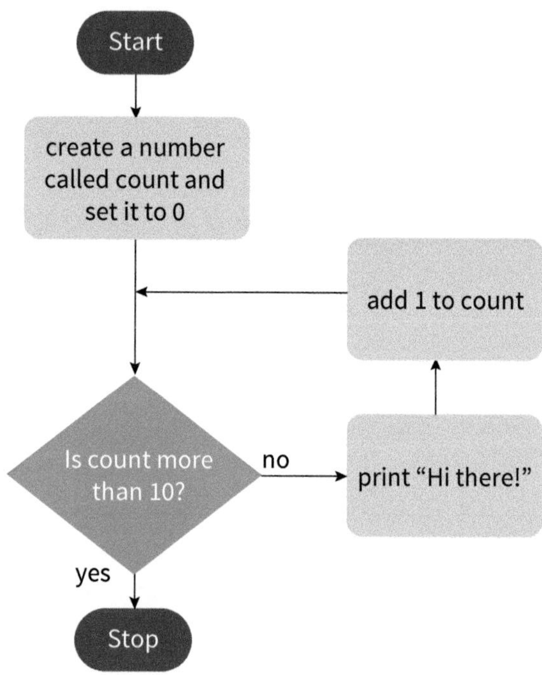

Figure 20.10: A flowchart describing a simple FOR loop.

Code

```
for count in range (0,10):
  print ("Hi there!")
```

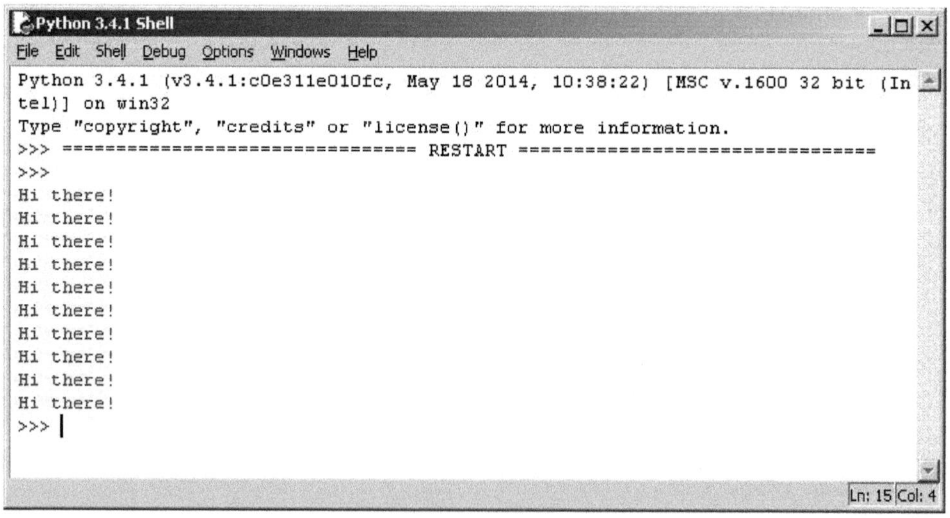

```
Python 3.4.1 Shell
File Edit Shell Debug Options Windows Help
Python 3.4.1 (v3.4.1:c0e311e010fc, May 18 2014, 10:38:22) [MSC v.1600 32 bit (In
tel)] on win32
Type "copyright", "credits" or "license()" for more information.
>>> ================================ RESTART ================================
>>>
Hi there!
Hi there!
Hi there!
Hi there!
Hi there!
Hi there!
Hi there!
Hi there!
Hi there!
Hi there!
>>>
Ln: 15 Col: 4
```

Figure 20.11: The output from the Python program from the code above.

WHILE loops are also used to repeat an instruction (or sequence of instructions), but whereas FOR loops execute instructions a set number of times, WHILE loops repeat an instruction until a condition is met, so they are also known as condition controlled loops. Figure 20.12 shows a flowchart for our simple guessing game, but this time, instead of ending the game after the first guess, the player must keep guessing until she gets the correct answer.

Code

```
import random

randomNumber=random.randint(0,10)

playerGuess=input ("Which number am I thinking of?")

while int (playerGuess)!= int (randomNumber):
  playerGuess=input ("Which number am I thinking of?")

print ("You win!")
```

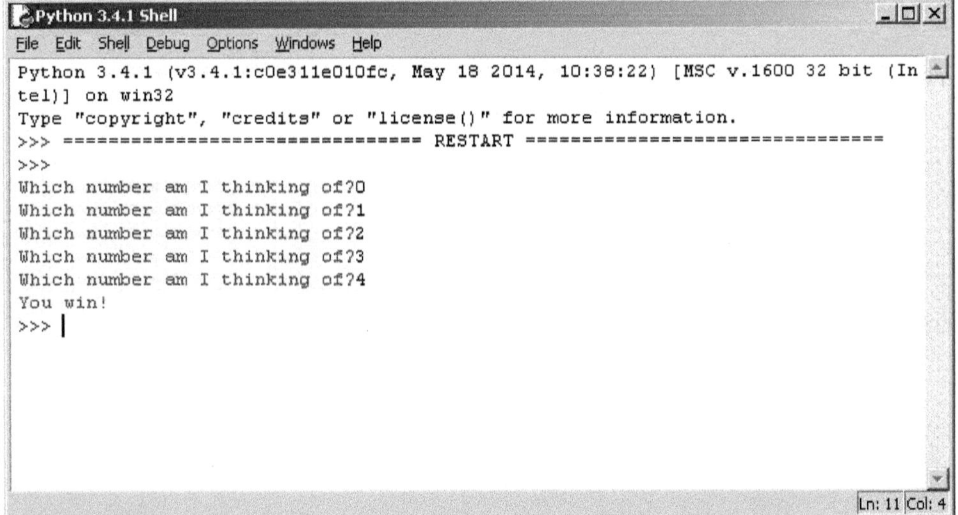

Figure 20.13: The output produced from the code above. Notice that the execution only stops when the user makes the correct guess.

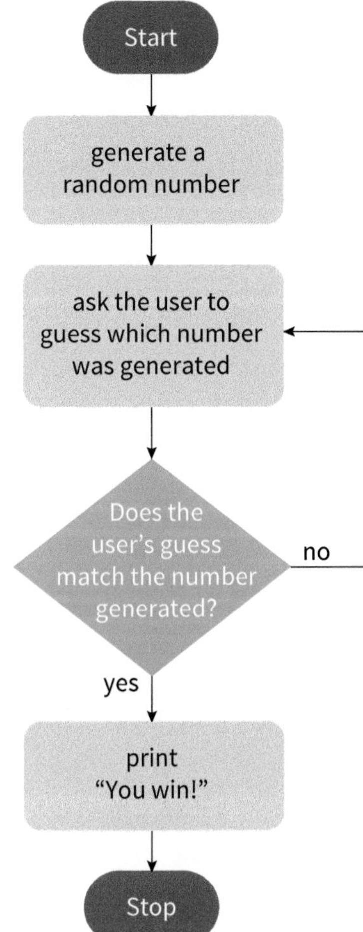

Figure 20.12: A flowchart which uses a condition controlled loop to ask the player to guess a random number until they get it right.

Nesting

Nesting is the name given to the practice of placing one construct within another. For example, you could have an IF statement nested inside another IF statement or a loop nested inside an IF statement. Figure 20.14 shows a more advanced version of the guessing game in which the user can choose whether to play again after each match.

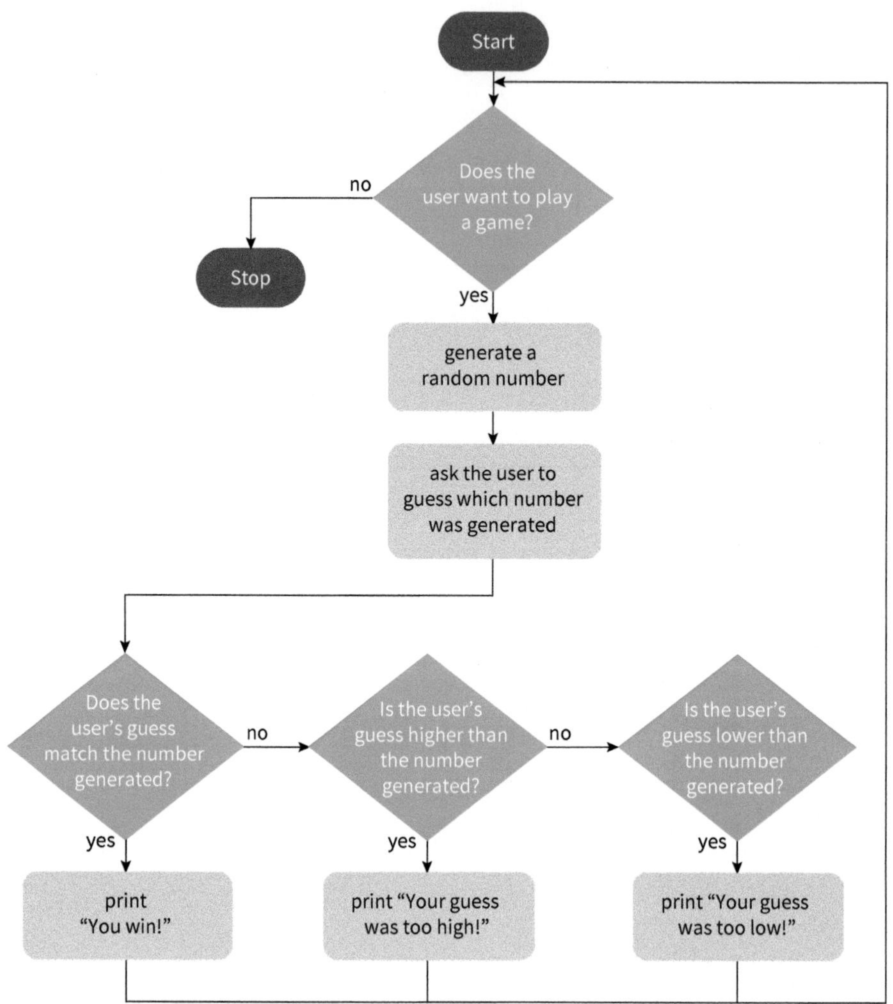

Figure 20.14: A more advanced version of the guessing game. Notice that the branching takes place within the iteration.

Code

```
import random
playerResponse=input ("Would you like to play a game?")

while playerResponse=="Yes":
  randomNumber=random.randint (0,10)

  playerGuess=input ("Which number am I thinking of?")

  if playerGuess == randomNumber:
    print ("You win!")
  elif int (playerGuess) > int (randomNumber):
    print ("Your guess was too high!")
  elif int (playerGuess) > int (randomNumber):
    print ("Your guess was too low!")

playerResponse=input ("Would you like to play a game?")
```

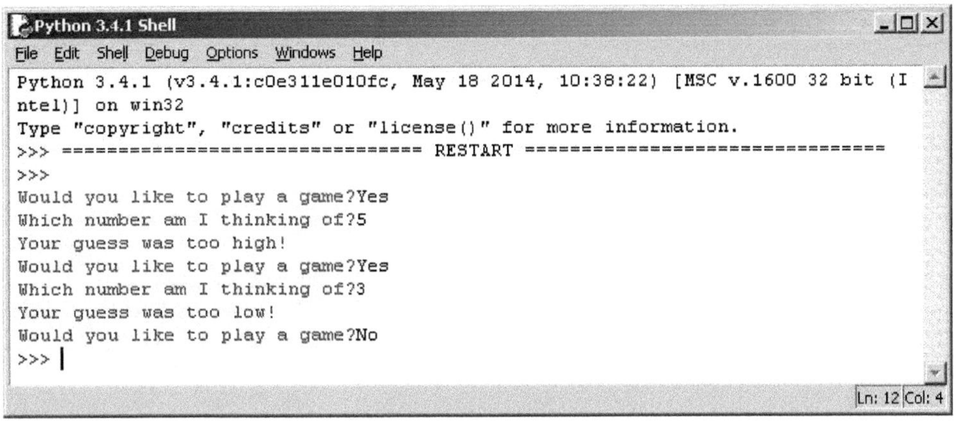

```
Python 3.4.1 Shell
File Edit Shell Debug Options Windows Help
Python 3.4.1 (v3.4.1:c0e311e010fc, May 18 2014, 10:38:22) [MSC v.1600 32 bit (I
ntel)] on win32
Type "copyright", "credits" or "license()" for more information.
>>> ================================ RESTART ================================
>>>
Would you like to play a game?Yes
Which number am I thinking of?5
Your guess was too high!
Would you like to play a game?Yes
Which number am I thinking of?3
Your guess was too low!
Would you like to play a game?No
>>> |
Ln: 12 Col: 4
```

Figure 20.15: The output produced by running the code above.

Recursion

A **recursive function** is one that repeatedly calls itself until a base case is met. This often provides an elegant way to carry out the same operation a number of times. Using the term 'elegant' implies that the code is very simple, maybe only a few lines, and therefore as minimal as possible.

The most common example of a recursive function is one that is used to calculate the factorial of a given whole number (integer). The factorial of any given number can be calculated by multiplying the number with all the whole numbers beneath it. For example, the factorial of 4 (shown as 4!) can be calculated as 4 × 3 × 2 × 1 or 24. Similarly, the factorial of 6 can be shown as, 6! = 6 × 5 × 4 × 3 × 2 × 1 or 720.

The calculation is carried out by repeatedly working out n*factorial (n-1). This recursive operation is repeated until n = 1, which is our base case, that is, the condition which when reached will stop the recursion (factorials don't use negative numbers) because it has a finite answer.

Using recursion, a function to calculate the factorial of a given number might look like the one in Figure 20.16

Code

```
def factorial(n):
  if n ==1:
    return 1
  else:
    return n* factorial(n-1)
```

Figure 20.16 shows the recursive function in action. The function calls begin at the top and the green arrows show the values being entered each time the function is called. The blue arrows show how the result from each function call is passed back up the chain once the base case has been reached. Notice that the base case (n == 1) is met at the bottom of the chain and the number 1 is passed back up to the instance before it.

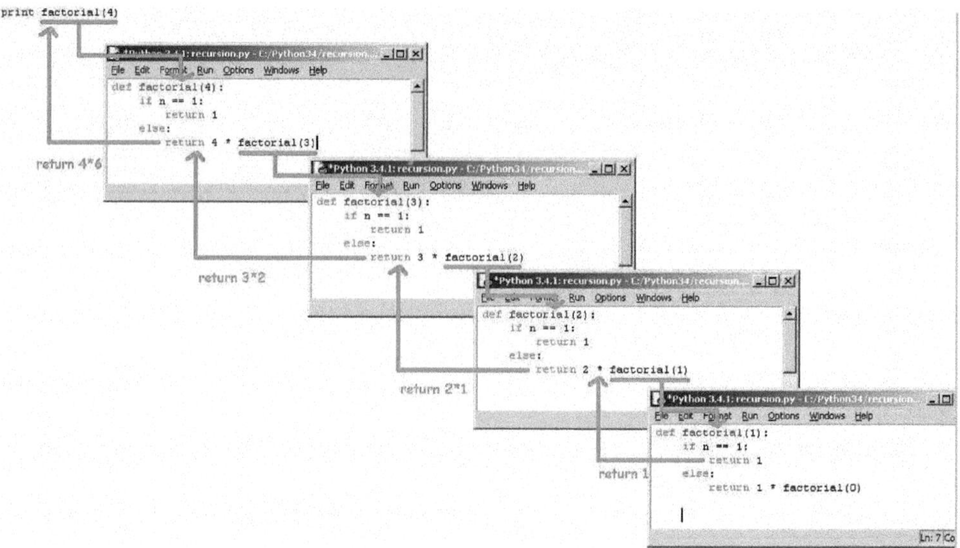

Figure 20.16: A recursive function for calculating the factorial of n is executed.

Recursion versus iteration

Given that recursion is used to repeat a set of instructions, there is clearly a crossover with the functionality provided by iteration. In fact, there is a whole series of languages (called functional programming languages) that don't support iteration, so a programmer must use recursion instead. The advantage of recursion is that people tend to think recursively, so they are happier applying the same procedure to different information than they are repeating some functionality a set number of times. This generally makes recursive code easier to understand. However, recursion has a big drawback in terms of the amount of memory it uses. Every time the function calls itself, a new copy of the function is created in memory. This is completely different from loops, in which the values of existing variables are simply updated.

Figure 20.17 shows two programs for calculating the factorial of the number 4. The one on the left uses recursion, the one on the right uses a FOR loop.

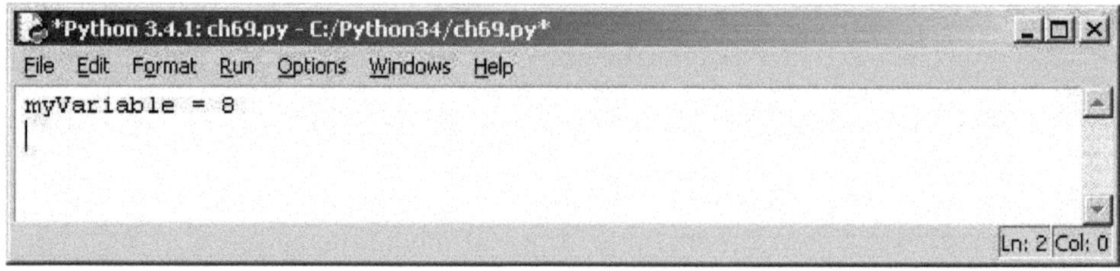

Figure 20.17: Recursion versus iteration.

They both use a similar number of lines but the loop version simply updates the values of i and factorial each time it is run. The recursive version, on the other hand, creates a new version of the variable n each time the function calls itself recursively; this increases the amount of random-access memory (RAM) that the program uses to run.

Tip

When it comes to programming, practice makes perfect. You can practise writing simple programs by registering with a website called Code Academy.

Variables

A **variable** is a named location in the computer's memory that a programmer can use to store data while the program is running. All the examples you have seen so far use variables.

All computer systems have some form of memory. You will probably be familiar with RAM as shown in Figure 20.18.

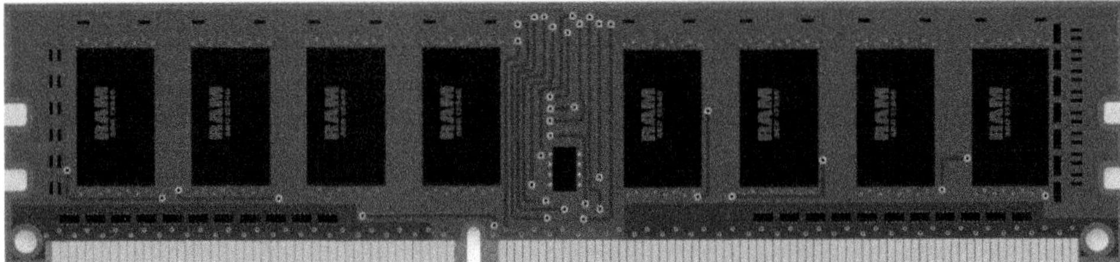

Figure 20.18: RAM.

You can think of a computer's memory as being made of lots of small storage boxes into which programmers can place an instruction or piece of data. Each storage box has its own unique address that can be used to access the instruction or data stored in that box. Figure 20.19 shows an illustration of this concept.

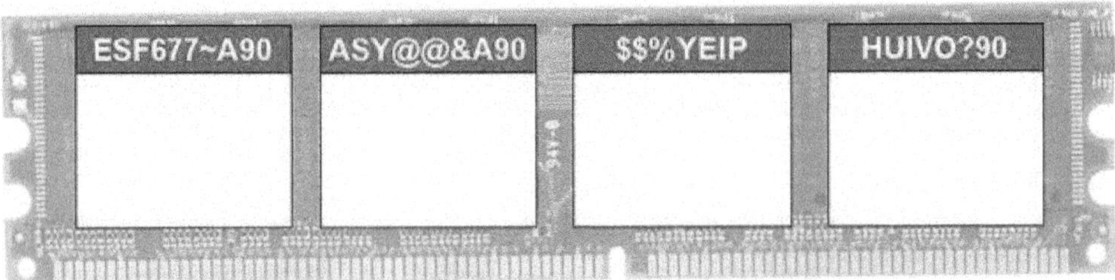

Figure 20.19: Storage locations in a computer's memory.

By default these storage locations have nonsensical names; for example, '$$%YEIP'. But as a programmer we can rename a storage location and use it to hold a value. We call this process 'declaring a variable'. Figure 20.20 shows how a variable can be declared in Python.

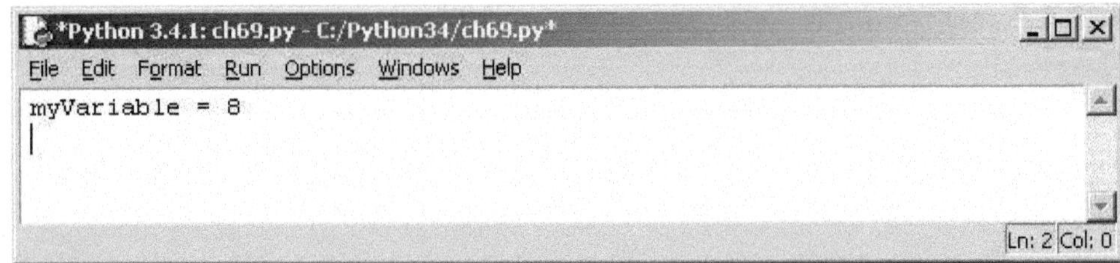

Figure 20.20: Declaring a variable in Python.

I have chosen to call the storage location 'myVariable' and have put the number 8 into it. Figure 20.21 shows the impact that this has had in our memory illustration. See that one of the locations has been renamed myVariable and now holds the number 8.

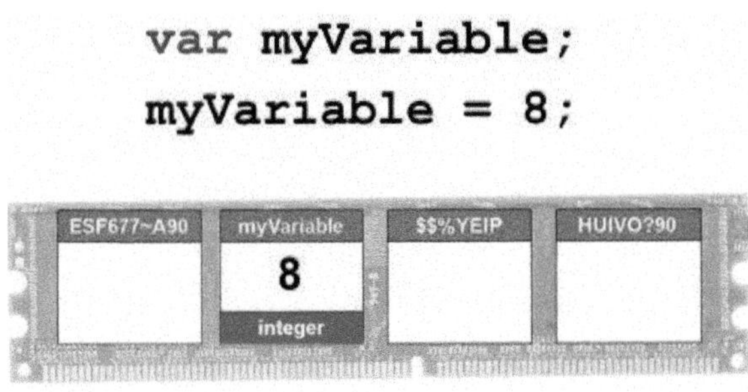

Figure 20.21: Variables in memory.

Data types

In Figure 20.21 you will notice that not only has the name of a storage location been changed to myVariable and the number 8 been put in it, but also that a blue label has appeared saying 'integer'.

When you declare your variable by giving it its name, the computer will want to know what type of data you are going to store in it: text, number, string, character etc.

There are many different **data types** but Table 20.1 shows you the most common:

Variable type	Description	Example
Char	A single character	a
String	A series of letters or numbers	Hello world
Boolean	Either TRUE or FALSE	TRUE
Integer	A whole number	35
Float	A decimal number	12.56

Table 20.1: Data types.

Python is a *weakly typed* language. This means it doesn't force you to say what type of data you will store in your variable when you declare it. Visual Basic is a *strongly typed* language – when you declare your variable in Visual Basic you do it like this:

Code

```
Dim myVariable as Integer
myVariable = 8
```

Notice that Visual Basic forces you to say that the variable is a particular data type – in this case an integer. The next line stores the number 8 in the location called myVariable. This is an assignment statement because it assigns a value to our newly created variable. If you try to store data of a different data type (e.g. myVariable = "Hello"), running the code will produce an error.

Python guesses what type of data you want the variable to hold based on what you put in it. If you write myVariable = "hello", it will assume the data type is a *string*. If you write myVariable = 8 it will assume the data type is an *integer*.

Being a weakly typed language makes Python code quicker to write but can lead to annoying bugs if it gets the data type wrong. However, it should also be noted that if you wish to represent a variable as a different data type during the course of a program, languages allow you to do this by casting. For example, in Python, the input function expects a string but if we want the user to type in a whole number, placing "int" outside of it will allow the user input to be stored and processed as an integer e.g. myNumber = int(input("Please enter a whole number: "))

Local variables

Local variables are those that can only be accessed by the subroutine they have been declared in.

The program in Figure 20.22 uses a subroutine to work out the value of adding two numbers together. It also uses the same variables to work out the addition and display it after the subroutine has run.

Code

```
Def Adding():
  intFirstNumber = 5
  intSecondNumber = 8

  intTotal = intFirstNumber + intSecondNumber

  print ("Result using the Adding procedure:")
  print (str (intTotal))

Adding ()

intTotal = intFirstNumber + intSecondNumber
print ("Result after using the Adding procedure:")
print (str (intTotal))
```

```
Python 3.4.1 Shell
File Edit Shell Debug Options Windows Help
Python 3.4.1 (v3.4.1:c0e311e010fc, May 18 2014, 10:38:22) [MSC v.1600 32 bit
(Intel)] on win32
Type "copyright", "credits" or "license()" for more information.
>>> ================================ RESTART ================================
>>>
Result using the Adding procedure:
13
Traceback (most recent call last):
  File "C:/Python34/localVariable.py", line 12, in <module>
    intTotal = intFirstNumber + intSecondNumber
NameError: name 'intFirstNumber' is not defined
>>> |
Ln: 11 Col: 4
```

Figure 20.22: Using local variables in a simple addition program.

The code produces an error because the variables intFirstNumber and intSecondNumber are local to the subroutine Adding. When they are called from the main block of code the computer can't find them.

Global variables

Global variables are available throughout the program to any subroutine. The program in Figure 20.23 is exactly the same as the previous example except that the variables intFirstNumber and intSecondNumber are declared as being global and are therefore accessible throughout the entire program.

Where in a program a variable can be accessed is called its scope. It is good practice to limit the scope of as many variables as possible in a program. The reason for this is to aid maintainability and code reuse. You should definitely avoid declaring global variables inside a function because this makes your code more difficult to follow and debug. Global variables should always be declared at the start of a program after any imported libraries.

Code

```
def Adding():
  global intFirstNumber
  global intSecondNumber

  intFirstNumber = 5
  intSecondNumber = 8

  intTotal = intFirstNumber + intSecondNumber

  print ("Result using the Adding procedure:")
  print (str (intTotal))

Adding()

intTotal = intFirstNumber + intSecondNumber
print ("Result after using the adding procedure:")
print (str (intTotal())
```

```
Python 3.4.1 Shell
File Edit Shell Debug Options Windows Help
Python 3.4.1 (v3.4.1:c0e311e010fc, May 18 2014, 10:38:22) [MSC v.16
00 32 bit (Intel)] on win32
Type "copyright", "credits" or "license()" for more information.
>>> ================================ RESTART ======================
==========
>>>
Result using the Adding procedure:
13
Result after using the Adding procedure:
13
>>> |
Ln: 9 Col: 4
```

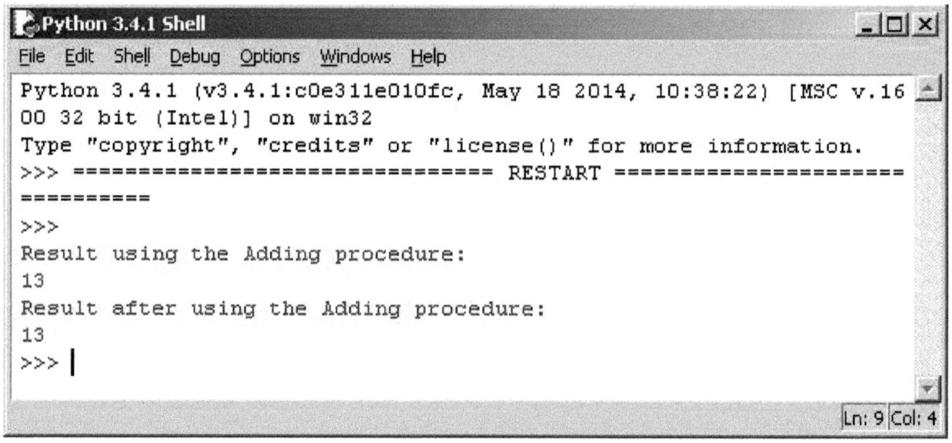

Figure 20.23: Using global variables in a simple addition program.

This time the program runs successfully because the variables being called are global and they can be accessed from any point in the program.

Modularity

When a sequence of instructions is going to be repeated a number of times at different points in the same program, it is often useful to put them in a separate **subroutine**. The subroutine can then be called at the relevant points in the program. This removes unnecessary repetition from a program and makes code easier to maintain.

Imagine a very security-conscious online store that wanted you to re-enter your username and password after every stage of your purchase. Figure 20.24 shows a flowchart that describes the process. Notice that the same sequence of instructions is repeated three times, making the flowchart long and complicated.

In comparison, look at the flowchart in Figure 20.25 which uses subroutines to describe the same process. Every time the 'Security' instruction is encountered, execution jumps to the Security subroutine and implements it. Notice how much simpler the code is; this

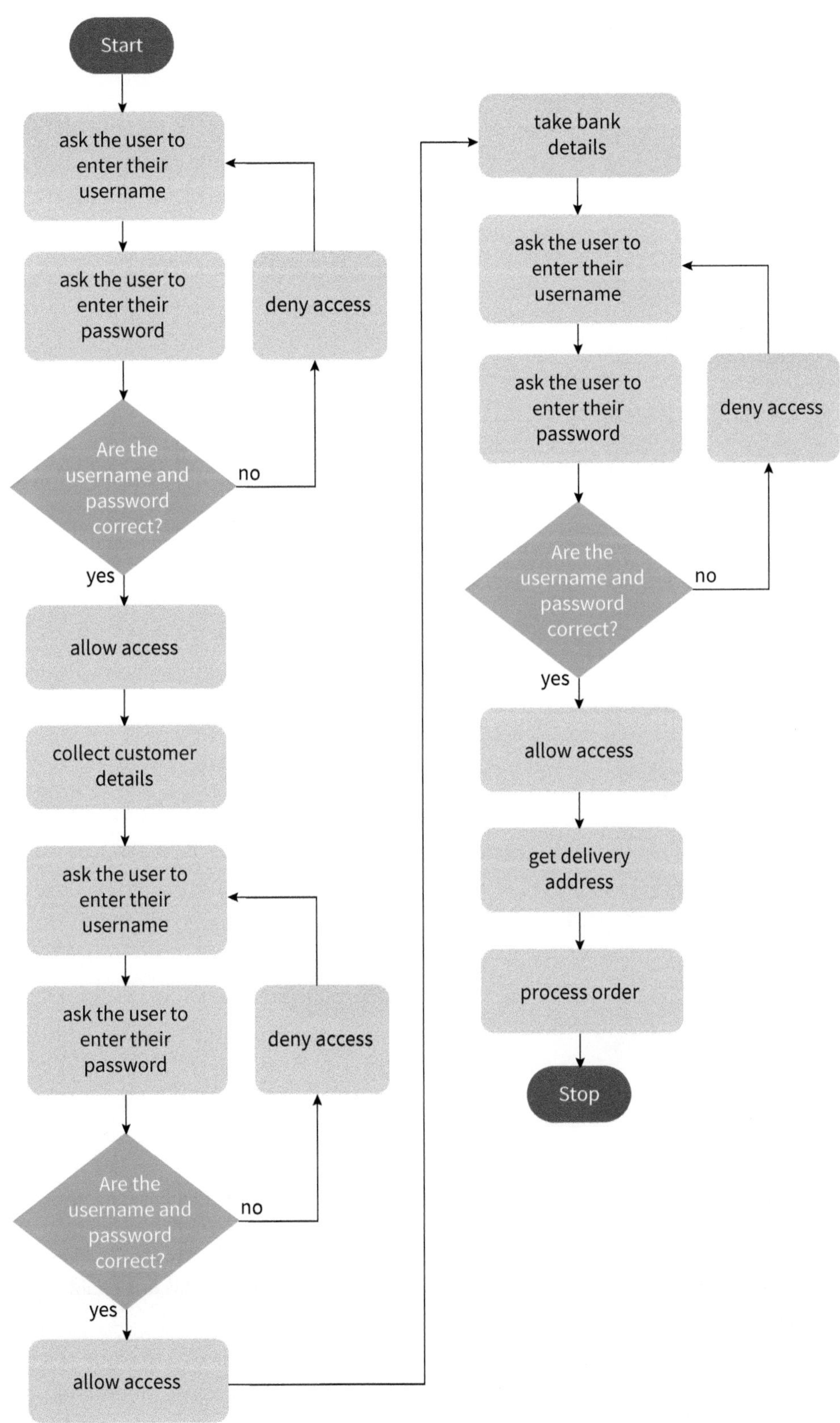

Figure 20.24: A long and complex flowchart that contains much repetition.

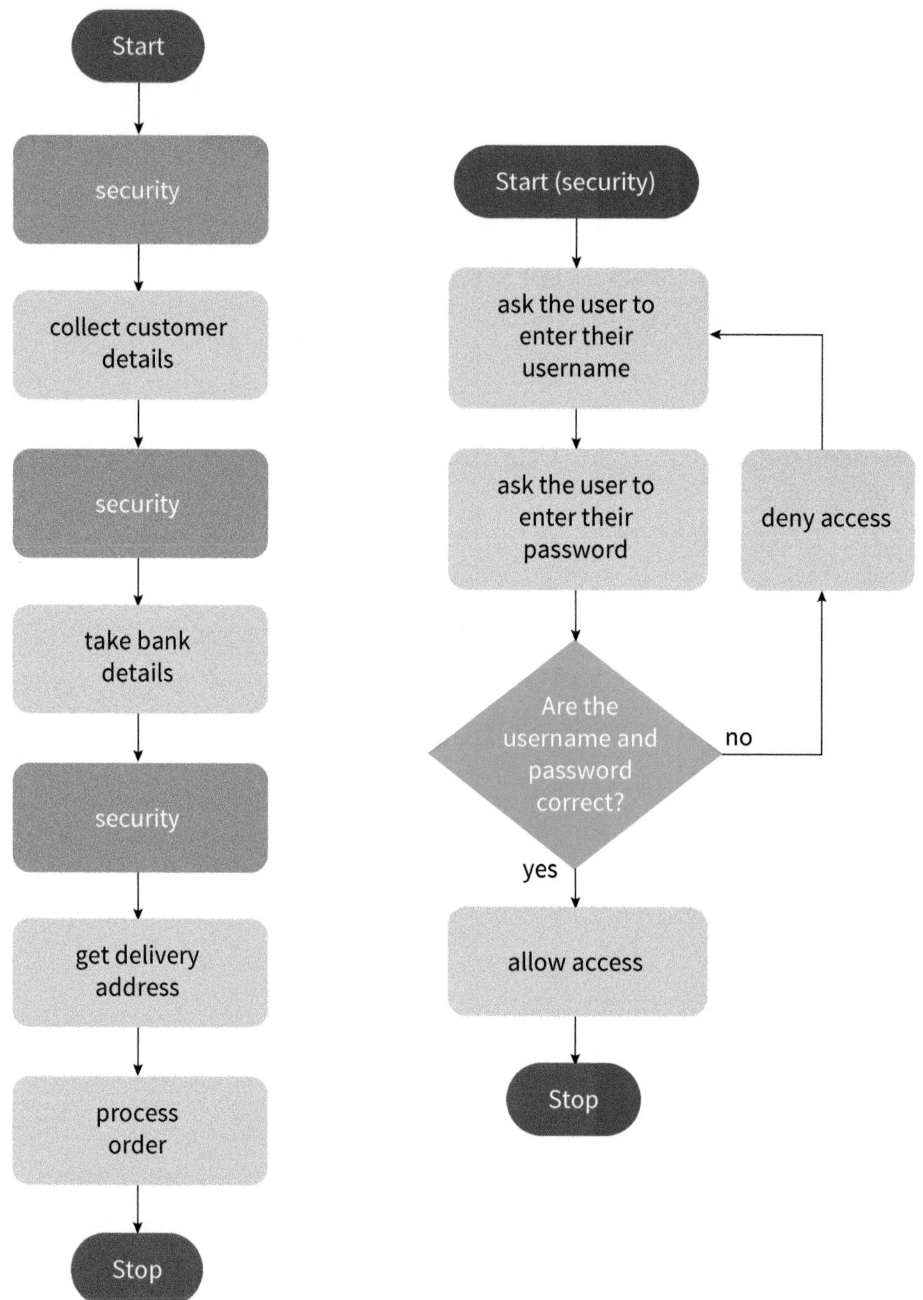

Figure 20.25: The same process as shown in Figure 20.24 but now much shorter thanks to use of a subroutine.

makes it less error-prone and easier to modify. In Python a change like this one could potentially save you writing hundreds of lines of code.

A subroutine can be defined as 'a named block of code that carries out a specific task'. Most programming languages make use of two types of subroutine: functions and procedures.

Functions

A **function** is a subroutine that returns a value.

In the Python example in the code below a function is created called funcArea. This function will take in two values (Height and Width) and return the area of a rectangle of those dimensions.

Code

```
def funcArea(Height, Width):
  Area = Height*Width
  return Area;

myArea = funcArea(2,5)
print (myArea)
```

Line 1 creates the function. The word 'def' (short for define) says that this is a function or procedure. The next part, funcArea, is the name of our function and is used when you want to call the subroutine. You can choose any function name you like but using names that describe the purpose makes your code easier to understand. The right-hand part of the instruction (Height, Width) says this function will accept two values that I've called 'Height' and 'Width' passed to it as parameters. Line 2 calculates the area of the rectangle by multiplying the two values together. Line 3 returns the Area to the program that called the function. Line 4 is blank to separate the two parts of the code. Line 5 is where the main program calls the subroutine. You can see the function name used is funcArea along with two numbers in brackets (2, 5); these values are called **arguments** and are the actual values that are passed to the subroutine. So 2 becomes Height and 5 becomes Width. Finally, line 6 tells the main program to print out the number that was returned when it called funcArea.

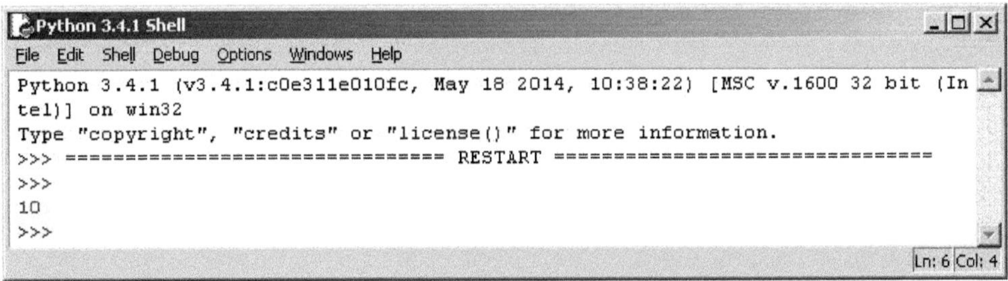

Figure 20.26: The result of running the code above.

Figure 20.26 shows the result of calling the function funcArea with the arguments 2 and 5. These have been multiplied together and the result returned to the main program. Finally, the result has been printed.

Computing in context: Bill Gates

Today Bill Gates is thought to be worth around $80 billion and in 2014 he was the richest man in the world. A self-made billionaire, Gates built his entire business empire on being able to write software.

It began in 1974 when he and a friend saw a magazine article about a new microcomputer, the Altair 8800. They called the company responsible for its manufacture and said they had coded their own computer language specifically for the device. The company's president said he was interested in seeing and potentially purchasing it. This gave Bill Gates and his friend a problem – they hadn't written anything! Working long hours in Bill Gates's garage, the pair finished the program and it worked perfectly first time!

On the back of their success, Bill Gates dropped out of university and established his own company, Microsoft. For many years the company did nothing except produce code. Its operating systems, such as MS-DOS, became standard around the world and by the year 2000 95% of all PCs and smartphones were running Microsoft software.

Today the company produces a range of software and devices from games consoles to tablets, but it all started from those humble beginnings writing code in a garage.

Procedures

Procedures are subroutines that don't return a value. They can display information to a user but they don't return any information back to the main program.

The example below shows a procedure being used to calculate the area of a rectangle. Line 1 remains the same as the function except that the name has been changed to procArea so we know that this is a procedure not a function. Line 2 also remains the same and simply multiplies two numbers together. Line 3, however, is different; the result is displayed straight to the user and not returned to the main program as it was in the function. Line 5 calls the procedure with the arguments 3 and 6.

Code

```
def procArea(Height, Width):
  Area = Height*Width
  Print (Area)

procArea(3,6)
```

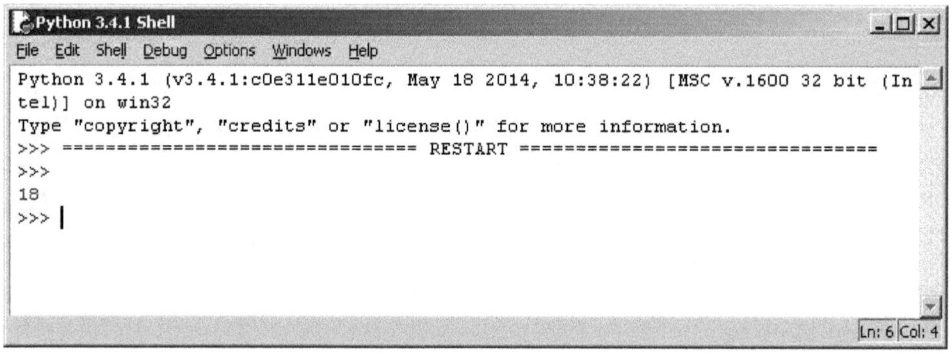

```
Python 3.4.1 Shell
File Edit Shell Debug Options Windows Help
Python 3.4.1 (v3.4.1:c0e311e010fc, May 18 2014, 10:38:22) [MSC v.1600 32 bit (In
tel)] on win32
Type "copyright", "credits" or "license()" for more information.
>>> ================================ RESTART ================================
>>>
18
>>> |
Ln: 6 Col: 4
```

Figure 20.27: The result of running the program in the code above.

Figure 20.27 shows the result of running our program. Execution begins on line 5 when the procedure is called and passed the values 3 and 6. The procedure then takes these values and calculates the area of the square before displaying the result (18) to the user.

Passing parameters by value

Parameters can be used to pass values into a subroutine. The example procedure in the code above uses two parameters, Height and Width. These parameters are replaced by copies of values, the arguments, when the subroutine is called. The function code may well change the values passed to it but it is important to note that the value in the procedure that called it will be unchanged.

Code

```
def procArea(Height, Width):
  Area = Height*Width
  Print (Area)

x = 7
y = 6
procArea (x,y)
```

For example, procArea(x,y) replaces the word Height with a copy of the value stored in x (7) and the word Width with a copy of the value stored in y (6) throughout the subroutine. The result is that the number 42 is displayed in Figure 20.28.

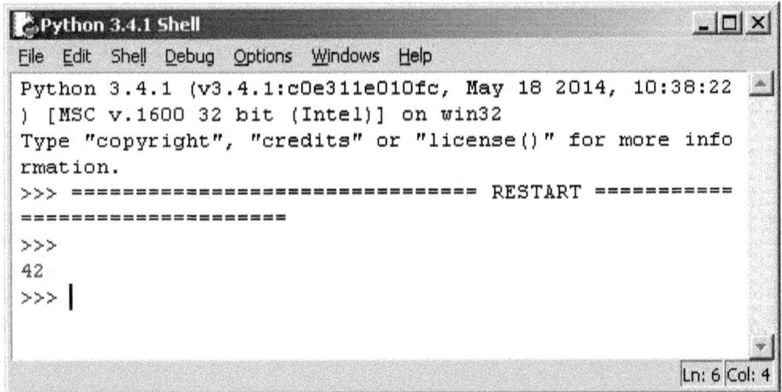

Figure 20.28: The result of running the program in the code above.

Parameters should be used in preference to global variables whenever possible, as they make code easier to read and maintain.

Passing parameters by reference

An alternative way of passing parameters into subroutines is to pass by reference: rather than making a copy of a variable, the subroutine is passed the address of the variable. The main difference is that when passing by reference, any change made within the subroutine will also affect the variable outside the subroutine (much like a global variable).

In these C++ examples the first passes by value, the second passes by reference. C++ uses the & symbol in the parameters to show that the value is being passed by reference.

Passing parameters by value and reference in C++ is shown in the code below.

Code

By value:

```
#include <iostream>
using namespace std;
Void procArea(int Height, int Width, int total)
{
  total = Height+Width;
  cout << "Total is:";
  cout << total << endl;
}
Inht main()
{
  int x, y, z;
  x = 7;
  y = 6;
  z = 0;
  procArea(x,y,z);
  cout << "z is:";
  cout << z << endl;
  return 0;
}
```

By reference:

```
#include <iostream>
using namespace std;
void procArea(int & Height, int & Width, int & total)
{
  total = Height+Width;
  cout << "Total is:";
  cout << total << endl;
}
int main()
{
  int x, y, z;
  x = 7;
  y = 6;
  z = 0;
  procArea(x,y,z);
  cout << "z is:";
  cout << z << endl;
  return 0;
}
```

Notice that *By value* prints out two different numbers because a copy of z is passed to procArea so the variable z in the main block of code is never changed. The *By reference* call prints out the same numbers because the address of z is passed to procArea, so when z is updated in procArea it is also updated in the main block of code.

Tip

You will be asked to write code in your answers to exam questions, which is very different from coding on a computer. Use the sample exam papers and mark schemes on the exam board's website to practise your technique.

Integrated development environments

Development

Integrated development environments (IDEs) are collections of tools that make a programmer's life easier. There are many different IDEs; some are free, some cost money, some support many languages, some just one – but there is some functionality that is common to all.

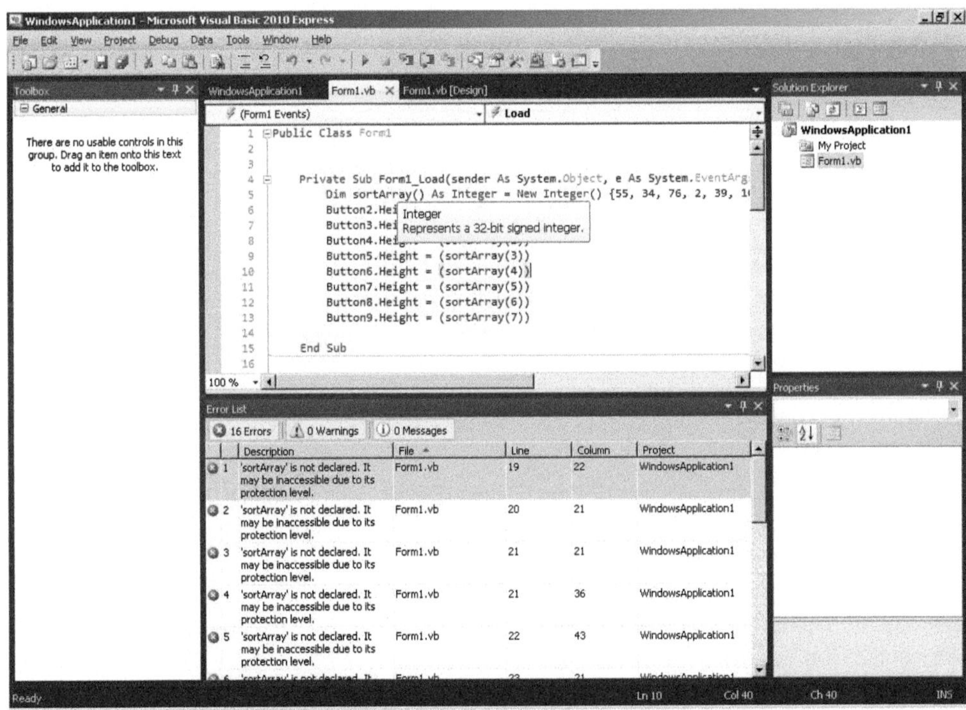

Figure 20.29: The free IDE for Visual Basic Express.

Most provide simple colouring that highlights keywords like if or def. They also provide automatic line numbering and some even draw lines to show which constructs (for example IF and ELSE) match each other. All these tools help make code easier to read.

The screenshot in Figure 20.29 shows some of the common tools available in an IDE. You can see that keywords have been highlighted and that hovering over them brings up an information box containing help text. Each line is also numbered, so it is easier to spot mistakes. The links to some free IDEs are included in the 'Further reading' section at the end of this chapter; most programmers have a favourite so it's worth downloading some and seeing which you prefer.

Debugging

As you've probably already found, programmers spend just as much time **debugging** as they do writing their code in the first place. IDEs come with a range of tools for helping programmers debug their code, including automatic error checking, error reports, breakpoints and stepping through. The next section will explain the function of these tools using a simple bubble sort algorithm as an example.

Computing in context: Bill Gates

Bubble sort is a simple sorting algorithm that repeatedly steps through the list to be sorted comparing each pair of items and swapping them if they are in the wrong order.

The list is run through repeatedly until no swaps have been carried out in a complete pass, at which point the list is assumed to be sorted.

1 Compare 6 and 3 and then swap them as 6 is larger.	6345
2 Compare 6 and 4 and then swap them as 6 is larger.	3645
3 Compare 6 and 5 and then swap them as 6 is larger. The pass is complete but 3 swaps were carried out so the list may still not be sorted.	3465
4 Start a new pass comparing 3 and 4. No swap is necessary.	3456
5 Compare 4 and 5. No swap is necessary.	3456
6 Compare 5 and 6. No swap is necessary. The pass is complete and no swaps were carried out so the list must be sorted.	3456

The algorithm gets its name from the way in which numbers (like 6 in the example above) appear to bubble up to the top of the list.

Bubble sort is simple to understand but is very slow and inefficient except for very small data sets. It is almost never used, except to explain sorting algorithms to students. It is discussed further in Chapter 22.

Automatic error checking

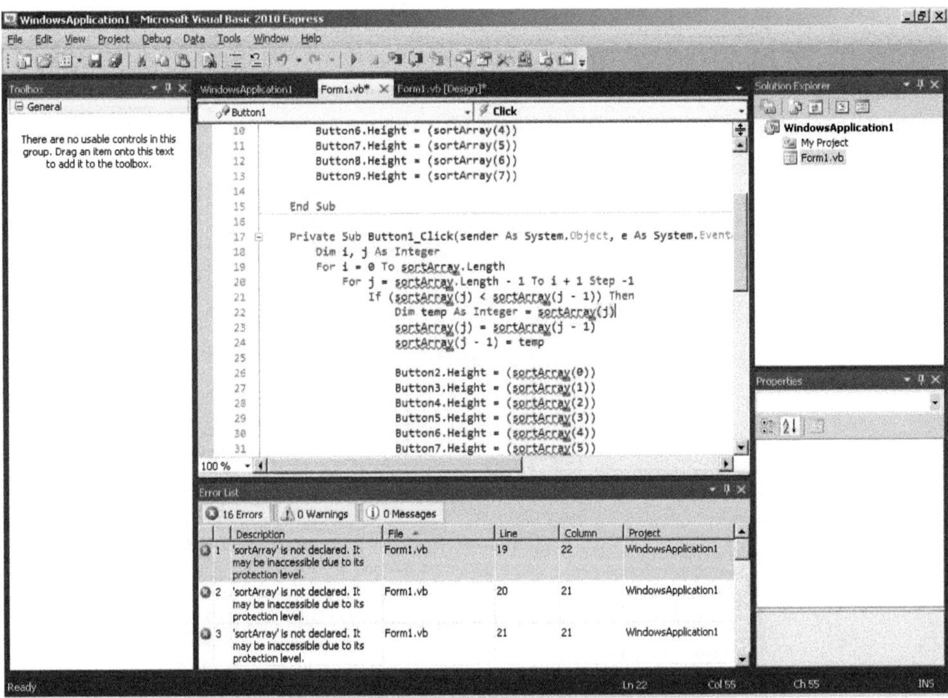

Figure 20.30: Automatic error checking in Visual Basic Express.

Figure 20.30 shows some of the code for a bubble sort program. The array that is being sorted (sortArray) has been declared as a local data structure in another subroutine, so the program won't work when it is run. Even before the program is run, the IDE has underlined all the instances of sortArray in blue to show that there is a problem with them. Clicking on the small red box next to each instance displays a more detailed description (Figure 20.31) of the problem along with possible solutions.

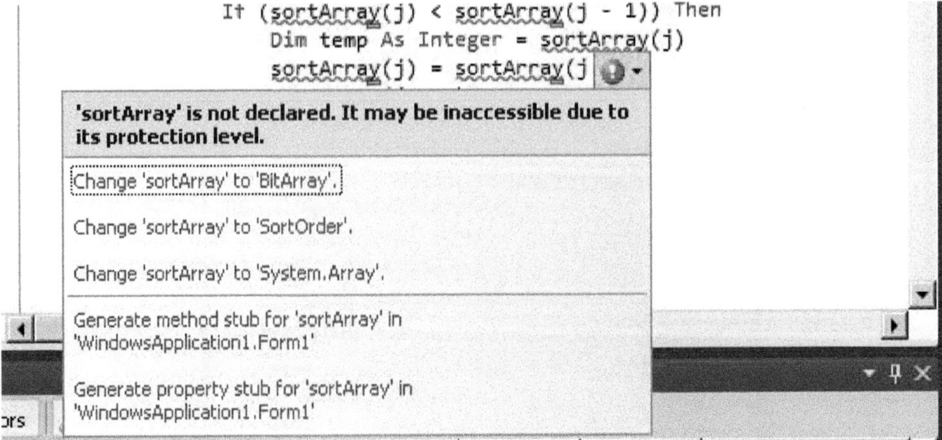

Figure 20.31: Possible solutions suggested by Visual Basic's automatic error checking.

IDEs tend to be very good at spotting mistakes, but you can see in the example in Figure 20.31 that although the IDE has noticed what is wrong, the suggestions for fixing it aren't very useful.

Error reports

As well as highlighting individual errors in the code, the IDE has also produced an error report at the bottom of the screen which shows a list of the errors that have yet to be fixed (Figure 20.32). Errors will stop the code from running successfully, and while the error report has entries the IDE won't let you run the program; instead it displays a warning message (Figure 20.33).

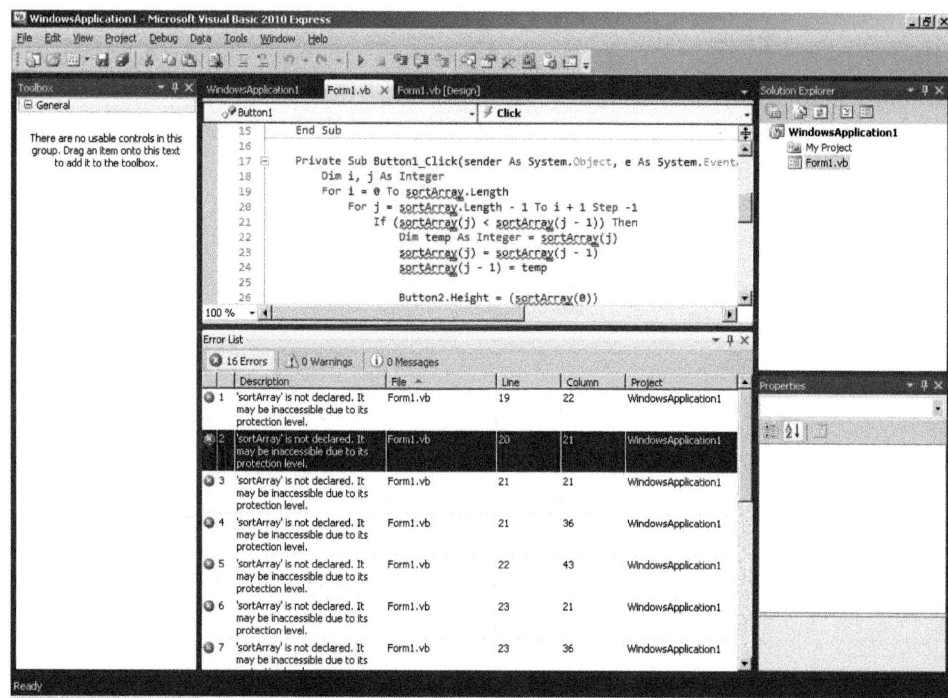

Figure 20.32: An error report in Visual Basic Express.

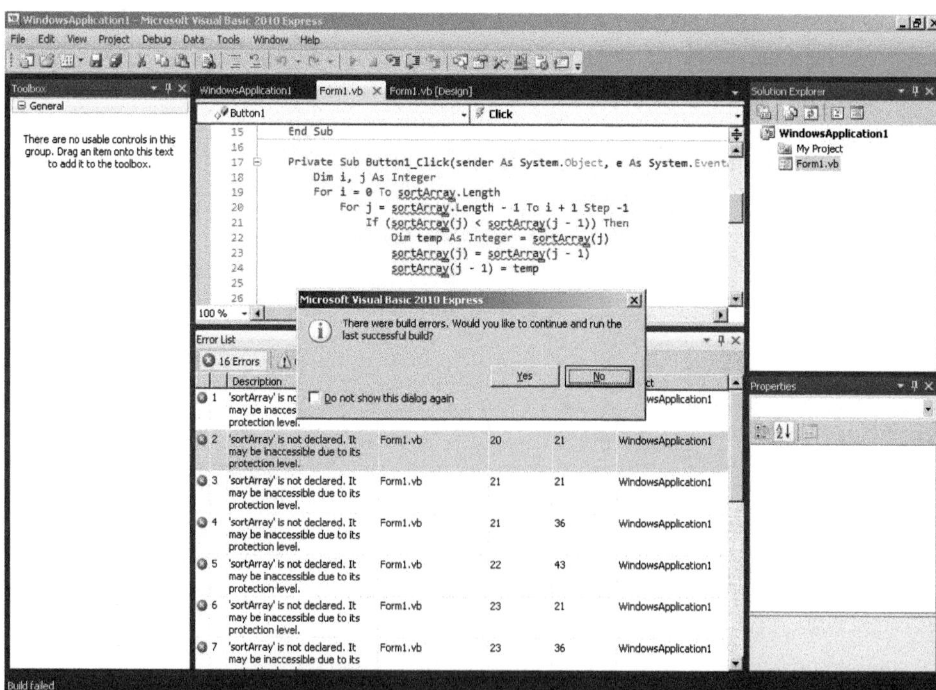

Figure 20.33: The Visual Basic Express IDE won't execute code that contains errors.

If the sortArray data structure is made global then all the error messages disappear and the program will run (Figure 20.34).

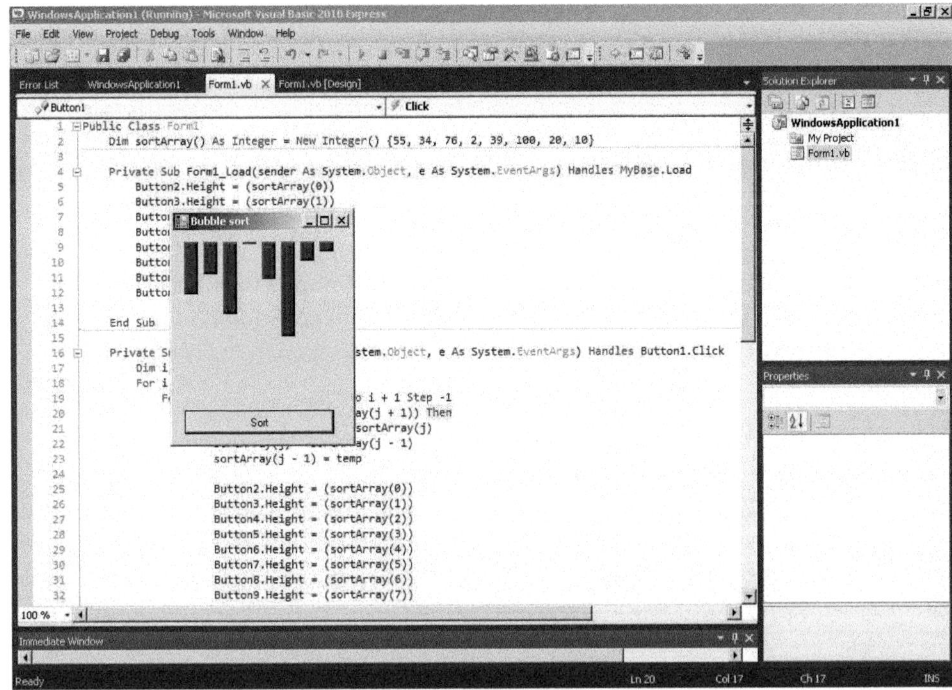

Figure 20.34: With the errors fixed the program will run.

However, the code still contains an error which will crash the program part way through execution. The IDE didn't pick this up during its automatic error checking or flag it up in an error report because the code was syntactically and structurally correct. However, once the 'Sort' button is pressed, the program quickly halts as the IDE spots the error, highlights where it occurred and explains some possible solutions (Figure 20.35).

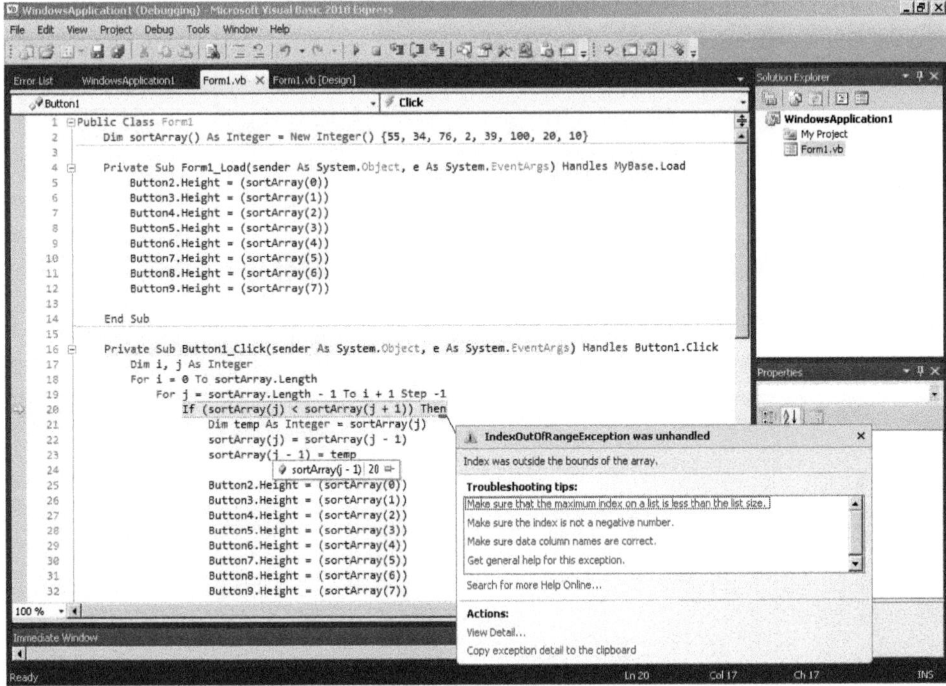

Figure 20.35: The IDE identifies the instruction that halted the execution and diagnoses the problem.

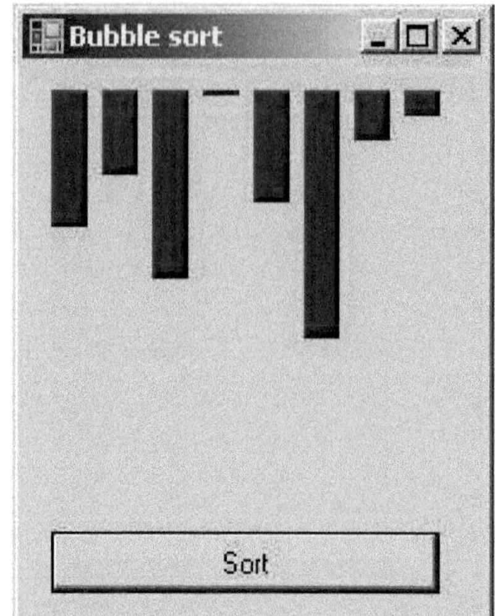

Figure 20.36: The program before the sort button is clicked.

Figure 20.37: The program after the sort button is clicked.

Fixing the problem that the IDE identified means the program can run through to completion without crashing.

Breakpoints

Breakpoints allow the programmer to pause the program at a specific point in its execution and look at the contents of variables to diagnose logic problems that are impossible for the IDE to diagnose.

For example, look at Figures 20.36 and 20.37. Figure 20.36 shows the bars before they are sorted; they are all different lengths. Figure 20.37 shows the bars after they are sorted and two in the middle are now the same length; something has obviously gone wrong.

The problem is occurring when the boxes are being sorted, so a breakpoint is placed on line 20 by clicking in the grey margin to the left of the instruction and selecting 'Breakpoint' (Figure 20.38). This will halt the execution there and help the programmer spot the problem, because when they hover the mouse cursor over any of the variables, they can see their current value (Figure 20.39).

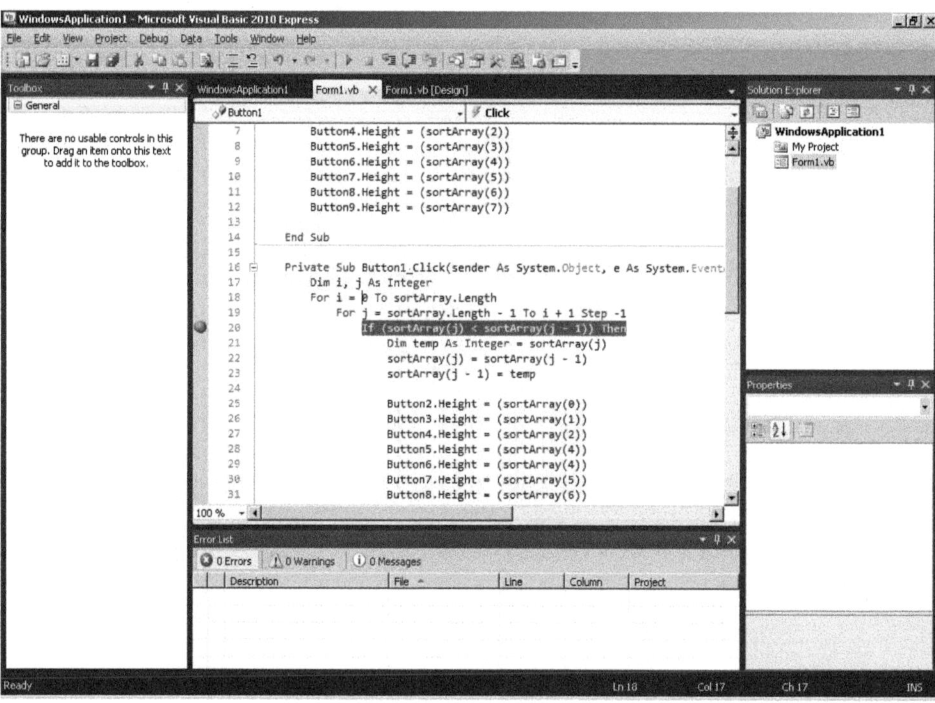

Figure 20.38: A breakpoint is placed on line 20.

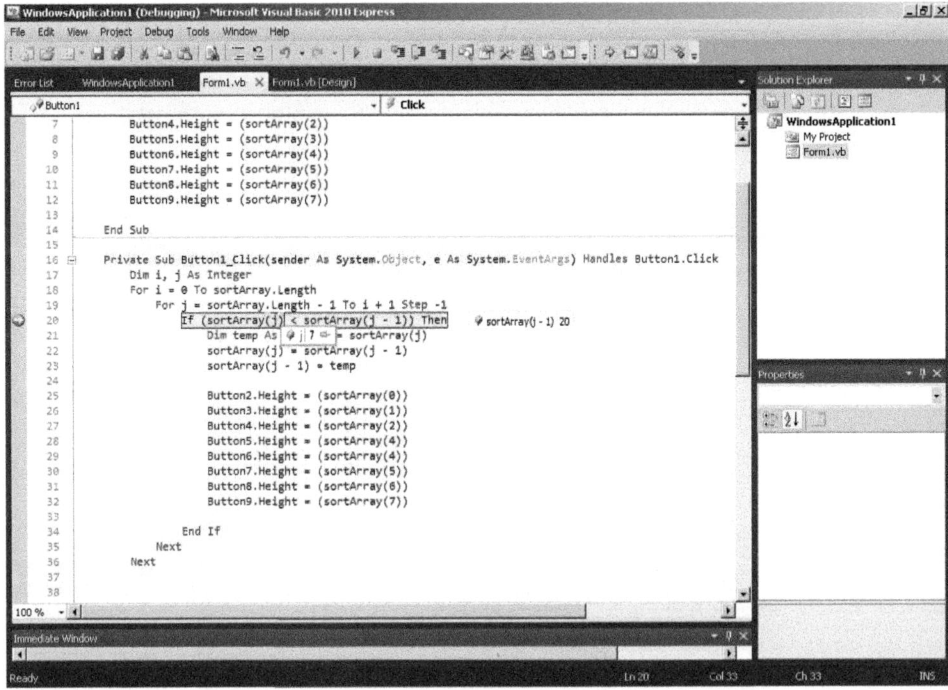

Figure 20.39: When the computer reaches a breakpoint, execution pauses, allowing a programmer to examine the contents of variables.

Unfortunately, everything looks normal, so the breakpoint hasn't helped find and fix the problem this time. The breakpoint can be repositioned later in the code and the code re-run until the problem is isolated, or we can go on to the next debugging technique.

Stepping through

Stepping through allows a programmer to place a breakpoint that pauses execution then click 'Step into' to execute the next instruction in the sequence, pausing before clicking 'Step into' again to repeat the process. It's the equivalent of having a breakpoint on every line in your program. In Figure 20.40 a breakpoint has been placed on line 28, so execution will pause when it reaches this point.

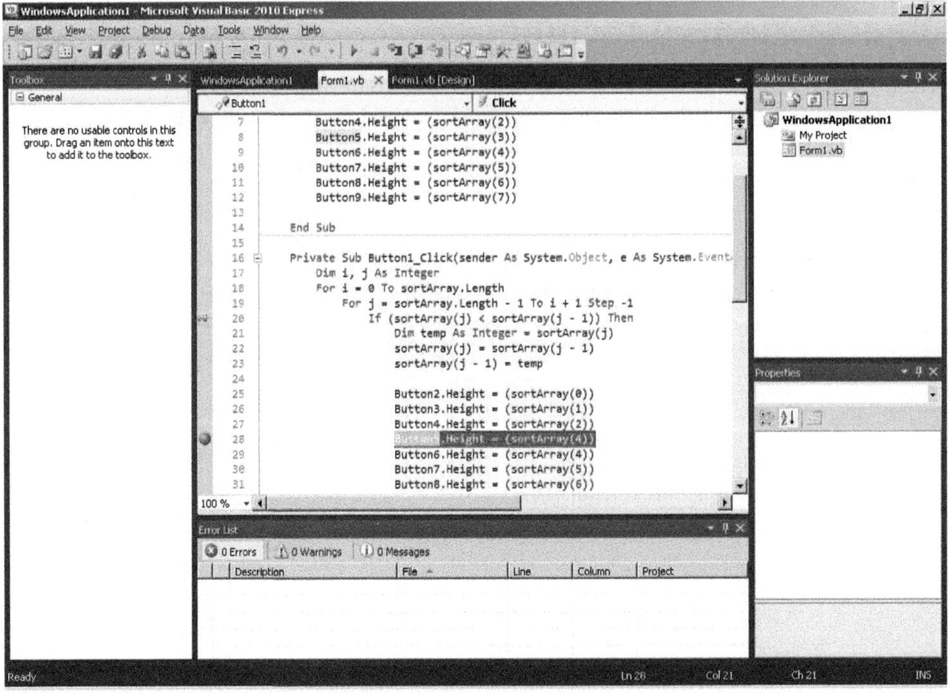

Figure 20.40: A breakpoint is placed on line 28.

Once execution has paused, the programmer can click 'Step into' (or press F8) to execute the next instruction, check the contents of variables and then 'Step into' the next instruction, as shown in Figure 20.41.

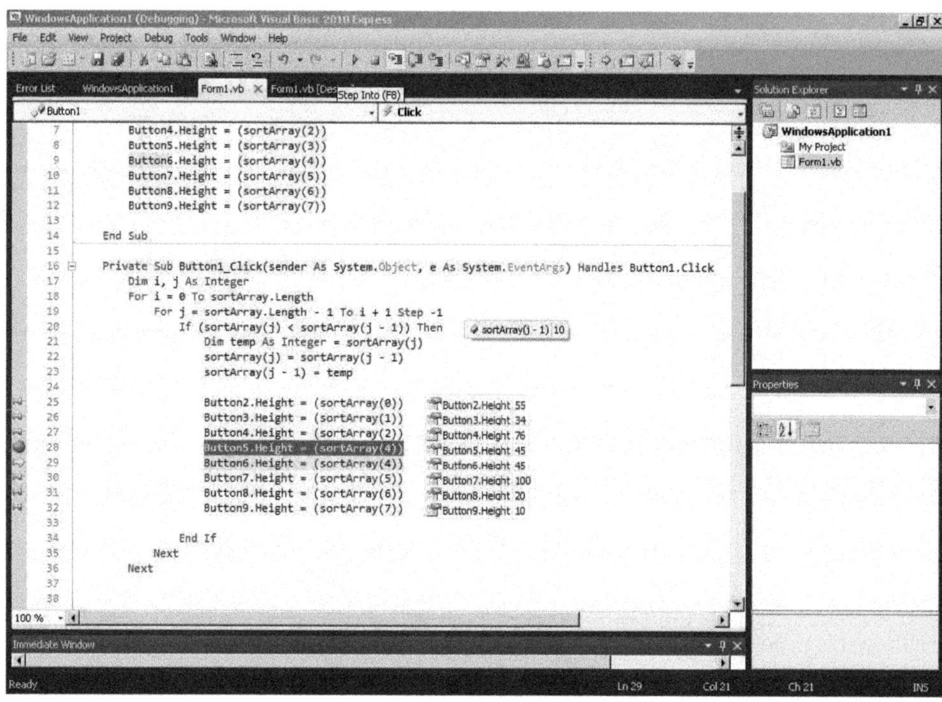

Figure 20.41: Stepping into the next instruction (yellow) helps to identify which variables are changing on each line.

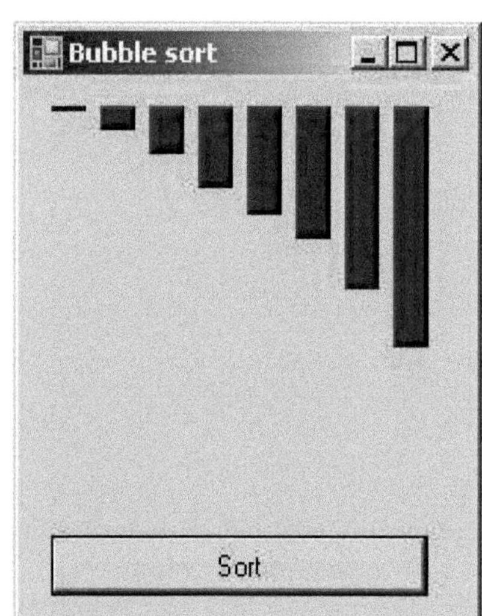

Figure 20.42: The bubble sort program produces the correct result.

Looking at the contents of the variables in Figure 20.37, we see that Button5 and Button6 both have the same height – we've found where the problem is. It's easily fixed by changing line 28 to read Button5.Height = (sortArray(3)), and now the program produces the correct output (Figure 20.42).

Object Oriented techniques

So far we have focused on the procedural programming paradigm. Many of the most popular programming languages such as Java, C++ and C#, use the Object Oriented Programming paradigm (OOP). In pure OO languages, every item that we use in a program is an object. The basic unit of any OO program is the class. A class defines all of the attributes that an object has and all of the operations that it supports. An object is an instance of a class. Even a very simple OO program must have one class and a main method. Below is an example of the classic Hello World program written in Java:

```
import java.util.Scanner;
import java.io.*;

public class First_Project {

    public static void main(String[] args) {
            System.out.println ("Hello World!");
            Scanner myScanner = new Scanner (System.in);

            System.out.println("Enter your name:");
            String name = myScanner.next();
            System.out.println("Hello" + name);
    }
}
```

This program has the added feature of allowing the user to enter their name to be added to the greeting. A public class or method can be accessed by any other class. The line: public static void main(String[] args)begins the main method. This may seem strange syntax but Java recognises this as the main method so knows that this is where execution should begin.

All of the basic constructs learnt so far for procedural languages can also be implemented in an OO one. Below is an example of Java's switchcase construct for handling multiple values for a decision:

```
public class switchcase {

        public static void main(String[] args) {
                                int grade = 3;
                switch(grade){
                case 1:
                        System.out.print("Well done!");
                        break;
                case 2:
                        System.out.print("Very good");
                        break;
                case 3:
                        System.out.print("OK");
                        break;
                case 4:
                        System.out.print("OK - ish");
                        break;
                case 5:
                        System.out.print("Try to do better");
                        break;
                }
        }
}
```

You may wish to modify this program to allow the user to enter in a fictional grade to receive the appropriate message.

Designing an OO program was discussed in Chapter 6. More complex OO programs make use of the core principles of inheritance, encapsulation and polymorphism. By understanding the hierarchy of classes and how methods and attributes are inherited, you will be able to write reusable code that inherits general points but also allows for specific features too. For example, in a game, the behaviour of sprite characters is generic. They will be able to run, jump, crouch and collect coins. However, we can create classes for a miner sprite who also has a method called dig, a diver sprite who supports a method called swim and a chef sprite who can toss pancakes while running. All of these sub classes would inherit the methods of the superclass sprite. As we have seen with procedural programming code, it is very important to design the program before you begin to code. This is especially true for OO programming, where inheritance can be used to reduce the number of lines that we need to write.

Once classes have been defined, we can create objects of it. A useful analogy is to visualise a class as a biscuit cutter and the objects as the biscuits that have been cut out. In an OO program, creating an instance of a class is called instantiation.

```
Scanner myScanner = new Scanner (System.in);
```

In this line, an instance of the class Scanner has been instantiated. Note the syntax and use of the keyword new.

A constructor assigns values to the attributes of an object. You can always spot a constructor in a program because it has the same name as the class.

```
public class Robot {

        int hitPoints;
        int initialSpeed;
        int initialStrength;

        Robot(initialSpeed, initialStrength){
                initialSpeed = speed;
                initialStrength = strength;
        }

Robot myRobot = new Robot(100, 50);

}
```

The constructor uses two values which are assigned when the object is instantiated. A robot object will have an initial speed and strength in this game. MyRobot specifically begins with the values 100 and 50.

Encapsulation only allows data to be accessed via methods. It is helpful to give methods names that identify their purpose. Traditionally, methods that manipulate data have names that start with get (to retrieve a value) and set (to set a value).

```
public void setDamage( int damage ){
                hitPoints = damage;
}
```

The above method sets the value of damage done in a battle.

If you wish to learn more techniques of Java programming, there are a number of excellent online tutorials including Oracle's extensive documentation.

Summary

- In this chapter you've learnt about some of the most fundamental programming constructs, including sequence, iteration and branching (selection). You've also seen how these can be implemented in Python using If statements and loops.
- You've learnt that global variables are accessible from anywhere in the code and that local variables are only available in the subroutine they were declared in.
- You've seen some of the advantages of modularity and learnt that a subroutine is a named block of code that performs a specific task. You've also learnt how to pass values to subroutines by value and by reference using parameters.
- Finally, you've seen some of the helpful tools provided by Integrated Development Environments (IDEs) including automatic error checks, breakpoints and stepping through.
- You've learnt that a recursive function is one that calls itself and the advantages and disadvantages of recursion compared to iteration.
- Object-oriented programming is widely used to develop programs and apps. OO programs are based around classes. Objects of a class are instantiated and assigned values via a constructor. Programs may consist of several related classes that inherit attributes and operations from the superclass.

Activity 20.1

Create a simple game in which a player must enter every letter of the alphabet in the correct order. The program should time how long it takes the player and give them a time at the end.

Activity 20.2

Create a simple game in which a player is shown a series of random words to type and the computer counts how many they can type in 30 seconds.

End-of-chapter questions

A **1** Describe what is meant by a 'recursive function'. [2]

A **2** Name **two** constructs other than recursion and iteration often found in programming languages. [2]

3 Describe what the term 'iteration' means. [2]

A **4** What is the main disadvantage of recursion compared to iteration? [2]

5 Explain the difference between a local and a global variable. [2]

Further reading

Bill Gates and OS development – http://www.computerhistory.org/atchm/microsoft-ms-dos-early-source-code/
Code Academy – https://www.codecademy.com/
Learn Python – search on the Code Academy website.
Java IDE – search on netbeans.org.
Notepad++ IDE – search for Notepad++.
Oracle – https://docs.oracle.com/javase/tutorial/java/javaOO/index.htm
Visual Studio IDE – search for Visual Studio from Microsoft.

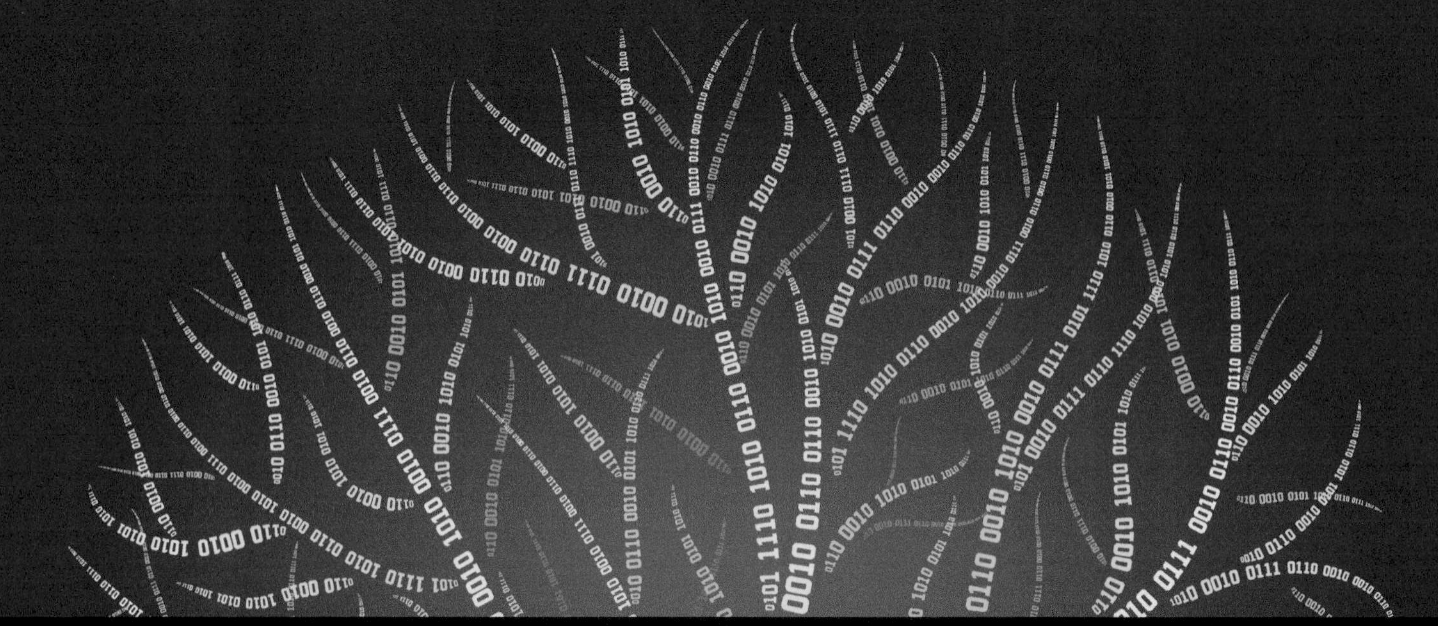

Chapter 21
Computational methods

A This chapter contains A Level content only

Specification points

2.2.2 Computational methods (A Level)

- Features that make a problem solvable by computational methods.
- Problem recognition.
- Problem decomposition.
- Use of divide and conquer.
- Use of abstraction.
- Learners should apply their knowledge of
  - backtracking
  - data mining
  - heuristics
  - performance modelling
  - pipelining
  - visualisation to solve problems.

Learning objectives

- To recognise the features that make a problem solvable by computational methods.
- To understand problem recognition.
- To understand problem decomposition.
- To understand the use of divide and conquer.
- To understand the use of abstraction.

- To apply your knowledge of the following to solve problems:
  - backtracking
  - data mining
  - heuristics
  - performance modelling
  - pipelining
  - visualisation.

Introduction

This chapter will further explore the computational methods you will have already been introduced to in your A/AS Level studies. Decidability and problem recognition will be covered, as well as why some problems are impossible to solve. In this chapter, you will also revisit ideas that you have come across already and develop a practical understanding of how they can be used to create algorithms.

In order to fully appreciate this chapter, you should attempt the activities and read over the exam questions in practise examination papers for Component 02 paper Programming and Algorithms. You must be able not only to understand the terms used in the chapter, but also to apply them under exam conditions.

Features that make a problem solvable by computational methods

Decidability

In order to understand what the features of a solvable problem look like, we must first define what we mean by a solution. To aid the discussion we will restrict the problems we are going to consider to decision problems. A decision problem is a logical problem which, for a given input, will return either true or false. A solvable decision problem can be formally specified by the following statement:

A problem belongs to the set of decidable problems if there exists a computable function f such that $f(x) = true$ if $x \in S$ and $f(x) = false$ if $x \notin S$.

For any given decision problem, we can say that a computational solution exists if the following axioms hold true:

- The output belongs to a set of natural numbers S.
- The algorithm will stop after a finite time.
- For any given input, we will arrive at an output which belongs to the set S.
- There exists a function (algorithm) which will take the input and produce the output.

As we know, binary can be used to encode many different types of data, from strings to images. Therefore, restricting ourselves to natural numbers is not an issue, as an encoding mechanism to represent different types of data can easily be found. Of course, algorithms in the real world do not use only natural numbers, but restricting the input domain helps to aid our understanding of what 'computable' means.

Computable functions are more generalised algorithms which are not restricted to a specific computational model such as a Turing machine. In the definition of a computable function, a sequence of mechanical steps must be followed, with an exponential amount of time and space available for the function to complete. This does not mean that an infinite amount of time and space is needed; rather that the function must have enough time and space available to reach its end point. There is, however, necessarily an upper bound on the amount of space a function can use for a given input. A problem is computable, therefore, regardless of the time complexity of that problem. Just because the time complexity of a computable function is exponential does not mean it is not computable.

Decision problems for which it is impossible to construct a computable function that will give a solution are called 'undecidable problems'. 'Partially decidable' problems are those where, if the solution is true, the function will stop. However, if the solution is false, then the function will run forever. These problems are themselves considered undecidable due to the fact they may, given some inputs, break the original axiom of a decidable problem that a solution will be computed in a finite amount of time. The **halting problem** is an example of an undecidable problem.

Consider a program, P, which is run to see if, at some point, it will stop and return an answer. If it does we say that it has the halting property. Imagine that we could write another program, H, which, when passed through the source code of P, would output if P had the halting property or not. Computing if a program has the halting property is known as the halting problem.

Computing in context: The Church–Turing thesis

In 1928, the German mathematician David Hilbert posed a challenge known as the *Entscheidungsproblem* which, when translated, means 'decision problem'. Given a problem defined in formal mathematics, the challenge is to create an algorithm that will answer 'true' or 'false' depending on the statements made. Essentially, David Hilbert was asking for an algorithm able to determine the truth of mathematical statements through the manipulation of symbols.

In 1936, both Alan Turing and Alonzo Church independently published papers showing that the problem was impossible to solve. Each of these mathematicians developed different computational models to allow them to represent computable functions. Turing developed the Turing machine, while Church came up with the lambda calculus (λ-calculus). Turing later determined that the two computational methods were in fact equivalent, which gave rise to the theory that all programming languages are no more expressive than a universal Turing machine.

The Church–Turing thesis states that a function is computable if, and only if, it can be computed by a Turing machine. Some problems are not computable by a Turing machine, for example the halting problem, which therefore means that problems exist that cannot be solved using algorithms. As the λ-calculus can be shown to be equivalent to a Turing machine, as are all programming languages, this has far-reaching implications for computer scientists.

Problem recognition

Features of computable functions

Solvable problems are computable, so it is possible to formalise their characteristics. A problem is deemed to be undecidable if the algorithm designed to solve it does not meet one or more of the following characteristics:

- The algorithm must be finite in length.
- Instructions must be precise and based on a formal language.
- The algorithm will be given a set of values as input and, after a finite number of discrete steps, will produce an output.

- For any given input the correct output will always be returned.
- The algorithm must work regardless of the size of the input.
- The algorithm must halt at some point and produce correct output.
- There is no limit to the amount of space (memory) needed when calculating a solution.

Some problems may not be solvable in all cases, but only for a restricted input. By restricting the input, it can effectively be handled on a case-by-case basis. This form of solution takes its input from a recursively enumerable set. That is, it will produce a correct output if, and only if, the input is taken from a recursively enumerable set which can be ordered and a positive integer number assigned to each member. This restriction provides very specific circumstances in which problems such as the halting problem can be solved. Formally, we can define a recursively enumerable set problem as:

$$f(x) = \begin{cases} 0 & if\, x \in S \\ undefined\ or\ does\ not\ halt & if\, x \notin S \end{cases}$$

When developing real algorithms, it is important to ascertain if a problem is solvable or not. If it is not solvable, can it be solved for the input you want to use and therefore take its input from a recursively enumerable set?

Problem	Explanation
Entscheidungsproblem	Given a list of mathematical terms, find out whether or not a solution exists.
Halting	Given a program, decide if it will halt or generate an infinite loop.
Checking if a context-free grammar is ambiguous	For a given context-free grammar, ensure that it generates the required set of valid strings.
Kolmogorov complexity of strings	For any given string, find a minimal way of representing it which is no more than a few bytes larger than the original string.

Table 21.1: Examples of undecidable problems.

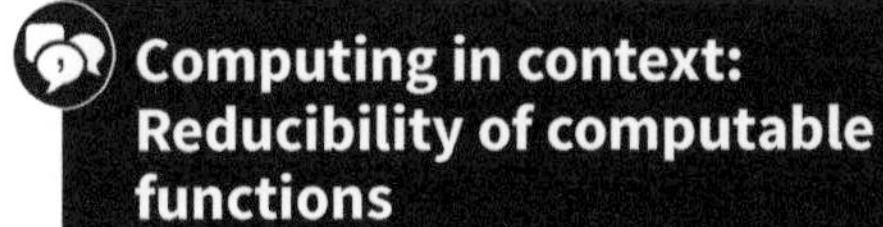

Computing in context: Reducibility of computable functions

A large number of problems are undecidable. To date, no computable function exists that can solve them completely. However, as looked at in the previous section, a partial solution may be found for a restricted domain. Some examples of undecidable problems include those listed in Table 21.1.

It is possible to reduce one problem to another through mathematical manipulation. Given two problems, A and B, if A can be reduced to B then any solution found for problem B could be used to solve problem A. Furthermore, solving A can be no harder than solving B. Conversely, if problem B was undecidable and problem A can be reduced to it, then problem A is also undecidable.

Reducing an algorithm to another is itself an algorithm. So, if an algorithm can convert problem A to problem B, then we say that A is reducible to B. In order to see how this works, let's look at a problem which, on the face of things, seems solvable.

Problem

Given any program, determine whether it will halt if the input value is blank (also known as the blank tape problem).

Imagine that a program that you have written has a validation rule which quits the code if the user enters nothing as input. Maybe it gives an error message saying 'please provide input'. Is it possible, given any program of this nature, to write an algorithm that can check if it will stop given no values? This problem can be represented in Figure 21.1.

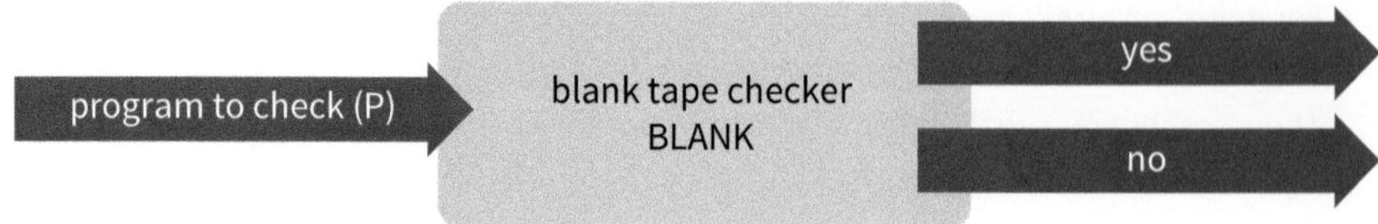

Figure 21.1: Diagrammatic representation of the blank tape problem.

Proof

Imagine that there exists a program that can determine if a program will halt given a blank input. In order to find out whether this problem is decidable, we need a way of reducing this down to the halting problem. If no way can be found to reduce it to the halting problem, or to any other undecidable problem, then a solution may exist. The halting problem requires two inputs: the program to be checked and the input we plan to put into that program. It is important to remember that some programs may only get into an infinite loop when faced with certain inputs.

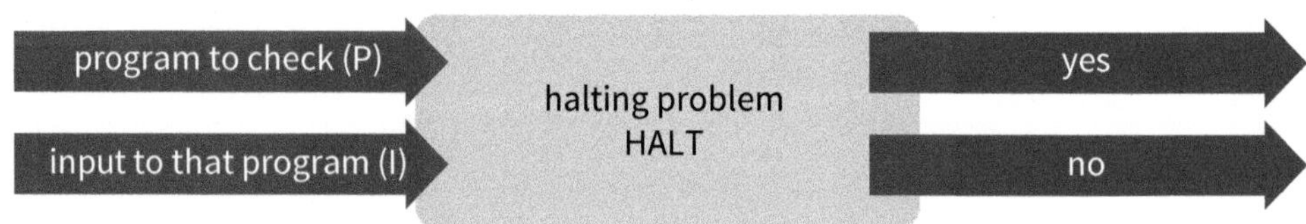

Figure 21.2: Diagrammatic representation of the halting problem.

In order to create an algorithm to reduce the blank tape problem to the halting problem, we need to create a new program using the program P and the input I. As it turns out, the reduction is actually very simple, and is shown below.

- If input is blank -> HALT
- If input is not blank -> run rest of the program using the input.

Imagine this in Python code where the program is being represented as a new function and passed as a parameter.

Code

```
def reduction(P,I,B = "blank"):
  if B!= "blank":
    quit()
  else:
    P(i)
```

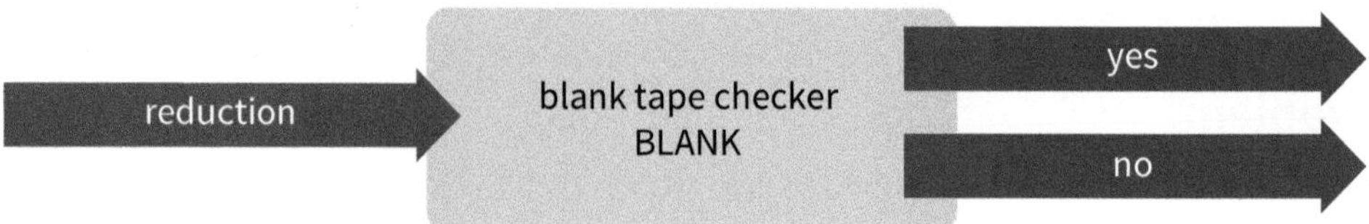

Figure 21.3: Blank tape reduction.

This new program 'reduction' is now passed to the blank tape checker, which will determine if it halts. However, as 'reduction' always starts out with a blank input and then runs a second function, we have essentially created a way of allowing the blank tape checker to test any arbitrary program and input. Our 'reduction' program essentially works the same way as the halting problem. As the halting problem is undecidable, we are left with a contradiction. Therefore, we can conclude that the blank tape checker problem is also undecidable.

Solving problems using decomposition, abstraction and divide and conquer

Using decomposition and abstraction

When dealing with a problem, the first step is to recognise what the computable parts of the problem are. This may involve conducting an initial decomposition of the problem and may even require some abstraction. Consider the problem of the game 'Snake', in which the player controls a snake which is always moving. As the snake eats dots on the screen, the player's score and the size of the snake increase. The game is lost when the snake collides with itself or any other obstacle.

On an initial decomposition of this problem we get the key ideas expressed in Figure 21.4.

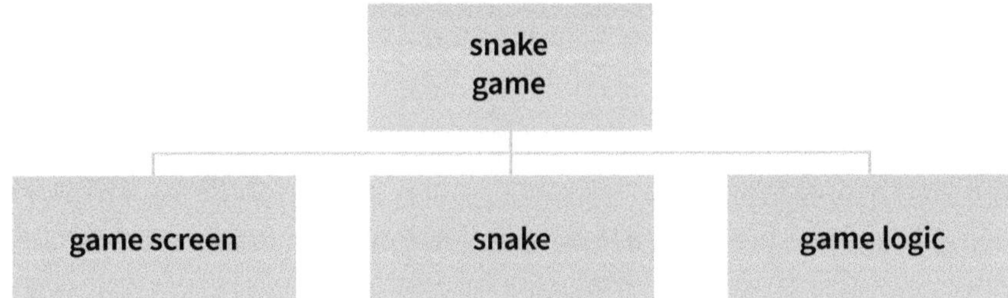

Figure 21.4: Example decomposition of a Snake game.

Each component can then be considered separately and an abstraction created. Consider the decomposition of the game screen. A game grid can be represented using a two-dimensional (2D) array to store the positions of the snake and the dots. This is an abstraction – a method of representing a visible interface as a data structure (Figure 21.5).

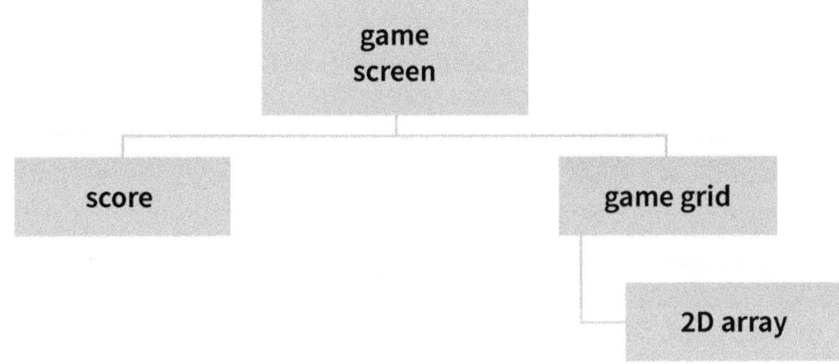

Figure 21.5: Further decomposition of Snake.

Going into more detail on the game grid, we could use numbers to represent the different elements found in the game as exemplified below:

- 0 – nothing
- 1 – dot (shown in green)
- 2 – snake (shown in grey).

0	1	2	3	4	5	6	7	8	9
1	0	0	0	0	0	0	0	0	0
2	0	0	0	0	0	0	0	1	0
3	0	0	0	0	0	0	0	0	0
4	0	0	0	0	0	0	2	0	0
5	0	0	0	0	0	0	2	0	0
6	0	0	0	0	0	2	2	0	0
7	0	0	0	0	2	2	0	0	0
8	0	0	0	0	0	0	0	0	0
9	0	0	0	0	0	0	0	0	0

Figure 21.6: 2D array representation of the snake screen.

The snake does not have to be a straight line, but should be able to weave around based on user input. Therefore it is important to consider how to abstract this behaviour, as well as a suitable data structure to use. An array is not suitable, as the snake needs to be able to grow, but a queue data structure could be an ideal abstraction. Queues work by adding data elements onto the end, which is exactly how the snake will work. Every time it eats a dot, the tail gets a bit bigger. If each square is abstracted to a grid coordinate, then we have a way of representing the snake. Figure 21.7 provides an example of the data we could store.

(7,4)	(7,5)	(7,6)	(6,6)	(6,7)	(5,7)

Figure 21.7: Linked list representation of the snake.

However, each time the snake moves, its appearance on screen is changed by adding the new position at the front and removing the last item. A queue does not allow this, therefore a more generic list structure must be used. When using computational methods, it is important to consider all aspects of the problem before finalising a solution. By taking an object-oriented approach to the snake we can define its methods and attributes.

Code

```
CLASS Snake INHERITS List
  public moveSnake(dx,dy)
  public growSnake()
  private getHead() # returns x,y
  private addHead(x,y)
  private removeTail()
  private addToTail()
```

Example algorithm for moving the snake:

Code

```
moveSnake(dx,dy)
  x,y = this.getHead()
  = x+dx
  = y+dy
  this.addHead(x,y)
  removeTail()
```

Using divide and conquer

In the previous section we looked at how abstraction and decomposition can be used to solve a problem. However, the algorithms required to develop the solution were too simple to require the use of divide and conquer. You have already seen many examples of divide and conquer, such as binary search and quick sort.

Divide and conquer is one of the simplest and most efficient ways to solve problems. Given any problem you attempt to split it into smaller, but similar, problems. This is then repeated until the problem becomes trivial to solve. At that point you can build up the answer by solving all of the smaller parts and combining the results. For example, binary search will split the problem by half every time (divide) until it finds the value or it fails to find the value (conquer).

This section focuses on spotting when it is necessary to use divide and conquer, using several examples.

Battleships

Consider a game of battleships against the computer. In a battleships game, a strategy must be employed rather than random placement of ships and random shots, assuming the computer does not cheat and look at your board. A battleships game grid is abstracted in Figures 21.8–21.10, showing a ship as 'B', a hit as 'X' and a miss as 'M'.

	0	1	2	3	4	5	6	7	8	9
0							B	B	B	
1		B								
2		B								B
3										B
4			B	B	B					B
5										B
6										
7										
8			B	B	B	B	B			
9										

Figure 21.8: 2D representation of battleships.

Activity 21.1

Design and create an algorithm that will decide if a snake has collided with itself. Once you have done this, try to implement a simple version of the snake game in a language of your choice.

On your first shot, you will either hit or miss. If you hit, then you know that an adjacent square must contain a ship. If you miss, you have no further knowledge to work with other than that you need to keep looking. However, assuming that the person or computer you are playing against is trying to outfox you, it is entirely possible that they have spread their ships around the board. This means a good strategy will be to spread shots around and take a methodical approach to the search. Also, by always trying different rows and columns, there is a higher chance of making a hit.

This problem can be made easier using divide and conquer. If we split the board into four quadrants, we reduce the search area, as shown in Figure 21.9. We can then split the problem down further by breaking the board down into four again, as shown in blue.

	0	1	2	3	4	5	6	7	8	9
0							B	B	B	
1		B								
2		B								B
3										B
4			B	B	B					B

Figure 21.9: Dividing the problem space.

As part of a strategy to win, we can implement the following search pattern.

- Pick the centre square, if not marked as hit or miss.
- If a miss, then try the four corners in a random order.
- If a hit, then try the squares immediately to the left, right, up and down (at random) until the next square of the battleship is uncovered. This will narrow it down to vertical and horizontal.
- Try either end until a miss is encountered or the length of the longest ship left to uncover is reached.

Once a search quadrant is exhausted, the algorithm should try the next search grid until either the computer or the human wins. The grid in Figure 21.10 shows the result of the algorithm running on the first quadrant.

	0	1	2	3	4	5	6	7	8	9
0	M	M	M				B	B	B	
1		X								
2	M	X	M							B
3		M								B
4			B	B	B					B
5										B
6										
7										
8			B	B	B	B	B			
9										

Figure 21.10: Sample run of the battleship algorithm.

If a further element of randomness is introduced, such that quadrants are visited in a random order, we eliminate the predictability of the winning strategy. This may not be the best strategy to use, but it is an example of how divide and conquer can be used as a computational method. The problem has been split down into smaller problems, with each problem having the same task to perform: find all of the battleships in that area.

Divide and conquer breaks a task down into smaller, similar tasks. Each smaller task has the exact same objectives but will be working on progressively smaller parts of the problem. It must not be confused with decomposition. Although decomposition similarly breaks a problem down into smaller parts, each part is different; with divide and conquer, each part can be solved using the same algorithm.

Divide and conquer when used with concurrency

Divide and conquer is particularly powerful when combined with concurrency. Consider a simple problem to sum the numbers in an array. Imagine that this array was large, of a magnitude of billions of values, meaning that anything that can be done to speed up the process would be welcome. Consider the linear solution below (as opposed to a divide-and-conquer solution), which has a time efficiency in Big O notation of $O(n)$.

Code

```
FUNCTION sumArray(A)
  total = 0
  FOR X = 0 to LENGTH(A)
    total = total + A[X]
  NEXT
  RETURN total
END FUNCTION
```

Now consider a situation in which there are multiple processors to enable concurrency. The above algorithm is designed to work on a single processor, so cannot take advantage of parallelism. Using divide and conquer, this task can easily be broken into smaller sub-tasks, as shown in Figure 21.11. The definition for the function is now sumArray(array, start, end).

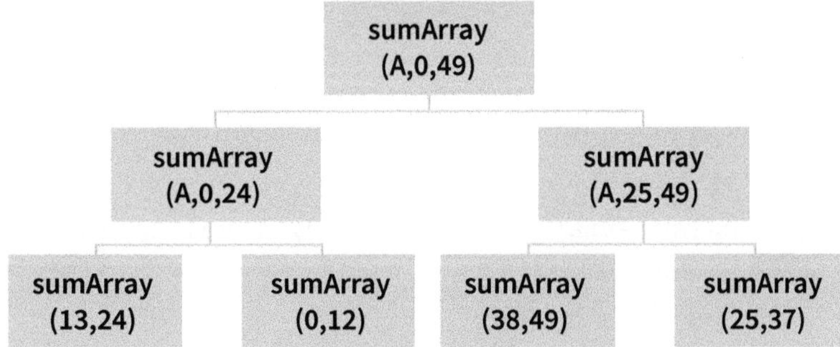

Figure 21.11: Adding up an array using divide and conquer.

The problem can be subdivided until we get to a situation where we either have end – start <= 1 or we have subdivided enough so that each processor has work to do. To calculate how many times to recurse for the latter situation, the equation $r = \log2$ P can be used, where P is the number of processors and r is the number of times the array should be split. It may be desirable to limit recursion, or the number of times we divide the problem, as, if we had 1 billion data items, we would need 30 levels of recursion, which would require 30 processors to do it all concurrently. If we only had eight processors then adding additional complexity of load-balancing processors, performing the split, adding a recursive call to the stack and finally performing a join could be counterproductive. The next stage is to create a new function called 'concurrentSumArray' which will, using divide and conquer, sum the values in an array.

In order to start designing an algorithm for concurrentSumArray we should consider the divide-and-conquer strategy known as 'fork/join'. This is a classic parallel approach to implement divide and conquer. The idea behind fork/join is very simple. When a task needs to be split across multiple processors a fork occurs, creating sub-tasks. Once all of these sub-tasks are complete the results are then joined together producing the final answer.

Let us consider the pseudocode for concurrentSumArray. To show that each recursive call of sumArray() will run on a different processor, a FORK object is created. You can assume that the FORK class handles the complexity of selecting a processor and executing the function on that processor. You can also assume that the return command will not run until each fork is completed and that the FORK.sleep() command frees up the current processor so it can be used to run further code.

Code

```
FUNCTION concurrentSumArray(A)
  P = number of processors
  R = log2P # decide on the number of levels
  Return sumArray(A,0, LENGTH(A), 1,R)
END FUNCTION
FUNCTION sumArray(A,start, end, level, maxLevel)
  # are we at the max recursion level?
  IF level == maxLevel OR end - start <= 1 THEN
    T = 0
    FOR X = start TO end
      T = T + A[X]
    NEXT
  RETURN T
ELSE
  # perform a fork - Tasks sent to different processors
    MID = ((end - start)/2) + start
  F1 = new FORK(sumArray(A, start, mid, level+1, maxLevel))
  F2 = new FORK(sumArray(A, mid+1, end, level+1, maxLevel))
    T1 = executeFork(F1)
    T2 = executeFork(F2)
    # suspend this code until all forks are completed
    FORK.sleep()
    # now join
    RETURN T1 + T2
  END IF
END FUNCTION
```

Divide and conquer is a very powerful technique for creating efficient algorithms. When combined with the fork/join method it can also allow problems to be solved concurrently.

Common computational techniques

You should be familiar with the techniques listed below. Although they bear little relation to one another, these are important computational techniques and you are likely to come across them in the future. Many of these techniques could be the subject of books in their own right, so the following should be used as an overview, not an exhaustive list. You could carry out your own research into one or more of these techniques.

Backtracking

Backtracking is a term used when programming in a declarative language (see Chapter 20). It refers to a situation in which a correct solution to a goal has been identified. The user must backtrack to find an alternative correct solution.

Look at the example code below:

Code

```
FACT: mouse(Micky)
FACT: mouse(Minnie)
FACT: mouse(Jerry)
FACT: cat(Tom)
RULE: Chases(A,B) IF cat(A) AND mouse(B)
RULE: Eats(A,B) IF cat(A) AND mouse(B)
RULE: Prey(A,B) IF Chases(B,A) OR Eats(B,A)
```

The goal Prey(Jerry,Tom)? returns True because Chases(Tom,Jerry) returns True. This answer is correct, but it is not the only solution. The same goal is also True because Eats(Tom,Jerry) is True. Given the original answer, this alternative solution can be identified by backtracking.

Confusingly, backtracking is also the name given to a slightly different technique, which is used for more complex problems.

Look at this example program:

Code

```
FACT: mouse(Micky)
FACT: mouse(Minnie)
FACT: mouse(Jerry)
FACT: cat(Tom)
FACT: dog(Buster)
RULE: Chases(A,B) (IF cat(A) AND mouse(B)) OR (IF dog(A)
AND cat(B))
RULE: Eats(A,B) IF cat(A) AND mouse(B)
RULE: Prey(A,B) IF Chases(B,A) OR Eats(B,A)
RULE: Enemy(A,B) IF Eats(A,B) OR Chases(A,B)
```

If we want to evaluate the goal Enemy(Buster,Tom). First we evaluate Eats(Buster,Tom) but we find that cat(Buster) returns False. So our goal has failed at the first hurdle. Rather than quitting, we backtrack to the most recent correct assumption and try an alternative route; for example, Chases(Buster,Tom). Here we find that dog(Buster) returns True as does cat(Tom). This enables us to see that Chases(Buster,Tom) is True so Enemy(Buster,Tom) is also True. In this instance, backtracking refers to the process of encountering the wrong answer and going back to the most recent correct answer to select another option.

Data mining

Computers have enabled corporations and governments to collect vast amounts of data. However, out of context or without a proper understanding of their relationship with other pieces of data, it can often be meaningless. Data mining is the process of finding new patterns in large data sets. Simply put, it is the process of identifying the relationships between different sets of data and setting it in the correct context. It is commonly used in conjunction with modelling to make predictions about the impact of new initiatives based on historical data.

For example, if a supermarket wants to increase the amount of profit it makes from selling milk, it could use the vast amount of data it has on different milk brands, prices, amounts and sales to look for patterns in consumer spending. If it finds that milk sales increase significantly when the price is 5p below that of its competitors, it is likely that setting the price at that level for the next month will increase its profits. It is exactly this kind of data mining that has led to the supermarket price wars over commodities like milk, bread and beans in the last few years.

Another common use of data mining is fraud detection. Credit card companies have to reimburse their customers if their card details are used fraudulently; this costs the banks a lot of money (an estimated $190 billion per year in the US alone). As a result, the banks have turned to data mining to try to solve the problem by spotting suspicious transactions and stopping them at source. The algorithms used are complex, but, essentially, if all your previous transactions have taken place in London and 98% of them are for items costing less than £100, a sudden one-off payment of £2,000 for a new TV in New York is likely to be flagged as a fraudulent payment (someone using your credit card details without your permission). By mining your purchase history, your bank has been able to spot new transactions that don't match the trend and stop them. Of course, this method isn't perfect and many people use their credit cards legitimately on holiday, only to find that their bank has cancelled the card!

Data mining requires fairly advanced technology. A large amount of storage is required to hold all the data, as well as a number of high-specification processors to search all the data as quickly as possible. Finally, complex algorithms are required to ensure that the patterns identified are reliable and represent useful information.

Heuristics

In computer science, heuristics refers to a problem-solving technique that is used when other (more traditional) problem-solving methods (like those in Chapters 15–19) are too slow. The main aim of a heuristic is to solve a given problem successfully in the least time possible. A heuristic solution will not normally be the most elegant or the most efficient solution to the problem, but it will be the quickest. A heuristic solution is also likely to present just one of many possible solutions to a given problem. A good example of this is the 'travelling salesman' problem.

The travelling salesman problem (TSP) asks a simple question:

Given a list of cities and the distances between them, what is the shortest possible route that visits each city only once and returns to the starting point?

This problem is of great interest in a number of applications, not least route planning in modern-day satellite navigation systems. The problem is simple to describe, but to date no general solution has been found (the problem is rated as non-deterministic [NP hard] in terms of computational complexity, so it is unlikely that a general solution will ever be found). However, there are heuristic algorithms that can provide adequate solutions in situations involving large data sets (millions of cities) and can do so in a reasonable time frame. These solutions are not the most efficient, but they are used because they consistently produce answers that are good enough for practical purposes. You can read more about this fascinating problem in the 'Further reading' section at the end of this chapter.

Another example of heuristics in use that you will almost certainly have come across is in virus scanners. Virus scanners work by matching a database of known viruses to files and flagging those files that match a known virus. The trouble is that new viruses are released all the time, so these virus databases need constant updates. However, many new viruses are in fact adapted versions of existing ones. This is where heuristics comes in. Heuristic algorithms can look at the structure of new files and see how closely they resemble known viruses. If the new file is a 90% match for a known virus then we can say with reasonable accuracy that the file is a virus. This heuristic approach is also responsible for false warnings from virus scanners.

Heuristic algorithms can also be used to analyse the behaviour of viruses. If a program is acting in a way that matches the behaviour of a known virus (even if it has a totally different structure), a heuristic algorithm may be able to spot this behaviour and contain the program responsible.

Performance modelling

Performance modelling is the title given to a group of techniques used to model and improve the performance of computer systems (commonly networks). These systems could be existing systems or simply designs for future systems. The focus of performance modelling is on achieving the best possible balance between system performance, cost and expected workload. Performance modelling is a vast subject and the tools and techniques used vary significantly, depending on the context.

As a general guide, performance modelling could include the following:

- Measurement: changing a facet of an existing system and measuring the resulting change in performance.
- Simulation: constructing a full computer simulation of a system and then measuring the impact of changing variables on system performance.
- Queuing theory: since computer systems work by executing sequences of instructions, any process that speeds up the execution of jobs stored in queues is likely to lead to an improvement in the performance of a computer system.

The main aim of performance modelling is to improve the performance of a system. It is most useful in large, complex systems where the potential gains are likely to be significant. You can find some simple examples of performance modelling in the 'Further reading' section at the end of this chapter.

Pipelining

Pipelining is a technique used in modern processors where the processor begins to execute the next instruction before the current instruction has been completed. A number of instructions are therefore 'in the pipeline' simultaneously, though they will probably all be at different stages of execution.

Pipelining does not reduce the time taken to execute individual instructions, but it does increase the number of instructions that can be executed in a given time frame.

A common analogy for pipelining is the process of building a car. Consider an assembly line in which all the workers stand in a row, each assigned their specific job. The first worker builds the chassis, the second adds the wheels, the third inserts the engine, and so on until the completed car rolls off the end of the production line. Without pipelining, the first worker would build the chassis then stand idle until the car was completely finished. Then he would build the chassis of the next car, pass it on and repeat the process. If it takes one day to produce a car the first worker would finish his job early in the morning and then wait until the following day before he did anything else. With the introduction of pipelining, however, once he has built the first chassis he passes it on to the next worker and immediately begins work on the next chassis. Each car still takes one day to make, but far more cars are produced each week.

Pipelining has exactly the same impact on the fetch–decode–execute cycle in a computer as it does on a car assembly line. All the instructions take the same length of time to complete but more instructions are executed.

Pipelining is a fascinating and complex operation. At A Level you only need to know what it is, but you can find out much more by looking at the resources in the 'Further reading' section at the end of this chapter. You can also find out more by reading the section on pipelining in Chapter 1.

Using visualisation to solve problems

Nearly everyone relies on some form of visualisation to solve problems. This can be in the form of diagrams or drawings, or as a mental image. For example, when asked a simple maths question such as: 'I have five oranges; how many oranges will I have left if I take away two oranges?' most children will create a mental image of five oranges, remove two and count the remainder. When children are very young, teachers will often assist them in visualising the problem by using pictures or actual oranges. As we become better at solving a particular problem, our reliance on visualisation lessens and the calculations become instinctive. However, when we encounter new, more difficult problems we often fall back on visualisation to help us solve them. This is why more abstract problems (which are more difficult to visualise) are generally harder to solve.

Visualising a problem can help us to model possible solutions by planning ahead. Look at the following simple problem.

> A man has to carry a fox, a chicken and a sack of corn across a river. He has a boat, but it only has space for him and for one other thing. If the fox and the chicken are left together, the fox will eat the chicken. If the chicken and the corn are left together, the chicken will eat the corn. How can he get everything across the river?

Trying to solve the problem by holding all the pertinent information in your head is difficult. Try to solve it by cutting out pieces to represent the different objects and you can quickly experiment with different options until the correct solution is identified.

Summary

In this chapter you've learnt that problems are only computable if they have an upper bound for both space and time complexity.

You've also seen how to recognise the key features of a computable problem, including:

- The algorithm must be finite in length.
- Instructions must be precise and based on a formal language.
- The algorithm will be given a set of values as input and, after a finite number of discrete steps, will produce an output.
- For any given input the correct output will always be returned.
- The algorithm must work regardless of the size of the input.
- The algorithm must halt at some point and produce correct output.
- There is no limit to the amount of space (memory) needed when calculating a solution.
- Decomposition is the process of splitting a problem up into smaller sub-problems which, in turn, can also be decomposed.
- Decomposition is used to make potentially difficult problems much simpler to solve.
- Divide and conquer is a classic computer science approach to solving difficult problems. Problems are split into smaller problems until they become trivial to solve.
- Backtracking refers to a situation in which a correct solution to a goal has been identified but a user can backtrack to find an alternative correct solution.
- Data mining is the process of finding new patterns in large data sets.
- The main aim of a heuristic algorithm is to solve a given problem successfully in the least time possible. This will not normally be the most elegant or the most efficient solution to the problem.
- Performance modelling is all about achieving the best possible balance between system performance, cost and expected workload.
- Pipelining is a technique used in modern processors where the processor begins to execute the next instruction before the current instruction has been completed. A number of instructions are therefore 'in the pipeline' simultaneously.
- Visualisation is the use of physical or mental images to solve problems. These can be in the form of diagrams, drawings or just in the mind.

End-of-chapter questions

1 Discuss what computing methods can be employed when trying to create an app which will perform route finding over Manhattan's tube network. [8]

2 Quick sort is an example of an algorithm that uses divide and conquer. Describe how the quick sort algorithm can be made concurrent. [6]

3 The tube map below shows part of the tube network.

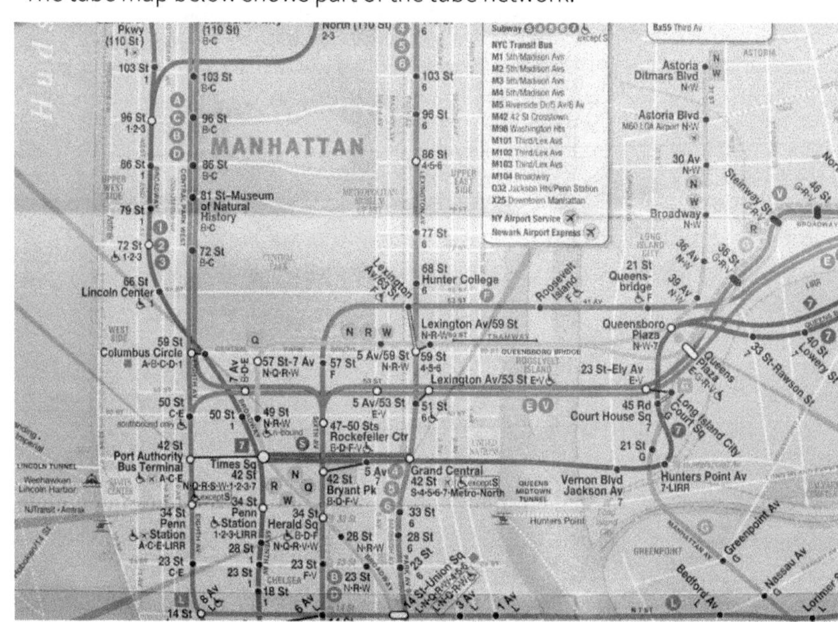

a What reusable components could be created from this map? [3]

b The map can be represented as a graph data structure. Create an algorithm which, given a station, will find the closest station with disabled access. [8]

Further reading

List of undecidable problems – search on the University of Texas at San Antonio's Department of Computer Science website.

Reducing to the halting problem – search on programming.dojo.net.nz.

Reducing the blank tape problem – search on the oaklandcse Youtube channel.

Fork/join in Java – search on the InfoQ website.

Backtracking in Prolog – search on WikiWikiWeb.

Data mining – search on the University of Texas at Austin's College of Liberal Arts' website.

Travelling salesman problem – search on +plus magazine's website.

Pipelining – search on Iowa State University's Computer Science website.

Visualising a problem – search on nrich.maths.org.

Chapter 22
Algorithms

Specification points

2.3.1 Algorithms

- Analysis and design of algorithms for a given situation.
- Standard algorithms, (bubble sort, insertion sort).
- Implement bubble sort, insertion sort.
- Implement binary and linear search.
- A Representing, adding data to and removing data from queues and stacks.
- Standard algorithms, (merge sort, quick sort, Dijkstra's shortest path algorithm, A* algorithm, binary search and linear search).
- Algorithms for the main data structures, (stacks, queues, trees, linked lists, depth-first (post-order) and breadth-first traversal of trees).
- Comparison of the complexity of algorithms.
- Compare the suitability of different algorithms for a given task and data set, in terms of execution time and space.
- Measures and methods to determine the efficiency of different algorithms, Big O notation (constant, linear, polynomial, exponential and logarithmic complexity).

Learning objectives

- To look at how algorithms are designed and analysed for a given situation or problem.
- To appreciate the suitability of algorithms for a given task with regards to execution time and space.

- To understand the complexity of algorithms using the Big O notation and use it to allow comparison between algorithms.
- To understand algorithms that are related to stacks, queues, linked lists and trees.
- To understand and use the following standard algorithms:
  - bubble sort
  - insertion sort
  - binary search
  - serial search.
  - merge sort
  - quick sort
  - Dijkstra's shortest path
  - A* algorithm

Introduction

So far you will have produced a number of programs to solve problems, some of which may have been fairly complex. In order to solve these problems, you may have needed to create algorithms. In this chapter you will be looking at how algorithms can be analysed in terms of their execution time and memory requirements. This analysis is crucial when deciding if your algorithm design efficiently solved the problem or if a different algorithm would perform better. When designing an algorithm the steps below must be followed:

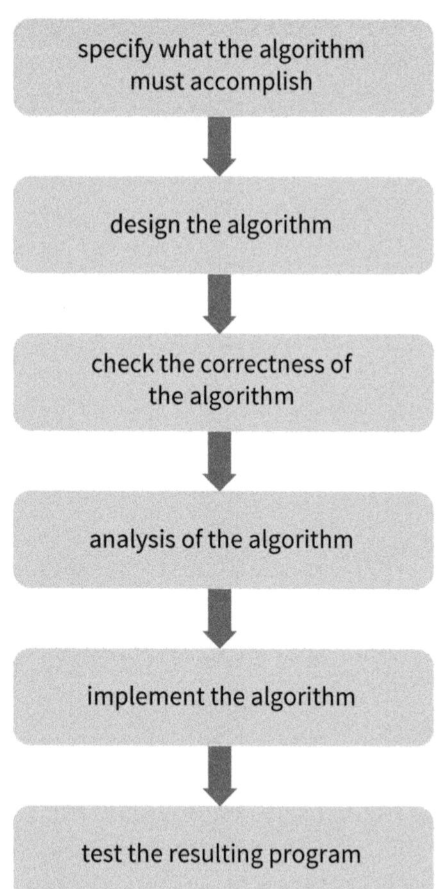

Figure 22.1: The steps that must be followed when creating an algorithm.

Define the problem, develop a model and design the algorithm

Before you can design and create an algorithm the algorithm must first be defined. This will include defining what inputs the algorithm will accept, what outputs it will produce and the scope of the algorithm. Essentially, an algorithm will map an input (or **set** of inputs) to an output. It does not stand true that given a unique input you will always get a unique output, unless the problem specifically requires it. However, it does hold true that for any given input then the same output will always be produced – we say the algorithm is repeatable and predictable. An algorithm can be thought of as a mathematical **function**, as shown below.

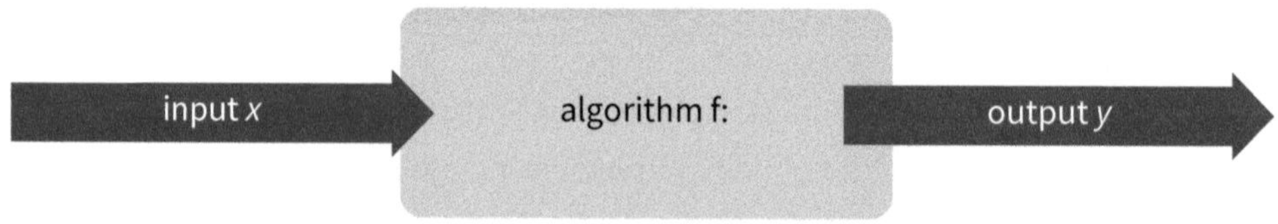

Figure 22.2: Diagrammatic representation of an algorithmic function $f(x)$.

Algorithms provide a mapping from the input values (known as the **domain**) to the output (known as the range). The set of values that could possibly come out of the algorithm, not necessarily what will come out it, is known as the **codomain**. This mapping can be shown using the notation $f: X \rightarrow Y$ read as 'the function *f* maps values from the domain *X* to the codomain *Y*'. This can also be written as $y = f(x)$. The input domain can be restricted to only allowable values within a set, which allows us to define the scope of an algorithm. A domain can be defined by specifying what values are acceptable for the algorithm. For example, we could define an algorithm's domain to be positive whole numbers (known as natural numbers) between 10 and 100. Natural numbers are represented using the ℕ symbol in maths. The domain, therefore, can be defined using the expression below. It is read as 'the set of all *x* such that *x* is an element of the set of natural number and *x* is greater or equal to 10 and less than or equal to 100'.

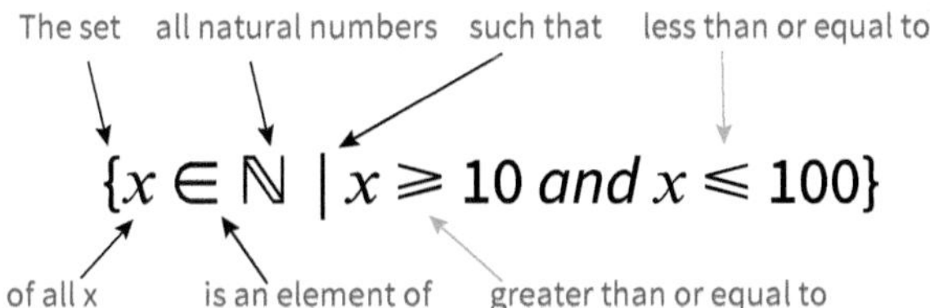

Example: tax calculator

When defining an algorithm formally we need to be able to define the **domain** and **codomain** as well as understanding how the algorithm will perform the actual mapping. Consider a concrete example of a tax calculator based on yearly salary. The **domain** would be decimal numbers, or real numbers, greater than 0. It makes no sense to try to calculate tax for negative numbers, so these will not be included in the **domain** and would be rejected by the algorithm come implementation. The **domain** and **codomain**, therefore, would be $\{x \in \mathbb{R} \mid x > 0\}$ where ℝ represents the **set** of all real numbers (decimal numbers). This is read as 'There exists an x in the **set** of real numbers such that x is greater than 0'.

$$f(x) = \begin{cases} 0 & if\, x \leq 9\,440 \\ 0.2(x - 9\,440) & if\, x \leq 41\,450 \\ 6402 + 0.4(x - 41\,450) & if\, x > 41\,450 \end{cases}$$

The above definition for a tax algorithm is based on the table below and taken from 2013–2014 values. Regardless of how much you earn, every taxpayer is entitled to pay no tax on the first £9440 of their salary. This is known as your personal allowance. After that, the remainder of your salary tax is paid at either 20% or 40%, depending on the amount. Between £9440 and £41 450, 20% tax is paid; anything over that is paid at 40%. Tax is not paid at 40% on all of your salary, only on the amount over £41 450. Some values have been mapped below to help exemplify this.

UK tax rate for 2013–2014	Amount/£
Personal allowance (no tax paid)	9440
20% rate	32 010
40% rate	41 450

Figure 22.3: Mapping salary to the amount of tax paid.

Example: Palindrome

Not all algorithms will have such easily identifiable domains and codomains and have a mapping that can be defined mathematically. This does not matter as long as you know what values it can work on, what it will do and what outputs will be produced. Above all, an algorithm must be repeatable and predictable. It is common to design algorithms using pseudocode, and if you look up common algorithms, such as bubble sort, you will see them defined. Consider an algorithm for working out if a word is a palindrome or not. A palindrome is a word that is spelled the same forwards as it is backwards, such as 'Hannah' or 'rotator'. The **domain** and **codomain** is defined below and the initial pseudocode shown.

Domain {*x* | *x is a word with an odd number of letters*}

Codomain {*True, False*}

Pseudocode

```
INPUT → word
start = 0
end = LEN(word) - 1
WHILE (word[start] = word[end] AND start!= end)
  start = start + 1
  end = end - 1

END WHILE
IF start = end RETURN TRUE
ELSE RETURN FALSE
```

NOTE: this algorithm will not work for the palindrome 'Hannah' and this is purposeful. This will be fixed in the next section when looking at the correctness of an algorithm. This is why the **domain** was restricted to words with an odd number of letters.

Checking the correctness of an algorithm

It is important that, before a single line of code has been written, the algorithm design meets the problem at hand. Testing done after the code has been implemented should test the correctness of the implementation rather than the correctness of the algorithm itself. This is an important distinction and one that is easily missed by students. If the algorithm is fundamentally flawed and this is not picked up until after implementation, then this could cause at best a delay in development or at worst a security vulnerability.

An algorithm can be considered correct when, for all valid inputs from the **domain**, the correct output is produced from the **codomain**. The mapping **function** $f: X \rightarrow Y$, regardless of the value chosen from the **domain** X, will always map correctly. When showing correctness, there is a big difference between testing and proving that the **function** is correct for all $x \in X$. In fact, testing will not prove the **function** works for all cases and there could be test cases that cause it to fail. Proving the correctness of an algorithm is outside the scope of A Level, so our remaining focus will be on testing.

Example: checking the correctness of the palindrome algorithm

The palindrome algorithm was introduced in the last section as a way of determining if a word is a palindrome or not. However, if tested with the word 'Hannah', we get a run time error (out of bounds). Running a trace quickly shows why.

Start	End	Word[start]	Word[end]
0	5	H	H
1	4	A	A
2	3	N	N
3	2	N	N
4	1	A	A
5	0	H	H
6	-1	Out of range	Out of range

Table 22.1: A dry run of the palindrome algorithm showing an error.

The trace lines shown in yellow are correct, while the lines in red should not have been executed and eventually result in an error. This shows that the previously defined algorithm is not correct for the **domain** {all words}. At most, when executing this algorithm, we should only compare half of the letters; after that, we know that the word is a palindrome. Below is an improved algorithm which works for the palindrome 'Hannah'.

Code

```
INPUT → word
start = 0
end = LEN(word) - 1
WHILE (word[start] = word[end] AND start <FLOOR(LEN(word)/2))
  start = start + 1
  end = end - 1
END WHILE
IF start >= LEN(word)/2 RETURN TRUE
ELSE RETURN FALSE
```

This code works for 'Hannah' and 'rotator'. The trace table below shows the above code working for 'rotator'. The line in red will not actually be run as it is not necessary. Comparing a letter to itself will always be true, so there is no need to run the comparison. When running a word that has an even number of letters, the loop will run once more than required.

Start	End	Word[start]	Word[end]
0	5	R	R
1	4	O	O
2	3	T	T
3	2	A	A

Table 22.2: A dry run for the word 'rotator'.

When designing algorithms, it is important to do dry runs like this for a range of values that will cover a spread of values in the **codomain**. For completeness, the trace table below shows that the word 'prop' is not a palindrome. The line in red shows where the while loop ends and, as start is not greater than LEN(word)/2, it will return false.

Start	End	Word[start]	Word[end]
0	3	P	P
1	2	R	O

Table 22.3: A dry run for the word 'prop'.

The above testing strategy is important for showing partial correctness of an algorithm, but does not ensure complete correctness.

Execution time and analysis of the algorithm

Code sample testing the physical run time of a list sort in Python

Code

```
from timeit import Timer
import random

l = []
for f in range(1,30000):
  l.append(random.randint(1,30000))

def test():
  global l
  l.sort()

print Timer("test()", "from cpuspeed import test").
timeit()
```

In Python there is a built-in function for lists that will sort their values. The above code shows how this method could be measured to see how long it takes to perform a sort on 30 000 values. The timeit module in Python will run the code 1 million times to get a good idea of the average run time for that function. However, if this code was run on multiple computers, the value returned would be different. In fact, if this code was run multiple times on the same computer then a different value may be returned. This can be due to many different factors, such as processor load, amount of free memory or even tasks scheduled by the operating system. Evaluating speed in this way is known as **benchmarking** and is not a reliable way to evaluate the effectiveness of an algorithm.

Execution time, or how long an algorithm takes to run, needs to be done in a more analytical way without resorting to benchmarking. When analysing an algorithm, we are looking at its complexity. By comparing the complexity of different algorithms we can make decisions on which algorithm would be best in any given circumstance. Complexity can be measured in two ways:

- execution time, which looks at how many steps an algorithm will take with a given input
- space, which measures how much memory is taken up during execution.

An algorithm could be efficient with regards to execution time but use memory inefficiently. The problem with this is that, if the size of input is large enough, then the algorithm could use an exponential amount of memory leading to using virtual memory or running out of memory.

Python code to find the smallest item in a list

Code

```
import random

l = []
for f in range(1,30000):
  l.append(random.randint(1,30000))

m = l[0]
for current in l:
  if current < m:
    m = current

print m
```

When looking at **time complexity**, we need a frame of measurement. The above code, ignoring the creation of the array, has a number of steps which are executed. Counting the number of lines of code executed is not a good measurement, as each line would ultimately be translated into machine code and thus be dependent on the efficiency of the compiler, the language and the CPU. A good measurement for this algorithm, on the other hand, is to look at the number of comparisons that need to be made. This will not give us an exact running time, but it will give a general idea. There are 30 000 numbers in the list and each number will be considered once, making 30 000 comparisons. Every time the loop runs, a comparison is made; therefore, the size of the list directly influences how many comparisons we make. If there were ten items then we would make ten comparisons. In the general case, if there were n items then we would run n comparisons. This can be written as a function $f(n) = n$ produces a straight-line graph. $f(n) = n$ is known as a linear equation.

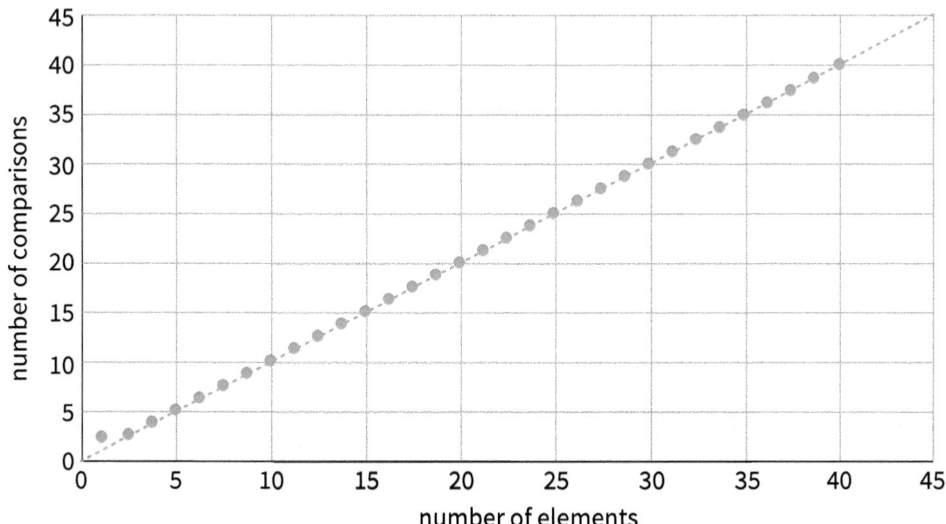

Figure 22.4: Graph showing the growth of a linear function for finding the smallest item in a list.

$f(n) = n$ shows us that this algorithm has linear growth. Time complexity, in computer science, analyses the growth of an algorithm. So as the input size grows, we can determine if an algorithm will still perform efficiently or not simply by looking at its time complexity. Consider the simple loop below.

Python code showing a nested loop

Code

```
def example(end):
  i=0
  total = 0
  while i < end:
    j = 0
    while j < end:
      if i < j:
        total = total + i
      else:
        total = total + j
      j + = 1
    i + = 1
  return total
print example(100)
```

The parameter end will determine how often the inner and outer loops will run for. The inner loop, when invoked with 100, will run 100 times every time the outer loop runs. As this also runs 100 times, we get a simple equation of 100^2 or more generally n^2. An equation that contains a square will grow more rapidly than one that is linear. This can be shown in Figure 22.5.

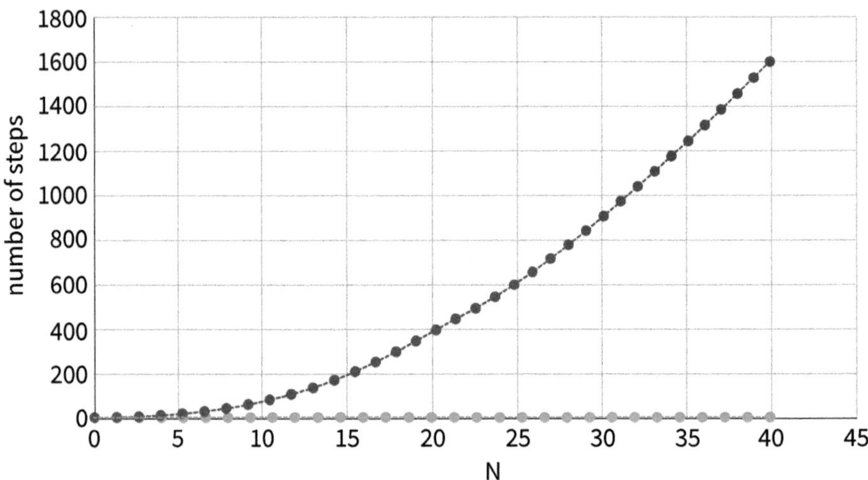

Figure 22.5: Comparison of linear (blue) and squared (pink) function growth.

As the value of n increases, the number of comparisons increases dramatically for the squared equation. By the time n becomes 40, there is a massive gulf between the linear and squared equations. As such, if we had two algorithms that did the same thing, then we could say that the algorithm with linear growth was more efficient.

Big O notation

In order to explain **Big O**, pronounced 'big-oh', we need to take a short look at the order of functions. Consider the two functions below.

$$f(x) = 2x$$
$$g(x) = 4x + 1$$

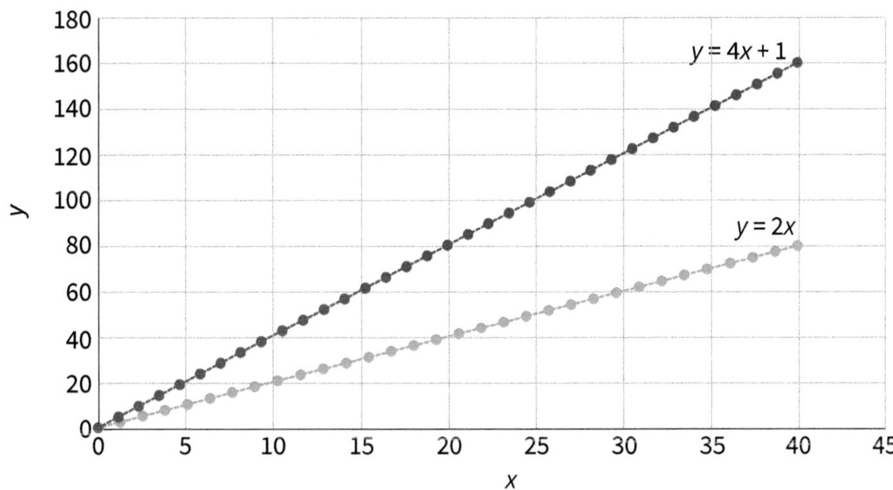

Figure 22.6: Two linear functions with different coefficients.

Both of these functions exhibit linear growth, even though $g(x)$ grows faster than $f(x)$.

Comparing a squared function to a linear one, we can see that the squared function grows faster. We can say that a squared function is of a higher order than the linear one. In fact, all squared functions are of a higher order than linear ones. This is regardless of the coefficients used, as eventually a squared function will outgrow a linear one. $f(x)$ and $g(x)$ below show these functions in their more general form.

$$f(x) = ax + b$$
$$g(x) = ax^2 + b$$

Consider the two functions below. The coefficients for $f(x)$ were purposefully made larger than those for $g(x)$. This way we can show that for some value of x in the result will be $g(x) > f(x)$. This can be clearly seen in Figure 22.7.

- $f(x) = 4x + 10$
- $g(x) = 0.5x^2 - 10$

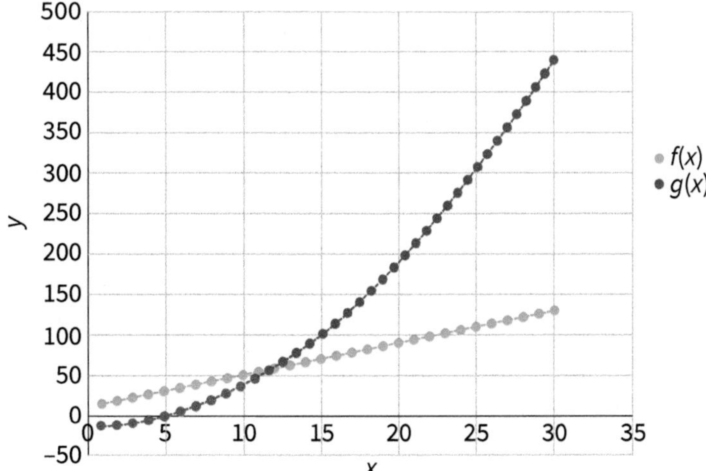

Figure 22.7: Graph showing how a squared function grows faster than a linear one regardless of the coefficients used.

Tip

You must know the order of growth of linear, squared, exponential and logarithmic functions. It's worth drawing out the graphs for your study notes.

Families of functions that share the same order can be classified using the Big O notation. That means that all linear functions can be generalised by the notation O (n) and all squared functions by the notation O (n^2). The key families of functions that are used in computer science are listed in order below, from the slowest growth to the quickest.

- O (1) constant time
- O ($\text{Log}_2\, n$) logarithmic time (note: logs are base 2)
- O (n) linear time
- O (n^2) squared time
- O (n^3) cubed time
- O (n^c) polynomial time
- O (n^n) exponential time.

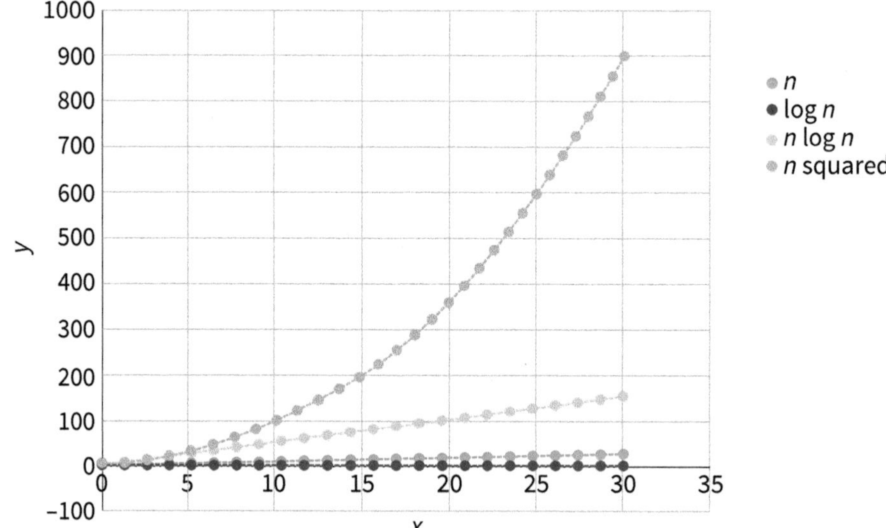

Figure 22.8: Chart showing comparison of different orders of functions.

We have already seen how a function can be derived to show the growth of an algorithm, based on the size of the input $f(n)$. Consider a function which has its efficiency modelled by the function $f(n) = 2n + 5$. We can more simply write O (n) as the algorithm will grow linearly based on the input. A number of standard algorithms will be introduced in the next section and their efficiency examined using Big O notation.

Computing in context: NP-complete problems

Most of the algorithms in this chapter have a time complexity which is, at worst, bounded by a polynomial function. These problems, for example sorting, form a set of problems which can be solved in polynomial time. There exists another set of problems, known as **non-deterministic polynomial problems**, where the solution could be quickly verified in polynomial time.

Non-deterministic polynomial (or NP) problems may or may not have an algorithmic solution to them that is bounded by polynomial time. The ones that do not are considered hard problems and form a set of problems called **NP-hard**. These are the hardest problems to solve and so far no one has found a general solution to one, although some special cases can be solved. A problem is considered to be NP-hard if there is a way to reduce or convert the solution into another NP-hard problem. This may seem confusing, but ultimately the definition is just showing that there is a link between all NP-hard problems, and those problems are difficult to solve.

NP-complete problems are those that are both NP and NP-hard. NP-complete problems are very common in computing (e.g. in cryptography), and so far no one has been able to solve them in polynomial time. There is a $1 million reward fund offered by the Clay Mathematics Institute for anyone who manages to show that an NP-complete problem can be solved in polynomial time. However, the implications of solving NP-complete are vast. Cryptography only works because decrypting a file without the key is an NP-complete problem and would take a massive amount of computing time to achieve. Should a solution be found in polynomial time it would leave cryptographic methods used by every website in the world useless.

Common algorithms

Bubble sort

One of the easiest sorting algorithms to both understand and implement is **bubble sort**. It takes a list or array of items as input and produces a sorted list at the end. In order for the sort to work, the items within must be of a comparable type. So given two items x_0 and x_1 it must be possible to test $x_0 > x_1$, $x_0 < x_1$, and $x_0 = x_1$. This might seem a trivial point to make, but it is crucial that we are formal in our definitions. For example, if you had a list {4, Fred, 8}, then sorting could not take place, as Fred cannot (in any meaningful way) be compared to numbers.

Figure 22.9: Input and output diagram for bubble sort.

Bubble sort compares the two left-hand items (0 and 1) and swaps them if necessary so the largest is on the right. It does the same with the next pair (1 and 2), and so on all the way to the end of the list. The result is that the largest number finishes up at the end of the list. This process is repeated until all the items are in order. Bubble sort derives its name from larger numbers moving up the list like bubbles floating to the top of a glass.

Pseudocode

```
FUNCTION bubblesort(list)
  REPEAT
  swapped = false
    FOR n = 1 TO LEN(list)
      IF list[n-1] > list[n] THEN
        temp = list[n-1]
        list[n-1] = list[n]
        list[n] = temp
        swapped = true
      END IF
    NEXT n
  UNTIL NOT swapped
RETURN list
END FUNCTION
```

Tip

You need to demonstrate your understanding of these algorithms by doing dry runs. You are not expected to memorise the pseudocode but you should be able to write out the key steps.

Bubble sort revolves around two loops. The inner loop will always run n – 1 times, where n is the size of the list. This has the job of moving the largest value in the list to the end of the list that has not already been moved, or is not already in the correct position. The outer loop will run if and only if no more values have been swapped in the previous run of the inner loop.

Initial unsorted list

	32	12	56	3	31	76	45	49	64
Index	0	1	2	3	4	5	6	7	8

First run of inner loop

	12	32	3	31	56	45	49	64	76
Index	0	1	2	3	4	5	6	7	8

After the first run of the inner loop we made eight comparisons, or n – 1, and were left with the largest number in position 8. Each swap moved the larger numbers to the higher indices.

Second run of inner loop

	12	3	31	32	45	49	56	64	76
Index	0	1	2	3	4	5	6	7	8

Third run of inner loop

	3	12	31	32	45	49	56	64	76
Index	0	1	2	3	4	5	6	7	8

By the end of the third loop we end up with a sorted list. As the third loop required a swap, we need to run the inner loop once more, but this time no swap will occur and the variable swapped will remain false.

Efficiency analysis of bubble sort

The inner loop for bubble sort will perform $n - 1$ comparisons every time it is run, where n is the number of items in the list. The key to working out the efficiency for bubble sort is to find out how many times the inner loop runs. In the previous example the inner loop ran four times or $f(n) = 4(n - 1)$ Creating a general case we end up with $f(n) = C(n - 1)$. However, based on the input, we could end up with a very different coefficient C for each invocation. Below are two lists which show the best-case and worst-case scenarios for bubble sort. In the best-case scenario the inner loop runs only once. This is because the list is already sorted, meaning no swaps occur. In the worst-case scenario, where the list is in reverse order, the inner loop must run eight times.

Best-case scenario

	2	4	8	10	16	20	24	32	45
Index	0	1	2	3	4	5	6	7	8

Worst-case scenario

	9	8	7	6	5	4	3	2	1
Index	0	1	2	3	4	5	6	7	8

First run

	8	7	6	5	4	3	2	1	9
Index	0	1	2	3	4	5	6	7	8

Second run

	7	6	5	4	3	2	1	8	9
Index	0	1	2	3	4	5	6	7	8

Eighth run

	1	2	3	4	5	6	7	8	9
Index	0	1	2	3	4	5	6	7	8

Generalising the best-case scenario we get $f(n) = n - 1$ as the inner loop only runs once. Generalising the worst-case scenario gives us $(x) = n(n - 1) = n^2 - n$. Bubble sort has a time complexity of $O(n^2)$, as the outer loop, on average, will have to run more than once.

Space complexity of bubble sort

Bubble sort is a very simple algorithm and makes little additional use of memory other than a few variables. Regardless of the size of the input, the additional memory footprint of bubble sort does not change. Therefore, as the space complexity is constant in both the best and worst cases, we can represent it as $O(1)$.

Space complexity is analysed in the same way as time complexity is analysed. If variables are used, but always the same number for each loop, then this has a constant space complexity. If we had a linked list to which we always added one each time through the loop, then we would have linear growth. As well as variables and abstract data types, we should consider the number of recursive calls, as each recursive call uses memory.

Python code for bubble sort

Code

```
import random

# generate a list of random items
l=[]
for f in range(1,30000):
  l.append(random.randint(1,30000))

# function to see the first and last
# items as a quick check for the result of
# the sort.
```

```
def displayfirstandlast(l):
    for i in range(0,5):
      print str(l[i])+",",
    print ".....",
    for i in range(len(l)-6, len(l)-1):
      print str(l[i])+",",
    print ""

def bubbleSort(l):
  swapped = True
  # will loop until no more swaps occur
  while swapped: # outer loop
    swapped = False # assume no swap
    x = 1
    while x < len(l): # inner loop always runs n times
      if l[x-1] > l[x]:
        # perform a swap
        temp = l[x-1]
        l[x-1] = l[x]
        l[x] = temp
        swapped = True # note that a swap occurred
    x += 1
  return l
# test bubble sort function
displayfirstandlast(l)
l = bubbleSort(l)
displayfirstandlast(l)
```

Insertion sort

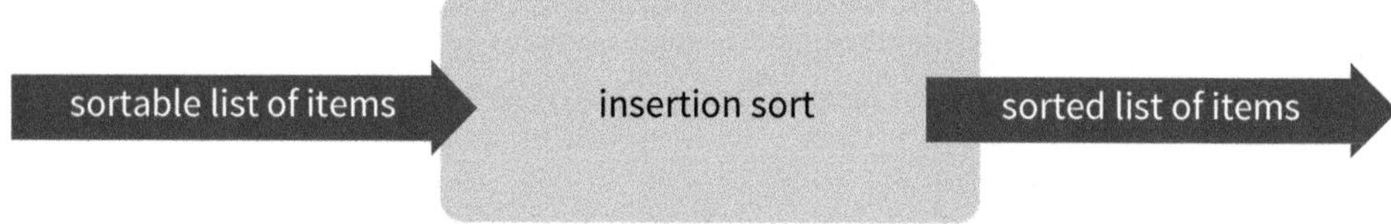

Figure 22.10: Input and output diagram for insertion sort.

Insertion sort draws its inspiration from how humans sort cards in their hand when playing a game. Consider a hand of cards which are not in order.

Figure 22.11: Unsorted hand of cards.

One approach to ordering cards that could be taken is to hold the cards in one hand and remove a single card with the other. That card can then be inserted into the correct position. This simple procedure is repeated until the hand is sorted. For example, the three of spades could be drawn by the player's right hand, leaving the following situation.

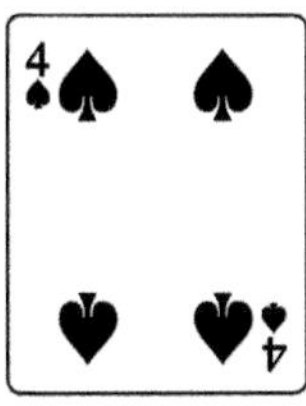

Figure 22.12: A single card removed, ready to be inserted back.

The three of spades can then be inserted into the correct position in the left hand by pushing all of the other cards to the right and placing the three of spades at the front. This simple example leads us to the fundamental principle of insertion sort, where we remove a single item and place it back into the list. Like bubble sort, insertion sort can only work on lists of items that are comparable to one another.

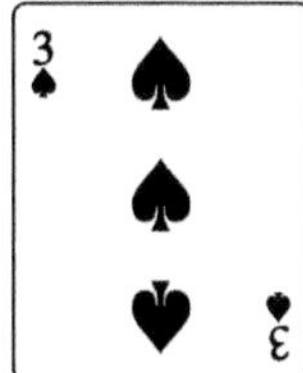

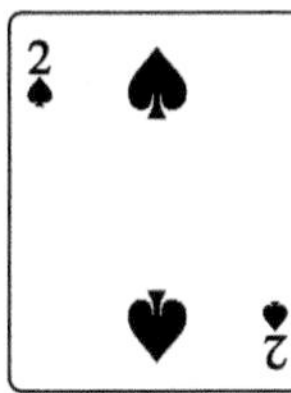

Figure 22.13: Card is inserted back into the correct position.

Initially, we assume that the first item in the list is in the correct position, regardless of how true that may be, and refer to it as a sub-list of size 1. In insertion sort we guarantee that the sub-list is always sorted. This means we can insert other records into that list in the correct position creating an ever-growing sorted list until all items have been inserted.

In the example below, the shaded boxes will show the progress of an alphabetically sorted sub-list.

Kiwi	Cherry	Apple	Orange	Melon	Lemon
0	1	2	3	4	5

Kiwi		Apple	Orange	Melon	Lemon
0	1	2	3	4	5

Temp = Cherry

Figure 22.14: Item removed from the list ready for insertion.

Insertion sort will start with the second item in the list and place it into a temporary space or variable. This will produce a hole in the list allowing us to safely shift items around without losing data. In order to add the removed item into the sub-list it is compared to the first item. If the value is less than the current element then all of the items below it are shifted along by one.

Cherry	Kiwi	Apple	Orange	Melon	Lemon
0	1	2	3	4	5

Temp = BLANK

Figure 22.15: Top item is shifted down and the removed item inserted back in.

Apple is less than Kiwi so that means that Kiwi must be shifted along into the hole. Once the shift has happened then Apple can be inserted into the correct position, creating a sorted sub-list of two items. The next item in the list becomes the current item and the algorithm is repeated.

Cherry	Kiwi		Orange	Melon	Lemon
0	1	2	3	4	5

Temp = Apple

Cherry		Kiwi	Orange	Melon	Lemon
0	1	2	3	4	5

Temp = Apple

	Cherry	Kiwi	Orange	Melon	Lemon
0	1	2	3	4	5

Temp = Apple

Apple	Cherry	Kiwi	Orange	Melon	Lemon
0	1	2	3	4	5

Temp = BLANK

Figure 22.16: Next step of insertion sort.

In the step shown in Figure 22.16, both Kiwi and Cherry had to be shifted up to make room for Apple. A shift, when it takes place, requires more steps than if the item is just placed at the back of the sorted sub-list. This is important to note, as it will impact the time complexity of the algorithm. Successive items in turn are moved into the correct position until the list is sorted.

Pseudocode

```
FOR p = 1 TO LEN(list)
  # remove the current item into a temp variable
  hole = list[p]
  z = p
  # keep shifting until we are at the end of the list
  # or found the point of insertion
  WHILE z > 0 AND list[z-1] > hole
    list[z] = list[z-1]
    z = z - 1
  END WHILE
  # insert the item into the correct position
  list[z] = hole
NEXT
```

Efficiency and analysis of insertion sort

Let

$L = \{x_0, x_1, x_2, x_3 \ldots.. x_n\}$	List of items to be sorted
$n = \|L\|$	The **cardinality** (length) of the list
S = {sorted sub-list}	

Each item in L must be removed from the list into a variable, apart from x_0, which means that insertion sort must run the outer loop at least $n - 1$ times, where n is the size of the list. In order to insert a value back into the list we must shift values, starting from x_0 going to x_i, where i is the position from which we removed the item. In the best-case scenario we do not need to perform any shifts, as the list is already sorted, which means that only one comparison needs to be made for every iteration of the outer loop. This leaves us with a linear function $O(n)$.

Value	6	2	1	7	3	7	9	14	15
Index	0	1	2	3	4	5	6	7	8
x_i	x_0	x_1	x_2	x_3	x_4	x_5	x_6	x_7	x_8

Figure 22.17: Initial list showing an unsorted list and the values of x.

To work out the time complexity of insertion sort for the worst-case scenario we must analyse the inner loop as it swaps values. During the first execution of insertion sort for the above list, we are checking to see if $x_0 > x_1$, or $6 > 2$, which means that we need to make one comparison leading to a shift. In order to make analysis of the algorithm easier, we shall only consider comparisons rather than considering swaps as well.

Value	2	6	1	7	3	7	9	14	15
Index	0	1	2	3	4	5	6	7	8
x_i	x_0	x_1	x_2	x_3	x_4	x_5	x_6	x_7	x_8

Figure 22.18: After the first iteration of insertion sort.

The second iteration, $x_0 > x_2$, leads to two comparisons, against x_0 and x_1. If p is the current item we are looking at and the inequality $x_0 > x_p$ holds true then we need to perform p number of swaps. In the worst-case scenario, which is where the list is in reverse order, we have to perform the maximum number of swaps each time the outer loop runs. Below are the stages of insertion sort for the worst case. The shaded columns show the number of comparisons made for each loop.

Let's switch to a shorter list to simplify the explanation.

Initial list

Value	10	9	8	7	6
Index	0	1	2	3	4
x_i	x_0	x_1	x_2	x_3	x_4

First run

Value	9	10	8	7	6
Index	0	1	2	3	4
x_i	x_0	x_1	x_2	x_3	x_4

Second run

Value	8	9	10	7	6
Index	0	1	2	3	4
x_i	x_0	x_1	x_2	x_3	x_4

Third run

Value	7	8	9	10	6
Index	0	1	2	3	4
x_i	x_0	x_1	x_2	x_3	x_4

Fourth run

Value	6	7	8	9	10
Index	0	1	2	3	4
x_i	x_0	x_1	x_2	x_3	x_4

The number of comparisons done on this list is $1 + 2 + 3 + 4 = 10$. Taking the generic case, we end up with the pattern $1 + 2 + 3 \ldots. + n - 2 + n - 1$. Although beyond the scope of this book, this pattern is that of triangular numbers. The sum of all triangular numbers $\sum_{k=1}^{x} k$ can be represented by the function $\frac{x(x+1)}{2}$, where x will be replaced by $n - 1$ as $n - 1$ is the last value in our pattern. Therefore, insertion sort's worst-case scenario will be as follows.

$\sum_{k=1}^{x} k = \frac{x(x+1)}{2}$	The equation for triangular numbers
$f(n) = \frac{(n-1)(n-1+1)}{2}$	Substituting n − 1 for x
$f(n) = \frac{(n-1)n}{2}$	
$f(n) = \frac{1}{2}(n^2 - n)$	

When looking at time complexity, we do not consider the coefficients, as we are only interested in the growth of the function. Therefore, the time complexity of insertion sort is an element of the squared functions:

$$\frac{1}{2}(n^2 - n) \quad \in 0(n^2)$$

Space complexity of insertion sort

Insertion sort is a very simple algorithm and makes very little additional use of memory other than a few variables. Regardless of the size of the input, the additional memory footprint of insertion sort does not change. Therefore, as the memory usage is constant in both the best and worst cases, we can represent it as O (1).

Quick sort

So far the sorting algorithms considered perform poorly on larger sets of data. However, they are simple to implement and perform well for small sets of data. Quick sort performs much more favourably for larger sets of data but is more complicated to understand and implement. Quick sort is a **recursive algorithm** which will apply itself to smaller and smaller sections of the list until the number of values being looked at is 1. The basic steps of quick sort are as follows.

1. Pick a single item from the list and call it the pivot x^p.
2. Reorder the list so all items that are less than the pivot come before it and all items that are larger come after it. Once this operation is complete, the pivot will be in its final position. This is known as the 'partition phase'.
3. Perform steps 1 and 2 recursively on all items less than x^p and again on all items greater than x^p. Keep doing this until the number of items smaller or greater than x^p is 1 or 0.

Most of the work for quick sort happens in the partition phase and is summarised by the algorithm below. There is more than one way to perform the partition and the one described below is the most documented method.

1. Swap the pivot with the item in the right-most position of the list.
2. Record the position of the left-most item in the list and store it in a variable storePosition.
3. For each item in the list (excluding the pivot):
   a. if the value of the item being looked at is less than the pivot:
      i. swap the item for the item in storePosition
      ii. add 1 to storePosition.
4. Swap the pivot for the item that is in storePosition.

In pseudocode, this algorithm can be written as follows.

Pseudocode

```
FUNCTION partition(array, left, right)
  Pivot = pick random index
  pivotValue = array[pivot]
  Swap array[pivot] and array[right]
  storePosition = left
    FOR j = left TO right
      IF array[j] < pivotValue THEN
        Swap array[j] and array[storePosition]
        storePosition ++
      END IF
    NEXT
  Swap array[storePosition] and array[right]
  RETURN storePosition
END FUNCTION
```

Initial unsorted list

	7	1	4	6	9	12	3	8	2
Index	0	1	2	3	4	5	6	7	8

The above partition algorithm, once a pivot has been chosen, will reorder the array so that all items with a smaller value than the pivot will be on the left and all items with a larger value than the pivot will be on the right. Numbers to the left and right may not be in numeric order, but they will match the property $x_{p-2}, x_{p-1} < x_p \leq x_{p+1}, x_{p+1}$. The best way to understand the above algorithm is to see a worked example. When picking a pivot, a random index will be used, as the choice of pivot is not crucial to how the algorithm works. However, it is crucial to the efficiency of the algorithm, and this will be discussed later. The pivot will be shown in red and values swapped in orange.

Step 1 – swap the pivot with the end of the list

	7	1	4	6	9	12	3	8	2
Index	0	1	2	3	4	5	6	7	8

	7	1	4	2	9	12	3	8	6
Index	0	1	2	3	4	5	6	7	8

By moving the pivot to the end of the list we are essentially moving it out of the way for the main loop of the algorithm. At no point do we want to compare the pivot to itself, as that makes no sense. Therefore, moving it to the right and ensuring the loop ends before it gets there (right – 1) we can prevent this from happening.

Step 2 – swap values if less than the pivot

	1	7	4	2	9	12	3	8	6
Index	0	1	2	3	4	5	6	7	8
StorePosition =		1		J =		1			

The first iteration will compare array[0] to the pivot resulting in no swap, as 7 is not less than 6. On the second iteration, however, a swap occurs, as 1 is less than 7. The swap, array[j] and array[storePosition] are shown above. Once a swap occurs, storePosition is incremented by one. What is really happening is that storePosition is keeping track of where the last number smaller than the pivot was seen, or where the pivot must be placed after the algorithm runs. Larger numbers are then swapped so their index is always greater than storePosition.

	1	4	7	2	9	12	3	8	6
Index	0	1	2	3	4	5	6	7	8
StorePosition =		1		J =		2			

	1	4	2	7	9	12	3	8	6
Index	0	1	2	3	4	5	6	7	8
StorePosition =		2		J =		3			

The next two iterations are shown above. Notice that all values in positions ≤ are less than the pivot. This property holds true throughout the execution of the algorithm.

	1	4	2	3	9	12	7	8	6
Index	0	1	2	3	4	5	6	7	8
StorePosition =		3		J =		6			

Both 9 and 12 are not less than the pivot, so we move past them without any swaps. A new property has emerged, which existed before but was not obvious. That is that all values between storePosition+1 and j have a value greater than the pivot.

Step 3 – swap pivot for the item in storePosition

	1	4	2	3	6	12	7	8	9
Index	0	1	2	3	4	5	6	7	8
StorePosition =		4		J =		7			

Once the final step has occurred, all values less than the pivot are now to the left while all values that are larger are to the right. This array is not yet sorted; however, it will be after we perform the recursive steps.

Quick sort recursion

Code

```
FUNCTION quicksort(array, left, right)
  IF left < right THEN
    p = partition(array, left, right)
    # quicksort lower values
    Quicksort(array, left, p-1)
    # quicksort higher values
    Quicksort(array, p+1, right)
  END IF
END FUNCTION
```

When the partition function runs it will return the position of the pivot in the array after reordering has taken place. In order for the array to be ordered, quick sort must be recursively run on both the lower and upper sub-arrays. Looking back at our example, partition would return index 4. This means that we repeat the quick sort algorithm on the lower numbers, quicksort(0, 3) and the upper numbers, quicksort(4, 8).

	1	4	2	3	6	12	7	8	9
Index	0	1	2	3	4	5	6	7	8
StorePosition =		4							

Quicksort(array, 0, 3) – pivot index 2

Running the partition function on the lower numbers, taking index 2 as the pivot, produces the following reordering after the partition algorithm has been run, returning index 2. After the partition, as 0 is less than 3, we need to run quick sort twice more. Quicksort(array, 0, 1) and quicksort(array, 3, 3). The next recursion of quick sort will be quicksort(array, 0, 1) as we always do the lower numbers first, regardless of whether we still have larger numbers to do. The full recursive tree can be seen in Figure 22.22.

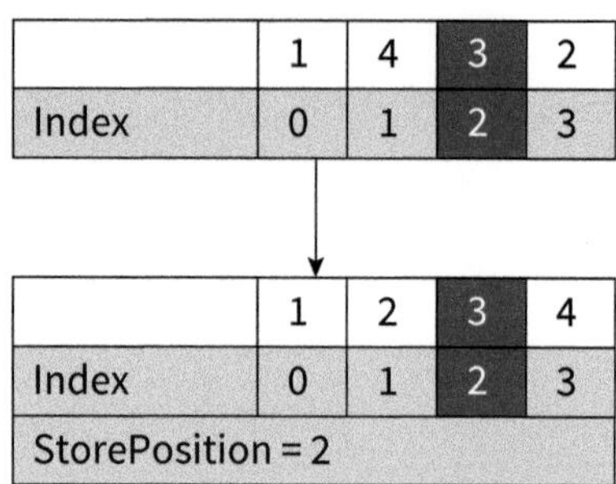

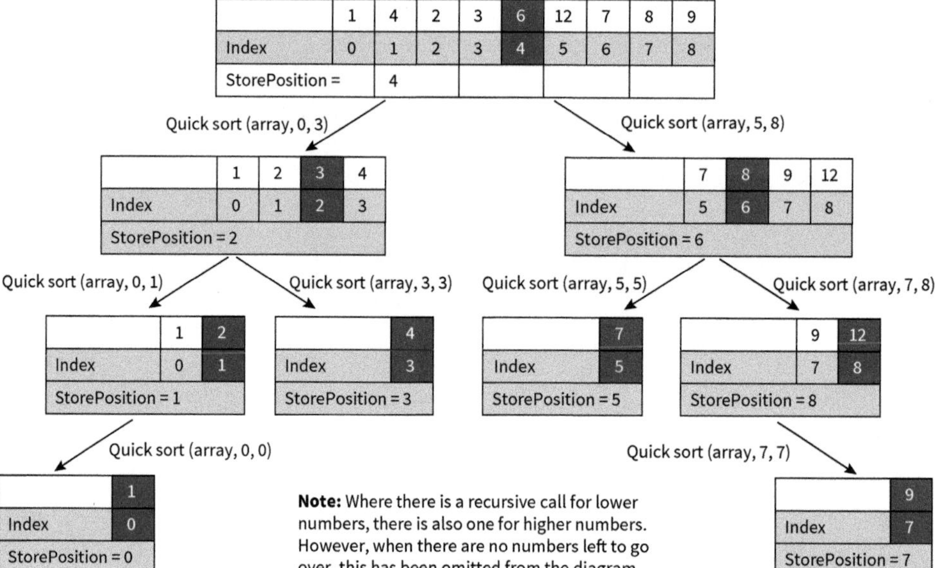

Figure 22.19: Full recursion tree for quick sort.

Time complexity of quick sort

Quick sort's time complexity can be shown to be $O(n \log_2 n)$, which makes it the most efficient sorting algorithm seen so far. Both insertion sort and bubble sort have a growth function of $O(n^2)$, which means that, as n gets increasingly larger, quick sort outperforms them by a substantial margin. In order to understand where $O(n \log_2 n)$ was derived from, we must first work out the time complexity for the partition function

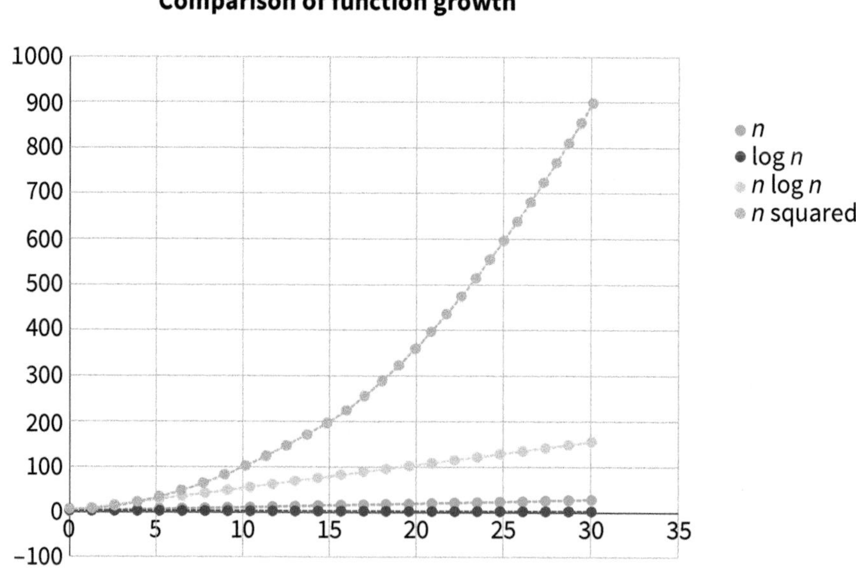

Figure 22.20: Comparison of function growth.

Code

```
FUNCTION partition(array, left, right)
  Pivot = pick random index
  pivotValue = array[pivot]
  Swap array[pivot] and array[right]
  storePosition = left
  FOR j = left TO right
    IF array[j] < pivotValue THEN
      Swap array[j] and array[storePosition]
      storePosition ++
    END IF
  NEXT
  Swap array[storePosition] and array[right]
  RETURN storePosition
END FUNCTION
```

To work out the number of comparisons the partition function will perform we can do a simple bit of arithmetic: right – left. The first time partition is called will be on the full array, which means that its time complexity will be n. However, for subsequent calls it will be based on the size of the partitions after reordering. This can be affected by the choice of pivot and the input.

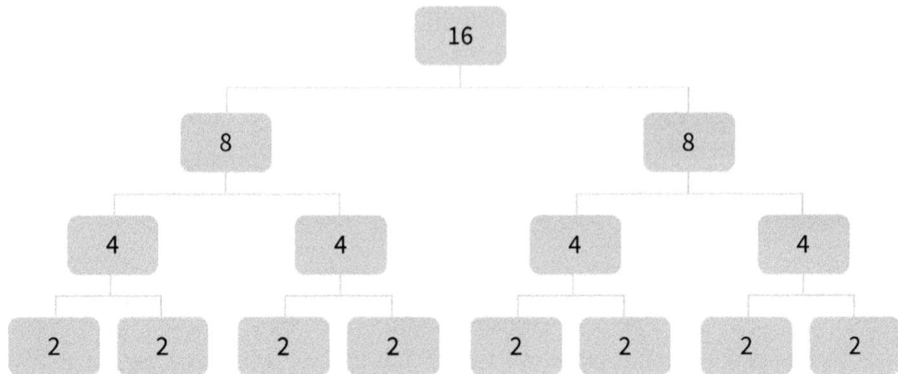

Figure 22.21: Splitting an array into equally sized chunks.

Consider the ideal scenario, where each partition is split equally, for an array of 16 items, as shown in Figure 22.21. We would need to have four levels of recursion, including the initial invocation, in order to fully sort the list. Following the same pattern for 32 items, we would require five levels of recursion, as shown below. In the general case, where the partition sizes are always halved on each invocation, we would need $\log_2 n$ levels of recursion.

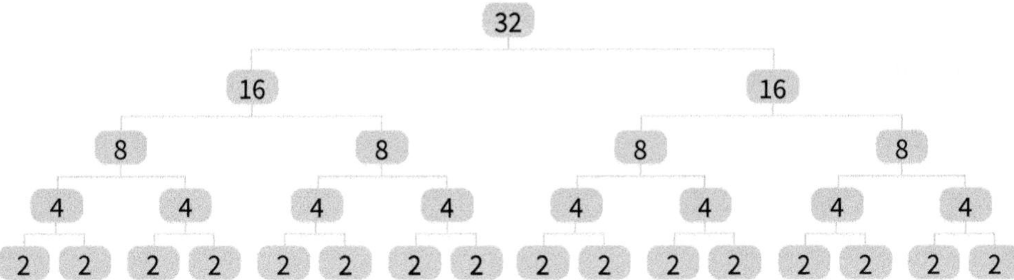

Figure 22.22: Splitting an array into equally sized chunks for an array with 32 elements.

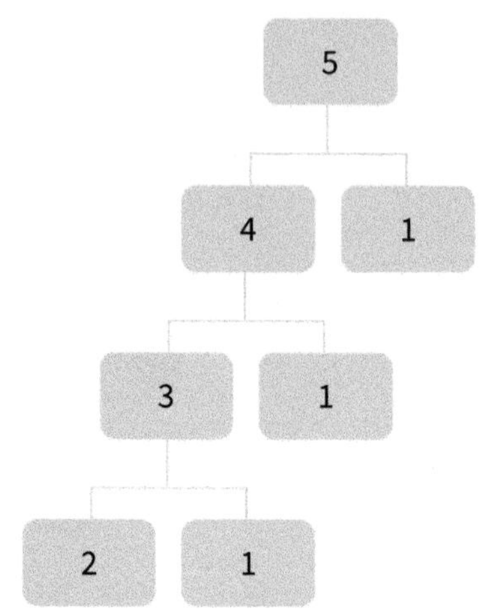

Figure 22.23: Splitting an array where one chunk is always 1.

At each level we will have many invocations of partition. However, at each recursive level we will always perform n comparisons. If an array of size 8 was split into two equal chunks of four, then partition will require four comparisons for each chunk. As we have $\log_2 n$ levels of recursion, each performing n comparisons, then the time complexity of n $\log_2 n$ becomes clear.

It will not always be the case that partition will split cleanly in half. As it turns out, on average, partition will still lead to $O(n \log^2 n)$ unless we get the worst-case scenario. In the worst-case scenario, as shown below, partition always splits the input so that one sub-array has a size of one. We end up with n levels of recursion rather than $\log_2 n$. We still, at each level, need to make n comparisons – this leads us to a worst-case time complexity of n^2.

Space complexity for quick sort

As quick sort is a recursive function, it requires memory every time a function is added to the call stack. As quick sort uses a constant amount of memory during partition, regardless of input size, for each function call we can work out the size requirements based on the number of recursive calls. In the best-case scenario we need to make $O(\log_2 n)$ calls as we equally split the list of numbers each time. In the worst-case scenario, where we always get a partition of size 1, we have to perform $O(n)$ calls.

With careful implementation, the number of calls on the stack can be limited to $\log_2 n$ even in the worst-case scenario. To limit the worst-case scenario, the partition with the smallest number of values should always be done first. That will guarantee the completion of that partition earlier and thus reduce the number of recursive calls that require further recursion. As space complexity is based on the number of recursive calls that have not yet completed, this trick enables quick sort to $\log_2 n$.

Merge sort

Figure 22.24: Input and output diagram for merge sort.

Merge sort is different from the other sorting methods used so far in the sense that it takes two arrays as input and produces a single array as output. Merge sort can also be used to sort and merge files. In order for merge sort to work it must have both arrays/files sorted prior to the execution of the algorithm. That means that a second sorting algorithm must be used if the arrays are not sorted initially, as shown in Figure 22.25.

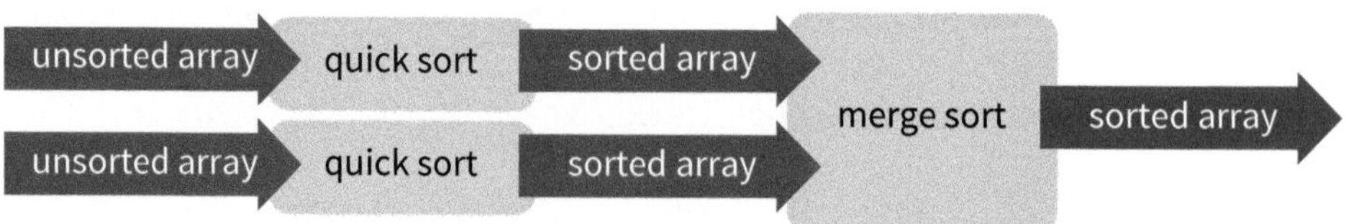

Figure 22.25: Input and output diagram for merge sort where the input must be sorted first.

Pseudocode

```
FUNCTION mergesort(A,B)
  i = 0
  h = 0
  r = 0
```

```
  WHILE i < LEN(A) AND h < LEN(B)
    IF A[i] <= B[h] THEN
      result[r] = A[i]
      i++
    ELSE
      result[r] = B[h]
      h++
    END IF
    r++
  END WHILE

  WHILE i < LEN(A)
    result[r] = A[i]
    i++
    r++
  END WHILE

  WHILE h < LEN(B)
    result[r] = B[h]
    h++
    r++
  END WHILE

  RETURN result

END FUNCTION
```

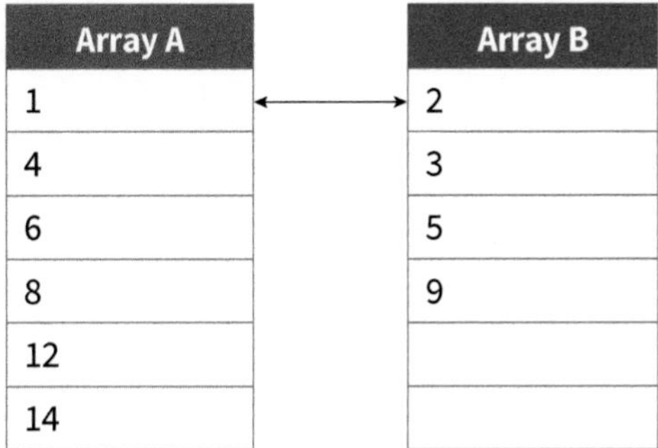

Figure 22.26: First loop of merge sort.

On the first loop of merge sort, the first values in both arrays are compared and the smallest added to the result list. Each array has its own variable to track the last index copied over to the result array, so whichever array had a value copied over will have its index incremented by 1. When the values are equal then it does not matter which one is copied over.

Figure 22.27 shows the next few steps of the merge sort algorithm. This process will continue until no more comparisons can be made. This occurs when one of the pointers is larger than the size of the array. At that point, whichever array still has items left over must have the remaining items copied into the result.

Time and space complexity for merge sort

There is only one loop with comparisons, which is based on the list with the fewest values. This makes merge sort's time **complexity** $O(n)$. For space **complexity**, because we require a new array which is based on the size of both lists added up, we still have a linear **function**. As such, the space **complexity** will also be $O(n)$.

> **Tip**
>
> You are expected to be able to justify your choice of sort in the exam. For example, quick sort is the most efficient but is also the most complex. It has no real benefit if the number of items is small.

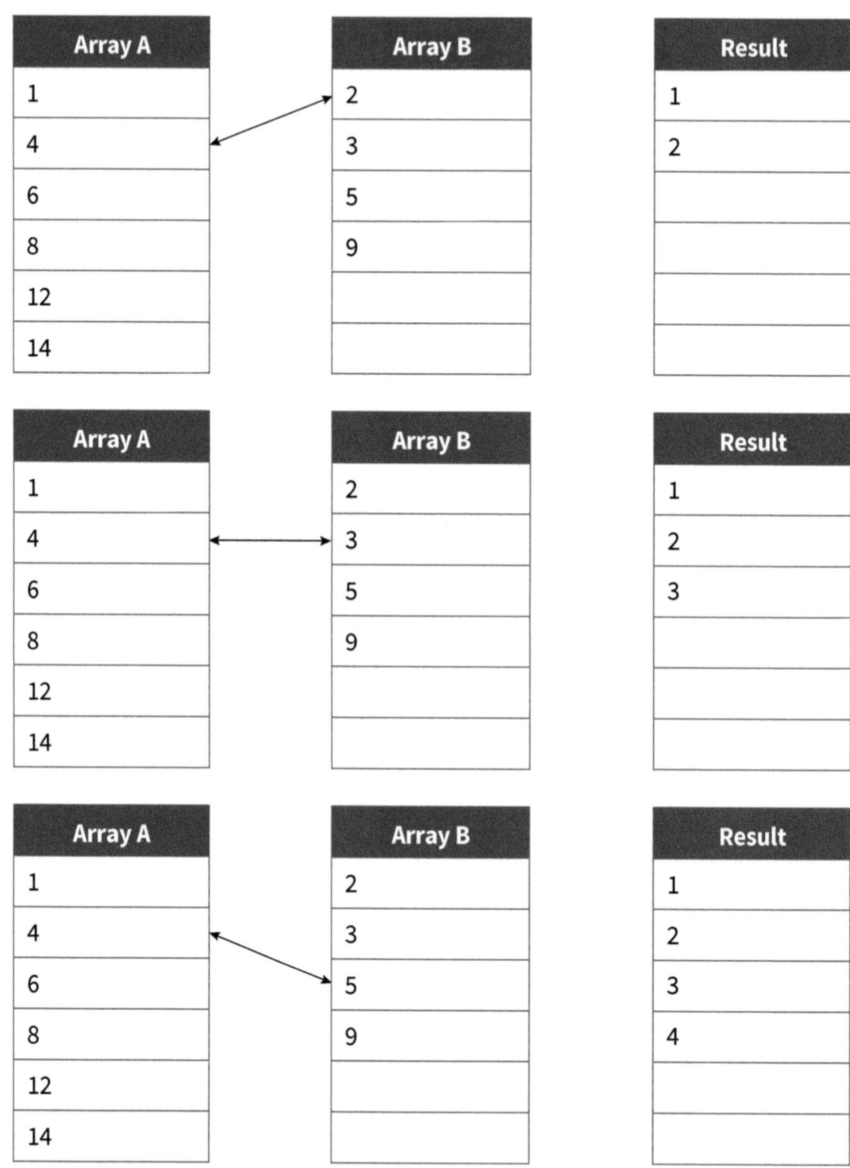

Figure 22.27: Next few iterations of merge sort.

Serial search

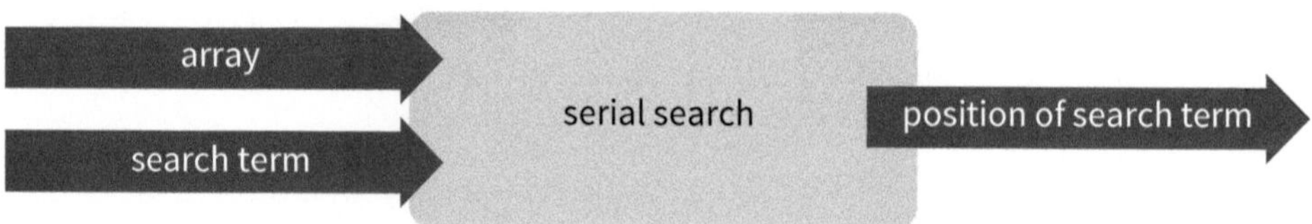

Figure 22.28: Input and output diagram for serial search.

Serial (or linear) search will, given an array and a search term, return the index of the first instance of that search term or −1 should the item not be found.

Code

```
FUNCTION serialSearch(A, searchTerm)
  l = 0
  WHILE l<LEN(A) and A[l]!= searchTerm
    l++
  END WHILE
  IF l == LEN(A) THEN RETURN -1
  ELSE RETURN l
END FUNCTION
```

Serial search will start at the first index in the array and compare the search term to every item until that item is found or the end of the array is reached. The loop has an additional comparison which will cause the loop to exit either at the end of the list or when the item is found. If we have reached the end of the array, where l = LEN(A), then −1 is returned to signify an error.

The time complexity of serial search in the best-case scenario, if the item was found immediately, will be 1. In the worst case, when the item is not found, it will take n comparisons. So on average, we have to make between 1 and n comparisons, meaning that serial search is $O(n)$.

The space complexity of serial search is constant or $O(1)$.

Binary search

Figure 22.29: Input and output diagram for binary search.

Binary search is a divide-and-conquer algorithm which requires the initial array to be sorted before searching. Binary search gets its name from the idea that after every iteration it will have halved the number of items to search through. As the initial array is sorted, each item in the array has the property $x_{i-1} < x_i \leq x_{i+1}$. Initially, binary search will look at the item in the middle of the array, x_m, and compare its value to the search term s. This leads us to three possible scenarios:

$$\begin{Bmatrix} x_m = s & \textit{Return } m \\ x_m < s & \textit{item is between } 0 \textit{ and } m-1 \\ x_m > s & \textit{item is between } m+1 \textit{ and } n \end{Bmatrix}$$

where n is the size of the array.

If the search term is smaller or greater than the value of the middle item then we can discount half of the array immediately. For example, if the search term was 44 and the middle value was 21, then there is no point looking at any values to the left of the midpoint, as all values to the left are less than the midpoint.

Pseudocode

```
FUNCTION binarySearch(A, searchTerm, left, right)
  mid = left + ((right - left)/2)
  IF right < left THEN RETURN -1
  ELSE
    IF A[mid] > searchTerm THEN
      RETURN binarySearch(A, searchTerm, mid+1, right)
    ELSE IF A[mid] < search THEN
      RETURN binarySearch(A, searchTerm, left, mid-1)
    ELSE
      RETURN mid
    END IF
  END IF
END FUNCTION
```

Initial list to search over

	4	15	23	26	32	39	45	56	57
Index	0	1	2	3	4	5	6	7	8

Binary search is a recursive algorithm which, at each invocation, will divide the problem in half by discarding half of the array each time. Using the above array and the search term '56', we can invoke binary search by binarySearch(A, 56, 0, 8). Finding the midpoint is done using the calculation Mid = left + ((right – left) / 2). Substituting values gives us the following answer.

```
Mid = left + ((right – left)/2)
Mid = 0 + ((8 – 0)/2)
Mid = 8/2
Mid = 4
```

This may seem overly complicated and you may wonder why we could not just use mid = right - left / 2. To understand this we need to look at the next invocation of binary search. As 56 > 32, left becomes 5 and right remains 8. So we recursively call binary search with binarySearch(A, 56, 5, 8) giving us the array below. Dark pink parts of the array will no longer be considered and the next midpoint is shown in light pink.

After the first iteration

	4	15	23	26	32	39	45	56	57
Index	0	1	2	3	4	5	6	7	8

If we stuck with the (right - left/2), or (8 - 4) / 2, this gives 2 rather than 6. In order to find the correct midpoint we need to add on left. Continuing with binary search, 45 is compared to the search term 56, which leads to the next invocation binarySearch(A, 56, 7, 8).

After the second iteration

	4	15	23	26	32	39	45	56	57
Index	0	1	2	3	4	5	6	7	8

```
Mid = left + ((right - left) ÷ 2)
Mid = 7 + ((7 - 8) ÷ 2)
Mid = (7 + 1) ÷ 2
Mid = 7.5
```

The above situation, when the range of indexes is even and there is no clear midpoint, leads to a fractional result for the midpoint. In situations like this, a decision has to be made to either round down (floor) or round up (ceiling). It does not matter which one is used as long as the choice is consistent. Commonly, floor is used to round down.

Time complexity of binary search

Binary search is more efficient than serial search, but does have the disadvantage that the array must be sorted. Given a sorted array, binary search's growth function is $O(\log_2 n)$. Every time we recursively call binary search one comparison is made. Therefore the time complexity of binary search is solely based on the number of recursions.

Every time binary search is called the range of values being considered will be halved. By halving the size for each call the worst-case scenario for an array of 32 items is five comparisons. For any n, the number of times we can halve a number before reaching 1 is $\log_2 n$. Therefore the time complexity of binary search, owing to only one comparison being done per recursive call, is $O(\log_2 n)$.

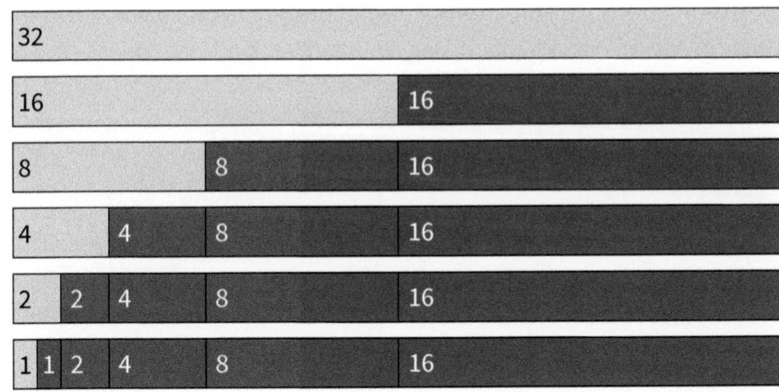

Figure 22.30: Diagram showing how the problem is reduced for every call to binary search.

Space complexity

Every time binary search is invoked we need a constant amount of space to run the function. As such, the space complexity for binary search is directly linked to the number of recursive calls we must make, which gives us $O(\log_2 n)$.

Dijkstra's algorithm

Note: before reading the following two algorithms, you should have made yourself familiar with the graph data structure. This information can be found in Chapter 12.

Introduction and definitions

Dijkstra's algorithm will find the shortest path between two vertices in a graph. The graph can be represented as an ordered pair, G = (V, E) where V = {set of all vertices} and E = {set of all edges}. In order to find the shortest path, each edge must have an associated cost,

Tip

Make sure you know how graphs link into real-world scenarios. For example, graphs are used extensively for route finding.

that is if $e \in E$ then $|e|$ is the cost of that edge. To help clarify the above mathematical definitions we can consider the example graph below. $a \in V$ is read as 'a is an element of the set of vertices V' and is one of the vertices in the graph below. That vertex has three edges, {a,b}, {a,d} and {a,g}, which have the associated costs of |{a,b}| = 7, |{a,d}| = 3 and |{a,g}| = 14. The length of the lines is not representative of an edge's cost.

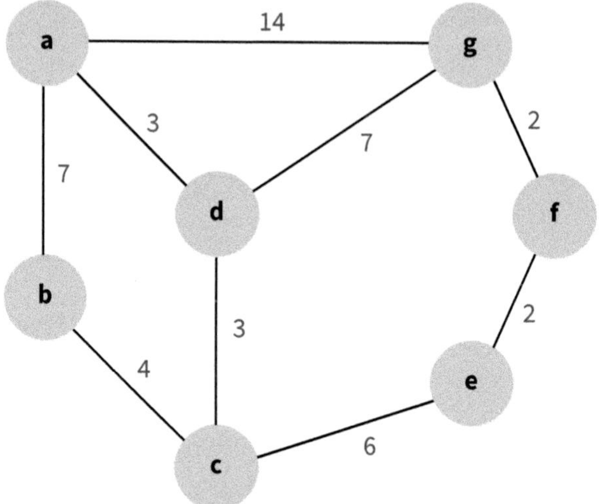

Figure 22.31: Example graph with weighted edges.

To understand what is meant by the shortest path, it is worth defining the cost of a path using the above graph as an example. Taking two vertices, c and g, there exists a path between them p = {c,e}, {e,f}, {f,g} with a cost |p| = 6 + 2 + 2 = 10. There is a second path q = {c,b}, {b,a}, {a,g} with a cost |q| = 4 + 7 + 14 = 25. Clearly |p| < |q| meaning that the path p is shorter. Considering all possible paths, p is the joint shortest path, with r = {c,d}, {d,g} having the same cost |r| = 10.

Considering the path between two vertices we can assign costs to the intermediate nodes to help show the shortest path. That cost will be the smallest sum of all edges followed from the initial starting node to the current one. Adding these costs, shown in green, to the previous example we get the graph in Figure 22.32.

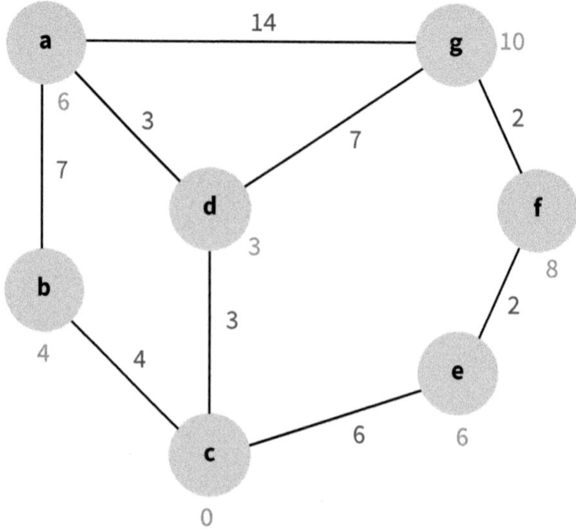

Figure 22.32: Example graph showing intermediate cost values.

When considering the path between c and a, there exists two possible costs which can be assigned to vertex a, which are |{c,b}| + |{b,a}| and |{c,d}| + |{d,a}|. The cost assigned to a vertex will always be the smallest sum, so as $3 + 3 < 4 + 7$ we assign the cost of 6.

Algorithm

1. Assign initial cost to each node of ∞ other than the start node, which is set to 0.
2. Add all vertices to a set of unvisited nodes and set the start node to be the current.
3. For each unvisited neighbour, u, of the current node, c:
   - **a** Add |c| to the cost of the connecting edge |{c,u}|
   - **b** If the new cost is less than |u| then replace the cost of u.
4. Remove the current node from the set of unvisited nodes.
5. Assign the unvisited node with the smallest cost from the unvisited set and make that the current node.
6. Repeat steps 3 to 5 until we mark the destination node as visited.

Figure 22.33 shows an example of this algorithm finding the shortest path from a to e.

Setup phase

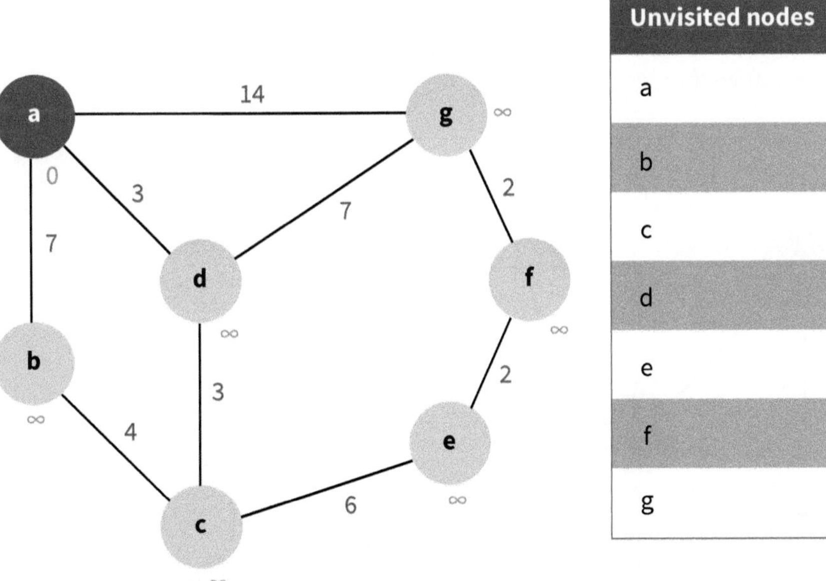

Unvisited nodes
a
b
c
d
e
f
g

Figure 22.33: Setup phase for Dijkstra's algorithm.

All nodes are added to a set of unvisited nodes and the cost of infinity is added to every node except the start node, which has the cost of 0. The current node is the start node, highlighted in orange.

Main loop

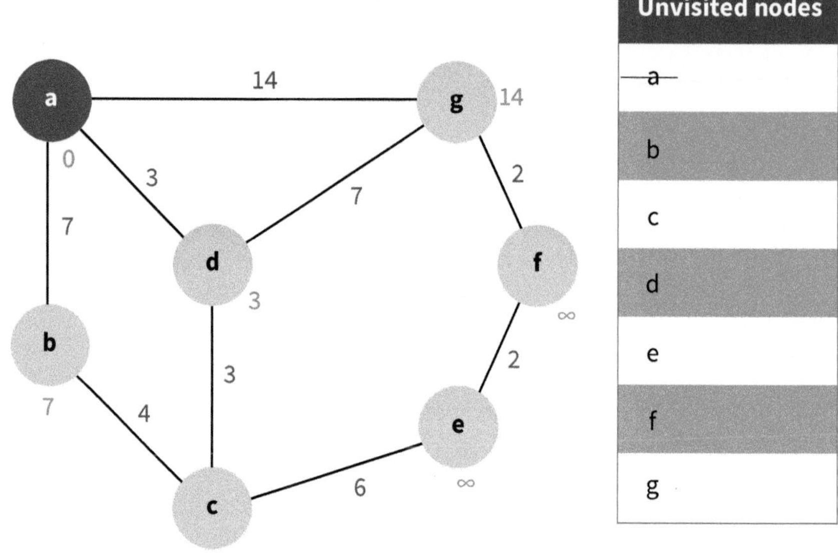

Figure 22.34: First loop of Dijkstra's algorithm.

Node a has three other nodes connected to it and their costs must be calculated.

$$|b| = 0 + 7$$
$$|g| = 0 + 14$$
$$|d| = 0 + 3$$

As $|d| < |b|$ and $|d| < |g|$ we set the current node to bed, as shown in orange in Figure 22.34. Node a has now been visited, shown in red, and can be removed from the unvisited set, shown as a strike-through.

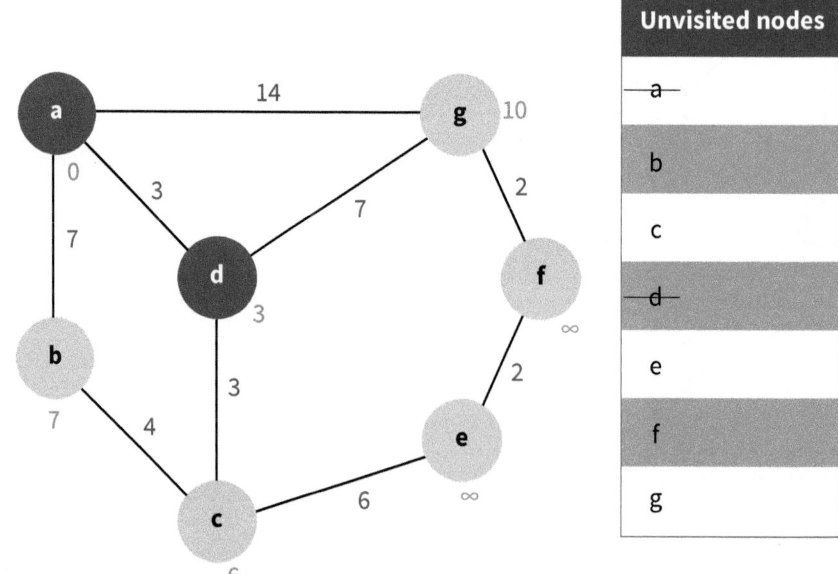

Figure 22.35: Second loop of Dijkstra's algorithm.

$$|g| = 3 + 7$$

$$|c| = 3 + 3$$

The cost of c is set to 6 as it was previously ∞. |g| was previously 14, which is greater than the new calculated cost of 10. Therefore the cost of g is replaced with the new lower value. Node d is then set as visited and the next current node becomes c, as it has the lowest cost so far.

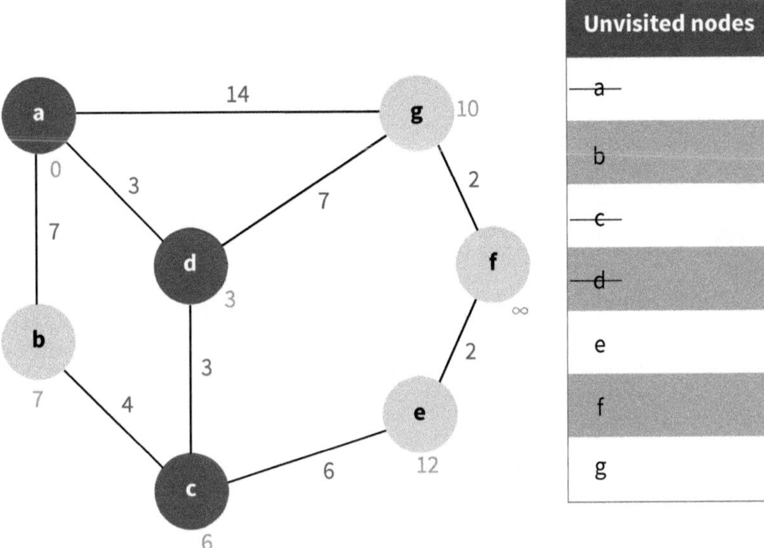

Figure 22.36: Third loop of Dijkstra's algorithm.

Node b has the lowest cost of all unvisited nodes, but does not have any connecting nodes which still remain in the unvisited node list. As such, we mark it as visited and make no further alterations to the graph. The next node with the smallest cost becomes g.

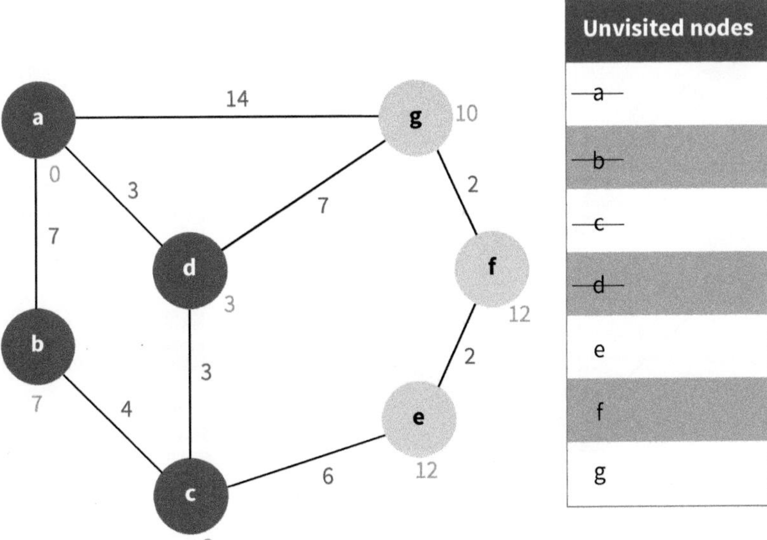

Figure 22.37: Fourth loop of Dijkstra's algorithm.

$$|f| = 10 + 2$$

We now have two nodes in the unvisited node set that have the same cost. It does not matter which one we pick, as we will still get the same result overall. Even though picking e would be the most logical choice, by looking at the graph, f will be chosen to exemplify the fact that the choice of node when costs are equal does not matter.

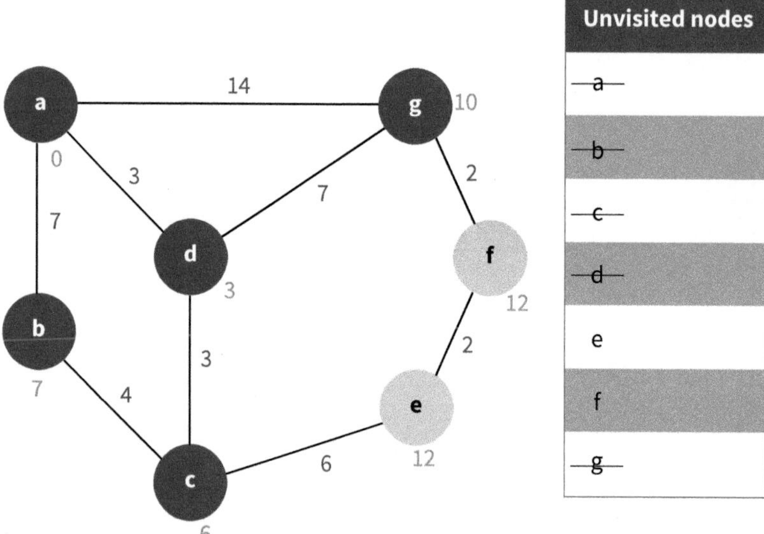

Figure 22.38: Fifth loop of Dijkstra's algorithm.

$$|e| = 12 + 2$$

Node e currently has a cost of 12, which is less than the new cost calculated above. As such, no changes will be made. Node f is marked as visited and e becomes the next current node.

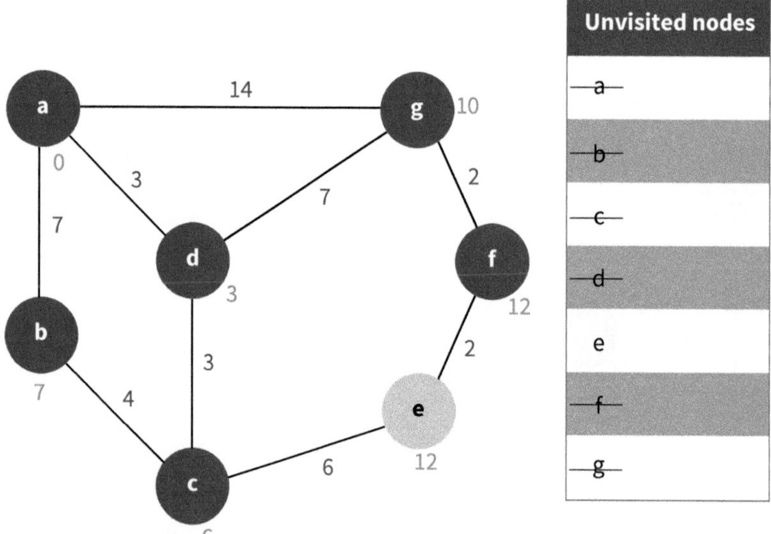

Figure 22.39: Final loop of Dijkstra's algorithm.

Finally, node e can be marked as visited, as there are no other nodes connected to it that exist in the unvisited set. The final cost was |e| = 12, which comprised the path {a,d}, {d,c} then {c,e}.

Pseudocode

G = graph to be searched

S = source node

D = destination node

U = unvisited set

```
FUNCTION dijkstra(G, S, D)
  # set up phase
S.cost = 0
  FOR EACH v in G
    IF v != S THEN
      v.cost = ∞
      v.previous = NULL
  END IF
  Add v to U
NEXT
# main loop
current = S
WHILE U NOT empty AND D is in U
  Remove current from U
  FOR EACH neighbour v of current IN U
    T = current.cost + length(current, v)
    IF T < v.cost THEN
      v.cost = T
      v.previous = current
    END IF
NEXT
  current = min_cost(U)
END WHILE
END FUNCTION
```

To work out the final route, we read the route in reverse using the previous nodes set. Every time a cost is set (when T < v.cost) we set up v.previous to be the current node, which means that we always store the lowest cost path as the algorithm progresses. To output the final route, we use the algorithm below.

Code

```
current = D
route = new Stack()
WHILE current.previous is defined
  route.push(current)
  current = current.previous
END WHILE
```

Time complexity

The time complexity for this algorithm is based on the implementation of the unvisited set and how finding the minimum cost within that set works. If the unvisited list is implemented as a simple linked list then the time complexity will be $O(|V|^2 + |E|)$ where V is the set of all vertices, E is the set of all edges and |V|,|E| represents the number of items in those sets (the cardinality).

The main loop will run |V| times, as we have to visit each node to find out the shortest path. Also, if the unvisited set is implemented as a list, we would have V| comparisons in that set to find the minimum cost. This gives us $|V| \times |V| = |V|^2$. The inner loop is based on the number of edges and runs once for each edge in the graph. Although it is repeated for every node, suggesting it should be multiplied to $|V|^2$, we never look at every edge in each loop. Each edge only needs to be considered once per run of the algorithm.

By using a heap to store the unvisited nodes, the time complexity can be brought down to $O(|E| \log^2|V|)$.

Space complexity

In order to run Dijkstra's algorithm we need to maintain a set of unvisited nodes which initially contain all vertices. As the algorithm proceeds, no additional space is required, meaning that space complexity is directly proportional to the number of vertices or O (n).

A* algorithm

A* is a search algorithm commonly used for graph traversal and path finding in games. It is similar to Dijkstra's algorithm in the sense that it computes costs for each vertex of the graph. However, it has one key difference in that it makes use of a heuristic function to help estimate the distance to the goal node. At any given point, A* will follow the neighbour which has the lowest overall cost using the function $f(n) = g(n) + h(n)$, where $g(n)$ is the cost from the start node to the current node and $h(n)$ is the estimated cost from the current node to the destination. The performance of the A* algorithm is directly linked to how well the heuristic function performs. If, for example, $h(n) = 0$ then we only consider the neighbours of the current node, meaning that it turns into Dijkstra's algorithm.

A* is a very versatile algorithm and can be used for many different problems. However, the heuristic function is problem dependent. For example, if you used A* to find the solution to a maze, then it may make use of the Manhattan heuristic, $h(n) = |x_2 - x_1| + |(y_2 - y_1)|$. This heuristic treats the maze as a grid and works out, from the current point (x_1, y_1), the number of steps needed to go horizontally and vertically, without going diagonally. Going diagonally would result in a heuristic h'(n), which would show a straight line distance or 'as the crow flies'.

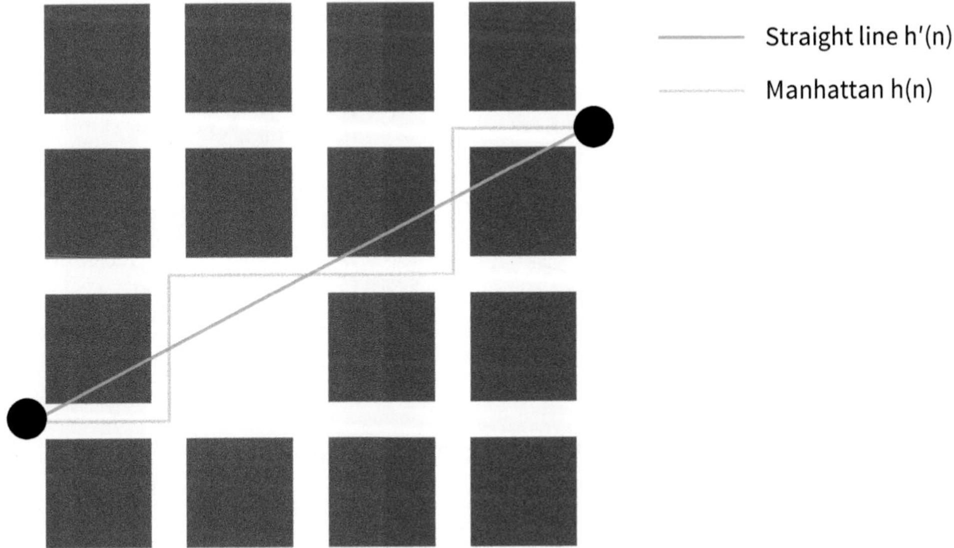

Figure 22.40: Manhattan heuristic exemplified.

To implement A* successfully, an admissible heuristic must be chosen that fulfils the property h (n) ≤ C (n), where C (n) is the true cost of the optimal path between two nodes. Essentially, this property is showing that h (n) is an underestimate of the true cost. While the heuristic is admissible a solution will always be found. As h (n) gets closer to C (n) the performance of A* improves. However, when h (n) > C (n) performance will improve but a solution may not be found.

Heuristics example

Figure 22.41 shows an example graph representing towns where each vertex represents a single town. Each edge represents a motorway that connects the towns together and the cost is the number of miles between two towns. Consider the situation where you're travelling from town a to town e and want to find the shortest route. If you could fly over all obstacles the shortest route would be directly from a to e and would take 64 miles. All of the straight-line distances are shown in the table in Figure 22.41. Each square on the grid, shown by dotted lines, is 10 by 10 miles. The distances have been approximated and assume that the motorways are perfectly straight.

Using this grid system, we can estimate the distance from any town to the destination. If a is in grid (0,0) and e is in grid (5,4) then the distance, d, can be found using Pythagoras' theorem:

$$d^2 = (x_2 - x_1)^2 + (y_2 - y_1)^2$$
$$d^2 = (5 - 0)^2 + (0 - 4)^2$$
$$d^2 = 25 + 16$$
$$d = \sqrt{41}$$
$$d = 6.4$$

As each grid is 10 miles, the final distance is 6.4 × 10 = 64. Our straight-line heuristic function, therefore, becomes $h(n) = 10(\sqrt{(x_2 - x_1)^2 + (y_2 - y_1)^2})$. Because, other than when we are in a neighbouring town, we can never take the straight line, there will not be a case where h (n) > C (n), meaning that this heuristic is admissible.

> **Tip**
>
> A* has no set heuristic. Without one it performs exactly like Dijkstra's algorithm. You need to know why the addition of a heuristic can make A* more efficient.

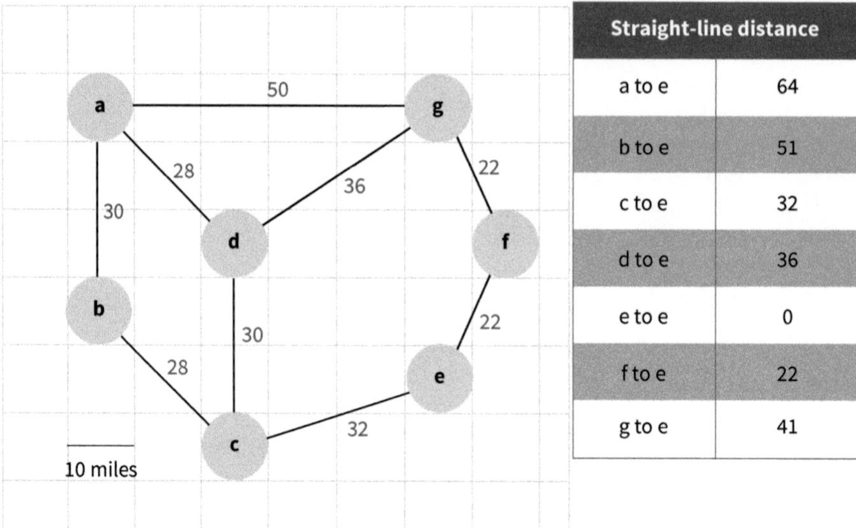

Straight-line distance	
a to e	64
b to e	51
c to e	32
d to e	36
e to e	0
f to e	22
g to e	41

Figure 22.41: Example graph with straight-line heuristic calculated.

A* pseudocode

Pseudocode

```
FUNCTION A*(G, start, goal)
closedset = empty
openset = start
start.g = 0
start.f = heuristic_function(start, goal)
WHILE openset is not empty
  current = min_f_score(openset)
  IF current = goal THEN RETURN constructed path
  Remove current from openset
  Add current to closedset
  FOR EACH n IN get_all_neighbours(current)
    IF n NOT IN closedset THEN
    g_score = current.g + dist_between(current, n)
  IF n NOT IN openset or g_score < n.g THEN
    n.g = g_score
    n.f = n.g + heuristic_function(n, goal)
    if n NOT IN openset
      add n to openset
    END IF
  END IF
END IF
  NEXT
END WHILE
END FUNCTION
```

Notes on the above pseudocode

- min_f_score(S) – will find the node with the smallest f (n) value in the set S.
- get_all_neighbours(p) – will return a set of nodes which are neighbours, or have an edge, with the node p.
- dist_between(a,b) – will return the edge cost between nodes a and b.
- heuristic_function(i, j) – will return a cost estimate between two nodes based on the admissible heuristic function in use for the implementation of A*. This function will be determined by the problem being solved.

Example run for A*

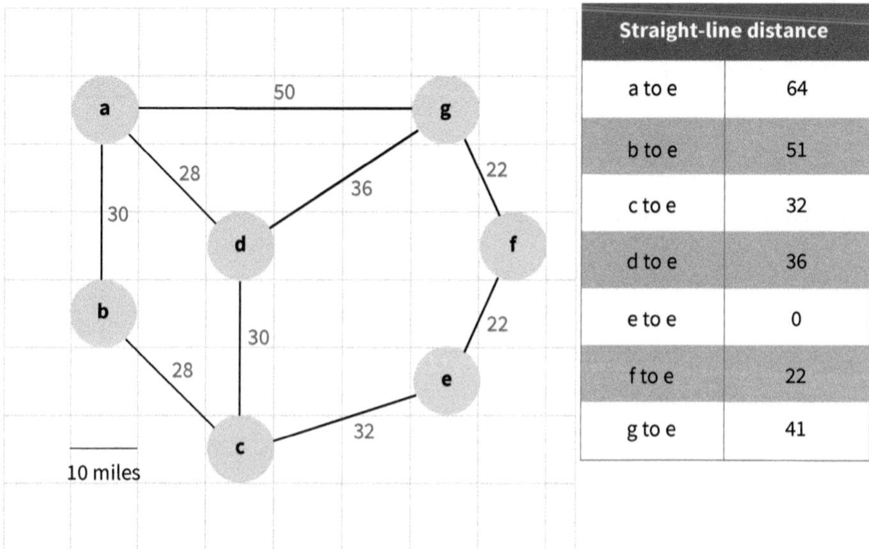

Straight-line distance	
a to e	64
b to e	51
c to e	32
d to e	36
e to e	0
f to e	22
g to e	41

Figure 22.42: Initial start point for A*.

To help explain how A* works, the graph used to explain the heuristic function will be used, including the straight-line heuristics with the results shown in the table in Figure 22.42.

Set-up for A*

Code

```
closedset = empty
openset = start
start.g = 0
start.f = heuristic_function(start, goal)
```

Two data structures are used, as in Dijkstra's algorithm, to keep track of which nodes should be considered and which ones should be avoided. The open set initially will only contain the start node, unlike Dijkstra's, which starts off with all nodes other than the start. The key behind A* is that it will only consider nodes if the heuristic function suggests the shortest path can be ascertained by considering them. Nodes only get added to the open set if they are to be considered rather than considering all nodes. The closed set, like Dijkstra's, stores nodes which have already been considered and should not be looked at again. Each node will contain two values, one for g (n) and one for h (n). g (n) stores the path so far, which is why it is initialised to 0, while h (n) stores the heuristic estimate to the goal. Initially, this estimate will be the distance from the start to the goal.

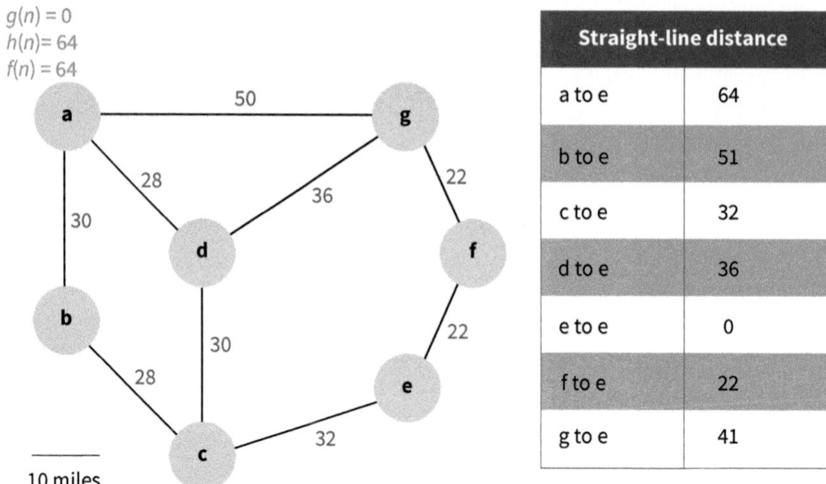

Straight-line distance	
a to e	64
b to e	51
c to e	32
d to e	36
e to e	0
f to e	22
g to e	41

Figure 22.43: Set-up with the start node assigned g (n), h (n) and f (n).

In this example we are going to search for the path from a to e. g (n) is 0 and h (n) is 64, as shown in the table. As a reminder, the straight-line heuristic function we are using here is:

$$d^2 = (x_2 - x_1)^2 + (y_2 - y_1)^2$$

Main loop

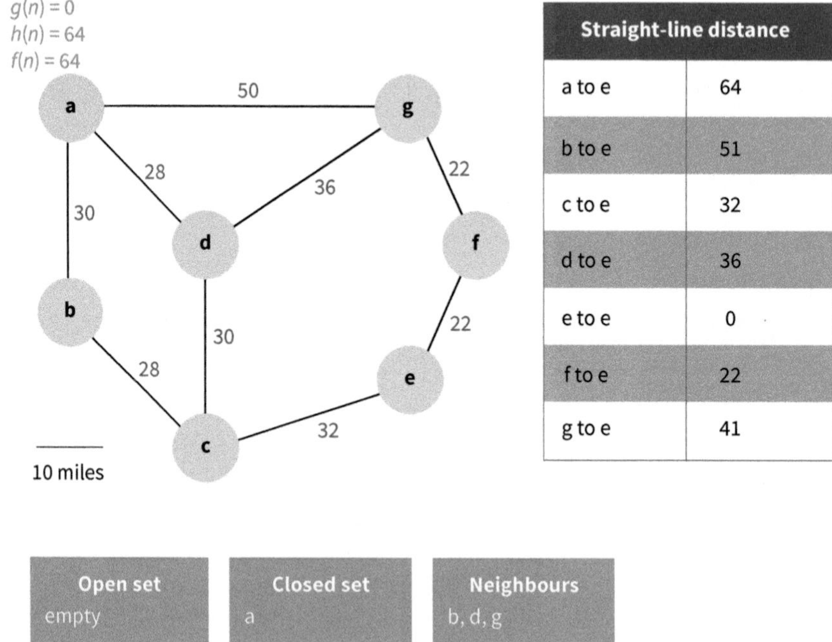

Straight-line distance	
a to e	64
b to e	51
c to e	32
d to e	36
e to e	0
f to e	22
g to e	41

Figure 22.44: Initial contents of the data structures before the main loop.

Node a has three neighbours and before each neighbour is iterated over we have the situation as shown in Figure 22.44. The current node is highlighted in orange and is selected by finding the node in the open set with the lowest f (n). Each neighbour that is not in the closed set will then have a new g (n) calculated and tested to see if it is not in the open set or if the new g score is less than the one already assigned. After the first loop we get the following result.

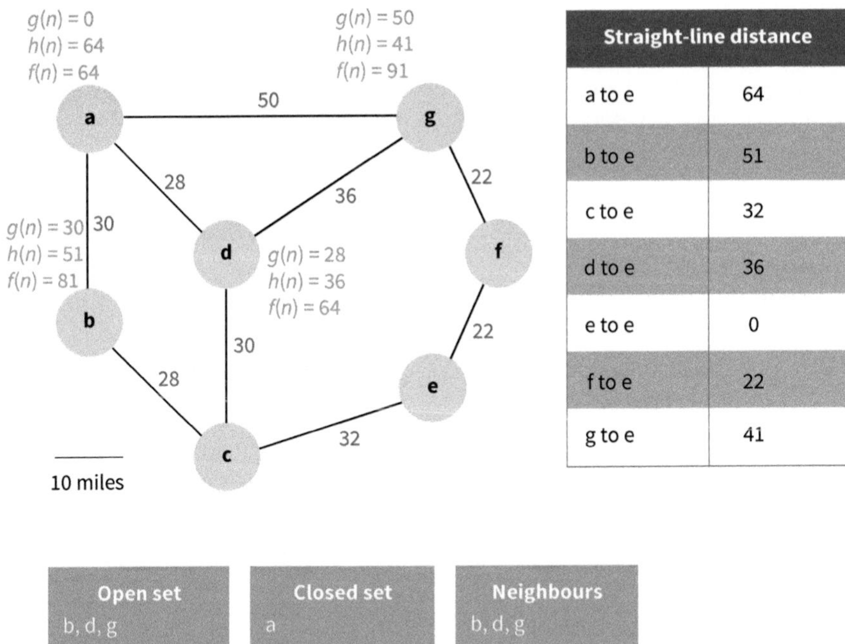

Straight-line distance	
a to e	64
b to e	51
c to e	32
d to e	36
e to e	0
f to e	22
g to e	41

Figure 22.45: Result of the first loop of A*.

In the second iteration there are three nodes in the open set, as shown in Figure 22.45. Node d has the lowest f (n) and therefore becomes the next current. Node d has the neighbouring nodes a, c and g. As a is in the closed set it will not be considered again; c will have values calculated and added to the open set. Node g, however, is already in the open set. In this scenario a new g (n) is calculated to see if it is less than the one currently assigned. The current node, d, has a g (n) score of 28 and the distance between |{d,g}| is 36, giving a tentative g (n) score of 64. This is larger than the g (n) already assigned, meaning that node g will not be considered.

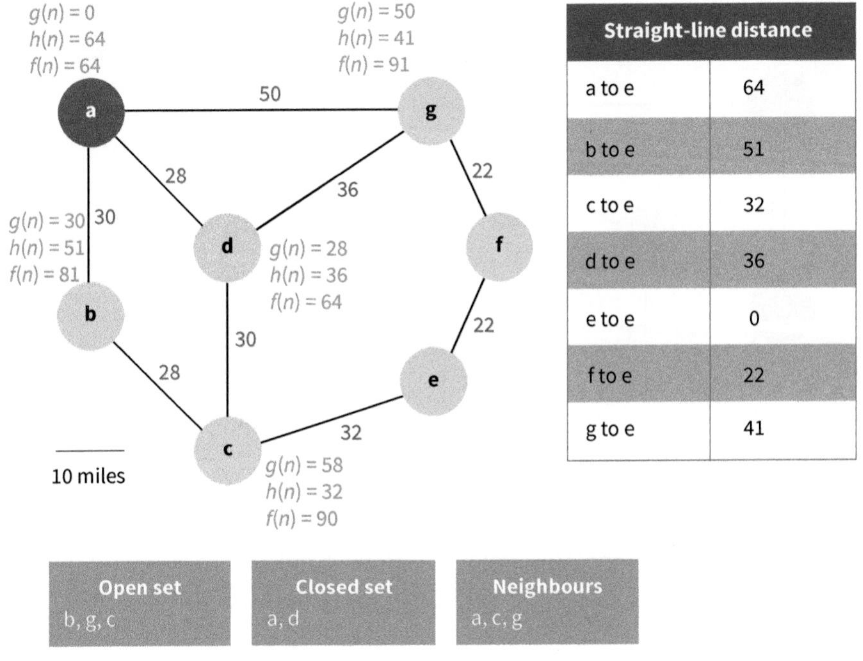

Straight-line distance	
a to e	64
b to e	51
c to e	32
d to e	36
e to e	0
f to e	22
g to e	41

Figure 22.46: Result of the second loop of A*.

In the next iteration, b has the lowest f (n) score. Again, as c is already in the open set, a new g (n) score will be calculated to see if it is less than the one currently assigned. In this case, they are equal to each other, meaning that it will not have its value changed. Therefore the only change to happen is that node b is added to the closed set.

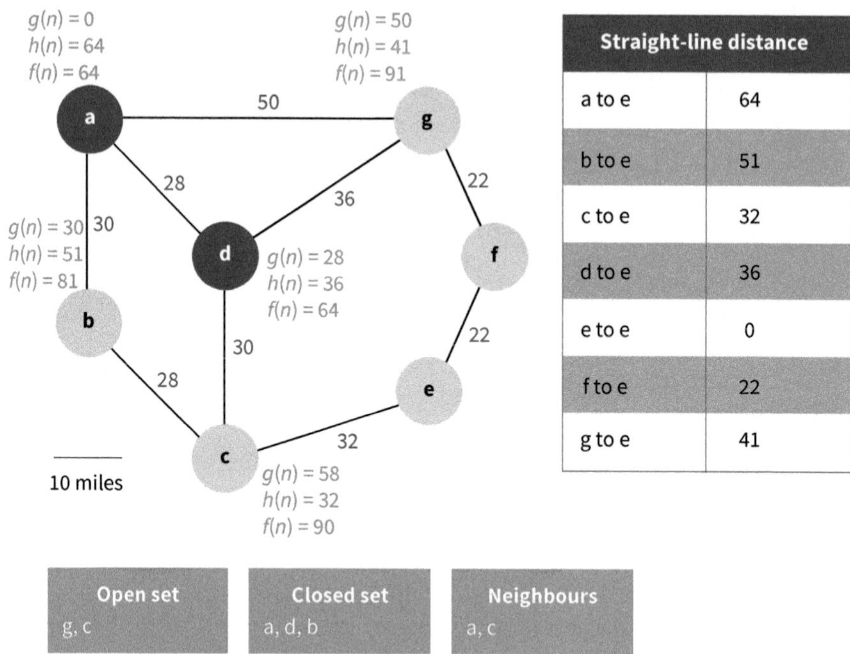

Straight-line distance	
a to e	64
b to e	51
c to e	32
d to e	36
e to e	0
f to e	22
g to e	41

Figure 22.47: Result of the third loop of A*.

In the next iteration, the node with the lowest f (n) in the open set is node c. Node e is the only neighbour that is not in the closed set, but it is also not in the open set either. Therefore it must have its f (n) and g (n) scores calculated and be added to the open set. Node e also happens to be the goal node, so the algorithm has found a solution.

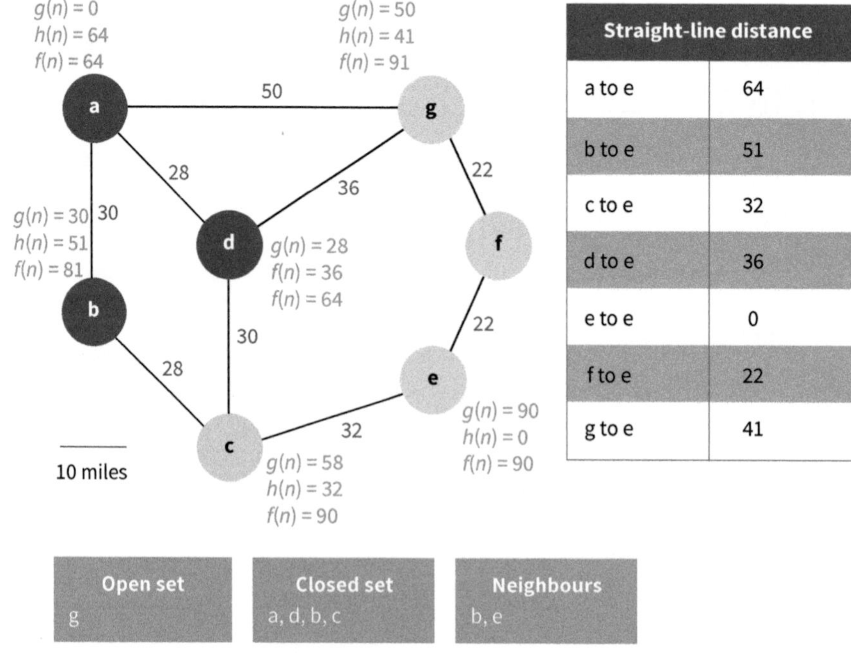

Straight-line distance	
a to e	64
b to e	51
c to e	32
d to e	36
e to e	0
f to e	22
g to e	41

Figure 22.48: Result of the final loop of A*.

In the last iteration, node e becomes the current node as it has the lowest f (n) score. As node e is both the current and goal then the algorithm is complete.

Time complexity of A*

The time complexity of A* is directly dependent on the heuristic used as this controls the number of nodes that must be considered. In the worst-case scenario, where the choice of h (n) is poor, we are left with $O(b^d)$, where b is the average number of times the algorithm considers other branches and d is the depth of the tree considered. It is the same function for the space complexity in the worst-case scenario.

Consider the perfect heuristic function, h*(n), which calculates the exact cost of a given node to the goal. In practical terms there is no way to produce h*(n), so we are left with the inequality $|h(n) - h^*(n)| = O(\log h^*(n))$. This essentially means that the closer h (n) gets to h*(n), the closer we get to logarithmic time.

Algorithms for data structures

Algorithms for the main data structures – stacks, queues, trees, linked lists, depth-first (pre-order) and breadth-first traversal of trees – were explained in Chapter 11.

Summary

- When designing algorithms you must consider not only how to solve the problem, but also the correctness of the solution and how efficiently it solves the problem.
- Every algorithm can have its efficiency analysed by considering the number of comparisons it can make and determining a function that grows with the size of the input.
- Review your understanding of data structures covered in Chapter 12 and be able to implement pseudocode to create the structure, search and sort data and insert and delete data items. For the AS examination you need to know: linear and binary searches and bubble and quick sort methods as well as the data structures: array, list, queue and stack. Although binary tree data structures are not explicitly listed, a basic understanding will help you to understand how a binary search operates.

- Functions used to determine efficiency are broken down into categories of functions.
- You should understand the algorithms used to search and sort data including those associated with the AS level course and additionally merge and insertion sort algorithms.
- Pathfinding algorithms include Dijkstra's and A*, which provide efficient graph traversal.
- Big O notation allows us to compare the growth of different algorithms and enables comparison.
- The time complexity of a given algorithm is directly related to the size of input.
- In this chapter you will have looked at a number of standard algorithms and seen their time and space complexity. Below is a summary.

Tip

Memorise the time and space complexities of all of these standard algorithms.

Algorithm	Time complexity	Space complexity
Bubble sort	$O(n^2)$	$O(1)$
Insertion sort	$O(n^2)$	$O(1)$
Quick sort	$O(n \log_2 n)$	$O(n \log_2 n)$
Serial search	$O(n)$	$O(1)$
Binary search	$O(n \log_2 n)$	$O(n \log_2 n)$
Dijkstra graph search	$O(\|V\|^2 + \|E\|)$	$O(\|E\| \log_2 \|V\|)$.
A* graph search	Based on heuristic	Based on heuristic

Activity 22.1

Design a simple algorithm which will take a size *N* as input and produce an array of items of size *N* containing random numbers as output.

Activity 22.2

Implement bubble sort and quick sort as functions. Test them using the algorithm produced in the first activity.

Activity 22.3

Add a counter to both bubble sort and quick sort that will count how many times a comparison is done within them. Have this value printed out before each function returns.

Activity 22.4

Run simulations for differing array sizes to see how many comparisons are made by both bubble and quick sort. Plot these on a chart to see if their growth is comparable to the theoretical growth discussed in this chapter.

Activity 22.5

Perform the same experiment for serial and binary search.

End-of-chapter questions

A **1** Explain the difference between logarithmic and exponential growth for a given algorithm. [3]

A **2** Define how heuristics can be used by a firewall to protect against hackers. [5]

3 A developer has been asked to create an app for a music festival that will create a high-score table based on the number of tweets each band have received. She was going to use quick sort to order the final output once all of the tweets had been added up. Explain why using quick sort would not be the best choice in this scenario. [5]

A **4** A balanced binary tree is one that ensures that every level is as full as it can possibly be. Explain why searching a balanced binary tree has a worst-case time complexity of log n while searching a binary tree would have a worst-case time complexity of n. [6]

Further reading

Quick overview of various algorithms and their associated complexity – go to bigocheatsheet.com.
How A* can be used for path finding – search on the Policy Almanac website.
Introduction to graphs for programmers – search on Algolist.net.
Algorithm analysis – http://interactivepython.org/courselib/static/pythonds/AlgorithmAnalysis/WhatIsAlgorithmAnalysis.html
Repository of algorithms (Facebook account needed to gain access) – go to www.daqwest.com.

Glossary

Artificial intelligence: Intelligence that has been built into a computer, enabling it to perform tasks normally undertaken by humans.

Assembler: A form of translator used when converting assembly code to machine code.

Association: The order in which logical connectives of the same type are used does not change the overall truth.

Attribute: A characteristic of an object.

Automata: Finite state machines created for each expression during lexical analysis.

Bandwidth: A measure of how much data can be fitted onto a cable at any point in time.

Biconditional equivalence: Both sides of the equivalence must be true.

Binary: A base-two number system that is used to represent information in computer systems.

BIOS: Basic input and output system – initialises and runs basic tests on connected hardware before running the boot loader to trigger loading of the operating system.

Bit rate: The rate at which data is sent over a network (bits per second). It is not a measure of speed, rather the amount of data that can be sent at a given time.

Blocked: A process that is waiting for a resource to become available. Blocked processes will not be moved into the running state until they unblock.

Buffer: Temporary memory used to store data to be saved onto slower storage or output devices. Use of a buffer enables the processor to work on other processes.

Cache: Memory that runs much faster than standard memory and sits in between RAM and the processor.

Centralised computing: Server model of computing where services are provided at a single point of contact.

Checksum: An error checking method used by TCP. It will perform a calculation on data, producing a short value that can be added to the packet for verification purposes.

Cipher text: The scrambled code produced by encrypting the plain text message.

Circuit switching: A route across the network is set up in advance and all packets are then sent down the same route.

CISC: Complex instruction set computer.

Client–server: Services, such as file storage, are made available on servers to which clients connect in order to access the services.

Client-side processing: Programs are executed by the client; a common example is a JavaScript file.

Clock cycle: One increment of the CPU clock.

Cloud computing: A system allowing companies and individuals to store all their data online rather than on their own computers.

Command line: A means of interacting with a program where the user (or client) issues commands to the program (command lines). Commands can take one or more arguments.

Commutation: The order of propositions combined using a logical connective does not matter and does not change the overall truth.

Compiler: Produces an executable file from source code. Commonly used when releasing closed source software.

Compression: A reduction in the number of bits in a file. Usually achieved by removing duplicated bits.

Conjunction: Used to combine propositions where both have to be true in order for the whole statement to be true.

Constructor: A special method called when a class is instantiated. Co-processor

Co-processor: An additional processor used for a specific task.

CPU: Another term for a processor. It stands for central processing unit.

CSS: Cascading Style Sheets contain the formatting information for HTML documents.

Cybercrime: Criminal activity carried out over the internet.

Data dictionary: A database that stores every item of data, the size of that data, the type of the data and a comment to explain what that data means.

Data link layer: Focuses on the transmission medium and ensures that a packet is packaged correctly for either wired or wireless transmission.

DHCP (dynamic host configuration protocol) server: Used by ISPs to assign an IP address to a device when that device connects to the internet.

Disjunction: Used to combine propositions where either can be true in order for the whole statement to be true.

Distributed computing: Services are spread across many computers, each of which plays a part in providing a single s ervice.

Distributed processing: In peer-to-peer networking, peers share the processing load for complicated calculations.

Distribution: Propositions, which are combined with statements in brackets using a different logical connective, can be expanded.

Double negation: A double negative always results in the original truth value.

Duplex: A method of transmitting data over a physical cable. Data can be sent in simplex, half duplex or (full) duplex.

Edge: A link between two items in a graph.

EEPROM: Electronically erasable programmable read-only memory

Element: The name given to a variable within an array. Usually accessed using its position in the array.

Encapsulation: The hiding of the implementation of a class and controlling access to its methods and attributes.

Fetch, decode and execute (FDE) cycle: Uses the cache to improve the processor's efficiency.

Flat file database: A single large table is used to hold all information.

Foreign key: The primary key of one table is included in a record in another table to link the two entities.

GPU: Graphics processing unit. A co-processor usually used to handle graphics but also suitable for a number of other tasks.

Handshaking: A process in which two communicating devices agree on a set of protocols to use.

Hash: A unique string of data.

Hash function: Used to produce the location in a hash table where a piece of data should be stored.

Heap: A large pool of memory.

Hertz (Hz): The number of clock cycles per second.

HTML: Hyper Text Markup Language, the language in which all webpages are written.

Identifier: A text name, not starting with a number, used to identify variables, constants or functions.

Implication: Given a logical statement we can infer further truth.

Increment: Adding to something; e.g. adding new functionality to a product.

Inheritance: The idea is that something is being passed down through some form of relationship.

Instantiation: The process of creating an object.

Intermediate code: Generic machine code for a general purpose computer. Used for languages that are both compiled and interpreted.

Interpreter: Reads source code in line by line, translating each line into machine code as it goes.

Interrupts: A signal sent to the CPU to inform it that an event has happened. Interrupts are recorded in the interrupt register, which is evaluated at the end of each Fetch–Decode–Execute cycle.

IP masquerading: Private LAN networks sharing a smaller number of external IP addresses to connect to the internet by using network address translation.

Iterative: Repeating an action; e.g. repeatedly improving the functionality of a product.

JavaScript: A scripting language commonly used with webpages.

Least significant bit (LSB): The rightmost bit in a byte, so called because it represents the lowest value.

Leeching: A term used in peer-to-peer networking, describing the initial stages of a file download process.

Literal: A hard-coded number or string found within source code.

MAC: Media access control layer. Hardware addresses used by the data link layer.

Machine code: Instructions in binary notation that can be executed by the CPU. Machine code instructions will only work on a specific machine architecture.

Method: A piece of code that implements one of the behaviours of a class.

Mission creep: A situation where objectives shift gradually during the course of software development, resulting in new, unplanned features and escalating costs.

Mnemonic: A symbolic name.

Mnemonics: A human readable representation of the machine code instruction set. A single mnemonic, such as ADD, would represent a single machine code instruction.

Model, methodology: A particular way of implementing the systems lifecycle.

Most significant bit (MSB): The leftmost bit in a byte, so called because it represents the highest value.

Motherboard: The main circuit board of a computer, which contains connectors for attaching additional boards.

Negation: Reverses the truth of any given statement. True becomes false and vice versa.

Network layer: Handles routing and is used to navigate the internet to get a packet to the correct destination.

NIC: Network interface card. Hardware responsible for placing packets onto network cables in the form of electronic signals, or bursts of light if the cable is optical.

Node: The part of a data structure that holds the data.

Normalisation: The process of converting a flat file database into a relational one.

Object: A combination of data and the actions that can operate on that data.

Opcode: A specific binary value that represents a single instruction from the processor's instruction set.

Overclocking: Increasing the speed of a processor beyond the manufacturer's specifications; it will probably void the warranty.

Packet: Data to be sent over a network containing additional data needed to correctly transmit the data.

Packet switching: Packets take independent routes through the network.

Page: A fixed sized memory block used when assigning memory to processes.

PageRank algorithm: Used to prioritise some webpages over others in the results provided by search engines.

Paging table: A table that maps virtual memory spaces used by processes to physical locations in RAM.

Parallel processor: An additional processor that works on the same task as the primary processor.

Parser: Reads text or tokens and provides context to that text. For example, parsers are used during syntax analysis.

Peer-to-peer network: Each computer, or peer, in a network has the same status as the others. No computer acts as a server, meaning that peers must work together to fulfil the required task.

Pipelining: The process of fetching one instruction while executing another, which enables higher throughput of instructions in the CPU.

Plain text: The original message prior to its encryption.

Pointer: A variable that holds a memory address, denoted with a * in many programming languages.

Polymorphism: The ability for an object of one class type to appear to be used as another.

Port: A point of contact for networking. Software ports have packets redirected to a specific application while hardware ports can be used to route packets.

POST: Power-on self-test - started when the computer boots and runs basic tests on connected devices. A report is generated and shown to the user as long as quiet boot has not been enabled.

Primary key: A unique piece of information used to refer to an individual record.

Process: A running program.

Processor: Runs instructions from memory and controls the rest of the computer.

Proposition: An atomic logical statement that can be either true or false.

Protocol: A set of rules that govern communication.

Protocol stack: A number of protocols chained together.

Prototype: A functioning but limited version of an application system, usually created to give the customer a rough idea of what to expect.

Recursion: A function that calls itself.

Relational database: A number of tables are used to hold information; these are linked together using primary and foreign keys.

Requirement: A key feature of a system that must be present in the final implementation.

Requirements specification: A document that contains the exact requirements of the new system.

RISC: Reduced instruction set computer.

ROM: Read-only memory – non-volatile memory that is used to store essential systems software.

Scheduling: Part of the operating system that is responsible for managing the order of processes and how they will be managed to achieve multitasking.

Scope: The lifetime of a variable. A variable can have either local or global scope.

Search engine indexing: A technique for speeding up the response time and relevance of search engine results.

Secondary key: A piece of information that can be used to sort a database or search for a group of items.

Segmentation: A variable sized block of memory that can be shared between processes. A common example would be the use of dynamic libraries.

Segmentation table: A table that stores the location of segments to map between virtual and physical memory addresses.

Server-side processing: Programs are executed by a server. Such programs are commonly written in server-side languages such as PHP.

Sign and magnitude: A method of indicating whether or not a binary number is negative using the MSB.

Source code: Human-readable code written to perform tasks. Must be translated into machine code before it can be run on any CPU.

SQL: Structured Query Language. A language created to help modify and query databases.

Strong encryption: Encryption that is very difficult to break.

Suspended: A process that has been moved to virtual memory.

Systems software: Software that manages the hardware and other software such as the operating system or system start-up software.

Tautology: Regardless of the truth values of the individual propositions, the overall value must always be true.

Translator: Software that takes source code and converts it into machine code. Examples of translators include assemblers, compilers and interpreters.

Transport layer: Has the choice of a reliable stream of data (TCP), or an unreliable 'fire and forget' datagram (UDP).

Two's complement: A way of displaying negative numbers using binary.

Unary operator: An operator with only one operand.

Unit tests: Tests created by programmers to ensure that the code they have written is working as expected.

USB: Universal serial bus – a common type of connection for external devices such as memory sticks, mice and keyboards.

Vertices: The set of all the values in a graph.

Von Neumann architecture: A software development model in which the different stages are arranged in order, with each stage cascading down to the next.

Weak encryption: Encryption that is easy to break.

WIC: Wireless interface card. Needed if the connection to the network is wireless.

Wireless access point (WAP): A device that allows wireless devices to connect to a wired network using Wi-Fi or another similar standard.

Index

W

X

Acknowledgements

Cover © 2013 Fabian Oefner **www.FabianOefner.com**

All images used in the chapter openings are courtesy of Shutterstock , except for Chapter 2 Jeffrey Hamilton/Getty Images; Chapter 4 Brent Lewin/Getty Images; Chapter 10 Yagi Studio/Getty Images..

0.3 Shutterstock; 1.1 SPL; 1.5 Alamy; van Neumann, Corbis; 2.4, 2.5, 2.6, Shutterstock; 2.10 SPL; 4.3 Alamy; Richard Stallman, Corbis; Alan Turing, SPL; 9.6 Corbis; 9.8, 9.11 Shutterstock; Department of Justice, Corbis; 14.2, 14.3 Aljazeera; Chapter 7, EoC Question 3, image of Manhattan Tube Map © MShieldsPhotos / Alamy.

Edited and revised for this print edition by Christine Swan.